Acclaim for *PARLIAMENT THE BIOGRAPHY VOLUME 1: ANCESTRAL VOICES*

'This magnificent book . . . Bryant is a fine historian. His understanding of political processes shines through. After this epic the next volume will be eagerly awaited' Leo McKinstry, *Express*

'A bravura "biography" of Parliament . . . both charming and important . . . A carefully constructed and lucidly written adventure story about the institution that – like it or not – still shapes our lives'
Roy Hattersley, *Telegraph*

'Admirably comprehensive . . . and written in the kind of lucid, elegant prose now rarely associated with our elective representatives'
New Statesman

'A fascinating study into the lives and reputations of those who, honourable or not, have sat as parliamentarians . . . compelling reading'
Chris Skidmore, *Times Literary Supplement*

'This book tells the story of our greatest national institution. It is well-written, contains much truth and a great deal of important information. It is a wonderful idea' Peter Oborne

'Lively . . . a warts-and-all account of how MPs have first survived and subsequently shaped and initiated policy' *The Lady*

'This is a wonderful, wry view of the history of parliament "from the inside". Chris Bryant is a great myth-buster. If you ever thought that modern MPs were more corrupt or worse behaved than their predecessors, then read on. You'll find it's not quite so simple' Mary Beard

'A remarkably readable and scholarly account of the emergence of the British Parliament over its first five hundred years or so' Ken Clarke

'A wonderfully iconoclastic yet affectionate history . . . Bryant tells the story with clarity and verve' Diarmaid MacCulloch, Professor of the History of the Church, Oxford University

'Worthy of its venerable subject' *Independent on Sunday*

'A colourful, eminently readable and enjoyable history of our country written by a serving Member of Parliament' *Choice*

'A clear and interesting account of Parliament before the seventeenth century' *Total Politics*

'A sweeping history of British Parliament. . . Enjoyably pacey'
BBC History Magazine

'[Bryant] at his best . . . most entertaining' *Sunday Times*

www.transworldbooks.co.uk

Chris Bryant is a British Labour Party politician who has been the Member of Parliament for Rhondda since 2001 and was the Minister for Europe and the Deputy Leader of the House of Commons in the previous Labour government. He was one of the two leading MPs who fought to expose the phone-hacking scandal at Rupert Murdoch's News International. Before entering parliament he was a priest in the Church of England. His previous books include biographies of Sir Stafford Cripps and Glenda Jackson.

Also by Chris Bryant

STAFFORD CRIPPS:
THE FIRST MODERN CHANCELLOR

GLENDA JACKSON:
THE BIOGRAPHY

POSSIBLE DREAMS:
A PERSONAL HISTORY OF THE BRITISH
CHRISTIAN SOCIALISTS

PARLIAMENT: THE BIOGRAPHY
VOLUME 2: REFORM

PARLIAMENT
THE BIOGRAPHY
VOLUME 1: ANCESTRAL VOICES

CHRIS BRYANT

BLACK SWAN

TRANSWORLD PUBLISHERS
61–63 Uxbridge Road, London W5 5SA
www.transworldbooks.co.uk

Transworld is part of the Penguin Random House group of companies
whose addresses can be found at global.penguinrandomhouse.com

Penguin
Random House
UK

First published in Great Britain in 2014 by Doubleday
an imprint of Transworld Publishers
Black Swan edition published 2015

A CIP catalogue record for this book
is available from the British Library.

ISBN
9780552779951

Typeset in 11/14 pt Minion by Falcon Oast Graphic Art Ltd.
Printed and bound by CPI Group (UK) Ltd, Croydon, CR0 4YY.

Penguin Random House is committed to a sustainable
future for our business, our readers and our planet. This book
is made from Forest Stewardship Council® certified paper.

MIX
Paper from
responsible sources
FSC® C016897

1 3 5 7 9 10 8 6 4 2

JCƆB

To be a good Member of Parliament, is, let me tell you, no easy task; especially at this time, when there is so strong a disposition to run into the perilous extremes of servile compliance, or wild popularity. To unite circumspection with vigour, is absolutely necessary; but it is extremely difficult.

Edmund Burke MP to the electors of Bristol,
3 November 1774

Contents

Acknowledgements   11

Prologue   15
1   The First Commoners   33
2   Subjected Thus   55
3   A House Divided against Itself   83
4   The King's Pleasure   117
5   An Outward Countenance   153
6   Freeborn Men   189
7   The Gathering Storm   209
8   The Vertical Turning Point   243
9   Court and Country   281
10   Ane Auld Sang   319
11   One Party State   355
12   Revolution and Reaction   387
13   Honourable Members   419
14   Ireland   441
Epilogue: The Wisdom of our Ancestors   475

Notes   481
Bibliography   514
Picture Acknowledgements   535
Index   541

Acknowledgements

I AM INDEBTED TO many people for their help with this book and its sister second volume. In particular, my agent Jim Gill steered me through the early stages, my editor Doug Young provided sage advice at every turn, Gillian Somerscales spotted errors and unintended ambiguities aplenty, Sheila Lee researched the illustrations, and several friends read individual chapters and put me back on the straight and narrow, including Professor Sir Diarmaid MacCulloch, Gregg McClymont MP, Chris Skidmore MP, Lynn Brown MP, Tristram Hunt MP, Jesse Norman MP and David Natzler. The printed and online publications of the History of Parliament Trust have been invaluable, as have several of its staff who also reviewed chapters, including Stuart Handley, Andrew Thrush, Stephen Roberts and Paul Seaward. While I have often relied on the scholarship of others, I have been fortunate in being able to access primary sources in the collections of the British Library, Lambeth Palace, the Middle Temple, the Bodleian Library at Oxford University, the National Archives at Kew and the Parliamentary Archives in the Victoria Tower, whose staff members Simon Gough, Adrian Brown and Caroline Shenton also cleared up some specific queries for me.

The House of Commons and House of Lords Library staff have been universally superb, especially Erkin Gozutok and Dora Clark.

An interest in history and religion was sparked in me by my parents Anne and Rees, and by three beautiful sisters who lived together all their lives and were my cousins twice removed, Isobel, Jean and Alison Gracie, but that interest was brought alive by many schoolteachers and college lecturers, including the Revd Sam Salter, Tim Pearce, Jack Ralphs, Tim Brown, Bill Simpson, Professor John Creaser and Professor Donald Sykes. Colleagues at Ripon College Cuddesdon, at ISEDET in Buenos Aires, and in the dioceses of Oxford and Peterborough weaned me off conservatism and schooled me in the pursuit of justice and freedom; they include Colin Manley, Jon and Penny Inkpin, Nicholas Cranfield, Wilfrid Browning, Christopher Evans, Michael Roberts, John MacQuarrie and Bishops Rowan Williams, David Willcox, Richard Harries, Richard Holloway and Peter Selby. And members of the Labour Party in High Wycombe, Northampton, Hackney and South Wales, and in the Christian Socialist Movement, made me realize that justice won't roll down like a river without the dedication of those who are prepared to deliver leaflets in the pouring rain, listen to speeches into the small hours, pay their party dues and turn up for the vote. Those volunteer members of every party are the rock and solid place on which our parliamentary system stands.

I am enormously grateful to those among my friends and family (and my office staff Rhys Goode, Kevin Morgan, Mark Norris, Jack Jones and Matt Reilly) who have put up with me while I have recounted endless parliamentary anecdotes at them or disappeared into the library for hours on end. Above all, I would not have been able to write this book without the forbearance of the people of the Rhondda, whose voice in parliament I try faithfully to be. In that, and in this, all mistakes are my own.

Civitatis Westmonasteriensis pars

Parliament House   the Hall   the Abby

Although parliament often met elsewhere in the middle ages, the Palace of Westminster was its normal home. The 'Hall', which was the scene of many parliamentary occasions including the deposition of Richard II and the trials for treason of William Wallace and Charles I, was already 550 years old by the time this image was drawn in 1647. The 'Parliament House', formerly the chapel of St Stephen's, was home to the House of Commons from 1547 until it burned down in 1834.

Prologue

IN ONE OF THE GRAND ROOMS in Speaker's House there is a vast walnut and gilt bedstead, with a crimson silk damask canopy reaching up to the ceiling. It purports to be the State Bed, reserved for the monarch on the eve of his or her coronation. It has never been used. It was commissioned in 1858, when the Victorians sought to cast Britain's magnificence in stone, building a deliberately ostentatious palace in the Gothic style to replace the higgledy-piggledy suite of medieval buildings at Westminster that had been engulfed in flames in 1834. Not only did they construct new chambers for the Commons and the Lords, both bigger and better than before, but the Lord Chancellor and the Speaker were provided with plush pavilions at either end of the Palace, overlooking the river. From the comfort of his library the Speaker, Evelyn Denison, could survey London's history. Down the Thames stood St Paul's Cathedral (completed 1708) and the Tower of London (founded 1066); across the water stood the Clink (built 1144) and St Thomas's Hospital (named 1173); a little further upstream was Lambeth Palace (established *c.*1200), and a short stroll away was Westminster Abbey (rebuilt in 1245). Surrounded by far older historic monuments, parliament affected antiquity of its own. Hence the State Bed – grand, opulent, but ultimately fake.

But then, self-aggrandizing exaggeration has been parliament's stock-in-trade for centuries. Elizabethan and Stuart antiquarians claimed the uniqueness of the English parliament. The Whigs of the eighteenth century preached the gospel of the Glorious Revolution. Without a scintilla of self-doubt, Winston Churchill declared in 1945 that 'we have the strongest Parliament in the world'.[1] Even today MPs place metaphorical hand on heart, summon up the blood and trot out the threadbare phrase 'the mother of all parliaments' with inordinate pride.

But this assumption of effortless superiority is nonsense, and it is time we dispelled such self-regarding mythology. For too long, successive historians have charted our supposedly ineluctable ascent from 'ignominious vassalage' to glorious liberty with excessive ease and we have lapped it up, mistily praising ourselves for our long-established independence of thought, our inalienable freedom from corruption and our elegantly evolved constitution.

Quite simply, we have got it wrong; and there is a real danger that a combination of misplaced patriotism and unalloyed cynicism will lead us to fetishize our past and encase our very imperfect modern parliament in aspic.

There are six core myths that these two volumes seek to dispel:

1 'Westminster is the mother of parliaments'

Nancy, Viscountess Astor claimed in her maiden speech in 1920 that it was the 'fighting men of Devon who dared to send the first woman to represent women in the Mother of Parliaments'.[2] It was a nice thought, but wholly inaccurate: though the phrase is often repeated and equally often misquoted, Westminster has never been the 'Mother of Parliaments'. Indeed, the originator of the phrase, a Victorian Liberal campaigner for parliamentary reform and universal suffrage, John Bright MP, coined it not to praise but to criticize England. Yes, he acknowledged in his speech in Birmingham Town Hall in 1865 that 'England is the ancient country of Parliaments', that its parliament had met more or less constantly for six hundred years and that 'England is the mother of Parliaments'. But his whole point was the terrible irony that the English 'are free to think, they are free to speak, they are free to write', so 'why is it that her people should not be free to vote?'[3] Far from eulogizing England's constitution and harking back to a glorious past, Bright was pointing to the country's abject failure to reform its political institutions. He was right. The 'Great' Reform Act of 1832 enfranchised only about 5 per cent of the population – and explicitly barred anyone but 'male persons' from voting.

The British like to think that the parliament at Westminster is the oldest representative democracy in the world, and yet it is quite a latecomer – in more ways than one. The oldest parliament in the world is the Icelandic Althingi (established 23 June 930), and the parliament of the Isle of Man, the Tynwald, came into existence in 979. Ireland's first known Act of Parliament, dated 1216, beats England's, enrolled in 1229. In modern times, too, we have lagged behind others. New Zealand was the first country to give women the vote, in 1893, followed rapidly by the Cook Islands (whose women narrowly beat the New Zealanders to the polls that same year). It was not until 1918 that universal adult male suffrage was introduced in the UK – and even then, only women over the age of thirty got the vote. Women had to wait until 1928 to gain the franchise on an equal basis with men – after their sisters in Norway, Denmark, Canada, Germany, Poland, the Netherlands, the United States and the Irish Free State. When Finland became the first European country to allow women to stand for its new Eduskunta in 1906, 19 (out of 200) seats went to women, a figure the UK was not to reach until 1945. By any criterion it is difficult to maintain the claim to parliamentary motherhood.

2 'The history of British parliamentary democracy has proceeded according to plan'

For many a nineteenth-century historian, the history of parliament was one of the central proofs of Britain's greatness. Like a barnacle-encrusted galleon, the constitution had sailed on through stormy waters towards her long-charted destination, modern constitutional monarchy. Just listen to the first sentence of Henry Hallam's *Constitutional History of England*, published in 1846:

> The government of England, in all times recorded by history, has been one of those mixed or limited monarchies which the Celtic and Gothic tribes appear universally to have established in preference to the coarse despotism of eastern nations, to the more artificial tyranny of Rome and Constantinople, or to the various models of republican polity which were tried upon the coasts of the Mediterranean sea.[4]

Few sentences encompass more prejudice and patriotism untainted by examination of the evidence, but this belief in the inalienable righteousness of British history was a consistent theme in most historical works on parliament well into the twentieth century. The Great Charter, the 'Model Parliament' of 1295, Henry VIII's Reformation by parliamentary statute, the Stuart wars of the three kingdoms, the Acts of Union and the Reform Act of 1832 were all stepping stones on the path towards the completed masterpiece that was the Victorian constitutional settlement. As Thomas Babington Macaulay, himself an MP and government minister, put it, his *History of England* would tell 'how, from the auspicious union of order and freedom, sprang a prosperity of which the annals of human affairs had furnished no example; how our country, from a state of ignominious vassalage, rapidly rose to the place of umpire among European powers'.[5] The drum roll of rising rhetoric proclaims its own patriotism.

But the evidence for an intelligent plan behind the development of parliament is extremely thin. Rather, this has been a great improvised experiment in which caprice has played every bit as important a role as any consciously pursued constitutional ideology. Sometimes the caprice lay in the accidents of birth and death. Often, in both England and Scotland, it was a contested throne that led to the summoning of an early parliament. So, had Henry VIII's or Charles I's elder brothers or William and Mary's child lived, or had Queen Anne brought forth an heir, the succession itself would have passed down a very different route. The uncertainty over who would succeed Elizabeth I encouraged parliament to flex its muscles, and Victoria became queen only because her grandfather, father, three uncles and three cousins all died before her own twelfth birthday. It is not just the sad stories of the death of kings, either, that have played a part in determining the pattern of our history. Had Pitt the Younger been his father's eldest son and inherited his title in the Lords, he would almost certainly not have become Prime Minister; and if Edward Wood's three elder brothers had not died in infancy, leaving him to inherit his father's title as Viscount Halifax in 1934, it might well have been he rather than Winston Churchill who took over from Neville Chamberlain in 1940.

Time and again the hazard of fortune has sat at the table as an extra player. The 1713 Place Bill, which would have taken all government ministers out of parliament and split the executive from the legislature, failed to get on to the statute book only because the vote on the third reading in the Lords was tied. The Reform Act of 1832 was later thought so good they named it Great, but on its second reading in 1831 was carried in the Commons by a single vote, as was the vote of no confidence in the government of Jim Callaghan in 1979 that led to Mrs

Thatcher's first election victory. Even more bizarrely, one of the key legal texts underpinning the freedom against arbitrary arrest, the Habeas Corpus Act of 1679, only got through the House of Lords by two votes when the teller for the Ayes counted a fat peer for ten votes. On forty-nine occasions since 1801 the Speaker has had to decide on a tied vote, including the occasion on 23 July 1993 when it was discovered that one vote had accidentally been added to the Ayes over the Maastricht Treaty.

So the history of parliament is not the tracing out of some hidden, intelligent design, but a story of the vagaries of chance – and indeed, it is in the detail of these moments of haphazard history that the real drama of that story comes to life.

3 'There is no going back'

The ability to stand on one's head has always been an important political skill. Witness the two parliaments of 1376 and 1377, which removed and then reinstated the king's ministers. The tergiversations of the Tudor parliaments of Edward VI, Mary and Elizabeth were even more dizzying, as Edward made parliament enact a fuller Reformation of the church than even his father had allowed for, Queen Mary had the whole of parliament beg forgiveness on bended knee before Cardinal Pole, and when Elizabeth became queen she demanded that parliament restore her brother's Reformed religion.

Some advances have stuck – free and fair elections, the rule of law, votes for women. But other forward steps have gone into reverse. Take the relative power of crown and parliament. At the end of the eighteenth century Edmund Burke and others complained vigorously about the corruption of parliament through the army of government placemen on salaries and pensions. Their numbers were cut, and any member appointed to an office of profit under the crown was compelled to fight a by-election. Yet when the two world wars were being waged the rules were relaxed and the crown was allowed to appoint ever more ministers, under-secretaries and parliamentary private secretaries. When you consider this alongside the nineteenth-century land grab that put the whole parliamentary timetable in the government's hands, it is difficult to argue that parliament achieved an unalterable supremacy over the crown. Indeed, the primary role of parliament today is not to scrutinize a government but to staff and sustain it.

So too with freedom of speech. Tudor and Stuart parliaments battled with the monarch over the right to debate whatever they wanted, and in 1641 the Long Parliament abolished the Star Chamber, which had acted as state censor. But its replacement, a monopoly exercised by the Stationers' Company, was equally restrictive. Newspapers had to be licensed before publication – and the rules were strictly enforced. That monopoly was ended in 1694, but fear of a French invasion or of internal insurrection inspired 'Gagging Acts' in 1795 and 1817 that made most publications financially unviable. Even the principle of habeas corpus was enacted in 1640, repealed at the Restoration, re-enacted in 1679, suspended in 1794 and 1817, and withheld for purposes of internment during both world wars and the Northern Ireland Troubles.

4 'There was a golden age of glorious independents'

Parliament has certainly had its standalone heroes: William Wilberforce campaigning for the abolition of the slave trade; Andrew Marvell refusing to take a post in a corrupt government; Simon de Montfort summoning knights and burgesses for the first time; Sydney Silverman securing the abolition of the death penalty through a private member's Bill in 1965. Often they have been neglected by the wider sweep of party political history. Take Samuel Plimsoll, the Liberal MP for Derby for twelve years between 1868 and 1880, who left school in Sheffield at the age of fifteen and battled with bankruptcy and destitution before refreshing his fortunes as a coal merchant thanks to a prosperous marriage. Plimsoll's campaign against the shipping rules that had seen overloaded ships go to the bottom with all hands came about thanks to a casual acquaintance with a shipbuilder on Tyneside, but he pursued it with vigour and not a little high emotion. First, in 1871, came a Merchant Shipping Survey Bill, which was lost by just three votes in the Commons. Then, in 1873, a polemic, *Our Seamen: an Appeal*, which made an emotive case for reform that Disraeli could not bring himself to refuse. A government Bill was introduced – and allowed to run into the sands, whereupon Plimsoll lost his temper, declaring that he was 'determined to unmask the villains who send [men] to death and destruction'. As MPs screamed 'Order!', the Speaker demanded five times that Plimsoll retract his accusation before he was forced to leave the House, shouting, 'Do you know that thousands are dying for this?' as he went.[6] Members were scandalized and he was forced to apologize, but within a year Disraeli was shamed into introducing a new Merchant Shipping Bill and in 1890 the Plimsoll Line was enshrined in law as an obligatory marking on all British merchant vessels.

The point about Plimsoll is that he was not immaculate. He was thrown out of his local church for his business practices, he was vain enough to make his own heraldic shield and he lost his seat in 1880. Even Lord Shaftesbury, who pursued his Factory Act and campaigns against chimney boys with just as much emotion, thought: 'He is proud of his own impetuosity and seems to think that no-one can be weary of it. I find him bold, earnest, rash. He will ruin himself and the cause by his violence.'[7]

Moreover, the modern-day lionizing of the individual parliamentary hero should not obscure the fact that the development of political parties has been one of the most important innovations in the British political system. Their growth from the simple congregation of like-minded MPs and peers in a Tudor tavern in London to the popular Exclusion campaigns in 1679–81, the inauguration of the political clubs such as the Reform and the Carlton, and then fully fledged parties with membership cards, enforced discipline and election manifestos is as important as the tales of individual talented politicians. Indeed, the strength of the political party system in the United Kingdom, with the 'whippers-in' enforcing discipline, has latterly made it far more difficult to buy a vote in parliament than in the US Congress.

5 'Today's parliament is worse behaved than ever'

The most frequent complaint about today's House of Commons is its resemblance to a children's playground. It is true that the noise level during Prime Minister's Questions is so high that without the microphones and speakers little would be heard. But it would be wrong to suggest that this is a recent phenomenon. Asquith was howled down as Prime Minister in 1911, and in 1863 'an angry and determined House' silenced a series of speakers, including Disraeli, over the purchase of the Great Exhibition building. Sometimes it was just a question of individual high spirits. We know from Samuel Pepys that 'Sir Allen Broderick and Sir Allen Apsley did both come drunk the other day [19 December 1666] into the House and did both speak for half an hour together, and could not be either laughed or pulled, or bid to sit down and hold their peace'.[8] Nearly three centuries later, on 4 April 1938, things got very heated during questions on Spain as the irascible Scottish Labour MP Manny Shinwell accused the Conservative minister Rab Butler of 'humbug' and, when jeered at by a Tory MP, stomped across the chamber and, in the words of Hansard, which rarely includes stage directions, 'struck the hon. and gallant Member for Cleveland (Commander BOWER) a blow on the face'.[9]

The worst moment of the modern parliamentary era came on the evening of 27 July 1893, when Gladstone and Joseph Chamberlain sparred over the Irish Home Rule Bill, which was coming to the end of its forty-seventh filibustered session in committee. Gladstone had already secured a guillotine motion, requiring all remaining questions on the Bill to be put at ten o'clock. Chamberlain ended his speech by taunting the Liberals with their apparent desire to do whatever Gladstone demanded. 'The Prime Minister calls "black," and they say, "it is good": the Prime Minister calls "white," and they say "it is better." It is always the voice of a god.' This was standard party political taunting, but then he added sardonically: 'Never since the time of Herod has there been such slavish adulation.'[10] This equation of Gladstone with Herod prompted the Irish MP T. P. O'Connor, who had sloshed back a fair amount of champagne that evening, to hurl his favourite term of abuse, 'Judas!', across the Chamber. Immediately the other Irish nationalists took up the chant and the Tory Vicary Gibbs could not even make himself heard as he tried to get the chairman to demand that the term be retracted. Chaos ensued as the division proceeded. The Liberal Sir John Logan, sitting down on the opposition front bench next to the Unionist Sir Edward Carson, was grabbed round the neck by Hayes Fisher, pummelled in the stomach by Sir Ellis Ashmead-Bartlett and bundled under the bench. Someone jostled Colonel Edward Saunderson, another Unionist, who took aim at the Labour Nationalist Eugene Crean, but instead landed a bloody punch on another Irishman, Michael Austin. Others were dragged into the battle, including the Unionist Colonel Robert Gunter and the Nationalist Tim Healy, and when Dr Charles Tanner arrived in the Chamber and launched himself at the maul, J. A. Pease leaped on his back 'and in an old Rugby Union style . . . collared and held him back on the floor of the House'.[11] Order was only restored when John Burns started tearing people out of the scrimmage and thrusting them back into their seats and the Speaker was summoned. (Memory plays tricks: James Lowther recollected that the clerk read out the title of the next business, 'Pistols Bill – Second Reading',[12] and everyone laughed. Sadly, there was no such moment, as the Bill's title had been read out three days earlier.)

6 'Today's MPs are the most venal we have had'

One of the most potent myths is that today's set of MPs is more vicious, self-serving and incompetent than any other. It's a charge that is difficult to substantiate. Look at one small slice of the Victorian era, 1889–92. In that short period, one MP, Colonel Hughes-Hallett (Conservative, Rochester) was forced to step down after he was discovered to have stolen £5,000 of his deceased first wife's first husband's daughter's inheritance; another, Captain Edmund Verney (Liberal, Buckingham) was convicted of procuring a nineteen-year-old girl for sex and was expelled from the Commons; a third, Samuel Wesley de Cobain (Unionist, Belfast East) fled the country when a warrant for his arrest was issued for committing gross indecency with a man named Allan, and was expelled when he refused to return; one George Hastings (Liberal Unionist, Worcestershire East) was expelled over a £20,000 inheritance fraud; and John Deasy (Nationalist, Mayo) stood down when he was convicted of an assault on his own maid. Other convictions were to follow, most notably that of Jabez Spencer Balfour (Liberal, Burnley) who fled the country, was brought back and in 1893 was sentenced to fourteen years' penal servitude for fraud on a massive scale. Any one of these stories would have press and public frothing at the mouth today; at the time, the *Morning Advertiser* commented with notable restraint: 'The chosen of the electorate in Parliament and elsewhere have not been turning out particularly well lately.'[13]

There were plenty more parliamentary rogues and unfortunates, too – like Sir Giles Mompesson, expelled from parliament for abusing his monopoly over the licensing of inns and taverns; or the Sadleir brothers, John and James, who were implicated in a series of Victorian frauds, and respectively ended their days with a draught of prussic acid on Hampstead Heath and shot dead after a mugging in Switzerland. Or John Mytton, who drank five bottles of port every morning and when that ran out supplemented it with eau de cologne. Or Lord Charles Townshend, killed on the way back from his election at Great Yarmouth in 1796 by either his own hand or that of his brother Frederick.

In fact, for much of its history the whole parliamentary system was soaked in corruption. Rotten boroughs with no real voters lasted well into the nineteenth century; pocket boroughs in the gift of local magnates were still being sold, and voters were still being bribed with cash, in the 1800s; and the likes of Sir William Paxton, who bought his Carmarthenshire seat with 11,070 breakfasts, 36,901 dinners and 25,275 gallons of ale, carried on treating the electorate with food and booze until a series of Corrupt Practices Acts in 1854, 1883 and 1885. Successive royal favourites and prime ministers bought political loyalty with secret service money, James I invented baronetcies and sold them to the wealthy to subsidize the royal purse, the Tories packed the Lords with extra peers to vote through the Treaty of Utrecht in 1713, and both Lloyd George and Austen Chamberlain sold peerages, baronetcies and knighthoods to raise money for their respective parties after the First World War. This is not to sanction corruption, simply to set more recent scandals in historical context.

There are many other parliamentary myths. The red lines in the carpet of the House of Commons are not two sword lengths apart and are a Victorian innovation. The phrase 'toe the line' is of nautical origin and does not come from the Speaker admonishing a member for overstepping the line. MPs were never required to wear hats. The two Houses did not first sit separately in Acton Burnell in 1283. The 'Model Parliament' of 1295 did not fix the composition of parliament. The Scots were not bribed to accept union with England (though the Irish were). The Great Charter of 1215 makes no mention of parliament. Owain Glyndwr did not hold a 'parliament' in Machynlleth in 1404: the one contemporary account, by Adam of Usk, maintains only that he 'held, or counterfeited or made pretence of holding parliaments',[14] and there is no evidence of anyone attending other than a council of nobles.

But perhaps the most dangerous myth of all is that politicians have only ever been out for themselves. You only have to knock on a few doors to hear the cynicism with which MPs are viewed. 'Typical, they only ever come round when they want your vote.' Or, better yet: 'If voting ever changed anything, they'd abolish it.' This two-volume history is written from a different perspective. In my experience most politicians have lofty aspirations – to change the world, to improve the human condition, to transform people's opportunities, to bring peace. Sometimes the most passionate have been the most dangerous. Often the quietest have been the most effective. Invariably they have proved to have feet of clay. Yet each twist of parliament's history has been driven by an attempt to improve upon what was already in place. It has been a constant experiment in making things better, pursued against many challenges and temptations. Edmund Burke put it well when he confessed: 'To be a good Member of Parliament, is, let me tell you, no easy task; especially at this time, when there is so strong a disposition to run into the perilous extremes of servile compliance, or wild popularity.'[15] This is why the Commons starts its business every day with a prayer that MPs 'may never lead the nation wrongly through love of power, desire to please, or unworthy ideals'.

It is impossible fully to comprehend the history of Britain or of parliament without examining the personal entrails of events. With its rowdy confrontations and angry altercations, its fierce antipathies and deep loyalties, its towering personal triumphs and its very public falls from grace, Westminster's parliament has always been a place of personal drama. Within the two-acre sliver of land between the Abbey and the Thames people have been tried, excoriated, humiliated, ostracized, executed and exiled from the body politic. Others have been lionized, risen to great office, performed great service to the nation and even on occasion died with the adulation of the crowds still ringing in their ears. In the main these have been uncommon individuals, imbued both with a vision of how the world should be and with a sense of their own destiny. Few were unambiguously noble. Many were as ambitious for themselves as for the common weal. Most are scarcely remembered today. But their lives, whether complicated or straightforward, were so intertwined with the history of the kingdom that if we ignore the deeply personal aspects of their contribution we miss the true driving force of politics.

That is why this history follows in detail the lives of so many people who passed through parliament – mitred abbots, prince-bishops, lords, knights, burgesses and clergy – because personal conviction, personal loyalty, personal antipathy have framed many of the key moments in that history. Indeed, it is the clashes between different opinions and contrasting personalities, the struggle between reaction and progress, the tension between preserving the past and forging the future, that have characterized the way these isles have made constitutional history – through a process of evolution, not the tidy or deliberate manufacture of a monolith.

PROLOGUE

This is a complex and densely populated story, so it has been divided into two volumes. The first deals with the different strands that came together to form parliament. Starting in 1258 with the first commoners to attend a parliament, it considers the often ignored but equally important parliamentary traditions of Scotland and Ireland and deals with early elections, the development of free speech, the civil wars and the separation of the two houses, ending with the establishment of the Parliament of the United Kingdom of Great Britain and Ireland, or the 'Imperial Parliament' as it was gazetted, in 1801. It takes us from Simon de Montfort to Pitt the Younger via Thomas Cromwell, John Hampden and John Wilkes. The second volume will recount the campaign for reform in the UK parliament, the development of the party system, the collapse of aristocratic dominance, the arrival of working men, the eventual admission of women, the radical effect of two world wars and the many attempts at modern reform. It will include chapters on financial corruption, and on the roles of alcohol and of sexuality. It ends with Margaret Thatcher.

Many have been cynical about parliament; and many still are. T. P. O'Connor (who began that Gladstonian brawl) complained of it that 'the tide of talk rolls on' – though that did not stop him sitting in it for fifty years. The novelist and Unionist MP John Buchan thought of it as a tedious form of opera. And after the Second World War Christopher Hollis MP wrote in *Can Parliament Survive?* that it would be 'cheaper to keep a flock of tame sheep and from time to time drive them through the division lobbies in the appropriate numbers'.[16] More recently, a lethal combination of apathy and anger has inspired profound distrust of politicians, deep scepticism about party politics and a significant fall in voter turnout in elections.

Others, though, have been overly sentimental about parliament and have accepted every Victorian reinvention of our history as gospel truth. One instance makes the point – that of the two red lines on the carpet in the Commons, which every tour guide will tell you are two sword's-lengths apart. It is patently untrue. MPs did wear swords in the Commons in the past. When the Great Remonstrance was agreed in 1641 several MPs reached for their swords. Lord North once managed to catch the wig of Welbore Ellis on his scabbard. General John Burgoyne was thought rather thin-skinned for grasping the pommel of his sword when someone insulted him in the chamber. Eighteenth-century court dress, which ministers were required to wear, included a sword, and when Lord North's government fell Sir Nathaniel Wraxall MP was amazed to see in April 1782 the former opposition members throw off their blue and buff uniforms and return from court as ministers, 'decorated with Swords, Lace and Hair Powder'.[17] But all these moments took place in the old Commons chamber, where there was no carpet and there were no red lines, both of which only arrived with the new Victorian chamber after the fire of 1834. By then nobody wore a sword in the Commons. In fact, the distance between the two benches owes more to the space required for the altar party of a crucifer and two candle-bearers to walk abreast to the altar in the old Chapel of St Stephen's. Yet misty-eyed nationalists, imbued with self-conscious patriotism, adhere to this and many other parliamentary myths as a new Thirty-Nine Articles of religion.

My argument – and the argument of these two volumes – is that neither cynicism nor sentimentalism serves us well, and that Robert Blake was right when he maintained in his history of the Conservative Party that 'all these efforts and struggles, these dramatic changes of fortune, do mean something; that the careers devoted to politics are not a complete waste of time . . . and that it may make a real difference which side prevails in the unending struggle for political power'.[18] The whole point of these two volumes is that when chance plays such a part that a government can be lost by just one vote, when a death or a birth or a love affair can change the course of history, the individual endeavours of so many thousands of men and women are the very stuff that change is made from, if only we combine.

The seal of Simon de Montfort, who in 1258 led the baronial campaign to force King Henry III to accept a set of 'Provisions' severely limiting his power. In 1264 he defeated the king at the battle of Lewes, took power into his own hands and summoned a parliament that included both knights and burgesses, elected as the representatives of the cities and towns of England. Although de Montfort's control of the kingdom did not last long, his vanquisher, later King Edward I, adopted many of his innovations.

1

The First Commoners

A BIOGRAPHY SHOULD BEGIN with a birth. But parliament's evolution in the maelstrom of royal demands, baronial complaints and feudal grievances had no single moment of conception, no instant when the infant came mewling and puking into the world. So let's start instead with a teenager from Denton in Yorkshire, Mauger le Vavasour, who in August 1258 was summoned to Westminster to attend King Henry III's council 'in parliament'. Not because he is the most important figure in the history of parliament. Not because he made a particularly noteworthy speech. But because in October that year he and thirteen others turned up; and we know they did because they had their expenses paid. Kings had conferred with their magnates before. They had debated with their prelates. But these were the first commoners.

The Westminster they encountered was an impressive oasis of architectural beauty in a country blighted by poor harvests, floods and pestilence. According to the contemporary monastic historian Matthew Paris, 'a large number of poor people died and dead bodies were found in all directions, swollen and livid, lying by fives and sixes in pigsties, on dunghills and in the muddy streets'.[1] The royal palace at Westminster, by contrast, was burgeoning. The Great Hall was already nearly 200 years old, its sturdy six-foot-thick stone walls plastered and decorated with ornate paintings and its gallery hung with sumptuous tapestries. Beside this, Henry had started to build a chamber for the queen, another – ostentatiously luxurious – for himself, and a new two-storey chapel in honour of St Stephen to rival the Sainte-Chapelle in Paris. And barely a hundred yards away his life's work, the rebuilding of Westminster Abbey, with its hefty pale Gothic stonework and its flamboyant shrine to Henry's antecedent and spiritual hero, Edward the Confessor, had been under way for thirteen expensive years.

All this extravagant building work could not hide the fact that the foundations on which Henry's reign rested were far from secure. It was not that the king with the drooping eyelid lacked vision. Indeed, he had a very clear idea of what he wanted: to defend or extend his overseas territories and secure England against attack from France or Wales; to increase his own and his family's wealth and influence; and to meet his religious duties as a monarch who showed pity to the poor and glory to God by feeding the hungry and building a magnificent cathedral. This ambitious agenda certainly did not include any such constitutional innovation as the development of a 'parliament'. Yet Henry lacked the personal, political and financial resources to achieve any of his goals. He was prone to sudden mood swings and regularly fell out with his barons, who resented his extravagance and the depredations of his half-brothers, the Lusignans from Poitou, and objected to the vast sums he had already spent on his failed attempts to regain Poitou in 1242 and Gascony in 1253–4. Strapped for cash, he had winkled money out of his subjects through fines and impositions, and closed that drooping eyelid to the abuses by his royal officials, so often that there were acerbic complaints in the 1255 royal assembly that 'there were so many petty kings [reguli] in England that the old times seemed to be renewed'.[2]

Those old times had been terrible. Henry's father King John had a peculiar talent for antagonizing his barons – debauching their wives and daughters (he sired at least twelve illegitimate children), demanding large amounts of their cash in lieu of military service and failing properly to defend the realm by losing Normandy. When he made one round of financial demands too many in 1215, forty barons categorically refused to pay and renounced their duty of homage to the king until he signed a Great Charter (in Latin, the Magna Carta) at Runnymede, guaranteeing a series of basic protections against royal exploitation and establishing both a royal council of twenty-four barons and the principle that general taxation could not be obtained without consent. The subsequent baronial war, which hinged on John's adherence (or otherwise) to the Charter, subsided on his death in 1216, whereupon the barons swung behind the nine-year-old (and therefore infinitely more malleable) Henry and saw off the marauding French in his name. If the barons had learned one thing, it was that they could bring a king to heel – and henceforth, should a future king misbehave, they would always have the Great Charter in their metaphorical back pocket.

When Henry assumed personal rule as an adult, the same grievances resurfaced and, after festering for more than thirty years, came to a head in 1258. Events conspired. The people were ravaged by famine; there was a violent insurgency in Wales; and by the time of the Hoketide meeting (a week after Easter) of the king's council, at which the monarch was joined by his magnates and prelates, on 10 April the English barons were in open revolt at Henry's latest demand. In a desire to extend his sphere of influence, he had unwisely accepted Pope Innocent IV's double-edged offer that Henry's second son Edmund Crouchback become king of Sicily, on condition that England contributed £90,000 towards the ousting of the pope's Hohenstaufen enemies. Henry's plan was not entirely wrong-headed – Sicily was wealthy, and an English candidate would effectively bar a French one – but there was no money in the royal coffers and no political will among the barons for any such expedition, so when Henry proposed finding the £20,000 down payment from a large national levy, the suggestion prompted a swift and forthright set of counter-demands. The barons made themselves plain. The king had lavished too much of the realm's sparse wealth on his foreign relatives, especially his own half-brothers and the queen's family from Provence and Savoie. He had despised and pillaged his subjects, to the ruin of the whole kingdom. As Paris recorded, 'It was also thrown in his teeth, that he was so needy, while others possessed money in abundance, that he could not . . . even check the injurious incursions of the Welsh, who were the very scum of mankind.'[3]

Leading the charge against the king was the charismatic earl of Leicester, Simon de Montfort. The ironies in this were many-layered. De Montfort's central complaint was the king's advancement of foreigners at the expense of the native English, yet de Montfort was himself French. His father's estates lay near Paris, and despite his intense religiosity (he regularly rose at midnight to pray through until dawn, knew the Psalter by heart and dressed with affected simplicity) he had no aversion to self-enrichment. Relations between the king and the earl had gone through many twists and turns over the decades. Henry had generously allowed him to take up his father's claims in Leicester when he arrived in England in 1230 as an importunate orphaned younger son. The king had also gone out of his way to protect de Montfort when he had secretly married Henry's sister Eleanor, against the conventions of the time and despite her recently made vow of chastity. The following year, though, Henry was incensed when de Montfort used the king's name in surety for a debt, and in the ensuing storm de Montfort and his pregnant wife had to flee down the Thames and across to France. Relations were soon repaired – in 1244 Henry gave the earl extensive lands, including Kenilworth Castle, and in 1248 put him in charge of Gascony – but when complaints multiplied about de Montfort's rule, Henry refused to pay his legitimate expenses, and in 1252 he put him on trial in the refectory of Westminster Abbey. Both men again lost their tempers; but as de Montfort had the backing of most of the barons, Henry let the matter drop. Yet again de Montfort left England in high dudgeon, and that same year was reputedly offered the French regency on the death of Queen Blanche of Castile. However, Robert Grosseteste, the bishop of Lincoln, a close ally of de Montfort and his spiritual mentor, intervened and persuaded him that, notwithstanding Henry's failings, de Montfort should remember the good the king had done him. Once again the two men were reconciled.

By the time the king's council met in April 1258, though, de Montfort's discontent had resurfaced – and he had plenty to complain about. Like many others he was opposed to the Sicilian enterprise, but more importantly the exorbitant enrichment of Henry's Lusignan relatives had blocked de Montfort's sons' marital plans; the provisions for the king's marriage to Eleanor of Provence, who came with no money but plenty of Savoyard relatives, had prevented Henry from paying his dowry debts for his sister Eleanor to de Montfort; and in late 1257 Henry's Lusignan half-brother William de Valence had attacked de Montfort's lands. What is more, de Montfort did not just have grievances; he also had allies, including members of the king's own family as well as a group of powerful bishops and barons.

The April council meeting ended with Henry mounting a retreat over his proposed Sicilian levy and making a solemn oath at the shrine of St Edward that he would 'fully and properly amend his old errors and show favour and kindness to his native born subjects'. Still not satisfied that the king would change his ways unless presented with a show of force, a group of seven barons, led by de Montfort, swore allegiance to one another on 12 April and then, armed and accompanied by a host of lesser barons and knights, confronted Henry in Westminster Hall with a demand that the realm henceforth be ruled by a special council of twenty-four men, twelve appointed by the king and twelve by the barons. It worked. Henry immediately caved in and agreed to hold a specially reconvened council at which the details of a new royal settlement would be agreed.

This new council began its deliberations on 9 June, this time in Oxford. The atmosphere here was very different from that of royal Westminster. Along with its usual population of scholars and clerics, many of whom supported attempts to constrain the monarchy, the town was temporarily host to 137 knights, who had been summoned as part of a great muster of troops for the impending war with the Welsh. It seemed as if the whole of England was present, from the most senior cleric to the lowliest squire. The barons felt emboldened and the resulting 'Provisions of Oxford', which Henry had little choice but to accept, went even further than de Montfort had hoped. The king's council would now be permanent, no longer requiring a royal writ of summons, and would consist of just fifteen members, only three of whom would be nominated by the king. In dealing with 'the common business of the realm and of the king', it would appoint the king's ministers and councillors and dispose of funds for both war and peace. There were other changes, too. A national justiciar was appointed (Hugh Bigod), independent of the crown, to provide fair redress for grievances. Sheriffs, the king's representatives in the shires, would henceforth serve for a single year only, and only in the counties where they held lands. Many foreign magnates were to lose the castles Henry had gifted them. And, most significantly of all, there would be three 'parliaments' a year, meeting on dates fixed in advance at intervals of roughly seventeen weeks – on the octave of Michaelmas (6 October), on the morrow of Candlemas (3 February) and on 1 June.

Which brings us to an important point. 'Parliament' was by no means a settled concept at this stage. Although the word (*parlement* in the official language of the court, Norman French) had acquired a mixed currency in the reign of Henry II, sometimes referring in contemporary literature to a general conversation and sometimes to a specially constituted meeting summoned by the king, the first known official use of the word in England was in relation to the deferral of a legal case in November 1236 until the following *parliamentum*.[4] Paris then used it to describe a meeting of bishops and earls in April 1239,[5] the Close Rolls referred to a forthcoming 'king's parliament' in June 1242 (which may never have taken place), and four contemporary annalists name the 1246 assembly of abbots, priors, earls, bishops and barons as a 'parliament'. In all, as the modern historian J. R. Maddicott has pointed out, 'the 23 years between 1235 and 1257 saw some 46 assemblies which could be regarded with reasonable certainty as parliaments, with another eight "possibles"'.[6]

The composition of these assemblies was far from fixed, even among the barons, as there was no fixed peerage guaranteeing an individual a right to attend, and while bishops and archbishops were always present, they were sometimes but not always complemented by priors and abbots, or on occasion by their representatives or 'proctors'. Not surprisingly, given these variations and uncertainties, no single title was used to describe these assemblies, which were severally referred to as the council, the convocation or the *colloquium*.

Another highly significant provision of the Oxford settlement was that the king's council would deal not only with affairs 'of the realm and of the king', but also with legitimate local grievances. To this end the Oxford council resolved that knights (rather than magnates or clerics) be appointed to investigate problems in each county and report back to 'parliament' later in the year. So, on 4 August 1258, Henry wrote to the sheriffs of the thirty-seven counties of England, sending to each a list of local knights from which a number were to be chosen 'to enquire touching excesses, trespasses and injuries committed in that county, and to bring their inquisition personally to Westminster by the octave of Michaelmas, for delivery to the council'.[7] In all bar one county four knights were nominated, but for Yorkshire there were six, giving a neat total of 150. Not all those originally summoned were to make it to Westminster. Peter de Montfort (no relation to Simon), who had presided over the Oxford meeting, sent word that three of the Shropshire knights were 'not fit'; so they were replaced. And when the sheriff of Devon pointed out that two of his were sick he was allowed to appoint substitutes. We can, however, be certain that some of them did attend the parliament, for the partially illegible gall-spattered Close Rolls of November 1258 show that the 'reasonable expenses of coming and returning' to the Michaelmas council were met for the knights from at least ten counties. In the cases of Lincoln and York the knights who attended are named[8] – and are the same as those summoned in August. A further seven counties' knights seem to have arrived later, as their expenses were also met, and again in the case of Huntingdon the names of the attendant knights are the same as those summoned.

So it was that Mauger le Vavasour, together with Robert de Cam (or Cambhou), Giles de Gousle, Simon le Lilling, William of Buketown (or Boketon) and William of Barton, attended the king 'in parliament' from Yorkshire. Let's be clear about what this means – and what it doesn't mean. It doesn't mean these were the first knights summoned to a royal council. As early as 1212 King John, fearful of a plot against his life, instructed his sheriffs to send from their bailiwicks 'six of the more lawful and discreet knights who are to do what we shall tell them';[9] and a year later he called knights, at very short notice, 'to speak with us concerning the affairs of our realm'.[10] The following year John summoned four knights from each county to Oxford for a general assembly, again 'to speak with us concerning the affairs of our realm'.[11] Likewise, in 1226 Henry III ordered eight counties to send four knights each to a meeting to discuss complaints against the king's sheriffs. The meeting was aborted, but a year later another writ was sent to thirty-five counties (the list omits Westmorland and Cornwall, almost certainly accidentally) instructing them to elect four members each, and the meeting went ahead. According to the Tewkesbury Annals, Henry III's *magnum colloquium* of 1237 included an even wider group of knights, freemen, citizens and burgesses – and agreed a tax. Henry's June 1245, February 1248 and May 1253 gatherings – at which, respectively, a common complaint was supported, the king's demand for a tax was refused and funding for the king's expedition to Gascony was agreed – all incorporated knights. In a couple of cases we even have the names of knights who were summoned to these councils. Yet we cannot be sure that any of them actually attended, and we know for certain that some of them refused the summons. So, for instance, on 14 February 1254 the king demanded that the sheriff of Middlesex elect two knights to attend him at Westminster on 26 April to consider a tax, to which the reply came that the only people the sheriff considered suitable were two men called Roger – de la Dune and de Bachewurth – and that both point blank declined to attend. They were not alone. That same year the sheriff of Essex had to substitute another knight in place of Walter de Bibbeworthe, who was too busy managing the king's forest. The contemporary records suggest that the two men who were asked to fill the Middlesex places in 1254 were William son of Reyner and John de Twynne, and that John de Eselington and John de Letewell were 'elected for the whole county of Northumberland'. We know the names of these knights, and we know they were either appointed by the sheriff or elected by the county court, but we cannot be certain that any of them attended Westminster. Indeed, Matthew Paris refers to the 1254 session as a congregation of magnates alone, which would suggest that in the end no knights attended.

All of which means that Mauger le Vavasour and the other knights named on the expenses writs of 1258 are the first commoners (or non-magnates) whose names we still have of whose attendance 'in parliament' we can be certain.[12]

What kind of men were they? By definition they were not magnates, that is to say nobles endowed with hereditary titles and territories. Nor were they rural 'villeins' or ordinary townsfolk. A knight had to have property that would generate an annual income of at least £20 but many were far richer. Several on the two 1258 lists were men of considerable standing within and without their counties. Mauger himself was a scion of a distinguished family. The Vavasours had a pedigree that stretched back to the Conquest. They had held the family seat of Hazlewood near present-day Tadcaster since the time of the Domesday Book and had been major ecclesiastical benefactors under Henry II; Mauger's grandfather, Sir Robert, had been sheriff successively of Lancashire, Nottingham and Derby. The family also had a rebellious, romantic streak to it. Mauger's aunt Maud had been dead for thirty years by the time he got the summons to Westminster, but her fame lived on. Not only had she married Theobald Walter, first Baron Butler, and through him founded a dynasty that would include Anne Boleyn and Elizabeth I, but on his death she married another wealthy figure well-connected at court, Fulke Fitzwarin. Many romantic stories have been written about Fulke and Maud, some of them conflating the histories of two Fulkes, father and son. The story that Fulke had grown up in the court of Henry II with King John but had fallen out with him over a game of chess is probably apocryphal, but it is likely that for at least a couple of years at the start of the thirteenth century

Fulke was outlawed by John, and that during this time he and Maud lived with a group of friends and allies in the forests on the Welsh borders, in striking similarity to the less verifiable tales of Robin Hood and Maid Marian.

Mauger's inclusion in the list of knights is therefore perfectly understandable. He was the younger son of an important Yorkshire family. He held in his own name lands of the requisite value. But, even more importantly, it seems that in the sharply divided kingdom he took the side of the rebel barons, and he may have been selected directly by one or other of the de Montforts. We have no evidence of what grievances he or any of the other knights reported back to the king in 1258, but we do know that in 1265 Mauger took up arms against his royalist father's lands in Addingham in West Yorkshire, and that as a consequence the king granted his father special protection.

Another knight summoned in 1258 was Fulk Peyferer (or Payforer) from Kent. He too had a distinguished pedigree and that year had just got married. His wife, Margaret de Leveland, had recently lost her second husband (and Fulk's near neighbour) Giles de Badlesmere in the war against the Welsh and was an important Kentish heiress in her own right, bringing with her the extremely lucrative hereditary joint positions of Warden of the Fleet Prison and Keeper of the King's House of Westminster, which Fulk held in her name until his death in 1277. In addition, Fulk was to be sheriff of Kent in 1258, 1264 and 1267, and had estates of his own in both Eslinge and at Colbridge in Boughton Malherbe, where the couple made their home.* Like

---

* For 600 years Fulk Peyferer's memorial lay in the south chancel of St Nicholas' Church in Boughton Malherbe, opposite a similar fine Bethersden marble figure of his wife. He disappeared at some point in a Victorian clearout, which means that the earliest remaining effigies of commoners who attended parliament are two statues in Lincolnshire, both of knights lying cross-legged in chainmail, one in St Peter's, Kingerby, and the other in St Peter's, Norton

Mauger, therefore, he was a man of means considerably beyond the £20 knighthood qualification; and he too was of the baronial party, in part, it seems, out of a personal sense of injustice. There was plenty to bind him to his near neighbours and his wife's first husband's family in Kent. Indeed, two generations earlier a Badlesmere had married a Peyferer, and later Fulk's son was to serve alongside Giles's grandson Bartholomew de Badlesmere at the siege of Caerlaverock in 1300 and with him at the Carlisle parliament of 1307. But in the 1260s Fulk was to quarrel incessantly with Gunceline de Badlesmere (Giles's son), and 'completely despaired of being able to sue out any writ against him' because 'Gunceline had so many allies and supporters, namely William de Valence and others of the King's Council'.[13] It is notable that while Fulk was summoned to Westminster in 1258, Gunceline was not.

The Michaelmas meeting of 1258 was, then, an exceptional event, providing commoners like Mauger and Fulk with an opportunity to present real and present grievances to the 'parliament' as newly constituted by the Provisions of Oxford. That is not to say that they were in any proper sense members of parliament, or that the participation of knights or any other non-magnates was yet a permanent feature of such assemblies. The Provisions determined how frequently and when parliament should meet, but not who should be party to it. There was no constant membership, and the gatherings that followed were predominantly meetings of the magnates and prelates exclusively.

Nevertheless, the Oxford assembly did give a wider group of people a hand in the government of the realm. In addition to the fifteen-member king's council, it set up two other bodies: a

Disney: they are of Sir William Disney, who came to Westminster with Fulk and Mauger in 1258, and of his son, also William, who sat four times as knight of the shire for Lincoln.

baronial committee of twelve and a commission of twenty-four that was to consider new taxation. The higher nobility and epis-copacy still loomed large in all three: the commission included three bishops, six earls, Peter de Savoy (Queen Eleanor's uncle) and the count of Aumale (Albemarle), and the king's council had two bishops and seven earls. But lesser property-owners also began to make their presence felt. The Oxford assembly seems both to have increased the powers of the barons whose titles were so established that they always attended the king, and to have brought to the fore lesser barons and knights. Indeed, the distinction between barons and knights may have been blurred more than has generally been accepted. Thus while Roger de Somery, who was on both the baronial committee and the tax commission, was undoubtedly already a baron, Richard de Grey was not summoned as such until 1299, but nevertheless sat on the king's council, as did Sir James Audley, a knight. Even Peter de Montfort, Philip Basset and Basset's son-in-law Hugh Despenser, each of whom owned lands worth more than £120 a year, were not unambiguously barons as yet. They were to play significant roles in the ensuing political turbulence and were of baronial families; but their status came not from ennoblement but from their wealth, their active engagement in the body politic and their personal connection to the leaders of the baronial party.

The bishops also played an important role at this point. One of the opening statements of the Great Charter was the declara-tion that the Church of England 'shall be free' and its rights inviolable, but the church was a constant battleground through-out the thirteenth century. It was wealthy, it held special privileges and it had the power to excommunicate those who refused the king's or the pope's authority. Consequently, as well as trying to exact taxes from the church, Henry regularly attempted to intervene in the election of bishops to impose his own candidates on the more pliable cathedral chapters. Nowhere did he try harder than with the important and asset-rich see of Winchester. First, in 1238, he put forward his half-brother William de Valence; then he tried his wife's uncle Boniface of Savoy, who at least had the advantage of being ordained, but was, according to Paris, 'totally incompetent for such a dignified position'.[14] Neither got past the chapter. However, in 1241 Henry managed to get Boniface elected as archbishop and eventually enthroned at Canterbury, and in 1250 another of his half-brothers, the barely theologically literate and as yet unordained Aymer de Valence, was elected bishop of Winchester (although he was never consecrated). All this ecclesiastical jiggery-pokery availed Henry little, though, as the Lusignan Aymer and the Savoyard Boniface did not see eye to eye. Indeed, one dispute between the episcopal outreaches of the royal family saw Lambeth Palace plundered in 1252, Archbishop Boniface's money, jewels and silver stolen and his servants taken hostage. The internecine strife reached its apogee in the Provisions of Oxford: Boniface was appointed to the council and readily signed up to the banishment of the Lusignans, including Aymer.

The only other bishop elected to the new king's council, Walter de Cantilupe, bishop of Worcester, was a very different figure. His father and elder brother had been fiercely loyal counsellors to King John, but Walter was a committed supporter of the nationalist and reformist principles espoused by Robert Grosseteste, the bishop of Lincoln, and angrily opposed the highhanded treatment of the English church meted out by successive popes. On Grosseteste's death in 1253 Cantilupe became chief ecclesiastical spokesman for the reformists – and in the second baronial war of the 1260s, their military chaplain. The Oxford assembly gave one other bishop a key role as a member of the baronial committee of twelve. Fulk Basset, whose younger brother Sir Philip was also on the commission, had become baron of Headington in 1241 when their elder brother Gilbert, himself a thorn in the royal flesh, was killed in a hunting accident. Elected bishop of London that same year against the king's wishes, Fulk Basset had, like Cantilupe, opposed extortionate papal demands for church taxes and also Boniface's attempts to enforce them (which included arriving at St Paul's Cathedral with a cuirass glinting under his archiepiscopal garb, striking the sub-dean of St Bartholomew's to the ground and trampling him underfoot). Fulk was a man of equal determination to the archbishop. When both pope and king were against him he is said to have declared that 'the king and pope, who are stronger than I, may take from me my bishopric, which yet they cannot do by right. They may take away my mitre, but my helmet will be left.'[15] Alarmed by his reformist sympathies, when Basset died of the plague the year after the Oxford assembly, the pope tried to introduce two extra papalist canons into the London cathedral chapter to ensure the election of a more malleable new bishop. The plan backfired: the pair were butchered by reformist Londoners.

Historians of this period have tended to focus on the barons' confrontation with the king or the bishops' with both king and pope, but accounts of the Michaelmas parliament of 1259 suggest that divisions lower down the social scale were just as strongly felt. According to the annals of the Benedictine abbey of Burton-upon-Trent, the 'community of bachelors' – which almost certainly means the knights – forcefully complained that the barons had as yet done little for the common good ('ad utilitatem reipublicae').[16] The protest led directly to yet more reforms. A new ordinance forbidding sheriffs from taking bribes was promulgated, and an improved set of Provisions was agreed, banning a wide range of exploitative practices including the *murdrum* and *beaupleder* fines (for accidental deaths and mistaken judgments) and limiting 'suit of court' (the power of a lord to insist that tenants attend his court). These were precisely what the towns and counties of England had been complaining about, and even though the knights are not expressly mentioned as attending the final ceremony in Westminster Hall in 1259 when these new Provisions of Westminster were declared, and when Boniface in full canonicals as archbishop of Canterbury proclaimed excommunicate anyone who did not adhere to them, it is likely that knights had a hand in the drafting and the likes of Mauger le Vavasour and Fulk Peyferer were present.

Henry had signed up to the Provisions. He swore an oath to uphold them. But from the outset he sought to undermine them. In 1260 he forced Hugh Bigod, the justiciar, to cancel the Hoketide parliament as he was in France. Then, after mounting a convincing reconciliation at the May parliament with his son Edward, who had temporarily supported the reformers, Henry submitted de Montfort to a second show trial in July. By January 1261 Henry was so opposed to the Provisions that he summoned parliament to the Tower of London rather than to Westminster – and the reformers refused to attend. By the summer he was in open defiance of his oath. Infuriated, the triumvirate of de Montfort, Richard de Clare and Bishop Cantilupe summoned three knights from every county to meet with them in St Albans on 21 September and were promptly trumped by the king, who insisted that the same knights come to him at Windsor. So far as we know, neither meeting happened, but the process of claim and counter-claim was now in motion, with both de Montfort and Henry seeking justification from the pope and making appeals to the body politic of England.

In 1264 came a confrontation that had been foreshadowed six years earlier. In July 1258 Henry had been caught in a violent thunderstorm on the Thames and forced to put ashore at the bishop of Durham's palace, where he met de Montfort. The earl asked what the king was afraid of, as the storm had already passed. 'Not jestingly and with a severe look,' Henry replied: 'I fear thunder and lightning beyond measure, but by God's head I fear you more than all the thunder and the lightning in the world.'[17] His suspicions were to prove well merited. Events moved swiftly at the beginning of 1264. The French king's attempt to reconcile the opposing sides failed, so de Montfort led the defenders of the Provisions against the king, allied himself with the Welsh prince Llewelyn ap Gruffydd to attack Roger Mortimer's lands on the Welsh borders and sacked the city of Worcester. This second barons' war was a bloody affair. Bishop Cantilupe negotiated a truce that ended the battle for Gloucester, but that did not stop Prince Edward from exacting a fearsome revenge on the city's people, who had supported the reformers. The battle for Northampton saw around eighty reformers captured by the king, including Peter de Montfort and Simon de Montfort's son. It was not, however, until 14 May that de Montfort and the king faced each other directly in battle at Lewes. Henry had far superior forces, but de Montfort's tactical overnight decision to range his troops along the ridge of the downs won the day. The royalists were routed; Henry and Edward fled to the town's Cluniac priory and were eventually taken prisoner. Within six weeks a new parliament had been called in Henry's name but with de Montfort's authority. It included prelates, magnates and six knights elected from each county to discuss 'our business and the business of our realm'. To all intents and purposes de Montfort now ruled England.

De Montfort's summoning of elected knights was innovative enough, but that December he went further. He cut the number of magnates by more than half to twenty-three by summoning only reformers, while also ennobling allies such as Hugh Despenser. He included a large number of prelates and other church leaders. And he cut the number of knights to two per county, but supplemented them with two burgesses (borough freemen) from each town. The precise list of towns to be thus represented for each county was to be decided by the county sheriff, and it was for the county courts to elect who should attend. The writ of summons is interesting. Sent on 14 December 1264, soon after the release of Henry's son Edward, it starts:

> To provide happily for his deliverance, and to confirm and finally complete the full security tranquillity and peace, to the honour of God and the advantage of the whole realm, and also for certain other matters concerning our realm, which we do not wish to settle without your counsel and that of our prelates and magnates, it is necessary that we should have discussion with them.

Those summoned were called 'to treat on these things' and 'to lend us your counsel'.[18] All in all, de Montfort's 1265 parliament – a long one, running from late January to early March – with its inclusion of a wide range of representatives and the emphasis on its consultative role, amounted to a fuller declaration of a monarchy constrained by a parliamentary constitution than anything else England was to muster for another 300 years.

The burgesses who attended this assembly were not, however, the first of their kind to be gathered in the service of the national administration. In 1204 Geoffrey Fitz Peter had gathered sixty burgesses from the Cinque Ports* in the king's name, and in 1213 King John again summoned the Cinque Ports' representatives, together with a group of magnates, to talk about

* The Cinque Ports of Hastings, New Romney, Hythe, Dover and Sandwich were considered so strategically important for the defence of the realm that under a Royal Charter of 1155 they held special privileges in exchange for the duty to maintain a fleet for the crown in case of war.

defending the realm. There was a similar assembly in Dover in 1235. In both 1231 and 1241 Henry gathered congregations of Jews from each city or county that had a Jewish population, and the January 1237 parliament included 'freemen' according to the Close Rolls and 'burgesses and many others' according to the Annals of Tewkesbury.[19] Nevertheless, this parliament of de Montfort's was the first occasion at which burgesses were elected to come and treat generally with the magnates, the prelates and the king, and it marked a tacit acceptance that the whole realm could not be fully represented by magnates or their scions alone. De Montfort was no fool. He knew the dangers inherent in effectively usurping the power of the king. He was keen to gather the whole of the reforming party to lend him a quasi-regal authority and give credence to the baronial grievances. Although some of the unnamed knights and burgesses may well have departed before the final ceremonies in Westminster Hall on 17 March at which nine bishops (again) proclaimed excommunicate those who opposed the Provisions, de Montfort had secured at least the semblance of national support.

It was not to last. His attempt to rule the country in line with the Provisions and in the name of a captive king might have succeeded, had not his own rapacious acquisitiveness undermined his moral argument and had he not failed to tackle the factionalism within his own ranks. As it was, de Montfort's days were numbered. Some of the bishops, including Boniface of Canterbury, abandoned him; the pope excommunicated the barons; Gloucester switched allegiance in protest at de Montfort's deal with the Welsh prince Llewelyn; Prince Edward escaped and mustered an army; and the marcher lords, including Roger Mortimer, rallied to the royalist cause. Within weeks de Montfort was cornered by the royal forces at Evesham in Worcestershire. The ensuing particularly bloody battle, fought on 4 August in a fierce summer thunderstorm, saw de

Montfort's forces easily overwhelmed. Little mercy was shown. De Montfort's son Henry led a list of knights and barons who, instead of being offered the customary opportunity to surrender, were hacked down, including Peter de Montfort and Hugh Despenser. In all at least 30 and maybe as many as 160 reformist knights were killed, along with several thousand other soldiers. A local monk complained that the chancel of the church was full of corpses and blood ran down the stairs into the crypt. As for de Montfort himself, un-horsed, he defended himself with his sword but was stabbed and cut down by Roger Mortimer; his hands, his feet, his testicles and his head were cut off by William Mautravers, who sent the gory head to Mortimer's wife Maud. Even the arch-royalist contemporary annalist Thomas Wykes of Oseney was shocked by the needless brutality.

Considering the lengthy agonies of the successive baronial plaints and rebellions that Henry had to contend with, he might have been expected, following his triumph at Evesham, to dismantle everything de Montfort had created. He didn't, partly because the battle of Evesham did not immediately end the war and partly because many of those who supported him against de Montfort nonetheless subscribed to the reformists' principles and objected to Henry's and the pope's exactions. So, although the surviving rebels were immediately dispossessed of their lands, Henry soon restored them, and in November 1267 held a parliament at Marlborough at which he volunteered a new statute, or codified law to be agreed by the king in parliament,* which in large measure retained the anti-exploitative measures of the Provisions of Oxford and Westminster but ditched the structure that had so limited the king's powers. As one

---

* The development of statute law in England would fill a book in itself, but the idea that the law would not just be promulgated by the king or developed through the accretion of precedents in case law, but laid out and codified in statute as agreed by the king and parliament, rapidly gained traction.

chronicler put it: 'The king conceded that the statutes of Oxford should be observed, except in a few things.'[20]

One other respect in which Henry may have followed de Montfort's lead is in summoning not just magnates but knights and even burgesses, as the Marlborough meeting was reported as including attendees 'from among the greater and the lesser men',[21] and in March 1268 Henry also summoned representatives of twenty-seven specially selected towns to a meeting at Westminster. As he had begun after Evesham, so circumstances now forced him to continue. When Prince Edward launched a new crusade in June 1268, Henry sought a new tax to pay for it at a parliament held in York that September, but was rebuffed on the grounds that although the nobles were present he needed the assent of lesser folk – probably the knights. A month later another assembly included the lesser clergy and knights from the shires, but still Henry did not get his tax, and it was only at the October 1269 parliament – which included knights and the lower clergy – gathered to witness Archbishop Walter Giffard of York's translation of the relics of St Edward the Confessor into the new shrine at Westminster Abbey that Henry made any headway. Even then, he had to deal first with the knights' grievances against Jewish moneylending, and the general tax was finally conceded at a parliament in April 1270, after Henry had reaffirmed and republished the Great Charter and its companion the Forest Charter of 1217. Henry would never acknowledge the debt his new style of government owed to the Provisions of Oxford, nor would his overarching statute refer to them; but the argument had been won that the king could not rule without regular counsel afforded him by a convened council[22] or parliament that included more than just his friends and family.

So many of the knights of the shires and burgesses representing the cities and towns of England were disputatious lawyers (such as these 'princes of the law' from a fourteenth-century manuscript) that several kings tried to exclude all men of law from the Commons. This was such a success at Coventry in 1404 that the session was known as the 'Illiterate Parliament' or the 'Parliament of Dunces'.

2

Subjected Thus

ON 2 MAY 1774 A GROUP OF antiquaries gathered with the dean of Westminster Abbey in the chapel that Henry III had built to house the shrine of his revered predecessor, Edward the Confessor. Their interest was in one of the plainest monuments: the long, unpolished stone coffin in which Edward I was buried. The lid came off with ease, as did the lid of a further marble coffin inside. The king, his shrunken body apparently intact, was dressed in cloth of gold and red silk and satin; he carried a long sceptre in each hand and an open crown on his head. The observers studied his collapsed, beardless face and measured him: six feet two inches exactly. It is not surprising that he was considered impressive in his time and nicknamed 'Longshanks'. But later generations garlanded him with even more impressive titles. To the seventeenth-century jurist and MP Sir Edward Coke he was the 'English Justinian' who had first codified English law; to Bishop William Stubbs, writing at the end of the nineteenth century, he was the architect in 1295 of the 'Model Parliament' who had introduced 'the self-regulating action of the body politic'.[1] If parliament had a father, so Coke and Stubbs would argue, it was Edward I.

Yet you don't have to be one of the 'hammered' Scots to see that this swarthy warrior king with a lisp was no saint. He had a fearsome temper. People thought him as brave as a lion but as duplicitous as a leopard. He subdued Wales and Scotland in pitiless and expensive wars, he treated the Jews with manifest cruelty, and he died penniless. He supported de Montfort in his early campaigns against Henry III and he summoned parliaments with elected representatives, but the eulogies are misplaced. Take the parliament of earls, barons, bishops, clerics, knights and burgesses that he summoned to Shrewsbury in the autumn of 1283 to witness 'the trial and condemnation' of Dafydd son of Gruffydd. It was a grisly affair. After a lifetime of switching allegiance between the English crown and his elder brother the Welsh Prince Llewelyn, Dafydd had been captured on 22 June at Nanhysglain and brought to Edward's camp at Rhuddlan. Within a week Edward had summoned parliament to meet at the end of September, by which time Dafydd had been hauled to Chester and then to Shrewsbury Abbey. The trial was swift. Three days later he was dragged through the town behind his own horse, hanged alive, then cut down and resuscitated so that he could witness his own bowels being ripped out and burned. Finally he was sliced in four and fed to the dogs. It was the first notable case of a prince being hanged, drawn and quartered for high treason. Edward clearly thought it suitable entertainment for a parliament.

This was not a matter of high constitutional principle. Nor was it part of any great plan. Thus far, no two of Edward's parliaments had been identical in personnel, in timing, in venue or in the business transacted. His first, held at Easter 1275 (three years after he inherited the throne), gathered earls, barons, prelates, four knights drawn from those who were more 'discreet [i.e. learned] in law' for each county, four or six burgesses for each town and the lower clergy: it considered petitions and a lengthy new legal code, the Statute of Westminster. His second omitted the burgesses, the next twelve were held roughly twice a year with prelates and magnates alone, and then came a two-year gap during which the king occupied himself with war on the Welsh and a backlog of private petitions and complaints accumulated. Edward, fully aware that convincing kingship required that he put on a good show, now needed a parliament that was both declaratory and businesslike, part trial, part military celebration, part national admonition to the king's enemies; so this time he gathered not just the magnates and prelates, but the knights of the shires and a smattering of burgesses from London and the twenty most important towns, to witness his public statement of ruthless intent. Shrewsbury fitted the bill by virtue of its proximity to Wales, but was neither large enough nor well enough provisioned to accommodate all those summoned, which included 110 barons and earls and 74 knights. So within a few days of the trial parliament decamped to the extensive ancestral home of Robert Burnell, the king's closest adviser, just 8 miles away in the village of Acton Burnell.

Burnell was a controversial figure. There were rumours that despite being a bishop he had a mistress called Juliana and had sired a series of daughters. Many in the church were equally critical of his greedy simultaneous acquisition of several lucrative ecclesiastical posts. Yet his closeness to the king was undisputed: he had worked in Edward's household since 1257 and served as one of his four 'lieutenants' while he was away on crusade. Edward tried to secure the archbishopric of Canterbury for him on three occasions, but was frustrated by the pope; so it was as mere archdeacon of York that Burnell was appointed Lord Chancellor of England*

* The Lord Chancellor, a role dating back at least as far as the Norman Conquest, was the king's principal adviser and minister, charged with running the Chancery (where all official documents were produced) and acting as chief spiritual confidant and Keeper of the Great Seal. When the House of Lords started to sit separately, the Lord Chancellor acted as its spokesman.

on 21 September 1274, although the following year he was made bishop of Bath and Wells. Burnell was the dominant influence in Edward's early reign, drafting and presenting the far-reaching Statutes of Westminster that were agreed in 1275, 1285 and 1290, establishing a pattern of parliaments meeting at Easter and Michaelmas, running the central departments of government while Edward was at war, removing the Chancery to Westminster, mounting a complete reform of the royal finances and administration, and attempting to resolve the question of who should rule in Scotland (a mission in the course of which he died). He also acquired a vast fortune, yet the evidence suggests he was unusually rigorous in dealing with corrupt officials. His administrative flair alone intimates that if Edward's parliaments had a midwife, it was Burnell.

It is difficult to be precise about the series of events at Acton Burnell in Michaelmas 1283, although it seems that Burnell, who had lost two brothers in the Welsh conflict, played a key role. Local tradition goes that when the parliament removed to Acton Burnell, the barons met together with the king in the recently enlarged manor house while the knights and burgesses gathered in a tithe barn on the estate to consider the Statute of Merchants. Henry Hallam, writing in 1853, presumed that the barons were sitting in judgment at Shrewsbury and that 'the Commons adjourned to Acton Burnell' and gave their 'consent' to the statute.[2] The implication is that this was the first meeting of the putative 'Commons', even though only twenty-one towns were represented. There are problems with this account, however. The king was already present at Acton Burnell from 29 September, the day Dafydd's trial began, and remained there for most of October. Moreover, the only supposed evidence for the 'Commons' meeting separately is the fact that on 12 October a statute was agreed, a function that was often reserved to parliaments that included non-magnates. Certainly several statutes were agreed in full parliaments. In addition to Burnell's first Statute of Westminster, which laid down among other things that 'elections ought to be free',[3] and was agreed in front of knights and burgesses, the Statutes of Jewry and of the Exchequer were both agreed at the second 1275 parliament, which included knights. In that it dealt with the problems of mercantile debts, the statute of 1283 would have pleased burgesses and knights. But there were other early statutes that were simply agreed by the king's council or the magnates, including the Statutes of Gloucester (1278), Mortmain (1279) and Religious Men (1279), the last of which was made 'on the advice of the prelates, earls and other faithful subjects of our realm, who are of our council'.[4] The king could and did make statutes either alone or without the benefit of knights and burgesses. So there is no definitive proof that the knights and burgesses first sat alone in 1283, and the Victorian historian Sir William Betham is probably right in commenting that 'no small portion of what we have been in the habit of calling history is romance'.[5]

What we can be certain of is that, in Shrewsbury at least, knights and burgesses were present at the parliament of autumn 1283. The records give us a hint of the kind of people selected to attend. Gloucestershire sent two knights, Sir Walter de Helyun (or Helion), who lived with his wife Alice at Much Marcle near Ledbury in Herefordshire and held lands in Edgeworth, and Roger le Rous (his family name supposedly referred to their ruddy complexion), who was born in Harescombe in Gloucestershire but established his family home 10 miles away at Duntzbourne-Rouse. Both had been itinerant justices under Henry III; both were men trusted in the law. The six representatives from London, by contrast, who had the task of taking Dafydd's severed head back to London to be displayed at the Tower, were a more motley crew. Henry le Waleys and Gregory de Rokesley, the sitting mayor and his predecessor, were both wealthy and often truculent merchants who dominated London's turbulent political life from 1273 to 1299. They were joined by two aldermen, John de Gisors (whose father had been a Montfortian mayor) and Ralph Crepyn, plus a tailor called Philip and a merchant called Joce. Two years later Crepyn was wounded in a violent brawl with one Laurence Duket over the attentions of a woman called Alice. When Duket sought sanctuary in Bow Church, Crepyn's friends found him, murdered him and dressed it up as suicide. When the truth came out, Alice was burned alive, sixteen others were hanged, and Crepyn was deprived of his aldermanry and left to languish in the Tower.

The Shrewsbury parliament was undoubtedly an experiment born of necessity, but then so was every one of Edward I's parliaments. Not that Stubbs saw it that way. For him, Edward's 1295 parliament – for which, exceptionally, a full set of returns naming every knight and burgess still exists – was the model, 'a pattern for all future assemblies of the nation', as it 'may be accepted as fixing finally the right of shire and borough representation'.[6] Tidy as the thesis was, it has subsequently been proved wrong in every particular. For the composition of parliament continued to vary long after 1295. Only four of Edward I's subsequent parliaments (in 1296, 1300, 1305 and 1307) had the same composition as that of 1295; in the last thirteen years of his reign knights and burgesses were included in just eleven parliaments out of twenty; and it was not until the start of Edward III's reign in 1327 that the Chancery writs of summons termed a royal assembly a 'parliament' only if it included representation from the counties and towns.

Nor was the attendance of the clergy settled. Although all twenty-one bishops of England and Wales had since 1164 been required 'to be present at the judgements of the king's court unless a case shall arise of judgement concerning life and limb' (that is, they were never allowed to take part in a decision that would occasion a death),[7] the role of the lower clergy was less clear. Fiscally significant because they alone could unlock much of the wealth of the parishes and cathedrals, politically powerful because of their dual allegiance to the pope and the king, and administratively useful because of their clerical skills, the nation's priesthood was a body of men that all three Edwards were keen to draw into their ambit. The church maintained that the king had no power to require them to attend a lay court, but Edward I ensured the 1295 parliament included thirteen cathedral deans, ten priors and sixty archdeacons, plus one proctor per cathedral and two proctors for the parish clergy of each diocese – a total of 148 men. Again, this did not permanently set their attendance, as the proctors of the lesser clergy reluctantly attended just five of Edward I's last twenty parliaments and by the end of the 1330s the two Convocations of York and Canterbury, which they also attended, had become the central bodies for considering clerical measures and taxation. Often the proctors were present more in spirit than in the flesh: in 1322 Master David Fraunceys stood in for his bishop, all four of his diocesan archdeacons, and the clergy of both cathedral and parishes – yet in one form or another the lesser clergy continued to attend parliaments late into the fourteenth century.

There was no concept of a fixed baronage, either. For the most part, once the king had summoned a magnate he continued to summon him or his male heir thereafter, but the second and third Edwards meddled with the list of lords, increasing the number of earls from six to ten, allowing additional individuals to crenellate their manors (a privilege reserved to barons), giving out senior titles to royal favourites and introducing the new title of 'duke'. In addition, some men who were summoned as barons seem later to have slipped down the aristocratic ladder, such as John of Wigton and Ranulf de Frescheville, both of whom were summoned as magnates to the Salisbury parliament of 1297, but attended parliament as knights in 1301.

Far from a 'model' being established in 1295, then, parliament was still very much an improvisation, and was to remain so throughout the era of the three Edwards to 1377, even as revolution frequently bared its teeth in parliament and thereby transformed parliament itself.

The first confrontation began between 1294 and 1297, when the king demanded not just new taxes but unpaid military assistance in France. Robert Winchelsey, the archbishop of Canterbury, and Roger Bigod, the 5th earl of Norfolk, led the opposition, producing a set of angry remonstrances and a demand for either a new charter or re-affirmation of the Great Charter of 1215 and the Forest Charter of 1217. With Edward away at war in Scotland, the regency government initially backed down and reaffirmed the old charters, but in 1298 Norfolk persuaded parliament to refuse the king's demand for a lay subsidy.* The row persisted, with Edward again being denied a tax at the very full Lent parliament of 1300 unless he adhered to a new set of charters. No parliament was held that autumn, but the same two knights and burgesses from each county and borough were summoned to Lincoln the following January for a new parliament, which started with Roger Brabazon, Chief Justice of the King's Bench, demanding a subsidy of a fifteenth on behalf of the king. The reply came, uniquely in this period, not from a magnate or a bishop, but from one of the Lancashire knights, who was now at his third parliament: Henry of Keighley,

---

* A lay subsidy was a direct tax levied on the laity (as opposed to the clerical subsidies levied on the church) as a percentage (a tenth or a fifteenth) of the assessed value of their estates. It was expected that lay subsidies, unlike other forms of royal financing, would only be sought in special circumstances such as war.

who presented a bill of demands which focused for the most part on the local administration of sheriffs and the county courts, but also included the now perennial insistence that the king observe the charters. It was a bold move, and he was lucky that there was no immediate reprisal for his insolence. Six years later, Edward finally got his way. Having persuaded the pope to remove Archbishop Winchelsey and to release him from his oath on the charters, he got the magnates, prelates and knights sitting together to agree to grant him a tenth, and the burgesses, sitting apart on this occasion, to fork out a twentieth. Having thus over-turned the parliamentary decisions of 1300 and 1301, Edward immediately took his revenge against the intrepid Keighley, imprisoning him for the best part of a year.

The second major confrontation started virtually the moment Edward II succeeded his father in 1307. So uninterested was the new king in the affairs of state, and so recklessly gener-ous in the gifts of patronage, money and power that he lavished on a series of personal protégés, that the barons were provoked into equal measures of envy, *amour propre* and righteous indig-nation. Political life rapidly came to be dominated by feuds between the barons on the one side and the king and his favoured counsellors on the other. Indeed, the battle lines had been drawn up before his accession, when Prince Edward had demanded that his father grant the lands of Ponthieu to his close confidant (and possibly lover), the humbly born Gascon Piers Gaveston. Infuriated or scandalized, the king tore out chunks of his son's hair and threw him out of his chamber and Gaveston out of the kingdom. On taking the throne, Edward II swiftly recalled Gaveston, thereby precipitating a new confrontation with the barons, who demanded and secured his exile in the April 1308 parliament. Edward allowed Gaveston to return the following year, whereupon the barons, led by Edward's cousin, Thomas, 2nd earl of Lancaster (who was particularly riled by

Gaveston's teasing of him as 'the fiddler'), resolved to bring the favourite down. Several nobles refused to attend the 1309 parliament if Gaveston were present and, once he was dismissed, forced Edward to set up a group of men to 'ordain' reform of the kingdom. When these 'Ordinances' were finally presented to parliament in 1311, they again included a demand that Gaveston be banished. Edward had little choice but to agree, and Gaveston left the country on 3 November – only to return in December and thereby precipitate another minor war with the barons, led by the earls of Pembroke, Lancaster and Surrey, who proceeded to chase down both king and favourite. When Gaveston was captured at Scarborough he was initially given safe escort by Pembroke but was then seized by the earl of Warwick, who had him run through and beheaded on the earl of Lancaster's land. It was a significant moment. With Gaveston dead, the barons' campaign lost its impetus, but Edward's problems were not at an end. Two years later his forces were crushed by the Scots at Bannockburn and he had to flee ignominiously by ship to England, where the barons finished off his humiliation at the York parliament of September 1314 by forcing him to accept the Ordinances and appoint Lancaster as regent.

No amount of constitutional reform could change Edward's personality, though, and by 1318 he was becoming more and more reliant on a new protégé, Hugh Despenser, for whom Edward tried to secure titles and land. What most incensed the barons, though, was Edward's tendency to take counsel exclusively from Despenser and his father. So the baronial faction, again led by Lancaster, this time with Humphrey de Bohun, the earl of Hereford, took their cause to the July 1321 parliament, where they secured the indictment and exile of the Despensers, against the wishes of the king. Their victory was brief, though: over the next year Edward gained the upper hand, and when Lancaster and Hereford took arms against the Despensers and the king at Boroughbridge in north Yorkshire, they were roundly defeated by troops led by Sir Andrew Harclay. Hereford's death was excruciating. As he led his troops across a wooden bridge under a hail of arrows, he was spotted by a pikeman who was hiding under the bridge and who thrust his pike up through the planks directly into Hereford's backside and twisted it into his intestines. Soon it was a rout. As for Lancaster, who had carried Edward the Confessor's sword at Edward II's coronation, the king allowed him to be beheaded rather than hanged, drawn and quartered as he was of royal blood.

Throughout these episodes parliament was an important venue for baronial feuding and reconciliation, for attempts to reform the monarchy and for the king's resistance. Some have taken this to mean that parliament and the elected representatives in particular were irrelevant. It is true that the Ordinances of 1311 were largely the work of the barons and represented their obsessions. But, despite the fact that there is no evidence that Gaveston was particularly hated outside the baronial circle, both the king and the barons were keen to recruit the wider populace to their cause – well aware that, as in 1283, a parliament that included knights and burgesses was a perfect setting to show that neither side was just settling private scores. Moreover, the articles for reform presented in April 1309 included a complaint that the knights and burgesses had nobody to whom they could present petitions in parliament, which strongly suggests that while the barons were doing the heavy lifting, the knights were at least involved in the ongoing disaffection.

Even if all the confrontations thus far were in essence baronial disputes, Edward II's final struggle gave parliament a dramatic new role. The French king Charles IV demanded that Edward pay him homage for Gascony. Edward, as pig-headed and capricious as ever, refused and instead sent his wife Isabella (Charles's sister) to mediate, followed by the young prince, his heir. Since Isabella had understandably been complaining for ages that Gaveston and the Despensers had mistreated her, this was a dangerous move – a danger exacerbated when Roger Mortimer, who was probably Isabella's lover, set off for Paris and joined her in planning an invasion clearly aimed at toppling her husband. They moved swiftly as soon as they landed, garnering support from the new earl of Lancaster who tracked down, hanged and beheaded the elder Despenser in revenge for his father. Edward fled to south Wales in the hope of raising an army alongside the younger Despenser, but was captured in November 1326 near Tonyrefail and taken to Kenilworth Castle.

With the country now under the control of Isabella and Mortimer, the question was what to do with the king. Isabella ruled out regicide, but with no prospect of Edward voluntarily relinquishing the throne, she summoned parliament in her husband's name to meet on 7 January 1327 and dispatched two bishops, Adam of Orleton (Hereford) and John Stratford (Winchester) to demand Edward's attendance, thereby recognizing that there could be no true parliament without the king. Edward, also aware of this, refused to budge, and by 12 January the bishops were back at Westminster. Orleton, a long-time opponent of the king who later alleged that he had committed sodomy, addressed the full complement of magnates, knights and burgesses, playing on their sympathy for the queen and asking whether they would prefer Edward or his thirteen-year-old son as king. There was no clear answer. The next move came at a magnificent feast that night, when a group of prelates and magnates drew up 'articles of accusation', and the following morning a great collection of magnates, prelates, knights and burgesses swore on oath at the Guildhall that they would support the Ordinances of 1311 and uphold Isabella's son Edward. With the groundwork for a possible parliamentary deposition thus laid, parliament itself was assembled in the Great Hall in the afternoon. Mortimer began proceedings by reading out the articles of accusation while his ally Thomas Wake, accompanied by a large crowd of intimidating Londoners, made encouraging noises. Orleton and Stratford then preached to further encouragement from Wake. Finally the unimpressive archbishop of Canterbury, Walter Reynolds, erstwhile Chancellor and confidant to Edward, who had initially excommunicated the invaders but had been terrified into support for Isabella when the bishop of Exeter, Walter Stapledon, was dragged from his horse and murdered by the London mob, read out the full indictment and urged that the teenage boy be proclaimed king, to which parliament apparently unanimously responded, 'So be it', before singing the Latin hymn 'Gloria, laus et honor'. Only the archbishop of York and the bishops of Lincoln, Rochester and Carlisle abstained. Two days later a group including knights and burgesses was sent to tell Edward that he had a choice of either abdicating in favour of his son or being deposed and having some other figure selected. After a stern lecture from Orleton, Edward buckled and, weeping bitter tears, agreed to his own deposition, before William Trussell withdrew the oaths of homage to the king 'on behalf of all those named in his proxy'.[8] Thus was a deposition transformed into an abdication, and parliament acquired the apparently legitimate power to remove a king.

Again, it can be alleged that this was merely baronial politics in action and that parliament was no more than the setting for the conflict. But after Boroughbridge and in the run-up to Isabella's invasion the elected representatives were more vocal than their baronial counterparts, presenting a series of petitions and amalgamating them into one document or 'bill' in three separate parliaments (February and October 1324 and November 1325). Moreover, while the elected representatives were only very rarely the prime movers in political matters at this stage, they were important observers. The very fact that Mortimer and Isabella resolved to orchestrate the deposition of Edward in parliament betrays their nagging guilt that they were acting illegally and their fear that without creating a perception of common assent their *coup d'état* would fail. Indeed, one historical account put that very thought in the mouth of the archbishop, who chose as the text for his homily to parliament the phrase 'the people's voice is the voice of God' (*vox populi vox dei*) and included the assertion that the deposition would only happen 'if you unanimously consent' (*si unanimiter consentitis*).[9] The very fact that parliament's consent was sought in 1327 granted it a power to anoint events that it had not realized it enjoyed.

One innovation of the 1327 parliament makes the point. The summons included the request that the justiciary of north Wales send twenty-four men from those parts – the first suggestion that Wales be represented at all. Among the names he returned (for Anglesey) was Hywel ap Gruffydd ap Iorwerth, whose nickname was *y pedolau* (of the horseshoes) because of his ability to bend horseshoes with his bare hands, and his brother Iorwerth (for Caernarvon). Mortimer was not impressed: Hywel was a thoroughgoing supporter of the king who had served in the Scottish wars. So Mortimer had the two brothers and eleven others imprisoned in Caernarvon Castle up until Edward's abdication, and we cannot be certain that any of the Welsh representatives attended the parliament. No Welsh members were to be summoned or returned again until the time of Henry VIII.

The deposition and enforced abdication of Edward II undoubtedly happened *in* parliament, but it was not done *by* parliament so much as by the bishops and the baronial party surrounding Isabella and Mortimer, while parliament looked on and nodded its approval. But by the end of Edward III's reign it would be impossible to make such a tidy distinction. The new teenage king had initially refused the throne until he was certain that his father had abdicated, so Isabella and Mortimer nervously made sure that his coronation suffered no delay. Within days, dressed in traditional blood-red samite, with orb and sceptre in his hands and Edward the Confessor's golden crown on his head, he received the fealty of the congregation from a gilded throne in Westminster Abbey and proclaimed the same fourfold oath his father had made in 1308, including 'to hold and keep the rightful laws and customs that the community of the realm shall choose, and to defend and strengthen them'.[10] It was an oath that many were now emboldened to believe they could enforce. After all, if a parliament could remove a king once, it could do it again.

Edward III was to be governed by his mother and her lover for the first three years of his reign, but in 1330 he dispatched Mortimer to meet his maker and his mother to respectable seclusion and set about ruling in earnest. He began to make war his métier, attempting to recoup the losses his father had sustained in Scotland and laying wild, inaccurate and expensive claim to the throne of France. It was a military exploit that led to the first major parliamentary crisis of the reign, when in late 1340 Edward was forced to abandon the siege of Tournai and sign the inglorious Treaty of Espléchin, largely owing to lack of funds. On his sudden, unannounced return to London, incensed into action by his steward John Darcy and the Keeper of the Privy Seal, William Killsby, he lashed out at those he believed had denied him the 'sinews of war', most especially the extremely savvy John Stratford, who was now archbishop of Canterbury, and his brother Robert, bishop of Chichester. Stratford had long been close to the king, alternating as Chancellor with his brother throughout the decade since the overthrow of Mortimer, but Edward knew of Stratford's role in his own father's removal and half believed rumours that he was plotting against his life. He now reproached himself for appointing so many clergy as ministers, rather than people whom he could 'if convicted of treason . . . cause to be drawn, hanged and beheaded'.[11] Edward now engaged in an orgy of recrimination, sacking the Chancellor and the Treasurer, William de Zouche, setting up committees of inquiry into the conduct of his ministers and launching a vituperative public accusation against the archbishop, whose presence he demanded in London. Fearful for his life, Stratford wisely refused to budge from Canterbury. The row raged for weeks. Stratford demanded that he be allowed to answer his critics in parliament, writing to the king that he was 'making unseemly process against the law of the land and against the Great Charter, which you are bound to keep and maintain by the oath you made at your coronation',[12] taunting him with the memory of what had happened to his father and excommunicating his own opponents. Edward in return accused the archbishop of being 'tumid in prosperity but timid in adversity', of urging the clergy not to pay taxes and of treasonous sedition.

Events came to a head during the days after parliament met in Westminster on St George's Day, Monday, 23 April. Stratford presented himself on the Tuesday morning but was turned away at the door by John Darcy and Lord Stafford, who told him that he had to report to the Exchequer, which he did.* Turning up again on Friday, he was again told to go to the Exchequer, but this time he forced his way in to join the other bishops in the Painted Chamber. On Saturday both sides were prepared for a major confrontation. Stratford, his brother and his nephew, the bishop of London, were now told by the Sergeant-at-Arms that

---

* The Exchequer – named after a chequered cloth on a large table which was used to make financial calculations – combined two roles, collecting revenue and adjudicating on matters regarding the king's finances. It was based next door to the Great Hall.

he had express orders to bar their entry, whereupon the three bishops refused to move unless they were directly ordered to leave by the king himself. Darcy then weighed in, taunting Stratford, 'May you stay there for ever and never depart,'[13] and accusing him of being unworthy of the cross he wore. A knight, Giles de Beauchamp, angrily added his two groats' worth with a claim that Stratford had fatally undermined the king's campaign in France. Genuinely affronted, Stratford imperiously issued a general archiepiscopal curse on them. Darcy and Beauchamp stormed off while the earls of Northampton and Salisbury, in more conciliatory mood, led the group to where the other bishops were gathered before congregating in the Painted Chamber with the king, where an acrimonious but inconclusive debate ensued.

The political situation was now extremely fluid. On the Sunday Darcy and Killsby brought a crowd of Londoners to parliament to condemn Stratford, and when he offered to clear his name in front of a committee of peers he was shouted down; but on Saturday, 5 May a delegation including all the bishops, three abbots, five earls, eight barons, the mayor of London and all the knights appealed to the king on behalf of Stratford, and the following Monday the lords charged with examining the claim found that the archbishop, like any lord, had the right to be tried by his peers in parliament. Edward was forced to capitulate, first to the archbishop, who was restored to favour, and then to parliament, which demanded a new statute upholding the ancient charters and laying down that the king's ministers were responsible to parliament.

It is difficult to see why the tide turned so quickly from abuse of the archbishop to support for his cause, but two things seem to have swayed parliamentary minds. First, the king's close confidants clearly overplayed their hand with their rough treatment of the archbishop. More importantly, though, the very crux of Edward's complaint was that he had been denied funds; but most of parliament was already weary of his constant demands and there were explicit complaints about exorbitant fines and taxes being levied twice over. Sympathy for the archbishop soon trumped deference to the king. Thus a new constitutional principle was determined: that the king alone could not try or condemn a peer. Other elements of the statute were not to survive, as Edward simply annulled them later that year, but he could not obliterate one key point: it had become clear that parliament could *in extremis* stare down the king.

One other innovation sprang from the Stratford case. There had been previous instances of parliament separating into its constituent parts: the barons, clergy, knights and burgesses voted for different rates of subsidy in 1297, the knights deliberated apart from the magnates and prelates in 1332, and the 1339 parliament began with separate charges to the lords and bishops on the one hand and the knights and burgesses on the other. Given the paucity of records during this period, it may also be that the knights and burgesses came together far more assertively in opposition to new taxes than we can now establish with any certainty. But the row over the right of the king to arrest Stratford as a spiritual peer clearly affected peers alone, so in 1341 for the first time the magnates and prelates sat expressly and definitively as a House of Peers and the knights and burgesses as the House of Commons.

These issues were to be replayed thirty-five years later, when Edward was already sixty-four. The glittering military victories at Crécy, Calais and Poitiers were now long behind him, many of his gains had been reversed, youthful vigour had subsided into complacent old age, many of his ministers were loathed, his hero son Edward the Black Prince was dying, and he was absorbed in the affections of a mistress, Alice Perrers. Conscious of the palpable sense of discontent and disillusionment in the realm, he delayed summoning parliament for nearly two and a half years, but eventually the exigencies of war again forced him to seek a tax and the necessary parliament was summoned, although Edward himself remained absent throughout, leaving his son John of Gaunt, duke of Lancaster, to represent his interests.

Parliament gathered on Monday, 28 April 1376 in the King's Chamber, but there were so many absentees that it was not until the following day that the Chancellor, John Knyvet, delivered the opening 'pronunciation' on the reason for holding the parliament, citing the danger England was in and urging 'aid and succour against [the king's] enemies' in the shape of additional taxes to pay for the defence of the realm.[14]

The next day parliament separated into its two houses, the peers meeting in the White Chamber and the Commons crammed together in the octagonal chapter house of Westminster Abbey, 'where they could take their counsel privately without being disturbed or bothered by other folk'. Although Knyvet had expressly urged the Commons to consider whether 'there was anything to redress or amend in the realm, or if the realm should be badly ruled and governed or treacherously counselled', the Commons were so fretful that it was not until everyone had sworn an oath of secrecy that one of the southern county knights felt safe enough to argue that England could not possibly afford any more taxes, suggesting that the king could live and govern the kingdom and maintain the war 'with his own revenues' as 'there are various people who have in their hands without the king's knowledge his wealth and treasure amounting to a great sum of gold and silver and have falsely concealed the wealth'.[15] Others followed him to the lectern and repeated his complaint until one of the Herefordshire knights, Peter de la Mare, rose to speak and summed up the whole discussion so well that the Commons asked him to speak on their behalf before the peers. The same pattern was followed on each subsequent day:

diatribes against the king's ministers followed by de la Mare's summation. Soon he was officially chosen as 'Speaker'. De la Mare's aptness for the role was no accident. He was steward to Edmund Mortimer, earl of March and the 24-year-old great-grandson of King Edward's mother's lover and co-conspirator. Mortimer had married wealthily and well into the royal family; his son would even have a claim to the throne. He had become intensely critical of the cronyism of Edward's court and of the conduct both of the war in Flanders and of specific ministers, including the Lord Chamberlain William Latimer, to whom he owed money. It was only natural that his steward should hold similar views.

That Friday de la Mare led the Commons to the White Chamber, where he proceeded to argue their case, namely that if the king 'had been well served by his ministers and had had his treasure spent wisely and without waste, there would be no need of such a levy; but that he has with him certain counsellors and servants who are not loyal or useful to him or to the realm'.[16] It was an incendiary, authoritative and brave performance. When challenged, he named the corrupt counsellors as Latimer, his son-in-law John Neville (Steward of the Royal Household) and Richard Lyons (Steward of the Royal Mint); and when they protested their innocence he ostentatiously read out chapter and verse of how the law had been violated from a book of statutes he happened to have to hand.

The next couple of weeks saw protracted disputes as the list of allegations grew, especially those relating to Alice Perrers, whose affair with the king had started before his wife's death and who had accumulated both fortune and influence as the king's new consort. As Thomas Brinton, the bishop of Rochester, put it: 'It is not fitting or safe that all the keys should hang from the belt of one woman.'[17] A committee of mostly sympathetic peers was set up to meet with the Commons, but when under John of

Gaunt's instructions the court party refused to accept that there had been any wrongdoing, de la Mare made it clear, on Saturday, 24 May, that the Commons would refuse even to consider taxation unless and until the king dismissed the Chancellor, the Treasurer and his mistress and appointed a new council of three bishops, three earls and three barons. The court was evidently isolated, so Edward, from a safe distance at Havering, reluctantly agreed; and parliament's choice of new ministers, including William Courtenay and William of Wykeham, respectively bishops of London and Winchester, and de la Mare's master and patron, Edmund Mortimer, were foisted on him. Parliament then proceeded to consider a lengthy charge list; when Edward refused to abandon Latimer, it invented a new form of parliamentary calling to account in which Latimer, Neville, Lyons and a string of others were 'impeached' by the Commons: that is, tried by parliament, deprived of their posts, fined and imprisoned. Parliament even dealt with Alice Perrers, who was reputed to have captured the affections of the king courtesy of the magical skills of a Dominican friar. Two knights, John de la Mare (no relation) and John Kentwode, tricked the friar by arriving at Perrers' house pretending to need a doctor. Hoping for a hefty doctor's fee, the friar let them in and was immediately arrested before being confined to an obscure priory. Much to Edward's distress, Alice too was forced to swear in front of all the bishops that she would never see the king again.

The clear-out of ministers was unprecedented, both in its scope and in its being led by the Commons, but the settlement was not to last. Whether it was the much-lamented death of the Black Prince on 8 June, the king's own desperation and ill health, or a change in policy on a mooted papal tax that swayed the sympathy of the barons and bishops back towards the court, we cannot know, but the new council barely survived three months. John of Gaunt, who was every bit as brutally rough-hewn as his elder brother could be, now took things roughly by the neck. He had underestimated the strength of the knights, and once referred to them as mere 'plebs', but he was not going to repeat the mistake. By Christmas Peter de la Mare had been arrested and thrown into prison in Nottingham Castle, Mortimer bullied into surrendering his new position, Wykeham dismissed, Latimer and Neville forgiven. Even Alice Perrers was admitted to the king, much to the consternation of the monastic chronicler Thomas Walsingham, who wrote: 'The whole populace desired Alice's condemnation when they saw that no action was being taken to remedy her wrongdoings, but realized that this evil enchantress, exalted above the cedars of Lebanon, was enjoying extraordinary favour and all the people of the realm passionately longed for her downfall.'[18] John of Gaunt's revenge was completed in January, when he ensured that a host of new members were returned to parliament and overturned all the actions of their predecessors of 1376. To add insult to injury, the new parliament also introduced a poll tax.

The 1376 'Good Parliament' was a completely different affair from the grisly assembly at Shrewsbury in 1283. By now parliament was an annual event. The knights and burgesses were summoned by right. They sat apart as the Commons. They formed a shared view and appointed a Speaker to express it to the full parliament.* The temptation is to see this development through the Edwardian century as steady and inevitable; but the facts point to a far more haphazard process. Often an occasional experiment turned into an accepted norm and then a settled convention. Each time the king required new monies for a war

---

* Each Speaker, once appointed, remained in post to the end of that parliament, unless he stood down or was given another appointment in the meantime.

and summoned knights and burgesses in the hope of an enforceable tax, he increased the expectation that common assent was required. Each time the Commons in return demanded redress of public complaints, and each time they got their way, they gained in confidence. With each new summons and with each extended session the king also increased the number of men with parliamentary experience who knew one another well enough to cooperate. There were sudden spurts of innovation – the separation of the two houses, the first impeachment of a royal minister, the deposition of the king, the move towards common petitions rather than private ones. There were also constant reverses, precipitated by success or failure in war at home and abroad. At times even a feeble, vacillating king like Edward II could gain the upper hand. The appointment of a Speaker, a Commons decision, in practice often depended on royal favour. But one overall trend was clear – while the elected representatives were rarely the protagonists in the baronial dramas, they were certainly more than just a silent chorus.

There were reasons for the Commons' emergence as an increasingly vocal and influential body. For a start, from the beginning of the fourteenth century many of those who attended parliament were people of substantial experience in their own communities who became frequent attendees. Take those who represented the important towns of East Anglia. Lynn elected Thomas de Massingham to twenty parliaments between 1318 and 1338, and Thomas de Morton later in the century for eleven. At Yarmouth the town clerk, William Ambrose, attended eleven parliaments (1307–30), Colchester elected Elias Fitz John sixteen times (1295–1328) and in Maldon William de Pakelesham was returned thirteen times (1332–44). Re-election was not guaranteed. Far from it. After parliament granted a large loan of wool to the king in July 1340 just three knights managed to get re-elected the following April. But with knights and burgesses writing back reports of events in parliament, they increasingly had a sense of a mandate.

Continuity was not inevitably a good thing. In some places there were fierce battles over the monopolization of political office. In Ipswich, Thomas Stace, the son of a tailor, and Thomas de Rente, a farmer and victualler, ensured that the burgesses and the bailiffs were drawn exclusively from their small clique from 1295 to 1321. Local complaints, including that these 'elections' had not been secret, led to Stace and de Rente being deposed as bailiffs in 1321, but they fought back two years later with a violent assault on the new bailiffs at the house of one of the other reformers, John de Preston – who, with John de Halteby and Geoffrey Costyn, proceeded to monopolize Ipswich politics much as their opponents had done. Although Halteby himself attended only one parliament, he was so hated for the brutal thuggery with which he exacted political revenge that when he was murdered in 1344 the town refused to arrest the perpetrators and the king was forced to seize government of the town into his own hands.

The kind of men being returned also changed. Most of the early knights were warriors, but increasingly after 1322 they included people who were, in the words of Peter Coss, 'would-be rather than should-be knights',[19] and as parliament dealt more and more with statutes and petitions the number of lawyers increased – indeed, Edward I expressly asked for people who were learned in the law. These included people like the 'loyal man of law' Robert de Warwick, and Justices of the King's Bench like William Ormesby (Norfolk, 1290; Great Yarmouth, 1307) and Robert Baynard (Norfolk) and of the Common Pleas like John Cambridge (Cambridgeshire, 1320–7). But by the time of Edward III the superfluity of petitioners led the king to rebel against this influx and it was decided that 'henceforth no man of the law following business in the king's court, nor any sheriff . . . shall be returned nor accepted as knight of the shires'.[20]

Lawyers made sure that this last innovation was soon more honoured in the breach than in the observance. There was good reason for this. One of parliament's early roles, after all, was that of a court of law, and it had grown out of the king's court. As Bishop Adam of Orleton put it in 1327, parliament was there 'in order to provide justice to all'. That increasingly meant settling litigation where justices had differed in their interpretation of the law or where the king's interest was expressly involved, and securing redress for injustices perpetrated by the king's ministers. In such a judicial context competing views needed keen debaters, petitioners required able advocates and the many different interest groups swirling around the court sought out men who could put their case knowledgeably and effectively. It is hardly surprising that more and more members of the Commons came from the ranks of lawyers who had studied at the Inns of Court that sprang up in the fourteenth century.

The Commons did not retain this judicial role for long, though. The upper house had already tried the Despensers in 1321, it had claimed the right to try a peer collectively in 1341 following Archbishop Stratford's case, and it had acted as the court for the impeachments prosecuted by the Commons at the Good Parliament in 1376. In 1399 this judicial role became the exclusive preserve of the peers, who would additionally act as the final court of appeal where a petitioner sought to overturn the decision of a lower court on matters either civil or criminal. At first the number of such petitions was so large that two committees of 'triers of petitions' had to be set up in each parliament to sift them and decide which ones should be heard. Over the centuries the number fell off dramatically, reaching a low point in the sixteenth century when just five such cases were heard between 1514 and 1621. Just occasionally the Lords would take on a case in the first instance, but this practice too came to an end when in 1675 the Lords heard the case of *Shirley* v. *Fagg*, which led to the Commons, of which Sir John Fagg was a member, to demand that the Lords respect the Commons' privileges. The appeal role of the Lords as a whole remained, however, until the Appellate Jurisdiction Act 1876 hived it off to twelve full-time judges known as the Lords of Appeal in Ordinary, who sat in committee in the main chamber until the Second World War, when they moved to a separate committee room. In theory they had full voting rights in the Lords, but they almost exclusively restricted their activities to legal matters and steered clear of partisan controversy. This too would eventually change when on 30 July 2009 the Lords of Appeal in Ordinary became the first justices of the new twelve-member Supreme Court.

Lawyers might come and go in the Commons and the role of the Commons in judicial (as opposed to legislative) matters might change, but by the time of Edward III's death on 21 June 1376 one thing was clear: the assertiveness of the Commons was an indelible mark on British political life.

This brass rubbing is taken from the tomb of Thomas Chaucer, son of the poet Geoffrey (himself a knight of the shire for Kent in the parliament of 1386), who attended fifteen parliaments as knight of the shire for Oxfordshire between 1400 and 1431 and was Speaker five times, a record not surpassed until Sir Arthur Onslow's tenure from 1728 to 1761.

3

A House Divided
against Itself

THE SERMON GIVEN AT the start of the 'Good Parliament' was delivered by one of the liveliest preachers of the day, the bishop of Rochester, Thomas Brinton. This clever Benedictine had forthright views. In 1377 he would preach that 'the rich and the poor are alike and equal'.[1] On this occasion, just months earlier, he roundly condemned Edward's government: 'It is not people who incline to virtue but those who lead vicious and scandalous lives who have long had the chief share in the government of this kingdom. We universally grumble and protest against the rule of such men, yet we do not have the courage to speak the truth as to the proper remedy.' Lest his point were not clear enough, he went on specifically to berate the Commons, exhorting the knights and burgesses: 'Let us be not merely talkers, but doers.' Otherwise they would be likened to the rats and mice in the fable, who were too cowardly and disorganized to face up to the cat that terrorized them.[2]

It was not the only political metaphor Brinton would have known. When a new pulpit was being installed in the choir of his solid Norman cathedral in 1840, the remnants of a six-foot-high warm-hued fresco were discovered, dating back to 1248. It shows a woman – Fortune – spinning a large wheel: one king sits atop the wheel in resplendent glory, another is climbing to power and a third is clambering on the treadmill. All that is missing is the fourth figure common to similar medieval depictions: the king who has fallen from power. The moral was simple and has its echo in every generation; as one rises, another falls; 'man, proud man, dressed in a little brief authority'[3]; 'pride goeth before destruction, and an haughty spirit before a fall'.[4]

Brinton might have had an inkling of how far-reaching the Good Parliament's clearout was to be – but he cannot have imagined how fast and how frequently the wheel of fortune was to spin over the years that followed it. As we have seen, under John of Gaunt's direction and with a new, more compliant Speaker, Thomas Hungerford, the 1377 parliament entirely undid everything that had been achieved just months earlier. But the gyrations were to become even more rapid when Edward III's grandson Richard of Bordeaux succeeded him that year at the tender and politically vulnerable age of nine.

The first turn of the wheel came in 1381. Richard's first parliaments had been surprisingly peaceable. A rumoured challenge to the succession from his uncle, John of Gaunt, never materialized and Richard secured parliamentary assent to three successive graduated poll taxes to pay for the latest ruinous (and fruitless) military campaigns. But the readiness with which the taxes had been granted belied the anger they would arouse across the country. By 1381 a feverish campaign to refuse payment had infected much of the south-east of England, and in June there was a real fear that the 'Peasants' Revolt', led by an unknown man from Essex, Wat Tyler, and the priest John Ball, would sweep away the government, the king, the church and feudalism itself.

Then came the moment that was to instil in Richard a dangerous sense of his own impregnability. The militant hordes were gathered at Mile End, east of the City of London; on Friday, 14 June they seized and beheaded both Simon Sudbury, the archbishop of Canterbury and Lord Chancellor, and Robert Hales, the prior of the Hospitallers and Lord Treasurer, on Tower Hill. It was an extraordinary act of militancy, taking out the two most senior members of the king's council. Nobody felt safe. But the next day, still aged only fourteen, Richard courageously rode out to meet Tyler, and in the midst of the ensuing melee, during which Tyler was killed, he defiantly told the rebels that he and he alone would now be their captain. Royal chutzpah won the day, and within weeks the revolt was crushed.

Richard's elation was not to last; nor was any kind of stability. His was to prove a vengeful, bipolar reign, a tone reflected only too clearly in parliament's proceedings. Almost as soon as the young king entered on his personal rule the wheel turned harshly against him. In 1386 his Chancellor, Michael de la Pole, earl of Suffolk, was impeached on largely trumped-up charges, and in 1387, enraged by what they saw as Richard's capricious and tyrannical rule and determined to oust his favourites and ministers, three of the chief magnates of the kingdom, the duke of Gloucester (Richard's uncle) and the earls of Arundel and Warwick, with support from Gaunt's son, the young Henry Bolingbroke, and Thomas Mowbray, duke of Norfolk, served a formal 'appeal' to parliament for the conviction for treason of Richard's ministers. When that failed they resorted to armed rebellion, defeating the king in December 1387 at the battle of Radcot Bridge and forcing him under threat of death or deposition to summon a parliament. That four-month assembly saw a blood-curdling purge, with summary trials in parliament followed by swift executions. Many of Richard's closest allies were dispatched, including the wealthy former mayor of London, Nicholas Brembre, and the Chief Justice, Robert Tresilian. After his parliamentary conviction without trial Tresilian was snatched by the London mob, who dragged him from his place of sanctuary, hanged him naked and slit his throat. Many others, including quite junior retainers and at least fourteen royal clerks, were caught in the maelstrom. John Beauchamp, steward to the royal household, who had been created Lord Beauchamp just the previous year, was executed, and Robert de Vere, Richard's much loved and newly elevated duke of Ireland, was cast into exile, along with the archbishops of York and Canterbury and the bishop of Chichester. When the king pleaded for another ally, Simon Burley, Gloucester shouted his nephew down with a demand for Burley's immediate execution. Even the poet Geoffrey Chaucer (who had been elected as a knight of Kent in 1386) was forced out of his position as Controller of Customs. The parliament was soon known as the 'Merciless'.

Richard's revenge was delayed a decade; but from the moment the Commons met in the Abbey chapter house on Tuesday, 18 September 1397 it was clear that the king had the upper hand. Two months earlier his once-triumphant uncle Gloucester had been arrested and murdered in Calais. As their Speaker, the Commons elected a Lincolnshire knight, John Bussy,[5] a man steeped in Richard's patronage. In 1388, as a close ally of John of Gaunt's son, Henry Bolingbroke, Bussy had supported the rebellion; but since then he had so steered his way back into royal favour that he was elected Speaker for the first time in 1393 thanks to Richard's support. An unapologetic supporter of Richard's extreme monarchist theology, Bussy was more a spokesman for the king than for the Commons, but as a veteran of ten parliaments he was also a highly effective fixer (and ardent royal flatterer). First he prepared the ground. The royal pardons previously granted to the three rebellious lords of 1387 were revoked, and the clergy, who seem to have sat separately, were persuaded to elect their own speaker, Thomas Percy, empowered to impose the death penalty.

Then Bussy sowed the king's revenge. The earl of Arundel, who had carried the crown at Richard's coronation, was dragged before parliament to be arraigned for treason by John of Gaunt, as steward of England. His response, that he had already been pardoned by the king twice, in 1388 and 1394, was thrown back at him by Bussy, who declared that the king had revoked the pardon with the assent of the lords and the 'faithful Commons'. An infuriated Arundel spat back at him: 'Where are those faithful Commons? I know all about you and your crew, and how you have got here: not to act faithfully, but to shed my blood. The faithful Commons of the kingdom are not here . . . while you, I know, have always been false.'[6] The barbed reference to the fact that Bussy had sided with the rebels in 1387 might have stung, but the accusation of hypocrisy sealed Arundel's fate, by further infuriating Richard. That same day Arundel was sentenced and beheaded, begging his executioner to use but one blow. His brother Thomas Arundel, the archbishop of Canterbury and former Chancellor, was exiled.

Bussy's duties were not yet over. When parliament reassembled in Shrewsbury in January 1398, he steered through the repeal of all the other Merciless provisions that restricted the royal prerogative, secured Richard a lifetime tax on wool and set up a commission of eighteen men to deal with outstanding petitions, including a quarrel between two of the rebels, Bolingbroke and Mowbray, who, it was decided, should resolve their difference in combat. Then Richard made a petulant, and fatal, mistake. When the two lined up to joust, he suddenly halted the tournament and proclaimed them both banished. Five months later, in February 1399, Bolingbroke's father John of Gaunt died, and Richard compounded his mistake by declaring Bolingbroke's inheritance forfeit. It was the beginning of the end. That summer, while Richard was fighting rebellion in Ireland, Bolingbroke defied the order of banishment, landed at

Ravenspur in Yorkshire and gathered a force, including the Percies from neighbouring Northumberland, with the ostensible aim of merely reclaiming his inheritance. Richard's lieutenant in his absence, his uncle the duke of York, made a feeble attempt to prepare against Bolingbroke, but soon defected to the Lancastrian forces and surrendered his troops at Berkeley Castle. Richard himself, meanwhile, made his tardy way back from Ireland only to be cornered by Bolingbroke in Conwy, where Harry Percy negotiated his surrender.

It was the end for Bussy, too. With the royalists in disarray, the instrument of Richard's parliamentary revenge was seized at Bristol Castle, and on 29 July 1399 he was beheaded. History has left us with a very partisan account of Bussy as ambitious, avaricious and cruel; but then, contemporary accounts, including the official records that were deliberately crafted and promulgated by Bolingbroke's supporters to support his claim to the throne, are equally skewed in their presentation of subsequent events. On the face of it the situation had remarkable parallels with 1327. By September Bolingbroke had the king under arrest in the Tower of London and, having summoned a parliament to meet on the last day of the month, a Tuesday, he sent a delegation on the Sunday evening after dinner and again on the Monday morning to ask Richard to abdicate. At the third time of asking, on the Monday evening, Richard, under harsh duress, acquiesced and signed a Bill of abdication, witnessed by Henry, a group of representative bishops and peers, and Thomas Gray and Thomas Erpingham for the knights.

Like Isabella and Mortimer in 1327, Bolingbroke was no slouch when it came to stagecraft. His chosen setting for the next scene was the Great Hall of Westminster, which was temporarily a building site. Richard had started rebuilding the 300-year-old hall, heightening and refacing the walls, reshaping the windows, installing a Purbeck marble floor and transforming the south wall into a royalist reredos with thirteen gilded statues of his predecessors installed in niches above the throne. Everywhere there were personal marks of the king, his emblem the white hart emblazoned on corbels and set in tiles. Most impressively, he had a vast new single-span hammer-beam roof created from 650 tons of oak, soaring effortlessly on the wings of carved angels.

That Tuesday, Bolingbroke took great care to ensure he would get parliament's support. First he went ostentatiously to mass at the Abbey. Then, just after midday, he processed into the Great Hall, his great jewelled sword carried in front of him by Erpingham. Keen not to be seen to presume upon the will of those assembled, he took his father's seat next to the bishop of Carlisle and left the throne empty, covered in cloth of gold. He had taken the precaution of filling the available space with supportive Londoners. As one contemporary put it, the hall was so full of 'prelates and lords, knights squires varlets and archers, with many sorts of folk who were neither noble nor gentle . . . in such great heaps . . . that the officers could scarcely enter'.[7] These were wise moves. In 1327 Edward had had a son and heir. Richard, by contrast, had no offspring, and his heir presumptive was not Bolingbroke but the seven-year-old Edmund Mortimer, earl of March. Neat footwork was vital if Bolingbroke was to assume, and secure, the throne.

The two archbishops led the charge, with York explaining the reasons for Richard's abdication and Canterbury asking the assembled crowd whether they agreed to the resignation and whether they were prepared to send a delegation to Richard to withdraw their homage. Each time came a hearty 'yes, yes, yes'. There remained the matter of who should reign in his stead. Henry then stood up, crossed himself and, in English, laid claim to the crown on the twin grounds of his royal descent from Henry III and 'the just cause which God of his grace [had sent him] for recovering the kingdom with the help of his kinsmen and friends'.[8] In other words, his conquest was his claim. When the archbishop again asked whether this was the people's will, the crowd shouted their assent and Henry was escorted to the throne. The following Monday, thanks to new writs issued by Bolingbroke, a new parliament met, and on 13 October King Henry IV was crowned.

According to the contemporary Bolingbroke loyalist Thomas of Walsingham, 'the lords both spiritual and temporal and all the estates of the realm unanimously agreed that the duke should rule over them,'[9] but this was an exaggeration. Thomas Merke, the bishop of Carlisle, spoke against the decision and was promptly arrested. Harry Percy, angry that Bolingbroke had used him to obtain Richard's surrender on false pretences, refused to attend the coronation dinner and four years later mounted his own rebellion. And Philip fitz Eustace supported the Percy uprising expressly because Henry 'was not elected by the magnates and the community of England but by the London rabble'.[10]

It was precisely this lack of unanimity that sent the new regime into propaganda overdrive. It lost no time in publishing a formal and decidedly partisan record of events, averring that Henry's claim was valid because 'there was a parliament summoned of all the estates of the realm . . . by cause of the which summons all the states of this land were there gathered'.[11] This view was supported for centuries. The authoritative nineteenth-century *Report on the Dignity of a Peer* concluded as much, declaring that 'the title of Henry the Fourth depended wholly on the authority of the Lords and Commons, summoned in the name of Richard to attend his parliament, assuming the character of representatives of the three estates of the realm'.[12] Bishop Stubbs even stated, as if from his episcopal throne, that it was parliament that had replaced the monarch and that henceforth 'the validity of a parliamentary title [was] indispensable to royalty'.[13]

But since Richard neither sanctioned the calling of parliament nor appointed a lieutenant to act in his stead, and had indeed resigned before it assembled, it is difficult to see in what sense the events of 30 September 1399 could possibly be regarded as a parliamentary decision. Properly speaking, parliament did not remove Richard. Nor did parliament appoint Henry. Henry craftily obtained simultaneously the benediction of the church, the approval of the magnates and the quasi-judicial authority of the realm as if in parliament, but his claim was really nothing more than that of the usurping victor to the spoils of war. He presented the assembly with a *fait accompli* and merely allowed it to assent.

Richard has suffered sorely from the invective of historians, who have variously described him as a 'pitiful neurotic', 'mentally unbalanced' and 'dangerously mad'.[14] But it is difficult not to sympathize with the lament Adam of Usk attributed to him just ten days before his deposition: 'My God, this is a strange and fickle land.'[15]

Many of those who sat in Richard's parliament would have agreed: politics at this time was a dangerous business, full of vicious reversals. The Scrope family saw a good few turns of the wheel. Richard, Baron Scrope of Bolton, was honoured by Richard II as Treasurer and Chancellor and then disgraced by him; his son William rose to be Treasurer and earl of Wiltshire, only to be executed immediately on Bolingbroke's return from exile. Richard le Scrope, the archbishop of York who called for Richard II to be replaced by Henry in 1399, was beheaded outside his palace at Bishopsthorpe just six years later, while Henry, 3rd Baron Scrope of Masham, became Treasurer under Henry V, but was then executed for treason.

It was possible to survive a change of regime, however, as

the case of William Bagot shows. Bagot first came to parliament as a Warwickshire knight at the Merciless session, when he supported the rebel lords, but in 1397 he helped the king secure his parliamentary revenge and raised troops against the Bolingbroke invasion. Although he was arrested and imprisoned in the Tower for a year, he managed to survive Henry's putsch, and in 1402 was re-elected and granted a £100 royal annuity. The ornamental brass in the Church of St John the Baptist in Baginton, Warwickshire, even portrays him wearing the 'Collar of Esses' that denoted a Lancastrian allegiance. Some might call him a turncoat or an opportunist, but at this vengeful stage in parliamentary history the ability to survive suggests a wise flexibility.

Henry sought to be a better and more popular king than Richard, not least because he feared the very blade that he had sharpened. There would be no more favourites. No arbitrary seizure of lands. No temperamental tyranny. Yet Henry was closer in spirit to his cousin than his public persona would admit. Richard emphasized the inviolability of an anointed king. But Henry too had his own theology of monarchy, as exemplified by his adoption for the first time of the closed, imperial style of crown that survives today. Richard had his 'creatures', but Henry brought with him a phalanx of new advisers.

The most striking beneficiary of Henry's immediate patronage was Thomas Chaucer. There were plenty of rumours about Thomas, most notably that his father was not the poet Geoffrey, but John of Gaunt. It was possible. His mother was lady-in-waiting to Gaunt's second wife and his aunt Katherine Swynford was Gaunt's mistress, who bore him four children. Either way, Thomas's four out-of-wedlock cousins (John, Henry, Thomas and Joan Beaufort) were made legitimate when Katherine became Gaunt's third duchess and were half-siblings to the new king. So the young Chaucer was at least half-cousin to Henry IV

and quite possibly his brother. Within three days of the coronation, Chaucer was made constable of Wallingford Castle; in
January 1401 he was elected to parliament for Oxfordshire; the
following year he was made butler to the king, a lucrative post he
held for most of the rest of his life; and on Tuesday, 25 October
1407 he was elected Speaker of the Commons, thanks to the
patronage of his Beaufort cousins Henry and Thomas, now
respectively bishop of Winchester and duke of Exeter.

It was a critical time to become Speaker. The previous year's
parliament had been the longest to date, and had seen long altercations. The political backdrop had been sour. The Welsh were
in open revolt under Owain Glyndwr, who had even attracted
the support of two bishops. Henry had quashed a revolt in the
north led by Mowbray and Archbishop le Scrope in favour of his
challenger, the teenage Edmund Mortimer, but when miracles
were reported at le Scrope's tomb and the king was seen to be ill,
superstitious people reckoned they could smell the stench of
decay. The parliament that had gathered in Westminster in
March 1406 had started well for Henry as the Commons elected
a trusted knight of his own chamber, Sir John Tiptoft, as Speaker,
but by April all had gone awry. The government was under attack
and the king was furious that members of the Commons had
made personal attacks on him. Tiptoft apologized and the king,
grudgingly, accepted, but after a break for Easter things got worse
as the Commons refused to consider Henry's demand for taxation until other matters had been addressed. In Tiptoft's
cautious words, they sought 'good and abundant governance'. In
practice, they wanted a say in royal spending and in who advised
the king. Twice earlier in the reign (in 1401 and 1404) they had
insisted that Henry name his council in parliament. But now
there was even more urgent cause to take matters out of the
king's hands: the king's increasingly unstable health. In 1405
Henry had suffered the first of a series of bouts of illness that

left him so completely incapacitated that he wrote to the bishops asking them to pray for him and to the sheriffs demanding that they arrest anyone spreading rumours that he was sick. Now, at the critical moment in the battle for new money from the Commons, the malady, which was referred to as his 'dis-ease' and 'une grande accesse', struck again. The king holed himself up at the London palace of his Chancellor, Thomas Langley, for whom Henry had very recently secured some £4,000 a year by making him bishop-elect of Durham. Langley had supported Richard's deposition and was to be Henry's executor at his deathbed, so there can be little doubt that even though Durham Place (*sic*) was just at the far end of the Strand, Henry felt safe here from the prying eyes of those who might consider a sick king a dispensable one. He duly remained there, incommunicado except by signet letter, between 4 May and 7 July.

In his absence Henry was forced to agree to a list of seventeen councillors to whom he handed over the day-to-day running of the realm on 22 May, even accepting a catch-all clause to the effect that the council could abrogate any other powers to themselves as they thought expedient. Even this was not enough for the Commons. When Tiptoft asked whether the councillors all agreed to serve, the archbishop of Canterbury (the now restored Thomas Arundel) sneeringly replied that they would do so as long as the Commons gave them enough resources with which to do the job. The Commons still refused to buckle, though, and delivered a lengthy complaint about the parlous state of the nation. Tiptoft was bold on their behalf. The king was deceived, his extravagantly wasteful household was full of 'rascals', and he must account to the Commons for his expenditure. Henry's haughty long-distance reply that 'kings are not wont to render account'[16] provoked another bout of Commons anger, and by the summer the king still had nowhere near enough to fund the military campaigns in Wales and France that the Commons themselves were demanding. On 19 June, in exasperation and exhaustion, Henry suspended parliament until 13 October.[17]

Little changed during the intervening months. Henry spent £4,000 on a dowry for his daughter Philippa's marriage to the king of Denmark and went on a slow pilgrimage round the country. The Commons, equally concerned about the rumours of the king's ill health and angered by the delays to the new session which, thanks to Henry's further indisposition, did not meet until 18 November, remained in no mood to compromise. Eventually the royal concessions came. First, on 8 December, Henry appointed Tiptoft as treasurer of the royal household, with permission to reassess royal spending. Then thirty-one articles were hammered out establishing the new council, stipulating among other things that the king should always be attended by members of the council and that he could no longer resolve disputes or make grants or appointments unilaterally. Henry had little choice but to accept these strictures, and on 22 December the new councillors swore to abide by the articles. The Commons promptly agreed to a slender set of new taxes to pay for defence and to a grant of £6,000 expressly for the king.

Looked at from afar, the articles seem a shocking incursion into the royal prerogative. They even stipulated that the king had to be accessible two days a week. They seem all the more surprising considering that, compared to any other medieval monarch, Henry had strong overt support in parliament. With both the crown lands and his own duchy of Lancaster in his possession, he had a myriad royal retainers and Lancastrian lackeys in the Commons, while the Lords had been cleansed of opposition after the rebellions of 1400, 1403 and 1405. Even the lords spiritual were aligned with Henry, as the two bishops who supported Owain Glyndwr (St Asaph and Bangor) were not invited and York had been replaced. In the Commons too, roughly thirty-six out of the seventy-five knights of the shires were Henry's servants or tenants, and several burgesses were express supporters. So Henry should have had little problem getting his grants and securing his own agenda.

Lancastrian propaganda later claimed that the articles and the continual council were all part of a great Lancastrian constitutional experiment and that Henry was a proto-democrat. But this is belied by the fury with which the two sides argued their cases and the reluctance with which Henry surrendered his prerogative. Nor is it consonant with what happened when Chaucer took over as Speaker at the subsequent parliament that gathered on the Welsh borders in Gloucester Abbey in 1407. For here the financial rows of 1406 were repeated and Chaucer, for all his royal connections, was every bit as forthright as Tiptoft.

The most significant altercation of the new session was to have profound effects on the development of parliament. It came about by accident. Henry, ever importunate, asked the lords, one by one, what resources and taxation they thought were needed, and then summoned twelve members of the Commons to tell them what the lords thought in the hope that they would persuade their colleagues to agree. Immediately all hell broke loose. The Commons were incensed – Chaucer said 'perturbed' – that they were effectively being presented with a *fait accompli*, and declared that this was 'to the manifest prejudice and derogation of their liberties'. It felt as if a proposal for taxation were being initiated in the Lords, whereas the Commons maintained that taxation could be initiated only by them. Again Henry was forced to back down, this time assenting that Lords and Commons should be allowed to 'discuss the condition of the realm and the measures needed to remedy it' in private, and that no report should be made to the king until 'the said Lords and Commons shall be of one accord and assent on the matter'. Quite specifically, money was to be 'granted' by the Commons and 'assented to' by the Lords. The Commons had wrung out of the king both their right to self-determination and their financial prerogative – principles that were codified much later in two resolutions of 1671 and 1678 which state 'that in all aids given to the King by the Commons, the rate of tax ought not to be altered by the Lords' and that it is the 'undoubted and sole right of the Commons' to deal with all public expenditure and revenues raised to meet that expenditure. The principles remain in force today.

It was not just the king's health that forced his capitulation in 1406 and 1407. Constellations of power were shifting. For one thing, these days even knights could have their own entourages in the Commons. Thomas Chaucer, for instance, could count on the loyalty in parliament at various times of his brother-in-law John Grenville, his wife's uncle by marriage Thomas Brooke and at least seven other associates, including a close drinking companion of the young Prince Harry of Wales. For another, the kind of people coming to the Commons was changing: many of the knights of the shires were now as grand as their lordly counterparts, living in great castles. Also, in several counties parliamentary lineages were by now well established. A comparison of the lists for 1295 and the 1400s makes the point. One Neville represented Leicestershire in 1295; in 1400 there were two. John de Popham and John de Fauconer were the two knights for Southamptonshire in 1295; between 1402 and 1411, John and Henry Popham and William Fauconer sat for the county.[18] The first Lowther appeared at this time, founding a parliamentary dynasty that would include representatives of Cumberland, Westmorland, Carlisle, Pontefract, Cockermouth, Haslemere and Penrith in virtually every generation up to James William Lowther, who was a Conservative Speaker from 1905 to 1921, ended his days as Viscount Ullswater and encapsulated centuries of parliamentary experience in his aphorism: 'There are three golden rules for Parliamentary speakers: Stand up. Speak up. Shut up.'[19]

At the same time as they were gaining in wealth and influence, the Commons were also beginning to hold a far wider variety of experience than previously. This was important for the Commons themselves, for the country and for the king. Wine merchants could provide wine for the parliamentary banquets and advise on duties. Ship-owners were vital to England's naval and merchant security. The pesagers who weighed wool for duty at the ports and the customs officers who oversaw the collection of tariffs were the very people the king relied on to harvest his taxes.

What is more, parliament was beginning to have a sense of its own importance. There were squabbles among the lords about the order of precedence: should the earl of Warwick sit closer to the king than the hereditary Earl Marshal? And what about the relative seniority of Lord Grey of Codnor and Lord Beaumont? These rows seem petty, but they show an increasing sensitivity to the importance of parliamentary hierarchy, as does the new fashion for parliamentary robes which saw the lords wearing special caps, coronets and scarlet gowns for new investitures. Specially graded robes were introduced for Henry IV's coronation – three bands of fur for earls and dukes, and two for barons.

All of which goes to explain how the combination of an incapacitated king, a parliament that in the main had no desire to oust him, and a determined minority of truculent knights and burgesses could lead to a significant parliamentary incursion into the powers of the monarch. Henry IV's own use of parliament to usurp the throne added to the sense that parliament was now an integral part of the king's government. That Henry managed to persuade successive generations of chroniclers and historians that he had a sound claim to the throne and that he had pioneered the principle of free speech is a secure indication that, in the term Shakespeare put in the mouth of Richard II, he was the ultimate 'politician'. It was no compliment.

Although Henry's health rallied enough for him to contemplate a campaign in the Holy Land, over the next few years he dwindled towards death. A final attack came when he was praying at Edward the Confessor's shrine on 20 March 1413; he was carried through to the Jerusalem chamber in Cheynegates, the recently built house of the abbot of Westminster, where he died, Thomas Langley at his side. As he stared at the ceiling he may just have been able to make out the letter 'R' for Richard embossed on the timbers.

Although the vigorous new King Henry V's reign was to scintillate with unexpected military triumphs at Harfleur and Agincourt, and Henry was to succeed where his predecessors had failed in claiming the French crown, he was no more able to assert his will in parliament than his father, as became abundantly clear in the session that started on Monday, 15 May 1413. The Commons were in a restive mood. Their chosen Speaker, William Stourton (Dorset), sarcastically told the king that although his father had regularly promised good government he was sure that the king was 'well aware of how this was subsequently fulfilled and carried out' – a presumptuous familiarity that provoked Henry into demanding caustically that henceforth Stourton put down any complaints in writing, to which Stourton agreed. Since the tradition had always been that the Speaker made his representations orally to the king or the Lords, so that they could be corrected if he strayed from what the Commons intended, his fellow members were furious, and three days later sent a different knight, John Doreward (Essex), to withdraw what Stourton had agreed. A week on, with Stourton ill in bed (he died soon after), the Commons formally appointed Doreward in his place. Again, almost by accident, a precedent was set: that the Speaker was primarily the creature of the knights and burgesses, not of the king.

Subsequent parliaments were equally querulous, Henry's lieutenants during his absences on campaign in France finding the Commons reluctant to grant new taxes. A session held in the Grey Friars Priory in Leicester in April 1414 agreed the traditional tonnage and poundage duties* under the speakership of Walter Hungerford, one of the military heroes of the Hundred Years War, but was far more interested in the suppression of the Lollards. A second session that year stumped up a subsidy but saw Chaucer (now Speaker for the fourth time) struggle to get wholehearted parliamentary assent to the war, even though many peers and MPs would go on to fight at Agincourt, including both Hungerford and Chaucer, who brought with him twelve men-at-arms and thirty-seven archers. When it came to Chaucer's fifth and final speakership in 1421 (a record not to be matched by any of his successors until Arthur Onslow, who was elected Speaker five times between 1728 and 1761), parliament point blank refused any more cash.

Henry's reign was cut tragically short by a bout of dysentery in 1422, but the real tragedy of his passing was the uncivil warfare that ensued; for the seedlings of the Wars of the Roses had been planted, manured and watered long before the first battle was enjoined at St Albans in 1455. There was Henry VI's contestable claim to the throne, which depended from his great-grandfather, John of Gaunt, *fourth* son of Edward III, and was therefore questioned by (among others) Richard, 3rd duke of York, who was descended on his mother's side from Edward's *third* son Lionel of Antwerp, 1st duke of Clarence, and on his

---

* Dating from the reign of Edward II, tonnage (or tunnage) and poundage were duties levied on every tun of imported wine and every pound of other imports or exports, and were normally granted to the king for life.

father's side from Edward's *fifth* son Edmund. There was also the problem of Henry VI's incapacity, the result of fifteen years of minority, regular bouts of insanity and a sheer inability to lead. And there was an ample sufficiency of headstrong, ambitious and vengeful figures such as the dukes of Suffolk and Somerset, the 'kingmaker' earl of Warwick and Henry VI's wife Margaret of Anjou. And then there was Henry V's will, which, in laying down that his younger brother Humphrey, duke of Gloucester, would direct the council of regency, but only while the elder of his brothers, John, duke of Bedford, was leading the English troops at war in France, was a charter for envious fraternal dissension. Even as Henry VI was hiccuping in his nurse's arms, competing loyalties and ambitions were rife. Only a kingdom of saints could have survived these inherent problems without going to war. England was not full of saints.

For all its intricacies and intrigues, the essential tale of the Wars of the Roses is quickly told. When the nine-month-old baby Henry inherited his father's throne, his court was immediately factionalized, with his two uncles, Bedford and Gloucester, competing for seniority. Things got no better when Henry came of age. First, his lack of mettle or political nous left him at the mercy of arch-machinators like bishop (later Cardinal) Beaufort and his nephew Edmund Beaufort, the duke of Somerset. When Henry began to flit in and out of sanity, a distant cousin, Richard, duke of York, who had an equal if not better claim to the throne, saw his opportunity and, in association with Richard Neville, earl of Warwick, sought first to gain the upper hand at court and, when that failed, to overthrow his incapable and inept Lancastrian relative. York was killed in battle at Wakefield in late 1460, but his son Edward immediately assumed the Yorkist mantle and, following his victory at the battle of Towton (fought in a snowstorm on Palm Sunday 1461), declared himself King Edward IV. Henry's magnificently combative wife Margaret of

Anjou led the fightback and, thanks to Warwick and Clarence changing sides, Henry was briefly restored in 1470 before his wife's troops lost their final battle at Tewkesbury the following year. Henry's son and heir was executed and he was murdered in the Tower. His wife Margaret was sold back to France for 50,000 crowns. Edward IV then reigned for twelve relatively peaceful years (apart from imprisoning George Neville, archbishop of York, and executing his younger brother George, duke of Clarence, for treason) before dying suddenly at the age of forty in 1483, to be succeeded for seventy-eight days by his twelve-year-old son. The young Edward V's uncle, Richard, duke of Gloucester, as if enacting a medieval version of *Kind Hearts and Coronets*, first had Edward IV's secret marriage declared illegal and his son deemed illegitimate, and then saw off all other potential claimants before assuming the throne himself as Richard III. In little more than two years he too was dead, vanquished by a distant Welsh relative, Henry Tudor, at the battle of Bosworth Field. Within a hundred years four English kings had been deposed and murdered.

It is tempting to think that most of this passed way over the head of the average knight or burgess. After all, whereas Edward I had called three parliaments a year, in the thirty-nine years between 1422 and 1461 only twenty-two parliaments were held, and many a commoner may have thought, as royal and noble claimants fought and intrigued, 'as flies to wanton boys are we to the gods'. Yet many of the key moments occurred in or around parliament. In 1422 parliament debated the creation of the regency council and came to its uneasy conclusion that Gloucester would not be regent but could exercise limited authority while his elder brother Bedford was occupied in France. In 1426 the ever-simmering animosity between Bishop Beaufort and Gloucester erupted into near-warfare in London, and Bedford, who had returned expressly to deal with the issue, banned weapons from the parliament that he summoned to the great hall at Leicester Castle (members decided to carry sticks or 'bats' instead: hence its nickname the Parliament of Bats). It was here that Beaufort was forced to bend the knee to Gloucester and resign the chancellorship in favour of John Kemp, the bishop of London, in return for permission to attend the pope to receive the cardinal's hat he had been denied by Henry V. The feud continued nonetheless. The 1432 parliament, which inclined towards Gloucester, forced Beaufort to give the king £6,000, while the mood at the following parliament swung back towards Bedford and Beaufort. When Henry began to rule in his own right in 1437, with Bedford now dead, the two arch-enemies battled to keep the king in check and themselves in lucrative power. Beaufort gathered a group of allies including Kemp (now archbishop of York), Henry's much-trusted William de la Pole, duke of Suffolk, and Adam Moleyns, who was both bishop of Chichester and clerk of the council, to support him in parliamentary attacks on Gloucester and then in 1441 on Gloucester's wife, Eleanor Cobham, who was accused of witchcraft.

When parliament was called in November 1449, though, the one thing on everyone's mind was the loss of Normandy, for which the blame fell substantially on Suffolk, who had acted as the king's virtual regent since the deaths of both Gloucester and Cardinal Beaufort in 1447 (there were rumours Gloucester was poisoned on his way to face charges of treason at a parliament in Bury St Edmunds). The first selection as Speaker in 1449, the Agincourt veteran Sir John Popham, turned it down, and his place was taken by William Tresham, who had already performed the role three times. It rapidly became clear that the Commons were sick of the Suffolk regime. First, Bishop Moleyns was eased into retirement (only to be murdered within weeks). Next, charges of treason were laid by the Commons against Suffolk himself: he had brought about Gloucester's death, enriched himself by extortion and fatally undermined the English campaign against the French. In March 1450, with the Commons baying for blood and the Lords at best divided, Henry took matters into his own hands and exiled the duke for five years, thereby hoping to save him from an indicted traitor's death. Suffolk was not to escape, however. En route for the continent he was captured in the Channel and beheaded with six blows of a rusty axe before being dumped in the sea.

The Commons' anger had now spread throughout the country, and parliament had to be ended to deal with a popular rebellion led by Jack Cade that sought to replicate the advance on London of 1381 and to bring Richard, duke of York, to the throne. Although in June another Suffolk ally, William Aiscough, bishop of Salisbury, was snatched while celebrating mass, dragged out and hacked to pieces, the popular rebellion was swiftly and brutally suppressed, and when a new parliament was summoned in November the dukes of York and Norfolk ensured that it had as strong a Yorkist contingent as possible so as to see off any charges of treason against York himself and to undermine Henry's remaining confidant, Edmund Beaufort, the duke of Somerset. York's chamberlain, Sir William Oldhall, was elected Speaker and the Commons petitioned against Suffolk's duchess, Alice (Thomas Chaucer's daughter). Large numbers of those gathered were still spitting with fury at the losses in France and wanted revenge on those they identified as the treacherous perpetrators. Armed Yorkists tried to capture the failed commander, Somerset, and the house of Suffolk's vile bullyboy and knight of the shire Thomas Tuddenham was attacked. In the confusion the former Speaker William Tresham was killed on his way to meet York.

Despite Oldhall's election, the king was not entirely outmanoeuvred. In 1449 he had sent Thomas Young to the Tower for saying in parliament that York should be heir presumptive. Now he so successfully managed to see off York's parliamentary attempts on Somerset that Oldhall was terrified the king would seek retribution and fled to sanctuary in St Martin's le Grand church in London. Normally this was a place of unconditional refuge, protected by ancient statute, but so furious was the Somerset party that an armed band of peers stormed the church after midnight and dragged Oldhall to the Tower. The courageous (and Yorkist) dean of St Martin's, Richard Cawdray, immediately demanded that the king honour the longstanding liberties of St Martin's under threat of excommunication, and two days later Oldhall was back at St Martin's – but the king twice had him indicted for treason, outlawed and, in the 1453 parliament, attainted.*

Parliament was, then, directly involved in the early skirmishes of Henry VI's reign; and the pattern was repeated through the Wars of the Roses right up until the battle of Bosworth as virtually every parliament now considered impeachment or Acts of Attainder. For the most part it was a follower of political fashion, not its master. York's son Edward took the throne on 4 March 1461, but it was his military victory, confirmed in spectacular style at the battle of Towton on 29 March, that proved his title, not the parliamentary debate that November. Again in 1470, it was the fact that Margaret of Anjou had wrested the kingdom back for her husband by force that

* Acts of Attainder, declaring individuals guilty of treason and depriving them and therefore their successors of their estates and livelihood, were presented by the king to parliament. Often they were agreed without dissent, but on occasion the Commons or the Lords quibbled about the terms of the attainder or the list of those included. Oldhall's first attainder was reversed in 1455 under the protectorate of York, but he was again attainted in 1459, gaining a reversal only a month before his death in November 1460.

enabled the new Chancellor, George Neville, brother to the 'king-maker' earl of Warwick, to preach to parliament on the text 'return, you backsliding children'. Richard III's declaration that 'the lords spiritual and temporal and the Commons of this land' had begged him to be king on 26 June 1483 is at best a post hoc rationalization, for in truth Richard seized the crown and didn't even bother to summon a parliament until January 1484. Since Richard's sole argument was that Edward IV's marriage was bigamous and therefore Edward V was illegitimate, which was a matter that could only be properly adjudicated by a church court, it is not surprising that he was reluctant to allow parliament to do any more than ratify the self-evident fact of his reign. So parliament did the constitutional mopping up after the change of regime, not the heavy lifting to bring it about. Even the duke of Clarence's trial in 1478 came as a sad parliamentary denouement. The only accusations came from King Edward himself; the only defence from his brother, the accused. In desperation Clarence offered to prove his innocence in mortal combat. Edward hesitated until the partisan Yorkist Speaker William Allington stormed in and demanded that Clarence be executed.[20]

The lords spiritual (the twenty-one bishops and a similar number of abbots) were thoroughly enmeshed in the political strife of the fifteenth century. They were guaranteed their seats in parliament, and because of their protection under canon law they tended to survive regime changes. They provided both the moral authority and the administrative backbone of a government: in all but eight of the eighty-four years between 1399 and 1483 clergy held the post of Chancellor, and seven clerics served as Lord Treasurer during the same period. Many of these senior churchmen, such as Thomas Arundel, Henry Beaufort and George Neville, were blood relatives of the protagonists; even those who were not were often strongly partisan. In 1470, out of the seventeen English bishops seven were undoubted Lancastrians (London, Durham, Norwich, Chichester, Coventry, Hereford, Winchester) and seven clear Yorkists (Canterbury, York, Bath and Wells, Ely, Rochester, Carlisle, Exeter). Indeed, so closely involved in the battles for supremacy were the higher clergy that when Edward IV was forced into exile in October that year and Queen Margaret was in a mood for revenge, at least three Yorkist bishops took refuge in St Martin's le Grand. They would have been in interesting company: one contemporary complained that the sanctuary housed common criminals, including 'subtle pickers of locks, counterfeiters of keys, contrivers of scales, forgers of false evidence . . . unto the common hurt of the people'.[21] The bishops themselves were often ambitious or corrupt. But even the most venal could do work of enduring value, endowing colleges at Oxford or Cambridge and building chapels and churches. Sometimes their real gift was political. John Kemp, for instance, was thoroughly ambitious and rose speedily up the episcopal ladder via Rochester, Chichester and London to York (1425), largely thanks to his partisan support for Beaufort and Bedford. He was negligent in his pastoral duties, visiting his diocese only once in seventeen years, and he was nepotistic, too, securing the bishopric of London for his entirely worthless nephew Thomas – but he was a competent and equanimous Chancellor for twelve years, and his sudden death (as the first cardinal archbishop of Canterbury) in March 1454, with Henry VI insane and York militating for change, contributed to the slide into disorder and the ensuing conflagration.

Loyalties, ambitions and fortunes varied just as much among the baronage – both between and within families. Take one family, the Courtenays, which consisted of two strands descended from sons of Hugh, 2nd earl of Devon. By the middle of the fifteenth century it had already produced an archbishop of

Canterbury and Chancellor in William and a bishop of Norwich in Richard. The senior branch of the family was Lancastrian and all three sons of the 5th earl were to lose their lives in the Lancastrian cause. Thomas, the 6th earl, was executed after Edward's victory at Towton; Henry Courtenay, after a few years of uneasy accommodation with the new regime before assisting in the rebellion of Sir Thomas Hungerford, was arrested and executed in 1469; and Sir John, who fled the country after Towton but returned for the brief restoration of Henry VI, was killed in the battle of Tewkesbury. By contrast, most of the Powderham Courtenays had strong Yorkist allegiances. Sir Philip Courtenay held regular royal commissions under Edward IV, his son Sir William was a Yorkist knight for Somerset, another son (Philip) sat in the Yorkist parliament of 1472–5, John joined in the attainder of Clarence, and Humphrey was well rewarded by both Edward IV and Richard III. Two other sons took a different tack. Sir Walter Courtenay assisted in the failed rebellion led by Henry Stafford, 2nd duke of Buckingham, in 1483, escaped and was rewarded by Henry VII, sitting for Devon in the 1495 parliament. The most prominent of Sir Philip's sons, though, was to be Peter, who first arrived in parliament under Edward IV as a dean and rose to be bishop of Exeter in 1478. He too joined Buckingham's rebellion, but fled to France and returned to England with Henry Tudor, who translated him to the far more significant and lucrative see of Winchester in 1487. In all, eight Courtenays were sent to parliament in the second half of the fifteenth century, four were executed or killed in battle and eleven were at some point or other declared traitors.

It is difficult, then, to argue that parliament was irrelevant to the course of fifteenth-century history. Between 1453 and 1504 parliament condemned 397 people to death or banishment,[22] and for years these proceedings dominated parliament. Attainder, bringing with it forfeiture of land, title, income and legal standing in perpetuity (or at least until pardoned), was a constant peril throughout this half-century, and many of those who fell foul of it were members of parliament. Many others were killed in battle or were executed. The Lancastrian Thomas Thorpe was imprisoned as Speaker in 1453 when he lost a legal battle against the duke of York, and was killed by a mob of angry Londoners on his way to join Margaret of Anjou in 1461. Thomas Tresham, son of the murdered Speaker, was executed as a Lancastrian after the battle of Barnet in 1471. And John Wenlock, a renowned turncoat Speaker, was ennobled but later killed at the battle of Tewkesbury by his own commander, the duke of Somerset, who smashed his head with a mace in anger at his feeble indecision.

Despite the constant political upheavals, the Commons showed a growing self-confidence, attested to by two significant developments: the amount of new legislation governing elections to parliament and the advent of lobbying.

Although some local government officers had long been elected – coroners, for instance, since 1194 – the precise method of election varied considerably, as it did in the selection of early parliamentary representatives. The writs of summons regularly stated that representatives had to come with full powers to act *plena potestas* (with full power) and that the choice must be registered *in pleno comitatu* (in the full [county] court), but often the local grandees called the shots. In 1318, for instance, Matthew Crawthorne complained that he had been nominated for Devon 'by the Bishop of Exeter and William, Lord Martin, by the assent of the other good men of that county . . . and presented to the sheriff in full county court' but that the sheriff had sent another in his stead. Similarly, for many years the sheriff and lawyers acting for the greatest local landowners, including the archbishop of York and the earls of Northumberland and Westmorland, signed off the returns for Yorkshire. There were irregularities, too. Lincolnshire and Cambridgeshire both complained in the 1330s that the under-sheriff had returned himself to parliament 'by his own virtue and without consent of the community' and it is clear they were not alone.[23]

These abuses and concomitant complaints had accumulated towards the end of the fourteenth century, and the first attempt to tackle the issue came in the Good Parliament, when the Commons petitioned that knights should be elected by common (or county) election by the best people ('soient esluz par Commune eleccion de les meillieurs Gentz'[24]) and that tough penalties be imposed on sheriffs who failed to hold proper elections. Still the abuses continued; there were regular complaints that John of Gaunt, Richard II and Henry IV all attempted to pack the Commons with their placemen. So in 1406 the Commons demanded and secured a new statute laying down that electoral returns had to include the signatures of those who had voted to attest that they had done so. These new returns make it clear that a substantial number of people were now taking part in the election process, especially considering that not all voters may have been able to sign their names. Oxfordshire had roughly 200 attesters in 1410, Gloucestershire and Lincolnshire had more than 100 attesters in 1427 and Buckinghamshire more than 200 in 1429.

Indeed, so much interest was there in many of these elections that the Commons returned to the issue in 1430, complaining that virtually anyone could now vote, including those who had no legitimate interest as they were indigent. A new statute stipulated that only those with an annual income of 40 shillings should vote, thereby enfranchising yeomen and wealthier husbandmen, giving a county like Nottinghamshire an electorate of about 650. It also laid down that where there was a contest the candidate with the most votes won. Presumably this was codified because other, more consensual, ways of election had been essayed in some areas, possibly the alternative vote or exhaustive ballot. Thus in 1430 was 'first past the post' made universal.

There was a further statute on elections in 1445, which insisted for the first time that only knights, or at least squires or gentlemen born in the shire, qualified for election as knights of the shire. This was an important change, as an increasing number of those elected were not resident in the areas they represented – especially in the boroughs, which by the time of Edward IV returned four outsiders for every three residents.

By now, although most 'elections' were consensual, there were contests aplenty and contenders fought hard to win. In essence, there were three avenues open to a candidate – and they were all used. First was packing the election. Thus in October 1427 Walter Tailboys of Goltho and Patrick Skipworth of Utterby secured the two Lincolnshire seats by ensuring that 106 of their neighbours from Lindsey voted, thereby providing the vast majority of the 119 attesters. A few years later Henry, Lord Grey of Codnor, bussed in 200 men for the Derbyshire election of 1433, only to be outdone by his opponents Richard Vernon and John Cockayne, who marshalled 300 supporters; and in 1439 Sir John Tiptoft alleged that Sir James Lemons brought 2,000 men to the Cambridgeshire election. Next was denigrating the opposition. Sir John Paston complained bitterly to his brother in 1470 that their rival 'will craftily send among you six or more people with the express intention of slandering your fellowship by saying that they are riotous people of no substance'.[25] Finally, there was straightforward bribery. The same John Paston complained about it in 1461 and 1472, and there were countless instances where candidates simply bought votes – though few could have done so as curiously as William Burley and Richard Legett, who handed out fish to the Shropshire electors in 1435. Quite why Burley had to resort to such tactics when he secured a seat in parliament on eighteen occasions it is difficult to see, but it didn't prevent him from being Speaker for the last few days of the March 1437 parliament and again in 1445.

Money didn't all go in one direction. There is clear evidence that parliamentary service could be lucrative, as individuals and organizations that wanted to secure a petition or parliamentary judgment would not only send representatives to hang around Westminster when parliament was sitting, but would often pay officers for help with their lobbying efforts.

Lobbying was by now a fixed part of the parliamentary process. In one sense it was predictable, and well established. Any individual or group that wanted to secure a new charter, legal redress for some ill done them, or a change in the law, had for some time made representations to the king, to his council and/or to parliament. One of the first tasks of each new parliament was to appoint a set of people to hear and adjudicate on these petitions, and 'common petitions' became more frequent. But only a fool would presume that a petition could sail through parliament without strong gusts of wind behind it. So petitioners sought out lawyers to advise them on what statutes already existed, entertained parliamentary clerks, paid MPs to advance their cause and bribed the king's councillors.

The Brewers' Company, for instance, one of the great merchant bodies in the City of London, sent three of their members to Westminster in 1432 to lobby parliament for a new charter. The next year they paid 'diverse persons of the parliament' in the attempt to push the charter forward, but disappointedly had it 'laid aside'. It was only when they paid the Chancellor the whopping sum of £40 and John Norris of the king's chamber a further £13 6s 8d in 1438 that their wish came true. The Tailors did the same, forking out £30 to Humphrey, duke of Gloucester, and £8 6s 8d (6s 8d was a 'noble') to Adam Moleyns, the clerk of the council, and making them members of the fraternity in return for their new charter; the Mercers paid John Whittocksmead a noble in 1455 'to be our friend in parliament'; and the Pewterers paid a noble to Thomas Bayon (or Bayen), the clerk to the Commons, 'to speed our bills to be read'.[26]

Bayon was also instrumental in the battle between the canons and the 'poor knights' of Windsor in 1485. Both sides were desperate for parliament to resolve the longstanding row over their original financial settlement. In order to oil the wheels, Canon Seymour not only entertained Bayon to a lavish breakfast but paid the porter at parliament twopence 'for his favour', the Sergeant-at-Arms another twenty pence and the Speaker, Thomas Lovell, a hefty 66s 8d. In addition John Vavasour, who was sergeant to the king, was paid to speak three times in the House of Lords on behalf of the canons, as were two MPs, Thomas Lymryk (Gloucestershire) and a man called 'Morden' (either the future Speaker John Mordaunt or Thomas Morton, a relative of the bishop of Ely).[27] In the end, though, it was a £100 gift to the king himself that sealed the deal.

Of course, for the most part towns would want to see their interests pursued by their representatives, but at the same time there was a growing reluctance to pay for representation, especially among those who had to contribute to the parliamentary wages but could not vote. There was a vicious circle here. It has been shown that almost a quarter of burgesses sitting in the 1422 parliament were not resident in the towns they represented, and that by 1449 almost a half lived elsewhere;[28] but since many towns were parsimonious in their payment of MPs' wages, it seems they often succumbed to the offer of free 'carpet-bagger' representation. The offer made by Ralph Neville, 2nd earl of Westmorland, to the burgesses of Grimsby that if they returned two of his advisers as their MPs they would still be able to raise any issues they wanted but would not have to meet their costs cannot have been unique.[29]

Although the 1406 and 1430 statutes regularized many issues in relation to the election of knights, the burgesses were virtually ignored by statute law. The parliamentary attendance fee of 2s a day for a burgess (4s for a knight) had been fixed in 1327, but it was a much dishonoured figure. Some paid far more. York gave a knight's fee to its burgesses, Bristol paid 5s and London laid out the truly princely sum of 40s a day when parliament met outside the capital in 1459 and 1464. But many others paid far less. Totnes, for example, said that Thomas Gille had been elected on the proviso that he would only be paid a noble (less than a week's fee) for however long the 1446 parliament sat. And the following year, when parliament met in Bury St Edmunds, the town of Liskeard decided it was too far to go and sent two men from East Anglia instead.

All of which goes to show that parliament did now matter. It adjudicated individual legal cases and petitions. It decided on taxes. It could force out ministers and kings. Common petitions touching more than just a narrow point could be enacted in statute and provide relief for a town, an industry or a trade. It was worth lobbying parliament. It was also worth stacking it with allies – as successive monarchs sought to do by securing seats for royal servants, who by 1478 made up nearly one in five members of the Commons. It was even worth creating a few more amenable seats like Wootton Bassett, Hindon, Westbury, Heytesbury and Gatton, all granted two burgesses each under Henry VI, and Grantham, Ludlow and Much Wenlock under Edward IV. Equally importantly, individuals could use a parliamentary career to build themselves personal fortunes and rise to the highest councils in the land. It was worth getting elected – and people fought hard for the honour.

From the very first parliaments the twenty-one archbishops and bishops of England and Wales sat in the House of Lords. The religious controversies of the sixteenth century saw many of them – and many of less exalted rank – executed for their faith. This print shows not only John Fisher, the bishop of Rochester and a leading defendant of papal supremacy, at the block in June 1535 for his refusal to assent to Henry VIII's self-declared title as 'Supreme Head of the Church of England', but other figures representing the many condemned to death on the gibbet or at the stake.

4

The King's Pleasure

EARLY ON THE MORNING of 24 April 1509 a former Speaker was arrested. Languishing in the Tower for more than a year, he devoted his hours to drafting a treatise on good government in the hope that it might secure a royal pardon. His theories were not particularly earth-shattering, but one can sense the personal anguish he was living through. Furious that he stood condemned on what he thought was false evidence, he lamented that there was no rule to 'punish perjury, for persons perjured be the uttermost mischief of all'. Bored to distraction, he inveighed against 'idleness, the very mother of all vice both in man and woman, both noble and un-noble, and the lineal grandma of poverty and misery'. It is his own capacity for stoicism in the face of almost certain death that most impresses, though. 'Yet look a little further on our selves. When we be dead, for all pomp and prosperity, what is our precious carcase, and what shall we have hence with us? Is our carcase any thing but a carrion most vile and abominable?'[1]

His words could easily have been his epitaph, for Edmund Dudley, staunchly loyal councillor to Henry VII, was, along with another Speaker executed on the same day, Sir Richard Empson, to go down in history as among the most abominable of politicians. A century after their death Robert Cecil would threaten the Commons with 'an Empson and a Dudley'.[2] There are plenty of rivals for the post of most hated Tudor councillor, but the hagiographers and martyrologists of early Tudor history that cast Thomas More as a saint, label Thomas Cromwell as a corrupt manipulator and suggest that parliament was stuffed with feeble yes-men have misled us. The sallow Henry VII and his ebullient son Henry VIII were avaricious, rapacious and self-centred; and yet, in one of the great ironies of British history, in using parliament for their own ends they strengthened it and gave it new authority.

In one sense the Tudor kings started off on a good footing in relation to parliament. The battle of Bosworth Field was meant to put a definitive end to the Wars of the Roses, so Henry rammed the message home. The dead king, scrawnier than his Plantagenet forebears, was stripped naked and hauled to a church in Leicester where everyone could see for sure that Yorkist rule was over. Such signs of victory were not enough, however. Henry was cautious and mistrustful by nature, and conscious that his claim to the throne was relatively weak. As Henry IV had done in 1399, he turned to parliament for that amalgam of legal certitude and moral authority that only its approval could afford.

Getting parliament to deliver the legal undergirding that Henry needed would be no mean feat, though. Richard III's parliament of 1484 had passed the statute *Titulus Regius*, declaring Edward IV's children bastards, and delivered four Acts of Attainder against Henry Tudor and 103 others. Henry was now demanding that what parliament had done, parliament must undo, which required either a change of mind or a change of personnel in both houses. Given the reputation his authoritarian son Henry VIII later acquired for manipulating parliament, one might have expected Henry VII to have gone in for wholesale change of personnel. It is true that in excluding the Yorkist peers Lord Audley, treasurer to Richard III, the earl of Westmorland, and Lords Grey of Codnor and Scrope of Bolton, he was the last monarch to refuse to summon lords who were entitled to be called. He also excluded the Yorkist bishops Robert Stillington of Bath and Wells and Richard Redman of St Asaph, elevated a few Lancastrians to earldoms and summoned three earls despite their being attainted. But in essence both the Lords and the Commons consisted of the same personnel who had gathered the previous year.

Henry's strategy was not to replace parliament but to persuade it to perform a U-turn, a task that was largely put in the hands of two figures, his new Chancellor and Speaker. Both were astute appointments. The chancellorship went to John Alcock, who had sat in parliament as bishop successively of Rochester and Worcester since 1472. Alcock had been an active supporter of Edward IV and tutor to his doomed son; he had even deputed for the detested Bishop Stillington as Chancellor and shared the chancellorship with Bishop Rotherham under Edward IV. Even so, Henry called him to open the parliament that was to meet, following the new king's coronation at the end of October, on 7 November, in recognition of the fact that his Christian faith seemed more than a mere adjunct to an administrative career. As one contemporary put it, 'having devoted himself from childhood to learning and piety, [Alcock had] made such a proficiency in virtue that no one in England had a greater reputation for sanctity'.[3] Henry knew a little sanctity could never go amiss.

For Speaker, Henry chose a man who had been with him in exile, Sir Thomas Lovell, a clever and efficient East Anglian lawyer who had joined the rebellion against Richard III in 1483 and been attainted for his pains. The fact of his attainder was referred to the law lords, who understandably ruled that since the king himself had also been attainted by Richard's parliament, Lovell could indeed be Speaker – as well as Treasurer of the King's Chamber and Chancellor of the Exchequer.

The appointment of Alcock and Lovell paid healthy dividends. Parliament annulled the *Titulus Regius* and deleted it from the record so that 'the matter might be and remain in perpetual oblivion for the falseness and shamefulness of it',[4] declared Richard a treacherous usurper and condemned his 'unnatural mischievous and great perjuries, treasons, homicides and murders'.[5] The majority of Richard's attainders and several of Edward IV's were reversed, and Henry presented his own set of twenty-eight new attainders, condemning among others five peers and Sir William Catesby, who had already been executed.[6] Since Catesby had been Speaker in Richard's sole parliament, there must have been members of the lower house who within the course of two years voted for him both to be Speaker and to be attainted.

Securing the parliamentary passage of these new attainders was not quite so easy. One contemporary chronicler observed that the Act of Attainder 'did not pass without much argument or, to be more truthful, rebuke for what was done',[7] a view echoed by the two burgesses for Colchester, Thomas Christmas and John Vertue, who wrote in their journal that when the Bill came from the Lords on 9 December, it 'sore was questioned with'. Nevertheless, Henry was not to be deterred; as Thomas Betanson told Sir Robert Plumpton, 'howbeit there was many gentlemen against it, . . . it would not be, for it was the king's pleasure'.[8] And it was a pleasure to which the king would repeatedly return. Whether it was a vengeful bent, an altruistic concern for the security of the realm or perpetual anxiety that inspired him, Henry was to prove a determined avenger, consistently responding to rebellion with robust retribution. The Stafford brothers were dragged out of sanctuary for conspiring with Viscount

Lovell in 1486: the elder brother was executed and the lord abbot of Abingdon, who had provided the sanctuary, was heavily fined. The earl of Lincoln, who sponsored the abortive revolt of 1487 in the name of Lambert Simnel, was killed at the battle of Stoke later that year, and the subsequent parliament saw a further twenty-eight attainders. Six more were executed after the Yorkshire rebellion in 1489, Sir James Tyrrell and Sir John Wyndham were executed for their support for the duke of Suffolk in 1502, and when Henry finally decided to deal with the earl of Warwick, whom he had kept incarcerated since Bosworth, the earl was allowed trial by his peers, but then executed for treason. Henry's last parliament in 1504 saw even more Acts of Attainder than any of its predecessors: in all there were to be 138 attainders during his reign, of which just 52 were to be reversed, compared to Edward IV's reversal of 86 out of 140. Henry was not without imagination in the punishments he meted out. When James Touchet, 7th Baron Audley, was convicted of leading a group of Cornish rebels to London in 1497, he was dragged from Newgate to Tower Hill 'clad in a coat of his own arms, painted upon paper, reversed and torn; and there he was beheaded'.[9]

Lovell proved his worth, securing Henry's desired attainders despite all objections and persuading the Commons to agree the customary grant of tonnage and poundage. On top of all this there was one other, less customary, but equally necessary, piece of parliamentary business to be done. Henry had promised while still in exile that he would seal the end of England's dynastic wars by marrying Elizabeth of York, Edward IV's daughter, who was now released from bastardy by the overturning of the *Titulus Regius*. The Commons humbly beseeched the king that he fulfil that promise; and one by one all the lords agreed. After a brief delay the marriage went ahead on 18 January 1486 and, after a further delay occasioned by a Yorkist rebellion, Elizabeth was crowned in Westminster while a new parliament was sitting in November 1487. Finally it felt as if the two houses of York and Lancaster, both alike in enmity, had been reconciled.

Having used parliament to secure his dynasty, Henry showed no great enthusiasm for it thereafter. In the twenty-four years of his reign he held only seven parliaments, most of which lasted for just a few weeks – and in the final twelve years he held just one. Parliament, it seems, was less a fixed part of the English constitution at the start of the sixteenth century than it had been a hundred years earlier. Indeed, Henry tried to argue that he was doing his subjects a favour by not calling it. As the preamble to a 1504 Bill put it, 'his highness is not minded, for the ease of his subjects, without great necessary and urgent causes, of longe time to call and summon a new parliament'.[10] Whether his subjects agreed with this is quite another matter. It is true that some men absented themselves from parliament – witness Thomas Thorisby and Robert Pilye, who were both elected for Bishop's Lynn* in 1489 but declined to attend, the latter because he had hurt his foot. Yet it cannot just have been the change of king in 1509 that made Archbishop Warham declare as Chancellor in 1512 that it was 'no less . . . necessary than healthy and useful in kingdoms and empires, at least when serious and pressing business is at hand, that subjects ought to assemble more often in parliaments or in general councils'.[11] There was an expectation that parliament should meet. But an expectation was all it could be; for it was almost entirely within the discretion of the king whether to hold a parliament, how long it should sit, who should be called by writ to sit in the Lords and which counties or boroughs should be represented. He could also decide whether to have a single parliament sit for several sessions across several years or to have a new parliament elected. There were

* Later King's Lynn.

early attempts to limit this power, but it was not until the civil wars that it was to be a definitive element of the constitutional battle.

Some have suggested that the deaths of Henry's wife and his eldest and third sons left him feeling isolated and lonely, and that his lurching decline into ill health left the reins of power in the less scrupulous hands of people who disdained parliamentary scrutiny. More importantly, though, Henry didn't really need parliament. Yes, he was acquisitive – the Venetian ambassador described him as 'a very great miser but a man of vast ability'[12] – and he turned to parliament early in his reign to raise funds for war and then in 1504 (unsuccessfully) to seek feudal aids* for the knighting of Prince Arthur and the marriage of Princess Margaret to James IV of Scotland. But he soon discovered far more effective ways of raising cash, not least smuggling Venetian alum and thereby circumventing the heavily taxed papal mono-poly. This was not quite 'govern[ing] England in the French fashion',[13] as the Spanish envoy Pedro de Ayala put it – Henry did not exact taxes at his pleasure – but some of the extra-parliamentary methods used were to create a sense of resentment.

It was Henry's second Chancellor, the exceptionally gifted John Morton, who was to start the restoration of the royal coffers that helped make parliamentary taxation redundant. Originally a committed Lancastrian, from 1456 he was Chancellor to the young Edward, prince of Wales, and after the battle of Towton he escaped to join Margaret of Anjou. He later came to terms with the Edwardian regime and pursued a twin-track legal and eccle-siastical career, becoming Master of the Rolls in 1472 and Dean of the Arches in 1474, while also holding the rectory of Shellingford. In 1478 Edward IV made him bishop of Ely, but

* That is, funds peers were required to provide to their prince as part of their feudal obligations.

under Richard III he was arrested, imprisoned and attainted again when he supported the Buckingham rebellion. A remarkable escapologist, Morton gained Henry Tudor's favour by securing the pope's support for his claim to the throne, and in 1486 Henry made him archbishop of Canterbury; the following year he completed a switch with Alcock, who surrendered the chancellorship and transferred from Worcester to Ely. In 1493 Morton was created cardinal priest of St Anastasia.

Cardinal Morton's fame rests largely on the way in which voluntary 'benevolences' were extracted from the wealthy in the 1490s. His neat catch-22 (extravagance betrays wealth whereas frugality implies savings, so either way you should contribute generously to the king) was later nicknamed 'Morton's fork' by Francis Bacon. Morton's gift for accountancy, his financial acumen and his political nous were evident from the moment he became Chancellor. It was the creation of the 'council learned in the law' in 1495, though, that was to prove the most effective means of do-it-yourself financing. This was the brainchild of Sir Reynold Bray, the rough, plain-speaking adviser to Henry's mother Margaret Beaufort, who assisted in Henry's invasion, was rewarded with appointment to the lucrative posts of Chancellor of the Duchy of Lancaster and Treasurer, and sat in three parliaments for Hampshire. Bray's entrepreneurial panache undoubtedly helped line his own and the king's pockets, but its operation was transformed by the promotion in 1504 to the council learned in the law of two former Speakers, Sir Richard Empson and Edmund Dudley.

They were a talented and ambitious pair. Both came from respectable stock. Empson's family held sway at Towcester; Dudley's father John was the second son of the first Baron Dudley and brother of William Dudley, Edward IV's depressingly feeble bishop of Durham. They both trained as lawyers and sat in parliament – Empson for Northamptonshire in at least the three parliaments between 1489 and 1495 and probably also in 1497 and 1504, and Dudley for Lewes (1491–2) and then Sussex (1495, 1504). They both served as Speaker – Empson successfully securing a hefty two-tenths and two-fifteenths impost for Henry's military campaign in 1491 and Dudley presiding over the disastrous 1504 session at which monarch and Commons were at loggerheads over proposed attainders and financial demands. They both also sat on the king's council and the council learned, with Dudley, uniquely for a layman, presiding over the former and Empson, as Chancellor of the Duchy of Lancaster from 1505, over the latter.

The council learned was ostensibly an advisory subcommittee of the king's council, but in practice its role was to ensure that every penny of the king's feudal dues was collected. That meant enforcing tough tenancy rules, fining delinquents, resolving legal disputes in the king's favour – and doing it expeditiously, without a jury. The complaints came in thick and fast. There were accusations that Empson and Dudley sold royal offices, pardons and marriage licences. Preachers condemned them, Perkin Warbeck called them Henry's 'low-born and evil counsellors', and their fashionable attire and grand entourages infuriated courtiers: Empson was accused of 'having his footmen waiting on his stirrups, more like the degree of a duke than a bachelor knight',[14] and it was said of Dudley that he 'became so proud that the best duke in this land was more easy to sue and speak to, than he was'.[15]

Empson and Dudley pursued their master's directions and interests aggressively, but they were not the only two members of the council learned. Roger Leybourne (bishop of Carlisle), Robert Sherborne (bishop of St David's, later of Chichester) and Sir James Hobart (Attorney-General) were all fixtures. And while Henry VII was acquisitive, in the way that only an indebted and impoverished peripatetic youth who falls on good times can be,

this thorough harvesting of the royal lands did mean parliamentary taxes were mostly unnecessary. Moreover, envy and
snobbery undoubtedly animated much opposition at court,
where it was far easier to attack the king's messengers than
the king.

When the king died, though, there was no protection for his
creatures. So, in search of a little popularity that was not gained
at the expense of his deceased father, Henry VIII ensured that
the latter's death, late on 21 April 1509, was kept secret for forty-
eight hours while preparations were made for the arrest of
Dudley and Empson. Dudley was convicted of treason first,
supposedly for having summoned troops to 'hold, guide and
govern the king and his council'. Empson's conviction followed,
but when parliament was pushed to attaint them the following
year, the Bill passed the Commons but fell in the Lords. It was
only when new complaints were made that Henry decided the
scapegoats had to die, and on 17 August 1510 they were both
beheaded on Tower Hill. It is difficult to avoid the sense that their
trespass was to have loved the old king not wisely, but too well.

Two other similarly loyal servants stood before the king in
April 1523 when he summoned a new parliament.

On this occasion Henry had travelled up the Thames from
one palace at Greenwich to another at Bridewell, and from there
processed in state to Blackfriars. It was quite a sight: the lawyers
and justices dressed in gowns with scarlet hoods and white linen
coifs on their heads, the mitred lord abbots in black, the bishops with ermine-lined capes, and the barons, earls and dukes in
their parliamentary robes. At the rear the royal party was led by
the Lord Lieutenant carrying the royal sceptre, the earl of Exeter
bearing the sword of state and the earl of Devonshire holding a
gold baton at the end of which hung the cap of state. Finally
came the king himself, dressed in a long narrow-sleeved gown of
plain crimson lined with ermine, over which he wore a crimson

cape and mantle lined with ermine and finished off with a long train. The luxurious pomp was designed to impress, and it had the desired effect; the Venetian ambassador wrote home that Henry looked 'very handsome and grand with his fine presence'.[16]

At Blackfriars, the five-acre home of the Dominican preachers, a Mass of the Holy Ghost was sung by the choir of the King's Chapel and presided over by the king's confessor, the scholarly and conservative bishop of Lincoln, John Longland. Prayers were said for divine inspiration for the king, his council and his parliament, everyone kissed the paxbred for peace in their proper order of precedence, and then the assembly withdrew to Blackfriars' two-storey hall, the large upper floor of which served as the frater or dining room for the friars but was so 'richly furnished with ornaments' that it was suitable for a parliament chamber.[17] Indeed, it had been used as such when the plague was thought to hover over Westminster in 1450, and Henry would later use it for his divorce proceedings against Katherine of Aragon.*

The preparations for the parliament were equally elaborate. The hall had to be 'trimmed' exactly as at Westminster. The floor was covered in tiles or a drugget painted in the same green-and-white pattern used in Henry III's Parliament Chamber in Westminster; on it stood a four-step-high dais with a throne covered in cloth of gold and bearing a fringed canopy. Tudor symbols were everywhere: the royal coat of arms, a carpet elaborately decorated with lilies and red-and-white roses, the royal blue cushion for the king's feet. On either side of the throne were

---

* It was also cavernous enough to accommodate, some years later, London's first indoor theatre with three galleries, serving as the venue for Shakespeare's late plays performed by the King's Men, *The Winter's Tale*, *Cymbeline* and *The Tempest*.

seats for the two archbishops, and a bench for their bishops and abbots. The dukes, viscounts and earls took their ordered places, followed by the prior of the hospital and the other barons. In the middle of the room there were four special benches for the justices stuffed with wool. All the benches were covered in expensive red say.[18]

The centre of attention was the king, but the man at his right hand commanded just as much fear and respect. This was Thomas Wolsey: Chancellor, cardinal archbishop of York, lord abbot of St Albans and prince-bishop of Durham. Wolsey was at the height of his power. Having slipped his way into the king's service as a protégé of the conservatively minded bishop of Winchester, Richard Foxe, he had risen with phenomenal speed, becoming a cardinal just twenty months after being consecrated bishop and then papal legate *a latere*. Many an archbishop had been Chancellor before, but what was special about Wolsey was his exclusive power to act directly not just *for* the pope but *as* the pope, a combination which rendered him virtually omnipotent.

On the other side of the throne sat the archbishop of Canterbury, the septuagenarian William Warham, who had been appointed under Henry VII and had already served the crown for nearly two full decades, eleven of those years as Chancellor. Since Wolsey had taken over as Chancellor and been appointed cardinal there had been tensions between the two men over who took precedence – the primate of all England or the papal legate. There were remarkable similarities. Neither came from an aristocratic background – Wolsey's father was a butcher and grazier from Ipswich; Warham had chandlers and carpenters in his family. Both men had qualified as lawyers. And neither was by any means an ascetic. Wolsey's extravagance was legendary, but Warham also lived grandly, sumptuously improving his predecessor's palace at Knole near Sevenoaks and building a new palace on a par with Wolsey's Hampton Court just a couple of miles away from Knole at Otford. There were also differences. Wolsey notoriously kept a mistress in his early years, Joan Larke, by whom he had a son, Thomas Wynter, for whom he regularly attempted to get preferment.[19] By contrast, the bookish Warham was a humanist supporter of Desiderius Erasmus, in adherence to whose principles he avoided many of the sins of the flesh to which his colleagues were attracted: women, dice, hunting, wine.

It was to be a fractious parliament. The king needed money to pay for another war against the French, but since parliament had not sat since December 1515 and the laity had only just been stung for £204,424 of 'loans' that it worried might never be repaid, the lower house was reluctant to comply. Clearly it would be vital to get the right man controlling the debates as Speaker, a post that had been keenly fought over in earlier years. Both king and cardinal ensured it went to someone who understood the crown's pecuniary predicament: the king's under-treasurer, Sir Thomas More.

This was not More's first parliament. According to his some-times inaccurate hagiographer and son-in-law William Roper, when only a 'beardless boy' he had been the improbable prime mover in the overturning of Henry VII's demand for feudal aids in 1504.[20] Certainly he had been elected in 1510 as a London burgess and was now one of the Middlesex knights determined to secure the king's demand of a tax of 4s in the pound, which Wolsey reckoned, incorrectly, would bring in £800,000.

The debate was rancorous. One contemporary wrote to the earl of Surrey that 'the highest necessity [was] alleged on the king's behalf to us that ever was heard of; and of the contrary, the highest poverty confessed as well by knights, squires and gentlemen of every quarter as by the commoners, citizens and burgesses'. Indeed, the blockage in the Commons was 'the greatest and the sorest' anyone had ever seen in parliament.[21] Wolsey decided to take matters into his own hands and on

29 April, with More's consent, himself stormed into the lower house. The king must have his £800,000. The next day More repeated Wolsey's demands. Still the Commons demurred, sending a delegation to tell Wolsey to his face that the king should accept a lesser sum. Wolsey snapped back that he would rather 'have his tongue plucked out of his head with a pair of pincers',[22] before dismissing them. Again he appeared before the Commons, and again demanded his £800,000. This time, for all his intimidating eminence, he was met with 'a marvellous, obstinate silence'. Wolsey demanded that members reason with him, but it was pointed out that it was the custom of the House 'to hear and not to reason, but among themselves',[23] whereupon Wolsey furiously went round the room, demanding of individual members that they support the king. The silence continued. Finally, More got down on his knees before the rampaging Wolsey and begged him to leave as 'it was neither expedient nor agreeable with the ancient liberty of the house' that he carry on like this.[24] For weeks the debate continued without resolution, and by the time of the recess on 21 May the best More could come up with was an offer of 2s in the pound, at which Wolsey 'was sore discontent'. With matters clearly going nowhere, the sittings were adjourned for three weeks while More and others tried to work on members away from the public glare. On their return there was another fortnight of rumbustious debate and behind-the-scenes arm-twisting.

Although it was an offence to speak publicly of parliamentary debates, the rumour in every alehouse in London was now that the king would not get his way. On 27 June, after another fortnight of debate, there was a vote. At this time divisions were extremely unusual: the Commons' usual method of declaring its decision was by 'acclamation', in which the Speaker put the question to the House, asking those in favour to say 'Aye' and those opposed to say 'Noe'. If the resulting shouts gave no clear result, there would be a division – which tended to work to the benefit of the opposition, as the usual practice was for those supporting a motion to leave the chamber while the Noes were counted and then be counted on their return. Invariably this gave the upper hand to the Noes, as some members were reluctant to lose their seats.* Indeed, later in the century Speaker Yelverton put the question three times in 1593 to try to help the government, but still got a Noe. In 1523 the result was convincing. The knights of the shire supported the king, but the burgesses voted en bloc to oppose the higher charge and to boot accused the knights of being 'enemies to the realm'.

Eventually, at the end of July, just before parliament adjourned from Blackfriars to Westminster owing to fears of the plague, the 'long persuading and privy labouring' bore fruit and a grant was agreed,[25] although at a rate lower than Wolsey had sought and barely higher than that which had been offered in May. It took some time to enact the agreed subsidy, so parliament was not eventually prorogued until nine in the evening on 13 August, when Wolsey declared, without so much as a hint of irony, that he was grateful to both houses for their 'long pain, travail, study, costs and charges'.[26] The young burgess Thomas Cromwell would have agreed, complaining (perhaps in jest) that he had

> endured a parliament which continued by the space of 17 whole
> weeks where we communed of war, peace, strife, contention,

---

* The king increasingly favoured divisions as they enabled him to see who approved and who opposed his proposals. The practice on divisions was subject to complex rules, with the Speaker ultimately deciding whether the Ayes or the Noes were required to retire to the ante-chapel or lobby once the doors to the Chamber as a whole had been locked for a decision on the motion in hand. All members in the Chamber, including the lobby, were therefore required to vote. Those outside could not.

debate, murmur, grudge, riches, poverty, penury, truth, false-
hood, justice, equity, dictate, oppression, magnanymity, activity,
force, intemperunce, treason, murder, felony . . . Howbeit in
conclusion we have done as our predecessors have been wont to
do, that is to say, as well as we might, and left where we began.[27]

Nevertheless, he reckoned that 'we have in our parliament
granted unto the King's highness a right large subsidy, the like
whereof was never granted in this realm'.[28] Even though it was a
mere fraction of what the king had sought, More was handsomely rewarded by Henry with an additional £100 for his
efforts.

Later events cast an ironic backward shadow. Wolsey was
disgraced; More was executed for refusing to assent to the king's
supremacy; Cromwell was executed for treason. But for the
moment all were stout enforcers of the king's will.

When Henry summoned the next parliament to Blackfriars
for 3 November 1529, most people wondered why he wanted a
parliament at all. The last one had hardly been a success, and he
had managed the ensuing six years without any more. True, a
great deal had changed. The king's affections for his son-less wife
Katherine of Aragon had dwindled, and he had begun his quest
to have his marriage annulled on the grounds that the pope
should never have granted extraordinary permission for him to
marry his dead brother Arthur's widow. The pope refused to
budge, so the battle at hand was now with Rome, not with France
– and Wolsey was its first victim. The French ambassador
thought that the parliament might be used to unseat Wolsey, but
in fact the cardinal, unable or unwilling to facilitate the king's
desire, was dismissed and replaced as Chancellor by Thomas
More just days before parliament congregated. Nobody, though,
would have expected that the question of the divorce could
possibly come before parliament. Religious and moral issues

were a matter for canon law. They were debated and resolved by the bicameral convocations* of the two provinces of York and Canterbury or adjudicated by the papal courts. The idea of parliament enacting laws on such matters was not just unthinkable – it was anathema.

Which makes the sequence of events in the 'Reformation' Parliament of 1529–36 and its successors in 1536, 1539–40, 1541–4 and 1544–7 all the more extraordinary. Indeed, many a modern chief whip would confess a sneaking admiration for Henry's phenomenal parliamentary accomplishment in securing radical reform not by royal fiat but by consent through statute law, albeit with a distinct whiff of burning flesh. In the popular imagination all this was possible because Henry was a vile, mendacious bully who threatened all and sundry with the block so as to drive through his entirely self-centred policies and parliament was stuffed full of spineless yes-men, but neither stereotype describes more than part of the truth. Although Henry was determined to secure his divorce – the king's 'great matter' – there is no evidence that he ever conceived of a coherent programme of reform. On the contrary, he proceeded very much by trial and error, and it was only with the advent of Thomas Cromwell as parliamentary strategist that any such programme was developed.

Moreover, just as in 1523, the new parliament had a mind of its own. The London alderman and draper Robert Fabyan reckoned in 1529 that this was 'a parliament for enormities of the clergy',[29] and he was right. Wolsey had been found guilty of *praemunire* (a 1353 offence of abrogating jurisdiction to a foreign power – in his case, the pope) and deprived of all greatness bar

---

* The Convocation of Canterbury normally met at the same time as parliament, with an upper house of 382 bishops, abbots and priors and a lower house of 120 archdeacons, deans and proctors of the clergy.

the palace at Esher, but even in his absence he cast a shadow over the proceedings. Indeed, More opened the new parliament with an attack on the cardinal's 'fraudulent juggling and attempts',[30] and the former Chancellor's downfall helped unleash a pent-up fever of anti-clericalism. Almost immediately after selecting a Speaker (the very malleable new Chancellor of the Duchy of Lancaster, Thomas Audley), the lower house began demanding legislation to deal with clerical abuses. Complaints against the clergy were manifold. Members resented the excessive probate fines and mortuary fees they charged. They maintained that when priests took on secular employment as stewards they deprived lay husbandmen of work, and when the church engaged in trade by running tanning houses and taverns they took business from merchants and kept prices artificially high. The fact that many clergy were permanently absent from their parishes meant that parishioners were never taught true religion, 'to the great peril of their souls'. Moreover, it was wrong that clergy often held several posts simultaneously and that anyone who criticized clerical lifestyles was immediately branded a heretic. The example of James Stanley, bishop of Ely (1506–15), was regularly cited: soldier, huntsman, pluralist and cockfighter, he quite openly kept a mistress at the episcopal palace of Somersham. Even More's scholarly friend Sir Thomas Elyot, who later sat for Cambridgeshire, wrote of the clergy that 'they digged the ditch that they be now fallen in'.[31]

With parliament in this mood, when Henry began to agitate for measures against the pope, he was pushing at an open door. The king and the lower house were at one in 1529 when anti-clerical statutes were suggested, provoking a furious response from the conservative end of the bench of bishops. When John Fisher, bishop of Rochester, fumed that the proposals were a 'heap of mischief' that would bring the church 'into servile thraldom, like to a bound maid, or rather by little and little to be clean banished and driven out of our confines and dwelling places',[32] the lower house sent a delegation of thirty members with the Speaker to remonstrate with the king, who forced Fisher to explain himself before pardoning him. His explanation merely antagonized the lower house, which triumphantly proceeded to agree legislation to tackle the worst clergy abuses of absenteeism, pluralism and lucrative secular employment. The lords spiritual harrumphed implacably but were outvoted by the other peers; and so the first pieces of the reformist jigsaw were slotted into place at the express demand of the lower house.

The next year Henry was the instigator of a quite different move against the church, making twin demands to the Canterbury Convocation for £100,000 to pay for the costs of his 'great matter' and for the clergy to recognize him as 'sole protector and supreme head of the Anglican church and clergy'. Convocation was understandably truculent, especially about the egotistical demand for a provocative new title. Fisher argued with incontrovertible logic: 'We cannot grant this unto the king . . . without abandoning our unity with the see of Rome . . . and so leap out of Peter's ship, to be drowned in the waves of all heresies, sects, schisms and divisions.'[33] A period of intense haggling between Warham and the king's counsellors eventually led to a face-saving amendment, adding the get-out clause, 'so far as the law of Christ allows'. Few in Convocation were happy with the outcome. When the weary archbishop sought a seconder for the amendment, the assembled clerics responded with a stony silence. Warham swiftly pronounced that 'he who is silent seems to consent', to which a lonely, courageously ironic voice replied, 'We are all silent then.'

In parliament the lower house's appetite for anti-clerical measures was still not sated, and in 1532 Audley presented a new set of grievances in the form of *A Supplication against the*

Ordinaries.* Henry replied rather coolly, merely acknowledging the apparent desire for 'a redress and a reformation',[34] but he too was busy pursuing in parliament his own claim to the money payable to the pope on the consecration of a new bishop, known as annates; and he had a new demand of the clergy in Convocation, that they abjure all right to legislate and submit themselves to his authority. The prelates in the Lords and the whole of Convocation were alike deeply opposed to these moves, and there was also resistance in the lower house; it required direct intervention from the king to carry the day. Audley was summoned with twelve members to be told by Henry:

> Well-beloved subjects, we thought that the clergy of our realm had been our subjects wholly, but now we have well perceived that they be but half our subjects, yea and scarce our subjects; for all the prelates at their consecration make an oath to the pope, clean contrary to the oath that they make to us, so that they seem to be his subjects and not ours.[35]

Within days parliament caved in and Convocation submitted. Two days later, on 16 May, certain that this meant a complete break with Rome, Thomas More resigned as Chancellor and resolved to keep his counsel in silence at home in Chelsea. On 22 August the much conflicted Archbishop Warham died.

By now the prime mover in many of these developments was the strategically brilliant and incorrigibly ambitious Thomas Cromwell, who had originally caught Wolsey's eye as a highly effective conveyancer and had acted as the cardinal's legal brain throughout the process of dissolving some of the monasteries where there were allegations of corruption and vice and

---

* An ordinary was a cleric, such as a bishop, who had ordinary jurisdiction over his diocese.

transferring their assets to Wolsey's proposed new colleges at Oxford and Ipswich. Cromwell, ever eager and resourceful, had been swift to act on Wolsey's fall. Standing by a window in the Great Hall at Wolsey's palace at Esher, he told the cardinal's secretary: 'I do intend (god willing) this afternoon, when my lord hath dined to ride to London and so to the court, where I will other make or mar or I come again. I will put myself in the press to see what any man is able to lay to my charge of untruth or misdemeanour.'[36] So he set about trying to find a seat, any seat, in parliament. He tried for Orford in Suffolk, but that had already been secured for another. Then he tried the Wolsey connection, asking Sir William Paulet, who was in control of Wolsey's rights as bishop of Winchester, whether he might be accommodated in one of the seats to which the bishop could normally nominate: Taunton, Downton or Hindon. At the very last minute, the day before parliament sat, Sir Thomas Wriothesley filled in Cromwell's name on a conveniently blank form for Taunton.

Almost immediately he made his mark. In February 1530 his friend Stephen Vaughan assured him, 'You now sail in a sure haven,'[37] and soon after Wolsey's death on his way to the Tower on a treason charge in November 1530 Cromwell was appointed to the king's council. By the time parliament embarked on the 1532 session he was drafting legislation and assisting Audley in getting business through the lower house. Cromwell now became indispensable in the management of parliament, drawing up a plan for completing the king's divorce and for the concomitant reform of the church. The following year he drafted the Statute in Restraint of Appeals that banned any appeal to Rome just as both Convocation and the new archbishop of Canterbury, Thomas Cranmer, proclaimed Henry's first marriage null and void, rendering him free to marry Anne Boleyn. Cromwell's drafting skills were again put to use in formulating the Act of Supremacy that followed in 1534, the terms of which astutely made clear that parliament was not granting but merely recognizing the king's supremacy (lest it ever think to take away that which it had granted). Cromwell proceeded to complete the break with Rome with the Act of Succession, the Act for the Submission of the Clergy and a new Statute in Restraint of Annates. Throughout, Cromwell ensured that every argument and every vote was won, granting permission for absence and holding proxies in the Lords, where from 1536 he sat as Baron Cromwell. Soon he was dignified as 'Vice-Gerent in Spirituals', a brand-new title which was never used again after his fall but concealed under the lay title the fact that the king had given him Wolsey's powers as papal legate, now exercised on behalf of Henry as the supreme head of the church in England. It was one thing to legislate for the king's supremacy, quite another to enforce it, but to this end Cromwell now introduced a requirement that peers make an oath of obedience and drafted a redefinition of treason to include the mere questioning of the king's title or good faith. The latter did not have an easy time in the lower house, where John Rastell said it was 'earnestly withstood' and Robert Fisher maintained that 'there was never such a sticking at the passage of any act in the lower house'.[38] Yet Cromwell secured the Bills, and on their back he was able to dispatch refuseniks such as the redoubtably courageous Bishop Fisher, who was sent to Tyburn on 22 June 1535, and the impressively and resolutely silent Thomas More, who followed him to the block in July.

Cromwell was far from secure himself, though, with both the reformist circle around Anne Boleyn and the more conservative allies of the duke of Norfolk seeking his downfall. In three remarkable weeks in the spring of 1536 he moved against Anne, charging her with adultery and her brother with treason. Both were executed. A similar fate befell Cromwell's conservative opponents. When Sir Geoffrey Pole, who sat for Wilton, confessed to plotting against the king and directly implicated his mother Margaret, 8th countess of Salisbury, his brother Henry, 1st Baron Montagu, his brother-in-law Edward Neville and William Courtenay, the marquess of Exeter, all four were beheaded and Sir Geoffrey tried to take his own life.

Cromwell's writ was to run through to 1540, by which time he had seen through a new statute to ensure heresy trials were held in public and that heretics had a chance to recant; the suppression first of the minor monasteries and then of the wealthier religious houses; the introduction of a new 'bishop's book of doctrine' based on broadly evangelical principles; a Protestant redrafting of the ten commandments to make explicit the condemnation of 'graven images', the statues that he had had removed from churches across the land; the introduction of the parish register of births, deaths and marriages; and the publication with £400 of his own money of Coverdale's Great Bible in English. In the political field, too, his reach was enormous. Ireland, the Council of the North, Wales were all bound firmly into the nation and there was a new, marginally more generous, poor law that placed an onus on parishes to look after the impotent poor.[39]

He did not always get his way. When he was ill for the opening of parliament in 1539, the duke of Norfolk, with Henry's backing, presented a set of six articles of faith of a decidedly conservative bent that were then agreed in both houses. It was not on the rock of faith that Cromwell was to founder, however. It was when he arranged the king's marriage to the Protestant Anne of Cleves and she turned out to be rather less to Henry's pleasing than her Holbein portrait that Cromwell was weakened just enough for Norfolk to be able to move against him. To everyone's surprise he was arrested at a Privy Council meeting and charged with heresy and treason. Cromwell had always had to put up with snobbery about his humble origins; now it was overlain with sheer hatred. One peer, Lord Darcy, had told him in 1537: 'I trust that or thou die, though thou wouldest procure all the noblemen's heads within the realm to be stricken off, yet shall there one head remain that shall strike off thy head.'[40] There was. Cromwell's last letter to Henry ended: 'Most gracious prince, I cry for mercy mercy mercy.' It was not forthcoming. On 28 July 1540, in a badly botched job, he was executed.

Henry's parliaments have had a bad press. Edward Hall, who sat for Wenlock, wrote that 'the most part of the Commons were the king's servants',[41] and Bishop Fisher's early biographer wrote that it was full of 'roysting courtiers, serving-men, parasites and flatterers of all sorts . . . lightly furnished either with learning or honesty'.[42] Many have also cited Cromwell's words to Henry, asserting that he 'and other your dedicated counsellors be about to bring all things so as to pass that your Majesty had never more tractable parliament',[43] as evidence of dastardly royal inveigling of members. And indeed, there were attempts to secure a pliable lower house. In 1536, for instance, when Cromwell was at the height of his powers, he sought and probably secured election for Richard Pollard, William Portman, Thomas Paulet, William Petre, Thomas Lee and Ralph Sadler for Taunton, Downton and Hindon. He asked the townsfolk of Buckingham to elect Thomas Pope, a former servant of Audley's, and George Gifford, a retainer of Norfolk's – and they did. When he tried to get Oxford to elect the lawyer John Latton and grocer William Flemyng, the mayor William Freurs replied that Flemyng was 'an aged man, and cannot well see nor go',[44] but nonetheless acquiesced. In Canterbury, Cromwell's instructions that the electors choose John Brydges and Robert Darknall, a member of the king's household, arrived too late; but, undeterred, Cromwell simply demanded a new election and the next morning the mayor John Alcock summoned the commonalty and ninety-seven men

'freely, with one voice and without any contradiction' agreed to
do as they were told.[45] Others did the same. The duke of Norfolk
worked his patronage hard, boasting that 'in all the shires in my
commission, sauf Lancashire, I have put such order that such
shall be chosen as I doubt not shall serve his Highness according
to his pleasures'.[46] So too in 1539 Sir William Fitzwilliam, earl of
Southampton and Lord Admiral, went on a progress round
vacant seats, sorting out suitable candidates for Midhurst,
Portsmouth, Guildford, Hampshire and Ludgershall. In
Farnham he was beaten to it by Stephen Gardiner, bishop of
Winchester, but he did persuade Sir Richard Weston, who
declared himself at death's door, to try to secure a seat for Sir
Anthony Browne, the king's new Master of the Horse, despite
the fact that he was described as 'a man most unreasonable . . .
and one whose words and deeds do not agree together'.[47]

Yet it is clear that throughout Henry's reign there were
members of both houses who held strong views and were
prepared to defend them. It is true that some of the more conservative bishops simply didn't attend much; but others – on both
sides of 'the king's great matter' – were vocal and active. Nicholas
West of Ely and Henry Standish of St Asaph incurred Henry's
wrath for arguing Katherine's case at Blackfriars and were subsequently charged with *praemunire*, while Fisher, of course,
manfully opposed Henry's every trick until his execution.
Similarly, there were those in the lower house who felt strongly
and spoke out. There were convinced conservatives such as Sir
Thomas Cheyne, who sat throughout Henry's reign for Kent and
served as Warden of the Cinque Ports. Later described as 'a timid
man, much addicted to worldly possessions',[48] Cheyne was
attacked by Cranmer for his 'threats at [as]sizes and sessions'
which meant that the 'people in Kent dare not read God's word',[49]
and was accused of treason by his own son in 1540 for having
images in his chapel, yet continued to attend council meetings

and featured in Henry's will. Another, Thomas Temys (Westbury), boldly told parliament that Henry's divorce was 'bastarding the Lady Mary, the King's only child', and directly urged the king to 'take the Queen again into his company', provoking a fierce reaction from Henry who said he marvelled that this had been raised at all in parliament as the 'matter was not to be determined there'.[50] And there were keen reformists too. Indeed, Norfolk noted during the 1532 session that there was an 'infinite clamor of the temporality here in parliament against the misusing of the spiritual jurisdiction'.[51] George Blagge, elected in 1545 for Bedford and affectionately nicknamed 'pig' by Henry, was sentenced to be burned for his denial of transubstantiation and escaped the stake only by virtue of the king's personal affection for him. Thomas Broke (Calais*) spoke against the Six Articles, called for communion in both kinds and declared transubstantiation 'a gross and foolish error'. Sadly he did so at such great length that the House 'wearied of him'. When he finally shut up, Sir William Kingston replied: 'I will bring a faggot to help to burn you withal,'[52] and Broke ended up serving more than three years in prison.

The case of one of the London members of the Reformation Parliament shows the level of suspicion and religious antagonism in the air at this time. Robert Pakington was first returned in a by-election of October 1533. A man of Protestant sympathies with close connections to Cromwell, he smuggled in English bibles, roundly condemned 'the covetousness and cruelties of the clergy',[53] and was described by his fellow MP Edward Hall as 'a man of great courage and one that could speak and also would be heard'. Re-elected for the November 1536 parliament, on the misty morning of 13 November he was murdered on his way to church. The reformist propaganda machine went

---

* Calais was briefly represented between 1536 and 1555.

into overdrive. John Foxe claimed him as a Protestant martyr, who had risen early to go to 'prayer' – omitting the fact that he was attending mass – and alleged that his murder had been commissioned by the bishop of London, John Stokesley, who had argued for Henry's divorce and his supremacy but remained in all other regards a theological conservative.

There was even some, albeit very limited, coordination among certain members in opposition to certain of Henry's policies, led in the Reformation Parliament by the Warwickshire knight Sir George Throckmorton. Once a close associate of Wolsey's, Throckmorton was advised by Fisher not to speak out against reform, and when he did so he was summoned to see Henry, where he repeated his opposition to the divorce. What finally saw him consigned to the Tower, however, first in January and then again in October 1537, was a botched and tangential involvement in the York rebellion known as the Pilgrimage of Grace and his younger brother's support for the exiled Cardinal Pole. He was lucky to leave the Tower alive. Throckmorton later confessed to Henry that he and a group of MPs 'did much use the Queen's Head [in Cripplegate] at dinner and supper',[54] meeting there to talk secretly about parliament. There were others, too, who pulled against the general trend of Henry's policy, and they did not go unnoticed. The ever-vigilant Cromwell made a list of MPs opposed to one of Henry's Bills in 1533 and another list of those who might be useful to pack a committee to ensure the passage of the Treasons Bill in 1534.

Nor was parliament concerned only with constitutional matters of church and state. Against a background of rising prices and static wages, petitions both to parliament and from parliament to the king led to new laws regulating trade in wool, worsteds, leather, pewter, baking and brewing. There was a Prices of Foreign Hats Act in 1529, followed by a Bridges Act and an Egyptians Act to 'expel the outlandish people' in 1530, a Foreign

Wines Act in 1531 and an Apparel Act (to regulate flamboyant attire) in 1532. Parliament also legislated to allow someone who killed a thief to escape the death penalty and to allow for the 'destruction' of crows, choughs and rooks. In 1533 it found time for a Buggery Act (part of the campaign against the clergy, whose celibacy could give rise to innuendo), under which sodomites were to be hanged.

It is clear enough from even this brief review that, far from being the monochrome subservient creature of a tyrannical king, Henry's parliament had a life of its own. This was a time when brilliant thinkers and administrators, many of them from humble stock, came to the fore. Yes, many wriggled on the hook of regal authority: it was both prudent and morally right that a subject obey his king, and the ensuing dilemmas left Thomas More battling with his conscience, Wolsey regretting his excessive compliance and Cromwell pleading for mercy. When Henry, by now morbidly obese and suffering from gout, died on 28 January 1547, his 37-year reign had seen religious, political and consti-tutional change, all the more extraordinary for being completely unexpected and largely unplanned. It is one of the ironies of history, however, that although Henry, ever the autocrat, saw parliament as little more than an adjunct of the royal prerogative, his personal circumstances drove him to use it in a way no previous king had done. The concatenation of the divorce, the royal supremacy and the need for a clear statement of the new religious settlement, along with Henry's frequent vacillation between conservative and reformist positions on clerical celibacy and the theology of the mass, and his deter-mination that parliament should decide and enforce these matters by statute, gave parliament an omnicompetence even Simon de Montfort had never dreamed of. Parliament came centre stage.

It saw structural change, too. In his father's time 74 knights and 222 burgesses were summoned. In Henry VIII's last parliament the numbers were 88 and 251: Lancaster, Buckingham, Preston, Thetford, and both the County Palatine of Chester and Chester city had seats for the first time; Wales got one knight per county and a burgess for each county town (apart from the borough and county of Monmouth, which got two each). From 1536, Calais returned two members.

The most dramatic change of all, though, came from the dissolution of the monasteries and the consequent departure from the House of Lords of the abbots and priors. For centuries the heads of the major religious houses of England had been invited to the royal councils because they held vast tracts of land under royal warrant over which they exercised their own special jurisdiction. But as monastic numbers dwindled towards the end of the middle ages, so too the number of abbots summoned to parliament first fluctuated (Edward I summoned sixty-seven in 1295 and eighty in 1301) and then fell. By 1341 the list had more or less settled at the heads of the two houses of Augustinian canons (Waltham and Cirencester), twenty-three Benedictine abbots, the prior of Coventry and the prior of the Hospital of St John (who, being a layman, was considered a temporal lord but nonetheless ceased attending parliament at the dissolution). Ironically, Henry VIII added the abbots of Tavistock and Burton-on-Trent.

The monastic lords were every bit as impressive as their episcopal colleagues. Their libraries were expensive oases of learning. Their chapels rang out with great music. They held court. They administered justice. They provided for the poor and ran infirmaries. They regularly hosted the king. And they were wealthy. Glastonbury was said to be worth £3,311 at the time of the dissolution; its main house alone covered 60 acres and its abbot kept home at the 300-acre estate of Sharpham Park. Similarly, in addition to its main house, Waltham Abbey had bought the 180-acre park at Copped Hall near Nazeing in 1350, added a further 120 acres and established a manor house that was so grand a 'mansion of pleasure and privacy' that Edward VI was later to think it suitable for his sister Mary's semi-imprisonment – and, once it had been reworked by the new owner Sir Thomas Heneage MP,[55] it was to be the scene of the first performance of *A Midsummer Night's Dream* in 1594. The abbeys were not universally grand; John Hamond presided over a much less prepossessing establishment at Battle, which was described with contempt: 'So beggary a house I never see, nor so filthy stuff . . . The revestiary [vestry] is the worst and poorest that is.'[56] But Westminster had a large abbot's house at La Neyte near Chelsea, Canterbury a splendid manor house at Sturry, and St Albans Abbey, where Wolsey had been abbot (in addition to his other posts), a treasure trove of tapestries, ornaments, ewers, candlesticks, chalices, censers and altarcloths.

The abbots themselves had a degree of independence, too. In theory, bishops were elected by their cathedral chapters and the pope could reject a nominee, but in practice English kings nearly always got their way and could virtually appoint the bishops who would then by virtue of their status enter parliament. With abbots it was slightly more difficult as, unlike the bishops, they almost invariably came from within their own houses or orders, and it was more difficult to overcome the entrenched internal politics of a small community. Having said that, many of the senior monks were bishops-in-waiting – Glastonbury produced six archbishops of Canterbury, and thirty-six members of religious orders were to become bishops after 1533.

Some of those who headed monastic houses come across as figures of true scholarship and spirituality – Richard Kidderminster, for example, abbot of Winchcombe for nearly forty years, a warm-hearted humanist antiquarian with a passion for learning. Others left their legacies in stone, like Abbot Kiston, who added the beautiful filigree fan vaulting to Peterborough; Abbot Bere, who built new lodgings for the king at Glastonbury, two new chapels and an imaginative stone St Andrew's Cross support for the creaking tower in the fashion of Wells Cathedral; and John Islip, whose great triumph is the glorious Henry VII Chapel at Westminster Abbey. They were not invariably holy, though. Even allowing for some of the politically motivated exaggeration and anti-clerical envy of Henry's investigators, some had clearly strayed from their vows of poverty, chastity and obedience. Archbishop Lee of York was deeply critical in 1534 of William Thornton, abbot of St Mary's, York, for allowing too much wearing of silk and spurs and 'indeterminate' intercourse with women.

The abbots, like their episcopal colleagues, were not particularly assiduous in attendance at Henry's parliaments, but they were far from indifferent to the proceedings. They made sure their voice was heard by nominating proxies among those who could attend. This did not necessarily work to the benefit of the monasteries; for example, the abbots of Hyde and St Benedict's, Hulme, who both supported the king's policy, held thirteen of these proxies between them. Indeed, many of the abbots seem to have conspired in their own demise. William Benson (or Boston), who attended the Reformation Parliament as abbot of Burton and returned in 1536 as abbot of Westminster, not only signed up to the royal supremacy himself but urged Thomas More to do the same.

Others made their own accommodation with what was becoming a political reality. The conservative William Rugge, abbot of St Benedict's, Hulme, from 1530 and bishop of Norwich from 1536, was allowed to subsume the one role into the other, which is why today's bishop of Norwich is still also abbot of Hulme. Gloucester Abbey became a cathedral and the abbot of Tewkesbury became its first bishop; the abbots of Westminster and Burton both became the first deans of new collegiate chapters. Large pensions were doled out: £200 a year each for the abbots of Abingdon, Cirencester and Thorney, more for Ramsey, Evesham and St Albans.

Not everyone caved in, though. The law stipulated that the crown could take the assets of all monasteries that voluntarily surrendered, or of those who had committed treason (which arguably covered any who refused to acknowledge the king's supremacy over the church). In September 1539 the abbots of Reading (Hugh Cook of Farringdon), Glastonbury (Richard Whiting) and Colchester (Thomas Marshall or Beche) were arrested. Cook – unfairly described by Edward Hall MP as 'a stubborn monk and utterly without learning' – had sat as a parliamentary abbot for sixteen years, but under pressure he seemed to affirm papal supremacy, which constituted treason. At Whiting's rigged trial in Wells the only allegation was that he had stolen from Glastonbury. Both were found guilty: on 14 November Cook was executed outside the gateway at Reading and the following day Whiting, now well into his seventies, was dragged through Glastonbury on a hurdle before being hanged, drawn and quartered. His body was dispersed around the local market towns. For dramatic effect each was accompanied to the scaffold by a couple of his own monks. Beche lasted a little longer, but he found it difficult to refute the accusations against him, namely that he thought the king's agents were 'wretched tyrants and bloodsuckers' and that he had said that 'all the water in the Thames would not slake the king's covetousness'. He too was executed on 1 December. Thomas More's sympathetic first biographer, Nicholas Harpsfield, suggested that the executions were enforced so as to make others 'so sore afraid that they soon entreated to yield over all to the king's hands',[57] but in truth by now all but a very few abbeys had already succumbed.

So who was the last parliamentary abbot? The last to attend

in person under Henry was John Chambers, who attended the morning and afternoon sessions on 28 June 1539 as abbot of Peterborough, and returned as the first bishop of Peterborough until his death in 1556, just as John Salcot, the abbot of Hyde, returned as bishop successively of Bangor and Salisbury until his death in 1557. Robert Fuller, the abbot of the Augustinian Abbey of Waltham Holy Cross, was the last to surrender his abbey, in April 1540. He held out not because he disagreed with the supremacy of the king – he had signed up to that; nor because he denied the Six Articles – he agreed with them; but probably in the hope of preferment, as there was talk of making the abbey a cathedral. In the end, the plan came to nothing and Fuller died before he could be preferred to another see.

But the last mitred parliamentary abbot of all attended some twenty years later. Queen Mary reconstituted the abbey at Westminster and appointed her confessor, the former monk John Feckenham, as the new abbot, sitting in parliament from January 1557.[58] Although Feckenham, who had been chaplain to the arch-Catholic bishop of London, Edmund Bonner, prepared Lady Jane Grey for her execution, he was reputed to dislike the bloodier aspects of Bishop Bonner's work and argued for Princess Elizabeth's freedom – although when she became queen he infuriated her by welcoming her for the opening service at the abbey for her first parliament with monks carrying liturgical candles, by opposing her religious Bills in the Lords and by refusing the oath of supremacy. When parliament agreed to abolish Mary's monastic institutions, the abbey was again dissolved in 1560, whereupon Feckenham was kept under various forms of house arrest for the best part of twenty-four years, ending his days in the care of Richard Cox, the bishop of Ely, at Wisbech Castle. The final time the rather gentle, devout Feckenham attended, on Monday, 8 May 1559, was then the last day on which a mitred abbot sat in parliament.

There was one strange parliamentary coda to the reign of the two Tudor Henries. On Christmas Eve 1545, the lecherous, adulterous Henry VIII summoned both houses of parliament and gave one of the most affecting parliamentary sermons of all, pleading for unity in religion and deriding the disputatious clergy. According to Sir William Petre, who was attending the Lords under a writ of assistance as one of the two secretaries of state, the king wept, as did many of those listening to him, as he complained that 'charity between man and man is so refrigerate'.[59] Edward Hall, who kept a more or less verbatim record, recalled Henry's complaint that 'the one calleth the other Hereticke and Anabaptist, and he calleth hym again, Papist, Yypocrite and Pharisey'. In one of Henry's most memorable aphorisms, he said it was a sign of the lack of charity in the church that 'some be too styff in their old Mumpsimus' while others 'be too busy and curious in their newe Sumpsimus'.[60]

Petre might have given a wry smile to hear Henry fret thus. As Cromwell's deputy, Sir William had claimed the right to chair Convocation in 1536; he had been a counsellor to Queen Katherine, he had been charged with interrogating Robert Aske after the Pilgrimage of Grace in 1537, he had overseen the surrender of twenty monasteries in 1538, he had been one of the commissioners who drafted the Six Articles on religion, and he had searched Cromwell's house following his fall. He knew very well the merry dance that Henry had led his country on the matter of religion, and he would retain his ability to stay on board through each chicane in England's road to the Reformation. In Edward VI's reign he would examine the imprisoned bishop of Durham, Cuthbert Tunstall, over his conservative views on religion; and he would continue to serve as secretary to Edward, Mary and Elizabeth. Petre himself benefited enormously from the change in religion, securing for himself at the advantageous price of £849 12s 6d the luxuriant former lands of the abbot of Barking at Ingatestone, where he built a fine mansion.

Edward Hall, too, might have been surprised by Henry's attack on the disputatiousness of the clergy. Many of his speeches as burgess for Wenlock and later for Bridgnorth had been about religion. He had supported the translation of the Bible into the vernacular. He had attacked those who opposed the split with Rome and joined in the criticism of the clergy. He had, in fact, been just as disputatious as the king.

But above all, both Petre and Hall believed in the majesty and the authority of monarchy. Neither was a man to rock the boat, both were intent on securing royal favour, and they followed the king's suit in matters divine. But while parliament might remain in thrall to the king, the battle over religion was far from over – and it was a battle that Henry had brought within the purview of parliament.

In this imagined (although probably accurate) depiction of Elizabeth I opening parliament, the queen sits with the Lord Chancellor standing on her right; in her absence he would sit on the empty woolsack. The dukes, marquesses, earls and barons are ranged before her in order of seniority on her left, the bishops on her right and the clerks and legal officers in the middle. At the bar of the House stands the Speaker, with the Sergeant-at-Arms and Black Rod on either side.

5

An Outward Countenance

FROM THE MOMENT EDWARD VI became king there was a new spring in the step of the religious reformers, who had itched with frustration at Henry's cautious conservatism. The archbishop of Canterbury, Thomas Cranmer, grew a beard and started living openly with his second wife Margarete, whom he had secretly married some fifteen years earlier in Nuremberg. Margarete had not had a particularly easy time of it hitherto – when Henry's Six Articles had confirmed the concept of clerical celibacy, she had been shipped abroad – but now, even before the new Edwardian regime moved to legalize married clergy, Thomas and Margarete lived openly as a couple.

Plenty of Cranmer's predecessors had taken mistresses, but now the Lords sprouted several married bishops. Cranmer's counterpart at York, Robert Holgate, married Barbara Wentworth at the advanced age of sixty-eight, in part so as to prove his reformist mettle. Cranmer's younger brother Edmund, archdeacon of Canterbury, had also married in secret as early as the 1530s, and his one-time chaplain, the accomplished theologian-cum-engineer John Ponet, was also married long before the law changed – and before he was made bishop of Rochester in 1550 and of Winchester the following year. (It turned out that this was a bigamous marriage as his wife was already married to a butcher from Nottingham; undeterred, he married again, at Croydon Parish Church on 25 October 1551, this time to the far more respectable Mary Hayman.)

If clerical marriage proved one's Protestant credentials, it deeply angered conservatives, who saw it as a sign of the licentiousness and depravity of the new religion. Nor was it universally approved of by Protestant peers, concerned that bishops could now enter the dynastic stream in their own right. William Barlow proved the point. Successively bishop of St Asaph and St David's under Henry VIII, he was an ardent ally of Cranmer's in opposing the use of relics and images. On being translated to Bath and Wells in 1548, he married Agatha Wellesbourne, by whom he had two sons, one of whom became archdeacon of Salisbury, and five daughters, every one of whom married a future bishop or archbishop.

Clerical marriage was just one of the dividing lines in the battle for England's soul. In the Protestant mind purgatory was an invention of the pope, designed to help the church enrich itself; statues, relics, rood screens and crucifixes all flouted the Ten Commandments' condemnation of graven images; the 'mass', celebrated by a priest dressed in vestments at an altar facing eastwards, reeked of superstition; the belief that the bread and wine turned into the very body and blood of Christ was ludicrous; and services held in Latin where only the priest received communion in both kinds were offensive to English anti-clericalism. Yet the majority of the country's population held firmly to the old religion, especially outside London and the south-east. They liked the blessing of baptismal water in the font, the rituals of Candlemas, Ash Wednesday and Whitsuntide. The seven sacraments helped people explain their fleeting lives and gave hope of a world beyond this vale of tears. To them, the whole new Edwardian regime must have seemed a hideous, dangerous and immoral nightmare.

That the majority of England held firm in the old faith – at least in private – is not in doubt. The Pilgrimage of Grace in 1536 had shown the allegiance of the north, and in 1549 the introduction of the Book of Common Prayer and the consequent ban on Latin rites led to armed revolt in Devon and Cornwall. Both uprisings had to be suppressed by force, and celebration of the mass started up again long before Mary restored the faith. The old religion ran deep. So how did Edward's England become so unequivocally Protestant?

For a start, the assertively Protestant and self-consciously populist Edward Seymour, uncle to the new nine-year-old king, was in command. It was not meant to have been thus. Henry VIII's will had determined that during Edward's minority a council should act corporately. Seymour, earl of Hertford, was to be just one among sixteen. But in Henry's dying moments one of his two secretaries of state, Sir William Paget, conspired with Seymour to add a clause that allowed the council to do anything they thought necessary for the good government of the realm. As Henry breathed his last, Seymour gathered the new king into his care and persuaded, bribed or coerced his fellow councillors into using the clause to accord him the title of Lord Protector.

Parliament had no place in Seymour's calculations. When the infant Henry VI had assumed the throne, parliament was in the ascendant. His uncles had battled for its approval, and there were debates about the role and powers of the regency. But with Edward VI everything was different. Although Seymour briefly considered having Henry VIII's will read out in parliament, there was never any suggestion that parliament should decide on the governance of the king's minority. This was particularly curious as Henry's final parliament was still in session when he died, and remained so throughout the three days when his death was kept secret while Seymour consolidated his position. On 31 January the regency council bypassed parliament, accorded Seymour the title he sought and awarded themselves a few additional titles while they were at it. Seymour became duke of Somerset and his younger brother Thomas a baron, while Paget received both the promise that he would be Somerset's first adviser and lands worth 400 marks.

The second reason for England's swing to the new, slimmed-down faith was parliament itself, where there was a considerable appetite for change in the Commons, even if the Lords was still full of Henry's conservative bishops. A new parliament did not meet until November, but it had plenty to do, not least because the Lord Protector and the archbishop of Canterbury were as one in wanting to recalibrate the national religion. Where Henry had trodden cautiously, they would march with determination. Some things could be done by the Protector or Council alone. Devotional candles, ashes, palms, hocking,* hognels,† public processions, Plough Monday gatherings, the dressing of churches on holy days and 'creeping to the Cross' on Good Friday were all abolished by decree. But other matters needed legislation.

Edward's two parliaments (1547–52 and 1553) sat for a total of just 292 days across six years, but the religious impact of these five sessions was immense. In the first session alone, which started on 4 November 1547, one Bill repealed the Six Articles and the 1543 Act for the Advancement of True Religion, which had restricted the reading of the English Bible to the clergy and the wealthy, and abolished Cromwell's Treason Acts; another reformed the doctrine of the 'sacrament of the altar' to allow for

---

* The extraction of money from innocent bystanders by gangs on the Monday and Tuesday after Easter.
† A similar practice at Christmastime.

congregations to receive communion in both kinds; another legalized clerical marriage. The second session, which lasted from 24 November 1549 to 14 March 1550, returned to the religious fray with the First Act of Uniformity, mandating church attendance and altering daily worship by imposing Cranmer's linguistically glorious new Book of Common Prayer. Not everything went smoothly. In the first session Somerset's major Bills were amended in both houses, while in the second there was a protracted row over transubstantiation between Somerset and Edmund Bonner, the traditionalist bishop of London, and eight bishops voted against the Act of Uniformity.

Oddly, it was a Bill that is really no more than an addendum in the volume of Edwardian religious legislation that had the toughest time in the Commons – and that was to have the most dramatic effect on the Commons itself. For the fourteenth Act of the 1547 session, 'whereby certain chantries, colleges, free chapels and the possessions of the same be given to the King's Majesty', was meant simply to replace an Act that had lapsed on Henry's death; but the burgesses of King's Lynn and Coventry kicked up a fuss about the income their respective towns would lose and dropped their objections only after a bit of judicious pork-barrelling.

The reason the Bill was so important to the history of the Commons, though, is that it disbanded the old College of St Stephen's in the heart of Westminster, and a year later Edward granted its chapel to the Commons for their permanent home. The old Gothic chamber immediately gave a distinctive tone to the Commons' proceedings and determined much of how the House did its business. A tall, narrow building, 90 feet long and just 26 feet wide, with two storeys of windows, it was divided into five bays with an elaborate screen (or *pulpitum*) between the second and third bays creating an inner and an outer chapel. The outer space served as a lobby while the inner chapel now became the Commons Chamber, with a personality of its own. The four raked rows of benches faced inwards and encouraged a confrontational style of debate. Although the chamber was roughly the same size as the Lords', which never had to accommodate more than sixty, there were now 379 MPs, far more than the chamber could comfortably accommodate, and so the practice of rowdy, jostling debate became part of the English parliamentary tradition. As John Hooker, MP for Exeter, wrote in 1571:

> Upon the lower row, next to the Speaker, sit all such Queen's Privy Council and head officers as be knights or burgesses for the House; but after, everyone sitteth as he cometh, no difference being there held of any degree, because each man in that place is of like calling, saving that the knights and burgesses for London and York do sit on the right side, next to the Councillors.[1]

The role parliament had played in Cromwell's statutory reform of religion ensured that although it had been irrelevant in determining the shape of Somerset's protectorate, it was by no means ignored by the upper echelons of the governing council. Indeed, when Somerset's envious and ambitious younger brother, the Lord High Admiral Thomas Seymour, tried to mount a coup he expressly sought to turn parliament against Somerset. As the charges laid against him put it, he had 'determined to have come into the Commons House [him]self and there with [his] favourers and adherents before prepared, to have made a broil or tumult and uproar to the great danger of the King's Majesty's Person'.[2] Appropriately enough, Seymour's own demise was brought about by a parliamentary Bill of attainder, which slipped through the Lords but was 'very much debated and argued' in the Commons, where he could count on the best part of a dozen loyalists. Eventually the Act was secured, and he was executed on 20 March 1549.

Somerset's own ascendancy was not to last. In many ways a brilliant leader of men, whose twin projects of religious reform and opposition to land enclosures seemed to betoken a genuine concern for the poor, his arrogance and total disregard for the rest of the council left him isolated. In consequence, when in 1549 those alienated by his political radicalism made common cause with those affronted by his religious radicalism, against the background of a costly and ill-fated war with Scotland and France, he was doomed. First, John Dudley, the newly elevated earl of Warwick, succeeded where the Protector had failed, in suppressing the rebellion led by Robert Kett in East Anglia; then he aligned himself with the conservative earls of Southampton and Arundel, who resolved in council to dislodge the Protector and have him arrested. At first Somerset holed up with the king at Windsor Castle, but after the council proved itself unanimous against him, he surrendered, to be succeeded by Warwick as Lord President of the Council. Although Somerset was allowed to rejoin the council, his fate was eventually sealed in 1552 when he had to face a double-headed trial, for the felony of seeking to imprison Dudley (by now further elevated as the duke of Northumberland), the marquess of Northampton and the earl of Pembroke, and for treason. William Paulet, the Lord Treasurer, ensured the trial was completed two days before the new parliament convened; when Somerset's peers acquitted him of the latter charge he was, as tradition required, escorted out of Westminster Hall with the Sergeant's axe facing away from him, indicating that he was not guilty of treason. The crowds cheered, ignorant of the fact that he had been convicted of the felony, for which on 22 January 1552, in the cold words of his nephew the king, he 'had his head cut off upon Tower Hill between 8 and 9 o'clock in the morning'.[3]

As the new parliament convened and set about its business it became clear that the drawn-out demise of Somerset had put the reins of power in the hands of a man who was every bit as committed to the Protestant cause. Indeed, his fervour matched the king's own faith, which was developing apace under the tutelage of John Cheke, the humanist classical scholar who sat as MP for Bletchingley throughout the reign. Under Northumberland the Reformation bandwagon gathered pace. Several of the more conservative and obstructive bishops were removed from office, including William Rugge of Norwich (resigned 1549), John Vesey of Exeter (resigned 1551), Edmund Bonner (deprived November 1549), Stephen Gardiner (deprived February 1551) and Nicholas Heath and George Day (deprived October 1551), all of whom were replaced with reformists.

In the Commons, too, there was a steady drift towards reform. In November 1551 William Cecil, the young MP for Stamford and now one of the junior secretaries of state, hosted a debate on the theology of the eucharist, effectively promoting the Protestant views of Cheke, who was his brother-in-law, of Edmund Grindal (later Archbishop of Canterbury) and of Robert Horne, the dean of Durham. His audience included Lord Russell, Sir Anthony Cooke, Sir Francis Knollys, Sir Thomas Wroth, John Harrington and one of the Protestant sons of Sir George Throckmorton, all of whom would later feature prominently in Elizabethan parliamentary debates. Another meeting was then held at the home of the MP for Wareham, Sir Richard Morrison, on the back of which Cranmer compiled a new canon law, a set of forty-five articles of religion (later thinned down) and a new, more decidedly Protestant prayer book, which replaced the old monastic hours with morning and evening prayer, deleted the vestigial references to the 'Mass' in favour of the 'Lord's Supper or Holy Communion', excised the exorcism and anointing with chrism from the baptism, and cut the prayers for the dead from the funeral service. The faithful were allowed to kneel to receive communion, but the last-minute addition of a special rubric made it clear that this in no sense implied a superstitious adoration of the elements.

When Northumberland presented parliament with the Second Bill of Uniformity in 1552, thereby giving legislative force to this new prayer book, there was scarcely a naysayer in the Commons. Indeed, the only measure that faced any difficulty in this session was the attempt to deprive one further prelate, the prince-bishop of Durham, Cuthbert Tunstall, which was carried in the Lords despite Cranmer's opposition but faced obdurate opposition in the Commons. Northumberland changed course and had Tunstall tried and deprived by a specially appointed commission rather than by parliamentary Bill.

The 1552 prayer book hardly had time to come into general usage, though, as Edward was already mortally ill with tuberculosis and all attempts at making the Reformation stick were focused on diverting the succession from his Catholic sister Mary to the Protestant claimant Lady Jane Grey. Edward died in his palace at Greenwich on 6 July 1553, still just fifteen. Almost immediately conservative clergy returned to their Latin rituals and their parishioners heard the words of the old Latin Mass again: 'hoc est enim corpus meum' to some, 'hocus-pocus' to others. The cautious and insinuating William Paget, who managed to survive as a minister under Henry, Edward and Mary, hit the nail on the head when he commented that 'the use of the old religion is forbidden by a law, and the use of the new is not yet printed in the stomachs of the eleven of the twelve parts in the realm, what countenance so ever men make outwardly to please them in whom they see this power resteth'.[4] Many would soon have to make yet another outward countenance to please the new power.

It was always going to be difficult for Mary. The first queen regnant of England, she was scarred by her parents' protracted and extremely public divorce and schooled in self-preservation. She had been declared a bastard by her father and by parliament, and her brother had sought to exclude her from the throne. She was thirty-seven and unmarried. Nothing was secure. Understandably but foolishly, she relied on a tiny coterie of advisers through whom she sought to achieve her primary aim, the restoration of Roman Catholicism in England. Emotionally attached to her mother's Spanish heritage, she was blind to the disdain she courted among her xenophobic subjects by her fixed intention to marry Philip, the heir to the throne of Spain.

Her first parliament, which she called within a month of her accession, was tough. There was an irony at the heart of the session, for in order to achieve her ends Mary had to use the very concept of royal supremacy over matters spiritual that she denied in her loyalty to Rome. There was considerable opposition in both houses to her signature Bill, repealing the Edwardian legislation on religion and turning the religious clock back to the last days of her father's reign. The treason law, which sought to repeal all existing treason laws and introduce a new offence of denying the legal title of her future husband, also struggled in the Commons, where it was debated for five days and a substantial minority of 80 voted against it (with 270 in favour). The Commons also boldly addressed the matter of the queen's marital intentions, sending the new Speaker Sir John Pollard on 16 November 1553 to demand not just that she marry, but that she marry an Englishman. As Mary had already secretly pledged herself to Philip, and as Pollard spoke in the next parliament in hearty support of that choice, there was an air of unreality about the whole proceeding, but Mary was nonetheless incensed at the impertinence. 'Parliament', she complained with a hint of feminist pique, 'was not accustomed to use such language to the kings of England, nor was it suitable or respectful that it should do so.'[5]

One thing Mary could do was change the bench of bishops. Those who had married were an easy target. Archbishop Holgate was deprived of his bishopric and sent to the Tower until he paid a £1,000 fine. Ponet was imprisoned and then fled the country, before assisting the Wyatt rebellion in 1554; he died in Strasbourg in 1556. Two other married bishops were treated relatively leniently, though. John Bird, successively bishop of St David's and Chester, was deprived but was allowed to continue as the married vicar of Dunmore until his death. Paul Bush, the bishop of Bristol, had married Edith Ashley; when she died three months into Mary's reign, he too was deprived but lived on as the widower rector of Winterbourne. Other grounds were found for removing mitres. John Taylor was deprived of his Lincoln see for refusing to attend the mass at the opening of Mary's first parliament, and died shortly thereafter. John Scory, of Rochester and then Chichester, was deprived for his views on the mass, though he returned as Elizabethan bishop of Hereford in 1559. In the places of those ejected, others who had been deprived under Edward were now restored: George Day, imprisoned in the Fleet for voting against the Book of Common Prayer, returned to Chichester; Bonner to London; Gardiner to Winchester; Vesey to Exeter.

Thanks in part to this change of personnel, and in part to the successful suppression early in 1554 of the rebellion against her betrothal to Philip, led by the belligerent one-time knight for Essex and son of the poet, Sir Thomas Wyatt,[6] Mary's second parliament, called in April 1554, was relatively quiescent. Even figures like Sir John Russell, who had sat as knight for Buckinghamshire but had joined the Lords as earl of Bedford and had promoted a series of Protestant MPs in the growing number of west country seats he controlled, opposed Wyatt, and in most things Mary got her way. The quiescence lasted through the wedding itself in July and into November, when Mary summoned another parliament for her intended *coup de grâce*, the restitution of union with Rome, for which she had recalled the exiled and attainted patrician Cardinal Reginald Pole.

Thanks to his family background, Pole had risen so swiftly as a young man that it was rumoured that he had been offered the archbishopric of York by Henry VIII at the age of thirty, only to be forced to leave the country when he unambiguously advised the king against his divorce in 1532. A cardinal since December 1536, he survived countless assassination attempts but in May 1539, following the Exeter rebellion, his Plantagenet mother and brother were both executed and he was attainted. He spent the Edwardian years in Italy and France, but was desperate to return to England under Mary. In November 1554 the call came, and on 28 November parliament was summoned to court to hear him declare in conciliatory mood: 'My commission is not to pull down but to build; to reconcile, not to censure; to invite but without compulsion.'[7] It was not Pole's normal style. Often abrasive, he missed out on the papacy by just two votes through refusing – out of either arrogance or humility – to plead his own case. Nevertheless, the following day a joint committee of the Lords and Commons drafted a petition to Philip and Mary asking that England be reunited to Rome, and in a carefully orchestrated event on 30 November MPs and peers, weeping abundant tears of contrition, presented the petition on their knees to Pole, who formally granted absolution to England. Only one brave soul spoke out against this: Sir Ralph Bagnall, the MP for Newcastle under Lyme, who two years later was indicted for treason. Whether the rest were merely making another 'outward countenance' we cannot tell, but although the temporal lords had refused to allow the burning of heretics in Mary's April parliament, now they agreed.

With Pole, Bonner and Gardiner now at the spiritual helm, Mary was able to proceed against the remaining recalcitrant bishops. First up was Robert Ferrar, who had opposed the Six Articles so vigorously that he was imprisoned by Henry and only released on Edward's accession. In 1548 he was appointed to the Welsh see of St David's and married Elizabeth, who gave him three children. Deprived by Mary and imprisoned in Southwark, he was sent for trial in Wales, where, on 30 March 1555, he was burned at the stake in the town square of Carmarthen. Next was the severe John Hooper. A follower of Zwingli, he was offered the see of Gloucester in 1550,[8] but was so incensed by what he saw as the overly Catholic terms of even the new ordinal, with its insistence on the use of vestments, that he refused to be consecrated. After long disputes with Nicholas Ridley – and a spell in the Fleet prison – he eventually agreed to a compromise and was consecrated, in vestments, in March 1551. By all accounts a devout although irascible man who cared passionately about the state of his diocese – he complained that several clergy could not even recite the Lord's Prayer in English – and about the poor, he too married and was imprisoned and deprived by Mary. On 9 February 1555 the green faggots placed around his feet in Gloucester took a painful eternity to light but by lunchtime he was dead.

Cruel as it now seems, there was method in the treatment of the Protestant bishops, evident as it came to a peak in the executions of Nicholas Ridley of London, Hugh Latimer, who had earlier been deprived of Worcester for opposing the Six Articles, and the archbishop, Thomas Cranmer. Mary truly believed that by demanding that they recant or burn she was saving not only their souls, but the souls of all of England. A painful death or a public recantation would discredit the new religion. Other executions throughout the year all reinforced the message, but the three bishops were reserved for the autumn of 1555, being held first in the Tower and then moved to Oxford. Latimer and Ridley were tried and predictably found guilty. On 16 October they were taken to Broad Street in the middle of Oxford and tied to the stake. Latimer quickly surrendered to the fumes, but Ridley lasted in agony as their friend Cranmer was forced to watch. Whether Latimer ever said the words attributed to him in Foxe's *Book of Martyrs* is uncertain, but the air of courageous defiance seems to have been genuine: 'Be of good comfort Master Ridley, and play the man: we shall this day light such a candle by God's grace in England, as (I trust) shall never be put out.'[9]

Which left Cranmer, the guiding light of the Edwardian Reformation. What a coup it would be if he were publicly to recant. Depressingly, after months of constant pressure, he succumbed. He attended Latin mass. He signed up to papal supremacy. And on 26 February 1556 he sought absolution for his sins in return for a full recantation. His allies must have been profoundly disillusioned. After all, others had held out. But the day that Mary had allocated for Cranmer's final humiliation did not quite end as she intended. For Cranmer started reading out the agreed text of recantation in the University Church, but then kept going with a fierce denunciation of all the 'bills and papers which I have written or signed with my hand since my degradation'. As he launched an attack on his deceased long-time adversary Gardiner, his captors dragged him out of the pulpit and into the pouring rain. The journey to Broad Street was short, but there was a large crowd who shouted at him on his way. In a triumphant girding of his dignity, as the flames took hold he shouted: 'Forasmuch as my hand offended, writing contrary to my heart, my hand shall first be punished there-for.' It was as elegant a piece of prose as the collects and exhortations of the prayer book that is his enduring legacy. In his own words, 'earth to earth, ashes to ashes, dust to dust'.

When summoning her third parliament Mary had tried to secure MPs of 'the wise, grave and catholic sort, such as indeed mean the true honour of God'.[10] It was an abject failure, but under Philip's pressing she returned to the matter in 1555, demanding again that the boroughs return Catholic burgesses. Again she failed. The Venetian ambassador Giovanni Michiel was scandalized, reporting that the Commons

> is quite full of gentry and nobility (for the most part suspected in the matter of religion) and therefore more daring and licentious than former houses, which consisted of burgesses and plebeians, by nature timid and respectful, who easily inclined towards the will of the sovereign, and yielded to it, whereas in the present house the opportunity for audacious licentiousness increases daily.[11]

Michiel was right in noting a diminution in deference, for the Commons did include a number of burgesses who were gentlemen with opinions on religion; and, just as there had been a small group of disaffected Catholic rebels under Henry VIII, so Mary had her proto-opposition, led by Sir Anthony Kingston, who met with a group of seven other 'right Protestant' MPs at Mistress Arundel's tavern in Poultney Lane. It was an interesting group, including William Cecil, who wrote of this time that 'I spoke my mind freely, whereby I incurred dislike'; Kingston's young step-grandson Sir William Courtenay of Powderham Castle, who was married to the granddaughter of Mary's Lord Treasurer, and his fellow MP for Plympton Erle, Sir Arthur Champernon; Sir John Pollard (not to be confused with his Catholic namesake, the Speaker in 1553), who sat for Exeter thanks to the patronage of the earl of Bedford and his friendship with Cecil; the belligerent Sir John Perrot, who was reckoned to be the illegitimate son of Henry VIII; and Henry Peckham. They were not the only dissenters. Four knights, Peter Carew, Edward Rogers, Nicholas Throckmorton and Edward

Warner, were involved in the initial rebels' meeting that led to the Wyatt rebellion as early as 26 November 1553.

It would be wrong to overestimate the importance of these meetings, but by 1555 some Protestants were feeling emboldened. Mary's marriage to Philip the previous year had as yet borne no fruit, either politically or genetically, and people could see a Protestant monarchy on the horizon. That year there were two major Bills at stake. The first was designed to restore the first fruits and tenths, which Henry had seized for the crown, to the church. Many were concerned at the principle of returning church property for the wholly unprincipled reason that they were themselves occupying former monastic lands. Others adopted a more theological defence of the status quo, but the end result was the same. The Commons disliked the Bill and tried to talk the third reading out. In retaliation Speaker Pollard locked the doors and kept them there until 3 p.m., long after their usual break; since sessions started at 8 a.m. and members stayed throughout the debate, this had some effect. Finally the Commons caved in and Mary got her First Fruits and Tenths Act. When it came to the matter of important religious refugees overseas who refused to return to England, however, the rebels were better prepared. This time Kingston used the Speaker's own tactic, grabbing the keys from the Sergeant-at-Arms, locking the doors and forcing a vote. The refugees Bill was lost and Kingston was sent off to the Tower.

Kingston was no great hero. He had tortured the heretic Anne Askew in 1545 and wrought a particularly cruel revenge on the Cornish rebels in 1549, killing two mayors and a series of priests; and when he was accused of adultery he assaulted the presiding bishop, John Hooper. The Cornish antiquarian and Elizabethan MP Richard Carew said of him, 'he left his name more memorable than commendable'.[12] He was not the only Arundel's rebel to see the inside of a jail: several were arrested for their involvement in an attempt to oust Mary the following year. Courtenay, Champernon, Pollard and Perrot were all imprisoned but eventually released. The most directly involved was Peckham, and he suffered retribution accordingly. An ardent Protestant, unlike his father Edmund and brother Robert who were both Catholic MPs, he plotted with his brothers-in-law, the Buckinghamshire knights and brothers Edmund and Francis Verney, and John, Baron Bray. In April 1556 the former MP John Throckmorton was executed for his complicity in the rebellion, and in July Peckham followed him. It was a fate that would almost certainly have befallen Kingston had he not died beforehand.

The ultimate flaw in Mary's plan to reclaim the country for her faith was the lack of a successor other than her Protestant sister Elizabeth. So when Mary died on 17 November 1558, after an eirenic session of parliament in January and while a second session was discussing a much-needed subsidy, all thoughts were that what had been done and undone by and in parliament would have to be done all over again, only more so. Yet another 'outward countenance' would have to be composed.

Elizabeth's parliaments should have been completely inert. Tudor government still consisted in personal rule. Ministers and the increasingly important Privy Council* were accountable to the monarch, not her parliament. The queen still called all the shots. True, the monarch could no longer unilaterally amend legislation, but she certainly retained the power of veto. She could ennoble peers and deprive bishops. She could create seats

---

* Derived from the king's council (or curia regis), the Privy Council was and is the body of senior ministers, clergy and politicians charged with advising the monarch on the use of the royal prerogative to provide judgments, enact orders in council or grant royal charters. During Elizabeth I's reign it grew significantly in power. Formally, the modern Cabinet is a subcommittee of the Privy Council.

in the Commons – and regularly did. She alone summoned parliament; and, as Sir John Puckering, the Lord Keeper, put it in 1593, 'Her majesty hath evermore been most loath to call for the assembly of her people in Parliament', a reluctance echoed by the scholar MP Sir Thomas Smith, who asked: 'What can a commonwealth desire more than peace, liberty, quietness, little taking of base money, few parliaments?'[13] In consequence it barely sat for 126 weeks in all her long reign, and twenty-six of those forty-four years saw no session at all.

There were other reasons why parliament might be expected to have been fairly and squarely under the royal thumb. More than two-thirds of MPs appeared for one parliament only; attendance was often sparse; only later in the reign were there many contested seats; and many members were clients of Elizabeth's senior ministers parachuted into borough constituencies without any local residency or connection. Ministers sat by the Speaker and whispered advice in his ear, ensuring their Bills were read out first. And they used that new means of getting helpful men elected, the parliamentary by-election, which Cromwell had initiated in the Reformation parliament when he ensured that the two Essex knights Sir Thomas Audley and Thomas Bonham, who had gone respectively to the Lords and the Lord, were replaced.

Given all these unpropitious circumstances, it is remarkable that in its thirteen sessions under Elizabeth I parliament acquired any traction at all. Yet on each of the key issues of her realm – the Protestant settlement, the succession, Mary Stuart, the Catholic threat, the Spanish threat, the royal monopolies – parliament had its say while simultaneously providing subsidies in all but one parliament, churning out a total of 433 Acts and featuring a string of bold, unapologetic and opinionated speeches.

What, then, were the reasons for parliament's surprising

potency? For a start, there was the tug of faith. For if the death of Henry VIII and accession of Edward had prompted a sense of Protestant relief, the death of Mary and the accession of Elizabeth as the self-confessed upholder of the Protestant faith inspired a heart-felt evangelical Hallelujah. The torment was over, and no instant must now be lost in bringing England round to the full unvarnished, demystified faith. The Commons had been truculent enough when Catholic reforms were mooted under Mary; now many in both houses clamoured for Protestant clarity and uniformity, and, believing Elizabeth to be broadly on their side, they were ready to press their case.

One group felt this more strongly than most. Elizabeth's first parliament harboured a group of émigrés, schooled in a new religion and zealous enough to risk pushing the bounds of what was permissible in parliament. The Catholic Bishop White of Winchester had predicted as much in his funeral sermon for Mary: 'I warn you, the wolves be coming out of Geneva and other places of Germany and have sent their books before, full of pestilent doctrines, blasphemy and heresy to infect the people.'[14] He was right. The Commons that gathered at the end of 1559 had at least twelve such returnees, including Sir Anthony Cooke, Sir Francis Knollys, Thomas Wilson, James Dalton and Francis Walsingham; and others were to join them in subsequent parliaments.

Moreover, thanks to Cromwell's revolution by statute, parliament was the cockpit where the battles over salvation and damnation had to be fought. Feathers certainly flew. Marian repression had turned many Protestant sympathizers into militant crusaders, and the pervasive fear of Catholic invasion from overseas was exacerbated by the self-evident fact that the nation had come to the end of the Tudor line. Its security now depended on a reliable succession. So the 25-year-old Elizabeth's refusal to countenance either marriage or a definitive statement on the succession not only infuriated MPs; it frightened them. Declared Protestants had already suffered once; they had no intention of doing so again.

Parliament had motive, then, to make a mark. It also had sufficient means. For even though the Commons was not in continuous session, family connections often provided a degree of continuity. Take the Kingsmills, who provided a Protestant faction all of their own. The eldest brother Richard sat for Calne in 1559 and Heytesbury in 1563, when he was joined by his émigré brother Henry, both of them having been attested Protestants by Robert Horne, the new bishop of Winchester. In both 1584 and 1586 Richard sat as knight for Hampshire alongside two more of his brothers, John and George, and their sister Alice married James Pilkington, another Marian exile, who became bishop of Durham in 1561 and claimed that the destruction of St Paul's Cathedral by lightning was a sign of God's fury at the nation's failure fully to adopt a reformed religion.

The Kingsmills were not alone. Sir Thomas Wroth, who served as one of the four principal gentlemen in Edward VI's privy chamber and whose grandfather was Lord Chancellor Rich, was one of the Middlesex knights under Edward, and for Elizabeth's first two parliaments sat alongside his son Sir Robert, who remained an MP until 1604 and inherited his father's reformism. The family bonds stretched between the houses, too – as did the religious rifts. Miles Sandys, who sat for eight different seats between 1563 and 1597, was brother to the evangelical archbishop of York and saw his son Edwin and son-in-law Thomas Temple both returned in the 1580s. The 3rd earl of Huntingdon and his two brothers Sir Edward and Francis Hastings were all convinced Protestants, despite the pronounced Catholicism of their other brother Sir George, who represented Derbyshire and Leicestershire before becoming the 4th earl. Similarly divided were the Throckmortons. Old Sir George had opposed Henry as a Catholic and his sons Anthony, John and Sir Robert followed suit, but his other sons Kenelm, Clement, George and Sir Nicholas were all 'favourers of the true religion', as were their relatives John, executed in 1556, and Sir Thomas; and all of them were MPs.

The significance of these parliamentary families was not that they provided clear factions – though sometimes they did. More importantly, they provided a continuity of parliamentary memory. The Marian refugee Sir Anthony Cooke, for example, was an influential Essex knight in both the 1559 and 1563 parliaments, where he was joined by his son; and three of his extremely well-educated daughters, Mildred, Anne and Elizabeth, cemented the Protestant lobby by marrying William Cecil, Nicholas Bacon and John, Lord Russell, son of the Protestant earl of Bedford.

This brings us to the key determining fact in the progress of Elizabeth's parliaments. Despite the fact that they were appointed by Elizabeth and might be expected merely to express her view in the parliament, several of her senior ministers were intimately involved in the surreptitiously militant Protestant circle. Indeed, on occasion they individually or collectively aided and abetted it. Since it was now more common for members of the Privy Council who were not in the Lords to seek seats in the Commons (whereas under her grandfather just two councillors had sat in the lower house), this body of men was a significant force. Sir William Knollys, one of the fugitives from Mary's England, was extremely active in leading the charge with Cooke in favour of a more Protestant Act of Supremacy in 1559; yet in 1572 he was made Treasurer of the Royal Household. Thomas Wilson had been tortured for his views in a papal prison in Rome, but on his return to England in 1560 was appointed Master of St Katherine's Hospital, and from 1577 was one of Elizabeth's two secretaries, yet argued and voted for a Protestant succession as a burgess. Robert Bell managed to antagonize the queen in the 1566 session when she described his push for a definitive Protestant settlement of the succession as 'unbridled', and in 1571 was hauled before the Privy Council for daring to question the dubious dealings of royal purveyors; yet he was knighted and nominated as Speaker with the queen's approval in 1572. Whether Elizabeth and her advisers intended to set a rebel Puritan to catch a house of rebel Puritans we cannot know, but what is clear is that the council and the Commons frequently saw eye to eye, even when the queen was busily frowning in quite another direction. Indeed, although the queen frequently expressed her opinion in unambiguous terms, her ministers did not necessarily agree either with her or with each other. So being a royal servant or even senior councillor did not preclude supporting the best endeavours of the parliamentary Puritans. At the pinnacle of this ministerial rebellion, Cecil, who became Lord Burghley in 1571, sought to manage the Commons more according to the religious predilections of the council than those of the queen, effectively giving the Commons its head as a means of shifting the queen's and the council's position.

Although it would be wrong to see parliament's Protestant voices as an embryonic political party, and although Sir John Neale's conception of a Protestant 'choir' led by Thomas Norton overstates the case, there was a steady stream of members who were prepared to sing from the same hymn sheet – and on occasion the Protestant *avant garde* was organized. At first led by the returning émigrés Cooke and Knollys and acting closely in accord with Elizabeth's ministers, they managed to improve the timid original drafting of Elizabeth's Supremacy Bill in 1559, ending up with an Act that gave Elizabeth the moderated title of 'Supreme Governor' rather than 'Head' of the church and the nation a new mandatory Book of Common Prayer, largely based on that of 1552. The Puritan ultras were far from satisfied. The highly articulate John Jewel, who was soon to be bishop of Salisbury and whose *Apology of the Church of England* was the first coherent exposition of the rationale behind the English Reformation, complained that people were 'seeking after a golden, or as it rather seems to me, a leaden mediocrity; and are crying out that the half is better than the whole'.[15] Many in the Commons agreed, and used every means of forcing the issue. In the Lords, though, the phalanx of implacable bishops (and the abbot of Westminster) made their views clear. Archbishop Heath thundered that as Elizabeth was a woman she was 'not qualified by God's words to feed the flock of Christ', and Abbot Feckenham opined that with the advent of the new religion 'all things are turned upside down . . . obedience is gone, humility and meekness clear abolished, virtuous chastity and straight living denied as though they had never been heard of in this realm'.[16] The harshest threat came from Viscount Montagu: 'In changing of religion we condemn all other nations, of whom some be our friends and many our enemies, open and ancient, who long time have, and no doubt do expect, an opportunity to annoy us.'[17] But the Commons persisted, almost certainly with council backing and tacit royal approval, and swept away Mary's laws on religion.

The Commons campaign was a blessing for Elizabeth, enabling her to break through the obduracy of the bishops' resistance in the Lords. If she had hoped that some of the bishops appointed under her sister would accept the new religious policy, she was to be disappointed. True, Cardinal Pole had died on the same day as Mary, and ten sees were vacant, but Elizabeth had even found it difficult to find a bishop who would crown her, Archbishop Heath having ruled himself out because he refused to use her English litany. Only one bishop was prepared to take part – Owen Oglethorpe of Carlisle – and even he insisted on raising the host for adoration at the sacring, which had prompted Elizabeth to storm out of a service in the Chapel Royal. It was a trick he had threatened to repeat at her coronation, so once he had performed the vital task of anointing and crowning, the dean of the Chapel Royal took over.

Now a new oath required that clerics swear 'that no foreign prince, person, prelate, state or potentate hath or ought to have any jurisdiction, power, superiority, pre-eminence or authority ecclesiastical or spiritual within this realm'. The bishops refused the oath and were deprived of their sees, including Heath, who politely begged to be 'disburdened' of his posts, Bonner, who had gained the nickname 'the bloody butcher of London' for his aggressive pursuit of Protestants, and old Methuselah himself, Cuthbert Tunstall, who had been prince-bishop of Durham for twenty-nine years. In all, fifteen bishops were replaced, including the provocative Oglethorpe. Several others died in captivity, among them Thomas Reynolds, who had still not been consecrated bishop of Hereford by the time of Elizabeth's accession and died in the Marshalsea prison, Thomas Watson (Lincoln), who ended his days imprisoned in Wisbech Castle, and Thomas Thirlby (Ely), who shuffled off his mortal coil under house arrest at Lambeth Palace. Only the avaricious and 'light-headed' Anthony Kitchin (Llandaff), originally a hearty opponent of reform, succumbed to Elizabeth's ecclesiastical charms. This meant that in the next parliament, which sat from 1563, Viscount Montagu was the sole opponent in the Lords of the Bill to impose sanctions on those who refused the oath, asking: 'What man is there so without courage and stomach, or void of all honour, that can consent . . . to receive an opinion and new religion by force and compulsion?'[18]

The weeding-out process was not quite so clear-cut in the Commons, although the 1563 Act for the Assurance of the Queen's Power extended the oath to new MPs at the next election, which came in 1571. In theory this should have disbarred all Catholics – and some were excluded, including James Courtenay, Sir Robert Throckmorton and John Talbot, who spent the best part of thirty years in some form or other of confinement – but in practice the Commons still contained a number of adherents to the old religion as the swearing-in process was so chaotic it was easy to slip through the net. Thus the oath didn't prevent wealthy Sir George Blount from being elected for Shropshire in 1571 or Much Wenlock in 1572, Sir William Courtenay being returned three times for Devon in 1584, 1588 and 1601, Francis Stonor sitting for Woodstock in 1586, or Oliver Manners and Tobias Matthew, who both became Catholic priests, getting elected.

In fact, although the Commons often had the air of a clan gathering of the zealots (all the more so after 1571, when the Commons resolved to recite the litany every morning followed by a 45-minute sermon at 7 a.m.), not everyone shared the same outlook. The irascible John Story, for instance, first got into trouble as MP for Hindon in 1549 when he lamented, 'Woe unto thee England when the king is a child,' as part of a general attack on Edward's prayer book. The Commons briefly imprisoned him and reallocated his seat, so he spent the rest of the reign on the continent before returning to be Bishop Bonner's belligerent Chancellor, in which capacity he took an eager part in the persecution of London's Protestants, arguing that 'the sharpness of the sword and other corrections have begun to bring forth that the word in stony hearts could not do, so that by discreet severity we have good hope of universal unity in religion'.[19] Under the new reign, he attacked Elizabeth's Supremacy Bill and excoriated the Catholic bishops for 'chopping at twigs, but I wished to have chopped at the root'.[20] It was not until he repeatedly refused to attend church and a denial of the oath of supremacy had been made a treasonable offence that he was imprisoned; having escaped for the Netherlands and declared himself a loyal subject of Philip II of Spain, he was ingeniously captured and brought back to be executed at Tyburn on 1 June 1571. The crowd, including the earl of Bedford, saw him fulminate at his executioner and roar in fear as he was grappled to the ground to be disembowelled.

It was not just in 1559 that the council and the Commons surreptitiously cooperated, albeit with varying success. In the 1563 and 1566–7 parliaments there were determined attempts on the part of both houses to force the queen into a declaration on the succession; and although after the events of 1559 she consistently refused to allow parliament to debate religion without her express warrant, bishops and Puritan MPs alike sought further change. By 1571 the Protestant parliamentary alliance was even stronger, as it had been augmented by a new set of bishops, and their lordships joined in the clamour for six Bills that would enforce the Thirty-Nine Articles defining the new faith (a slimmed-down version of Cranmer's forty-two), change canon law and impose discipline on the clergy. The initiative foundered when the Protestant 'stinger' William Strickland, MP for Scarborough, tabled his own purist Bill and Elizabeth vetoed all but two of the measures.

Strickland was now one of the most prominent of the avant-gardists, along with Thomas Norton. Norton, the son of a grocer, was a man of no little courage. He became tutor to Somerset's children just as the duke fell from power and married Cranmer's daughter Margaret around the time of the archbishop's execution. Yet he managed to get 'elected' to Mary's last parliament, having secured the Gatton seat thanks to his colleague Thomas Copley, whose mother Lady Copley was widowed in 1549 and who now held the sole vote for the borough's two seats. Unlike Copley, however, who died in exile as a Catholic, Norton was to become ever more trenchantly Protestant throughout his life, arguing in successive parliaments for a complete, though moderate, revision of canon law and for the swift execution of both Mary, Queen of Scots and the duke of Norfolk.

In Norton we can see the paradox of the Elizabethan parliaments laid bare, for he estimated his own contribution in two apparently contradictory ways. On the one hand he hoped God would bless him and the 'poore hod upon [his] back among the mortarbearers in the work of God, or rather the caryers away of dung and rubish to make roome for workmen and bylders in the house of Jesus Christ the church of England'.[21] Yet this same humble, ardent, independent Protestant also confessed that 'all that I have done I did by commandment of the House, and especially of the Queen's Council there, and my chiefest care was in all things to be directed by the Council'.[22] It would be wrong to see Norton as some kind of double agent for the crown – like many other MPs, he believed passionately in the new religion – but he knew that cooperation with members of the council was essential to success, and they in turn knew that his apparently uncompromising independence was an asset in their attempt to push the queen towards the path they wished her to take. So he and the other Puritan outriders, men such as William Fleetwood, Thomas Digges, Thomas Dannett and James Dalton, were licensed to roam.

The same strategy applied to the thorny problem of the Scottish queen, Mary Stuart. In 1572 the council wanted both her and the duke of Norfolk executed, considering both direct Catholic threats to the throne and therefore to their own security, but Elizabeth demurred. So Burghley was delighted that both the Commons and the Lords demanded that they be put to the sword. This time Elizabeth acquiesced in regard to Norfolk only, but following the revelation of Mary's involvement in the Babington plot in 1586 Burghley prevailed on the queen to hold a parliament. As he wrote to Walsingham: 'We stick upon Parliament, which her Majesty mislikes to have, but we all persist, to make the burden better borne and the world abroad more satisfied.'[23] When the newly elected Commons convened, everyone piled in to denounce Mary. Christopher Hatton called for 'the cutting of her off, by the course of justice', Sir Walter Mildmay said she was 'the very root from whom all the other lewd weeds do spring', and ancient Sir Ralph Sadler added that she was a 'most wicked and filthy woman'. These were all royal servants, but the real vituperation was left to the newly elected Puritan member for Warwick, Job Throckmorton, who called her 'the daughter of sedition, the mother of rebellion, the nurse of impiety, the handmaid of iniquity, the sister of unshamefastness' and argued that killing her would be 'one of the fairest riddances that ever the church of God had'.[24] Both houses agreed without a single dissentient voice that Mary must die. Finally, after another bout of royal prevarication, council and parliament prevailed; Elizabeth signed the warrant and Mary was executed on 8 February 1587. Burghley had used parliament, where he knew people would speak freely, to force the queen's hand. It was the only occasion on which they fell out.

Such cooperation had its limits, though. By the 1580s there was a sharp divide between the most extreme Protestants, who sought a bishop-less church using a Genevan Book of Prayer, and the defenders of a reformed but still liturgical and hierarchical church, headed by John Whitgift, the new archbishop of Canterbury, and John Aylmer, bishop of London. So when Anthony Cope (Banbury) presented his Presbyterian 'bill and book' in February 1587 it had little chance of success, the coalition of Puritans and council having collapsed. Cope and the four MPs who supported his Bill were all sent to the Tower for their effrontery, and Lord Chancellor Christopher Hatton extended the prohibitions that applied to recusant Catholics to include Puritans.

Elizabeth's last two parliaments, in 1597 and 1601, saw

skirmishes of a quite different kind as the Commons took on the issue of the monopolies granted by the queen to individuals and corporations to produce goods at a price of their choosing – the principal means whereby she could reward loyal subjects at no cost to herself. The matter had first been raised in 1571 by Robert Bell, and in 1589 the all-important salt monopoly was debated, to the embarrassment of the clerk to the Privy Council and burgess for Southampton, Sir Thomas Wilkes, who profited from it. On both these occasions the matter was dropped, but the dire economic background to the debates in 1597 and 1601 made for far more obstreperous complaints. The wars with Spain and France and a rebellion in Ireland had required England and Wales to fork out very substantial sums in subsidies. In just fifteen years Kent alone found £107,000. The monopolies covered many household items, so when fear abroad was capped by calamity at home with four years of bad harvests, the return of the bubonic plague, and bread riots in London in 1596 and 1597, their effect on the cost of living was the central concern of many knights and burgesses. As one unnamed MP put it,

> the eyes of the poor are upon this parliament, and sad for the want they suffer. The cries of the poor do importune much, standing like reeds shaking in every corner of the realm. This place is an epitome of the whole realm: the trust of the poor committed to us . . . we sit now in judgment over ourselves.[25]

These were curiously hobbled debates. On the one hand stood those fiercely opposed to the very concept of a monopoly. William Spicer referred to his town of Warwick being 'pestered and constantly vexed with the substitutes or vice-regents of these monopolitans',[26] and John Davies, a poet who was subsequently and controversially Speaker of the Irish parliament and Attorney-General in Ireland, demanded: 'Send for them and their patents, cancel them before their faces, arraign them as in times past at the bar and send them to the Tower, there to remain until they have made a good fine to the Queen and made some part of restitution to some of the poorest that have been oppressed by them.'[27] Davies' one-time brawling companion, the witty and boozy lawyer Richard Martin, over whose head Davies had once broken a cudgel, agreed, arguing that 'the principal commodities both of my town and country are engrossed into the hands of those blood-suckers of the common wealth'.[28]

On the other hand stood those who held monopolies themselves. The buccaneeringly irresponsible Sir Walter Ralegh with his thick Devonian accent held monopolies for tin and playing cards and was seen to blush when the latter was debated. Michael Stanhope, who had four brothers in parliament, held the monopoly for importing Spanish wool for felt hats – not that that stopped one of his brothers, Sir Edward, from attacking the very idea of monopolies. Sir Henry Neville held one for the production of ordnance; the earl of Leicester that for sweet wines. Even the keen defender of parliamentary freedom Sir Edward Hoby held a monopoly for the purchase of wool.

In both 1597 and 1601 the House was genuinely divided on what to do, not least because the issue touched the queen's prerogative very directly. The Commons could proceed either by humble petition to the queen (acceptable but probably ineffectual) or by statute (inflammatory and effective only if not vetoed). It was the age-old battle between the purists and the pragmatists, which even saw those closest to the council divided, with Burghley's younger son Robert, now secretary of state, opposed to any action, Robert's elder half-brother Thomas lobbying for a petition and his cousin Robert Wingfield attacking monopolies at full throttle. When Elizabeth promised to reform the system in 1597 the Commons gave way, but by the time of the next parliament, while some monopolies had been abolished others had been created – a point made by Sir Robert Wroth, who listed currants, iron, powder, lead, bags, glasses, bottles, aniseed, salt and smoked pilchards. William Hackwell quipped that bread must surely be included soon, and Wingfield pointed out that the queen had not really kept her side of the bargain as 'the wound . . . is still bleeding, and we grieve under the sore and are without remedy'.[29] Yet again there was a debate about whether to impose reform through statute or beg that Elizabeth attend to their grievances. Yet again deference won the day, and when Her Majesty indicated that she would take another look at the matter there was a general sense of relief. Sir George More thought her graciousness 'inestimable', and even Davies welcomed it as 'glad tidings', only insisting that since the gospel was written down, so too should the queen's determination be minuted. Clearly parliament knew how to push its luck, but like a naughty schoolboy it expected and even hoped to be reined in.

One other reason why parliament gained traction was that it was teeming with men of vigorous ambition and idiosyncratic ability. There were scholars and poets aplenty, such as John Donne, and explorers such as Francis Drake, fresh from his circumnavigation of the globe. Although the lower clergy no longer attended the Commons as a body and the House dispensed with Charles Mathew when he became a minister of religion, there were a few churchmen: John Foster was MP for Hindon in 1563 though ordained; the former archdeacon and proctor of the clergy for Exeter in Convocation in 1562, Robert Lougher, was MP for Pembroke boroughs in 1572; and James Bisse managed to be poetically MP for Wells and rector of Mells at the same time. Then as now, of course, neither ability nor clerical status guaranteed moral rectitude. Thomas Martin, who sat for various seats between 1553 and 1558, was accused of living with a syphilitic priest and committing buggery; George

Acworth, son-in-law of Bishop Horne, held several clergy livings but was 'put from his place for the dissolute life he led';[30] Richard Topcliffe so delighted in the practice of torture that he drew gallows in the margins of books; William Darrell had an affair with Sir Walter Hungerford's wife and threw his own wife's maid's newborn baby on the fire; Christopher Perne stole gold buttons, was sent to the Marshalsea for 'pickery' and was deprived of his seat of Grampound in 1566 as a 'lunatic'; Francis Keilway stole his mother-in-law's silver; Sir Richard Rogers and Robert Gregory were pirates; Walter Lee was a notorious swindler; Lewis Lashbrook was a forger and blackmailer; and John Killigrew's reputation for cattle rustling, trafficking and smuggling while sitting for Penryn embarrassed his older, wiser and duller diplomat brother Henry, but was easily exceeded by his son John (also Penryn), of whom it was said: 'He kept not within the compass of the law, as his father now and then, from fear of punishment, did.'[31]

Against this chequered background shone a series of talented royal councillors, many of whom came to the Commons from relatively modest backgrounds. None were more impressive than the Cecils, William and his younger son Robert. William's descendants would include two prime ministers and countless peers and MPs, but he was not the fount of the parliamentary lineage: his father Richard and grandfather David had attended parliament six times for Stamford by the time William took over the seat in 1542. His career could all have gone horribly wrong at an early stage, for his first public role was as secretary to the duke of Somerset, whose disgrace he survived with masterly skill by transferring his allegiance to the earl of Warwick and becoming third secretary of state and a member of Edward's Privy Council. Always at the heart of the Protestant clique – his first wife was John Cheke's sister Mary, his second Sir Anthony Cooke's daughter Mildred – he just managed to keep on the right side of the Marian regime and was appointed secretary by Elizabeth on the first day of her reign. It was to be a close and mutually dependent relationship that spanned forty years. In 1571 he was created Baron Burghley and the following year Lord Treasurer, a post he held until his death in 1598.

There were matters on which Burghley disagreed with his royal mistress. He was infuriated that she refused to marry. He loathed her procrastination. He wanted Mary Stuart executed. Often Elizabeth overruled him, refusing assent to Bills that he had sponsored or drafted. But Burghley's closeness to Elizabeth – and her combination of wilfulness and indecision – enabled him to do something not even Thomas Cromwell could do: use parliament to advance his policies independently of, or indeed contrary to, the queen's own views. While still in the Commons in 1559 he actively helped draft the religious settlement in terms that Elizabeth fervently opposed but eventually had to accept. He supported clear action against Mary Stuart as early as 1566, and ensured the election of Speakers Bell and Puckering in the hope that they would help advance the same policy. With personal control of about two dozen seats, he promoted supporters. Once in the Lords, he attended assiduously and worked through his fellow councillors in the Commons to ensure the success of his pet Bills.

Parliament, in short, mattered to Burghley in a way that it had never done to any previous royal minister, as it was his primary way of subtly pushing the queen to support his policies. He could be sycophantic but he was far from humble. He accumulated wealth, in large part thanks to his lucrative post as Master of the Wards, and he spent it in Wolseian style, constructing palaces to rival Hampton Court at Burghley (in the shape of an Elizabethan E) and at Theobalds. For some time Burghley jousted for primacy with that more amorous suitor for Elizabeth's affections, the earl of Leicester, but when the earl died in 1588 Burghley and his son Robert, who now helped his father in the role of secretary that the elder Cecil refused fully to relinquish when he became Lord Treasurer, were left as the pre-eminent royal councillors.

Robert was to prove as industrious as his father, a great secretary and a competent manager of his queen, but a far less successful manager of parliament. First elected for Westminster in 1584 and subsequently one of the Hertfordshire knights until his elevation to the Lords in 1603, Robert was made councillor in 1591 and secretary in 1596, effectively taking over from his father as Elizabeth's closest adviser. Unlike his father, he had little feel for the Commons, and indeed let four Commons sessions pass by before he opened his mouth. He was a methodical manager, though, contriving to have some thirty friends and allies elected in 1597 and 1601, despite committing the elementary mistake of trying to secure seats in Doncaster and Durham, neither of which was enfranchised.

Robert Cecil's manner with the Commons verged on the surly, which served him ill in the 1593 subsidy debate. He could also be phenomenally preachy. In the midst of the tough 1601 parliament, he lectured all and sundry:

> I have been . . . a member of this House in six or seven parliaments, yet never did I see the House in so great confusion. I believe there never was in any parliament a more tender point handled than the liberty of the subject, that when any is discussing this point, he should be cried and coughed down. This is more fit for a grammar school than a court of parliament.[32]

When a motion was later lost by a single vote, 106 to 105, and several members claimed that some had been persuaded to stay in the seats (and therefore vote No) by a deft tug on their sleeves,

Robert lambasted those who were trying to help his cause with the prim opinion that 'he whose voice may be drawn either forward or backward by the sleeves like a dog in a string may no more be of this House'.[33] Indeed, he only rescued the moment when someone suggested that the Speaker should have been allowed to vote, thereby again aiding the government. His unusually gracious answer settled the matter for ever: 'Mr Speaker hath no voice and though I am sorry to say it, lost it is, and farewell to it.' Henceforth the Speaker would not vote unless there was an equality of votes on either side (in contrast to the Lords, where the Lord Chancellor voted in his own right and a tied vote was decided according to the rules of the House).*

In 1597 a father wrote: 'As my son is as it were entering into the world and to those years that may fit his service . . . I am minded to advise him to stand to be knight of the shire for Surrey against the next parliament.'[34] It is a piece of advice William Cecil himself could have given, for although parliament was no stronger by the time of Elizabeth's death in 1603 than it had been a hundred years earlier, yet it was clear a man could make his way in life, could even make a mark, just by entering it.

* In the Commons this eventuality is now governed by three interlocking principles: that the Speaker should vote so as not to decide the question and to allow further debate; that he or she should ensure that any motion is carried only by the majority; and that in a division on a Bill he or she should vote to leave the Bill in its existing form.

The struggle for freedom of speech both inside and outside parliament was intense. When the MP John Wilkes heavily criticized George III and his chief minister, the earl of Bute, in the North Briton, he was arrested and expelled from parliament, only to be re-elected and re-expelled three times. Here the bookseller John Williams, who had re-published the offending issue of Wilkes's periodical, is pilloried in Palace Yard outside Westminster Hall.

6

Freeborn Men

ON 23 MAY 2011 JOHN HEMMING, a wealthy midlands Lib Dem MP, looked nervous but determined as he stood to ask a question of the Attorney-General. His anxiety sprang from the fact that he was about to flout a 'super-injunction' issued in the High Court that forbade newspapers to run a story about a footballer's extra-marital affair. Even the fact of the injunction could not be mentioned, let alone the name of the footballer who had secured it. So when Hemming named Ryan Giggs he was directly defying the court. He had done so before, when he had named Sir Fred Goodwin as another holder of a super-injunction, and in 2009 a Labour MP, Paul Farrelly, had cracked open the legal confidentiality around a super-injunction regarding toxic waste allegedly dumped by Trafigura in Côte d'Ivoire. Both MPs were using an old parliamentary privilege, as a result of which the press would be able to cite their words in full without fear of being sued.

On 8 February 1576 Peter Wentworth, the godly and earnest burgess for Tregony, became a candidate for earliest and indeed most forthright advocate of parliamentary free speech when he rose to speak at the very beginning of the newly reconvened parliament. He had thought long and hard about whether to make his speech. Indeed, he had drafted it three years earlier and had been waiting ever since for parliament to sit to give him the chance to deliver it – and even then he paced up and down in the garden trying to decide whether to go ahead.

To an extent he was following in the footsteps of his brother Paul, who had posed tough questions to the Commons in 1571. Frustration that Elizabeth had denied parliament the right to sit had irritated Peter, and he felt himself duty bound to warn his queen of the danger he believed she faced. Speaking with the certainty of the preacher, he was bold in his assertions. He detested, he said, the rumours and messages that passed around the Commons, intimating that you should 'take heed of what you do' or insinuating that 'the Queen's majestie liketh not of such a matter'. He disliked all royal inhibitions issued to the House, such as the command in the last session not to deal 'in any matters of religion but first to receive it from the bishops'. All such messages should be 'buried in Hell'. By contrast, 'all matters that concerne God's honour through free speech shall be propagated here and sett forward and all things that doe hinder it removed, repulsed and taken away'. Although some of the queen's councillors were good and faithful, some were 'traitors and undermyners of her Majestie's life and safety'. Above all, he believed that

> in this House which is tearmed a place of free speech there is nothing soe necessary for the preservacion of the prince and state as free speech, and without it, it is a scorne and mockery to call it a parliament house for in truth is it is none, but a very schoole of flattery and dissimulacion and soe a fitt place to serve the Devill and his angels in and not to glorify God and benefitt the commonwealth.

Elizabeth needed free and open discourse in the Commons so that she could be well counselled. And to cap it all: 'None is without fault,' he said, 'no, not our Noble Queen.'[1]

As he continued, his colleagues visibly recoiled and he acknowledged later that he was briefly cowed, but still he ploughed on until the House finally seized the initiative. He was howled down, arrested by the Sergeant and dragged off to appear before a special committee in the Star Chamber that same day.*

Wentworth's long brooding had steeled him to the fight. He refused to recognize the committee's jurisdiction, except as members of a committee of the House; and he demanded the right to speak his mind, 'for I am now no private person, I am a publick, and a Councellor to the whole State in that place where it is lawful for me to speak my mind freely and not for you (as counsellors) to call me to accompt for anything that I doe speake in the House'.[2] The next day, with Wentworth standing at the bar of the House, the committee recommended that he be sent to the Tower. Nobody demurred, not even the MPs of the same puritanical bent as himself. The impasse might have lasted for years, but when he quietly asked the queen's pardon she suggested that the Commons release him and his month-long stay in prison was ended. In essence, Wentworth got away with a deliberately incendiary speech.

This was not the first time that an MP had demanded freedom of speech. Early medieval Speakers demanded certain rights on behalf of the knights and burgesses when they were officially

---

* The Court of Star Chamber, so named because of the gilded stars on the dark ceiling of the room where it sat, consisted of privy councillors and judges and from the late fifteenth century functioned as an alternative court trying those considered too powerful to be found guilty by a common court. Its flexible approach to the law, its convention of sitting in secret and its practice of dealing only with written evidence gained it a reputation for arbitrary and tyrannical justice.

presented to the monarch at the start of a new parliament. After some self-deprecatory guff, the Speaker would issue a formulaic request for the right of access to the king and freedom from arrest before going on to beg that the king should not take offence at anything he might say as it would not be intentionally offensive, and that if his colleagues disagreed with anything he said he should be allowed to correct himself. In the fractious 1406 parliament, when there were said to be vicious rumours that members had been critical of Henry IV, Speaker Tiptoft made the same protective point seven times.

Yet in 1451, in the heat of the Wars of the Roses, when Thomas Yonge presented a petition on behalf of his Bristol burghers that the duke of York should be declared heir to the throne, he was sent to the Tower for his impudence. Yonge was released a year later and knighted in 1471, but he did not let go of the point of principle, arguing in parliament in 1456 that from time immemorial the Commons had enjoyed the liberty and freedom 'to speke and sey in the Hous of their assemble, as to theym is thought convenient or reasonable, without eny maner chalange, charge or punycion therefore'.[3]

Sir Thomas More, as Speaker in the 1523 parliament – and still a fiercely loyal royal servant – added to the traditional demands by pleading that Henry VIII

> give to all your commons here assembled your most gracious licence and pardon freely, without doubt of your dreadful displeasure, every man to discharge his conscience and boldly in everything incident among, declare his advice, and whatsoever happeneth any man to say, it may like your noble Majesty of your inestimable goodness to take all in good part, interpreting every man's words, how uncunningly soever they may be couched, to proceed yet of a good zeal towards the profit of your realm and honour of your royal person.[4]

Built at the end of the eleventh century and fitted with its magnificent hammer-beam ceiling in the fourteenth, for centuries Westminster Hall housed the royal courts, the state trials for treason and many parliamentary occasions. It is still standing today, the oldest surviving building on the site of the Palace of Westminster.

Above: Expenses for attending parliament were already being paid in the thirteenth century. Here is the writ for costs incurred by Bartholomew de Badlesmere (boxed) and Fulk Peyferer in 1309.

Above: Sir William Disney represented Lincoln at four parliaments under Edward I and II. His tomb is the earliest known surviving image of a commoner parliamentarian.

Below: Finance was a central interest of parliament. Ireland's Court of Exchequer was created in 1299 and used the same green chequered board as its English counterpart.

eftre ledit colier vendu engaige dóne ne aliene pour
necefsite ou caufe quelconque que ce foit

Alexander rex
Scotie

lewellin
princeps

English kings had consulted their barons and bishops from the earliest times,
but by the time of Edward I (**above**) the archbishops, bishops, mitred abbots,
lords and law officers were parliamentary fixtures. All six of Edward IV's
parliaments also included the Commons (at his feet, **below left**). Central to
parliament were the king's ministers, such as the notorious Richard Empson
and Edmund Dudley, seen with Henry VII (**below right**).

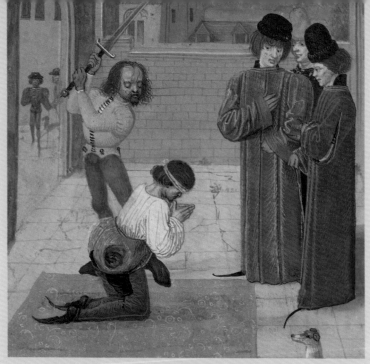

Medieval parliaments acquired significant power. When the Merciless Parliament found the judge Robert Tresilian guilty of corruption in 1388, he was hauled from sanctuary and executed (**above**). In 1399 (**below**) Henry Bolingbroke ostentatiously left the throne vacant until the shortest parliament on record had rubber-stamped his seizure of the crown from Richard II.

MPs Sir Francis Walsingham, Henry Carey, William Cecil and Walter Ralegh (**above, left to right**) prospered under Elizabeth I, but Ralegh was executed for treason under James VI and I, whose favourite George Villiers (**left**) was made a duke but was assassinated in 1628. In 1641 Thomas Wentworth, earl of Strafford, was convicted for treason by the Long Parliament by an Act of Attainder (**below**).

The wheel of fortune (**left**) was a medieval allegory of political fortunes that applied equally to the careers of the two Cromwells, Thomas (**above**) and Oliver (**opposite, far right**), and to Charles I (**above, right**), executed on 30 January 1649.

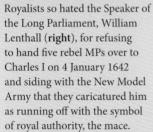

Royalists so hated the Speaker of the Long Parliament, William Lenthall (**right**), for refusing to hand five rebel MPs over to Charles I on 4 January 1642 and siding with the New Model Army that they caricatured him as running off with the symbol of royal authority, the mace.

Religion was a constant focus of parliamentary battles, with bishops regularly being deprived or executed. In 1688 seven (**below**) were imprisoned by James II and famously acquitted.

Even Charles II's five 'CABAL' ministers (**above**) were split by religion, as Thomas Clifford and the earl of Arlington (first and second from left) were Catholics, but the 2nd duke of Buckingham and Anthony Ashley-Cooper (third and fourth from left) organized mock processions and pope-burnings (**left and below**) during the Exclusion crisis of 1679–81.

More's remarks went further than his predecessors' and established a pattern. Both Sir Thomas Gargrave in 1559 and Thomas Williams in 1563 spoke in very similar vein, begging 'that the assembly of the lower house may have frank and free liberties to speak their minds, without any controlment, blame, grudge, menaces or displeasure, according to the ancient order'.[5]

The trouble was that this vaunted claim to free speech rested on two very shaky pillars.

The first was the rule of communal secrecy, which is why one of the first things the knights and burgesses did in the Good Parliament of 1376 was agree to a code of *omertà*. This was vital. It meant individuals could speak with impunity. They could criticize the policies of the crown. They could even demand the impeachment of ministers. Only the Speaker would relate the House's views to the Lords or the crown, and since he would be speaking for all, the views of individual MPs would be veiled from view. Throughout the fifteenth century this code was observed religiously. (Indeed, it is one of the reasons why we have few direct accounts of proceedings for the period.)

But in the sixteenth century the system broke down. As Commons petitions became less important than statute law, the monarch became more interested in the passage of laws through the Commons, and as more councillors sat in the Commons the very concept of secret deliberation became a fiction. At the same time, the Throckmorton and Kingston tavern gatherings were declared in clear breach of communal secrecy. This arrant hypocrisy was laid bare on Saturday, 15 February 1589, when the 28-year-old Sir Edward Hoby moved that 'speeches used in this House by members of the same be not by any of them made or used as table-talk, or in any wise delivered in notes of writing to any person or persons whatsoever not being members of this House',[6] and the Speaker duly admonished all members. The following Monday Hoby exposed the reason for his concern.

Following his speech introducing a Bill attacking the Exchequer the previous Friday, a 'great personage' who was not a member of the Commons (probably his uncle Lord Burghley) had 'very sharply rebuked' him about something he had said in the House.[7] Needless to say, he could not have done so without having been told what had transpired there. Nevertheless, the hypocrisy was maintained: in 1601 Robert Cecil had the cheek to maintain he was shocked to hear about parliamentary matters in the street – notwithstanding assiduous attempts by the council under both Cecils to plan and manipulate debates in the 'nether House'.

The second distinctly shaky pillar of free speech was the longstanding tradition of freedom from arrest for all members and their servants – and this is where individuals forced the Tudors to cede territory.

In Henry VIII's reign it was almost invariably religion that got MPs into trouble. Thus in 1539 Thomas Broke, the burgess for Calais, courted the king's wrath by speaking at length in favour of communion in both kinds and in consequence spent the whole of the third session of the parliament in jail in Calais. Similarly, John Gostwick was forced by Henry to apologize to Cranmer for calling him a heretic in the Commons, and in April 1543 the licentious Sir John Clere and the very Catholic William Stanford, respectively burgesses for Bramber and Stafford, were sent to the Fleet for eating meat in Lent. In each of these cases the Commons acquiesced.

A rather different case, though, accidentally changed the rules of engagement. George Ferrers was well read and well connected. He had been a servant to Thomas Cromwell and a page of the king's chamber, and had been responsible for editing and translating *The Great Boke of Statutes*. In March 1542, though, he was arrested for a debt of '200 marks or thereabouts' on his way to the Commons. Infuriated, the Commons sent the

Sergeant to effect his release. The sheriffs refused, and when the Sergeant's mace was broken in the kerfuffle the Commons summoned Ferrers' creditors and the sheriffs to the House before committing them to the Tower for two days. In this case the Commons took its freedom from arrest seriously, and the king reinforced the message, declaring: 'Whatsoever offence or injury during [parliament] is offered to the meanest members of the House is to be judged as done against our person and the whole court of Parliament.' In one respect this case echoed that of the brothers Edmund and Charles Fox, the burgesses for Ludlow, who the previous year had been sent to the Fleet by the council for mounting a wholly unsubstantiated attack on Rowland Lee, the bishop of Coventry and Lichfield, in his capacity as president of the Council in the Marches. Despite the completely unscrupulous nature of their campaign, they claimed the privilege of freedom of arrest as MPs and the council released them. But the Ferrers episode was different in one key respect: this was the first time the Commons itself freed a member from arrest.

The House also soon started to take into its own hands the corresponding power to discipline members. As already noted, John Story was sent to the Tower for opposing the first Edwardian Act of Conformity and shouting: 'Woe to the realm whose king is a child'; and the House took such offence when Thomas Copley (Gatton) used 'unreverent' words about Queen Mary that it took him into custody and asked her to adjudicate.

From the start of Elizabeth's reign the tussle between the royal prerogative and MPs' freedom of speech became an issue in its own right. Elizabeth forbade the Commons to debate matters she believed were her business and hers alone – and kicked up a fuss when she heard tell that the prohibition had been flouted, as Sir Nicholas Bacon, replying for the crown, made clear in 1563 with schoolmasterly condescension. The Commons' freedom was only conditional, he averred, so members should be 'neither unmindful or uncareful of their duties, reverence and obedience to their sovereign'.[8] It was a 'thus far and no further' formula that Elizabeth would constantly reassert. As the Lord Keeper put it in 1593,

> for libertie of speech her majestie commaundeth me to tell yow, that to say yea or no to Bills, god forbid that any man should be restrained, or afraide to answer according to his best liking, with some shorte declaracion of his reason therin, and therin to have a free voice, which is the verye trew libertie of the house, not as some suppose to speake there of all causes as him listeth, and to frame a forme of religion, or a state of government as to theyir idle braynes shall seeme meetest.[9]

But between these two seas of complete licence and restricted freedom there was a vast territory of dissent, disagreement and debate, and a steady stream of cases started to set precedent for a far broader doctrine of parliamentary privilege than the monarch could possibly tolerate.

The most prominent case related to a far less politic style of MP than Bacon, William Strickland. By the time he was elected for Scarborough in 1558 he had sailed to the New World with Sebastian Cabot and introduced the turkey to England. A convinced Puritan, he took the lead in the 1571 campaign to reform the Book of Common Prayer, delivering a long speech on 6 April on 'God's goodness', tabling a motion to introduce six evangelical Bills two days later and then, on the last day before the Easter recess, 14 April, introducing his own Bill to reform the prayer book. The House was sympathetic, so he was allowed to read the Bill out; but, conscious of Elizabeth's fierce injunction that the Commons should refrain from any discussion of religious matters, the councillors did their level best to put an end to the debate. In the end a compromise was reached: the queen's permission would be sought for continued discussion of the Bill, and the House adjourned.

But during the recess Strickland was summoned before the Privy Council and banned from returning to his seat in the Commons. When the Commons reassembled on 20 April this gave the Puritans new allies, for while most moderate MPs might be content to leave the prayer book alone, they were scandalized that an MP had been deprived of his seat. What price freedom of speech? Speaker after speaker condemned the high-handedness of the council, asserted the historic liberties of the House and demanded Strickland's return. Finally the councillors 'whispered together' and the following day Strickland reappeared in triumph. His victory was so complete that 'in witness of their joy' that he had been restored to them his colleagues immediately nominated him to a committee. It would not be the last time that an over-reaction by the government would turn a maverick into a popular hero.

The council did not learn its lesson, though. Later in the session Robert Bell was similarly reprimanded for a speech in which he argued that the Commons should grant further monies to the crown only if some of their complaints were addressed. On this occasion the council's strictures had some effect. Paul Wentworth reckoned that many MPs were terrified of saying anything controversial for at least a fortnight. And in 1572 Francis Bacon returned to the 'thus far and no further line', acknowledging 'that speech fit for the state well placed and used in matters convenient is very necessary', but demanding moderation as 'there is a difference between staring and stark blinde'.[10]

The free-speechers might affect pure liberty, but even they drew the line at Arthur Hall's outburst in 1572, when he defended Mary, Queen of Scots. So incensed was the House that he was summoned to the bar to apologize for his 'lewd' speeches. It was not to be Hall's last brush with the sensitivities of the

Commons. The following year he quarrelled at the gaming table with the magnificently named Melchisedech Mallory, who was then physically attacked by Hall's servant, Edward Smalley. When Mallory's brother had Smalley arrested for a fine of £100, he sought the traditional protection of the House as a member's servant. Janus-like, the House looked both ways. They ordered Smalley's release, thereby reinforcing the Commons privilege, but then had him re-arrested by the Sergeant and forced Hall to pay the debt. Like a fool, Hall refused to let the matter rest and wrote an angry account of the events for private circulation in which he referred to the Commons becoming 'a new person in the Trinity'. Parliament did not gather again until 1581, but when it did a furious Thomas Norton demanded that Hall be punished for his direct affront to the Commons, which duly imprisoned him for six months and expelled him from the House. In making Hall the first MP it expelled, the Commons again staked out its constitutional claim, but also made it clear that freedom of speech had boundaries.

Peter Wentworth was not finished, though. In 1586 the Speaker was told by the queen 'how she found fault both in our negligence in coming to the Parliament House and departing before the rising of the House;* and also that she heard how Parliament-matters was the common table-talk at ordinaries, which was a thing against the dignity of the House'. MPs were so furious that the Speaker had been to see the queen without their consent that they responded with asperity, claiming that it was none of her business, as at 'sundry times many of them met in private sort to devise how they might salve this sore so grievously inflicted upon them'.[11]

The following year, immediately after the reading of Cope's

---

* Members were not meant to leave while the Speaker was still in the chair and the session in progress.

Bill seeking a Puritan-inclined reform of the prayer book, Wentworth returned to the matter, provocatively posing ten questions to the House, all of them relating to the freedom of speech. It was brave stuff. Question five demanded 'whether it be not an Injurye to the whole state, and against the law, that the prince or priuie councell should send for any member of this howse in the parliament tyme, or after the end of the parliament, and to checke, blame or punishe them for any speache used in this place, except it be for trayterous words'. Yet again this was deliberately incendiary, so Speaker Puckering, acting on the prompting of the Essex knight Sir Thomas Heneage, dispatched Wentworth for another spell in the Tower, where he was joined by four other MPs, each of whom was supposedly arrested for his extra-parliamentary activities, not his Commons contributions: Anthony Cope, Edward Lewknor, Ralph Hurleston and Robert Bainbridge, the last of whom left a memento, scrawling in the wall the grammatically incorrect words *Vincet qui patitur*: he who suffers, conquers.

He was right, of course. This was yet another glaring instance of the crown winning the battle but losing the war. The crown could certainly still arrest MPs. But the furious Wentworths were furnished with new allies. The lawyer Edward Fenner, who had supported an early execution of the duke of Norfolk but had defended Arthur Hall in 1572, was now joined by the godly Nicholas St Leger, who had previously supported silencing the 'leprosy' of Hall's views. And the gloriously uncompromising Job Throckmorton declared sarcastically: 'Ye shall speak in the Parliament House freely, provided always that ye meddle neither with the reformation of religion nor the establishment of the succession.'[12]

The tussle continued. In 1593 Peter Wentworth came forward with a scheme for discussing the succession, and in the ensuing debate one member argued that 'there is no greater enemy to good council than fear, when men speak either in fear, or fear to speak';[13] but it was to no avail. Wentworth was packed off to prison yet again – this time along with three new recruits, Richard Stephens, Henry Bromley and William Walsh – and yet again the pretence was maintained that this was not for any activity in parliament.

Clearly freedom of speech was still far from unfettered, but by the end of the sixteenth century the Commons had won for itself the right to imprison or release an MP for any activity within the House and to determine whether a member had overstepped the mark. The rule of communal secrecy was increasingly ignored, and even though the Commons regularly took action against 'licentious' speech, Wentworth and his ilk got away with little more than brief spells in the dungeons.

Free speech *inside* parliament continued to be disputed throughout the early Stuart era, and the question would only be properly resolved in the 1688 Bill of Rights declaration 'that the freedom of speech and debates or proceedings in Parliament ought not to be impeached or questioned in any court or place out of Parliament'; but it was quite another matter to enshrine freedom of speech *outside* parliament. With the advent of printing, successive Tudor monarchs resorted to strict censorship. Henry VIII's Court of Star Chamber decreed in 1538 that nobody could publish without the express permission of the Privy Council; eighteen years later Mary incorporated the Company of Stationers and required it to examine and license books before publication; and although Elizabeth's list of proscribed books was different from Mary's, she ensured that unlicensed publications, especially those deemed profane or seditious, were dealt with mercilessly. In an attempt to limit the growing Puritan book trade, her Star Chamber decreed all printing outside London, Oxford and Cambridge illegal in 1586. The ban was flouted, not least by the anti-episcopal satires that appeared in the name of 'Martin Marprelate' and were probably written by the MP Job Throckmorton, but state censorship persisted: even when parliament abolished the Star Chamber in 1640, a brief three-year period of publishing freedom was ended by a licensing order that appointed twenty-seven new pre-publication licensing officers. The measure was deliberately ignored by the poet John Milton and furiously attacked in his thesis *Areopagitica: A Speech for the Liberty of Unlicensed Printing*, but it remained in place and was further tightened at the Restoration, so periodicals such as the *Tatler* and the *Spectator* were only able to flourish in the eighteenth century after a hotly contested parliamentary decision in 1694 to let the licensing order lapse.

Even after 1694 the bounds of free speech were tightly drawn. The achievement of greater freedom would require the scabrous spleen-venting of a master craftsman in satire – a libertine described by many as the ugliest man in England: John Wilkes. Born the son of a malt distiller and a tanner's daughter in 1725, he first arrived in the Commons in 1757 and was for a while a government supporter, but when Bute replaced Pitt the Elder as Prime Minister he went on the offensive, launching the *North Briton* in 1762 expressly to lampoon the government, mounting an acerbic commentary on George III's own speech from the throne, and continuing to satirize the ministry when Bute was replaced by George Grenville the following year. Suddenly the limits of free speech were made all too apparent as the government arrested Wilkes under a 'general warrant' that named no one person but could be used to bring in any 'authors, printers and publishers' the authorities felt like detaining; and while Grenville's estranged elder brother Lord Temple funded a legal campaign to challenge the disreputable 'general warrants', Wilkes had to rely on his membership of the Commons to secure his freedom.

Wilkes was far from safe, though. On 15 November 1763

John Montagu, the 4th earl of Sandwich and Secretary of State for the Northern Department, read out one of Wilkes's poems, entitled *Essay on Woman*, to the House of Lords. The text was thick with genitalia, as were the illustrations in the limited printed edition, but Sandwich proceeded with determination, intending to expose Wilkes as a peddler of obscenity. He had his own private, hypocritical reasons for enjoying the discomfort he was affording Wilkes. For when they had both been members of Sir Francis Dashwood's orgiastic private club the Monks of Medmenham, Wilkes had embarrassed him by bringing along a baboon. Their mutual enmity was intense. On one occasion Sandwich was said to have quipped: 'Sir, I do not know whether you will die on the gallows or of the pox,' to which Wilkes replied: 'That depends, my lord, on whether I embrace your lordship's principles or your mistress.' Wilkes's wit would often get him out of a hole. In this case, though, the poem was a concatenation of affronts. Written with the grandson of an archbishop, Thomas Potter, its cover claimed a commentary by the Reverend Dr Warburton. The real-life Dr Warburton, the bishop of Gloucester, was livid. So too was George Stone, the archbishop of Armagh, who, so Wilkes claimed, was 'frequently in the anus of the intrepid hero George Sackville'. The calumny seems baseless, but since Stone was a handsome unmarried political cleric and Sackville was a member of both Westminster and Dublin parliaments and his father, the duke of Dorset, was Lieutenant of Ireland, it seemed clear enough that the real target was the crown.

That day the Commons resolved the *North Briton* was seditious; on the sixteenth Wilkes fought a duel with Samuel Martin MP in which he was so badly wounded that he was not present on the twenty-fourth when the Commons ruled that parliamentary privilege did not cover him for sedition. By the end of the year he had fled the country; in January 1764 the Commons expelled him and, convicted in court for seditious libel in his absence, he was outlawed and remained abroad for four years. His return in 1768 was courageous as there was no hint of a pardon, but after coming seventh out of eight candidates for the City of London seats in the general election, he stood for Middlesex and was elected even as he was given a two-year sentence for sedition and obscenity. So began a cycle of election, expulsion and re-election that was repeated three times as the government's majority in the Commons dwindled and Wilkes's majority in Middlesex increased. By the time he completed his sentence there was a new Prime Minister, Lord North, and Wilkes's name was synonymous with liberty, not least because of the proliferation of newspaper reports of his trial and tribulations. In a final attempt to close the whole Wilkes phenomenon down, the government threatened to arrest all the other publishers, at which Wilkes sought the support of the City of London, which was dominated by his allies. The City jealously guarded its right to arrest, so when Wilkes and the other printers relocated to within the City limits, they were given sanctuary by the City authorities even as they manifestly flouted the law by merrily publishing details of events in parliament. By the time Wilkes returned to the Commons in 1774 the law of parliamentary secrecy had lapsed and the public had the right to know what was being said in their parliament.

This was not quite the end of the battle. In 1810 a tall baronet with an aquiline nose and receding hair, Sir Francis Burdett, who was described by his family chaplain as an 'implicit follower of Robespierre',[14] was sent to the Tower by the Commons for a 'libellous and scandalous paper reflecting on the just privileges of the House', even though all he had done was criticize the decisions to exclude reporters from the debates over military expeditions in 1809 and to jail the radical John Gale Jones. Refusing to be arrested, Burdett barricaded himself in his house and Admiral Thomas Cochrane MP offered to defend him by force, but he was seized on 9 April and imprisoned until the end of the session on 21 June. He was unrepentant, and when in 1819 he was found guilty of seditious libel for condemning the 'Peterloo massacre', in which cavalry had charged into demonstrators demanding parliamentary reform, he went through the whole saga again, spending three months in the Marshalsea prison, from which, like Wilkes, he was re-elected.

By then francophobic hysteria fuelled by the French Revolution and Napoleonic wars had given successive ministries an excuse to bring in a series of 'Gagging Acts'. In 1795 there were two: the Seditious Meetings Act prohibited any assembly of more than fifty people, and the Treason Act introduced a new offence of bringing the king or the government into contempt, on pain of transportation for seven years. In 1819, with another mass panic tearing at the body politic, there were six. Habeas corpus was suspended, further limits were introduced on public meetings (the preamble to the 'Six Acts' stated that 'every meeting for radical reform is an overt act of treasonable conspiracy against the King and his government'), extra duties were levied on newspapers that made them economically unviable and the Home Secretary, Lord Sidmouth, ordered the arrest of all printers thought responsible for seditious and blasphemous material. It was not until 1824 that Liverpool's over-long government finally abolished the last of these measures.

That was not to say that parliament was suddenly an ardent advocate of free speech in every aspect outside parliament. The Irishman John Croker, who was Tory Secretary of the Admiralty from 1809 to 1830, suggested in 1829 that a Cabinet minister should be put in charge of the 'instruction' of the press, as he believed that 'the regulation of public opinion' was 'one of the most important duties of the state'.[15] Fortunately the idea never caught on, even though politicians regularly gnawed at that bone. In 1827 the duke of Devonshire got his secretary, Thomas Young, to tour the newspaper offices in an attempt to persuade editors of the Whigs' cause, and on the other side of the fence Wellington complained in 1830 about 'the corrupt press in the pay of the government' just three weeks after leaving government himself.[16] Despite the fixed alignments of several papers, the press remained remarkably immune to such attempts at management, and although *The Times* had backed the Whigs since 1820, it switched to Peel when Melbourne's government fell in 1834 and viciously attacked the Whigs for 'interfer[ing] with the independence of the press and endeavour[ing] to make it a tool of government'.[17]

Spin doctors were not recognized as such for another 160 years, but once the liberty of the press was secured, politicians in every generation sought to influence what the papers printed, by means fair or foul. Both the Trades Union Congress and Churchill as Chancellor of the Exchequer published their own newspapers during the General Strike of 1926 (respectively, the *British Worker* and the *British Gazette*), and in 1931 Stanley Baldwin was so furious with the two press barons Lords Rothermere and Beaverbrook that he drafted in his cousin Rudyard Kipling to craft him a neat phrase to encapsulate the role of the press in their hands: 'power without responsibility, the prerogative of the harlot throughout the ages'.

The most ferocious twentieth-century political effort to determine what the press wrote was waged, however, by the government of Neville Chamberlain in the 1930s. Conscious that Hitler was, in the words of the British ambassador, 'unreasonably sensitive to press criticism', the Lord Privy Seal, Lord Halifax, promised Hitler in November 1937 that 'His Majesty's government would do everything in its power to influence the press to avoid unnecessary offence'. He was true to his word. He personally met with the proprietors of the *Daily Herald*, Lord

Southwood, and the *News Chronicle*, Sir William Layton. The *Evening Standard* was asked to tone down its anti-Nazi cartoons. The Home Secretary, Samuel Hoare, complained in no uncertain terms to the editor of the *Daily Telegraph* about its coverage of the Czech crisis in 1938, and even after the Munich agreement Chamberlain's press secretary George Steward (often cited as the first government spin doctor) met secretly with his German counterpart, Dr Fritz Hesse, with a view to developing a shared press strategy designed to make Britain more sympathetic to the Nazi government. This strategy undoubtedly paid some dividends. The *Observer*, the *Daily Mail*, the *Express* and *The Times* were all broadly supportive of the appeasement policy and critical articles from Berlin correspondents were often toned down, cut or simply excised. When *The Times'* Berlin correspondent, Norman Ebbut, was expelled from Germany no complaint was made. Not all the papers acquiesced, and several changed their mind after Munich, the *Daily Telegraph* declaring on 4 October: 'It was Mr Disraeli who said that England's two great assets in the world were its fleet and its good name. Today we must console ourselves that we still have our fleet.'

The management of the nascent BBC and of cinema newsreels was even more direct. The BBC was forbidden from mentioning Germany or Italy when Eden resigned in February 1938, it was told to bear in mind the sensitivities of Hitler and Mussolini when reporting German and Italian events, and the anti-appeasement National Labour MP Harold Nicolson was expressly barred from referring to the Czech crisis in a broadcast on 5 September 1938. Cinema audiences were even more sheltered from events. Chamberlain's preposterously triumphant arrival at Heston airport was one of the first deliberate photo opportunities of British history. He waved his piece of paper for the cameras and the moment was shown in every cinema in the land. So too were the supportive crowds outside Downing

Street; but not the far greater numbers at the anti-appeasement demonstration in Trafalgar Square. This was, as one historian of the era has put it, 'propaganda without the facts',[18] and one of the last moments when politicians could truly determine how the country got its news.

And then there was the theatre, which was long to remain the most strictly censored of all literary forms, with the Lord Chamberlain, in addition to his duties in the Cabinet and as head of the royal household, responsible for licensing plays for public performance under the Licensing Act of 1737. The Act had originally been designed to limit satirical portrayals of Walpole's corrupt government, but even when it was replaced by the Theatres Act in 1843, although the Lord Chamberlain could no longer refuse a licence without reason, he retained the right to ban a play if he thought it 'fitting for the preservation of good manners, decorum or of the public peace so to do'. For more than a century he remained the sole moral arbiter of theatrical taste and decency. Despite a series of parliamentary inquiries in 1866, 1909 and 1966, this provision remained in place until free speech campaigners finally secured its repeal in 1968.

When Milton was battling against parliament's new brand of censorship in the 1640s he cited Euripides' play *The Suppliant Women* in his own translation: 'This is true Liberty, when freeborn men, / Having to advise the public, may speak free,' and cried out: 'Give me the liberty to know, to utter, and to argue freely according to conscience, above all liberties.'[19] The intertwining aspirations of free speech within parliament and far beyond its walls have, like every other aspect of parliamentary history, proceeded in a dance of two steps forward, one step back; and the undoubted truth is that the nourishment of liberty depended very largely on the courage of a few volatile, extravagant figures.

But Parliament once call'd then Giles was brough
Unto account, contrary to his thought :
There to the Serjeant ward hee was committed,
Which made him much to feare, hee should be fitted
For all those former wrongs, that hee had done;
Which from his keeper made him here to runne;
Hee outlawde therefore was and baniſht quite
And also judg'd to be no more a Knight :
Not only ſo but jnfamous inroul'd ————,
Although(before) hee Iuſtice ſeat controul'd.

Elizabethan and Jacobean parliaments, exasperated by the corruption, nepotism and royal favouritism that were endemic in the English political system, repeatedly tried to strike down royal monopolies and curb the power of royal intimates. When the most notorious monopolist, Sir Giles Mompesson, was found guilty of extortion in 1621, he fled the country to escape his sentence and was declared by parliament an 'eternally notorious criminal'.

7

The Gathering Storm

THE STUART ERA THAT BEGAN in 1603 was conceived in treason. For, two years before Elizabeth's death, her secretary of state Robert Cecil began plotting the accession of her neighbour King James VI of Scotland to the English throne. Elizabeth knew nothing of this – indeed, she had expressly banned any such speculation. Nor was she aware that he was working in tandem with Lord Henry Howard, whose father the earl of Surrey had been attainted and executed in 1547 and whose elder brother, the 4th duke of Norfolk, had been executed for supporting and seeking to marry James's mother, Mary, Queen of Scots. Howard had been imprisoned five times for his pro-Catholic and pro-Scottish views, but when his close ally the earl of Essex spectacularly self-combusted in his abortive coup of 1601 Howard transferred his allegiance to Cecil just as Elizabeth's secretary became convinced of the need to ensure a smooth transition of the crown. The two men could not have been more different. Cecil, the second (though favourite) son of a first-generation peer, had grown up in steady prosperity, but had had to triumph over the pronounced curvature of his spine and his innate reserve to prove himself as deserving of respect, and as prudent and reliable a councillor, as his father. Howard, by contrast, was an aristocrat dispossessed of a fortune, who learned to rise to what he considered his proper station by flattery, insinuation and conspiracy. Cecil married, happily, but lost his wife in 1597 and never remarried. Howard, who preferred the company of men, remained unmarried. So a crypto-Catholic and an arch-Protestant complotted the accession through a steady two-year flow of secret, illegal and treasonable correspondence with James.

Cecil and Howard were taking a phenomenal risk. After all, nobody would have argued that James's claim was adamantine. It depended on Henry VIII's sister Margaret's first marriage to James IV of Scotland – but Henry's will had specified the succession through his younger sister Mary, duchess of Suffolk. Arguably, the Suffolk candidate, Edward Seymour, Viscount Beauchamp, had the stronger claim, even though he had been born in the Tower of London as his parents had married clandestinely. One might have expected Cecil to have taken the issue of the accession to a parliament as soon as possible, but the plague intervened and it was not until March 1604, eight months after James's coronation, that it was convened. Things got off to a terrible start. The moment the singularly unimpressive Sir Edward Phelips had been installed as Speaker on 22 March, Sir William Fleetwood, the junior knight for Buckinghamshire, complained that his friend Sir Francis Goodwin had been deprived of the other Buckinghamshire seat by the Court of Chancery on the spurious grounds that he had been outlawed over some debts several years earlier, and that his seat had been taken by the 71-year-old Sir John Fortescue in a by-election the previous day. This sounds a minor issue but it was to prove explosive, not least because Fortescue was a royal councillor; and on examination, a Commons committee concluded that the disqualification was wholly unjust. Their evidence was damning.

'A clerk, lately come to that office, hath now, many years after the time, and since this election, made entries, interlined with a new hand, that he was outlawed.'[1] In other words, it was a fraudulent royal stitch-up – hardly likely to endear the new king to the Commons.

There was a wider issue at stake than a single manipulated result, however. The combative new Lord Chancellor, Lord Ellesmere, had included in James's writs of summons the usual provision that sheriffs were to file their returns in the Court of Chancery; now it seemed that he was intent on using this provision to wrest the determination of contested elections from the Commons and put it in the hands of the crown. The attempt was to backfire spectacularly, though, as, quite unexpectedly, several key royal retainers in the Commons failed to support the election of Fortescue: among them were Francis Moore, who was reputed to be Ellesmere's eyes and ears among MPs, and Cecil's cousin Sir Robert Wingfield, who condemned the king's 'many misinformers' for leading him to be 'seduced by ill counsel'.[2]

What ultimately did for Ellesmere's plan, though, was the fact that the particular case at hand was also a personal grudge match, as there had been parliamentary enmity between the Goodwins and Fortescues in successive Buckinghamshire elections. Goodwin was a convinced Protestant, while Fortescue's father had been attainted with Cardinal Pole and executed; on occasion the enmity had become violent, as when Fortescue was beaten down from his horse by Goodwin's father-in-law Lord Grey of Wilton. Yet Fortescue was no political parvenu. He had been Elizabeth's Chancellor of the Exchequer and Keeper of the Great Wardrobe, and James kept him on as Chancellor of the Duchy of Lancaster and privy councillor until his death, even though he so disliked him that on one occasion he ostentatiously farted on leaving Fortescue's house to show his displeasure. All of this meant that Ellesmere – and therefore the king – was faced with a triple problem: the facts were against him, the Commons were damned if they were going to allow the crown to determine elections, and Goodwin had more and better organized Protestant friends than Fortescue. So, eager for the Commons to move on to other matters, the king suggested a compromise: that both Goodwin and Fortescue be set aside and a third election be held. The Commons acquiesced, Sir Christopher Piggott was duly elected, and other seats were found in 1606 for both Fortescue and Goodwin.

It was a significant victory. The Commons had already expelled members and would continue to do so, reluctantly expelling Piggott himself (ironically enough) at the king's insistence in 1607 for bad-mouthing the Scots, removing Thomas Sheppard for an obstreperous attack on the Puritans in 1621, and in 1628 declaring Sir Edmund Sawyer 'unworthy ever to sit as a Member of this House' because he had tampered with a witness.[3] But now it had the right to determine disputed elections as well.

In itself the Buckinghamshire saga was relatively unimportant, but like the jackdaw that flew into the chamber on the last day of May and frightened MPs into voting down a measure, it seemed to presage ill, as it exposed fundamental flaws in James's government. The king had appeared gauche and his council divided. Most importantly, the Commons had proceeded entirely devoid of any council leadership. In part this was James's fault. In a flurry of patronage at and immediately after his coronation, he made 300 new knights and virtually doubled the number of lay peers, catapulting many key councillors out of the Commons and into the Lords: plain Robert Cecil became Lord Cecil, Viscount Cranborne and in 1605 earl of Salisbury, Sir Thomas Egerton became Baron Ellesmere, and both Sir William Knollys and Sir Edward Wotton became barons. Leaving aside the resentment this caused among more established nobles, the end result was that James had just two councillors in the 1604 Commons. Neither cut a dash. Sir John Herbert, the second secretary, spoke regularly but to little effect, and there is no record of Sir John Stanhope, the Vice-Chamberlain, speaking at all. So, although two councillors, Sir Thomas Parry and Sir Julius Caesar, were found Commons seats in 1610, and although Cecil remained in control of the council up until his death – and indeed, along with the three Howard family earls of Northampton, Nottingham and Suffolk, ran the kingdom while his monarch toured the deer parks and palaces of England – it was clear from the ominous outset that the Commons lay beyond the king's reach.

It was not just that there was little clear leadership from the council; what leadership was on offer was maladroit. This became all too clear when the Commons came to deal with James's pet project, the union of Scotland and England. Many were deeply sceptical. Might not the poorer Scots 'flood' into England? If the name Great Britain were adopted, would all England's laws lapse? Which laws would have precedence? These were knotty enough conundrums, but the sheer ham-fistedness of the king's allies rapidly became apparent. An anonymously published pamphlet abruptly criticizing the Commons' objections to the union was quickly discovered to have been written by the newly appointed careerist bishop of Bristol, John Thornborough. The Commons immediately took umbrage at what they reckoned was a royally sanctioned attack, and when James then suggested that the Commons' privileges were not theirs by right and demanded that the Commons not be 'transported with the curiosity of a few giddy heads',[4] they feared that the king was seeking to undermine the very principles of parliament. So a committee of MPs, led by Sir Thomas Ridgeway and Sir Edwin Sandys (the son of the former archbishop of York), drafted a remarkably unapologetic *Apology and Satisfaction* for presentation to the king, in which they complained of the 'misinformation' he had received and argued that 'our privileges and liberties are our right and due inheritance, no less than our very lands and goods; that they cannot be withheld from us, denied or impaired, but with apparent wrong to the whole state of the realm'.[5]

The *Apology* was a clear attempt to put the Scottish king in his place, but although its theme was one to which the Commons was regularly to return, not all MPs were prepared to sign up to it immediately. In the debate Sir Francis Bacon and Dudley Carleton (both future peers and respectively future Lord Chancellor and secretary of state) persuaded the Commons not to submit it. But the air of general mistrust persisted, with the result that all James could extract from the Commons in his first session in relation to the union was the setting up of a committee to consider English–Scottish relations, and even after two further years of wrangling the Commons would countenance only the repeal of the oldest and most violently anti-Scottish laws. James was not happy. He ended the 1604 session complaining to the Commons about their 'pertness and boldness', and suggesting that even though there were some wise men among them, 'so was there a roll of knavery'.[6] It was maladroit schoolmasterly stuff, and it undoubtedly grated on the ears of those who felt they understood the ways of the English parliament far better than he did.

James had another flaw that unsettled the Commons: his extravagance. It did not help that the crown was broke even before he arrived in London, as Elizabeth had amassed large debts and ran an annual deficit. The royal revenues from feudal sources were much diminished, making it difficult for any monarch to live off her or his own normal income, and exceptional parliamentary subsidies had barely been reformed in decades. So even parliamentary income brought in far less than once it had. At this point James arrived from the far poorer kingdom of Scotland. Bedazzled by the wealth of the English, like a suddenly wealthy maiden aunt in a sweetshop he doled out gifts to his eager subjects – the more humble (and the more Scottish), the more grateful. A patent here, a monopoly there, acres of deer park, forests, land. For a while those who had complained about Elizabeth's parsimony were content to share in the aureate glow, but the situation rapidly became unsustainable. As his debts rose from £100,000 to £600,000 in just five years he complained to his Privy Council that 'the only disease and consumption which I can ever apprehend as likeliest to endanger me is this eating canker of want'.[7]

In private Salisbury was forthright. 'It is not possible for a king of England', he told James, 'to be rich or safe, but by frugality . . . this I write with dolour but have beheld with fear and terror.' Indeed, he saw it as his job to show the king 'demonstrably how the storm comes before it breaks'.[8] Admirable prudence, but not entirely without hypocrisy, for Salisbury was just as addicted to conspicuous consumption as his employer. He was an avid gambler, and an enthusiastic property developer: on exchanging Theobalds, the rambling Cecil mansion with a vast deer park, with James's Hatfield, he had three-quarters of it razed to the ground so that he could replace it with a more compact, though even more lavish palace. His palace at the Savoy in London was similarly opulent. It is little surprise that he left his estates heavily indebted, owing £37,867 at his death.

Nevertheless, Salisbury tried to come to the king's financial rescue, assuming the double role of secretary and treasurer in 1608, when he apparently found 'the Exchequer a chaos of confusion', with debts of £300,000 or £400,000, 'but which were good, which were bad, which sperate, which desperate, no man knew'.[9] Recognizing that the Commons was reluctant to grant

James any subsidy (Peter Wentworth's son Thomas had asked in 1607: 'To what purpose is it for us to draw a silver stream out of the country into the royal cistern, if it is daily run out thence by private cocks?'[10]), Salisbury launched a severe economy drive instead, and, on tenuous legal authority, introduced new 'impositions' on imported goods, which started to net the crown roughly £70,000 a year. These extra-parliamentary Empson-and-Dudley style tariffs raised hackles in the Commons, and as soon as the fourth session of the 1604 parliament began in 1610 the lawyer Nicholas Fuller enthusiastically condemned them. Bacon and Carleton again spoke for the king, as did Henry Yelverton, the son of Sir Christopher, who was keen to ingratiate himself; but the day belonged to the king's critics. Richard Martin asserted scathingly that it would be quite wrong to grant 'an arbitrary, irregular, unlimited, and transcendent power' to the king, as 'the King of England [was] the most absolute King in Parliament, but of himself, his power is limited by law',[11] a point that was reiterated with a plethora of historical references by the affable lawyer and antiquarian Sir James Whitelocke.

This was all very well, but the king was still financially embarrassed. Salisbury's pruning had cut the deficit, but still there was a shortfall and massive historical debt; so Salisbury came up with his most imaginative suggestion yet, a 'Great Contract'. The much disliked traditional sources of royal income, wardship (whereby the estates of minors who inherited were managed – and fleeced – by the crown) and purveyance (whereby trades provided goods cheap to the crown under duress), would be abolished in exchange for a £200,000 annual allocation and a one-off grant of £600,000. Yet again the Commons baulked. The sums were enormous, and there was a sneaking doubt that if the king had a guaranteed parliamentary income in perpetuity he would never again call parliament.

The upshot was a paltry one-off grant of just £100,000.
James angrily dissolved parliament and wrote to Salisbury:

> There is no more trust to be laid upon this rotten reed of Egypt,
> for your greatest error hath been that ye ever expected to draw
> honey out of gall, being a little blinded with the self-love of your
> own counsel in holding together of this parliament, whereof all
> men were despaired (as I have oft told you) but yourself alone.[12]

In truth, Salisbury himself was now something of a broken reed.
Left with few options for raising cash, he resorted to selling the
new title of baronet, a hereditary knighthood, eighty-eight of
which were sold in the second half of 1611 at £1,095 a piece. It
was a grubby business, but it briefly helped stem the outflow. In
December, having always suffered from ill health, but now struck
with abdominal cancer, Salisbury was forced to hand over much
of his day-to-day responsibility to Sir Julius Caesar, the
Chancellor of the Exchequer. Everyone now expected Salisbury's
death at any moment. Ever the treasurer, even he proclaimed,
'My audit is made, let me come now, O Jesus,' at the beginning
of May 1612; and then on the twenty-fourth, just forty-nine
years old, he died. As if a dam had burst, envious libels suddenly
trashed his reputation. Bacon disparaged him to the king,
Northampton confessed he hated him, there were rumours of
sexual depravity and infection, and there was even a local
demonstration when his funeral was held in the elegant chapel
at Hatfield House with its remarkably un-Protestant stained
glass.

The leadership of the council now lay in the hands of
Northampton. In the Commons, though, the key figure was
Francis Bacon, the academically brilliant philosopher and
lawyer of such a constantly curious bent that he asserted: 'I have
taken all knowledge to be my province.'[13] Now past fifty, he had

been born in 1561 in York House, the son of the Lord Keeper Sir Nicholas and his wife Anne, daughter of the Puritan MP Sir Anthony Cooke. A younger son, like Salisbury and Northampton, he had been fortunate to have the early patronage of his uncle Burghley and secured a Commons seat in 1581. Though desperate to be Solicitor-General he blotted his copybook with Elizabeth with some unhelpful comments about subsidies in 1593 – defending himself by arguing that 'there is variety allowed in counsel, as a discord in music, to make it more perfect'.[14] It was not until 1607 that the job came his way, to be followed in 1613 with the post of Attorney-General.

Bacon was an instinctive parliamentarian. He relished debate and knew that James's financial aspirations could only be met by parliamentary grants. Indeed, his opposition to the impositions hinted as much. Northampton, by contrast, maintained a patrician's disdain for parliament. By the spring of 1614, though, even Northampton had to accept that royal indebtedness made parliament a risk worth taking, and so new writs were sent out for an assembly on 5 April.

Yet again it was monumentally mishandled. The very first piece of business in the Commons after the election of Randolph Crewe as Speaker was an attempt, led by the Tavistock burgess Edward Duncombe and the Shropshire knight Sir Roger Owen, to exclude Bacon from his seat on the grounds that as Attorney-General he should attend the Lords under a writ of assistance, rather than the Commons.* Although a compromise was found whereby Bacon was allowed to stay, but any subsequent Attorney-General would be excluded, against this background

---

* Law officers such as the Attorney-General and Solicitor-General, the Lord Chief Justice and the Master of the Rolls, were issued special summonses termed 'writs of assistance' to attend the Lords, not for life but ex officio.

of mutual distrust the request for an immediate vote on a large grant by the new secretary of state, Sir Ralph Winwood, sitting as an extremely nervous MP for the first time, was unlikely to succeed. His task was made all the more difficult by the fact that the other councillors, including Bacon and Caesar, did not fully back him up. Things were no better after the Easter recess. The House was troubled by rumours that the rotund, red-headed old parliamentary hand and Shropshire knight Sir Henry Neville had undertaken to organize matters to the king's advantage and secure a more pliable Commons than in the previous parliament. Owen angrily denounced these 'undertakers' for packing the Commons, complaining that one peer had secured sixty seats, and John Hoskins added that it had all been orchestrated by papists. During the debate on the attempted rigging of the elections, which took up several days, Sir William Herbert (a cousin of the Herbert earls) and Sir Robert Killigrew (a kinsman of Neville) were reprimanded by the House for physically attacking Owen in the Chamber; and on 10 May the Commons expelled the 72-year-old Sir Thomas Parry on the grounds that he had threatened voters. Since Parry was Chancellor of the Duchy of Lancaster and a councillor, his expulsion was a potent sign of the Commons' incipient anger.

From the start of the parliament the Commons had also been advocating a Bill that would ban the impositions. Things now went from bad to worse when MPs demanded a conference on the matter with the Lords. This was hotly contested in the upper house between the crown's supporters and a group of opposition peers. Yet again one man's hyperbole made any possibility of harmony impossible as Richard Neile, the fiercely anti-Puritan and royalist bishop of Lincoln, said that he was bitterly opposed to any such conference as 'the Lower House was known to be composed of such turbulent and factious spirits as, if they should give way to a communication or treaty with them, they were likely to hear such mutinous speeches as were not fit for those honourable personages to lend their hearing to'.[15] It is true that there had been some wild talk in the Commons. Sandys alleged that 'it is come to be almost a tyrannical government in England',[16] and Thomas Wentworth pointed out that Henri IV of France, who had recently been assassinated, 'had died by a knife like a calf'.[17] But when Bishop Neile's speech was reported to the Commons, there was uproar. Phelips, whose father was now inexplicably Master of the Rolls, weighed in, followed by Hoskins, Owen and Christopher Neville (no relation), who complained: 'There are those [who] to please the king care not what they say to hurt the country . . . they are their master's spaniels, but their country's wolves; their tongues cut like a sharp razor to cut all from the commonwealth.'[18] Another member summed up the views of many: Neile should 'have his head set on Tower-Hill'.[19]

The session was now completely ungovernable. Even Sir Walter Chute, the king's sewer, who had tentatively spoken against the 'undertakers', now poignantly complained that 'some erect great and stately buildings but let the king's poor servants want' and boldly announced that 'he would never yield to give the king anything till we were righted in this'.[20] Hoskins brought it all to a tumultuous head on Friday, 4 June, when he complained about the many Scots who surrounded the king and urged him, like King Canute, who had sent his Danish compatriots home when he became king of England, 'to send all strangers home to their country'.[21] He ended with a reference to the Sicilian Vespers, the bloody insurrection of 1282 against French rule in Palermo. The implication was clear: if the Scottish king persisted in his impositions, his English subjects might slaughter his allies. James was now convinced that no good could come of letting the debates continue, so on Monday, 7 June he dissolved parliament and had Hoskins arrested and imprisoned along with Christopher Neville, Thomas Wentworth and Sir Walter Chute.[22]

What is surprising about this 'Addled' Parliament is that the council should have so completely lost control of the Commons despite there being more than 150 members who were councillors, courtiers or royal officials. In large measure this was due to the deliberate machinations of one group, led, extraordinarily, by Northampton, who had been secretly received into the Catholic Church in February. Like a prop forward who deliberately collapses the scrum, the Howard family willed the parliament to fail, for if the king had no money he could not fight Catholic Spain and would be obliged to provide Prince Charles with a Spanish match. Northampton's advice might not hold sway in the council, but by helping the Addled Parliament collapse he ensured there could be no war. The day after parliament was dissolved he paraded through London with one of Hoskins' accomplices in his coach, an improbable connection but one that betokened Howard complicity in the addling process. It was Northampton's last hurrah, for a week later he died.

At the time James confided to the Spanish ambassador that 'the House of Commons is a body without a head', but the real problem lay within his divided council, which offered double-headed, cack-handed leadership. Incapable of seeing this, and surprised that his ancestors should ever have permitted such an institution as parliament to come into existence, he moaned that 'I am a stranger and found it here when I arrived, so that I am obliged to put up with what I cannot get rid of'.[23] All he could do was not summon it, which is what he chose to do for the next seven years, the longest period without a parliament since 1523.

James held out as long as he could, but by 1621 he had little choice but to recall parliament. England had been at peace throughout his early years. He had even negotiated a peace treaty with Spain in 1604. But now war was on the horizon. For in 1613 his daughter Elizabeth had married the leader of the Protestant Union, Frederick V, Elector Palatine, who was then also offered the crown of Bohemia in preference to a Habsburg. The Holy Roman Emperor's retaliation was swift: Frederick and Elizabeth were expelled from both Bohemia and the Palatinate in 1620, leaving troops fighting in the Rhenish Palatinate. James had been opposed to accepting Bohemia and was a reluctant warrior, but was now determined to reclaim the Palatinate – to the delight of English Protestants, who viewed James's hopes of a Spanish wife for his son more as Catholic appeasement than as godly counsel.

There was another complication. For the tectonic plates underpinning the council had shifted massively in the interven-ing years. The process had started almost immediately after the 1614 parliament was dissolved, with a small group of peers antagonistic to the Howards hatching a plot in April 1615 at Baynards Castle in London to try to cut the king's favourite, the earl of Somerset, down to size. They knew this would be no easy task. If James had one indelible trait it was his tendency to invest his emotional energy on a single, young, male intimate. It had started in Scotland, when he had become infatuated with Esmé Stewart, whom he made duke of Lennox. Others had passed in and out of favour, but in 1607 the handsome Scot Robert Carr had caught the king's attention in dramatic style when he broke his leg during ceremonial tilting, and by 1614 he so dominated the king's affections that he had been made Viscount Rochester and earl of Somerset and appointed Lord Privy Seal in England, Treasurer in Scotland and Lord Chamberlain.

Removing Carr would clearly be impossible. So the plotters, led by the two Herbert brothers, William, 3rd earl of Pembroke, and Philip, earl of Montgomery (both, to varying degrees, earlier royal favourites), and the unmarried archbishop of Canterbury,

George Abbot – all confirmed Protestant members of the council – decided to bring to the king's attention another, more biddable young man. They were lucky. On a visit to the Mildmay residence at Apethorpe Hall in Northamptonshire the previous summer James had been introduced to George Villiers, whose widowed mother had recently married Sir Thomas Compton, the light-witted brother of William, Baron Compton of nearby Castle Ashby. People rhapsodized about Villiers. 'He had a lovely complexion; he was the handsomest bodied man of England; his limbs so well compacted, and his conversation so pleasing and of so sweet a disposition,'[24] said Bishop Godfrey Goodman; according to Sir John Oglander, 'he was one of the handsomest men in the whole world'.[25] Within weeks the two had become inseparable and the diplomat Sir Henry Wotton wrote that the king had taken such a liking to Villiers 'that he resolved to make him a master-piece and to mould him, as it were, Platonically, to his own idea'.[26] Now the Herberts and Abbot helped promote Villiers, providing him with the latest fashionable apparel and even persuading the queen to beg James to knight 'his' George on St George's Day 1615. James needed little encouragement. It was a relationship – and, so the private letters between the two would suggest, a physical love affair – of phenomenal strength that was to dominate the remaining years of James's reign and the first years of his son's. As James declared: 'I love [him] more than anyone else ... Christ had his John, and I have George.'[27]

By 1621 Villiers had been made a knight (1615), Baron Whaddon and Viscount Villiers (1616), earl (1617) and then marquess of Buckingham (1618); and in 1620 he married Frances Manners, the daughter of the encrustedly wealthy earl of Rutland. The titles and the marriage brought land with them, but the real power lay in Villiers' almost complete mastery of the king's affections, a process made complete in 1615 when Somerset and his wife were revealed to have plotted the murder

223

of Somerset's one-time friend Sir William Overbury, and both the earl and his countess were committed to the Tower.

It was connections that had brought Villiers to the king's attention; but connections have a nasty habit of getting one into trouble, and so he was to find in 1621. For within moments of sitting, the Commons decided that their main concern was the matter of monopolies. They had two men in their sights: the entrepreneurially greedy 36-year-old burgess for Great Bedwyn, Sir Giles Mompesson, who shared a patent for licensing inns and taverns with Buckingham's brother Christopher Villiers, and whose brother-in-law was Buckingham's half-brother Sir Edward Villiers, the newly elected MP for Westminster; and Sir Francis Michell, who shared in the alehouse patent and also held a monopoly for the production of gold and silver thread jointly with Edward Villiers.[28] Plenty of other MPs were patentees. Sir Robert Lloyd had a patent for engrossing wills, Sir Robert Mansell one for making glass. Sackville Crowe provided guns to the merchant navy under patent and Giles Bridges was directly involved in Mompesson's abuses. But it was Mompesson who was the first target when William Noy launched the Commons attack on 19 February. He had charged exorbitant fees, he had licensed 'disorderly alehouse-keepers and innkeepers' for cash, he had dubiously prosecuted 3,320 inns so as to exact hefty fines for himself. Other MPs piled in. Sir Dudley Digges complained that the patent holders 'had a virgin's face . . . [but] their hands were like griping talons'.[29] The next day a committee of the whole house unanimously condemned Mompesson, and within a week he was begging the House's mercy in the custody of the Sergeant-at-Arms.

Buckingham had been warned that the monopoly issue would crop up. Bacon (since 1618 Lord Chancellor) expressly told him in late 1620 that some of his lordship's 'special friends' might well be involved in matters that would be 'stirred' in the lower house and that he would be well advised to 'put off the envy of these things'.[30] Neither Buckingham nor the king took much notice at that point, but by the time parliament opened James admitted that he had been 'much deceived in doing many things hurtful to myself and prejudicious to my people in point of grant',[31] and when he saw the vitriol with which the Commons debates were proceeding he realized he needed to make far more of a concession. So on 26 March he promised to strike down the Mompesson and Michell monopolies.

At this point the story took a completely unexpected turn, largely thanks to two men, one in each House. The first was Sir Edward Coke (pronounced Cook). By now aged sixty-nine, he had made a first fortune by marrying Bridget, the daughter of John Paston of Suffolk, who provided a dowry of £30,000; another as Solicitor-General and then Attorney-General in the 1590s; and a third just six months after Bridget's death in 1598 when he married the beautiful widow of Sir William Hatton. For all his legal pre-eminence – he sat as Chief Justice of the Court of Common Pleas from 1606 and of the King's Bench from 1613 – the cantankerously arrogant Coke was less assured as a courtier and was dismissed from the King's Bench in 1616. In a cynical bid to restore himself to favour, he agreed the following year to marry his daughter Frances to Buckingham's elder brother Sir John Villiers, who had only an occasional grasp of his own sanity. Coke's forceful wife, in whom the Hatton family fortune was entailed, was so opposed to the match that she abducted Frances and refused to open the door when her husband arrived with a search warrant signed by Secretary Winwood. Undeterred, Coke smashed down the door and dragged Frances away. After lengthy legal wrangling the marriage went ahead late in 1617 and a grateful Buckingham had Coke restored to the council.[32]

In 1621 Coke was elected for Liskeard. Despite being a royal councillor, he was remarkably free with his views, demanding tougher action against recusants and declaring that the king was not in quite the financial mess he maintained. So outspoken was he that he was asked to chair the committee on monopolies, prompting the blunt Colchester burgess Edward Alford to comment that this was 'the first parliament wherein he ever saw the councillors of state so ready to do the commonwealth service'.[33] Coke got the bit between his teeth and brought forward a Bill to 'kill the serpent in the egg' by banning all new patents,[34] which eventually reached the statute book in 1624. (His questioning of patentees was as brusque as some of his earlier legal interrogations. Indeed, on occasion it was too aggressive for his own good. When he demanded of the monopolist John Lepton who had given him his patent, Lepton looked sheepish and eventually replied that it was the very best counsel in England. Infuriated, Coke demanded that he answer the question. Reluctantly Lepton replied, 'the attorney'. Again Coke attacked him for his evasiveness, whereupon Lepton had to own up that it was the former Attorney-General, one Edward Coke.)

What Coke spotted in the spring of 1621 was that although the Commons could discipline Mompesson for his activities as an MP, they could not tackle his abuse as a monopolist without resorting to the old process of impeachment. This required the cooperation of the Lords, an even larger number of whom were direct beneficiaries of the patents. Cooperation was forthcoming, though, thanks to the active determination of one peer: Henry Wriothesley, the consciously flamboyant earl of Southampton, who, with his deep auburn hair and sharp blue eyes, remains a colourful but intriguingly opaque figure. His recusant father had died when he was just eight and he had consequently grown up as a ward in Burghley's house; by 1621 he was a figure of national fascination. He had been imprisoned for his involvement in the Essex rebellion and released on James's accession. There were rumours that he had bedded a Captain Piers Edmonds while on campaign in Ireland. Equally confident as a man of war, a patron of the arts and a clothes-horse for the latest fashions, after James he was the most painted figure of his era. He was also an active member of the Lords, opposing the union with Scotland so overtly in 1604 that he was briefly arrested. Like many others who hoped for ministerial office, he came to an accommodation with Somerset and Buckingham and was made a councillor in 1619, but his most enduring alliances were with Sandys and now with Coke. Indeed, Sir Lionel Cranfield, the MP for Arundel who had been a minister since 1613, moaned that Southampton had consorted with younger peers and MPs who 'were most stirring and active to cross the general proceedings and to asperse and inflame the present government'.[35]

Southampton's campaign secured the Lords' support for the impeachment, and on 27 March the Lord Chief Justice declared Mompesson's punishment. The Commons had already expelled him from the House; now he was to lose his knighthood, be dragged up the Strand with his face in a horse's anus, fined £10,000 and imprisoned for life. Wisely he had already fled the country, leaving Michell to suffer the ignominy of having his knighthood stripped from him in Westminster Hall.

Buckingham hoped that Mompesson's despatch would trammel up the consequences, but he was wrong, as it was discovered that the primary referee for the Mompesson patents was the then Attorney-General, Francis Bacon. Coke, who had lost out twice to Bacon on promotions and once on a lucrative marriage proposal, was delighted. After some aggressive digging, it was established that Bacon had accepted two cash payments from litigants who were appearing before him in court. No matter that he had found against them – or that his record as Lord Chancellor was one of impeccable impartiality and administrative reform: it looked like a bribe. Bacon now desperately sought support from the king. All he got was studied indifference.

When James appeared before the Lords on 10 March he lavished praise on Buckingham, poured scorn on the monopolists and casually stated that he left the Chancellor 'to answer for himself and to stand and fall'.[36] Thus abandoned, Bacon pleaded 'I am guilty of corruption' before the Lords and was fined £40,000 and imprisoned at the king's pleasure. These would have been severe punishments if enforced; but the king released him after just three days' sojourn in the Tower and he was never required to pay his fine.

None the less, the outcome of the episode was harsh, ruthless and unfair. Michell later claimed that he had acted as a screen for the real targets of the Commons' anger, namely the Villiers family, telling the king that after 'failing against Cedars [the Commons] then oppressed your supplicant, a poor shrub, to his utter undoing'.[37] Bacon could easily have argued the same.

Although the monopoly issue had pitted the Commons against the king and his favourite, the debates had been relatively calm and the outcome satisfied even the most belligerent MP. The sense of harmony was not to last. First, having secured a grant of £160,000 for his Palatinate campaign, James threatened to prorogue parliament. Immediately MPs fretted, in the words of the godly Sir Richard Grosvenor: 'When we come into the country, what will they think of us? We have given subsidies, and have brought home nothing for them. I pray God we be not subjects of their fury.'[38] Then, having been forced to allow parliament to reconvene after an adjournment, James sacked Coke from the council and arrested the people he reckoned to have led the parliamentary campaign against the monopolists: Sandys, Southampton and the habitually debauched hereditary Lord High Chamberlain, Henry de Vere, the earl of Oxford.

The arrests aggravated the Commons, and on parliament's return in the autumn a third element came into play. Many wanted a strong, godly policy on all fronts. That meant defending the Palatinate, abandoning treaties with Spain and above all securing a Protestant marriage for the prince. Thus Sir Robert Phelips reckoned that it was the 'great wheel of Spain' that kept the smaller wheel of Germany going round and Coke urged people to be on their guard, as England had been considering treaties with Spain when the Armada was sent. So seized was he of an anti-Catholic patriotism that he even attributed sheep rot and venereal disease to the malign influence of Spain. Consequently, when Sir George Goring, Buckingham's unofficial spokesman in the Commons, moved a belligerent motion that called on the king not to declare that he would never fight Spain, Phelips added a sentence demanding that 'our most noble prince [Charles] may be timely and happily married to one of our own religion'.[39] Sir Edward Sackville, brother to the earl of Dorset and nephew to Suffolk, countered that 'it is the privilege of princes to marry where they list', but the Commons held firm. Since James still believed that his great balancing act of matrimonial diplomacy – a daughter married to a Protestant, his son to a Catholic – would maintain the peace, Phelips' demand was incendiary, and James wrote to the Speaker complaining about the 'fiery, popular and turbulent spirits' in the Commons and threatening that he was 'very free and able to punish any man's misdemeanours in parliament as well during their sitting as after; which we mean not to spare hereafter'.[40] This inevitably precipitated another bout of recriminations that culminated in the Commons issuing a 'Protestation of its Rights'. Within hours of its being drafted and entered in the *Commons Journal*, James angrily adjourned parliament indefinitely; within days he staged a symbolic tearing out of the Protestation and arrested Coke, Phelips, William Mallory and John Pym.

The next time parliament gathered, the atmosphere could not have been more different – all thanks to Spain. For when Prince Charles and Buckingham travelled incognito to Madrid in 1623 to seek the Infanta Maria's hand, it became clear that the Spanish had no intention of signing a marriage treaty. A disconsolate prince and angry Buckingham (who extraordinarily, and without his asking, had just been created the first non-royal duke since 1551) returned to London keen to see off the objections of Lionel Cranfield, now treasurer and earl of Middlesex, and others in the council who were still opposed to war, and to lead a new 'patriot' coalition. Buckingham and the prince thought parliament indispensable to this enterprise. Indeed, Buckingham expressly recruited the new parliament that gathered on 19 February 1624 to his cause, giving a highly partisan account of events in perfidious Madrid to a joint session of both houses, while Charles nodded assent. Everyone flocked to him. In the Lords, the earls of Pembroke and Southampton both urged his case, and in March 1624 the house declared itself prepared to 'assist His Majesty with our persons and fortunes'.[41] The Commons were a bit slower to give their wholehearted support. John Glanvill, for instance, made the wise point that there was no point in providing for war unless and until the king actually proposed it. But for once James let the debates run, and the Commons resolved that 'in pursuit of our advice we will be ready, upon His Majesty's declaration to break off both the treaties [with Spain], to assist, both with our persons and abilities, in a parliamentary manner'.[42] On 23 March, just a month after opening, the 'happy' deal was struck. James would break off both treaties in exchange for a Commons award of three subsidies and three-fifteenths, to be overseen by parliamentary commissioners. Just to allay any fears, Charles also let it be known in the Lords that 'whensoever it should please God to bestow upon him any lady that were popish, she should have no further liberty but for her own family, and no advantage to the recusants at home'.[43]

Buckingham still had important parliamentary business to

do. In particular, he was keen to remove, or at least disable, the two key remaining advocates of a Spanish match: John Digby, the headstrong earl of Bristol, who was ambassador in Madrid, and Treasurer Middlesex. The former he had recalled from Spain and confined to his estate. As for the latter, when Sir Miles Fleetwood, the Receiver-General of the Court of Wards and MP for Launceston, who had been accused of corruption in 1621 by Lionel Cranfield, laid charges against Middlesex, Buckingham did nothing to help the Lord Treasurer. Indeed, he and the prince actively conspired in his downfall. A stern, even stubborn man, Middlesex had few friends in the Commons, and when Coke and Sandys laid charges of bribery and corruption against him, the king's prediction came true: 'All Treasurers, if they do good service to their master, must be generally hated.'[44] As with Bacon, this was shamefully unjust. Middlesex had certainly made himself a quiet fortune, sometimes straying close to the edge of the difference between a bribe and a gratuity, but he had proved himself the king's most effective treasurer, and the Commons' demand for impeachment and the Lords' decision, announced in May 1624, to deprive, fine and imprison him owed more to courtly intrigue than to justice.

There remained the important question of a bride for Charles. The French proved every bit as tough as the Spanish in the negotiations for the hand of Henri IV's daughter Henrietta Maria, insisting on her freedom to worship as she pleased and far greater latitude for English Catholics in exchange for a £120,000 dowry and a nebulous offer of military support for the Palatinate. So it was only on 12 December that James arthritically and secretly signed a marriage treaty, to which parliament would almost certainly not have assented. Parliament stood conveniently prorogued until February 1625, when it was presented with a very French *fait accompli*, but by now James was ill. On 24 March he confirmed his faith, surrounded at Theobalds by his son, Bishop Williams of Lincoln and Buckingham, and three days later Charles was dragged out of his bed very early in the morning to witness his father's final moments.

The Church of England still celebrates the feast of 'Charles I, king and martyr', so it is all too easy to detect the distant drums beating out a remorseless rhythm on the road to the regicidal scaffold from the moment he ascended the throne. But it is a mistake. For Charles's first parliament could so easily have been harmonious. Charles had played an active part in parliament before his accession, and the single overriding national issue remained one that bound the 'patriot' alliance of Charles and Buckingham to parliament: the Thirty Years War. But instead of harmony, there was instant discord – not helped by the fact that the plague was raging in London, so that when MPs and peers gathered in the capital in May they were kept hanging around until 18 June before the session was opened by the king. Charles and Buckingham were complacent. The case for munitions and money was made, but in the most nebulous of terms, and the Commons insisted on granting the king his tonnage and poundage duties for a single year, during which a full audit of royal finances would be undertaken, rather than for life. Charles was understandably perplexed, and moaned to Buckingham: 'I have, in a manner, lost the love of my subjects. What wouldst thou have me do?'[45] The duke's answer was to reconvene parliament on 1 August in plague-free Oxford, where he tried to repeat his 1624 trick by addressing both houses, reminding them of the 1624 parliament when he 'had the honour to be applauded' and begging them to 'put the sword into [the king's] hands and he will maintain the war'.[46] It was to no avail. At first the opponents of any new tax steered clear of direct attacks on the duke, but the undercurrent of anti-Buckingham sentiment was so strong that when Edward Clarke objected to members' 'bitter invectives' against the duke, the Commons handed him over to the Sergeant-at-Arms, and as the debates progressed first Sir Robert Mansell and then Sir Francis Seymour (brother of the earl of Hertford) 'took off all vizards and disguises in which their discourses had been masked' and openly attacked Buckingham.[47] With no prospect of any further movement, Charles took a leaf out of his father's book and dissolved parliament.

However uncomfortable parliament might be, though, Charles had to face the inconvenient truth that war required money and money required parliamentary assent; and he had to face it the more urgently when the abject failure of an adventurous (hare-brained) attack on Cadiz two months later cost him another £250,000. So he was forced to summon a new parliament for February 1626, having taken two precautionary measures: creating a few extra earls ('so many cardinals to carry the consistory',[48] said the once loyal but now increasingly critical MP Benjamin Rudyerd) and naming the four trickiest knights (Coke, Wentworth, Phelips and Seymour) as sheriffs so as to exclude them.

Summoning parliament at this point was to prove a fatal mistake, as the antagonized Commons now sought to impeach Buckingham – who had only himself to blame. In 1621 he had surrendered Bacon to exculpate himself. In 1624 he had assisted Middlesex's downfall, and in 1625 his allies had taken a pop at Bishop Williams, which eventually bore fruit in his dismissal from the post of Lord Keeper by the king in October. Those who live by the sword, die by the sword. What was more, with the exclusion of the four troublesome knights the stage had been cleared for a far more dangerous foe, his erstwhile ally Sir John Eliot, the fervid, contumacious burgess for St Germans, who thus far had been a loyal client of Buckingham, at whose bidding he had called for the investigation into Williams and described Middlesex as a 'strange and prodigious comet . . .

whose substance is corruption'.[49] Buckingham had been generous to Eliot in return, appointing him vice-admiral for Devon
and protecting him from charges of piracy. But some time in
1625, quite possibly when two other Buckingham clients were
promoted ahead of him, Eliot defected.

He was not the only worm to have turned. The man who
had led the Baynards Castle plot to promote Villiers, the bookish patron of the arts William Herbert, 3rd earl of Pembroke,
had also turned against his former protégé and quietly lined up
MPs to support Eliot, who had found in the failed Cadiz expedition the perfect excuse to attack his former patron. In debate
after debate he launched an increasingly overt assault: 'Our
honour is ruined,' he said, 'our ships are sunk, our men perished,
not by the sword, not by an enemy, not by chance, but as the
strongest predictions had discerned and made apparent beforehand, by those we trust.'[50] He called for a full investigation into
the expenditure granted in 1624, arguing that the king's only
shortage was of good advice, and persuaded the Commons to
set up a Committee for Evils, Causes and Remedies, which
produced a list of accusations against Buckingham. Charles told
Buckingham: 'It is not you they aim at, but it is upon me that
they make their inquisition,'[51] but his reaction inflamed the situation. When he said that his councillors, including Buckingham,
had only ever acted 'by special directions and appointment', and
that 'parliaments are altogether in my power for their calling,
sitting and dissolution',[52] the Commons met his intransigence
by moving to impeach Buckingham on a lengthy charge sheet
that accused him of holding too many posts, of selling titles and
even of poisoning King James. Buckingham should have been
safe. He still had the clear backing of the king. But Pembroke had
been joined by other former Buckingham allies in the Lords,
who dealt the duke a blow when they pushed through a motion
to restrict the number of proxies held by any one peer at a time

to two, thereby ending Buckingham's block vote of thirteen. Buckingham was in danger of following Bacon and Middlesex; so yet again on 15 June Charles dissolved parliament early.

The decline in Charles's relations with parliament focused on one other, even more potent issue – religion. James's reign in England had been remarkably quiescent on this front. The arrest of Guy Fawkes and his Catholic 'powder plot' associates on the eve of the 1605 session of parliament had cemented the body politic in a fervid fear of Catholics. An elegant royal version of the Bible had been published in English and James had managed the conflicting theological strains astutely. But Charles did not share either his father's theological subtlety or his unequivocal Protestantism, as became shockingly apparent when he removed James's favourite cleric, Bishop Williams of Lincoln, as Lord Keeper and had the bishop of St David's, William Laud, preside at his coronation. This was a bold statement. Laud had supported the rector of Stanford Rivers in Essex, Richard Montagu, when his tract *A New Gag for an Old Goose* had been denounced by John Pym in James's last parliament as 'full fraught with dangerous opinions of Arminius', even though this was a direct accusation of crypto-Catholicism. The Dutch theologian Jacobus Arminius had sought to redefine Calvinism by suggesting that 'prevenient grace' was available to both the elect and the non-elect. In other words, God had not predestined every soul either to heaven or to hell. All had free will. For many Puritans and Evangelicals, this was dangerous papist heresy, so the Commons had complained to James, who had referred the matter to the evangelical Archbishop Abbot, who had told Montagu off. Little comforted, the Commons committed Montagu to the Sergeant-at-Arms in Charles's first parliament, whereupon Charles tactlessly made him one of his own chaplains, even as he promoted Laud to Bath and Wells. Moreover, Laud was hardly a master of tact. In his sermon to parliament he declared that the king was God's vice-regent and that the sole function of parliament was to furnish the king with financial support: 'The King is the sun. He draws up some vapours, some supply, some support, from us. It is true he must do so: for if the sun draw up no vapours, it can pour down no rain.'[53] These words encapsulated a fundamental clash between Protestant parliamentary liberty and Catholic-acting royal autocracy.

The Arminian views of Laud and Montagu soon became even more unpalatable to the Commons when Charles took a series of emergency measures after the calamitous 1626 parliament. First he wrote to all the justices of the peace seeking a loan, which he hoped his people would lend him 'lovingly, freely and voluntarily'; and then, when they mostly refused, he decided to enforce the loan on pain of imprisonment. This predictably raised the legal, constitutional and religious stakes. Seventy-six gentlemen and the earl of Lincoln refused to fork out and were imprisoned, five knights argued in court that the king had no legal power to arrest them without giving due reason, and when the former Speaker, now Chief Justice of the King's Bench, Sir Randolph Crewe refused to provide legal backing for the loan he was dismissed. Then, most toxically, Charles sought benediction for the enforced loan by encouraging clergy to preach adherence to the king's will. Montagu was first at the crease, followed by Robert Sibthorpe, whose assize sermon at Northampton called for absolute subjugation to the will of the monarch. That led to a major rupture with Lambeth Palace, as Abbot refused to license the publication of Sibthorpe's address and was consequently dismissed from the council and deprived of most of his powers.

It was against this background that Charles summoned his third parliament on 16 March 1628. It was a perfect storm. Military ignominy had been compounded when the Buckingham-led attempt to seize the Île de Ré had ended with a forced retreat, the compulsory loan followed by imprisonment of those who had refused to pay seemed to betray English parliamentary freedom, and the incense of 'damnable [papist] danger' was wafting through parliament thanks to the absolutist, pro-loan preaching of another royal chaplain, Roger Maynwaring.[54] No wonder Rudyerd reckoned: 'This is the crisis of parliaments. By this we shall know whether parliaments will live or die.'[55] The antagonists could hardly decide which issue to deal with first. The military danger meant that generous supply was on offer – both tonnage and poundage and five subsidies – but the Commons insisted that the king first allow a new statute restating the historic principles of the Great Charter. The debate raged between the king's diminished band of loyalists, who wanted to assert the royal prerogative, and those who feared an unfettered autocratic monarchy. With Charles threatening to veto any statute that advanced any new principle, Coke now pulled off a juridical masterstroke, sidestepping the prohibition on a new 'statute' by suggesting 'a petition of right to the King for our particular grievances',[56] which, unlike a mere 'petition of grace', would be legally enforceable and would include legal redress for the two houses' specific complaints. Coke presented the petition to the Lords on behalf of the Commons on 8 May, and although Charles had a phenomenal capacity for intransigence he conceded that so long as there was no statutory limitation on his prerogative, he would guarantee that he would never arrest people for not lending money to the crown. But by now the petitioners were confident of their majority in both houses, so Thomas Wentworth pressed for more, arguing that the king's concession was all very well, but 'not in a parliamentary way. I doubt not but it is a letter of grace, but the people will only like of that which is done in a parliamentary way.'[57] At the end of the month the Petition of Right was presented to the king on the understanding that Charles would signify royal assent in the traditional Norman French words: *Soit droit fait comme il est désiré.*

If only. For some reason Charles hedged his approval with yet more verbiage about the prerogative. When the Commons heard of this they vented their fury on Buckingham. It was Coke who broke the dam, declaring that 'the duke of Buckingham is the cause of all our miseries' and (unfairly) blaming him for the king's intransigence. Immediately everyone cried out 'It is he!' and set about drafting a new document, a remonstrance against the duke. Catching wind of this, Charles urged them not to enter into any new business or 'to cast aspersions on the state, government or ministers thereof', but the Commons' response was a cacophony of passions, with 'some [MPs] weeping, some expostulating, some prophesying of the fatal ruin of our kingdom'.[58] With the clamour at full pitch (and the coffers still empty), Charles finally succumbed: on 7 June he summoned both houses and had the clerk read out full royal assent for the Petition of Right. 'It is not possible for me to express', said one commentator, 'with what joy this was heard, nor what joy it does now cause in all this city, where at this hour they are making bonfires at every door.'[59]

The political turbulence did not end there, though. Parliament still had to agree a subsidy, and on 13 June a mob hacked to death a known Buckingham associate, the astrologer John Lambe, just a day after the Commons agreed another remonstrance against the favourite. Yet again Charles acted to protect the duke. As soon as the subsidy was agreed he prorogued parliament on 26 June. Charles now tried to calm things down. He restored the earls of Bristol and Arundel to favour and made Wentworth a baron. But even as he made these conciliatory gestures he further inflamed parliamentary fury with a set of religious appointments. In the course of the single month of July, he made Montagu bishop of Chichester and promoted Laud to

London, Neile to Winchester and Howson to Durham. With Laud and Neile also now on the council, the much-derided Arminians had full control of the church.

It seems certain that if parliament had continued to sit Buckingham would have been impeached, but in a bizarre quirk of fate there then followed an event that laid bare the Commons' disingenuousness. On 14 August the duke arrived in Portsmouth as Lord High Admiral to prepare for another naval expedition, and set up camp at the Greyhound Inn. On Saturday, 23 August he was passing through the crowded hall of the inn after break-fast on his way to give Charles the (inaccurate) news that La Rochelle had fallen. As he leaned forward to speak with one of his colonels a man lunged at him with a dagger and stabbed him in the chest. In the confusion, the fatally wounded Buckingham was laid out on a table, his wife and sister-in-law at his side; when the assassin was apprehended, he turned out to be a disgruntled soldier called John Felton, who had served in the Île de Ré expe-dition and who said that it was the Commons' remonstrance that had convinced him that by 'killing the duke he should do his country great service'.[60]

It was the most significant assassination in English history. Although formally he was only Lord High Admiral and Master of the Horse, Buckingham was to all intents and purposes first minister. But the real significance of his death was that it denied the government's critics their convenient scapegoat. While Buckingham lived they could attack the king's policies without attacking the monarch. Even Eliot had taken care to emphasize, when supporting the remonstrance, that 'we have no ends but only his majesty's honour and safety and that we do not, or will not, lay any aspersion on his Majesty's government'.[61] With the duke dead, though, they could no longer pretend unconditional fealty to the king while attacking all his policies. In the end the Commons' anger would find its real target.

For all the fulminations of Sandys, Eliot and Coke, there was at this point nothing like an organized opposition party with a coherent ideology. There were antiquarians, men who collected historical precedent and thought they knew the rules of parliament better than the king; but politics was still very fluid, with individuals chopping and changing and acting more out of instinct than out of adherence to a party line. Some abandoned their support for the king, but the traffic was not all one way. The Cornish lawyer William Noy, for instance, could often be rude and abrasive. He frequently opposed grants of supply, he condemned the forced loan, and he argued for the Petition of Right. Yet he owed his seat in 1624 to Charles's patronage and became his Attorney-General in 1631, prompting Thomas Carlyle, busily grinding his own Whiggish axe in 1845, to call Noy a 'morose, amorphous, cynical Law Pedant, an invincible living heap of learned rubbish; once a Patriot in Parliament, till they made him Attorney-General and enlightened his eyes'.[62] But this is to write history with the benefit of hindsight. There was as yet no party to betray, no party line to breach; and even when opposing one or other of the king's policies, none of these men conceived of themselves as 'in opposition'.

Much of the vilification of Buckingham is unmerited, too. Yes, he was ambitious and acquisitive. He enriched himself and his friends. He abandoned allies to protect himself. But he was also an engaging individual; he eschewed cruelty and he regularly extended olive branches to his enemies. What is more, many of those he patronized were genuinely competent, and the parliamentarians who wanted a godly war but remained unrealistic about paying for it were every bit as much to blame as he for England's military failures. Some had hoped that when Charles came to the throne he would dismiss his father's favourite, but Buckingham's intensely personal relationship with the first two Stuart monarchs was in many ways the glue that held the court together. The enduring strength of this relationship was never more apparent than in Charles's reaction when he heard that his much-loved George was dead. At first the king managed to control himself, barely showing his emotions through morning prayers. But as soon as he got to his room he 'threw himself upon his bed, lamenting with much passion and with abundance of tears'.[63]

THE
World turn'd upfide down:
OR
A briefe defcription of the ridiculous Fafhions of thefe diftracted Times.

By T. J. a well-willer to King, Parliament and Kingdom.

The civil wars in all three kingdoms saw every aspect of government turned on its head. The bishops were deprived of their sees, the Lords were abolished, the king was executed and Oliver Cromwell became Lord Protector of the Commonwealth of England, Scotland and Ireland for life. Cromwell's subsequent experiments included a parliament chosen for its religious purity, followed by a unicameral protectorate parliament and a second protectorate parliament that incorporated his own personally created 'other house'.

8

The Vertical Turning Point

THERE WAS A DRAMATIC CODA to the parliamentary skirmishes of the 1620s. Even after Buckingham's death his critics were determined to rein the king in, not least because he was still collecting tonnage and poundage without parliamentary say-so. So when, forced by poverty to re-summon parliament on 20 January 1629, Charles immediately ordered the arrest of John Rolle, a merchant who had refused to pay the duty, the Commons leaped to Rolle's defence. Charles had made a poor choice of victim, for Rolle, the burgess for Callington, was brother of the lawyer Henry Rolle MP and a friend of the most truculent royal critics, most notably Sir Edward Herbert, John Selden and Sir Edward Littleton. Members denounced the arrest as a breach of parliamentary privilege and refused to countenance consideration of tonnage and poundage until the issue was resolved.

As before, religion provided another string to the discontents' bow. Many had been infuriated by the previous year's ecclesiastical appointments, so a committee was set up to examine the state of the church; on 24 February it condemned the 'subtle and pernicious spreading of the Arminian faction' and asked that the king 'be graciously pleased to confer bishoprics, and other ecclesiastical preferments with the advice of his privy council upon learned, pious and orthodox men'.[1] So febrile was the atmosphere by this point that the king decided to force the Commons to adjourn so as to cool their heels. At first they agreed, suspending sittings from 25 February to 2 March; but far from calming down, the discontents intensified their activities, and two secret meetings were held at the Three Cranes tavern with Selden, Eliot, Denzil Holles, Benjamin Valentine, Walter Long, William Coryton, William Strode, Sir Miles Hobart and Sir Peter Hayman in attendance. So when the king's loyal Speaker, John Finch, announced after prayers on 2 March that the king demanded a further adjournment, the rebels were prepared and started to shout their refusal to adjourn. Eliot stood up to speak. At this Finch barked out that the king's clear instructions were that the House was to adjourn without further ado. Indeed, if anyone should attempt to speak he was to vacate the chair and thereby end the session. Determined that the Commons should be able to transact three final pieces of business, Holles and Valentine grabbed hold of Finch and forced him back into his chair so that Eliot could speak.

The chamber was now in tumult. Coryton hit an MP and Eliot threw a piece of paper to Sir William Fleetwood, who handed it to the clerk, and one after another the rebels demanded that the Speaker read it out. Again Finch tried to leave; again he was restrained. Strode told Finch that he must either be servant of the House or of the crown, and Finch's reply, 'I am not less the King's servant for being yours,' sparked off yet more fury. There were calls for the Serjeant to lock the doors, and when he refused Hobart seized the keys and did the job himself. Thus secure, Eliot delivered a long, coruscating speech, declaring that those who brought in Arminian innovations or collected tonnage and poundage without parliamentary authority were 'capital enemies to the king and kingdom' and that those who paid the duties were 'accessories to the rest'. Eliot then surreptitiously threw his paper into the fire and Holles read out three pre-arranged resolutions from his own copy, each of which was greeted by a mighty roar of approval. Their work done, the House adjourned until 10 March and Hobart unlocked the door.

Charles speedily dissolved parliament, condemning 'the undutiful and seditious carriage in the Lower House', where 'some few vipers among them did cast this mist of undutiful-ness over most of their eyes',[2] and on 3 March sent nine of the 'vipers' to a variety of prisons. Few were particularly brave. Coryton and Hayman made their peace fairly quickly and Selden denied that he had ever supported Eliot's paper. Only the recently widowed Eliot, one-time ally of Buckingham, now recal-citrant hero, held out to the end; he died at two o'clock in the morning on 28 November 1632, after three and a half years in the Tower.

Charles had had his fill of parliaments. The best he could say on the matter was that he would 'be more inclinable to meet in parliament again when our people shall see more clearly into our intents and actions'.[3] Which was tantamount to saying that he would not summon another session unless he absolutely could not avoid it, and he managed to avoid it for eleven years. Notwithstanding the antagonism this 'personal rule' built up, it might have been sustainable while England was at peace, or even while there was discord in just one of his three kingdoms; but when Charles started meddling like an absentee landlord with the religious settlement in Scotland, events conspired against him.

The Scottish Reformation of 1560 had been more extensive than its English counterpart. The Scottish parliament had not only expressly condemned the Catholic trinity of papal author-ity, transubstantiation and indulgences, but had enjoined the church to order itself along Presbyterian lines, dismantling the hierarchy of royally appointed bishops and replacing them with ministers and elders elected by their own congregations. King James, unlike his Catholic mother, who had refused to assent to these provisions, had been a comfortable Protestant, but had nevertheless hankered after the revitalization of the dormant Scottish episcopacy, which he achieved, to limited effect, in 1610. Charles, though, with the same religious predisposition towards orderly worship and royal authority over the church as Laud, who was by now his archbishop of Canterbury, wanted to go further. Not content with insisting that *English* churches place communion tables altar-wise back against the east end surrounded by communion rails, Charles decided to seek a parallel reform of the Scottish kirk, and in 1637 required that every Scottish church adopt Laud's new prayer book.

Charles had hideously misread his Scottish subjects' attachment to Calvinism and their preference for the old pre-1610 Reformation. Many ministers condemned the new prayer book, there were demonstrations across Scotland, and on Sunday, 23 July a market trader called Jenny Geddes was so incensed when she heard David Lindsay, the bishop of Edinburgh, read from the new prayer book in St Giles' Cathedral that she threw a folding stool at his head. The law of equal and opposite force kicked in with remarkable precision. In February 1638 Scottish Presbyterians signed a Scottish National Covenant, decrying the prayer book; in July Charles demanded obedience and threatened force; in November the general assembly of the kirk decided to do away with bishops again; Charles raised an army and marched against the Scots; and the opposing forces met in a series of skirmishes at the border. This stand-off was concluded with the Pacification of Berwick in June 1639, at which point Charles would have been wise to withdraw. Sadly he was not yet finished with the Scots' kirk, and back in London he decided to return to the field, better equipped.

For that he needed cash – and that in turn necessitated the parliament that was summoned for 13 April 1640. This summons, too, was misconceived. The English bishops' relentless ritualism had antagonized a new generation of English MPs and peers, many of whom now actively supported the Scottish Covenanters. Moreover, although many of the old rebels had died, there were enough who remembered the 1620s to brew up a storm.

The undoubted leader of the discontents was the 56-year-old burgess for Tavistock, John Pym. First elected in 1614, Pym was no great orator, nor was he ever accused of subtlety, but he was courageous and had, as Edward Hyde put it, 'a very comely and grave way of expressing himself, with great volubility of words, natural and proper'.[4] He had lost his wife, his stepfather and his eldest son in 1620 – all from natural causes – but he had a ready-made band of Commons followers including his half-brother Francis Rous, his nephew Anthony Nicoll and his stepbrother-in-law John Upton.

When the parliament began on 13 April 1640, then, the opposition's quiver was full of arrows. Within a week Pym furiously threw in the king's face the arrest of the nine members in 1629, the spread of Arminianism and the tyrannous eleven years of personal rule, and demanded that these grievances be addressed before the House even think about new taxes. One particular example of the king's tyranny that rankled was his extraction of ship money (traditionally levied on coastal towns) from land-locked counties, which one normally moderate royal critic, Sir Francis Seymour, and the lucid and brave knight for Buckinghamshire, John Hampden, had refused to pay. Hampden's trial in 1637 had ended with a victory for the crown, but the bench of judges, led by former Speaker and now Lord Keeper Finch, had split seven to five, so when Seymour, Hampden and his lawyer, Oliver St John, acerbically attacked the king's demands in the new parliament, they were feted as brave parliamentary martyrs. Within three weeks the acrimony was all too reminiscent of previous failed parliaments and on 5 May Charles drew stumps, yet again complaining that 'it hath been some few cunning and some ill-affectioned men that have been the cause of this misunderstanding'.[5]

This ended the 'Short' parliament, but it did not bring Charles's problems to a close. The trouble was that he had now exposed himself on two fronts: the Scots were in no mood to let matters rest, seizing Northumberland and County Durham in the summer of 1640, and the English parliament refused to come to Charles's aid financially unless he capitulated on arbitrary taxation, ministerial incompetence and religious innovation. If he remained intransigent, all that was needed to bring about his undoing was for his opponents to unite. Which is precisely what they did. In August the king was in York, preparing to take on the Scots, when his closest advisers gathered intelligence that secret meetings were being held in London between Pym, Hampden and a group of like-minded peers, and on the twenty-eighth Edward, Lord Howard of Escrick, and Edward Montagu, Viscount Mandeville, turned up in York with a petition, signed by twelve peers, demanding a parliament. The signatories were a tight-knit group – eight of them had formerly sat as MPs, several were related by marriage, all had close connections with Pym and Hampden – and, with many of the great families of England represented among them, they had an impressive pedigree. At first Charles conceded only a September meeting of peers in York, but when he came to a humiliating new settlement with the Scots that required him to pay their substantial daily expenses, he had absolutely no choice but to summon a new English parliament.

In the annals of British history this would come to be known as the Long Parliament, as it was only dissolved in 1653 and did not finally vote itself out of existence until 1660. When it opened on 3 November 1640, expectations were high. When the Short Parliament had collapsed, Edward Hyde, the prim burgess for Saltash, had presumed Oliver St John, 'who had naturally a great cloud in his face and very seldom was known to smile', would be downcast. In fact, he had been remarkably cheerful, explaining 'that all was well; and that it must be worse before it could be better; and that his Parliament could never have done what was necessary to be done'.[6] Others were more apprehensive. Benjamin Rudyerd reckoned: 'I have often thought and said that it must be some great extremity that would recover and rectify this state, and when that extremity did come, it would be a great hazard whether it would prove a remedy or ruin. We are now . . . upon that vertical turning point.'[7] He was right; the vertical turning point span fast as Pym, Seymour and Hampden were re-elected and set a plan in motion to keep parliament in session. Within three months parliament forced Charles to assent to a Triennial Act that determined that a parliament lasting at least fifty days must be called at least every three years, and then in May it passed another Act that meant parliament could not be dissolved without its own consent. These were powerful harbingers of a major assault on the royal prerogative.

Its first business, though, was to deal with those it reckoned to be the prime cause of all their grievances, the king's councillors – in Rudyerd's words, the 'subverting, destructive counsels, for they ring a doleful, deadly knell over the whole kingdom'.[8] First up was Thomas Wentworth, the earl of Strafford. The Commons' immediate concerns about the earl focused on his autocratic rule as Lord Deputy of Ireland and the threat that he might bring Irish troops to England to see off the king's several enemies. But feelings about Strafford had a longer pedigree. He had sat as an anti-war Yorkshire MP throughout the 1620s, he had been imprisoned for refusing to pay the forced loan, and he had argued for the defence of 'our ancient, sober, vital liberties' in the debates on the Petition of Right. Moreover, his father-in-law was John Holles, earl of Clare and a prominent critic of Charles. However, following his own ennoblement in 1628, Wentworth had performed an abrupt volte-face, becoming one of the mainstays of the personal rule. Some MPs felt personally slighted by him. He gave evidence against his father-in-law, thereby antagonizing the earl's son Denzil Holles, and on returning to England from Ireland at the king's behest in 1639 to lead the charge against the Scots, he was simultaneously made earl of Strafford and baron of Raby, even though Raby Castle was owned by the recently appointed secretary of state, Sir Henry Vane. In the popular imagination Strafford was a new Buckingham, and when Pym persuaded a tightly packed chamber to impeach him on 11 November on a charge sheet that had not even yet been drawn up, Strafford was forced to kneel at the bar of the upper house before being led away to custody. Two weeks later he was sent to the Tower, supposedly for trying to introduce 'an arbitrary and tyrannical government against law'.[9] Two others followed in quick succession. The other secretary of state, Sir Francis Windebank, was accused of protecting Catholic priests and fled to France, and when Lord Keeper Finch was attacked for his ship money judgment against Hampden, he mounted a stoical defence on 21 December, but that same night stole away to The Hague.

This left Archbishop Laud, who was, according to Sir Harbottle Grimston, 'the root and ground of all our miseries'.[10] Laud had hardly shied away from controversy. He had tried to make Scottish clergy wear surplices and the English bow to the altar, in 1625 he had breathtakingly declared that 'the power which resides in the King is not any assuming to himself, nor any gift from the people, but God's power',[11] and in 1628 he had lectured the Commons that they should stop meddling with the church, sit less and 'remember that the law of God, which gives kings aids and subsidies, may not be broken by them without heinous sin'.[12] His Catholic-inclined theology, his ritualism and his theocratic support for the personal rule all led to Sir John Hotham's call for his impeachment, which the Commons willingly agreed on 18 December.

Strafford's trial in the Lords commenced in March 1641, but when it became clear that he had always acted under the king's command, which meant that any attack on him was an indirect but treasonous attack on Charles, Pym, who was in charge of the prosecution, invented a new concept, 'constructive treason', which, unlike other treasons that were 'against the rule of law' was 'against the being of the law'.[13] This was a legal nonsense, and Strafford knew it, demanding to know how the sum total of his actions could be considered treason if none of the individual deeds was treasonous. There was another problem. Thus far Pym had only one witness against Strafford, but the Bible and the law required at least two. Then the younger Sir Henry Vane, notwithstanding the fact that his father was still secretary and he was Treasurer of the Navy, produced evidence that seemed to incriminate Strafford. This was not enough to convince the Lords, many of whom preferred to heed the earl's warning: 'Let me be a Pharos to keep you from the shipwreck, and do not put such rocks in your own way';[14] so Pym swiftly abandoned the impeachment and drafted a Bill of Attainder, which required no trial. Despite a large number of absentees, it was carried convincingly in both the Commons (200 to 59) and the Lords (26 to 19). When Charles had summoned Strafford to London, he had promised to protect his faithful servant's life, but when the earl magnanimously (or naively) wrote to release him from his oath, the king treacherously assented to the attainder and on 12 May 1641 Strafford was executed, the only grace afforded him being a beheading.

Proceedings against Laud were far slower, but followed the same relentlessly unjust pattern. Dubious charges were presented by the Commons, a trial began in the Lords in March 1644 and, when it proved impossible to make the charge of treason stick, the Commons abandoned impeachment in favour of attainder, which was reluctantly agreed by the Lords on 4 January 1645. When the archbishop mounted the scaffold six days later, Pym's Irish brother-in-law Sir John Clotworthy, another MP, taunted Laud so sharply that the archbishop turned to his executioner 'as the gentler and discreeter person'.[15] Two centuries later Macaulay, expressing the hatred for Laud shared by many of his contemporaries, condemned him as 'the ridiculous old bigot' for whom he entertained 'a more unmitigated contempt than for any other character in our history'. Any other reaction, he felt, was due to 'the perversity of affection which sometimes leads a mother to select the monster or idiot of the family as the object of her special favour'.[16] But while Laud supported Charles's theocratic absolutism, it is difficult not to respect his passionate defence of bishops and his espousal of a reverential, ordered liturgy. Few would argue that either Strafford or Laud's execution was anything other than a travesty of justice. Parliament had harried them to their deaths.

Up until late 1640 there was a large measure of consensus in the Commons. Even future royalists such as Edward Hyde and Lucius Cary, Viscount Falkland,* who was MP for Newport on the Isle of Wight, supported Strafford's attainder. Religion, though, was to fracture the consensus. For many were not satisfied with the mere removal of Laud. They wanted his

---

* Although English peers have always been barred from the Commons, a Scottish or Irish peerage did not preclude membership of the lower house, nor did courtesy titles granted to the sons of peers. Viscount Falkland was a title in the Scottish peerage. After the Irish Act of Union, Irish peers such as Viscount Palmerston could still sit for non-Irish seats.

Arminianist colleagues ousted and the church converted to Scottish-style bishopless godliness. First, a public petition calling for 'root and branch' abolition of the bishops, bearing 15,000 signatures, was presented to the Commons in December 1640, just as the Commons demanded that Matthew Wren, the bishop of Ely, be imprisoned for setting up 'idolatry and suspicion' in his diocese. Then came an acrimonious two-day debate on the petition in which Falkland, who had vigorously attacked ship money and laid charges against Finch, nevertheless argued that it was not 'fair to abolish, upon a few days debate, an order which hath lasted . . . in most churches these sixteen hundred years'.[17] Undeterred, the Commons moved on to Roger Maynwaring, who was now bishop of St David's and had antagonized Puritans and royal critics alike so comprehensively that even Bishop Williams of Lincoln urged that his bishopric be taken off him as 'he roved from alehouse to alehouse in disguise'.[18] As soon as he heard of the proceedings against him, Maynwaring took flight to Ireland with his young wife. Next, Laud's close ally in Wales, Morgan Owen of Llandaff, was added to the list of impeachable bishops, along with Richard Montagu at Norwich, who only evaded almost certain conviction by dying on 13 April 1641.

Still determined to find a more permanent solution to the 'popish' bishops, Oliver St John (newly appointed Solicitor-General in an act of royal conciliation) then surreptitiously helped the younger Vane and the 42-year-old MP for Cambridge, Oliver Cromwell, to draft a Bill for the 'utter abolishing of bishops, Deans, Archdeacons', which was presented by Edward Dering on 27 May 1641. The Commons debates at both first and second readings were fierce, ending with only narrow votes in favour, but by the time the Bill faltered in the Lords, another flank had been opened up when on 3 August the Commons sought the impeachment for treason of all the bishops who had agreed a new body of canon law at the Convocation of May 1640, which the Commons reckoned to have met unconstitutionally after parliament had been dissolved.

The religious temperature was already quite warm enough when October brought news of a Catholic rebellion in Ireland. Members of the vulnerable Protestant minority were apparently being murdered and raped. Suddenly people feared a 'popish plot' and suspected the king's hand in it. Immediately the attack on his policies and personnel intensified. A new Bill to exclude the bishops from parliament was produced, together with a lengthy Grand Remonstrance against the king, drafted by Pym, celebrating parliament's recent abolition of the tyrannical Court of Star Chamber, the banning of illegal taxes and the provisions for regular parliaments. When this was debated on 22 November 1641, the depth of the fracture in the Commons rapidly became apparent. Hampden and the younger Vane spoke in favour but Falkland was opposed, forcing the debate to last, quite exceptionally, well past midnight. When the vote came the result was close: just 159 votes in favour to 148 against. Two opponents, Hyde and Sir John Colepeper, tried to complain, but some members threw their hats in the air in delight and others 'took their swords in their scabbards out of their belts and held them by their pommels in their hands'. One MP feared that opponents were set to sheathe their 'swords in each other's bowels'.[19] Such was the animosity that former allies fell out. Lucius Cary, 2nd Viscount Falkland, the MP for Newport on the Isle of Wight, had supported reform of the church earlier in the year, but now voted against the remonstrance, prompting Oliver Cromwell to tell him angrily that if it had been defeated he would have sold all he had the next morning and never seen England more. In parliament there was a sense of crisis; but when the remonstrance was presented to Charles on 1 December, he procrastinated for three weeks before returning a noncommittal answer on 23 December – at which point Pym and his allies instantly voted to exclude the bishops from the House of Lords. Five days later a mob tried (but failed) to bar the way to bishops attending the Lords, shouting 'no bishops, no bishops', prompting the royalist veteran Sir John Strangways to point out that the privilege of parliament was 'utterly broke if men might not come in safety to give their votes freely'.[20]

The bishops themselves were furious, and two days later a formal 'protest' was signed by twelve of them, led by the only archbishop at liberty, John Williams, who only weeks earlier had been translated to York. Williams was no disciple of Laud. Far from it. Nor was the poet and satirist bishop of Norwich, Joseph Hall, or the small, sprightly, 76-year-old bishop of Durham, Thomas Morton, or John Owen of St Asaph; but they were joined in the protest by committed Laudians. Godfrey Goodman of Gloucester, who had regularly been condemned for 'popery', signed up. So did the aggressive John Towers of Peterborough, along with Wren of Ely, William Piers of Bath and Wells (condemned by parliament in December 1640 as a 'desperately profane, impious, turbulent Pilate'),[21] Robert Wright, the avaricious 80-year-old bishop of Coventry and Lichfield, who insisted on people bowing their head at the name of Jesus, Morgan Owen, the bishop of Llandaff, who had constructed the ornate portico to the University Church in Oxford adorned with a Virgin and Child, and Robert Skinner of Oxford, who advocated confession. One remaining signatory was a straightforward royalist, Secretary Sir John Coke's incompetent brother George, bishop of Hereford.

The 'protest' was incendiary, as it declared illegal anything done in the Lords in their absence, so the Commons gave them short shrift, insisting that all twelve be arrested. According to Edward Hyde, the only MP to tender even a smidgen of support to the bishops argued that they were not guilty of high treason, but were 'stark mad and therefore desired that they might be sent to Bedlam'.[22] The eleven still at liberty were arrested and dragged on their knees to the bar of the House of Lords; Wright and Morton, by virtue of their age, were consigned to the care of Black Rod* and the rest were sent to the Tower.

Of all Charles's many misguided moves, his next was the worst conceived. For on 1 January 1642 he appointed two of his supporters in the Commons, Falkland and Colepeper, as councillors, and two days later he demanded that the Attorney-General Sir Edward Herbert declare six opposition ringleaders – Pym, Hampden, Holles, Sir Arthur Haselrig, William Strode and Viscount Mandeville – traitors, despite the fact that they clearly enjoyed significant support in both houses. This became abundantly clear the next day, 4 January, when Viscount Saye's son, Nathaniel Fiennes, spoke eloquently on their behalf in the Commons, which decided that their arrest warrant was a 'scandalous paper' in breach of privilege.

Charles then compounded his folly by making his way with a 'great company' of about four hundred armed men from Whitehall to Westminster to try to arrest the five MPs. News of this reached the Commons at about three o'clock, whereupon four of the five immediately escaped via the river. Strode, who had spent the eleven years of the personal rule in prison, reckoned that being single he was prepared to die if necessary, and so refused to budge until his Dorset friend Sir Walter Erle virtually dragged him out of the Chamber. When Charles arrived a few moments later with his nephew Charles Louis, Elector Palatine, having left an armed guard outside in the lobby, the atmosphere was, to say the least, strained. The MPs dutifully took off their hats and the Speaker, William Lenthall, stood nervously in front

---

* The post of Gentleman Usher of the Black Rod has existed since 1361. He acts as Sergeant-at-Arms, chief doorkeeper and jailer to the Lords, and as personal attendant to the monarch in the Lords. His modern duties include summoning the Commons at the State Opening of Parliament.

of his chair. Charles, who was barely five feet tall, was hardly a commanding presence in a packed room, but started, 'Mr Speaker, I must for a time make bold with your chair,' before looking round the chamber for the five traitors. He asked whether Pym was present. There was silence. Holles? Again, silence. He pressed the Speaker. Terrified, Lenthall got down on his knees and said: 'May it please your Majesty, I have neither eyes to see nor tongue to speak but as the House is pleased to direct me, whose servant I am.'[23] There was a sharp inhalation at this. Speakers had occasionally stood up to the king before, but never before had so unambiguous a doctrine of fealty to the Commons been articulated. But then, never before had there been so flagrant a breach of the Commons' privilege, or so incompetent a royal intervention. An audibly deflated Charles muttered, 'Well, well, 'tis no matter, I think my eyes are as good as another's,' turned on his heel and left, declaring: 'I see the birds have flown.'[24] Lenthall was condemned by later royalists as 'obnoxious, timorous and interested';[25] but whatever his flaws of character may have been, it was the last time a member of the royal family entered the Commons.

The story of 4 January 1642 is so frequently told that it is easy to forget its significance. It is clear that, had the five members been present in the Commons Chamber, the king had intended to remove them, if necessary by force. Indeed, Sir Simonds d'Ewes reckoned that the king's intention was to pass through the lobby and to give full rein to his eighty or so 'ruffians', who were armed 'all of them with swords and some of them with pistols ready charged, [and] were so thirsty after innocent blood as they would scarcely have stayed the watchword'.[26]

The immediate reaction of both Commons and Lords was to cry 'privilege' and to seek the Attorney-General's impeachment; more importantly, seeing 100,000 men armed with halberds demonstrating at Westminster and 200 barges appearing on the Thames, Charles realized that he was no longer safe in London, and on 10 January he moved to Hampton Court and thence to Windsor and York. Some eighty or so peers joined him and, bereft of most royal supporters, the remaining Lords voted through the Exclusion Bill barring bishops from parliament on 5 February, with only bishops John Warner of Rochester, Walter Curll of Winchester and John Prideaux, newly appointed to Worcester, objecting.

Thus far the breach between king and parliament was not total – Charles even signed the Bill into law eight days later, which left a bishop-less House of just twenty Lords – but the ultimate rift was not far off. For the rebellion in Ireland required the recruitment of a new militia, which the Commons insisted should be accountable to them rather than the king, lest he direct it against them. When the king point blank refused to assent to the Militia Bill as originally mooted by Haselrig, the now even more tightly knit rebels in the Commons, on dodgy antiquarian advice provided by Sir Simonds d'Ewes, declared that parliament's ordinances, even if not assented to by the king, were as valid as statute law; and on 5 March a Militia Ordinance was agreed allowing parliament to appoint its own military leaders. Sir John Hotham, the MP for Beverley, was dispatched to take Hull, where munitions had been stored for use against the Scots, and here on 23 April, together with the town's MP Peregrine Pelham, he refused entry to the king.[27]

This was still not quite a decree absolute, but with Charles's critics in undisputed charge of both houses of parliament it certainly felt like a trial separation, and reconciliation seemed less and less likely. Parliament signed off a lengthy new ultimatum in the form of nineteen propositions, demanding that the king surrender to it the power to appoint ministers and determine religion. It appointed the earl of Warwick as Admiral of the navy and the jowly, fleshy and slow-to-move Robert

Devereux, 3rd earl of Essex, as Captain-General of the army. And it established a Committee of Safety comprising five peers and ten MPs, including Essex; Warwick's brother, the earl of Holland; Viscount Saye and his son Nathaniel Fiennes; Pym, Holles and Hampden; plus Sir Philip Stapleton, Sir William Waller, John Glynn, Sir John Merrick, William Pierrepoint and Henry Marten. To all intents and purposes the king was now surplus to parliament's requirements, an irritating irrelevance, as parliament had seized control of both the military and the civil power. All that was left was for Charles to reassert his marital rights by force; so while the queen sought money and materiel in Holland, Charles summoned his nephews, the Princes Rupert and Maurice, and on 22 August hoisted his royal standard on Castle Hill at Nottingham, calling on loyal Englishmen to rally to him. Some thought it an ill omen that the standard was blown down by the fierce wind of a summer storm and could not be hoist again for two days.

England had been torn apart by war before. But nothing quite matched the four-year conflict that now rent the country asunder. In previous civil wars few people had to make conscious decisions of which side to support – they were vassals of one feudal lord, members of one family or another. But this time everyone had to choose.

Most MPs and peers stuck to their family allegiances. Witness the Vanes, father and son, Sir William Strickland and his younger brother Walter, Henry Darley and his brother Richard, James, Edward and John Ashe, all of whom followed family suit. Ferdinando Fairfax, who was a Scottish peer but sat in the English Commons, and his son Sir Thomas both took the parliamentary side. Spencer Compton, the 2nd earl of Northampton, joined the king, fought at Edgehill and Banbury, and led three of his sons into battle at Hopton Heath, where he was killed in 1643. Just a year later his son and heir, James, led the king's cavalry at the first battle of Newbury and in 1644 relieved his younger brother under siege at Banbury. Likewise Sir John and his son Giles Strangways both fought for the king, and saw a further generation of Giles's three sons, Thomas, John and Wadham, sit for Dorset after the Restoration. So too the St John family, stemming from Oliver, Baron St John of Bletsoe Castle in Bedfordshire, produced a suite of parliamentarians in the shape of Oliver, the earl of Bolingbroke, his son Oliver, his three knighted brothers Alexander, Anthony and Beauchamp (all MPs), and Hampden's lawyer, also Oliver.

But some families were split apart by the war. At the battle of Edgehill the royalists William Feilding, earl of Denbigh, and Henry Carey, earl of Dover, both led cavalry against their own sons. Likewise Sir William Waller shared his parliamentary allegiance with three cousins, Sir Philip Stapleton, the Independent army officer and regicide Sir Hardress Waller and Francis Lennard the 14th Baron Dacre; but another cousin, the poet Edmund Waller, was an equally ardent royalist, and Thomas Waller was excluded from the Commons as unsound in the army's hollowing-out of parliament that came to be known as Pride's Purge. So, too, while William Pierrepoint was an early critic of ship money and a member of parliament's initial Committee of Safety, his royalist elder brother Henry joined the Lords in 1641, became a councillor and was made marquess of Dorchester. Sir Edmund Verney, who swore that he had eaten the king's bread and served him nearly thirty years and would not do 'so base a thing as to forsake him', had the task as knight marshal of raising the king's standard and died at Edgehill, but his son Ralph took the parliamentary Protestation, much to the consternation of his younger brother Edmund. And Henry Grey, the earl of Stamford, had one son who joined him in the parliamentary cause, but another, Anchitell, who fought for Charles.

Most tragically, the war split people's consciences. For some, the decision to take up arms was easy: Holles fought at the siege of Sherborne Castle, at Edgehill and at Brentford; Waller captured Portsmouth and after Edgehill had a string of victories in early 1643 before being made Major-General of the West, in which capacity he defeated his one-time friend Sir Ralph Hopton in March 1644; and Hampden led troops at Edgehill, Turnham Green and Reading before dying on 23 June 1643 from wounds suffered at Chalgrove. But many others found themselves in a very public quandary. William Seymour, for instance, made a complex political journey. Having inherited his grandfather's earldom of Hertford in 1621, he had been a prominent supporter of the Petition of Right in 1628 and one of the twelve peers who demanded a new parliament in the summer of 1640, along with his brother-in-law Essex. When Essex sided with parliament, though, Hertford, newly promoted to marquess by Charles, refused parliament's demand that he return to London and stayed with the king. An even more tortuous route was taken by Denzil Holles's elder brother John, the 2nd earl of Clare: having been a vocal critic of the king, he joined Charles in June 1642 but switched his allegiance to parliament when war was declared, only to rejoin the royal forces for the battle of Newbury when the Commons rejected peace and finally return to the Commons in protest at the king's own intransigence.

Back in the summer of 1642 one choice loomed above all others: war or negotiation? Factions soon began to appear within the Committee of Safety, with Essex, Holles and Stapleton advocating negotiations with the king, Waller rabidly demanding as fierce a prosecution of the war as possible, and Hampden, Pierrepoint and St John adopting a moderating position.

Pym, who had long kept up a very active correspondence with Presbyterian leaders in Scotland, was the first to realize that the parliamentary cause would be lost without a second front from the north, but it was not until September 1643 that he could persuade his English colleagues to do a deal with the Scots – a Solemn League and Covenant whereby the Scots would attack Charles in exchange for a promise of 'the reformation of religion in the kingdoms of England and Ireland, in doctrine, worship, discipline, and government, according to the word of God and the example of the best reformed churches'. This last thoroughly ambiguous phrase sits well in Britain's long tradition of fudged and evasive manifestos. The Scots thought kirk-style Presbyterianism would be ushered in forthwith, but in practice all they got was the appointment of a Presbyterian Commons chaplain and the decision that parliament would sit on 25 December (as they did not recognize such papist innovations as Christ-mass), a promise the Commons fulfilled in 1643 and thereafter until 1656. In exchange, the Scottish army under Alexander Leslie, earl of Leven, and David Leslie (later Lord Newark) crossed the border in January 1644 and made its way to York, where it joined with Lord Fairfax and the earl of Manchester (formerly Lord Mandeville) to defeat the royalist forces under Prince Rupert and William Cavendish, the marquess of Newcastle, at Marston Moor on 2 July. It was to prove the turning point Pym had hoped for, but he was never to see it: struck down by a cancerous abscess, he had died on 8 December 1643.

Battlefield victory was not all that was at stake, though, for the prospect of an authoritarian brand of Presbyterianism held little attraction for many in England who now hoped for a degree of (non-popish) independence of religious thought and worship. The Baptists, Congregationalists and Anabaptists, together with an infinite variety of standalone congregations, were flourishing. Prime among their important supporters was the Independent Oliver Cromwell, who had demonstrated exceptional military ability as Lieutenant-General of Horse at Marston Moor. When Cromwell's commanding officer, the

Presbyterian earl of Manchester, failed to capture Charles at the battle of Newbury on 27 October, Cromwell spotted a sudden opportunity to seize control. It was all too easy to attack Manchester's aristocratic incompetence and unpalatable theology, and in December Cromwell persuaded parliament to adopt a Self-Denying Ordinance that would require all members of both houses (apart from Cromwell himself, his son-in-law Henry Ireton, and the two commanders in Cheshire and north Wales) to resign their commissions within forty days and thereby establish the army on a new, professional basis without either Essex or Manchester. The ordinance was agreed in the Commons on 19 December, and on 6 January 1645 the New Model Army was created under a sole commander, Lord Fairfax's son Sir Thomas, with a stronger cavalry under Cromwell, better pay and a distinctive religious ethos informed by Cromwell's belief that 'if you choose godly honest men to be captains of horse, honest men will follow them'.[28]

What was godliness, though? For Manchester and Essex it required faithfulness to the Presbyterian Covenant with the Scots. But increasingly in the army it meant Independence, allowing the many radical Protestant sects and independent congregations who elected their own preachers to flourish. This was not just Cromwell's faith. Other colonels appointed by Fairfax were equally ardent in their support for a freelance faith. Edward Montagu, later the earl of Sandwich, was a supporter of the independent sects, and John Pickering preached so fervently to his troops that his regiment was known as one of the 'chiefest praying and preaching regiments in the army'.[29] The Presbyterians in parliament, led by Holles and Manchester, were scandalized. They banned lay preaching and nearly had Montagu and Pickering cashiered. They could hardly quibble with the army's results, though, for on 14 June it swept to victory at Naseby, in July Charles's troops were crushed again at Langport and in September Montagu took the news of Bristol's surrender to the Commons in person. Charles could still flee, but he could barely fight, so in May 1646 he put himself in the hands of a Scottish army in Southwell, who handed him over to parliament on 30 January 1647.

This gave Holles and Manchester a triple headache. Should they come to an accommodation with the king and if so, on what terms? What should they do with the army? And how could they effect a lasting Presbyterian religious settlement? Presbyterians had enjoyed a healthy majority in the Commons ever since royalist Anglicans had rallied to Charles. They had gained adherents, too. Sir William Waller joined their ranks when the Self-Denying Ordinance deprived him of his military commission, and Edward Massie and Richard Browne were both elected, or 'recruited', to replace royalist MPs in 1645. With such a Presbyterian parliamentary majority the answer to all three questions should have been simple: negotiate with Charles, enforce kirk-style religion and disband the army.

It was not to be so easy. Charles proved recalcitrant, and the self-appointed army council opposed an enforced Presbyterian code of religion and laughed at parliament's demands that its numbers be slashed, not least because vast arrears were owing to the troops. In June the army council published its own manifesto and demanded that parliament suspend eleven Presbyterian members on the grounds of their religious allegiance and their opposition to the army: Holles, Waller, Stapleton, John Glyn, Sir John Maynard, Sir William Lewis, Sir John Clotworthy, Edward Massie, Walter Long, Edward Harley and Anthony Nichol. Although the Commons objected, the eleven themselves at first took fright and nervously withdrew, but then on 26 July organized a flash mob to burst into parliament in their defence, demanding the disbanding of the army and the return of the monarch. The following day eight peers and fifty-seven MPs joined the army at its camp on Hounslow Heath. Days later, on 6 August, Sir Thomas Fairfax secured London for the army, restored the sixty-five members and, amid calls for a thorough purge of parliament, re-ousted the eleven Presbyterians, of whom Holles, Stapleton, Waller, Massie, Lewis, Clotworthy and Long fled the country. Meanwhile Henry Ireton published another set of army demands, the Heads of Proposals, calling for a written constitution and the abolition of rotten boroughs.

This thrust the Scottish Presbyterians into the open arms of Charles, now in custody on the Isle of Wight, who promised to make Presbyterianism the established religion of England in exchange for Scottish military support. In early 1648 a second civil war commenced with insurgencies against parliament in England and Wales, and on 8 July the Scottish army under the duke of Hamilton crossed the border. Neither the English insurgents nor the Scottish forces were any match for the New Model Army, and this second conflict ended with Cromwell's decisive victory at Preston in August.

By the middle of 1648, while there was still a substantial majority for the Presbyterians in the Commons and the Lords was almost evenly divided, the army – which now had its own Independent allies in parliament – had developed a political mind of its own and was getting restless. In the autumn of 1647 it had held a series of internal debates in Putney about the future constitutional settlement, with Cromwell in the chair. By this point some in both the army and parliament were agitating for an end to monarchy, for universal male suffrage and for biennial parliaments, and Colonel Thomas Rainsborough, the MP for Droitwich, argued that 'the poorest man in England is not at all bound in a strict sense to that Government that he hath not had a voice to put himself under'.[30] The army leaders' predisposition towards religious tolerance and congregational autonomy inclined many towards personal autonomy and republicanism, and their sense of the army's military achievements made them determined to see its will enacted. They had beaten Charles, whose improbable alliance with the Scottish Presbyterians proved that he was a man of blood. And all they that take the sword, so the good book said, shall perish with the sword.

So it was that calls that Charles be tried for treason built in a crescendo towards the end of the year. In November the army agreed a remonstrance arguing that Charles, as 'the capital and grand authour of our troubles',[31] had to be brought to book for the treason, blood and mischief of which he was guilty, yet even when the army intimidatingly occupied London on 2 December there was still, after a 24-hour debate three days later, a 129:83 Commons majority in favour of negotiating with the king. At this the army's patience snapped, and early on the morning of 6 December, having secured Palace Yard and Westminster Hall, Colonel Thomas Pride took up position at the entrance to the Commons with a list of MPs acceptable to the army. Of the 470 elected members, about 180 were excluded and 45 arrested, among them William Prynne, Massie and William Waller (whose cousin Hardress stood with Pride at the Commons door). About a hundred stayed away, including Holles and Glyn who fled the country, again.

With the Presbyterians excluded by Pride's Purge, the path was open for the Independent-dominated Commons. On 2 January they sent an ordinance up to the Lords demanding that Charles be put on trial. The Lords rejected this out of hand, so two days later the Commons decided to dispense with that member of the parliamentary trinity, declaring that 'whatsoever is enacted and declared for law by the Commons in parliament assembled has the force of law . . . although the consent and concurrence of the King and House of Lords be not had thereunto'.[32] Having thus unencumbered themselves, the Commons set up a tribunal of 150 commissioners to try the king, including peers, army officers, MPs and judges, which began meeting in the Great Hall on 20 January. Six days later Charles, who refused to acknowledge the authority of either the court or the purged parliament, was found guilty of 'high treason, and of the murders, rapines, burnings, spoils, desolations, damage, and mischief to this nation' because he had 'traitorously and maliciously levied war against the present Parliament, and people therein represented', and had sought 'to erect and uphold in himself an unlimited and tyrannical power to rule according to his will, and to overthrow the rights and liberties of the people'. The following day, a Saturday, the presiding judge, John Bradshaw, gave Charles a tongue-lashing for forty minutes before ordering that his sentence be read out. Fifty-nine of the commissioners signed the death warrant and, without a further word (as was traditionally allowed for condemned prisoners), the king was led away, to be executed three days later outside the sumptuous Banqueting House in Whitehall. Inside the Hall, the ceiling was adorned with a gloriously preposterous painting by Rubens, *The Apotheosis of James I*, a testament to Charles's father's 1609 declaration to parliament that 'kings are not only God's Lieutenants upon earth and sit upon God's throne, but even by God himself they are called gods'.[33] Outside, Charles I wore two shirts so that he might not shiver in the winter cold, and thereby seem to be trembling with fear, as he took his place on the scaffold. Declaring himself 'the martyr to the people', he told his faithful bishop of London, William Juxon: 'I go from a corruptible to an incorruptible crown; where no disturbance can be, no disturbance in the world,'[34] and his head was severed from his body in one neat blow.

The regicides presumed that Charles's execution would bring stability to the realm, but in practice the next eleven years were to see a constant whirligig of constitutional experiment. It began with a sudden spurt of innovation. In February the purged, ardent Rump Parliament of 210 MPs decided, without so much as a vote, that the Lords was 'useless and dangerous, and ought to be abolished',[35] and elected a 41-strong council of state; and on 19 May it declared England a 'Commonwealth and Free State', incorporating Scotland and Ireland for the first time.

Colonel Pride's attempt to bring uniformity to parliament was likewise confounded during these years of interregnum. For a start, there was a wide miscellany of viewpoints on offer in the purged House, as, in the words of the lawyer Bulstrode Whitelocke, 'everyone almost . . . endeavoured or expected to have his private fancy put in motion'.[36] Some seemed far more interested in their private causes than in the revolution; witness Sir John Danvers, who stopped attending the council of state once he had secured the overturn of his brother's will. Others were out of sympathy with elements of the new regime, yet remained in parliament and cooperated with it. Thus Whitelocke, like his lawyer friend Sir Thomas Widdrington, was opposed to the purge and stayed at home on the day of the execution, yet returned to parliament, was appointed to the council of state and, although opposed to the abolition of the Lords, nonetheless drafted the Bill that effected it.

At the other end of the scale there was a group of hard-liners for whom the regicide was an essential precondition for the establishment of a republic. They were led by the sharp-faced Buckinghamshire attorney and spymaster Thomas Scott, who held that anyone who drew his sword upon the king 'must throw his scabbard into the fire' and reckoned that it was impossible to keep the king alive for, 'so long as he was above ground, in view, there were daily revoltings among the army, and risings in all places'.[37] Having played a significant role in organizing the king's trial, he was to be equally as vocal a republican critic of Cromwell in all three protectorate parliaments. Alongside him was the convinced social radical Henry Marten, whose reputation for heavy drinking and keeping a 'lady of delight', Mary Ward, in addition to his wife, barely dented his effectiveness as a parliamentary performer; as his contemporary John Aubrey noted, he could turn the whole House's mood, being 'of an incomparable wit for repartees; not at all covetous; humble, not at all arrogant, as most of them were; a great cultivator of justice, who did always in the House take the part of the oppressed'.[38] Marten had expressed his republican views as early as 1643, and been removed from the House by the then Presbyterian majority; but, having been returned in the place of his brother-in-law Sir George Stonehouse in 1646, he was elected to the council of state in 1649 as a straightforward opponent of one-man rule, a view he continued to espouse when Cromwell assumed the protectorate.

Also militating against stability was the incontrovertible fact that the Rump's authority diminished with every passing month. No parliament had ever sat this long; it was losing legitimacy even before the advent of the recruiter members, the voluntary exodus of the royalists and the enforced departure of the Presbyterians, and as time passed more and more people were convinced that it had sat too long. Yet as parliament's authority waned, the army's waxed, for when Charles II crossed the border at the head of a new combined Scottish and royalist force in the summer of 1651, the army, led by Cromwell and General John Lambert, comprehensively defeated them at Worcester.

The army's growing power and prominence gave a particular edge to the problem of what should replace the Long Parliament. Many feared, as Whitelocke did in December 1649, that if attendances fell the parliament would be dissolved 'and thereby the whole power . . . [would be] given up into the hands of the army', which is why he wanted to consult 'about settling the kingdom by the parliament, and not to leave all to the sword'.[39] Some members were so convinced that they were doing God's work that they felt they should be allowed to remain in post. This self-serving line of argument infuriated virtually everyone else. Presbyterians disputed that the Rump was doing God's work, the Levellers under John (brother of MP Robert) Lilburne reckoned that God's work was not being advanced fast enough, and royalists contested that God's work could only be done in the name of the rightful king, Charles II.

Cromwell had his own critique. MPs were full of 'pride and ambition and self-seeking', they were 'engrossing all places of honour and profit to themselves and their friends', they were seeking to 'perpetuate themselves',[40] and 'the nation loathed their sitting'.[41] Under pressure, the council of state and army council agreed in January 1653 that a new parliament had to be elected, but when Cromwell discovered on 20 April 1653 that the Commons was proceeding with what one wit called a 'Perpetuation Bill', he stormed down to Westminster with a troop of musketeers. At first he quietly took his seat, but after a quarter of an hour, when the motion was about to be put, he embarked on a speech of his own – calm and measured at first but then suddenly angry. Pacing up and down, he ranted at the members. The parliament must dissolve. 'Some of you are drunkards,' he said, staring full square at Chaloner, before charging Henry Marten and Sir Peter Wentworth with being whore-masters 'living in open contempt of God's commandments'. Having finished these unsubstantiated (though true) attacks on individual members, he resorted to a general assault: 'How can you be a parliament for God's people? Depart, I say and let us have done with you. In the name of God, go!'[42] At Cromwell's command Thomas Harrison, who had already forced the expulsion of Lord Howard of Escrick for bribery and of Gregory Clement for adultery, opened the doors to let in the musketeers. Cromwell's longstanding ally Vane tried to complain, but Cromwell would have none of it. 'O Sir Henry Vane!' he cried, 'Sir Henry Vane! The Lord deliver me from Sir Henry Vane!' Harrison now helped the arch-survivor Speaker Lenthall down from his chair and pushed Algernon Sidney out of the Chamber while Cromwell turned to the mace, the symbol of royal power still present at every Commons sitting, and asked one of his captains, 'What shall we do with this bauble?'[43] Throughout all this Scott and Haselrig, who had supported the purge, but now resented the purge of the purge, were furious, but under duress they trooped out of the Chamber, which was locked behind them. The following day a note was to be found on the Commons door: 'This House to let – unfurnished.'[44] The Long Parliament had been forcibly dissolved and martial law asserted in a scene that could so easily have featured Charles I.

The constitutional carousel continued to spin. A new council of state was appointed that April, consisting of nine army officers and four MPs, and it in turn instituted an assembly of 140 men, chosen by Independent (non-Presbyterian) churches and army officers, all of them 'persons fearing God, and of approved fidelity and honesty'.[45] The assembly (soon named 'Barebone's Parliament' after its millenarian London member, lay preacher and leather-seller Praisegod Barbon) opened for business on 4 July and elected the 74-year-old veteran of the battles against Laud, Francis Rous, as its chairman – not Speaker, there being no longer a king to whom to speak. Hopes were high. Members looked for 'the long-expected birth of freedom and happiness',[46] and they managed to introduce some important legislation: civil marriage was instituted, along with registration of births, deaths and marriages and better care for 'lunatics'. Even saints can be divided, though, especially when it comes to money; and a yawning gap opened up on 10 December, when the millenarian members got a slender majority of 56 to 54 in favour of the abolition of tithes. Rous was not impressed. He had always been a pragmatic Presbyterian, and in supporting the legitimacy of the Commonwealth he had written in 1649 that 'when a person or persons have gotten Supreme Power, and by the same excluded all others from authority, either that authority which is thus taken by power must be obeyed, or else all authority and government must fall to the ground and so confusion (which is worse than titular tyranny) be admitted into a Commonwealth'.[47] Two days after the tithes vote, while the radicals were elsewhere at early morning prayers, he started a debate on a motion to dissolve the assembly and hand power to Cromwell. When the radicals began to join them, Rous left the chair and stomped off to Cromwell with his cohort of moderates and a deed of abdication for the assembly. Whether the motion was formally carried was immaterial, as the twenty-seven radicals left in the Commons could not form a quorum and were thrown out by the army. In another spin of the constitutional carousel three days after that, the army council adopted an Instrument of Government whereby power would be vested in a Lord Protector and a parliament; the latter would be elected every three years, would sit for at least five months and would hold four hundred newly constituted seats that included the growing towns of Manchester, Leeds and Halifax and thirty each from Ireland and Scotland, but excluded moribund boroughs like Old Sarum.

Two such protectorate parliaments were summoned, but Cromwell again resorted to remarkably Stuart-like tactics in dissolving the first on 22 January 1655, before its members could enact a measure that would prevent its adjournment, prorogation or dissolution without its own consent. The second protectorate parliament, summoned for September 1656 to raise money for a new war with Spain, continued the pattern of constant churning reform. Even before it met, the army major-generals decided to exclude as 'ungodly' ninety-three of its duly elected members, including Haselrig and Scott. When the motion to exclude them was carried, another fifty absented themselves out of sympathy with the ninety-three, while the Commons went on to debate (and refuse) additional taxation and to consider a Humble Address and Remonstrance, under which a new 'Other House' would be created and Cromwell would be crowned. This too was carried, by 123 to 62, in March 1657; but, aware that if he were king he would be subject to the very historical precedents that had so irked James and Charles, requiring him to hold parliaments if he wanted finances, Cromwell rejected the crown in favour of confirmation as Lord Protector for life, with the power to nominate his successor. In June he was right royally reinstalled as Protector under a new constitution, the Humble Petition and Advice, which also created the 'Other House' and allowed the Commons to resume its right to determine its own membership. When the re-empowered parliament met on 20 January 1658, its ninety-three excluded members were reinstated – at which point they immediately clamoured for an end to the protectorate and the abolition of the Other House. After just two weeks Cromwell summarily dissolved it, saying: 'Let God be judge between you and me.'[48]

On 3 September 1658, the anniversary of his victories at Dunbar and Worcester, Cromwell died, probably, though not certainly, having nominated his eldest surviving son Richard as his successor. Lacking his father's military reputation and personal magnetism, Richard Cromwell was never to enjoy a secure hold on office. His sole parliament, which he summoned to meet on 27 January 1659, should have passed off without contention, considering his allies' attempts to pack it, but was no happier than his father's sessions. Vane, who had spent the last six years in enforced rustication, managed to get elected despite fierce attempts to have his return nullified, and immediately cooperated with Haselrig, who had angrily denounced the

'Other House', saying that 'the Commons of England will quake to hear that they are returning to Egypt', and openly opposed Richard's appointment. Over the coming months, despite losing every vote, these republicans waged a war of attrition against the protectorate, moving that army members be impeached or removed and trying, in Edmund Ludlow's words, 'to lengthen out their debates, and to hang on the wheels of the chariot, that they might not be able to drive so furiously'.[49] Nor did Richard get much succour from the army, which lobbied for his brother-in-law Charles Fleetwood to lead in his stead. When the Commons voted that the army be barred from meeting while parliament was in session, and that its officers be required to swear that they would never prevent the Commons from sitting, the army, in the shape of Fleetwood and Richard's uncle Major-General John Desborough, demanded that Richard dissolve parliament, which he sought to do on 22 April. Not for the first time, the Commons expressed its fury by slamming the doors shut before the king's – or, in this case, the Protector's – message arrived; and behind the closed doors Vane unburdened himself of a stingingly acerbic attack on Richard. 'One could bear a little with Oliver Cromwell', he said,

> though, contrary to his oath of fidelity to Parliament, contrary to his duty to the public, contrary to the respect he owed to that venerable body from whom he received his authority, he usurped the government. But as for Richard Cromwell, his son, who is he? Where are his titles? We have seen he has a sword by his side, but has he ever drawn it? . . . For my part, I declare, Sir, it shall never be said that I made such a man my master.[50]

The day after the enforced dissolution, Vane and Haselrig tried to get past the military guard and retake their seats, but the army was still on constitutional manoeuvres. First Richard was forced to abdicate; two weeks later, under a deal with Vane and Haselrig, all seventy-eight still living and eligible members of the purged unicameral Rump parliament were re-summoned. Despite Vane's leadership, the forty-two who turned up showed no more unity than before. It was difficult to avoid the sense that the nation was adrift.

Yet again personal differences came to play a signal role in the developing crisis, for the loquacious Haselrig became steadily more suspicious of General Lambert and managed to get him cashiered, along with seven other army officers, in the autumn of 1659. With alacrity the army (for the seventh time in eleven years) took matters into its own hands by expelling the Rump on 13 October and setting up its own new Committee of Safety, with Vane but not Haselrig among its members, to run the nation. Yet again the country was in real danger of civil war as Haselrig pitched parliamentary camp in Portsmouth, the devout Presbyterian General George Monck, who had effectively run Scotland since 1654, declared that he too would support the 'liberty and authority of Parliament', and General Fairfax seized York for parliament. The Committee of Safety's reaction was first to dispatch Lambert to attempt to see off Monck's march south-wards, but once he had left they succumbed and again summoned the Rump to sit on 26 December, when Haselrig was appointed to head the new council of state. Lambert's troops were half-hearted at best and soon faded away as Monck steamed down to London, arriving on 3 February 1660.

With the advantage of military might, Monck insisted on both the re-admittance of the purged members of the bicameral Long Parliament and its dissolution within a month, to be followed by fresh elections. So the Long Parliament finally voted itself out of existence on 16 March 1660 and a Convention Parliament was called. The newly reinstated MPs were largely Presbyterians and swiftly recreated the Presbyterian church settlement, but Cromwell's Independents and the army's series of putsches having thrust them into the arms of the royalists, it was scarcely surprising that the election focused entirely on the matter of whether to restore the monarchy. Even so, when the new parliament gathered on 25 April, a 'Presbyterian knot' of MPs and peers, including Denzil Holles, William Pierrepoint and the new Speaker of the Commons, Sir Harbottle Grimston, tried to insist that tight Presbyterian conditions be imposed on the new Charles II if the monarchy were to be restored. In the revived Lords, the new Speaker, Edward Montagu, now sitting again as Lord Mandeville and hoping to be restored as earl of Manchester, went further, trying to bar those younger peers who might vote for an unconditional restoration from attending. Both stratagems failed: the vast majority of members of both houses made unambiguous and unfettered encomiums to Charles, to which he responded from abroad with the cleverly drafted Declaration of Breda, which arrived in parliament on 1 May. A week later both houses declared that Charles had been legitimate king ever since his father's death, and on 29 May King Charles II triumphantly arrived back in his capital. The carousel had come full circle.

With restoration came retribution. It was enacted most swiftly against the regicides who had signed Charles I's death warrant. Many were long dead. Cromwell, Ireton, Bradshaw and Pride were disinterred, their corpses either hanged, drawn and quartered at Tyburn or thrown into a common grave. Forty-nine of those still alive were sent to the Old Bailey for virtually trial-less sentencing. Thirteen had their sentences commuted to life imprisonment. But Harrison, Scott, John Carew, Gregory Clement, and John Jones Maesygarnedd were all executed in October 1660. A couple more – Simon Mayne and Sir John Bourchier – died before their execution. Others fled the country: Edward Whalley, his son-in-law William Goffe and John Dixwell to America, Will Say, Will Cawley and Edmund Ludlow to Switzerland, Daniel Blagrave and Valentine Walton to Germany, and Thomas Chaloner, Thomas Wogan, John Hewson and Sir Michael Livesey to the Netherlands. Exile was not sufficient security for all, though. John Okey fled the country but was captured by his one-time fellow MP in the protectorate parliament, Sir George Downing, and brought back to face justice, along with another former MP, Miles Corbett, and the military commander John Barkstead. All three were executed in 1662.

Apart from the Presbyterians, just one of the parliamentary protagonists of 1640 survived Charles II's return: Oliver St John, who narrowly avoided an Act of Attainder in May 1660 and got off with merely being debarred from office for life. For a while he resided at the elegant home he had built out of the ruins of the bishop's palace near Peterborough, Thorpe Hall, but in 1662 he left England with his third wife Elizabeth for the Protestant continent, staying in Basel and Augsburg, where he died on New Year's Eve 1673.

What of the Lord Protector of the Commonwealth whose statue now greets visitors to parliament? Although for some Oliver Cromwell was the modern Moses who had liberated his people from arbitrary Stuart rule and protected the Protestant faith, immediate history dealt roughly with him. Some saw him as a man who had merely taken monarchical power for himself. Others distrusted him as an intriguer. After the Restoration, Edward Hyde declared that he would 'be looked upon by posterity as a brave bad man'. The battle over Cromwell's reputation went on down the centuries. In the eighteenth century, the Whigs tried to recruit him to their cause as an incipient supporter of parliamentary rule. In the nineteenth, Thomas Carlyle edited his speeches and letters with evident admiration for a heroic figure. And in 1901, Samuel Rawson Gardiner condescendingly excused much when he wrote in similar vein that 'the man—it is ever so with the noblest—was greater than his work' and openly praised his 'effort to make England great by land and sea'.[51] But when Lord Rosebery wanted to commission that statue in Parliament Square in the 1890s he had to pay for it himself; and when Churchill wanted to name a battleship after him in the First World War, George V forbade it. The king had a point. Cromwell may have been driven by a passionate desire to build a land fit for godly people and by a proper hatred of tyranny, but it is wrong to ignore the brutality of his repression of Ireland, or his remarkably Stuart impatience with the elected Commons, or his failure to establish a republican settlement that could properly outlast his own death. As with so many in this book, his achievements were heroic and flawed.

So what did it all achieve, this maelstrom of constitutional revolution? Some things stuck. The Triennial Act's requirement to hold parliaments, for instance. There was something more nebulous, too: a sense that arbitrary rule and absolute monarchy imposed by martial law with undemocratic financial exactions was a tyranny to be resisted. But this was a message that still had to be whispered quietly and in private, as Harry Vane found when he stepped onto the scaffold on 14 June 1662. Having been sent first to the Tower and then to the Scilly Isles (where habeas corpus did not apply), he had been dragged back to London to face trial for treason. Vane had defended himself in court with elegant serenity and had refused to beg for mercy, so it was little surprise to him that he was to be marched out to Tower Hill. Indeed, he declared: 'I value my life less in a good cause, than the king can do his promise.'[52] What he had not reckoned with was that the Governor of the Tower would forbid him from making any criticism of the king in his address to the crowds. Undeterred, Vane made some oblique comments about the judges in his trial. Immediately the Governor's trumpeters and drummers tried to drown him out. He tried again, talking of the

Solemn League and Covenant and begging that he might be suffered to speak. The cacophony began again and the Governor forced those who were taking notes to hand them in. Finally, Vane gave up, surrendered his papers and prayed. Turning to his executioner, he told him he had a blister on his neck. It would be nice if he could avoid it. And with that he knelt down, placed his head on the block and spread his arms to die. The kingdom was not yet ready for the radical thoughts of Sir Harry Vane.

The frontispiece to a royalist work of 1660 celebrates the Restoration with a composite image of perfect religious and political harmony. Charles II sits in the Lords with his two brothers, the dukes of York and Gloucester, on either side. Below them, the Speaker sits in the Commons and the bishops, also restored but dressed in Protestant preaching gowns, use the prayer book; meanwhile the regicides are tortured and executed, and heretics are banished.

9

Court and Country

ACCORDING TO HIS CONTEMPORARIES, Edward Hyde was a
pompous prig. Jealous and insecure, he inspired envy in many,
and his prickliness and self-conceit were legendary. He prided
himself on his solemn sobriety, an attitude that irked the hedon-
istic king and provoked ribaldry from the royal mistresses, and
he boasted that the queen thought him 'so far from making
promises, or giving fair words, and flattering her, that she did
verily believe that "if he thought her a whore he would tell her of
it"'.[1] Royalists had plenty of reason to doubt him. Having landed
the seat of Wootton Bassett in the Short Parliament courtesy of
the St John family, he had attacked ship money and failed to
defend Strafford, and it was only when the Commons introduced the new Exclusion Bill and war loomed in late 1641 that
Hyde unambiguously stepped into the royalist camp – and even
then he was a constant advocate of a negotiated settlement. Such
conciliatory views availed him little with his former fellow
Middle Temple students, Bulstrode Whitelocke and Harbottle
Grimston, and so, condemned by parliament as one of the
authors of the civil war, he joined Charles I in Oxford, and later
Charles II in exile in Jersey, in the Hague and in Paris, where his

diligence helped him rise in the council, becoming Chancellor of the Exchequer to Charles I in 1643 and Lord Chancellor to Charles II in 1658. By the eve of the Restoration, he had made himself indispensable to the 29-year-old king, and when the Convention's call finally came, he drafted the Declaration of Breda, accompanied Charles on the triumphant trip back to London and, as Lord Chancellor, was given extensive delegated powers while Charles got on with the serious business of enjoying being king. To the common eye, Hyde was the political embodiment of the Restoration.

After the dissolution of the Convention in late 1660, Hyde's first duty was to summon a new parliament. The royalists expected that they would be able to show the revolutionaries a clean set of spurs. Statistically they should have been right. Only 92 Long Parliament MPs were re-elected, as 390 had died, and a clear majority of the new Commons (330 out of 507) had shown some royalist sympathy. Just fifty-six of those returned in 1661 had fought for parliament or continued to attend the Commons after 1642, a mere half dozen were extremely contrite Independents who had sat on in the Rump, and even the Presbyterians, who had held sway so confidently in the Convention, had melted away. In the Lords the figures were even starker. Of the 175 peers, 123 were royalists while just thirty had betrayed a parliamentary allegiance. The Presbyterians who remained in the Lords could be counted on the fingers of one hand, and the Commons could muster only seven. So heavily were the numbers stacked against them that Algernon Percy, the Presbyterian earl of Northumberland, moaned that 'all things' were like to pass through the House 'very unanimously'.[2]

Hyde, though, was clear in his mind that this was not a winner-takes-all Restoration. Charles had not vanquished his foes; they had invited him back. The constitutional slate had not been wiped clean, and the Long Parliament reforms of 1641 to which the king had reluctantly given his assent were legal until repealed. So he cautiously guided Charles to appoint a mixed council that included the two former parliamentary commanders Manchester and Monck (now the duke of Albemarle), as well as the zealous Scottish Covenanter the earl of Lauderdale (in charge of Scotland), the Commonwealth's General at Sea, Edward Montagu (earl of Sandwich), and Anthony Ashley Cooper, who had served on Cromwell's council of state and was now a baron and Chancellor of the Exchequer. The envy of disappointed royalists was palpable. George Digby, the talented but conflicted 2nd earl of Bristol, was vituperative: barred from office as a Catholic, he tried desperately (and with some success) to insinuate protégés such as Sir Henry Bennet into the king's affections. The 27-year-old Henry Cary, Viscount Falkland, complained bitterly when he heard he might not become Lord Lieutenant of Oxfordshire, and died, 'his heart . . . broke with the pure despair of his fortune'.[3]

The upshot was that when the new parliament met on 8 May 1661, although there was a clear royalist and Anglican majority in both houses, there were just enough members with long memories and chips on their shoulders to make a nuisance of themselves, especially in a poorly attended session. Even within royalist ranks there was a diversity of political opinion, and old grudges long harboured from the years of exile produced a grouping that was intent on Hyde's destruction.

The single most important issue confronting the new parliament was the vexed matter of the Church of England, which royalists wanted returned to bishop-led uniformity underpinned by parliamentary statute. This was to prove a far more complex issue than anyone suspected. The king inclined privately towards Catholicism, but many of his subjects had turned to other denominations. Some wanted to enforce uniformity *outside* the Church of England and opposed a policy of 'comprehension' to incorporate into the Anglican hierarchy Covenanting clergy who had been ordained *within* the temporarily bishop-less Church of England. So multi-layered were the religious sensitivities involved that this was bound to be a keenly fought argument.

The king's ministry took two precautionary measures in the run-up to the parliament. First, Charles replenished the episcopal bench. Only nine bishops had managed to survive the revolution: Wren at Ely, Roberts at Bangor, Skinner at Oxford, William Piers at Bath and Wells, Henry King at Chichester; Brian Duppa, a septuagenarian, who had been the new king's tutor as a child and was now promoted from Salisbury to Winchester; 'Wily Warner of Rochester', who, though seventy-nine, was nursing a grievance that he had not been translated to a richer see; the evangelically named Accepted Frewen (his brother was called Thankful), who was made archbishop of York; and the former Lord Treasurer William Juxon, who had managed to sit out the interregnum as bishop of London and was now elevated to Canterbury despite also being in his seventies. That left seventeen vacancies; so, on 28 October 1660, a first batch of royalist, and uniformly Laudian, bishops were consecrated at Westminster Abbey, followed by another batch on 2 December. Most had been deprived of their livings by parliament; Brian Walton of Chester had been attacked for his 'lowly incurvation and bowing towards the altar',[4] but was now triumphantly ushered into his new diocese in September 1661 and saluted 'in the language of soldiers with several volleys of shot'.[5] Second, although Charles sought a religious consensus, one of the new bishops, Gilbert Sheldon of London, pursued a different line, hosting a special conference at his lodgings at the Savoy to determine the new ecclesiastical settlement at which consensus was clearly not on offer: twelve bishops pounded into the Presbyterians represented by eleven divines and a solitary bishop, Edward Reynolds of Norwich.

Within days of its first sitting the new parliament gave the hard-line bishops a fillip, commanding that the Solemn League and Covenant be burned by the public hangman and that all MPs take communion according to the rites of the Church of England in St Margaret's Church. Days later the Savoy conference ended with a hard-line declaration of commitment to Laud's (marginally amended) Book of Common Prayer, and in July the two houses voted to restore the bishops to the Lords. The royalist Anglican dominance of parliament seemed complete.

Yet all was not well, for the debate on a new Uniformity Bill showed up a sharp divide between those who supported a degree of religious toleration and those who demanded inflexible adherence to the one church. Charles himself was inclined towards toleration; his Declaration of Breda had stated: 'We do declare a liberty to tender consciences, and that no man shall be disquieted or called in question for differences of opinion in matter of religion which do not disturb the peace of the kingdom.'[6] These last words, though, were the problem, for high Anglicans, convinced that security lay in uniformity, demanded both a Corporation Bill to ensure that all office-holders took Anglican communion and a new Uniformity Bill to eject nonconformists from the church.

This fierce Anglicanism went much further than that of the king, who made an explicit call for toleration when the Uniformity Bill came up for debate in the Lords on 17 March 1662. Yet despite his intervention and a string of moderating amendments sent down to the Commons, the few who argued for toleration in the Commons lost every vote and the amendments were summarily rejected. After a protracted stand-off the tolerance-free Act was passed, leading to the ejection from the Church of England of more than two thousand clergy whose 'tender consciences' would not allow them to sign up to the new

Book of Common Prayer. The Presbyterian MPs Birch and Love and their tolerant allies could only look on in sadness.

All of this was a major headache for Hyde, who was charged with managing parliament. Hyde was no naïf. He held daily meetings when parliament was sitting with a small crew of cronies who enjoyed a 'mutual confidence in each other'. But as fast as he could bind a group of court loyalists together, others lined up to attack from either the aggressively Anglican or the toleration-minded side of the House – all while Bristol and Bennet, now joined by Sir Richard Temple, were conducting a personal campaign against him for failing to secure the king's declared policy.

Steadily, positions became entrenched. Bishop Sheldon drove a Quaker Act through parliament that required loyal oaths of allegiance to the king. Charles's Declaration of Indulgence of December 1662, announcing that he hoped to suspend the laws against nonconformists and Catholics, was sharply rebuffed the following February by the Commons, who retorted that this was 'a thing altogether without precedent', that it was 'inconsistent with the methods and proceedings of the laws of England', and that 'for ought may be foreseen [it] may end in popery'.[7] Even Sir John Holland, who favoured latitude for Presbyterians, reckoned that if the Bill for Indulgence had been passed, 'then the doors would have been set so wide open, that no man could foresee what might or might not be brought in thereby'.[8] Still not content, the Anglican royalists put further bands of adamantine round uniformity in 1664 with a Conventicle Act outlawing any non-Anglican religious gathering of more than five people who were not in the same family and in 1665 a Five Mile Act which prevented nonconformist preachers from coming within five miles of any major town.

The row over religion infected other aspects of government policy, for in exercising their independence on toleration MPs also discovered their voice on constitutional and financial matters. Thus when between 1662 and 1664 Charles sought the repeal of the Triennial Act to which his father had reluctantly granted assent in 1641, the royalist majority expected little dissent. Indeed, Secretary Sir William Morrice argued that parliaments were 'the physic of the nation, not the food, to be summoned but in times of sickness and want of help in affairs not at any fixed periods'.[9] But Sir Richard Temple, Sir Thomas Meres and John Vaughan all spoke up in opposition, arguing that parliament was essential to liberty, that Edward III had stipulated annual parliaments, and that repeal would take the nation back to autocratic rule.

By now Hyde's position had been considerably weakened and he was accumulating enemies. He had alienated many royalist Anglicans by not delivering the king's desired toleration. He had attracted envy on being made earl of Clarendon. He had caused consternation in the court when his daughter Anne married the king's brother James, the duke of York and heir to the throne. When he refused to deal with the king's mistress Barbara Villiers, the countess of Castlemaine, he infuriated the king, who wrote to him: 'Whosoever I find to be my Lady Castlemaine's enemy in this matter, I do promise, upon my word, to be his enemy as long as I live.'[10] And throughout 1666–7 a new George Villiers, the 2nd duke of Buckingham, waged an obstructionist campaign against him. But it was the second Dutch war that precipitated Clarendon's downfall. He had worked hard to secure parliamentary cash for the war, but a suspicious Commons had insisted on a statutory review of the royal finances, and the negotiations had concluded too late to provision Medway, which lay unprotected when the Dutch sailed in on 10–13 June 1667. Panic ensued in London and Clarendon suddenly proposed a new forced loan, but just four days after parliament was summoned on 25 July to provide emergency cash it was prorogued, a treaty having hurriedly been signed with the Dutch. The immediate danger was over, but anti-Clarendon sentiment ran high. While Buckingham, Sir Henry Bennet (now Baron Arlington) and Sir William Coventry called for his removal, a gibbet was set up by the mob outside his extravagant Clarendon House in Piccadilly. August 1667 proved to be a miserable month for Hyde. On the ninth his wife died, and soon even his old ally Sheldon made clear that he had never much cared for him, writing to the duke of Ormond: 'God knows for these divers years I have had little reason to be fond of him . . . I am sure we owe the confusion we are in to his ill management of our affairs, and of himself.'[11]

So, having lost favour with king and public alike, but hoping for a quiet retirement, on 30 August 1667 Clarendon resigned. He had not expected the demands for his impeachment that came in the Commons in October and were backed by Charles. On 26 October Sir Edward Seymour opened the attack, followed up the next day by Littleton, Temple, Vaughan and Sir Thomas Osborne (who was to suffer similar proceedings later). On 6 November a committee chaired by Littleton produced a list of formal charges, which were debated for presentation to the Lords. Clarendon still had a degree of support – his son Lord Cornbury spoke up for him, along with the Presbyterians Birch and Swinfen and old William Prynne – but the majority of MPs were for impeachment, and on 15 November the Commons sent charges up to the Lords, whose seeming procrastination wound the militant anti-Clarendon group into a frenzy of constitutionalism. 'The people', claimed Edmund Waller, 'are at home nowhere but in the House of Commons, knock when you will.'[12] Clarendon himself broke the log-jam by setting sail for France in November, prompting Temple to comment that 'Lord Clarendon makes the fire betwixt the two Houses and goes away in the smoke'.[13] In the New Year a Bill to banish him was amended to allow him to return and face trial, but by then the earl was happily completing his two great, fluid, opinionated historical works, the *History of the Rebellion* and his *Life*, and was not to be lured out of his ivory tower.

What did for Clarendon? His own prickliness contributed. But more importantly his reliance on parliament to refashion the Church of England by statute and his acceptance that the Restoration had not given the king a *carte blanche* established that parliament was at least an equal partner to the crown in the constitution. He had created a rod for his own back.

If Clarendon was the epitome of the rule of law, the duke of Buckingham was a law unto himself. Brought up in the royal nursery after his father's assassination, he had joined Charles II's council in exile in 1650 and fought and fled with the king at Worcester; but in 1657 he had returned to England and inveigled his way into the affections of Mary Fairfax, who had the dual attraction of being both beautiful and, as the sole daughter of the parliamentary commander Thomas Fairfax, heir to the considerable Buckingham estates that parliament had confiscated to him. So opportunistic a match Britain has rarely seen. Charles refused to reappoint Buckingham to the council in 1660, but the bonds of nursery, the Villiers wit (his play *The Rehearsal* was a much produced and copied hit) and their shared hedonism (Buckingham had a longstanding affair with the countess of Shrewsbury and introduced Charles to Nell Gwynn) ensured him a place in the king's circle of intimates. What made Buckingham more than a rakish irrelevance were three personal traits that gave him an unexpectedly important role in the history of parliament: his hatred of living by other people's rules, his mischievous presumption on the affection of the king and his love of intrigue (he coined the phrase 'the plot thickens') combined to make him a key figure in the development of the first political party.

Buckingham always had enemies, especially Clarendon. He had a fight in the Lords with the marquess of Dorchester and threatened the duke of Ormond's son, the earl of Ossory, with a duel. But in a bizarre twist it was when two of his enemies over-played their hand that he was thrust into the front rank of politics. First Arlington accused him of 'being of a caball with some discontented persons of the late House of Commons, and opposing the desires of the King in all his matters in that House; and endeavouring to become popular'.[14] Then Arlington and Clarendon alleged that he had persuaded an astrologer to predict the king's death, and on 25 February 1667 his arrest was ordered. Forewarned, Buckingham went into hiding until Clarendon's star began to wane and then, on 27 June, handed himself in, thereby presenting himself as the leader of a popular anti-Clarendon opposition. As the storm raged around Clarendon, the allegations against Buckingham subsided and by the end of 1667, despite his inability 'to keep and observe those hours and orders of sleeping and eating as men who pretend to business are obliged to' (Clarendon's words), Buckingham's 'new strata-gem to make himself great in parliament, and to have a faction there' had succeeded,[15] and he was established as one of the king's foremost ministers.

Historical shorthand has referred to the succeeding six years as the era of the C-A-B-A-L ministry, named after Clifford, Arlington, Buckingham, Ashley and Lauderdale, the five members of the powerful Committee for Foreign Affairs, but any show of ministerial unity was no more than a chimera, for there were profound enmities among the five. Arlington and his protégé Clifford had actively sought Buckingham's arrest for treason and opposed Clarendon's impeachment, which Lauderdale, Buckingham and Ashley supported; and even Arlington and Clifford fell out when the latter was made Lord Treasurer. There was also a profound difference of view about religious toleration. For Arlington was rumoured to be a Catholic, Clifford had supported the attempted 1662 Declaration of Indulgence in the Commons, and both were to negotiate and sign the secret version of the Treaty of Dover in June 1670 that guaranteed that Charles would declare his conversion and ensure liberty of worship for English Catholics in exchange for a hefty subvention from the French king – a fact that was kept from the others. By contrast, Lauderdale was a Covenanter, and Ashley and Buckingham were disconcerted by the anti-dissenter provisions of another Conventicle Bill in 1670 – and, once they were aware of the Catholicism of Charles's brother, the duke of York, campaigned for the legitimization of the king's oldest bastard (but Protestant) son, the duke of Monmouth. This religious divergence infected foreign policy, as Charles sought to abandon the Triple Alliance with the Netherlands and Sweden in favour of an Anglo-French assault on the Dutch, and that in turn made the court's anti-Catholic and anti-French opponents determined to seek a dissolution of parliament and new elections. With the CABAL thus fractured, this was a centre that could not hold.

The final split came with the third Dutch war in 1672, which prompted Clifford to urge a stop on the exchequer and the king to issue a new Declaration of Indulgence to ensure the willing cooperation of Protestants against their Dutch co-religionists. By the time the oft-prorogued parliament was convened in February 1673, Ashley had risen from Chancellor of the Exchequer to Lord Chancellor and had been made earl of Shaftesbury, but the Commons was doubly angry with him for the irregular stop on the exchequer and for issuing writs to fill thirty-six Commons vacancies during the prorogation. Yet again there was a stand-off. The Commons declared the by-elections void and offered £1.26 million for the war, but only if the Declaration of Indulgence were withdrawn; when Charles backed down it pressed home its advantage, demanding a Test

Act that would require all civil and military office-holders to take Anglican communion and swear the same oath against transubstantiation that had already been enforced on corporations. This last measure put Clifford, who was described by the diarist John Evelyn as 'a little warping to Rome',[16] in a quandary, which he finally resolved on the last day allowed for by the Act, resigning his offices on 19 June 1673 and subsequently worshipping as a Catholic. Just four months later he was dead, quite possibly having strangled himself. Far more significantly, the duke of York was also caught by the Act: he refused to take Anglican communion that Easter and resigned as Lord High Admiral. That autumn, as if to rub it in, he married by proxy his second wife, the obviously Catholic Mary of Modena.* Anti-papist feelings now ran very high, and when parliament convened on 20 October, a wooden shoe was found in the Speaker's chair with 'the arms of the king of France carved on one side and those of his Britannic Majesty on the other, with a crown and a crucifix', and a note saying 'of one of the two',[17] suggesting that whichever way the shoe fell so too would England. Outside parliament, crowds burned effigies of the pope on Guy Fawkes' Day, 5 November, on the anniversary of Elizabeth I's accession on 17 November, and on the day Mary of Modena arrived in England, 26 November. At Westminster, York was keen that parliament be prorogued as soon as possible, but Shaftesbury, who had supported the Test Act and was worried that York might now produce a Catholic heir, deliberately kept the Lords sitting, thereby giving the Commons plenty of time to draft a petition demanding that the marriage not be consummated. It was a risky, populist defiance of the royal family, and provoked Charles into demanding that Shaftesbury surrender his seals of office.

Buckingham, meanwhile, whose sole official post was that

* His first wife, Anne Hyde, had died in 1671.

of Master of the Horse, had maintained his reputation as a rake. Having fought a duel with his mistress's husband, the earl of Shrewsbury, who died from the wounds received at Buckingham's hands, he took the widowed countess into his home at Wallingford House (to his wife Mary's understandable chagrin), and when their illegitimate child died had it buried in the family vault in Westminster Abbey. When parliament convened in January 1674, the young earl of Shrewsbury demanded that the Lords censure Buckingham for his 'scandalous life' with his mother: he was required to abjure her, and within a week the Commons moved on to demand that Charles dismiss him, which he did. All of which provided the personal and political momentum for one of the most significant political developments of the seventeenth century, as Shaftesbury and Buckingham began meeting regularly with a set of like-minded peers at Lord Holles' house. The group included two of Cromwell's military commanders – Charles Howard, earl of Carlisle, and Thomas Belasyse, 2nd Viscount Fauconberg – as well as the young James Cecil, 3rd earl of Salisbury, and Shaftesbury's nephew George Savile, the newly ennobled Viscount Halifax. On 24 January 1674 they made their first move, demanding that the royal children be educated as Protestants and that nobody in the line of succession be allowed to marry a Catholic without parliamentary assent.

As for Arlington, he blithely took the Test oath despite his true faith and managed to limp on as secretary of state into the new year, when a rowdy House of Commons moved to impeach him for 'popery' and ambition – Buckingham, in an attempt to save himself, having laid all the ills of the ministry at his door. Although Arlington rarely spoke, even in the council, in any more than 'private whispers', and there is no record of his speaking at all in his four years in the Commons, he was a talented linguist and poet, and also a cautious pleaser, always ready 'to make himself acceptable to any man who loved to hear himself commended and admired'.[18] This talent for quiet flattery served him well in January 1674 when he easily saw off the proceedings against him, especially as Charles, worried about the troublesome new alliance of peers, prorogued parliament early on 24 February. Thereafter, following his unvarying motto 'patience and shuffle again',[19] in September Arlington sold the secretaryship for £6,000 and took himself into semi-retirement as Lord Chamberlain, remaining thus comfortably until his death in 1685.

With the passing of the CABAL, the government was in the hands of Buckingham's one-time protégé, the former MP for York Thomas Osborne, who was made Lord Treasurer on Clifford's resignation and earl of Danby in June 1674. Danby's strategy was simple. In the words of Shaftesbury's 15,000-word pamphlet entitled *Letter from a Person of Quality*, it was to construct a party 'of the High Episcopal Man and the Old Cavalier'.[20] The tactic was first advanced when, after several prorogations, parliament reassembled in April 1675, and took the shape of the Test Bill, which Danby and the bishops presented in the Lords and which would require all office-holders, including MPs, to swear that it was unlawful 'on any pretence whatsoever' to take arms against the king or his ministers or to attempt 'any alteration in the government in church or state'. On the face of it, this was not so very different from the policy the Commons had forced on Charles earlier in his reign, and could be used as a defence against any attempt by a future monarch to reintroduce Catholicism. But to Shaftesbury's mind it smacked of arbitrary rule, and he and Buckingham attacked it throughout the seventeen days of debate in the Lords, many of which continued well into the night. One division was secured by just a single vote, but eventually Danby got his Bill through the Lords. It was a different matter in the Commons, where opponents procrastinated so successfully that Charles prorogued parliament on 9 June and the Test Bill lapsed, only to be resuscitated in the October session, when Shaftesbury again returned to the crease, accusing the bishops of believing that the king was king not by law but by divine right. In which case, he argued, 'our Magna Charta is of no force, our laws are but rules among ourselves during the king's pleasure . . . [and] all the properties and liberties of the people are to give way, not only to the interest, but the will and pleasure of the crown'.[21] It was not the only cause of dissension between the two houses: Shaftesbury used an innocuous dispute between the royal physician Dr Thomas Shirley and Sir John Fagg MP to generate an angry altercation between the Lords and Commons over the respective rights of the upper and lower houses in the hope of getting a dissolution and a new, less royalist parliament. Then, on Saturday, 20 November Lord Mohun, backed by the duke of York, the Catholic peers and Shaftesbury's supporters, moved that parliament be dissolved, a motion that was lost by just 50 votes to 48. Two days later, though, Charles, fearing that any newly elected parliament might be even more difficult to control, decided instead on yet another prorogation, this time for fifteen months to 15 February 1677.

Danby was nothing if not determined. He had spent the summer of 1675 compiling lists of loyalists and trying to build a larger alliance in the Commons. Now more and more MPs were given jobs or granted government pensions; but, rather than attempting to recruit respected individuals to his cause, in the words of Bishop Burnet, he 'reckoned that the major number was the surer game; so he neglected the great men who he thought raised the price too high, and reckoned he could gain ten ordinary men cheaper than one of those'.[22] It was a mistake: for, in attempting to build a paid court party, Danby was in danger of forcing the excluded to combine as well, and in focusing on quantity was driving quality to the opposing side.

Moreover, in at least one case he both misread his target and incensed a highly articulate opponent. For one of the MPs he tried to woo was the free-thinking poet Andrew Marvell, the son of a vicar, who had represented his home town of Kingston upon Hull since 1659. Having written both an elegy on Buckingham's younger royalist brother Francis Villiers after his death in battle in 1648 and (conversely) a eulogy of the Lord Protector, after the Restoration Marvell became a sharp critic of court policy, calling the Conventicle Act 'the Quintessence of Arbitrary Malice' and acting as teller in favour of banning MPs from accepting government offices. It is difficult to see why Danby could possibly have thought Marvell would be for hire. Yet he turned up at Marvell's lodgings near the Strand to offer him a post and, when it was declined, surreptitiously left behind a note for £1,000. As soon as Marvell realized, he stormed down into the street and piously told the earl that he already had enough to eat dinner by, so 'I live to serve my constituents; the ministry may seek men for their purpose; I am not one.'[23] Not long after this abject failure on Danby's part, Marvell published his most overtly political pamphlet, An Account of the Growth of Popery and Arbitrary Government, which opens with cool defiance: 'There has now for diverse Years, a design been carried on, to change the Lawful Government of England into an Absolute Tyranny, and to convert the established Protestant Religion into down-right Popery.'[24]

In total, Danby spent well over £252,467 on 'secret service' payments over the years 1676–9 and managed to sign up something like 200 MPs, delivering him a decent vote of supply in 1678; yet his most enduring return was the creation of a stubborn, recalcitrant, bloody-minded opposition, as during the long and resented prorogation between November 1675 and February 1677 Buckingham led calls for a *new* parliament on the grounds that the members who had now been sitting, albeit with considerable interruption, for sixteen years 'look upon them-selves as a standing senate and as a number of men picked out to be legislators for the rest of their whole lives'.[25] When the *old* parliament was finally re-summoned in 1677 Buckingham, Shaftesbury, Salisbury and Lord Wharton declared that it was *ipso facto* dissolved because it so ostentatiously flouted a statute of Edward III – and were dispatched to the Tower for their effrontery. Three of them were released fairly shortly thereafter, but Shaftesbury, refusing to apologize, stayed in jail until 25 February 1678. By then he had compiled a comprehensive list of peers and MPs, each noted as W for 'worthy' or V for 'vile'. This was not yet a fully fledged party system. Far from it. But the idea of combining and organizing so as to win votes was certainly in people's minds.

On 17 October 1678 the prominent London magistrate Sir Edmund Godfrey was found dead in a ditch on Primrose Hill, strangled and run through with his own sword. To use a new-coined word of Milton's, *pandemonium* broke out in political London. The coffee-houses and clubs buzzed with the news, as only weeks earlier Titus Oates and Israel Tonge had presented supposedly incontrovertible evidence to Godfrey of a plot to kill the king, and now he himself was dead. No matter that of all the manifest lies that have littered history, this alliteratively titled Popish Plot was the most nefarious and was propagated by the least pleasant character; London lapped up every fabricated detail. Oates expanded his 'evidence' daily and labelled anyone who refused to believe him an Irish outlaw, a *tórai* or 'Tory', a term that soon caught on. The royal assassination was suppos-edly plotted at a meeting at the White Horse Tavern near the Strand; several hundred Jesuits had been involved and five Catholic peers had assisted, namely William Herbert, the earl of Powis; William Howard, Viscount Stafford; Henry, 3rd Baron Arundell of Wardour; William, 4th Baron Petre; and John, Baron

Belasyse. Or so it was maintained. Parliament took action the moment it was in session. The peers were arrested, the Commons demanded their impeachment on 1 November and on 3 December they were charged with treason.

Paranoia seized hold of the city. The anti-Catholic Green Ribbon Club had met at the King's Head Tavern since 1675. Now it met four times in a week, and another club was set up at the Swan in Fish Street by a group of opposition peers committed 'to address the king for the certain sitting of the Parliament at the time approved'.[26] Although Shaftesbury and Buckingham had been complaining about the prevalence of papists in every nook and cranny of the court since their ejection from office in 1673, there is no evidence that they helped manufacture the Plot; even so, as Shaftesbury himself admitted, 'I will not say who started the Game, but I am sure I had the full hunting of it.'[27] So, ably assisted by three one-time royalists turned scabrous critics of the court, William Harbord, Thomas Bennett and William Sacheverell, Shaftesbury ensured Commons committees were set up to investigate Godfrey's death and to consider means of better protecting the king; on 24 October the Commons proposed a Bill to bar papists from both houses (unlike the previous Test Act, which had applied only to the Commons); and on 4 November another of Shaftesbury's allies and prominent member of the Green Ribbon Club, William Lord Russell, son of the 5th earl of Bedford, argued in the Commons that far too little had been done 'for the safety of religion' and it was time people made clear that 'all our dangers proceeded from the duke of York, who is perverted to Popery, and from him only'.[28] This was the nub of the matter. The heir to the throne was a Catholic, and while most bishops and arch-royalists believed that the hereditary principle was more important than the denominational allegiance of the monarch, the Popish Plot kindled such anti-Catholic passions that doubt about James II was sown in enough minds to dismantle the Danby coalition, whose new Test Bill, with an exemption for the duke of York, scraped through the Commons by just two votes.

Danby's sigh of relief can barely have escaped his lips, though, when a new MP, Ralph Montagu, the former ambassador to Paris who had recently been sacked when he fell out with both Danby and the king's mistress the duchess of Cleveland, produced papers proving that Danby had been in secret correspondence with the French even as he had supposedly been demanding parliamentary supply for a war against France. The charge was doubly dangerous for Danby, as William, Lord Cavendish, son of the 3rd earl of Devonshire, pointed out in the Commons on 19 December 'that the war with France was pretended, for the sake of an Army, and that a great man carried on the interest of an Army and Popery'.[29] Suddenly Danby was at the mercy of the Commons. Again Harbord and Bennett worked in alliance with Shaftesbury, forcing a series of votes, each of which was lost by Danby's court supporters. Although the opposition had only loosely coalesced over the preceding five years, it was now remarkably united. Charles's response was to prorogue parliament yet again on 30 December, thereby letting the proceedings lapse; then, on 24 January 1679, he dissolved the longest parliament in England's history and called new elections.

It was a risk, but Charles still needed money and he reckoned on the provisional support of some of the Presbyterians, still led by the fussy (and now 81-year-old) Holles, who guaranteed their votes, just so long as York was sent into exile and Danby into retirement. But out in the country, politics had changed. At the start of the century, counties and boroughs had almost universally proceeded to elect their MPs by consensus. Occasionally there were local set-tos, but in the main the great and the good settled early upon a candidate and expected him to carry the day unopposed. It was a code of deferential honour, summed up by Sir Henry Poole's 1621 view that 'men should not stand to be knights, but they should be chosen whom the county chooses of itself, not they that desire it'.[30] To covet a seat was vulgar, so boroughs like Chipping Wycombe sought to ensure that 'no canvassing or persuasion of any sort was to be practiced in favour of any candidate for parliament or for the mayoralty before the actual electoral assembly'.[31] But the century had seen an explosion in the number of candidates – and quite often they were so determined to stand that they could not be dissuaded. In 1660, for instance, Robert Eyre was asked to stand aside for Sir John Curzon in Derbyshire, but held that 'I could not be taken off but by the major vote of the county . . . By God's grace I am resolved to try it out . . . I am engaged; I will never shrink.'[32] In like manner Anchitell Grey was so eager to find himself a berth in 1665 that he commented that the MP for Derby, Roger Allestry, 'is yet living, but is on the point of expiring every hour. While it pleases God to continue him I can make no further progress than give the corporation their fill of sack and tobacco.'[33]

The cost of getting elected also rose rapidly, especially after 1660, when personal donations to voters and a general feast for supporters became the norm. Sir Richard Temple forked out for a meal in Buckingham, the agent for Danby's son Lord Dunblane doled out cash at Corfe Castle, Sir William Drake spent £40 a day on 'treatments' in Amersham and Henry Northleigh spent £460 at Okehampton. Bribery did not always work, of course. Sir William Ellis lent Grantham £1,000 and still failed to get elected, while Samuel Pepys similarly wasted £700 at Castle Rising. Nevertheless, spending, especially at by-elections, rose astronomically. One such 1668 contest in Hertfordshire came in at £1,200, and the Winchelsea by-election in early 1678 cost the two opponents Sir John Banks (for the court) and Cresheld Draper (for the 'country' opposition) £4,500 and £11,000 respectively. Ironically, Banks won, only to be thrown out by the Commons on Draper's petition. Public attitudes to all this conspicuous expenditure were mixed. John Evelyn derided the fact that at his brother George's election in Surrey voters 'ate and drank him out near two thousand pounds by a most abominable custom',[34] but Lady Roos was entirely philosophical about John Grey's costs, which ran to £800, reckoning that although it was 'a great sum, yet being we carried it's not so much as the least repined at'.[35]

Treating was necessary, but not always sufficient. The Dover by-election of 1673, for instance, saw a bitter campaign between the governor of the castle, Admiral Sir Edward Spragge, and the dissident victualler of the navy, Thomas Papillon. Spragge poured ale down the voters' necks with abandon and promised the town £500 for a wet dock and a further outright gift of £300. Papillon refused to engage in such blatant bribery, arguing that he could not 'but think such things unlawful that occasion persons to neglect their families and callings to spend their time in tippling houses'. Papillon had seen nothing yet, though, for the newly elected mayor of Dover, Captain Richard Jacob, who supported Spragge, appointed an additional fifty-three men as voting freemen of the borough at an extraordinary meeting of the town corporation held at short notice behind closed doors on the eve of poll. The electoral shenanigans became apparent when Jacob, as was the local custom, started reading out the names of voting freemen one by one, starting with the longest sitting, and recording their votes. This meant that the hastily created new freemen would come last. Before their vote was tallied, though, Papillon had 137 votes to 106 for Spragge. Papillon's supporters cried out 'No faggots, No faggots, Mr Papillon is fairly chosen,' but as the irregularly appointed new freemen (or 'faggots') voted, the tally changed. Forty-seven of them voted 'and every one voted for Sir Edward Spragge'.[36]

The century had also seen the emergence of contests that were about more than just court rivalries. As early as 1640 one candidate, Mr Stephens, promised the voters of Gloucestershire that he would oppose ship money; in Lincoln the rival candidates' manifestos were summed up in a rhyming ditty, 'Choose no Ship Sheriff nor court Atheist / No Fen drainer, Nor Court Papist / But if you'd scour the Pope's armoury / choose Dallison and Dr Farmery';[37] and in 1656 the New Model Army's major-general Hezekiah Haynes worried that the 'honest men' in Suffolk 'will be compelled to take in with the Presbyterians to keep out the malignants'.[38]

But the elections of 1679 took on a far more clearly partisan hue. Danby's own fortunes were at stake, and he pulled every string to get allies elected. It was an uphill task: he struggled even to ensure seats for his sons Lords Latimer and Dunblane. What was more, even once elected several court candidates, Dunblane among them, fell foul of the intensely partisan Commons committee of elections, which could declare an election null and void for what were often entirely arbitrary reasons. In London the court only dared to put up a candidate for one of the four seats, hoping that Sir Joseph Sheldon, brother of the late arch-bishop, would trump Sir Thomas Player, a close associate of Shaftesbury. Player won as easily as his three opposition allies, though, and next door in Westminster the ardent anti-papist and Green Ribbon Club man Sir William Waller came close to unseating Sir Stephen Fox when the number of his supporters, which at first seemed 'a cloud no bigger than a man's hand', grew so fast that 'before night it covered the whole heavens, so great is the merit of priest-catching and so little the credit of a courtier among the mobile'.[39] With all the writs back in, Shaftesbury's new lists showed that he could be certain of a decent Commons majority: 153 were marked as old and worthy and 149 as new and honest, a total of 302 'country' to 158 'court'.

The king then played directly into the opposition's hands by refusing the Commons' almost unanimous choice of Edward Seymour for Speaker, in favour of the crown and mitre royalist Sir Thomas Meres. Seymour had been one of the prime agitators against the court in 1667, but was enticed into the royalist camp in 1670 and had lucratively become Treasurer of the Navy and Speaker. He was a commanding manager of Commons business, and opponents had threatened to hold him in the chair like Speaker Finch when he summarily adjourned parliament on royal orders on four occasions, but Danby blamed him for the collapse of his support in the final months of the old parliament and pushed hard for Meres, who had just arranged a lucrative marriage for Danby's nephew Lord Willoughby, courtesy of Meres' half-brother John Dolben, bishop of Rochester. Charles's refusal of Seymour was unprecedented; the House stood its ground, whereupon the king had to prorogue parliament for two days while a third candidate was found, the wholly ineffectual William Gregory. Charles and Danby may have seen this as an important battle; but the delay and the removal of Seymour needled uncommitted MPs, who became as determined as Shaftesbury to see Danby prosecuted for treason. Montagu and the recently sacked Solicitor-General Sir Francis Winnington led the Commons in demanding his attainder, which the Lords agreed by 39 votes to 36 (with seven bishops supporting Danby and six withdrawing to avoid voting) on 14 April. By now it was becoming clear that the king was not going to get his much-needed supply, so at Easter, with Danby in the Tower, he tried a more conciliatory approach, appointing a wholly new council with Shaftesbury as its Lord President. It was too late for such insincere gestures, though, as the Commons was fixated on the fortunes of the duke of York, and on Sunday 11 May Sir Thomas Player proposed an unambiguous Bill for the exclusion of Catholics from the succession. Some of the veteran oppositionists, such as Littleton and Henry Powle, demurred, but feisty comments from Edward Boscawen, who felt the king's promises to put limits on a Catholic successor 'look like gold, but are leaf-gold when you touch them',[40] helped the exclusionists, and by midnight the Green Ribbon Club was lighting celebratory bonfires as the Bill got its second reading in an unusually well-attended House by 207 votes to 128. Despite his attempts at coalition, then, Charles was still facing legislation to exclude his brother from the throne, the attainder of Danby and the trial of the Catholic peers. So on 27 May he prorogued parliament until August, and in July he dissolved it.

The parliament had largely been a waste of time, but one important piece of legislation sneaked through. Commons had been arguing for a habeas corpus Bill for some time, and on the morning of the prorogation it was debated in the Lords. According to Bishop Burnet, the teller for the Not contents was Lord Norris, who 'being a man subject to vapours, was not at all times attentive to what he was doing',[41] so when the teller for the 'Contents', Lord Grey of Warke, jokingly counted a very fat peer for ten votes and Norris failed to complain, it was agreed that the Bill was carried by 57 votes to 55, even though the *Lords Journal* recorded only 107 peers as attending that day. Allowing for four tellers, the result should really have been 48 to 55 and the Bill should have been lost. The Act remains on the statute book as one of the principal defences against arbitrary arrest.

There were plenty of tricks available to either side in the elections of July 1679. The returning officer could choose whether to insist on (or omit) the obligatory oath (and thereby exclude or include Quakers) during the full 'poll' that could be conducted when the initial 'view' taken by the returning officer was not definitive enough. Or he could refuse to record the poll correctly, as happened in Abingdon when the mayor was regaled all the way home with shouts of 'a cheat, a cheat' after deliberately declaring the wrong winner. The returning officer could also choose the venue for the poll. The Buckinghamshire election, for instance, was suddenly moved from Aylesbury to Buckingham, closer to the support base of the court candidate Sir Andrew Hackett. It did not stop the assembled crowd of country supporters, led by the duke of Buckingham himself, from ploughing across the county through an overnight downpour to elect their man. In Surrey, though, the sheriff was even slipperier, calling the election the instant the country candidates had gone to look for shelter from the pouring rain. Similarly, despite clearly being in a minority, the court candidates in Essex insisted on a poll of every voter, which would take several days, in the hope that the opposition supporters would have to leave to tend to the harvest. Resolve among the latter was strong, though, as they declared 'they would rather trust God with their corn than trust the Devil to choose their Parliament men'.[42] The duke of Albemarle must have been furious, as he had turned up with a claque of 200 willing clergy.

That summer and autumn of 1679 saw several alarums. First Charles was ill and, in fear of a coup by the duke of Monmouth, the duke of York returned to England, only to be sent off into exile again, this time to Scotland. Meanwhile another supposed plot was 'revealed', named the Meal Tub, whereby Catholics were purportedly planning to frame Shaftesbury. The lies were soon exposed, but when Charles procrastinated with prorogation after prorogation, Shaftesbury, who had again been removed from the council in October, first delivered a demand in the name of sixteen peers for parliament to meet and then launched a mass petition, which was signed by some twenty thousand members of the public. The campaign was sustained through the winter months into 1680, so that by the time the new parliament was finally allowed to sit, in October, things were self-evidently even worse for the court than before. Shaftesbury had become the undisputed leader of a more united opposition, and several of those who had opposed exclusion the year before now backed it. The court was in manifest retreat and a new Exclusion Bill sailed through its third reading in the Commons on 11 November. It hit the rocks in the Lords four days later, though, for while Shaftesbury managed to get the new secretary of state, Robert Spencer, the earl of Sunderland, to vote for the Bill, he fell out spectacularly with his relative George Savile, the new earl of Halifax and royal councillor. The Bill was lost by 63 votes to 30 and Shaftesbury's only victory was the long-delayed start of the trials of the Catholic peers. Stafford had the misfortune of being dealt with first; rapidly found guilty after a patently unfair trial, he was executed on 29 December. Three weeks later the king dissolved parliament, thereby ensuring that the trials of the other four were so delayed that although the exhausted Petre died in the Tower, Powis, Arundell and gout-ridden Belasyse were all released when history overtook them in 1685.

Despite receiving a hefty subsidy from the French, Charles still needed parliamentary supply and, thinking that a third roll of the dice might deliver a better outcome, he called yet another set of elections, this time for a parliament to meet in royalist Oxford on 21 March 1681. Shaftesbury and his allies were so incensed by this choice of location that he, together with two members of the council (James Cecil, the 3rd earl of Salisbury, and Arthur Capell, the earl of Essex) and thirteen other peers petitioned the king to return to Westminster. At the same time Shaftesbury attempted to have the duke of York indicted as a recusant by a grand jury at the Old Bailey. These elections were even more acutely focused, with Buckingham and Shaftesbury making guest appearances on behalf of their candidates, and towns and counties drawing up mini-manifestos requiring their MPs to vote for exclusion. Charles declared himself open to anything that might 'remove all reasonable Fears that may arise from the Possibility of a Popish Successor coming to the Crown',[43] and Shaftesbury demanded that Monmouth be declared the heir to the throne. When the new, barely altered Commons presented its third Exclusion Bill on 26 March, Charles decided to dissolve parliament for his fourth and last time and went on the offensive, assembling a largely Tory council and starting legal proceedings against leading exclusionists. Shaftesbury was arrested in July and committed for trial in October. Fortunately for him, the majority of London jurors favoured exclusion and found for him, and he was released on 28 November; but Charles was resolute in his support for the 'abhorrers' of any attempt to overthrow the succession and over the next four years, buoyed up by peace with France, which rendered parliamentary taxes unnecessary, he achieved a remarkable reversal of fortunes. Tories seized the offices of sheriff and mayor of London in 1682, and in 1684 Charles's duumvirate of confidants, Laurence Hyde, the earl of Rochester (Clarendon's second son), and Robert Spencer, the 2nd earl of Sunderland, was complemented by a new pair of younger Tory ministers, Sidney Godolphin (aged thirty-nine) and Charles, the 2nd earl of Middleton (thirty-four). By the time of his early death on 6 February 1685, Charles II could confidently pass into his brother James's care not only his French Catholic mistress, the duchess of Portsmouth, and his English Protestant one, Nell Gwynn, but his crown.

For Shaftesbury and Buckingham, the two most prominent members of the first loosely organized party of opposition, self-styled as the 'country party' but satirized as Scottish Covenanting cattle drivers, 'whiggamors', or 'Whigs', the remaining years of Charles II's reign held only eclipse. Shaftesbury did not see them out: fearing the Tories in charge of the London courts, by the end of November 1682 he had left the country for Amsterdam, where his health rapidly failed him and on 21 January 1683 he died. His passing was noted exuberantly by Charles's ambassador Thomas Chudleigh: 'Lord Shaftesbury is gone to answer in another world for all the villainies and treasons he committed in this.'[44] Buckingham, by contrast, survived a political charge of sodomy in May 1680 but when parliament met that autumn was ill during the opening moments of proceedings and thereafter retired to his extensive but increasingly impoverished estates in Yorkshire. It was here that he died after catching a chill when he fell from his horse out on the moor in 1687. Both men have suffered the disdainful opprobrium of men who led tidier lives. Both had more than a little of the rogue about them. But it is difficult to see how the next stage of British history could have unfolded without them.

At the beginning of April 1685 three curtained galleries, a stage and a pair of thrones were installed in Westminster Hall for the massive banquet to celebrate the coronation of James II and Mary of Modena, which was held on 23 April. At the king and queen's table alone ninety-nine cold dishes and forty-six hot ones were served as the first course and another thirty hot dishes for the second. That morning the choir at the Abbey had premiered Henry Purcell's soaring introit 'I was glad', but in truth, while Charles had achieved a stunning ascendancy in his last four parliament-free years and James ascended the throne to the sound of willing fanfares, it felt as if the lady did protest too much. For even on the day of the coronation there were problems. James could not take Anglican communion, so a special Latin service was held the day beforehand in Whitehall and Archbishop Sancroft heavily curtailed the service in the Abbey. At the Tower, meanwhile, the royal standard was torn in the wind. Among the population there was so little love for the new king that although Francis Sandford spent two years compiling a beautiful illustrated book detailing every aspect of the day's events he was barely able to recoup his costs and died a pauper.

James can have been under no illusions about the problems he would face. The elections for Charles's last three parliaments had repeatedly delivered a House of Commons in which the brothers could count their supporters in the scores not the hundreds, yet James, like every other king at the start of his reign, needed parliament to grant him money; and in addition he wanted parliamentary approval for the latitude he wished to afford to his Catholic and dissenting subjects. So, conscious of the risks, within a month of his coronation he summoned a new parliament. Leaving little to chance, he tried to ensure that supporters were returned in as many places as possible. In many places 'great tricks and practices were used', according to Narcissus Luttrell, 'to keep out those they call whigs or trimmers'.[45] Ministers wrote to boroughs telling them whom they should elect. As had happened under Charles, corporations had their charters changed so as to angle the franchise in the government's favour, as in St Albans, where the two exclusionists who had been elected in 1679 and 1681 were both dispensed with as the electorate was slashed from 600 to 100. The political climate had changed as well: for the revelation of the Rye House Plot against the royal brothers in 1683 had undermined popular support for exclusionists. The MPs Algernon Sidney, William, Lord Russell and Sir Thomas Armstrong had been arrested and executed for their involvement, the earl of Macclesfield and Baron Grey of Warke had narrowly escaped with their lives and a distraught earl of Essex had slit his own throat in the Tower. Thereafter the exclusionists were in retreat, and now, with James patently *in situ*, the composition of the new Commons was dizzyingly reversed. Only 57 of the 513 seats went to Whigs.

To be thus is nothing, but to be safely thus . . . James, like Macbeth, was to find security elusive, for his twin policies split his coalition of support asunder. True, the Commons, which met on 19 May, did loyally vote through the same financial support that Charles II had enjoyed at the Restoration and bumped it up with three additional grants. But just three days in, the former Speaker Seymour quibbled at the results of the elections and pointed out that 'the people of England were strong in their aversion to the Catholic religion and were attached to their laws', which could all too easily be altered 'when there was a parliament dependent on those who had that end in view'.[46] The next day 330 MPs resolved to demand that the king put 'the laws in execution against all Dissenters whatsoever from the Church of England'. The Commons rapidly backed down, but it was not to be the last skirmish, for within weeks there were simultaneous rebellions by the duke of Monmouth in the west and the earl of Argyll in Scotland. Both fizzed brightly, but were easily suppressed by James's professional and rapidly growing army, and their leaders were executed.

Herein lay a new danger. For while parliament was happy to see the rebellions put down, it was far less content to see the size of the army that did so rise from 8,565 soldiers under Charles to 19,778 by the close of 1685. Moreover, James's decision to appoint Catholics as army officers was in manifest breach of the Test Act of 1673. Halifax was so angry that he had to be replaced as Lord President by Sunderland; the duke of Ormond, the earl of Bridgwater, Viscount Fauconberg and Henry Compton, the bishop of London, refused to attend the council; and when parliament resumed on 9 November James was given a drubbing for his patently untrue declaration that nobody had taken exception to his illegal appointment of Catholics. In the Lords, Halifax sarcastically thanked him for revealing what he was up to, and in the Commons Seymour condemned the existence of the standing army. On the sixteenth the Commons declared the Catholic appointments illegal and proceeded to slice

James's demand for £1,200,000 down to £700,000, most MPs feeling, as Thomas Christie put it, that they owed 'a duty to our country, to leave our posterity as free in our liberties and properties as we can' and that the appointment of Catholic officers 'greatly flats my zeal for it [the subsidy]'.[47] The Lords then took up the baton, with the Whig earls of Devonshire and Anglesey, Baron Mordaunt and even the ultra-royalist bishops led by Henry Compton demanding adherence to the Test Act.

James's reaction? He dismissed Compton, prorogued parliament and proceeded down a course that was doomed to fail. It had been bad enough when his supposedly Anglican brother had espoused religious toleration, thereby alienating his core loyalists, the Anglicans, without garnering the support of the Presbyterians and Calvinists who hated any relaxation of the anti-papist laws. But when the openly Catholic James attempted to issue his own Declaration of Indulgence in April 1687 he was creating a triad of enemies: those who hated popery, those who wanted a clear fence around the Church of England and those who believed that only parliament could suspend or amend the laws of the land. James decided to get himself a new House of Commons – but not before he had toured the country extolling the virtues of toleration and Catholicism and had conducted a three-question poll of virtually every courtier, former MP and official in the land, asking whether they would, if elected, vote for the repeal of the penal laws and Test Acts; whether they would vote for candidates pledged to repeal them; and whether they would live peaceably with people of all religious views. The poll was a disaster. Many refused to subscribe to the policy of toleration as demanded by the king – and many more refused to answer at all or absented themselves. So James resorted to a relentless purge of office-holders, removing magistrates, liverymen, lieutenants and even whole corporations, in an attempt to rig the electorate.

The one group he had not yet messed with was the clergy, but in May 1688 he demanded that every bishop have his reissued Declaration read out in every church on two successive Sundays. This amounted to demanding that the bishops disown their church; and so on 13 May William Sancroft of Canterbury and Thomas White of Peterborough met with Compton at Lambeth Palace and resolved to present the king with a defiant Memorial, which was presented to a furious James five days later by Sancroft, White and five others. Piling legal ineptitude on top of political folly, the king then had the seven bishops arrested and tried for seditious libel, doubtless expecting an easy victory. But when the trial opened in Westminster Hall on 29 June, the public turned up in their hundreds, not only to heckle the compliant and corpulent bishop of Gloucester, who was reckoned 'to have the Pope in his belly', but to kick the recent Catholic convert Secretary Sunderland very hard in the backside. After a day of wrangling and mixed advice from the three judges, the jury came to a swift verdict of 'not guilty', the crowds cheered and James's authority was shredded. That same day Edward Russell, naval officer and brother of the 5th earl of Bedford, and the alcoholic former MP Henry Sidney, both of whom had seen close relatives executed by James, persuaded five members of the Lords – Compton, the earls of Devonshire, Danby and Shrewsbury, and Richard, Baron Lumley – to sign a letter to James's son-in-law William of Orange inviting him to invade England.

William, the 38-year-old stadtholder of the Dutch United Provinces, had been watching these events very closely, primarily because he feared that if England were to re-embrace Catholicism it might enter into alliance with the French against the Dutch, but also because as the husband of James's eldest daughter Mary (to whom he had been married by Compton) and the only son of Charles's and James's sister Mary, he had a claim of his own to the English throne – a claim challenged by the birth to Mary of Modena in June 1688 of a son and Catholic heir. So, at the behest of the seven, William published a conciliatory manifesto (drafted by Danby), prepared his fleet and landed at Tor Bay on 5 November. Thereafter things moved remarkably swiftly. Within weeks William's force had steamed up the country from Brixham to Exeter and Wincanton, where there was a brief skirmish, and by the end of the month James's army had disintegrated and even his loyal commander John Churchill had deserted him. There were widespread demands for a free parliament, backed even by James's few remaining supporters, who saw it as the only way of guaranteeing his preservation. James at first refused to consider these demands unless and until William left England; then, when his support collapsed, he tried to escape to France on 10 and 11 December, dumping the Great Seal in the Thames and disbanding his army, only to be captured by some seamen and sent back to London. By now the country was completely leaderless, with riots and attacks on anyone thought to have backed James. In the general mayhem James's brother-in-law, the sacked Lord Treasurer Rochester, who had balefully refused James's constant requests that he convert to Catholicism, summoned the Lords, who decided to form a provisional government in hopeful anticipation of William's calling a free parliament to restore order. William arrived in London on 18 December and gathered the Lords at the Queen's Presence Chamber in St James's on the twenty-first, but could get no agreement on how to summon a parliament while James was still in the kingdom; so two days later a blind eye was conveniently turned while the dislodged king slipped away to France, thereby enabling the Lords on Christmas Day to call on William to rule the country *pro tempore* and summon the remaining MPs who had sat in the Oxford parliament (those from James's 1685 parliament were thought too compromised) to meet the next day. This less than legitimate assembly then summoned a Convention to meet on 22 January.

When the Convention gathered it was clear that the Whigs and Tories were in roughly equal proportions in the Commons. Indeed, in some cases boroughs had intentionally returned one of each. Although there were 183 new members, many were well-known faces, among them Edward Seymour, who again failed to get appointed as Speaker, losing to the moderate Whig Henry Powle. The constitutional debate that then ensued was tangled. On the one side stood those, like Rochester, his brother the 2nd earl of Clarendon, the earl of Nottingham and the majority of the bishops, who believed intrinsically in the hereditary principle and proposed a regency to govern in James's name, since, as Bishop Turner put it, 'the King was in being and so was his authority'. By contrast, a diverse group including Compton and Gilbert Burnet (who was soon to be made bishop of Salisbury) argued that James had not only abdicated by fleeing the country but had un-kinged himself by acting unlawfully; and in the Commons Gilbert Dolben, the son of the old archbishop of York, stated that the king was 'demised' in that he had deserted, forsaken and abandoned his post, Robert Howard insisted that he had abdicated and the lawyer Henry Pollexfen stated that he had forfeited his right to the crown even before he left the country. Others took a yet more radical line. John Wildman, an old associate of Buckingham, and John Hampden, the grandson of the ship-money hero, posited that with the complete collapse of government the whole constitution needed revision, so that a monarch should at least be required to summon regular parliaments.

These radicals also had some support from royalists. When the Commons came to talk about who should assume the throne, Anthony Cary, Viscount Falkland, proposed that England needed to protect itself from arbitrary government and urged his colleagues: 'Before you fill the Throne, I would have you resolve, what Power you will give the King, and what not.'[48] Falkland was an Anglican Tory, but he was backed up by Whigs such as William Garroway and Hugh Boscawen, who maintained that 'Arbitrary Government was not only by the late King that is gone, but by his Ministers, and farthered by extravagant acts of the Long Parliament,'[49] and by Seymour, who demanded of his colleagues: 'Will you establish the Crown, and not secure yourselves?'[50] The point was well made, and the Commons set up a committee under the Whig Sir George Treby to draw up a list of grievances that needed to be addressed if the monarchy should be entrusted to new hands.

The Convention was making much heavier weather of this crisis than the 1399 parliament had of Richard II's 'abdication', but the old half-digested disputes of 1628 and 1641 lay heavy on the stomachs of a generation of men determined to do a better job of constitutional wrangling than their immediate forebears had done in 1660. Nevertheless, the Lords' quibbles with the Commons over whether James had abdicated (or indeed could abdicate) or merely deserted, and whether the throne was therefore vacant or just temporarily unoccupied, brought about delay just when the country needed clarity. So on 3 February William decided to break the log-jam by telling Halifax and Danby that if the matter were not soon resolved he would return to Holland. Three days later the Lords finally agreed with the Commons that James had abdicated and the throne was vacant, on the eighth it was agreed that the crown should be offered to William and Mary, with William exercising sole authority, and on the twelfth (the day Mary finally arrived in England after waiting for the frozen Dutch ports to thaw) the text of a Declaration of Rights, encompassing the Heads of Grievances drawn up by Treby's committee, was agreed as a statement of the historic rights and liberties of the English people. The following day the Convention gathered in the Banqueting House and Halifax had the Declaration read out to William and Mary before offering them the crown. For some it was a new contract, for others a simple restatement of the old law. Either way, ten days later William III and Mary II proclaimed the Convention to be their first parliament and by the end of the year the Declaration of Rights had become a Bill and then an Act, ambiguously proclaiming that the new monarchs had accepted the throne 'according to the resolution and desire of the said Lords and Commons contained in the said declaration'. Henceforth it was established in law that no Catholic could become monarch, nor could a monarch marry a Catholic; that taxes, laws and the maintenance of a standing army could only be imposed or amended with the consent of parliament; that parliament should be regularly summoned and freely elected; and that its members should enjoy freedom of speech.

The Whigs rejoiced. John Hampden, for instance, had been elected in both the 1679 parliaments and again in 1681. He had been tried for treason for his involvement in the Rye House Plot and, although pardoned when he confessed, he had lost his goods, his estate, his wife and his reputation. For him the events of 1689–90 were indeed, as he told a committee of the House of Lords in autumn 1690, a 'Glorious Revolution'. But not everyone was happy. Several of the bishops felt honour bound to stand by their oaths to James, among them Sancroft, who refused to conduct the coronation on 11 April 1689 and let Compton take his place. In all, eight bishops refused to swear allegiance to William and Mary and were dismissed from their posts on 1 February 1690, together with 400 clergy. We get a sad glimpse of how much that schism hurt from the tale of the last of the nonjuror bishops to die, the pious hymn-writer Thomas Ken, who continued to sign himself bishop of Bath and Wells for years. He was eventually reconciled to the new Church of England after

James II's death and was even offered his diocese back on the death of his successor (or 'supplanter' as he called him); but when he died he was buried with little pomp under the east window *outside* the parish church in Frome. The original memorial was a series of brutish iron bars topped with a mitre and crozier, but in the nineteenth century high church clerics built him a small Gothic chapel, open to the elements and still outside the body of the church.

This 'Glorious Revolution' would later be presented as inevitable. Charles James Fox would call Charles II 'a disgrace to the history of our country',[51] and Macaulay would portray James II as a villainous absolutist and William of Orange as a selfless deliverer. The myth that the Bill of Rights changed the law (rather than restated it) and established for once and for all the supremacy of parliament over the monarch acquired a potency that helped entrench it as accepted fact. But the seeds of that idea – that parliament must have its way – were sown by Clarendon's insistence that the Restoration had to be effected by parliamentary statute, watered by Buckingham and Shaftesbury's creation of the 'country' party and constantly nourished by the curious serendipity of uncontrollable events.

*The Scots fought hard to maintain their legal and parliamentary
independence from England, even when the two crowns were joined
in 1603. This satire of 1707 shows an English politician reading
Machiavelli's* The Prince *while riding an ass face to face with a fool in
spectacles. A Scotsman watches on and comments that the Scots had
'made 'em buy the U[nio]n pretty dear'.*

10

Ane Auld Sang

ON THURSDAY, 14 MARCH 1689, while English MPs were debating William's exorbitant invoice for his Dutch invasion of their shores, the bishops, lords and commissioners for the shires and burghs of Scotland gathered as the Scottish Convention of Estates in the Parliament Hall in Edinburgh. At first sight the assembly seemed evenly balanced between Williamites and Jacobites. As in England, James had only recently re-ordered the franchise in Scotland in order to deliver himself more support-ive commissioners and, according to the thirty-year-old Presbyterian Sir James Montgomery of Skelmorlie, the Episcopalians had 'bestirred themselves more vigorously about elections', riding hither and thither in the pursuit of votes and resorting to 'all the indirect ways imaginable'.[1] There were plenty of members who wanted to recall James, not least the bishops, the Catholic duke of Gordon (who was still holed up in Edinburgh Castle refusing to surrender its governorship) and the Episcopalians Colin Lindsay, earl of Balcarres, and John Graham, Viscount Dundee. Difficult members of the 1686 Convention, such as Alex Milne, the provost of Linlithgow, were no longer present. Moreover, James could rely on longstanding

Scottish connections, having successfully managed the 1681 Convention as his brother Charles II's commissioner. Yet since then relations between the crown and the northern kingdom had soured, and in 1686 James's attempt to suspend the Scottish penal laws against Catholics had foundered.

The first sign of how the Convention might swing came with the election of its president, in which William Hamilton was pitted against James's ally John Murray, the marquess of Atholl, who (against his wife's pleading) was just about the last and most reluctant Scottish lord to venture south to welcome William in January 1689. Hamilton had served on James's Scottish Privy Council, but had won himself a name as leader of the opposition to the repressive rule in Scotland of the king's commissioner to the estates, John Maitland, duke of Lauderdale; he had been corresponding with William of Orange for some time and privately hoped for a Presbyterian revolution. The result was close, but Hamilton won by fifteen votes and within days Atholl was plotting an alternative, Jacobite convention to meet in Stirling.

Meanwhile the Convention of Estates proceeded to business – and did so more radically than its English counterpart. First James's sacked Lord Advocate Sir John Dalrymple, whose father had recently returned from self-imposed exile as a Protestant in Holland, proposed a full-blown union with England, which was roundly condemned. Then, on 4 April, with just twelve votes to the contrary (seven of them cast by bishops) the Convention agreed with Dalrymple that the throne was vacant as James had 'forfaulted the right to the crown', and a week later drafted a Claim of Right, which deprived the king of any power to determine religion, demanded free and frequent parliaments, and abolished for ever two of the major parliamentary bugbears of the Presbyterians and Whigs: the Scottish bishops, who had invariably voted with the monarch, and the main instrument of royal manipulation of the estates, the committee known as the Lords of the Articles, which had determined the business of each session. Three men were then sent to London – Dalrymple, Archibald Campbell, the 10th earl of Argyll (another Dutch exile), and Sir James Montgomery – to offer the Scottish crown to William and Mary on the basis of the Claim of Right, which they accepted on 11 May.

As in England, not all were happy. Fifteen ordinary members, six bishops and nine earls permanently absented themselves from the Convention at the end of March, and Viscount Dundee led a Jacobite rebellion that scored a victory at Killiecrankie on 27 July 1689 (where Dundee himself was killed). But within a year the rebellion was crushed, and the second session of the estates restored the presbytery as the kirk's method of governance and the aggressively anti-Catholic Westminster Confession as its creed – or at least its doctrinal *cri de coeur*.

The body that gathered in Edinburgh in 1689 was a very different entity from its English counterpart. The Convention of Estates, like the parliament at Westminster, had developed out of the royal councils, but it had remained unicameral, with bishops and nobles consorting with representatives of the burghs and shires. Its meetings were less frequent – and shorter. It never acquired a Speaker.

Yet there were similarities. Just as a Frenchman, Simon de Montfort, helped forge the early English parliament, so in Scotland it was a young Norwegian girl who unwittingly provided the impetus for its Scottish counterpart. For although Alexander II of Scotland held what he referred to as a *colloquium* with his barons at Kirkliston in 1235, there is little hard evidence of further such meetings for another fifty years. But when his son Alexander III's son and heir died on 28 January 1284, the king called thirteen earls, twenty-four barons and three other magnates to a 'parliament' in Scone to decide formally who should be his heir; and they settled on Alexander's baby grand-daughter Margaret, daughter of the king of Norway. When two years later Alexander himself died, on 19 March 1286 after a fall from his horse, another meeting of magnates and clerics was held within a fortnight at Scone, at which the crown was settled on Margaret, even though she was just three years old and had never visited Scotland; and six Guardians (two bishops, two earls and two barons) were elected to manage the kingdom until she came of age. Parliamentary, or at least corporate, decision-making had poked its head over the Scottish battlements.

England's Edward I, meanwhile, was watching Scotland's hereditary travails intently. In an attempt to resolve the conflict between two other rival claimants for the throne, John of Balliol and Robert Bruce (5th Lord of Annandale and grandfather of Robert the Bruce), the Guardians summoned a parliament of bishops, earls, abbots, priors and barons to the tiny town of Birgham, where, in two open-air sessions in March and July 1289, they negotiated at considerable length with Edward's ambassadors the twin treaties of Salisbury and Birgham, whereby Margaret would marry Edward's son Edward of Caernarvon and thereby unite the two crowns, but the Scots would retain their kingdom as 'separate and divided from England according to its rightful boundaries, free in itself and without subjection', and the Scottish parliament would remain separate. It was an ambitious master-plan, which might have advanced the creation of Great Britain by four hundred years, but it came to nothing when Margaret died soon after landing in the Orkney Islands en route for Scone in September 1290, and the Guardians formally assumed the government of Scotland.

Margaret's death left a vacuum at the heart of an already turbulent state and William Fraser, bishop of St Andrews, who was one of the Guardians, wrote to Edward to ask him to arbitrate between the remaining candidates. Edward seized the advantage, first summoning the Scottish lords to Norham in England rather than Berwick in Scotland, and then demanding that they accept him as 'Lord Paramount of Scotland'. Robert Wishart, bishop of Glasgow and the other episcopal Guardian, was incandescent, not least because the Scottish church had been arguing for its own independence from the archbishop of York since 1174; but after long wrangling a formula was agreed and the Scots reluctantly swore fealty to Edward as 'the chief lord and guardian of the kingdom [of Scotland], until a king was provided',[2] whereupon Edward presided over a series of meetings of 'auditors' who were to decide on the succession. On 17 November 1292 they awarded the throne to the remarkably English John of Balliol. Edward had not yet finished meddling with Scotland, though: in 1294 he dragged John down to London and demanded that he provide Scottish troops for war with France. Back in Scotland, John called a parliament at Stirling, which decreed that the king 'could do no act by himself' and appointed a special council of four earls, four barons and four bishops, who resolved instead to sign a treaty with France, the 'Auld Alliance', guaranteeing mutual support for an assault on England. This incensed Edward, who stormed north, sacked Berwick, routed the Scots at Dunbar, forced John to abdicate on 10 July 1296, ceremonially tore the royal insignia from his tabard, carted him (and the Stone of Destiny from Scone) off to London, and forced all the Scottish nobles and freeholders to pay homage to him at a new parliament at Berwick.

Scotland was now in effect a vassal state to England, governed by the lazy and uninterested John de Warenne, 6th earl of Surrey, who received the seal of Scotland from Edward with the words: 'A man does good business when he rids himself of a turd.'[3] The vanquished Scots did not give up, though. First Bishop Wishart, backed by the earl of Carrick Robert Bruce, the new bishop of St Andrews William Lamberton and James the Steward,* led a short-lived rebellion in the summer of 1297, which saw Wishart imprisoned and Bruce forced to capitulate. Still the battle for independence went on, with the accomplished military leader Sir William Wallace defeating the English at the battle of Stirling Bridge and appointing himself Guardian, only to surrender the post a year later after his comprehensive defeat at Falkirk. Having narrowly escaped capture, Wallace sustained a spirited guerrilla resistance through to 1305, when he was finally taken and brought to Westminster Hall for his brutal execution as a traitor on 23 August.

Edward now resolved at an English parliament with Scottish representatives that the aged Surrey should be supported as Governor by a council including Bishops Wishart and Lamberton and the two new principal claimants to the Scottish throne, Robert the Bruce and John Balliol's nephew, John Comyn (the younger). The fact that both Bruce and Comyn at times flattered Edward may have blinded him to their commitment to Scottish independence and their intense mutual rivalry; in any event, Edward's Scottish council never came into being, as on 10 February 1306 Bruce and Comyn started a heated quarrel in Greyfriars Kirk in Dumfries, which ended in Bruce assaulting Comyn, fleeing the scene and sending his henchmen round to finish him and his uncle off later. Within seven weeks Bruce had gained absolution from Bishop Wishart and had himself installed as King Robert I at Scone by Lamberton, before launching another campaign against the English. Initially defeated and sent into hiding, Bruce returned to the fray once England was in

---

* The Steward or High Steward of Scotland was a hereditary title created in the twelfth century which often went hand in hand with guardianship of an under-age monarch. The family became known as the Stewarts or Stuarts. When in 1371 Robert Steward inherited the crown as Robert II, the title of High Steward became a subsidiary title of the Scottish heir apparent. It still is.

the far more tender hands of Edward II, and secured some stunning Scottish victories, not least at Bannockburn in 1314.

By the time Robert I seized the throne, then, there was a clear expectation that major issues that touched everyone, including the resolution of dynastic quandaries, should be addressed by representatives of the whole community gathered in parliament. Thus the summons to the 1293 parliament included the provision that 'everyone with a complaint [should] show the injuries and trespass done them by whatsoever ill-doers . . . and receive for them what justice demands'; and the fortnight-long Candlemas parliament of 1294 even included discussion of who should be the new bishop of Whithorn. Robert I was no sentimentalist, though, and had little intention of honouring a system of collective decision-making that he believed had paralysed Scotland. For him, Scottish royal authority was paramount. Yet even the great Scottish warrior king paid obeisance to the parliamentary model, not least because he found congregations of lords, especially when accompanied by bishops in a parliament, a good means of undergirding his own precarious authority. So he held at least twelve parliaments and seven other assemblies in his nineteen years on the throne, many of them producing ragman rolls, similar to statutes, with the seals of nobles and bishops attached. This was parliament as a public relations exercise, shoring up not just royal authority per se, but Bruce's own claim to it. Thus, in 1315 he summoned a meeting in Ayr parish church to resolve the perennial issue of the uncertain succession, which was settled on his brother Edward Bruce, and, most famously, in 1320 he sought to have his papal excommunication (for murdering Comyn in church) lifted and the independence of Scotland proclaimed by virtue of the ringing tones of the Declaration of Arbroath, drafted by the local abbot and signed and sealed at a mass assembly of lords: 'For, as long as but a hundred of us remain alive, never will we on any conditions be brought under English rule.'[4] Little matter that it was not a formal parliament; the lords' seals proved Robert had support.

For all Robert the Bruce's courageous belligerence, his legacy was not to be so very different from that of Alexander III, for when he died in 1329 his heir was another child, the five-year-old David, whose reign – again, by chance rather than design – reinforced the role of the Scottish parliament. For although the young king was married in 1328, aged just four, to Joan, the daughter of England's Edward III, his kingdom was subject to constant English incursions in the name of Edward Balliol (son of the deposed King John) and in 1334 he was forced to seek refuge in France, leaving Scotland in the hands of two Guardians, John Randolph, earl of Moray, and his nephew, Robert the Steward, who was eight years older than the king. After Moray's death in 1338 the Steward ruled alone until David's return in 1341, so when five years later the English again routed the Scots at Neville's Cross and David was taken south into captivity, the Steward readily slipped back into power. Yet again the childless king had no clear heir other than the Steward, who might be expected to predecease him; so David made several attempts at securing his freedom in exchange for a commitment that the Scottish crown would pass on his demise to an English king. Successive Scottish parliaments robustly rejected these proposals, and it was only in 1357 that David was allowed to resume his reign in Scotland under the terms of the Treaty of Berwick, which stipulated payment of a ransom of 10,000 marks a year for ten years, equivalent to about £67,000 sterling, and settled the succession on the English king Edward III, a measure that even then had little public support in Scotland. Yet again parliament had proved itself decisive.

Up to this point there was little that was fixed about a Scottish 'parliament'. It moved from place to place – and would continue to do so until 1639, when the Parliament Hall in Edinburgh was completed. It met largely on an ad hoc basis, when the king or the Guardians wanted something debated or ratified, especially the ending of a minority or the signing of a treaty. Its composition varied, too. Thus the parliamentary ratification of the Auld Alliance at Dunfermline in February 1296 was witnessed by the usual combination of bishops, barons and earls, as well as the 'communities of the towns of Scotland' as attested to by the seals of six burghs. Likewise, in 1326 Robert was in such financial difficulty that in addition to the bishops and barons who agreed that the succession should go to the infant David, he invited burgh representatives to Cambuskenneth as he wanted to be granted an annual tenth for his lifetime; and two years later a similar financial embarrassment (the need to pay England for the peace treaty of 1328) meant that burgh representatives were summoned again, this time to Edinburgh. This hardly represented a mass enfranchisement of the common people; the royal burghs were summoned solely because they had a fiercely guarded monopoly on foreign trade and they alone could be taxed. But the expectation that the burghs should be represented was steadily gaining currency, and in 1357 the term 'the three communities' was used for the first time in relation to parliament. In 1373 it was rendered as 'the three estates', namely the clergy, the lords and the burgh representatives, known as 'commissioners'.

David II died in 1371 after years of mutual distrust between him and his successor, the 55-year-old Steward, Robert II, who had the good fortune to sire a rugby squad of at least nineteen offspring – sons and daughters, legitimate and illegitimate. Despite Robert's virility, however, his designated heir John Stewart, earl of Carrick (who reigned not as John II but as Robert III), was a physical and intellectual weakling, and in 1388 parliament determined that he was not fit to govern. At first Robert

III's younger and more ruthless brother Robert Stewart, the earl of Fife, ruled as Guardian with parliamentary support, and in 1399 the council deprived the king of all power, handing it to his son, David, the duke of Rothesay, as Lieutenant, ruling with a council of twenty-one under Fife (made duke of Albany) as Governor. Three years later Rothesay was dead in suspicious circumstances, and in 1406 Robert III himself died, not long after hearing that his second son and new heir James, aged twelve, had been captured by the English. Albany now ruled Scotland and was in little hurry to secure his nephew's release. Indeed, his sole concern was the return from captivity of his own heir, Murdoch Stewart, who followed in his father's footsteps as Governor on his death in 1420. When James I eventually gained his freedom he had himself crowned at Scone in May 1424 and the following year had Murdoch and his two sons Walter and Alasdair tried at a one-week parliament in Stirling and beheaded. James did not need the estates only for the exaction of revenge, though; the parliament that met in the month of his coronation gave him a hefty grant to pay an English ransom, and in each of the next three years the king returned to parliament for more.

James was never secure as king, and in October 1436 he was directly contradicted in a bid for more financial support by the spokesman of the estates, Sir Robert Graham, who was servant to Walter Stewart, James's uncle and earl of Atholl. Graham's challenge to James did not succeed, and the king got his money; but early the following year James was staying at one of the by now regular venues for the Scottish parliament, the Blackfriars church in Perth, when on the night of 20–21 February Graham led a group of armed men into the king's chambers, dragged him from his hiding place in a drain and killed him. This coup, led by Atholl, left Scotland in the hands of yet another minority under the six-year-old James II. This time the infant king's mother Joan took charge.

Although parliaments were still often one-day ad hoc affairs, they were debating all manner of things. The selling of salmon to foreigners was banned; the see of Glasgow was made an archbishopric; nobody was allowed to wear 'clothes of silk, nor furs of pine-martens, beech-martens, purray* nor great or richer furs, except only knights and lords';[5] Lollards were to be prosecuted; beggars were to be branded on the cheek; lords were to care for their castles, fortalices and manors, live in them and spend their monies locally; and legal cases were heard by the Lords Auditors of Causes and Complaints. As of 1455 the king was under oath 'neither to add to nor diminish the law, custom and statutes of the realm without the consent of the three estates, and nothing to work nor use touching the common profit of the realm without consent of the three estates'.[6] Yet even more than in England the three estates remained an instrument of royal authority. James II summoned them in 1445 to dispatch his baronial opponents using the Scottish equivalent of an Act of Attainder; in 1488 James III tried to shore up his unstable authority at another parliament in January, failing so miserably that he was killed by his barons at the battle of Sauchieburn in June; and his son James IV held one in October to reinforce his claim. Only one thing placed power unambiguously in the hands of parliament, and that was a prolonged minority – to which Scotland was submitted yet again when James IV went into battle against England out of loyalty to the Auld Alliance, despite being married to Henry VII of England's daughter Margaret Tudor, and was slaughtered ignominiously on Flodden Field in 1513. Yet again Scotland had an infant king, the seventeen-month-old James V, and during the long minority general councils and parliaments intervened at several key moments, initially granting governorship to James's English mother under the watchful

* A pure or bleached form of white miniver.

eye of a council of Scottish magnates; then removing her from the regency when she married Archibald Douglas, the earl of Angus; demanding that the French baron John Stewart, duke of Albany, come to Scotland as Governor in July 1515; backing Margaret when she took advantage of Albany's absence in France to 'erect' James V in his own right in 1524; and supporting her exiled husband Angus against her in 1525. When James finally began to rule in his own right in 1528 his stepfather was exiled into England, but yet again, as under his father, parliament played no great part in his rule.

The defining period of the Scottish parliament came about thanks to a six-day-old girl, for both of James V's sons died in infancy, so that when James himself died on 14 December 1542, the sole heir was another child, the infant Mary, daughter of James's French second wife, Mary of Guise. A brief dispute over the regency between the cardinal archbishop of St Andrews, David Beaton, and the next in line in the succession to young Mary, James Hamilton, earl of Arran, was resolved in January in favour of Arran, but the following years saw Arran and Mary of Guise constantly pitted against each other. It was a fractious time. Henry VIII, having unsuccessfully harried James V to abandon Catholicism, now saw an opportunity to seize the Scottish crown by marrying his son Edward to young Mary and taking her into English care. At first Arran agreed, but in December 1543 Beaton and Guise persuaded parliament that the Auld Alliance with the French was a safer haven, prompting Henry to engage in a seven-year campaign of 'rough wooing', which saw constant incursions into Scotland. The war ended in 1550, but by then Beaton and Guise had persuaded parliament to sign the treaty of Haddington, whereby young Mary would marry the French dauphin. Having completely overturned Arran's policy and secured for him the French dukedom of Châtelherault, all that was left was to oust him as regent, which Mary of Guise finally accomplished on 12 April 1554, when parliament made her queen regent.

Her achievement of this position of dominance was remarkable. A foreigner and a woman, she had another flaw: she was Catholic. For more than three decades now, Scotland had been feeling the chill winds of bitter religious disputes. Parliament had banned Lutheran teaching in 1525; three years later the 24-year-old lay abbot of Fearn Abbey, Patrick Hamilton, had been martyred for the Lutheran faith in St Andrews; and in 1541 parliament had categorically upheld the Catholic faith. But Protestantism was undoubtedly on the rise. When Cardinal Beaton brought about the execution of the Protestant preacher George Wishart in 1546, retribution came swiftly in the form of a band of Fife lairds who murdered the cardinal in his own castle on 29 May. Likewise, the very thought of Mary, Queen of Scots marrying a Catholic sparked a Protestant revolt. On 3 December 1557 a group of Protestant nobles not only made their objections to the French match clear but pledged themselves to work and, if necessary, fight to make Scotland Protestant. The regent hastily secured the marriage, which took place on 24 April 1558, but that autumn there were anti-Catholic riots in Edinburgh on St Giles's Day, and by mid-1559 it was clear that armed confrontation was inevitable. Now styling themselves 'the Lords of the Congregation', the group gained important adherents, including both Châtelherault and his son, the 3rd earl of Arran. On 27 February 1560 Elizabeth of England signed another Treaty of Berwick with the Congregation, who demanded an end to the Guise regency and the removal of French troops from Scotland, and in May called for a parliament at which all these matters might be settled. Yet again the religious dispute had become constitutional.

Then, on 11 June 1560, after several months of illness, Mary of Guise died. Suddenly the Catholic party collapsed; from Paris,

François and Mary agreed to the Lords of the Congregation's terms, and parliament was summoned for 10 July (although the session was actually delayed until 1 August). By now the Catholic bishops were distraught, not least the archbishop of St Andrews, John Hamilton, who was Châtelherault's half-brother. But the Lords of the Congregation were in effective control. When Thursday, 1 August came there was another delay as too few nobles had appeared, but finally, on Friday, 9 August, the three estates gathered: 8 bishops, 21 abbots or lay commendators,* 32 nobles and 22 burgh commissioners, plus, controversially, 99 largely Protestant lesser, untitled barons and lairds claiming a dubious 1428 right to attend. The initial votes all went the Congregation's way. Indeed, the election of the Lords of the Articles delivered such a landslide that the only clerics elected for the ten 'clerical' seats were the bishop-elect of Galloway, Alexander Gordon, who was brother of the Protestant leader George Gordon, the 4th earl of Huntly, and the bishop of Argyll, James Hamilton, who was another (illegitimate) half-brother to Châtelherault. All the other 'clergy' were Protestant lay commendators.

Prior to the session, the Congregation had commissioned the reformist clergyman and friend of Calvin, John Knox, and four others to draft a new Confession of Faith, which was presented to the Lords of the Articles on 15 August. Within just forty-eight hours the three estates gathered in plenary to hear the Confession clause by clause, with its denunciations of Rome as the 'kirk malignant', the 'horrible harlot' and Satan's 'pestilent synagogue'. So strong was the consensus that the estates dispatched business with celerity. The Treaty of Berwick was ratified, a proposal that Elizabeth be asked to marry Châtelherault

---

* Unlike in England, as Scottish monastic lands came into lay hands the religious abbots and priors' seats were taken by lay 'commmendators'.

was agreed, baronial representation (a fourth estate) was regularized and the Confession of Faith was assented to. Even the Catholic bishops held their silence. Lord Lindsay emotionally proclaimed that as the oldest baron present he was so pleased to be able to do so 'worthy a work' that he felt he could now say with Simeon: 'Lord, now lettest thou thy servant depart in peace.' The parliament was not yet done, though. On 24 August the jurisdiction of the pope in Scotland was annulled, all previous anti-Protestant acts were repealed, the mass was abolished and the governance of the kirk was put in the hands of a new General Assembly of the Church of Scotland, which met later that year and approved a new Book of Discipline. Queen Mary did not grant her assent to any of this, but in short order the estates, acting entirely independently of the crown, effected a far more radical religious revolution than in England.

The Scottish Reformation undoubtedly reflected public opinion across the main swathe of lowland Scotland, and unlike in England where it had been a royal project, here it was a parliamentary one; but it would be difficult to argue that the events of 1560 proved Scotland's democratic credentials. Yes, there were elections as early as 1437, when Linlithgow elected its commissioner 'by the whole common council', and the carpetbagger was to be a much rarer attendee in Scotland than in England. But as often as not the burgh commissioners were still 'nominated' on the recommendation of the local magnate or prelate, and would continue to be so for much of the seventeenth century. Fullblown Scottish democracy was still barely a twinkle in the firmament.

Thus far, such occasional bouts of Scottish parliamentary assertiveness as had occurred had been occasioned almost entirely by moments of dynastic uncertainty. Now the catalyst was Mary's marital problems. For on 5 December 1560 François died; within nine months Mary had returned to Scotland, where in 1565 she married her first cousin, Henry Stuart, Lord Darnley, who was Catholic and English, and, like Mary, had a claim to the English throne. Darnley soon turned against his wife, murdering her private secretary David Rizzio in front of her, only to be assassinated himself by the Protestant earl of Bothwell, who became Mary's third husband in 1567. By now Mary enjoyed little support from her nobles, twenty-six of whom combined to force Bothwell into exile and Mary to sign a 'voluntary demission' in favour of her one-year-old son, James VI. So, although christened a Catholic, the cradle king was crowned a Protestant, to the accompaniment of a sermon by John Knox, on 29 July 1567 in the parish church in Stirling, and the estates gathered to approve Mary's begrudging nomination of her illegitimate half-brother, James Stewart, the earl of Moray, as James's regent. He was proclaimed at a meeting of nobles, barons and commissioners in Edinburgh on 22 August and, as one of the devoutly Protestant Lords of the Congregation, he happily signed assent to the 1560 Reformation Acts.

If Mary was unlucky with her husbands, James was unfortunate in his regents. Moray was assassinated in January 1570; his successor Matthew Stewart, the 4th earl of Lennox, was killed a year later; the third regent, John Erskine, the earl of Mar, died of a sudden illness in October 1572; and the fourth, James Douglas, the 4th earl of Morton, was first removed as regent by the Convention of Estates in 1578, then reinstated, then supplanted in James's affections by the first of many male favourites, Esmé Stewart, then executed in 1581 for murdering Darnley. But the real problem for James was that, with his mother in captivity in England ever since the throne had passed to him, his minority was dominated by a civil war which saw successive parliaments swing this way and that. The May 1571 session, for instance, held in the Canongate, saw the estates meet under such fear of attack from the castle that it was known as the Creeping Parliament. Even the abduction of James by a gang of peers led by William Ruthven, the Protestant earl of Gowrie, in August 1582, which saw Gowrie seize control of government from the Catholic-seeming duke of Lennox and enforce a far more thoroughgoing Protestantism via a convention, was then condemned at another convention the following year, only for the Ruthven raiders (other than Gowrie himself, who was executed in 1584) to be reinstated at a meeting of parliament in 1585.

As in every other period of Scottish history, the lack of a resolute adult king allowed these internecine factional struggles to flourish, but James had a larger matter to contend with: the continuing battle over religion. Since 1560 it was the General Assembly, with its three tiers of nobles, clerics and burgesses, that managed the kirk, but the bishops had been allowed to retain their seats in parliament. Some, notably the archbishop of Glasgow, James Beaton (the Cardinal's nephew), and the bishops of Ross (John Lesley) and Dunblane (William Chisholm), fled the country as Catholics; others transferred their allegiance to the kirk and remained on sufferance and two-thirds pay until such time as they shuffled off their mortal coil. This fudge lasted until 1572, when a mixed assembly of the kirk and the regency agreed a concordat at Leith, which stipulated that bishops and archbishops could remain in parliament but would be subject to the General Assembly. The uneasy balance was rocked when Morton as regent appointed as archbishop of St Andrews his chaplain, the ambitious minister of Paisley, Patrick Adamson, who, despite having sworn that he would not accept any appointment without the advice of the General Assembly, now refused to submit himself to the kirk. By now a rising tide of open Presbyterianism, most effectively articulated by Andrew Melville, the Moderator in 1578 and from 1590 rector of St Andrew's University, was sweeping the Assembly, which condemned the office of bishop in itself and complained that bishops should 'not vote in Parliament in name of the Kirk without commission from the Kirk'.[7] When the duke of Lennox cynically appointed Robert Montgomery to Beaton's see of Glasgow, thereby replacing an absent Catholic bishop with a very present Presbyterian one, there were anti-Catholic riots and the kirk started to demand its own representation in Parliament.

In 1584 James began to rule in person. His later ardent advocacy of episcopacy and the right of kings to rule the church, as summed up in his expostulation 'no bishop, no king', is well known, but in these early years of his personal rule religion was in a state of constant flux in Scotland, as exemplified by the career of David Lindsay, the minister of Leith. A friend of Knox who had helped compile the kirk's exceedingly Presbyterian Second Book of Discipline, Lindsay was elected Moderator of the General Assembly on six occasions. When James was busy driving through the 1584 parliament a series of Acts (known as the Black Acts) that reinstated the authority of bishops and ceded overall control of the kirk to the crown, Lindsay attempted to storm parliament and was incarcerated in Blackness Castle for forty-seven weeks for his pains. Yet three years later he, alone of the ministers present, prayed for Mary, Queen of Scots as she awaited execution, and in 1589 he accompanied James to Oslo, where he married the king to Anne of Denmark. James's religious sensitivities then swung back towards a moderate Presbyterianism that saw him legally recognizing the presbyteries in the Golden Act of 1592, adding ministers such as Lindsay to the Privy Council and in 1594 banishing the prominent Catholic earls of Huntly, Angus and Errol. The pendulum swung again in January 1596, though, when James appointed a commission of eight men, known as the Octavians, charged with securing the royal finances. This incensed many Presbyterians, who not only disliked the new taxes being imposed but suspected several of the Octavians, including Alexander, Lord Seton, of being Catholics. So on 17 December they attempted a coup, forcing the king to flee the capital for a fortnight. It was to be a short-lived victory, for when James restored order, he abruptly changed religious tack, declaring at the 1597 General Assembly that henceforth he would be filling the vacant episcopal sees. His excuse was that this would formally give the kirk seats in parliament and guarantee that the old episcopal income came to the kirk, but in truth he had now decided that the only way to maintain religious order was to restore the episcopacy. After protracted discussions, during which one minister, David Calderwood, argued that James's plan was a classic Trojan horse, aimed at persuading the kirk to 'receive that in their honour and welfare which served for their utter wreck and destruction', and another reckoned he could 'see the horns of his mitre',[8] James got his way. In 1600 he appointed three new bishops: Lindsay went to Ross, George Gladstanes, minister of St Andrews, went to Caithness and Peter Blackburn to Aberdeen, where he was already the minister. All of them took seats in parliament. By calling the kirk's bluff, and by initially appointing suitably Presbyterian ministers of whom the kirk approved, James had craftily secured the restoration of the clerical estate to the Scottish parliament. In the July 1606 session in Perth a full set of parliamentary bishops was able to help vote through both the wholesale 'Act anent the restitution of the estate of bishops' and the final transformation of the old abbacies into temporal lordships, and in 1610 another parliament fully restored bishops to their religious offices. It was a religious settlement of kinds, agreed by parliament but definitely driven by the king.

When James VI left Scotland in 1603, he faithfully promised that he would return every three years. It was a promise he signally failed to keep: he only ever saw his native land once again, in 1617. Given Scotland's propensity for parliamentary agitation in times of uncertain leadership and the frequency with which the estates continued to be summoned, one might have expected this period of monarchy *in absentia* to lead to renewed parliamentary insubordination. Far from it. If anything, the remaining years of his reign – and the first decade of Charles I's – saw the king enjoy unprecedented mastery of the three estates (which since 1587 had included elected shire commissioners). True, his plans for union made no headway, but that was largely down to English intransigence, and in other areas he won real victories. In 1612 he secured the complete restitution of Scottish bishops, and nine years later he persuaded parliament to ratify the controversial Anglican-sounding Five Articles of Perth (kneeling for communion, private baptism and communion for the sick, episcopal confirmation and observance of holy days). Some fifty members opposed the measures, but considering the strength of Calvinist thought in Scotland, this showed extraordinary acquiescence to the royal diktat.

There were reasons. James's new-found English wealth enabled him to distribute emoluments to his Scottish subjects, especially the nobility. He could also rely on the procedural device of the Lords of the Articles to secure the exclusive consideration of matters that he and his ministers deemed important. Even his absence, which necessitated the creation of a new post, the king's commissioner to parliament, meant that any criticism was deflected from the king onto the commissioner. So John Graham, the 58-year-old 3rd earl of Montrose, absorbed the complaints about the proposed act of union in 1604; at the 'red' parliament in Perth in July 1606, George Keith, the eminently Protestant 4th Earl Marischal, helped drive through the changes of 1612; and James Hamilton, the 2nd marquess of Hamilton (of whom one contemporary said that 'he was more subject to the pleasures and company of women than to priests'[9]), ensured the Articles of Perth were adopted in 1621.

The apogee of royal management of the Scottish parliament was reached – and the seeds of its destruction sown – in the parliament of 1633. The session followed directly on from Charles I's Scottish coronation on Tuesday, 18 June, which was conducted by William Laud in a ceremony that many Scots thought smacked of popism. Charles had done everything possible to ensure he got his way at the parliament, which was originally summoned in 1628, but had been prorogued eight times without sitting. Former members who had not supported the Articles of Perth had been excluded, others who had, had been promoted, and proxy votes had been secured by the court. Honours had been doled out to helpful members of parliament: Patrick Ogilvie of Inchmartin was knighted, as was Patrick Hamilton of Little Preston; Sir George Forrester of Corstorphine was made a peer. To cap it all, as the session began, the election of the Lords of the Articles was rigged. All this was done to secure three things: a generous tax deal; an Act of Revocation, whereby royal or church lands held by the nobility would be restored to the king; and new religious laws that gave full authority in matters religious to the king and expressly allowed him to determine clerical apparel. The Lords of the Articles completed their business on 27 June, and the next day the package of measures was presented to the full parliament, while the king looked on. Each member was required to declare assent to the three Acts. When it came to the last of these, on religion, there was substantial opposition, and John Leslie, the 6th earl of Rothes, challenged the clerk register when it was announced that the Act was carried. Charles fumed at him that he should sit down unless he wanted to be prosecuted for treason.

Charles had got his way, but the ill-feeling engendered when he brandished a list of members and said, 'Gentlemen, I'll know who will do me service and who will not, this day,'[10] was to prove far more long-lasting than his legislation. For when in 1637 he tried to secure the replacement of Knox's Book of Discipline by the Laud-inspired Book of Canons and Book of Prayer, the leaders of the Covenanting movement, including Rothes, John Campbell, the first earl of Loudon, and Archibald Campbell, marquess of Argyll, not only made religious demands, but also sought to put an end to royal manipulation of parliament. With the signing of the National Covenant in February 1638, it was clear that any meeting of parliament or General Assembly would be dangerous for the king and his commissioner, Hamilton. So it proved at the Glasgow Assembly in November (the first such meeting for twenty years). Hamilton desperately attempted to dissolve the Assembly, but when Rothes, Loudon and Argyll kept it in session, it declared the bishops abolished and excommunicated and the Articles of Perth repealed, all in open defiance of the king.

When parliament next met, ironically enough in the splendid new Parliament House in Edinburgh commissioned by Charles in 1632, the new national leadership pushed through a string of measures without royal assent, enacting the abolition of bishops, disbanding the Lords of the Articles and barring foreigners (such as English peers with Scottish lands) from parliament. Whereas previously each shire was entitled to two commissioners but only one vote, each commissioner was now given his own vote, doubling the political weight of the Scottish gentry, the lairds or lesser lords, at one fell swoop. A Triennial Act prescribing mandatory elections was passed and, most radically, the powers of the much-derided Privy Council were put in the hands of a new Committee of the Estates.

The subsequent decade saw the Scottish parliament stand entirely on its own two feet. Two triennial parliaments were summoned (1644–7 and 1648–51) and a library of statutes was agreed. The leadership was predominantly noble, but not exclusively so, for the burgh commissioners happily provided finance for the Covenanting revolution. Moreover, the shire and burgh commissioners clearly played the decisive role in the 1643 decision to join with the English parliament in the Solemn League and Covenant: for when the Convention of Estates decided to appoint a 27-man committee, while its 19 Scottish noble members were overwhelmingly royalist, the remaining commissioner members were convinced Covenanters. So it was the likes of Robert Barclay, John Semple and Alexander Douglas, all burgh commissioners, who carried the day in the committee and then again in the Convention up against the nineteen nobles. The guiding spirit of the estates, though, was the marquess of Argyll, clan chief of the Campbells, who negotiated with the English and welcomed Cromwell into Scotland in 1648. Argyll had his enemies, most notably James Graham, the marquess of Montrose, who, despite taking the Covenant, fought courageously for Charles throughout the 1640s and was eventually executed at parliament's command, his four limbs scattered to Glasgow, Perth, Stirling and Aberdeen and his head spiked outside the Tolbooth. A similar fate awaited Commissioner Hamilton, who was captured in late 1648 and executed in London in February 1649, his newly granted English earldom of Cambridge having enabled the application of English law against him.

Scotland had toyed with backing Charles I when he proffered a commitment to Presbyterianism, but the Independents' purge of the Presbyterians from the Long Parliament and the king's execution in January 1649 produced such revulsion in Scotland that the Scottish parliament, still led by Argyll, was happy to go to war for the man it proclaimed Charles II on 5 February 1649, who took the Covenant on 23 June 1650 and was crowned by Argyll at Scone in January 1651. Cromwell's victory over Charles at Worcester in September, though, also meant defeat for the Scots. For the first time political union between the two nations was enforced as Cromwell created a single parliament with just thirty seats reserved for carefully vetted Scots. Ten years later, however, came a total reversal of fortunes that was more symbolic of Scotland's permanently changing fortunes. After General Monck's march south at the head of a Scottish army had seen off Lambert in late 1659 and enabled Charles II's return, on 11 May 1661 an extraordinary funeral was held in St Giles's Church in Edinburgh, at which royalists gathered around the coffin of the old marquess of Montrose, whose torso had been disinterred, his limbs recovered and his head removed from the spike outside the Tolbooth. Sixteen days later, despite having placed the crown on Charles's head, Argyll was executed on the Scottish Maiden for his connivance with Cromwell and his head was placed on the vacant spike. The royal restitution was even more assured in Scotland than in England and all the paraphernalia of authoritarian government were put back in place. The new Scottish parliament that sat in January 1661 required a fresh oath of allegiance for all those in public office, the bishops and the Lords of the Articles were restored, and parliament assented to the king's right to make war and peace, to appoint ministers and to summon parliament as and when he chose.

Charles II's new Scottish Secretary, John Maitland, the earl of Lauderdale, was to be the incarnation of absentee royal supremacy north of the border. At the outset Lauderdale was a Covenanter, but when the first Scottish plan to combine with Charles I so as to secure a Presbyterian England, known as the 'Engagement', which he supported, was overturned in the Scottish parliament, he joined the young prince in exile and thereafter became an ardent royalist; taken captive at Worcester, he spent the remaining years of the protectorate in a variety of prisons. He did well out of the restoration, regaining his lost family lands, acquiring a dukedom, and becoming Scottish

Secretary and the king's closest Scottish companion. Few other than Charles had a kind word to say about him, though. Gilbert Burnet, who became a derisive opponent of the duke, said of him that 'he made a very ill appearance; he was very big, his hair was red, hanging oddly about him, his tongue was too big for his mouth, which made him bedew all that he talked to, and his whole manner was rough and boisterous and very unfit for a court'. And it was not just his appearance that Burnet disliked. 'He was haughty beyond expression; abject to those he saw he must stoop to, but imperious, insolent and brutal to all others.'[11] This showed itself most clearly in his dealings with the Scottish parliament, to which he was made commissioner in 1669. In an attempt to clear the way for Charles's threefold plan for a Supremacy Act, the establishment of a national militia and agreement to political union, Lauderdale bribed several peers handsomely and flouted convention by demanding both that the Lords of the Articles be appointed before contested elections had been decided and that they then meet in closed, secret session, lest the meetings become 'tumultuary' and 'unfit for consultation and contriving'.[12] This provoked fury, but Lauderdale still got his way: a full slate of royalists was elected (with just one exception, the 3rd duke of Hamilton) and did the king's business swiftly and slavishly.

Back in parliament, however, Lauderdale had a more difficult time. Archbishop Alexander Burnet of Glasgow had been deprived of his see because he had contested the king's Scottish Declaration of Indulgence of 7 June, so it was left to James Sharp, the deeply conflicted archbishop of St Andrews, to mount the opposition. Having started life as a convinced Presbyterian and then antagonized all his one-time allies by accepting the archiepiscopate, Sharp had so few friends that even when an assassination attempt was made on him in broad daylight in 1668, nobody came to his defence. So too in parliament he was left without an ally as the Act of Supremacy sailed through. Sharp's opposition did not regain him any of his old Covenanting friends. Andrew Melville ranted that 'that old dragon (the devil) had so stinged him with avarice and swelled so exorbitantly that he threatened the destruction of the whole body if he were not cut off'.[13] This was the kind of disdainful venom meted out to all the former Presbyterian Scottish bishops, summed up in the accusation levelled at the twice married bishop of Aberdeen, Patrick Scougal, that he had not only become 'prelatical, but even a very prelate!'[14] A special venom was reserved for Archbishop Sharp, though, who was so hated that in 1679 he was dragged out of his coach on the Magus Moor outside St Andrews and butchered in front of his daughter Isabella by a group of disaffected religious dissenters from Fife.

Charles got his way on the Supremacy Act in 1669, but Lauderdale's political thuggery earned the monarchy plenty of enemies, and when he resorted to similar measures in the parliamentary sessions of 1670 and 1672 he effectively incited a country party into existence. At its head was William Douglas, 3rd duke of Hamilton. A man full of contradictions, Hamilton had been brought up a Catholic heir to the Douglas lands, then had forsworn his religion and changed his surname in order to marry the old duke's niece, Anne Hamilton, who was duchess in her own right. A man of military courage, he could also be remarkably precious, on one occasion exclaiming to Lauderdale that although Charles had granted him the dukedom in his own right in 1661 and taken him into the council, yet he was regarded as 'insignificant . . . neglected and misrepresented'.[15] By the start of the 1670s, though, Hamilton's search for position was far outweighed by his antagonism to Lauderdale's repression of the Covenanters, and in the 1672 parliament, while still sitting on the council, he moved into open opposition, demanding the estates settle the people's many grievances before they could proceed to consider Lauderdale's demands, a move which prompted Lauderdale to adjourn the session.

Determined not to be silenced so swiftly again, Hamilton prepared carefully for the November 1673 parliament, so that when he again demanded that the grievances of the people be considered first, he was backed by twenty others, including Sir James Dalrymple of Stair, the president of the session. This time Lauderdale was 'struck as one almost dead' by this patent insubordination and immediately responded with a threat of the royal veto, to which Sir Patrick Hume of Polwarth retaliated with a defiant request for a vote on whether this was in any sense a free parliament. Since Lauderdale had by now lost the support even of his once loyal ally and fellow minister, John Hay, the marquess of Tweeddale, and was soon to add Alexander Seton, 3rd earl of Dunfermline, and John Geddie of St Nicholas, the commissioner for St Andrews, to his list of opponents, he was clearly outnumbered, and in a sustained series of fits of pique he adjourned parliament six times in less than three weeks. By 1678, though, the king's commissioner was back in numerical control, and although guerrilla warfare by Hamilton's party managed to delay proceedings, Lauderdale secured a grant of 1.8 million Scottish pounds for the repression of the conventiclers at the July meeting of the Convention of Estates. All the duke could do was lead a mass walkout – and even that defiance did not last long. When James, duke of York, arrived as commissioner in Scotland in 1681, hell bent on getting a Scottish Test Act through and avoiding any kind of Exclusion crisis, Hamilton genuflected and with him the Scottish 'country' party subsided.

It is difficult to comprehend how the Scottish parliament came to vote for the Act of Union in 1707 that incorporated it into Westminster. For every previous attempt to unite the two parliaments – in 1606, in the 1650s and in 1689 – had won even less support in Scotland than in England. What was more, by the time William fell from his horse and died on 8 March 1702, relations with Scotland had been steadily embittered by a series of economic disasters. Scottish harvests had failed, prices had risen and hundreds had lost their lives in the ensuing famine. In addition, Scotland had fallen foul of English commercial jealousy in setting up the Company of Scotland, aimed at trading on a monopoly basis with Asia, Africa and the Indies. In particular, the Company's attempt at setting up a new colony of Caledonia in Panama, known as the Darien Scheme, had collapsed, leaving two thousand prospective colonists dead and the Scots humiliated and out of pocket to the tune of £1.8 million. Scottish naivety, poor planning and sheer incompetence had contributed to the fiasco, but as a quarter of Scotland's liquid capital mouldered in a foreign ditch, much of Edinburgh's élite unfairly blamed the English.

Things got no better when Queen Anne, the second daughter of James II, came to the throne with her high Anglican and Tory predilections barely obscured. Indeed, her initial actions, most especially her refusal to call the new elections required by the 1696 Scottish Act of Security, so infuriated a wide body of Scottish opinion that the leading noble, Hamilton's son, the quixotic 4th duke, whose mother had invested heavily in Darien, dramatically declared the session of William's old parliament that Anne had re-summoned illegitimate and stormed out, to the accompaniment of seventy-nine other members and a cheering mob. By now the delicate matter of the succession was paramount in most political considerations. Despite her countless pregnancies, Anne's only putative heir, William, the eleven-year-old duke of Gloucester, had died in 1700 and the Protestant end of the Stuart dynasty was clearly running into the hereditary buffers. The English parliament had accordingly provided for the throne to pass to James VI and I's granddaughter, the Electress Sophia of Hanover,* in the 1701 Act of Settlement, but in doing so without consulting the Scots had further inflamed nationalist sentiment north of the border. So, while Jacobites still looked to Mary of Modena's son, the prince of Wales James Francis Edward (James II having died in September 1701), as their true king, many Scots opposed union with England.

When Anne's Scottish ministers, led by James Douglas, the duke of Queensberry, called elections for a new parliament to meet in May 1703, the court party of ministers, pension-holders and Presbyterian supporters of the 1689 revolution was trounced. Jacobites, Cavaliers, Scottish Episcopalians and ardent nationalists took more than half of the elected seats, and without the benefit of bishops, the court could barely count on a hundred loyalists. Queensberry found himself fending off demands for a new Act of Security, led by James Hay, the 2nd marquess of Tweeddale, and the irascible virtually republican Andrew Fletcher of Saltoun – and he failed. On 13 August the Act of Security passed with a majority of nearly sixty, the estates thereby declaring that the Scottish crown should pass to a separate, Protestant monarch, unless England agreed terms that guaranteed the 'honour and independency of the crown of this kingdom'. A month's legislative tussle ensued in which the estates refused to grant supply in retaliation for Queensberry's withholding of royal assent for the Act, and the session collapsed in recriminations on 16 September.

Things did not improve the following year, even though by then Anne had replaced Queensberry with Tweeddale. If anything, matters deteriorated as Queensberry, smarting from his fall from favour, managed to peel off significant numbers of

* Sophia died aged 83 just two months before Queen Anne in 1714, thus narrowly missing becoming monarch of a realm she had never visited.

members who should have voted with the court party, including several with government pensions and emoluments. The eventual compromise – royal assent in exchange for six months' supply for the War of the Spanish Succession – was a clear defeat for the court. At this point the exasperated English parliament persuaded Anne's austere Lord Treasurer, Sidney Godolphin, that if wooing would not work then bullying might, and in February 1705 ministers encouraged the Commons and Lords to pass the Aliens Act, under which all Scots living in England would be treated as aliens and Scottish sheep, black cattle, coal and linen would be banned. Extraordinarily, the Act was to come into force on 25 December 1705 and last until 'the successors to the crown of Scotland be settled by Act of Parliament in Scotland'. In other words, Anne's ministers would barter trade for political union.

Scottish blood was up by now, so when Anne reshuffled her deck again, putting John Campbell, the 25-year-old no-nonsense militaristic 2nd duke of Argyll, in charge of relations with the Scottish parliament, with a restored Queensberry at his side, they had to face a third initially hostile session of the Scottish parliament with the Scots smarting under threat of further penury. Some baubles had been doled out to previously disaffected nobles in the shape of knighthoods of the Thistle, and Argyll's brother had been made Lord Treasurer with a seat in the estates, but there were few members who openly advocated union, and Hamilton's continued popularity as leader of a broad coalition of opponents helped defeat the court's initial attempts to have the succession settled. Yet always at their back was the threat of the Aliens Act. As Sir John Clerk of Penicuik, the commissioner for Whithorn, put it later: 'It would be hard for anybody to tell how we could be in worse circumstances than we were at the time.'[16] So, slowly, the opposition began to succumb, and on Saturday, 1 September the estates agreed to start negotiations on a treaty uniting the two kingdoms, barely rescuing their honour by demanding that the Aliens Act had to be repealed first. Hamilton, who had reluctantly come to the conclusion a year earlier that 'our independency is now a jest',[17] not only voted for the negotiations, but tabled a separate motion that the queen, rather than the estates, should appoint the thirty-one Scottish negotiating commissioners. Despite the opposition of a string of nobles and arch-conservatives such as George Lockhart of Carnwarth, who called it 'the commencement of Scotland's ruin',[18] the motion was carried by a handful of votes.

So, in April 1706, the Scottish commissioners, almost all hand-picked for their amenability, met in closed sessions with the English at Whitehall. Here the English offered a major concession – 'full freedom and intercourse of trade and navigation within the . . . United Kingdom and plantations thereunto belonging' – a long-held Scottish aspiration. In addition an 'equivalent' of £398,085 10s sterling was to be paid for the costs of ministerial arrears, compensation for Darien and some nebulous private compensations. In return, Scotland would send thirty-eight MPs and sixteen peers (to be elected by the Scottish peers every parliament) to Westminster. The Scottish commissioners argued forcefully about the terms of the treaty, but after a few amendments (including an extra seven MPs) a text was happily presented to Queen Anne on 23 July and on 3 October Queensberry, re-installed as commissioner, led the traditional ride from Holyroodhouse to the Parliament Hall in grand pomp and circumstance for the parliamentary session that he hoped would resolve what he described as 'an affair of the greatest concern and import'.

Now began the real heavy lifting. From the moment the parliamentary session was planned, ministers set about evening up the numbers. Argyll's brother was given an earldom, and potentially helpful itinerant Scottish nobles like the earls of Abercorn and Deloraine were persuaded to return home. (Not all the itinerants were helpful: Patrick, Lord Olliphant, was brought back but voted against the court.) More controversially, Queensberry was granted an additional £20,000 with which to pay off salary arrears – which Lockhart condemned as nothing short of bribery. Lockhart was unfair. The seventeen members we know to have received payments were indeed owed substantial sums in arrears, and several of them were men who already ardently supported the union. That is not to deny that the threat of non-payment might act as an inducement to support the court, but the longstanding Scottish nationalist belief that the union was bought for filthy lucre, which largely depends on the Lockhart attack, is difficult to substantiate. True, the leader of the *squadrone volante* group of non-aligned Scottish peers, Tweeddale, who had switched sides during the civil wars more frequently than a Premiership footballer and had voted against the queen's right to appoint the Scottish treaty commissioners on 1 September, received £1,000 in arrears and eventually voted for the Act of Union, but the arch-opponent of union, Hamilton, had proposed the September motion, so it is difficult to lay a direct charge of corruption even against Tweeddale. Moreover, as another of those who was paid, the earl of Cromartie, put it, nothing could 'alter me from being a Scotsman and a Briton, and for the union';[19] the earl of Atholl received £1,000 but consistently voted against the treaty; and Viscount Teviot, who could have expected £8,900 in arrears, did not even turn up.

All this parliamentary management was necessary, for there was still widespread public antipathy to union, exemplified by a slew of public petitions that came in bearing some 20,000 signatures. Indeed, when the treaty was published on the first day of the parliamentary session the public reaction was so fierce that John Erskine, the inconstantly Jacobite but presently Whig earl of Mar, thought 'the mob of this town are mad and against us',[20] the church bells at St Giles rang out to the tune 'Why should I be so sad on my wedding day?', and throughout October there was a tense stand-off between government troops and crowds supporting the opposition. On 23 October Daniel Defoe, despatched to Edinburgh as a spy by Robert Harley, the English secretary of state, witnessed the storming of the house of one of the commissioners, the Lord Provost Sir Patrick Johnston, which was soon followed by an invasion of the Parliament House itself, and although matters calmed somewhat in Edinburgh there was talk of violent insurrection further north and burnings of the treaty in both Dumfries and Stirling. At the end of the year Hamilton, Atholl, Lockhart and Fletcher coordinated a mass demonstration in favour of calling a new parliament and reject-ing the union, but Defoe reckoned that 'the women are the instructors and the men are mere machines wound up'.[21]

In parliament the debates were ferocious. Queensberry put his best case for the treaty and received the backing of Archibald Primrose, the earl of Rosebery, who thought that 'nothing will ever make this country easy but an entire complete union with England', as without it Scotland would become 'the most unhappy people in the world'.[22] But the opposition was fierce. Andrew Fletcher ranted that 'our trade . . . will be only an incon-siderable retail, in a poor, remote and barren country, where the richest of our nobility and gentry will no longer reside'.[23] John Hamilton, Lord Belhaven, brought himself to tears with his tirade against the despond into which Scotland would decline if the union were effected, Lord Balmerino demanded a respite while commissioners consulted the country, Atholl invoked the Declaration of Arbroath, the earl of Kincardine complained that England's system was patently corrupt as Old Sarum, 'where there is not one house, but a shepherd's coalhouse,' still sent two men to parliament, Viscount Kilsyth claimed that only one in two thousand Scots supported the treaty, and Hamilton dragged Robert the Bruce's removal of the English John Balliol into the fray. Queensberry held firm, and on 4 November won the vote on the first article by thirty-two votes.

He was still not out of the woods, though, for while the dogmatic Presbyterian *squadrone volante* member Patrick Hume, earl of Marchmont, thought that union was 'the only sound substantial and durable way for attaining what a Protestant free man . . . ought to desire and aim at',[24] the General Assembly had declared itself firmly opposed to the treaty, with its lack of protection for the Presbyterian kirk and its provision that sixteen Scottish peers would sit in a house alongside twenty-six contaminating bishops. Many estates members feared that a united parliament with a Tory Anglican majority would restore bishops in Scotland and destroy the kirk. Keen to reassure Presbyterians and split them off from Jacobites, Anne first declared she would take robust action against Catholics in Scotland and on 16 November gave royal assent to her ministers' emollient Act for Securing the Protestant Religion and the Presbyterian Church Government. Not everyone was satisfied, but the polymath pro-union antiquarian Sir John Clerk of Penicuik reckoned that at this point the 'trumpets of sedition fell silent'.[25]

In the end, though, the biggest consideration was financial. Clerk was not alone in taking the view that, given Scotland's current economic plight, refusal was simply not an option. So it was that not just the hard and fast court party, which included some seventy-eight government office-holders and pensioners and nineteen serving army officers, voted each article through, but invariably they were joined by the two dozen *squadrone volante* members, led by Tweeddale, Rothes and Haddington.[26] Also, by the time it came to the final vote to ratify the treaty on 16 January 1707, many opposition members had lost their stomach for the fight, and the likes of Sir David Ramsay of Balmain and William Johnson of Sciennes had drifted away to their homes. Hamilton remained, though, and when the vote was announced – 110 votes in favour to 69 against – he bellowed out 'No!' He was not alone. His namesake John Hamilton, Lord Belhaven, had moaned on 2 November: 'I think I see our Ancient Mother Caledonia, like Caesar sitting in the midst of our Senate, ruefully looking around her, covering herself with her royal garment, attending the Fatal Blow, and breathing out her last with a *Et tu quoque mi fili*.'[27] Lockhart was less apocalyptic, but just as angry, reckoning that 'everybody [was] enraged and displeased' because 'the union was crammed down Scotland's throat'.[28]

The deed was done, though, and all that was needed was for Westminster to go through the same process, which it did in such swift measure that on Tuesday, 25 March 1707, Queensberry addressed the estates:

> I am persuaded that we and our posterity will reap the benefit of the union of the two kingdoms, and I doubt not that, as this parliament has had the honour to conclude it, you will in your several stations recommend to the people of this nation a grateful sense of her majesty's goodness and great care for the welfare of her subjects in bringing this important affair to perfection, and that you will promote a universal desire in this kingdom to become one in hearts and affections as we are inseparably joined in interest with our neighbouring nation.

The Chancellor of Scotland, James Ogilvy, earl of Seafield, was more poetic: 'There's ane end of ane auld sang.'[29] There was nothing left to say.

A satire on George II's reluctance to accept a coalition or 'broad-bottomed' government. As the Whig Prime Minister Henry Pelham and his elder brother Thomas, the duke of Newcastle, try to stuff the Tory John Hinde Cotton MP into his mouth, other former opposition MPs look on, while the king has just evacuated a string of former ministers.

11

One Party State

THE HOUSE OF COMMONS SAT late on Tuesday, 12 March 1695, so late that candles had to be brought in. It was an uncomfortable evening, for the previous Wednesday the House had set up a committee to investigate allegations that MPs had been bribed to help ease legislation through the Commons. The Speaker, Sir John Trevor, a lumbering bull of a man, was both one of the accused and now chairman of the debate on the committee's findings. Trevor was renowned for his capacity to survive against the odds. A Welshman, he had worked his family connections hard, gaining a place in his uncle Arthur's legal chambers, and a knighthood and promotion thanks to his cousin Sir George Jeffreys, before inheriting his father's estates in Brynkinallt near Chirk when his elder 'lunatic' brother Edward died. First elected to parliament when he effectively bought the seat of Castle Rising for £60 from the Howard family in 1673, Trevor was a keen Tory anti-papist, yet his vote against the First Exclusion Bill and his declaration that, if carried, it would 'dispose of the most valuable thing in the world, the crown of England',[1] endeared him to James II, who made him Speaker, Master of the Rolls and councillor (just as Jeffreys was made Lord Chancellor). William's revolution temporarily relieved Trevor of high office, but having secured a seat in the Convention through a by-election, he wheedled his way into the Tories' affections and declared himself their effective leader. By the time of the 1690 parliament he was indispensable and was elected Speaker unopposed. Patronage continued to flow his way, landing him a post as First Commissioner of the Great Seal and renewed membership of the Privy Council.

All of which may well have told against him when, against the background of widespread Commons concern about the cost of the Nine Years War, MPs were told on 7 March 1695 that it was bruited abroad that 'both public and private business came to market [in the Commons] and neither could be done unless paid for'.[2] In other words, you could buy any legislation you wanted if only you knew whose palm to grease. Sir Orlando Gee made the specific allegation in the House that John Brewer MP had taken thirty guineas for promoting a Bill, a charge Gee probably made in the hope of dissuading Brewer from his campaign against Gee's brother Richard, who was said to have taken bribes in granting hackney carriage licences. The charges against Brewer were soon discarded, but the word on the street was not so easily silenced, and the suggestion persisted that 'there is something working in the House of Commons that don't yet appear; not but that it is sufficiently talked of without doors, particularly against the Speaker for having taken money to promote private bills'.[3] And indeed, when the committee report came out on 12 March it became known that the City of London had paid Trevor 1,000 guineas for getting the Orphans Bill (which benefited the City rather than the orphans) onto the statute book. Trevor's argument that no improper influence had been involved cut no ice. When he called the vote, his friends kept silent and the House declared him guilty. Considerably abashed, Trevor took to his bed for two days, thereby preventing the House from sitting, whereupon king and Commons united in declaring a vacancy for the speakership; and as soon as his replacement was chosen, Trevor was expelled from the House, the last Speaker so to be dismissed.

Trevor was probably no more nor less corrupt than many of his predecessors or contemporaries. Many previous Speakers accepted payments expressly to further a particular parliamentary cause, and it was standard for the promoters of private Bills to pay the Speaker a 'gratuity'. In 1671 Speaker Edward Turnor was 'blown in the House of Commons' for having taken 50 guineas from the East India Company, but survived. Moreover, the two witnesses in this case, Sir Robert Clayton MP and Sir James Houblon, got off pretty lightly: Clayton escaped censure by pretending to be ill and was re-elected on five further occasions, and Houblon entered the House as a prominent London member in 1698. Yet Whig distrust of Tory corruption played against Trevor, and although he avoided impeachment thanks to the prorogation of parliament and was to continue as Master of the Rolls up until his death (earning £4,000 a year), the general view seemed to be that he had been fairly expelled, 'so just a horror, so noble an indignation had this august assembly for his crime'.[4] Trevor left a legacy, too, as he had a pronounced squint. Thus far MPs had relied on 'catching the Speaker's eye' when they wanted to speak. Henceforth Speakers would always call them by name.

Most importantly, Trevor's indiscretion was downright paltry compared with Whig financial chicanery, the pinnacle of which was reached with the abuse of the South Sea Company. At its foundation in 1711 the company's explicit aim, as a Tory rival to the Bank of England, was to exploit a monopoly of trade with South America, contingent upon the successful completion of the War of the Spanish Succession; but the director of the company, John Blunt,* came up with the imaginative idea of

---

* Sir John Blunt on being made a baronet in 1720.

exchanging a large chunk of the national debt incurred by the war for company stock. This met with such warm government support from the Chancellor of the Exchequer, John Aislabie, that by 1719 the company held nearly £12 million of the £50 million national debt. So far, so good. True, Blunt had furnished a few government ministers with some 'free' stock in exchange for helpful legislation, but the company was secure. Then, in 1720, in a deliberate attempt to boost the share price, Blunt fanned speculation about massive profits. The price leaped: £128 in January, £175 in February, £330 in March and £550 in May. Then the government gave the company a further boost by requiring any competitor company to be licensed – and the share price rose even further, to £890 in June and £1,000 in August.

When the bubble burst with the abrupt collapse of the share price in September, the many thousands of people who now faced bankruptcy were keen to rescue what they could financially, and to pick over the political entrails of the scandal. For MPs and ministers had been involved at every twist. Such was the outcry that the ministry reluctantly recalled parliament in December 1720. The Whig leadership in both houses was under simultaneous attack. For Charles Spencer, 3rd earl of Sunderland and First Lord of the Treasury, and James, Earl Stanhope, the Northern Secretary, had led the government in the Lords since 1718, and in the Commons Chancellor Aislabie and the Southern Secretary, James Craggs the younger (whose father, also called James, was Postmaster-General), held the ministry reins.*

* The post of royal secretary had existed since the middle ages. By the end of Elizabeth's reign there were two 'secretaries of state', and in 1660 they were denominated secretaries for the Southern and Northern Departments. The former had responsibility for the Catholic states and the Muslim world; the latter, which was normally considered the junior post, had responsibility for relations with the northern, Protestant states. In 1782 the posts were reorganized and renamed Secretary of State for, respectively, the Home Department and the Foreign Department.

All four were implicated. So too were several MPs who were directors of the company, including Sir Theodore Janssen, a naturalized Frenchman of Huguenot descent who was a wealthy director of both the South Sea Company and the Bank of England. The December debates in the Commons were rowdy, not least because several MPs had made a fortune and others had lost one. The Tory William Shippen pointedly stared at Craggs as he argued that he knew some ministers who were more guilty than the directors of the company, thereby provoking Craggs into offering him satisfaction in a duel. Soon the whole House was in uproar, and was restored to calm only when it was agreed that a committee should investigate further. Things looked perilous for the ministry as the court-backed slate of members for that committee failed to get elected. Those who did performed their task swiftly: on 23 January the Scottish Tory General Charles Rosse told the House that they had 'already discovered a train of deepest villainy and fraud that hell ever contrived to ruin a nation',[5] and in the following days the four MP directors of the company were expelled from the House. Fate then intervened. For on 4 February the ever-tempestuous Stanhope was engaged in a ferocious row with another peer when he suffered a stroke in the Lords. The next day he was dead, and eleven days later fellow Secretary Craggs died of smallpox.

These two deaths did little to abate the public anger, but within political circles there was now a clear desire to limit the fallout so far as possible. So, when a resolution was moved in the Commons alleging that Stanhope's cousin Charles, who was MP for Milborne Port and Secretary to the Treasury, had received £50,000 in bribes, the court went into overdrive, King George I begging influential members not to vote; and, despite his patent malfeasance, Stanhope survived, by just three votes. Without such overt royal support, Aislabie was not to be so lucky, and in early March both he and Sir George Caswall MP, who was a director of the Sword Blade Company that had been used to channel monies to MPs, were expelled from the House and deprived of their fortunes, to be joined in May by Aislabie's brother-in-law, Thomas Vernon, who had tried to interfere with the committee of investigation. This left Sunderland, who managed to survive a ferocious debate in the Commons on 15 March by a relatively comfortable 233 votes to 172, but even he soon tendered his resignation; and the next day, on the eve of giving evidence to the House, Craggs' father died, probably of a deliberate overdose of opium.

Throughout the episode, parliament's justice was capricious. On the one hand, as the historian Edward Gibbon, whose grandfather Edward was also arraigned in 1721, wrote, 'instead of the calm solemnity of a judicial inquiry, the fortune and honour of thirty three Englishmen were made the topics of hasty conversation, the sport of a lawless majority'.[6] On the other, several crooks got off scot-free, Charles Stanhope and the earl of Sunderland were guilty as charged, and despite the brief public obloquy several of those involved went on to prosper. Stanhope, for instance, continued to sit until 1741, Vernon was returned in the 1722 election and even Aislabie, who was otherwise rarely blessed with good luck, losing his father in a duel and his first wife and daughter in a house fire, was allowed to keep £119,000 out of his £164,000 fortune. The public was less inclined to tolerance. Caswall was savagely attacked in the street, and in August investors came to the Commons in their droves to demand justice; but by then the political waters had covered over the scandal, most MPs had absented themselves, and the ministry was able to see off calls for a further inquiry by 78 votes to 29 before threatening the new Riot Act on the protestors. As they filed out, one was heard to protest, 'You first pick our pockets and then send us to gaol for complaining,'[7] but the government's South Sea Sufferers' Bill took just three days to sail through the Commons. Despite losing four of their most senior ministers, the Whigs had survived.

One man was central to their survival. Sir Robert Walpole, MP for King's Lynn, who stage-managed the government's response to the crisis, not only managed to exculpate himself and screen his old enemy Sunderland from censure, but in making himself indispensable to a string of Whig politicians bound them to him so closely that by the spring of 1721 he was able to take Sunderland's post as First Lord of the Treasury and install his brother-in-law Charles, Viscount Townshend, to replace James, Earl Stanhope, as Northern Secretary,* beginning the longest period of personal political ascendancy this country has yet seen.

To comprehend how Walpole was to achieve his twenty-year mastery of British politics, it is important to understand how the Whigs themselves gained so unassailable a grip on power. For the Whig hegemony was far from inevitable. William and Mary had an understandable predilection for those Whigs who had helped them to the throne, but there were Tories too who had preferred the anti-papist security guaranteed to the Church of England by James's 'vacating' the throne in 1688. Moreover Anne, an ardent Anglican, made little attempt to hide the fact that such high church Tories were her kind of people. Yet in neither reign did the monarch choose a straight slate of Whig or Tory ministers.

There was another element in play here. Later generations of historians branded this an era of 'constitutional monarchy', but in truth the government was still entirely a creature of the monarch. Whether the two parties gained or lost seats at a general election still made little difference to the choice of those

* Stanhope had also served briefly as Chancellor of the Exchequer from 1717 to 1718 – the last peer to do so.

appointed as ministers. It was the monarch who formed the administration, and there was no sense of a government depending on a majority in the Commons. The first eight general elections of the new era saw big swings: in both 1695 and 1698 the Whigs came out on top, but in the election of January 1701 the Tories managed a slender win, only to lose the advantage in another election at the end of the year, and regain it more convincingly the following year in Anne's first parliament. The Tories then won narrowly in 1705, but lost again in 1708 when the Whigs had roughly 268 seats to the Tories' 225. But up to this point the complexion of the Commons was almost irrelevant to who held the monarch's favour and office.

The Whigs then made a massive miscalculation. For the ministry was led by two nominal Tories: the grave and laborious Lord Treasurer, Sidney, earl Godolphin, whose financial expertise had made him indispensable to all three previous monarchs; and the headstrong military leader of the War of the Spanish Succession, John Churchill, now the duke of Marlborough. But they were increasingly dependent on and allied to a group of Whigs who unambiguously supported the new war effort, unlike many Tories. Known as the Whig Junto, the five peers (John, Lord Somers; Thomas, earl Wharton; Charles Montagu, Baron Halifax; Admiral Edward Russell, earl of Orford; and Marlborough's son-in-law Charles Spencer, the 3rd earl of Sunderland) had prospered under William III and been dismissed on Anne's accession (she described them as the 'five tyrannising lords'). Four had been reappointed – Somers was Lord President of the Council, Wharton Lord Lieutenant in Ireland, Orford First Lord of the Admiralty and Sunderland Southern Secretary. But in 1709 the Junto sought to capitalize on the Whig strength in the Commons to secure Anne's undivided attention.

Their strategy was to split the Tories over religion, so when the stentorian high church Anglican cleric Henry Sacheverell delivered himself of a bold ninety-minute rant against 'sectarists and schismatics of whatsoever wild, romantic or enthusiastic notions' and claimed that thanks to 'false brethren' the Church of England had become 'not only a den of thieves but a receptacle of Legions of Devils',[8] and that the Glorious Revolution had not involved a righteous resistance to an unrighteous king, they pounced. To Whig minds this was seditious stuff, and Sacheverell's speech seemed a golden opportunity to type Tories as dangerous traitors; so John Dolben was put up to demand Sacheverell's impeachment, to which the Commons readily assented in December 1709. But the Whigs had made a mistake. For when the matter reached the Lords, there were riots on the eve of the trial, and when Sacheverell made a well-argued defence, although the Lords found him guilty they handed down only a token punishment in the form of a three-year ban on preaching. With public dislike of the Whigs now manifest and Anne herself keen on destroying the power of the Marlboroughs, the queen dismissed a series of Whig ministers in the early months of 1710. When the Tories secured a massive 329 seats to the Whigs' 168 in that autumn's election,[9] the transformation was complete, and Anne could appoint the Whig-turned-Tory Robert Harley as Chancellor of the Exchequer and the arch-Tory Henry St John as secretary of state. (The election did not, of course, change the numbers in the Lords, which remained stubbornly Whig, despite Anne's appointment of Tory bishops; so in 1711 she had to add twelve Tory peers merely to carry the unpopular Treaty of Utrecht.)

The 1710 election was hard fought: 131 seats were contested, windows were smashed in houses that did not visibly celebrate the Tory victory, and Walpole, who had been Secretary of War since 1708, stood in Norfolk, was pelted with dirt and stones, and came last. Even dirtier, though, was the Tories' revenge, for within a year they pressed charges against Walpole (who had insured himself against losing Norfolk by taking the King's Lynn seat) for accepting a bribe and the Tory Commons found him guilty in January 1712 of 'a high breach of trust and notorious corruption'. Although confined to the Tower, he was re-elected by a comfortable majority in the subsequent King's Lynn by-election, only to have the Commons declare that he could not be re-elected to a parliament from which he had been expelled. He therefore had to sit the rest of the parliament out, but with steely composure he wrote to his sister: 'This barbarous injustice being only the effect of party malice, does not concern me at all and I heartily despise what I shall one day revenge.'[10] The Sacheverell debacle and the Tories' abuse of the system had taught Walpole a clear lesson: ruthless manipulation of the electoral system and determined use of the ensuing parliamentary majority, together with an astute eye for public opinion, could bring one to power and keep one there.

So it was that when George I arrived in 1714 as the first Hanoverian king, the Whigs were remorseless in persuading him that they and they alone had supported his accession. The Scottish novelist Tobias Smollett betrayed his own Tory outlook when he argued that it was 'a very great prejudice to the nation' that George had been 'misled into strong prepossessions against the Tories, who constituted such a considerable part of his subjects', but he was simply stating the facts when he noted that 'the whole nation was delivered into the hands of the Whigs',[11] who did indeed seize every post going. James Brydges, the newly ennobled earl of Carnarvon, noted that hardly a Tory was left, 'not even a mean one', and for decades Tories were excluded from every element of patronage in the magistracy, the ministry and the pulpit.

If George had arrived with 'prepossessions', though, he was soon confirmed in them, for the ludicrously conceived and incompetently effected rebellion of 1715, which saw significant Tories like St John, whom Anne had made Viscount Bolingbroke, revealed as Jacobites, proved to the unloved Hanoverian that Whig absolutism was the only means of keeping the nation secure. So he actively threw his weight behind them, replacing the Triennial Act of 1694 with a Septennial Act, thereby extending parliaments to seven years, and using cash and influence to ensure a helpfully Whig Commons. The latter enterprise proved to be remarkably simple, as although the eighty shire seats had large electorates and open contests, the 146 boroughs together had just 3,500 voters, many of whom were extremely susceptible to royal influence. By securing the boroughs, the Whigs could win a majority of the seats, even if the Tories retained a majority of the votes, as happened in every election bar 1727 up until 1747.

The Whigs faced one other challenge: themselves. For they liked falling out with each other. George's first administration had Walpole as Paymaster to the Forces and then in October 1715 Chancellor of the Exchequer, and his brother-in-law Townshend as Northern Secretary. Before long Sunderland opened up a schism in Whig ranks by allying himself alongside the Southern Secretary, Stanhope, in a move to oust Walpole and Townshend and seize the key offices of state. From March 1718 Sunderland was First Lord of the Treasury and Stanhope was Northern Secretary, consigning Walpole and Townshend to three years in vituperative Whig opposition. Whig on Whig action could be ferocious. When Walpole and another Whig, William Pulteney, attacked William, Baron Cadogan, for corruption they did so with such vehemence that Walpole got a nosebleed, and Edward Harley wrote that Walpole 'bore harder upon the Court than any Tory durst attempt to do'.[12] When Sunderland, as First Lord of the Treasury, attempted to limit the number of new peers that could be created to just six in 1719, Walpole sneered at his erstwhile fellow minister Earl Stanhope for having got himself into the House of Lords and now wanting 'to shut the door after him'.[13]

But by the time Walpole was screening his colleagues from public opprobrium in 1721, he had learned not only the value of keeping the Tories at bay but also the equal value of keeping the Whig ship in one piece. He had come back on board as Paymaster in 1720, and although he would not have agreed with Arthur Onslow's comment that there had never been 'so corrupt a time', he had certainly witnessed Sunderland's often desperate efforts to secure votes at a time when 'men set their own price and had it, as he and they knew their value'.[14] Walpole was to take all these measures to new heights. A sociable man, he would wine and dine friends and allies. He would spot individual members who were still unaligned and recruit them to his cause. John, Viscount Perceval, who held an Irish peerage and an English seat, perspicaciously described Walpole's modus operandi: 'Sir Robert, like the altars of refuge in old times, is the asylum of little unworthy wretches who, submitting to dirty work, endear themselves to him, and get his protection first and then his favour.'[15] So, with George I's willing acquiescence, Walpole doled out seats and sinecures in a spree of political patronage. As Edmund Burke put it, the court could not only furnish 'all honours, offices, emoluments' and 'every sort of personal gratification to avarice or vanity', it could also provide 'the means of growing, by innumerable petty services to individuals, into a spreading interest in their country'. The end result, then, was that a man 'can procure indemnity from quarters [creditors]. He can procure advantages in trade. He can get pardons for offences. He can obtain a thousand favours, and avert a thousand evils.'[16]

Walpole also took every opportunity to portray his opponents in the Tory party as unpatriotic zealots. In this he was blessed, as most leading Tories, for all they might deny it, held true to the Stuart cause, and as a result regularly acted as most willing accomplices in their own misfortune. Bolingbroke, indeed, despite several attempts to ease himself back into Hanoverian favour, admitted as much when defining the Whigs and Tories in 1739: 'The Whigs have always looked on the Protestant succession, and the Tories on the restoration of the Stuarts, as a sure means to throw the whole power of Government into the hands of one or the other of them, and to keep it there.'[17] His close ally Sir William Wyndham MP led the Tories in avowing Hanoverian loyalty, but regularly corresponded with Cardinal Fleury and the 'Pretender', Mary of Modena's son James. And Francis Atterbury, the bishop of Rochester, nobly argued for the Tory cause while Anne was still on the throne, but after George's accession soon became bitter and increasingly sharp in his attacks on the Hanoverians in the Lords. When his incompetent conspiracy with the Pretender was discovered in 1721, both the Commons and the Lords voted to deprive and banish him under a Bill of Pains and Penalties. Walpole could not have wished for a better emblem of Tory treachery.

There were some important constitutional changes during these years of Whig hegemony. From the start of William's reign parliament met regularly, not least thanks to the financial demands of war; and the Commons took greater interest in the minutiae of government expenditure, setting up the Commissioners of Public Accounts in 1691. Charles I had briefly referred to his 'Cabinet Council', but when William was abroad senior ministers were charged to meet as a 'Cabinet'; in 1695 they met even though he was in the country, and ten years later the Regency Act formally enacted meetings of the 'Lords of the cabinet council'. When the Hanoverians arrived the Cabinet eclipsed the Privy Council. Anne's reign was the first not to include a single Act of Attainder or Pains and Penalties, the former MP for

Northumberland, Sir John Fenwick, being the last to be so dispatched (for a Jacobite conspiracy) in 1697. Monarchs had always enjoyed the right to veto a Bill – a right Charles II and James II had used six times between them – but when William III rejected a Triennial Bill in 1693, Bishop Burnet noted that the intervention, 'though an unquestionable right of the crown, has been so seldom practised that the two Houses are apt to think it a hardship when there is a bill denied'.[18] When Anne refused the Scotch Militia Bill in 1708 little fuss was made, but it was to be the last such occasion. Thereafter even royal assent was just a formality.

But for every democratic reform there was a repressive measure. True, the 1713 Commons motion that no charge on the public finances could be made except on the motion of a minister of the crown, which still prevents the opposition tabling amendments to tax rates, was a Tory one; but the 1711 Land Qualification Act, which significantly increased the landholding requirement for MPs to £300, the Septennial Act, the suspension of habeas corpus, the Riot Act, the licensing and regulation of theatres, all came from Whig loins, and though they did not return to Acts of Attainder the Whigs resorted instead to Acts of Pains and Penalties. Some thirty-one statutes extended the death penalty to a wide range of crimes, including merely being caught blacked up or disguised in a forest, which was deemed tantamount to intent to poach. The passage of each of these measures relied on the manufactured Whig majority in both houses, further aided by the arrival of the Scottish representative peers, who were almost invariably elected straight from a list of sixteen preferred government candidates, and by the new dominance in the Lords given to the influential Chairman of Committees. Barring incompetence or internal division, it was almost impossible to lose a vote.

Walpole did not always get his own way. His Excise Bill for

tobacco limped through the Commons with such a wafer-thin majority of 36 in 1733 that he withdrew it before sending it up to the Lords, and weeks later a Tory motion in the upper house to investigate what the government had done with the estates of directors of the South Sea Company was tied on 75. Walpole was regularly satirized in the burgeoning print media, and seating patterns in the Commons betrayed the growth of opposition. For whereas MPs had sat wherever they liked under the Tudors and Stuarts, the only distinction being that ministers and London MPs were reserved the seats closest to the Speaker, on his right, by the 1740s those in opposition to the ministry, of whatever party, sat on the Speaker's left. This was not an absolute rule. William Pulteney, for instance, who led a growling and growing group of discontented oppositionist Whigs from 1725, sat close enough to Walpole to engage in a bet with him on whether he had correctly cited a Latin tag in a 1741 debate. But in general the opposition now sat opposite the government in what was, with the advent of the Scottish MPs and despite Sir Christopher Wren's enlargement of the gallery in preparation for the new Scottish MPs in 1707, an even more crowded house.

In addition to Pulteney, there was a small but talented and effective band of Whig oppositionists coordinated by Richard Temple, Viscount Cobham, who had entered politics as a Whig but by 1734 was an opponent of Walpole's. These 'Cobham's Cubs' met regularly at Cobham's estate in Stowe and at the Beefsteak Club in London; three of them delivered their maiden speeches on the same day, 22 April 1735.[19] It was a closely knit group, in blood as well as politics: its members included Cobham's nephews Richard and George Grenville, and George Lyttelton along with his brothers-in-law Thomas Pitt and Thomas's younger brother William. The group grew with the addition of two more relatives each of Lyttelton and Grenville as MPs. But what gave them real political cachet was the involvement, from 1735, of George II's estranged and discontented son Frederick, the prince of Wales, to whom Lyttelton acted as equerry. The group referred to themselves as the 'Boy Patriots', but they were as self-serving as any other set of ambitious young men on the political make – and as opportunistic in their opposition as Walpole had been in his own sojourn out of power. Indeed, it is a depressing fact that even while pretending piety, as one writer put it in describing the situation in 1715,

> self-interest and corruption have reached such a pitch in this nation that few people act on principle pure and simple . . . There are members of both Houses of Parliament who, if they are not employed, will always be of a different opinion from that which they would have held had they been in office and though on the whole they may follow their party, will hurt the Crown in important debates by taking some popular pretext for differing from it or even by abstaining.[20]

Although Walpole could manipulate democracy, he could not entirely evade its consequences. His problems started to multiply in 1737, when his great ally Queen Caroline died, and thereafter, what with the costs of the 1739 War of Jenkins' Ear, the unpopular new treaty with Austria and the renewed opposition of Cobham's Cubs and their new-found readiness to work with the Tories, it was unclear how long Walpole could maintain his grip on power. He had managed to survive an opposition Whig motion of personal censure in each house in February 1741, as Tories had refused to support anything other than the dismissal of the whole ministry, but when the May–June 1741 election results were in it was clear that while he had increased his share of the vote in the shire seats he had lost ground in the boroughs, in part thanks to the intervention of the prince, who held many seats in his grasp as duke of Cornwall. Walpole could now rely on just 286 members, while Pulteney commanded 131 opposition Whigs and the Tories could muster 136. Parliament did not sit until December, but the first sign that Walpole was in trouble came with the election at the beginning of the session for the chair of the Committee of Elections (described late in the previous century as 'the most corrupt court in Christendom'[21]). The two sides dined apart before gathering in the Commons, whereupon Walpole proposed the re-election of Giles Earle, one of the Lords of the Treasury. Earle was reckoned to have left rather too many members smarting from his acerbic wit, so by a majority of just four the House preferred the opposition Whig Dr George Lee. All was not yet up, though, for a few days later the ministry managed to win (by three votes) the division on foreign policy, even though the Patriots had managed to exclude three government-supporting invalids by pouring sand in the keyhole of the door from the Speaker's chamber where they awaited the vote.

Ironically, it was the opposition's attempt to rig the election in Chippenham on 4 May 1741 that dealt the final blow to Walpole. Two opposition Whigs, Edward Rolt and Sir Edmund Thomas, were narrowly elected after bringing a large number of armed men into the town and arresting the government-supporting sheriff. When the ministry tried to use its majority in the Commons to overturn the election, it lost a procedural motion by a single vote on 28 January 1742. Although the business in hand had absolutely nothing to do with his own conduct, Walpole treated it as a personal matter and tendered his resignation to the king, just as news of the British defeat at Cartagena in the war against Spain broke in London. He left office with political and military defeat ringing in his ears – but with an earldom and an annual pension of £4,000 for life in his pocket.

Walpole was astute, a good parliamentary performer, an engaging host – and corrupt. His contemporaries knew it. Philip

Stanhope wrote of him that 'Money, not prerogative, was the chief engine of his Administration; and he employed it with a success that in a manner disgraced humanity . . . When he found anybody proof against pecuniary temptations, which, alas, was but seldom, he had recourse to a still worse art; for he laughed at and ridiculed all notions of public virtue.'[22] He also presided over an era of financial scandals. In 1723 John, Viscount Barrington, was expelled from the Commons for his fraudulent involvement in the Harburgh lottery; in 1725 Thomas Parker, the earl of Macclesfield, was impeached for taking £100,000 in bribes as Lord Chancellor; in 1732 Dennis Bond and John Birch were expelled from the Commons when their fraudulent management of the forfeited estates of James Radcliffe, the earl of Derwentwater, was discovered, while Walpole's close ally Sir John Eyles was allowed to get away with a mild reprimand; and later in the year George Robinson, Sir Robert Sutton and Sir Archibald Grant were thrown out of the Commons for embezzling funds from the Charitable Corporation.

Parliament has seen plenty of sibling partnerships. Walpole sat in the Commons alongside his brothers Horatio and Galfridus; George Grenville, First Lord of the Treasury from 1763 to 1765, had three brothers sitting with him in the House; and William Cavendish, the 4th duke of Devonshire, who was Prime Minister for seven months in 1756–7, sat in the Lords while his younger brother John sat in the Commons. Often, like the Miliband brothers or the twin Eagle sisters, siblings have served in the same government. But no two brothers have so dominated the political landscape as the two Pelhams did for the fifteen years following Walpole's resignation. They did not take over immediately; Walpole's immediate replacement as First Lord of the Treasury and nominal head of the administration was Spencer Compton, the younger son of the 3rd earl of Northampton, who had been Speaker and became the earl of Wilmington in 1730, while one of Sunderland's protégés, John, Lord Carteret, became the dominant force in the administration as Northern Secretary and Samuel Sandys became leader of the House of Commons and Chancellor of the Exchequer. But on 2 July 1743 Wilmington, one of just four unmarried prime ministers in British history, died at the age of seventy, while Carteret was in Hanover with the king. Pulteney, who had bizarrely abjured office when Walpole fell (in favour of an earldom), sought the premiership, but he had missed his chance: George II settled on a Pelham instead.

The elder Pelham was the tall, irascible, unpredictable and frequently lachrymose Thomas. Born on 21 July 1693, he inherited the considerable estates of his maternal uncle, John Holles, duke of Newcastle upon Tyne, in July 1711, and seven months later those of his father, Thomas, Lord Pelham of Laughton, leaving him at the age of nineteen a baron with an annual income of at least £32,000 and a considerable power of patronage over a string of seats. The younger brother, by contrast, was the affable and prudent Henry, born just fourteen months later but endowed with little more than £5,000 a year. From an early age both men were engaged in politics: Thomas took advantage of his seat in the Lords and in both 1717 and 1722 got Henry elected to the Commons. Both prospered under Walpole, but it was the younger brother who gained a Cabinet post first, becoming Secretary at War on 3 April 1724, eleven days before Newcastle was appointed as Southern Secretary. Again in 1730 the brothers' careers moved in parallel, for when Townshend resigned as Northern Secretary and was replaced by William Stanhope, Lord Harrington, Newcastle became the effective leader of the Lords, just as Pelham became Paymaster-General. Neither man cared for the oppositionist Whigs such as Carteret, who resigned in 1730, but when Walpole fell in 1742, the two brothers remained in post and managed to rub along with

Carteret when he was appointed Northern Secretary, even though Newcastle reckoned that 'our active Secretary, will at last find out, that dexterity with princes, to seem to promise all, and intend nothing, will as little do, as with private persons'.[23]

When Wilmington died, it was Pelham rather than Newcastle who became Prime Minister, partly thanks to his calm geniality and partly thanks to a growing consensus that it was better that an MP take the all-important post of First Lord of the Treasury, which he did in August 1743, becoming Chancellor of the Exchequer as well in December. It was a pattern that was soon to become normative as Walpole, Pelham and Pitt proved themselves in the Commons, while the Wilmington, Newcastle and Devonshire premierships flopped. But nothing was easy about this administration. Carteret's disdain for Pelham was palpable. Indeed, he acidly and arrogantly complained that Pelham 'was only a chief clerk to Sir Robert Walpole, and why he should expect to be more under me, I can't imagine: he did his drudgery and he shall do mine'.[24] Carteret was soon replaced by Harrington, but this did not smooth the way entirely, for even the relationship between the two brothers could often swing wildly from high regard to intense animosity. So, Newcastle said that Pelham had 'all the prudence, knowledge, experience, and good intention, that I can wish or hope in a man',[25] and paid him an annual pension of £1,000. Yet his brother's prominence rankled, and on another occasion he snootily declared: 'I do apprehend that my brother does think that his superior interest in the Closet, and situation in the House of Commons, gives him great advantage over everybody else. They are indeed great advantages, but may be counter-balanced, especially if it is considered over *whom* those advantages are given.'[26] So angry did he get with Pelham in 1745 that he announced that he would call on him every morning. 'There', he declared with a hint of menace, 'the scheme of the day shall be settled, to be handed out

to others afterwards, as shall be necessary; and a frequent intercourse with ease, at each other's houses, and at all hours and
times, will also make this very easy to us.'[27] Such peremptory
missives are perhaps the cross a younger but senior brother has
to bear, and a later letter from Pelham shows his calming style at
work: 'We cannot change our natures nor add to our understanding; we must therefore be satisfied with each other and
convinced that if we do differ, it is what we can't avoid, and
endeavour that those differences shall have as little effect upon
the Public and be as little known as possible.'[28]

The peacemaker throughout these tempestuous passages
was Philip Yorke, the earl of Hardwicke, who had risen with
impressive speed through the legal ranks, becoming Attorney-
General in 1720, aged twenty-nine, after just four years as a
barrister, and then progressing to Lord Chief Justice of the King's
Bench in 1733 and Lord Chancellor four years later. Hardwicke
was a man of his times. He happily led the attack on Atterbury
and gave legal opinion that slavery was lawful. Yet, despite having
been tutor to Macclesfield's son and progressed thanks to his
patronage, he seems to have been unsullied and resolutely
impartial in his legal dealings. He was also sage, spotting that the
kind of sums that the war required would mean regular sessions
of parliament and that while 'in times of peace, sometimes a
session of parliament may be played with, and events waited for
. . . in time of war . . . the case is quite different'.[29]

With Carteret out of the way, the triumvirate could act in
close concert. In February 1746, hot on the heels of the victory
over a second Jacobite rebellion that had started in Scotland and
been barbarously bludgeoned to death there at Culloden,
and fed up with the king's constant intimations that he would
prefer a different set of ministers and policy, Pelham demanded
the appointment of one of Cobham's Cubs, William Pitt,
as Secretary at War. When George refused, Newcastle and

Hardwicke staged a mass resignation of ministers. It was impressively successful. First the two secretaries resigned, followed by Pelham and Hardwicke. The resignations gathered pace, with Henry Fox, one of the Lords of the Treasury, and William Cavendish, the 3rd duke of Devonshire, soon joined by the whole slate of treasury, admiralty and trade ministers. At first unabashed, George looked to Pulteney, now earl of Bath, to form a new administration, but after forty-eight hours and forty-five minutes he had managed to secure the support of only a single figure – Carteret – and was ignominiously forced to restore Pelham, turn his back on all the Pulteney allies and make Pitt, if not Secretary at War, then Vice-Treasurer in Ireland and after a few months Paymaster-General. Hardwicke attempted to console George by telling him that ministers were merely his instruments of government, but the monarch bitterly retaliated: 'Ministers are the kings in this country.'[30] The king was right. It was a significant development. Kings and queens had always been free to appoint whomsoever they chose, but the Pelham brothers and Hardwicke had cowed the king into submission, dragged much of the younger anti-Walpole Whig faction into their broad-bottomed government, and isolated Carteret with the tiny remaining grouping of Tories. To complete their tactical victory, Pelham called an election a year early in 1747 – and won it handsomely.

For all Pelham's natural talents, it was as much an accident of birth that denied Newcastle the premiership in 1743 and gave it to his commoner brother, but when Pelham died unexpectedly on 6 March 1754 there was a general consensus that it had to go to the duke this time. It was to be an unmitigated disaster.

Not everything had passed off smoothly in his brother's period in office. The Jewish Naturalisation Act of 1753, for instance, which made a very moderate accommodation for the growing number of Jewish financiers in England, was so unpopular that it had to be repealed within nine months of its passage. And although Pelham himself made little personal profit from office, his secretary, a Mr Roberts, later admitted that his master had helped maintain his dominance by bribery, as Roberts was charged with distributing significant retainers to MPs – often as much as £800 – standing in the Court of Requests on the day of the prorogation of parliament and conveying the money 'in a squeeze of the hand'.[31]

But at least Pelham was competent. Newcastle was not. Out of some misguided belief in his own powers, he took the Treasury into his own hands and depended on the less than exciting talents of his old schoolmate, Thomas Robinson, to lead the government in the Commons as Southern Secretary rather than calling on either of the far more able MPs Henry Fox or William Pitt. It was a foolishly sentimental decision. Robinson had declared to Newcastle that since he had 'a habitude of thinking more than of speaking . . . nothing but a good heart and the mite of a single vote is to be expected from me',[32] and the opposition in the Commons, led by Pitt and Fox, immediately set about ridiculing his peculiar voice and his attempts at oratory with such success that even his friends could not keep a straight face. Within a year he gratefully retired with a healthy pension and Fox took his place. By now the piqued Pitt was on permanent harassment duty and mockingly described Fox and Newcastle as being like the two French rivers, the Rhône and the Saône, that come together at Lyons, the one a 'gentle, feeble, languid stream, and though languid of no depth', the other 'a boisterous and overbearing torrent'.[33] Just weeks after Pelham's death Newcastle had won another general election victory, with the Tories and opposition Whigs securing just 148 seats to Newcastle's 368, so parliamentary heft was never the problem. What eventually did for Newcastle, though, was his lack of capability in foreign affairs – in either might or insight. For his foreign policy had hinged on wooing Austria into an anti-French alliance, but when Austria sided with France, and both started harassing British colonies in north America, opinion turned sharply, especially when the French managed to seize the British garrison of Fort St Philip on Minorca on 29 June 1756. Newcastle was forced into political retreat and parliament was constantly prorogued until December, by which time both Newcastle and Fox had resigned.

The loss of Minorca occasioned a great deal of nauseating opportunism and national hysteria. In search of a scapegoat, the public landed on the figure of Admiral John Byng, head of the British navy at Minorca and MP for Rochester, who, despite an appeal for clemency from Pitt and the Commons, was shot on 14 March 1757 on board HMS *Monarch*, in Voltaire's famous words 'pour encourager les autres'. Ironically, the Minorca debate saw one otherwise odious creature partially redeem himself. For George Bubb, who had assumed his uncle's name of Dodington when he inherited his estate, was a notoriously inconstant ally who at various times sought Walpole's patronage, urged Wilmington to supplant Walpole and begged Walpole to sack Wilmington. He secured profitable office as Treasurer of the Navy under Pelham, but soon jumped ship, backing Prince Frederick's Leicester House oppositionists in the hope of a peerage. By the time of the 1754 election he had represented Bridgwater for thirty-two years, but his reputation was such that an excoriating attack on him, probably penned by Lord Egmont, had labelled him 'the most tawdry man in the nation' and Horace Walpole called him 'the reprostituted prostitute'.[34] After what he described as three days 'spent in the infamous and disagreeable compliance with the low habits of venal wretches',[35] he lost to Egmont at Bridgwater and transferred himself to Weymouth and Melcombe Regis, the unique four-berth cabin that he virtually controlled. Amazingly, Newcastle brought him back to his old post at the navy and in 1761 he was granted a peerage. John Tucker, a fellow MP for Weymouth, whom Dodington appointed as his cashier at the navy, wrote of him in 1742 that 'All Great Men are alike. The only difference is that some are less scrupulous to avow themselves than others.'[36] But Dodington did have one moment of genuine greatness, for while many were demanding Byng's execution, Dodington made what Horace Walpole called a 'humane and pathetic speech' in his defence.[37]

Political squabbling brought about another constitutional innovation in 1756–7. Newcastle commanded the majority of Whigs and, despite being nominally a Whig, Pitt held the respect of the Tories and the Leicester House set (led after the prince's death in 1751 by the dowager princess of Wales). Yet both Newcastle and King George loathed Pitt – and Pitt refused to serve with Newcastle, who had so ignominiously overlooked him. The temporary result was an inherently unstable adminis-tration reluctantly agreed to in December 1756, in which the duke of Devonshire became nominal head of the government and Pitt was made Southern Secretary and leader of a House of Commons in which he could not command a majority. Pitt was very confident of his own ability. He even told Devonshire, 'I am sure I can save this country, and no one else can,'[38] but the administration foundered once parliament began to sit and in April George dismissed Pitt, leaving Devonshire to totter on without a government spokesman in the Commons. Then came a decisive moment. With public concern about Bourbon and Prussian successes in the Seven Years War growing, corporation after corporation granted the sacked Pitt the freedom of their city. As Horace Walpole put it, 'it rained gold boxes'. Clearly the Commons or the king might not want Pitt to lead, but the public did – and for the first time public opinion determined the premiership. In July George reached for the only remaining option, a Pitt–Newcastle administration, brokered by Hardwicke, with Pitt as secretary of state, the duke at the Treasury, Fox as Paymaster, George Grenville as Treasurer of the Navy and his brother Richard (now Lord Temple) as Lord Privy Seal. Of the Cobham Cubs, only George Lyttelton was now out of office; perhaps his compensatory peerage was adequate consolation as, according to Horace Walpole, his 'warmest prayer was to go to heaven in a coronet'.[39]

Once again the Tories were entirely excluded from office, but this wartime coalition government was as successful as the standalone Newcastle ministry had been a failure. Tradition has it that Pitt was the political hero of the hour, as he had charge of foreign and war policy and Newcastle was restricted to home affairs and the Treasury. In Temple's words, Pitt was 'minister for measures' and Newcastle 'minister for numbers'. Yet even the tempestuous Newcastle could be invaluable when he deployed his Commons troops to good effect and he now played his subservient role well, furnishing Pitt with the financial resources he needed to prosecute a fierce war effort. In North America Louisburg, Fort Niagara and Fort Carillon were taken, Quebec was held and the French surrendered their last hold on Canada at Montreal. With victories secured by Robert Clive at Plassey and Sir Eyre Coote at Wandiwash, followed by the surrender of the French capital Pondicherry, India was British. Even the inso-lent French attempt at an invasion of Britain in 1759 was prevented by dramatic naval victories at Lagos (where British forces were led by Edward Boscawen MP) and Quiberon Bay.

Despite the innovative role of public opinion in raising Pitt to the premiership, it was not military failure, political folly or public opinion that ended the Pitt–Newcastle ministry, but the whim of a new king. For on 25 October 1760, at the age of seventy-six, George II died and his place was taken by his 22-year-old grandson. George III had little time for partisan politics and retained an inordinate affection for his tutor, John Stuart, the Scottish earl of Bute, whom he made Northern Secretary. Pitt had previously been aligned with the Leicester House group led by the new king's father and mother, but he was the first of the ministry to depart the scene when his plan to declare war on Spain was opposed by Bute and the king in October 1761. Newcastle followed soon after, tendering his resignation to George amid many tears on 26 May 1762. He attempted one final heave that autumn, when he tried to get those of his allies who remained in office to resign their posts in opposition to the peace treaty which both he and Pitt felt was far too generous to the French, but when few did, Bute exacted the 'massacre of the Pelhamite innocents'. Newcastle was not quite done with public office yet, though, for when Charles Watson-Wentworth, the 2nd marquess of Rockingham, was asked to form a new ministry in 1765, Newcastle was still the unofficial chairman, if not the leader, of the Whigs and was made Lord Privy Seal. The ministry lasted just twelve months and seventeen days before Pitt was back again – at which point Newcastle, who had been in office now for the best part of five decades, stepped into the strange shadows of opposition.

Early in 1768 parliament lost one of the century's dominant figures: Arthur Onslow, who in 1727, like his uncle and another forebear, rose to be Speaker – and who, unlike any of his predecessors, was re-elected in 1735, 1741, 1747 and 1754, thereby achieving the longest period in office of any Speaker thus far. The caprice of history has portrayed him as a man of outstanding probity in an era of pervasive corruption. He would have agreed. Indeed, he proudly declared: 'I loved independency, and pursued it. I kept firm to my original Whig principles, upon conscience, and never deviated from them to serve any party cause whatsoever.'[40] It is true that through his thirty-three years as Speaker Onslow regularly proved himself his own man, voting

381

against his great friend Walpole's ministry. Moreover, according to Philip Stanhope, the calculating 4th earl of Chesterfield, he 'made himself many personal friends in the minority',[41] so much so that Horace Walpole reckoned that 'the Opposition, to flatter his pretence to popularity and impartiality, call him their own Speaker'.[42] He also carried himself with authority in the role and developed a belief 'that the forms of proceedings, as instituted by our ancestors, operated as a check and control on the actions of ministers; and that they were, in many instances, a shelter and protection to the minority, against the attempts of power'.[43] And he was an innovator. The Commons had resolved in 1693 that any member officially 'named' by the Speaker would be subject to the House's censure, but it was Onslow who started regularly naming unruly members, and from him stems the still extant tradition that a 'named' member should withdraw from the House or be removed by the Sergeant-at-Arms. But Onslow was no constitutional saint. He proclaimed that he was not moti-vated by 'employments or riches', only admitting that he courted 'fame and respect' too much.[44] Yet while Speaker he took the lucrative post of Treasurer to the Navy for nine years and contin-ued to receive gratuities from the promoters of private Bills; and when he retired he ensured he left with a pension of £3,000 a year not just for his life but also for that of his son.

Onslow died at his home in Great Russell Street in London on 17 February 1768, while Newcastle was still struggling on, weighed down by enormous debts occasioned by a habit of financial recklessness that had seen him throw extravagant parties, treat thousands of voters and extravagantly refashion his homes at Claremont and in Lincoln's Inn Fields. Out of office, he suffered a stroke in December 1767, and though he limped back to London for the following autumn's session of parliament, on 17 November 1768 he died at home.

Historians have tended to see Walpole as a corrupt megalomaniac, Onslow as a parliamentary saint, Pelham as a mediocrity and Newcastle as a manipulative buffoon. But the more important reality beyond these caricatures is that the constant majority guaranteed to the Whigs in both houses kept the public at bay and ensured that politics remained a private competition for favour and position. The one-party state was to change, but not yet.

One election demonstrates quite how undemocratic parliament still remained. The general election that began when parliament was dissolved on 11 March 1768 saw just eighty-three contests. One, in Preston, was particularly violent. The Commons had determined in 1661 that Preston's electorate consisted of 'the inhabitants' of the borough, but for a long time this had been presumed to mean just the resident freemen, a much smaller number, and in consequence the corporation had effective control of the borough's two parliamentary seats. James Smith Stanley, Lord Strange, who was the eldest son of the 11th earl of Derby and sat in the Commons for Lancashire for thirty years from 1741 to 1771, wanted Preston to return two MPs who would support the government in which he was Chancellor of the Duchy of Lancaster, namely his brother-in-law, Colonel (later General) John Burgoyne, and another Lancashire ally, Sir Henry Hoghton. After voting began on 21 March it became clear that the corporation's two candidates, Sir Peter Leicester and Sir Frank Standish, were winning a narrow majority among the freemen. Immediately Strange demanded that there be a poll of all the 'inhabitants at large' and drafted in some of his father's local colliers to make mayhem in the town. Such was the atmosphere that when Burgoyne heard that the mayor had been doling out weapons from an arsenal at the town hall to corporation supporters in an attempt to prevent the freemen having 'an alien palmed upon [them]', he turned up himself with a loaded pistol in each hand and an armed guard. One voter claimed in the

March edition of the *Gentleman's Magazine* that the town was in 'imminent danger' and worried that 'tonight or tomorrow will be fatal to many. This is shocking work in a civilized country.' The mayor continued to insist that only freemen were entitled to vote and duly declared Leicester and Standish elected; but after the first short session of parliament that met in May and June, he was forced to hold a second poll of all inhabitants on 11 September, which put Burgoyne and Hoghton ahead by more than two to one (even when twenty-eight 'papists' were illegally allowed to vote for the corporation candidates). When parliament sat again that November a Commons committee, dominated by the administration, determined that Burgoyne and Hoghton had been duly elected. That was not the end of the matter, though. The following year Burgoyne was prosecuted for inciting violence at the election. He was fined £1,000 and narrowly escaped the prison sentence that his three sergeants and drummers were given. And yet such was the administration's support for Burgoyne that the Prime Minister, the duke of Grafton, not only paid the fine but also gave him the well-paid post of Governor of Fort George in Scotland. Electoral chicanery, bribery, tight government management of the Commons committees for electoral returns, even violence: eighteenth-century Britain was no beacon of Enlightenment.

Above: Politicians including Thomas Cromwell and the earl of Shaftesbury produced whipping lists of supporters and opponents before key divisions. This list of lords dates from 1703.

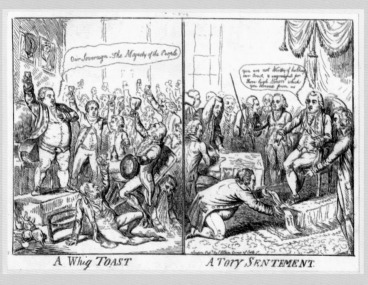

Rivalry between Whigs, derisively named after Scottish cattle-drivers or 'whiggamors', and Tories, equally contemptuously named after Irish robbers or *tóraí*, dominated parliament between 1680 and 1850.

The Scottish parliament, which came into existence in 1235, sat as a single house incorporating the 'three estates' of bishops, lords, and burgh and county commissioners (**above**, in the procession or 'Riding' to the Parliament House). It was persuaded to vote for the Act of Union in 1707 (**below**) only after the financially disastrous Darien Scheme.

Above: As of 1707 Scotland sent forty-five MPs and sixteen representative peers to Westminster. They were often treated with contempt by the English, as in this satirical print of 1784.

Below: Henry Grattan addresses the Irish House of Commons in 1780 to demand the repeal of repressive English legislation.

The political longevity of some eighteenth-century figures was phenomenal. Sir Robert Walpole (**opposite, above**, addressing his Cabinet) was Prime Minister for twenty-one years. The duke of Newcastle (**opposite, below left**, with his nephew, the earl of Lincoln) succeeded his younger brother as Prime Minister and was a minister for nearly forty-five years. Arthur Onslow (**right**, in a drawing by George Townshend MP) was Speaker from 1728 to 1761, and William Pitt was a minister for fifteen years and an MP for thirty-four before joining the Lords, where he collapsed on 7 April 1778 (**below**) before dying one month later.

Above: Corruption was endemic in contested eighteenth-century elections. Voters were wined, dined and bribed at extraordinary cost, as here in William Hogarth's version of the Oxfordshire contest of 1754.

Below: Parliamentary dynasties were common. Both William Pitt and Henry Fox were ennobled after years as MPs, and had younger sons who followed in their footsteps – and in loathing one another.

Published for the History of the Westminster & Middlesex Elections. Nov.' 1806.

The far from secret election of two MPs for
Westminster was often fiercely contested.
In 1784 the Duchess of Devonshire (**top**)
led supporters of Charles James Fox, who
came second to the Tory, Admiral Samuel
Hood. The hustings scene at Covent Garden
in November 1806 (**above**) shows the 'state
of the poll', with another Admiral Samuel
Hood leading James Paull and Richard
Brinsley Sheridan.

The concept of parliamentary honour
was felt so strongly that it prompted many
MPs to fight duels well into the nineteenth
century, or even to take their own lives, as
Lord Castlereagh did (**right**).

The chapel of St Stephen's, remodelled by Sir Christopher Wren, was the overcrowded, poorly ventilated and noisy scene of rumbustious battles. The atmosphere of apparent calm in this depiction of William Pitt the Younger's call for war against France in 1793 is not reflected in contemporary accounts of the occasion.

The Stamp Act of 1765 was so resented in the North American colonies that the Prime Minister, George Grenville, was replaced by the marquess of Rockingham, who was committed to its repeal. This satire, commissioned by Rockingham, shows the supporters of the Stamp Act gathered for its funeral.

12

Revolution and Reaction

WHEN THE DEVOUT, RESTRAINED young George III came to the throne in 1760 he decided 'to put an end to those unhappy distinctions of party called Whigs and Tories, by declaring that I would countenance every man that supported my Administration and concurred in that form of government which had been so wisely established by the Revolution'.[1] After the luxurious corruption of the era of one-party hegemony, this sounds like magnificent wisdom. But in truth, by 1760 neither party was much more than a hollowed-out husk. The Tories, once united and strong in their quasi-Jacobite ideology and their opportunistic association with George's father Frederick, the prince of Wales, entered the new era blinkingly excited that they were no longer to be excluded from office. But they were few in number – just 113 were elected in the 1761 parliament – and after so many years of cooperating with oppositionist Whigs their views were barely distinctive or coherent. Indeed, one of their number, Sir Roger Newdigate, rejected the term 'Tories' for the group that had engaged in the 'sisyphian labour' of opposing 'a 50 years Whig administration', reckoning they should more properly be termed a 'country party in opposition to administration'.[2] Nor could the Whigs claim any greater coherence as a political force, as among their ranks the strongest loyalties were not to party but to person. Newcastle, Grenville, Pitt, Rockingham, Fox: all commanded their own parliamentary platoons and rarely stood united. So a pronounced political fluidity was the order of the new Georgian day, with political principles taking a back seat behind considerations of personal advancement and remuneration. Politics had deteriorated into a quasi-medieval style of parliamentary feudalism, with new 'barons' holding sway. To quote W. B. Yeats, in such circumstances all too often 'things fall apart; the centre cannot hold', for 'the best lack all conviction, while the worst / Are full of passionate intensity'.[3]

In practice, George's determination that he should be free to appoint whomsoever he wanted meant bringing in his old tutor, mentor, surrogate father and rumoured lover to his mother, John Stuart, earl of Bute, first as Northern Secretary alongside Pitt and then, once Newcastle and Pitt had left office, as First Lord of the Treasury in May 1762. Bute was amiable enough, although his shyness often came across as haughtiness and he was so noncommittal as a politician that, having been elected as a representative Scottish peer in 1737, he failed to stand again in 1741. All this endeared Bute yet more to the young king, but it meant that without any political base in either the Commons or the Lords, his position was entirely dependent on royal favour. So within a year the combined forces of Pitt and the remaining old corps Whigs under Newcastle had so undermined him that he only just managed to scrape through an Excise Act incorporating a duty on cider promoted by Sir Francis Dashwood, his Chancellor of the Exchequer. It was a victory Bute would have been better off without, for those who still considered themselves Tories disliked any new duty and Whigs railed against the provisions that allowed excise officers to enter people's homes. There were widespread public demonstrations. Frederick Keppel, the bishop of Exeter, was hissed and pelted with apples for having voted for the duty, and Sir John Philips MP was dragged out of his carriage in Monmouth and forced to plead for mercy. The issue also forced the Tory MP William Dowdeswell to switch party allegiance, and he ended up as the Whig Chancellor in Rockingham's administration, which repealed the duty in 1766. But for now, despite the opposition of some 120 MPs and 39 peers, the cider excise was carried. With mass national opprobrium being heaped on him daily in lampoons and sketches, Bute resigned, ceding the way to the man he had removed as leader of the Commons, George Grenville, the second of Cobham's Cubs to become First Lord of the Treasury.

The terrain facing Grenville as the new First Lord was strewn with rocks. The king still resorted to Bute for advice, manifestly disliked Grenville and resented what Henry Fox described as his lengthy orations, complaining that 'a dose so large and so nauseous often repeated was too much for anyone's stomach'.[4] Grenville had also fallen out with Pitt and his own brother, Lord Temple, in 1761. Moreover, the cider excise was still needed to balance the books. As Grenville asked Pitt in the Commons, 'Let the honourable gentleman tell me where you can lay another tax, let the honourable gentleman, I say, tell me where.' Pitt, on cruel form, then started to mimic his brother-in-law, murmuring the popular ballad, 'Where, gentle shepherd? Tell me where?' Grenville went apoplectic, but as Pitt bowed contemptuously, the Commons erupted in laughter. Grenville was stuck with the cider excise – and with the epithet 'gentle shepherd'.[5]

One of the ironies of being in opposition is that all too often the government policies that you most detest and most vociferously condemn are the very policies that come back and embarrass you. Sometimes that is because governments lay intentional booby-traps, but such conspiracies are far more rare than the genuine political cock-up – which is the best description of the stamp duty of 1765. The rationale was understandable enough. The North American colonies were expensive to defend, and the people of Boston, Massachusetts were as subject to British law as those of Boston, Lincolnshire; it was time they contributed more towards their own defence. The answer, so ran the Grenville line, was 'a Bill for granting certain Stamp Duties, and other Duties, in the British Colonies and Plantations in America; and for applying the same towards further defraying the Expenses of defending, protecting, and securing such Colonies and Plantations'. Grenville had met with the four agents for the colonies, Benjamin Franklin, Jared Ingersoll, Richard Jackson MP and Charles Garth MP, to discuss the matter, but in the absence of any other ideas, ploughed on with the Bill, which came to the Committee of Ways and Means on 6 February 1765. The debate was heated. Two MPs who had substantial plantations in Jamaica, William Beckford and Rose Fuller, questioned the wisdom of proceeding with the duty. But Charles Townshend, who it was reckoned 'knew his superiority over all men, and talked of it',[6] led with his chin, asking whether 'these Americans, children planted by our care, nourished by our indulgence until they are grown to a high degree of strength and opulence, and protected by our arms, will they grudge to contribute their mite to relieve us from the heavy weight of that burden which we lie under?'[7] Within months his support for the government was to be rewarded with the post of Paymaster-General, but in the debate he was shot down by a spontaneous fusillade from Colonel Isaac Barré, a Dubliner of French Huguenot extraction who had fought at Louisbourg and lost an eye in the attack on Quebec:

They, planted by your care? No! Your oppressions planted them in America. They fled from your tyranny to a then uncultivated and unhospitable country where they exposed themselves to almost all the hardships to which human nature is liable . . . They, nourished by your indulgence? They grew by your neglect of them . . . They, protected by your arms? They have nobly taken up arms in your defence . . . God knows I do not at this time speak from motives of party heat, what I deliver are the genuine sentiments of my heart . . . The people I believe are as truly loyal as any subjects the King has, but a people jealous of their liberties and who will vindicate them if ever they should be violated.[8]

It was one of the great Commons rebuttals – but it did not win the vote when Grenville submitted the Bill to the full House eight days later. Indeed, the opposition could only scratch together forty-nine votes on 27 February 1765, and on 5 March the Lords agreed it without amendment. The Stamp Act received royal assent by commission (as George III was ill and unable to attend parliament) on 22 March 1765, to take effect on 1 November.

When George recovered he was so incensed by the Regency Bill that Grenville had proposed that he replaced him in July with Rockingham, who despite wishing to repeal the stamp duty then bore the full brunt of the ferocious anger that rapidly swept America. There were riots in New York, Boston and Newport. British officers were hanged in effigy. The legislatures sent official protests and the colonies started to combine their efforts, holding a special Stamp Act Congress in October. British merchants complained that their trade was at risk, while the new government was in agonies over how to extricate itself from the Grenville-made mess. Some now argued that the Stamp Bill had been easier to oppose before its enactment than it was to repeal now it was law. After all, the Commons had the legal right to impose taxes across all its dominions, and even Whigs who ardently proclaimed the principle of 'no taxation without representation' were reluctant to abjure Commons sovereignty. From the opposition, Grenville and his fellow former ministers defended their old legislation with the active support of the king, who demanded that his friends oppose any repeal, even if his own government proposed it. Yet others were not only frightened by the evident American antipathy, but felt that the American cause was a new battle for liberty. Pitt openly rejoiced that America had resisted, arguing that 'America, if she fell, would fall like the strong man. She would embrace the pillars of the state and pull down the constitution with her.'[9]

For months Rockingham sucked his pencil while gently encouraging British merchants to make their problems with the Act known. When he finally came down in favour of complete repeal of the Act in the new year, it was only to find himself thwarted by the king's friends in the shape of Bute, the old Tory families and the former ministers, who helped carry a motion in the Lords by a hefty majority on 6 February endorsing armed enforcement of the Act. The same motion was tabled by an overexcited Grenville the next day in the Commons, but the new Southern Secretary Henry Conway was assisted by another Whig general, George Howard, who had fought at Fontenoy and Culloden; both now argued that they would hurt themselves before they would attack Americans 'contending for liberty'. With such opposition, the motion was easily defeated by 274 to 134. Buoyed up by this Commons support, Rockingham furiously objected to George about his intolerable royal interference and threatened resignation, but when the king failed to appoint another ministry, Rockingham came up with a classically elegant but politically naive British compromise. Two new Bills were agreed on the same day, one repealing the Stamp Act, the other reasserting the sovereignty of the British parliament over the

American colonies and its right to impose taxes upon them 'in all cases whatsoever'. Only Pitt and a very few others voted against this 'Declaratory Act', but although the merchants gathered outside Westminster cheered and the bells rang out in London, nobody was ultimately satisfied. The colonists now had a cause to fight for, the government had a hole in its budget and the king had so irretrievably fallen out with his ministry that Rockingham had to go. In a curious quirk of fate it was Pitt, in a deal with the duke of Grafton as First Lord of the Treasury, who took over the administration from the strange vantage point (for the self-proclaimed 'great commoner') of a seat in the Lords as earl of Chatham and Lord Privy Seal.

Pitt's administration was no more stable than either of its predecessors. Edmund Burke described it as 'utterly unsafe to touch and unsure to stand on',[10] and public opinion soon showed itself a fickle mistress as a dinner to celebrate Pitt's premiership was cancelled when it was known that he had accepted an earldom. But many of the problems lay inside Pitt himself. Grafton thought that, despite his superior talents, 'he did not possess that of conciliating mankind'.[11] His arrogant sense of his own accomplishments in the Seven Years War, his refusal to engage in the day-to-day management of parliament and his rejection of party factionalism left him without allies and he started losing important votes. At the heart of the problem, though, were recurrent bouts of mental illness that left him in 'tears and trembling' when anyone mentioned business,[12] and reduced him by the end of March 1767 to 'the lowest dejection and debility that mind or body can be in'.[13] Nineteen miserable isolated months later he resigned, and although he returned to the parliamentary fray he was never to return to political office.

In an early portrait of Frederick, Lord North, by Pompeo Batoni (which hangs in the Committee corridor of the Commons) he looks contemplative, at ease with himself and modishly *distrait* in his attire. In another, painted just a few years later by Sir Nathaniel Dance (who went on to be an MP), he cuts a very different figure. In this one, North is thrust back in his chair as if astounded at something he has glimpsed over the viewer's left shoulder. He is only forty, yet his jowls are full, his skin pallid, his eye alarmed. Not a man in whom to put one's confidence. Yet, extraordinarily, North was to remain First Lord of the Treasury from 1770 for twelve years and two months, bringing stability to the political terrain after six years of constant shift. North has suffered in the history books as the royal marionette who lost America through intransigence and poor strategy, but his well-covered frame, his physical similarity to the king and his general air of affable bewilderment belied a self-aware and an often witty politician, who was only too conscious of his own limitations. He had an easy way with him which he explained to the Commons:

> It was the etiquette of the Minister, if he could not grant the favour asked of him, at least to send home the person refused in good humour. This was well understood by courtiers; but for such ignorant honest country gentlemen as the Honourable Member, he thought it right to explain, that, when he only nodded, or squeezed the hand, or did not absolutely promise, he always meant No.[14]

True, North also had a habit of nodding off, as when he fell asleep during a lengthy Grenville speech detailing every aspect of the history of the constitution. But even then he was witty. Awoken by a particularly loud passage, he complained: 'You have wakened me nearly one hundred years too soon!'[15]

Having started life relatively poor, as the eldest son of Francis, earl of Guildford, North found himself a seat at the age of twenty-two and soon gained office, but only really started to make his name through his very determined pursuit of Wilkes and his support for the Stamp Act. North has been labelled a Tory, but more than anything he was a political survivor. Appointed to the Treasury Board in 1759 under Newcastle, he survived under Bute and Grenville and had just a year in opposition under Rockingham before Chatham made him Paymaster-General in July 1766 and he joined the Privy Council in December. The next September, on the premature death of the quixotic Chancellor of the Exchequer, Charles Townshend, Grafton, who had effective control of the government given Chatham's mental illness, breathed a sigh of relief as he appointed dependable, reliable North in his stead as the government's lead spokesman in the Commons. And when the ministry's latest attempt to quell Wilkes failed in January 1770, Grafton stepped down and North took over.

North's most immediate problem was the worsened situation across the Atlantic, but with the king adamant that no concessions should be made to the colonists and a clear majority in both the Commons and the Lords supporting a robust defence of the constitutional right of parliament to enforce laws on America, North was hideously ill equipped to face the impending storm. His own intransigence didn't help. When the Cabinet had met in 1769 to discuss what to do about a range of duties that had been instituted by Townshend to replace the stamp duty, North had voted, against Grafton and with the majority of five to four, in favour of retaining the duties. So in 1770 he presented a compromise: all the other duties would be repealed because they affected British manufacturers, but the duty on tea, which was a good source of revenue, would be retained. This was bad enough, but the colonists could just as easily buy illegally imported Dutch tea, which might not have so good a flavour but at least tasted of liberty. Sales of British tea fell dramatically, and soon the East India Company had full

warehouses and empty order books, so in 1773 North introduced a new Tea Act aimed at helping the British East India
Company sell off its vast stocks of surplus tea in London warehouses by loosening the legal restraints on the company and
thereby undercutting illegally imported tea in North America.
Campaigning colonists smelled a rat, and soon the government
had a rerun of the Stamp Act riots on its hands, when on 16
December 1773 a group of colonists known as the Sons of
Liberty (a term first coined by Barré in the Commons stamp
duty debate) from the city that paid the most duty, Boston, cast
three shiploads of tea into the harbour.

North was incensed, telling the Commons that 'the
Americans have tarred and feathered your subjects, plundered
your merchants, burnt your ships, denied all obedience to your
laws and authority'. But the political conclusion he drew was
utter folly. Arguing that Britain's conduct had been 'so clement
and so long forbearing', he urged MPs that it was now incumbent
on them 'to take a different course', insisting that 'whatever may
be the consequences, we must risk something; if we do not, all is
over'.[16] Many pointed out the dangers. But North's 'different
course' was rapidly adopted, in the shape of a series of retaliatory
measures, or 'Coercive Acts'. The Boston Port Act closed the
harbour until such time as compensation should be paid for the
tea. The Massachusetts constitution was summarily altered by
Westminster statute. Frigates were threatened. There was fierce
opposition to these measures in the Commons. James Adair
described them as 'the most violent, the most unjust and tyrannical, that ever disgraced the annals of any civilized nation',[17] and
Frederick Bull bemoaned 'those cruel and arbitrary measures,
which were recommended and have been fatally carried into
execution by an unfeeling, an unrelenting administration, who
have dared to abuse the throne by their wicked and sanguinary
councils, and whose whole conduct has proved them entirely

destitute of every principle of justice, humanity and the religion of their country'.[18] The American reaction was all too predictable. The other colonies backed Massachusetts and the fledgling Congress declared that Westminster had no right to legislate for America. Equally predictable was the counter-reaction: an even stronger determination of North and his allies to resolve the matter by force. In April 1775 battle was joined between British troops and local militias at Lexington and Concord, and on 23 August King George declared the American patriots traitors, thereby pushing them towards independence, which they eventually declared on 4 July 1776. Political mistakes were now compounded by military ineptitude when George Sackville, Lord Germain, the MP for East Grinstead, took over as American Secretary in November 1775; and when France and Spain added their battalions to the colonists' cause in 1778 and 1779, Britain was left fighting not just for its colonies but for its honour.

Westminster was far from impervious to events across the Atlantic. Rockingham's platoon of oppositionists might be paltry in number, but it had consistently warned against an obstreperous response to American claims and steadily gained adherents as the news of Saratoga, the Franco-Spanish invasion fleet in the Channel and other reversals came through. Some argued explicitly that the colonists' cause was that of liberty, that independence should be granted willingly and that the modern concerns of the colonists should be addressed with the principles of 1688, not the arbitrary tactics of the Stuarts. Thus John Dunning, the precise and scholarly MP for Calne, tabled two simple resolutions in the Commons on 6 April 1780, the latter of which was carried: 'That the influence of the Crown has increased, is increasing, and ought to be diminished.' For a government to lose such a motion today would mean instant resignation, but North, who still had the royal purse to hand, decided instead to call an early general election, which was held in September and October. When the results were all in he had splashed out an eye-watering £50,000 on candidates (£17,000 of which George expected him to meet himself) and lost a few seats, but he still had a majority in the Commons. What he did not have was victory in the war.

When the news of General Cornwallis's surrender to George Washington at Yorktown spread round Westminster on 25 November 1781, North knew that British rule in America was effectively over, even if his king and his American Secretary refused to give in. Indeed, so embarrassed was he by Germain's continuing in post that he refused to sit on the Treasury bench beside him on 14 December. Still George kept North, even as he lost a vote on continuing offensive war on 27 February. The final blow came when, after just scraping together a majority of ten on 8 March and nine a week later, North was visited by a group of independent MPs who came to tell him that they would not support him in a vote of confidence planned for 20 March. North had already tried to resign several times, but now made clear to the king 'that the fate of the present Ministry is absolutely and irrevocably decided'. Finally, leaving no room for doubt, he wrote to the king with equal clarity and elegance that 'Parliament have altered their sentiments, and as their sentiments whether just or erroneous, must ultimately prevail, your Majesty having persevered as long as possible, in what You thought right, can lose no honour if you yield at length . . . to the opinion and wishes of the House of Commons'.[19] In return the king viciously condemned his act of 'desertion', writing: 'If you resign before I have decided what I will do, you will certainly for ever forfeit my regard.'[20] On 20 March North arrived at the Commons for the debate and faced an orchestrated barracking from the opposition who were there to back the no confidence motion tabled by Charles Howard, the son of the 10th duke of Norfolk and

MP for Carlisle. For more than an hour the Speaker, Charles Cornwall, found it impossible to bring the House to order; when North was finally allowed to speak, he begged that it adjourn instead of proceeding with the humiliating motion, confessing that 'his Majesty has come to a full determination to change his ministers'.[21] Thus North resigned, the first Prime Minister to be forced out by the threat of a vote of confidence.

By this time North had outlived most of his rivals for the premiership. Newcastle had died in 1768 and Grenville in 1770. The next to fall was Chatham, the great orator, political shape-shifter and occasional genius, called by Hardwicke 'the great actor',[22] ridiculed by Barré as 'the gentleman, with solemn looks, with eyes uplift to heaven, one hand beating on his breast, and formally contradicting and disowning the principles he had maintained the day before',[23] and decried by Edmund Burke for his tendency 'to keep hovering in the air, above all parties, and to swoop down where the prey may prove best'. But Chatham had been prescient about America, and came to the House of Lords on 7 April 1778 to reply to the duke of Richmond's motion that peace should be concluded with America on any terms. This was painful, personal stuff for Chatham. He took pride in his conduct of the Seven Years War and could see the government squandering his legacy. Ever the tragedian, after a rambling, often incoherent speech tinged with moments of brilliance, he uttered his final words to parliament: 'My Lords, any state is better than despair; if we must fall, let us fall like men.'[24] Moments later in the debate he realized he had forgotten an important point and rose to speak again, but was suddenly convulsed with pain and collapsed into the arms of his son.* A month later on 11 May, he died.

* The eldest son of a peer was (and indeed still is) allowed to sit on the steps of the throne in the Lords.

With the field thus thinned out, the immediate choice for successor to North in 1782 was the leader of the old Newcastle faction, Rockingham; but on 1 July, just fourteen weeks after taking over and still only fifty-two years old, he too died, in an outbreak of influenza. Which left William Petty, the 2nd earl of Shelburne, Barré's old military companion and parliamentary ally and Rockingham's Home Secretary. Few others had a good word to say for him. His social equals disliked his radical attitudes and many of his potential allies feared his violent mood swings. Shelburne described Bute in words that many others might have applied to him: 'insolent and cowardly . . . he was rash and timid . . . he was ready to abandon his nearest friend if attacked'.[25] Nevertheless, in July 1782 Shelburne was the only man who could possibly take over from Rockingham in the final moments of the war. Like many ministries built on the *faute de mieux* principle, his was hampered from the outset by further royal interference, yet it managed to limp through the winter, divided and unhappy, before finally succumbing in April 1783, its sole achievement being a set of over-generous peace terms offered to the Americans.

It was time for a new generation, and the two men who led it would dominate parliament for twenty years and transform the political system. The elder of the two was the young Charles James Fox, as full of hatreds as his father Henry, but far more able as a speaker and less convinced that politics was just about holding office. Burke thought the young Fox 'one of the pleasantest men in the world, as well as the greatest genius that perhaps this country has ever produced',[26] and even William Wilberforce, whose religious enthusiasm might have made him critical of Fox's louche lifestyle (he twice gambled himself into bankruptcy and his dalliances with actresses, society beauties and the duchess of Devonshire were all well publicized), considered debates without him 'insipid and vapid'. Not that Fox cared much what others thought. As he said, 'he never cared what was said of his person. If he was represented ugly and was not so, those who knew him would do him justice, and he did not care for what he passed in that respect with those who did not'.[27]

The one person whose opinion did matter, though, was the king, who took a violent dislike to Fox, blaming him for every bout of debauchery indulged in by his own son, Fox's drinking companion the prince of Wales. Nevertheless, heavily promoted by his father, Fox prospered as a young man. Elected to parliament in 1768 at just nineteen years of age, he was a member of the Admiralty Board two years later and the Treasury Board in 1772, and the only barrier to further rapid promotion seemed to be his propensity for resigning: he stood down from the Admiralty over the Royal Marriages Act, and from the Treasury in high dudgeon that North refused to turn his nephew's title of Baron Holland into an earldom. Out of office just as the American war hove into view, Fox took a distinct turn away from his father's studied ministerialism, and just two months after his resignation was excoriating North and telling the Commons that 'countries should always be governed by the will of the governed'.[28] Soon he was leading the opposition charge in the Commons alongside Rockingham in the Lords, and in 1782 he accepted Rockingham's offer of the newly created Foreign Office. It was to be another short spell in government as Shelburne, then Home Secretary, won a vote in Cabinet overturning Fox's foreign policy just before Rockingham's death, whereupon Fox, Burke and John Cavendish resigned. Suddenly the old foes Fox and North were on the same side in opposition to Shelburne's ministry, and from this position North was as radical as Fox, declaring that 'the appearance of power is all that a King of this country can have'.[29] So, on the principle that my enemy's enemy is my friend, the two men attempted the boldest of coalitions.

This was an extraordinary turn of events. After all, Fox had been phenomenally rude about several of North's supporters, not least the MP William Adam, whom he called 'a Beast of Nature', a 'pest of Society' and a 'Libeller of Mankind',[30] and had taken a bullet in the stomach from him in a duel. Not surprisingly, the young William Pitt poured incredulous scorn on Fox for his self-serving volte-face, but Fox argued that, given the 'sacrifice of our chief possessions in America, Asia and Africa', it was clear the 'situation of the country required a coalition of parties'.[31] The crunch came in the shape of two debates in the Commons, both of which Shelburne lost, forcing him to resign on 24 February 1783. After a month of uncertainty the coalition government was formally constituted on 1 April, with Fox back as Foreign Secretary, North as Home Secretary and William Cavendish-Bentinck, the duke of Portland, as nominal head of the administration and First Lord of the Treasury. For the first time it was clear that losing a vote in the Commons could end a ministry, whatever the Lords or the king thought.

This administration might have been conceived in mutual hatred of Shelburne and distrust of King George, but its dissolution came about at royal command and under the instruction of the other dominant political figure in these closing years of the eighteenth century: Chatham's younger son, William Pitt. An MP at twenty-one and Chancellor of the Exchequer under Shelburne at twenty-three, he was a shrewd man who was keenly aware that while North and Fox could resolve all they wanted about the formal power of the throne, George III could always deliver a fatal blow to a ministry. So, when Burke and Fox proposed an East India Bill to rein in the corrupt practices of the East India Company, Pitt urged George to weigh in by telling his friends in the Lords that he would consider anyone who voted for the measure an enemy. Along with some twenty-six others, the newly appointed archbishop of Canterbury, John Moore, was persuaded to withdraw his previous support for the Bill, which was lost in the Lords by nineteen votes on 17 December 1783.

The rhetoric hit the fan. Pitt had already denounced Fox's argument that the India Bill was needed to prevent the complete collapse of the company with the stinging words: 'Necessity is the plea for every infringement of human freedom. It was the argument of tyrants; it was the creed of slaves.'[32] But now Fox had an even better chant: 'The deliberations of this evening must decide whether we are to be henceforward free men or slaves: whether this House is a palladium of liberty or the engine of despotism; whether we are prospectively to exercise any functions of our own, or to become the mere echo of secret influence.'[33] Pitt, desperate to deny any royal involvement, blatantly lied – and got his reward. George sacked Portland, Fox and North by letter at midnight the next day, and on the nineteenth the Commons gathered to hear the Solicitor-General, Richard Arden, announce in a comically high-pitched voice that there was to be a ministerial by-election as Pitt had accepted the twin offices of First Lord of the Treasury and Chancellor of the Exchequer. The immediate reaction of the Commons was to laugh at the effrontery of it all, but Pitt calmly turned his back on them to form a Cabinet from outside the House.

He did not have great material to work with. A few friends were brought in, many of them bibulous dinner companions, but with so many senior established political figures refusing to join what seemed like a doomed venture, he had to make do with the likes of Newcastle's great-nephew, Thomas Townshend, who was bumped up from the Commons to the Lords as Lord Sydney, and Francis Osborne, the marquess of Carmarthen, respectively for Home and Foreign Secretary, despite both men generally being reckoned to be 'unequal to the most ordinary business of their own offices'.[34] They were not the only ciphers. Pitt's tiny Cabinet of seven members was to be a singular venture, containing no member of the Commons – nor any man of substance – apart from himself. Little wonder Fox's friend Mrs Crewe thought that it was a 'mince-pie' administration that would not last out the Christmas season.

Unabashed by his unorthodox and downright unseemly route to power, Pitt proceeded to use every trick in the Hanoverian book to remain there. One friend whose father commanded several Commons seats was shunted up into the Lords. So were a cousin, Thomas Pitt, and Sir James Lowther, and Lord Weymouth's brother – all with the express intention of overturning the Fox–North majority by the time parliament gathered on 12 January, by which time Pitt was newly re-elected as MP for Appleby. Fox had confidently predicted a Commons majority of more than a hundred, but Pitt lost the first two divisions of the new session by just 39 and 54 votes, so clearly the steady drip of patronage was having its effect. Yet Fox still had the upper hand and managed to win three successive votes of no confidence. The irony of all this was that on so many issues Fox and Pitt had identical views. They were both still Whigs, and it is difficult to avoid the impression that the only real difference between them was that one was in office and the other was not. Certainly this was the view of many of the seventy or so independent MPs who gathered for a series of meetings in the St Albans Tavern in February under the leadership of Charles Marsham, Thomas Grosvenor and Thomas Powys, who called on Fox, Pitt and Portland to form a grand coalition government on the grounds that 'a union which was not founded in principle would be fallacious and injurious to the interest of the public'.[35]

The overtures to Pitt went unheeded because he was successfully wearing the opposition down, so that by 8 March the Foxite majority had dwindled to a single vote. Moreover, while Pitt had initially been reluctant to call an early election, by the spring he was ready. The king's cash was lubricating the wheels of an impressive electoral machine, and the new peers and converts were exercising their influence in favour of helpful candidates. An intimation of the campaign to come had been afforded on 28 February, when Pitt was granted the freedom of the City of London, to the accompaniment of a eulogy by Wilkes for Pitt's 'noble act of disinterestedness in favour of the public' in creating a broadly based administration.[36] Pitt's supporters were so excited that they drove Pitt and his brother, the new earl of Chatham, back through the streets of London and insisted on demonstrating outside the prince of Wales's residence at Carlton House. This left the two Pitt brothers provocatively stuck in their carriage just outside Brooks's club, known as a gathering place for Foxite Whigs – whereupon some of the loyal Foxite waiters and members of the club poured out deploying bludgeons and broken sedan chair poles to attack the carriage and try to drag Pitt out into the street. The Pitts managed to escape to the nearby refuge of the more congenial White's club, but Chatham later acknowledged, unsurprisingly: 'I never went to Brooks any more.'[37]

The general election was conducted in similar turbulent style. Indeed, Pitt told one ally to 'tear the enemy to pieces'. The attacks on Fox were ferocious. He was portrayed as Guy Fawkes, Satan and, even worse, Oliver Cromwell. Had there been an award for 'liberty campaigner of the year', it is difficult to know who would have won, with Pitt standing for reform of borough representation and Fox for reform in India and restraint of the royal prerogative. But the victor's crown went to Pitt. In Cambridge, he and his friend George Fitzroy, Lord Euston, ousted Fox's close friend John Townshend and the coalition's Solicitor-General James Mansfield in the two university seats. Elsewhere, not only did Pitt's allies see off the former Chancellor of the Exchequer, John, Lord Cavendish, in York and the unofficial Foxite whip George Byng at Middlesex, but some ninety-six coalition supporters were either frightened into not standing or lost their seats, and Pitt secured himself a majority of ninety-seven in the first division of the new parliament. As for Fox's own election in Westminster, the battle lasted for forty full days, with the running totals for each of the candidates being published every day and the prince of Wales, along with the great society beauty Georgiana, duchess of Devonshire, touring the streets in support of their friend. So bountiful was the treating by all the candidates that a Westminster voter can scarcely have wanted for food, wine or entertainment for nearly six weeks. The result was not clear until parliament was about to assemble. Admiral Hood came top with 6,694, Fox was second with 6,234 and Pitt's supporter Sir Cecil Wray came third with 5,998. Pitt still had a trick up his sleeve, though, for Wray immediately demanded a full scrutiny of the vote, which could take years, during which Fox would be excluded from taking a seat. Not to be outdone, Fox had hitched up a safety net, getting himself made a burgess of Kirkwall in Orkney (which he had never visited) to qualify for the distant Scottish seat of Tain Burghs.*

Pitt's success in the 1784 election was to be mirrored in his long mastery of the Commons and his dominance of the country's political affairs. For although he was to remain a deeply private person and a single man, his political style and administrative drive were to keep him in power for the longest period of any Prime Minister thus far since Walpole. In this he was considerably assisted by Fox and the French. For Fox had never had the political tidiness gene. Obsessive on the question of royal interference in the administration, which he would blame for every evil under Pitt's sun, Fox could often be lazy and selfish. At key moments, he was often distracted or absent. During the regency

---

* As things turned out, he didn't need it, eventually being allowed to take up his Westminster seat.

crisis of 1788–9, while George III was laid low by insanity probably caused by porphyria, Fox was at first abroad in Italy, only returning home three weeks after the crisis had erupted, and then insistent on taking lengthy periods of convalescence of his own from a series of minor illnesses, before making a complete fool of himself by demanding the rapid installation of his close friend the prince of Wales as regent with completely unfettered power. Since this flew straight in the face of his proudly declared hatred of royal despotism, Pitt just laughed. Fox was also prone to start things in an impressive blaze of colour, but fail to drive them through to a conclusion. So it was with his campaign to impeach Warren Hastings, the governor of Bengal, on charges of corruption and mismanagement. At first, in 1787, Fox was one of the core participants, along with the roistering Irish playwright Richard Brinsley Sheridan and the diligent Burke, but by the end he was a very rare attendee at the proceedings and Burke would sit alone to hear the legal arguments that came to an end with Hastings' acquittal on 23 April 1795.

The defining moment for the seventeen-year Pitt administration, though, came in 1789 with the French Revolution. Whigs had been reflecting smugly for decades that at least Britain was not as bad as France, where a despotic and luxurious king ruled his people without any pretence of consultation. So when the French Estates General were summoned for the first time since 1614, giving a voice to a Third Estate that looked rather like a French House of Commons, and when this led to the creation of the National Assembly, all good Whigs rejoiced. Even the storming of the Bastille on 14 July 1789 and the incarceration of the French royal family in the Tuileries, signalling the complete collapse of the French monarchy, was greeted with wild applause by every British political leader. Fox was exhilarated, writing that it was 'by much the greatest Event that has ever happened in the world'.[38] Pitt, too, thought that the revolution would lead to 'freedom rightly understood' and that it would render France 'less obnoxious as a neighbour'.[39] It was a state of grace that was to last at least until the start of 1792, when Pitt declared in his budget speech that developments in France proved that 'unquestionably there never was a time in the history of this country, when, from the situation of Europe, we might [more] reasonably expect fifteen years of peace, than we might at the present moment'.[40]

But by then two major splits had developed in the opposition ranks. For although Fox praised the new French constitution as 'the most stupendous and glorious edifice of liberty which had been erected on the foundation of human integrity in any time or country' (proving that hyperbole is the statesman's besetting sin),[41] his friend and ally Burke shied away in horror from what the revolutionaries were doing, and reckoned the French had shown themselves 'the ablest architects of ruin that had hitherto existed in the world'.[42] Burke hastened to get his arguments down in print, and in 1790 published an influential pamphlet, *Reflections on the Revolution in France*, asserting the priority of established rights such as that to private property over what he considered the entirely speculative rights to food or medicine espoused by the revolution. To many it was a flimsy argument. His account of the treatment of Marie Antoinette was described by his close friend and fellow Whig MP Philip Francis as 'pure foppery',[43] and when he insisted that 'we fear God, we look up with awe to kings; with affection to parliaments; with duty to magistrates; with reverence to priests; and with respect to nobility . . . because when such ideas are brought before our minds, it is *natural* to be so affected',[44] he inspired Thomas Paine to respond with his *Rights of Man* and Mary Wollstonecraft to pen *A Vindication of the Rights of Woman*. Fox, who never much bothered with religion, also disagreed, and matters came to a head in a Commons debate on 6 May 1791, when Burke responded to Fox's fulsome praise for the revolution with a declaration that while he had no desire to provoke enemies or to give his friends occasion to desert him, he felt he had to adhere to the traditional principles of the British constitution by condemning the events in Paris. Looking straight at Fox, he admitted that he was acting in the full knowledge that he had done his duty 'at the price of my friend', and added: 'Our friendship is at an end.'[45] Soon both men were in tears. Pitt was exultant. His opponents were divided.

They were also divided over the inauguration in April 1792 of the 'Society of the Friends of the People, Associated for the Purposes of a Parliamentary Reform'. This was the brainchild of a trio of leading Whigs, Sheridan, Charles Grey and Philip Francis, but expressly did not include Fox, who was troubled by any emphasis on constitutional change just as France was engaging in the constitutional equivalent of self-immolation. When the storming of the Tuileries and arrest of Louis came in August, followed first by the massacre of thousands of political prisoners in September, and then by Louis' trial and execution on 21 January 1793, Pitt's reaction was far more akin to that of Burke three years earlier. Now he feared both French aggression abroad and violent republican sentiment at home. These were not unreasonable fears. A dinner to celebrate the second anniversary of the fall of the Bastille had led to five days of riots in Birmingham. There was a harsh recession. The harvest had failed. So Pitt started to take what he termed 'necessary precautions', suspending habeas corpus, strengthening the army, hurrying an Aliens Bill through parliament and expelling the French ambassador. Again, this prompted open warfare within the Foxite contingent. For some, this was repressive despotism; for others, the homebred calls for reform were a disturbing sign of emerging Jacobin republicanism. The dividing lines were clear in the Aliens Bill debate in the Commons, when Burke claimed in a melodramatic speech that the country was already seething with Frenchmen armed to the teeth – and threw a knife to the floor as if to demonstrate his point. The shock was keenly felt, but Sheridan was quick to bring Burke down to earth. 'Where's the fork?' he demanded – and the House collapsed in laughter.

The fragmentation of the Foxite party gained pace when France declared war on Britain on 1 February, for while Fox remained adamantly pro-revolutionary, many of his erstwhile allies now deserted him. Burke was joined by Portland; by Rockingham's wealthy nephew and heir, the Earl Fitzwilliam; by James Harris, the earl of Malmesbury; and by William Windham, the bald-pated MP for Norwich. All were Whigs, but either through real anxiety about France or through personal disaffection with Fox, they were easily peeled off by Pitt. Fox summed up the disagreement in a letter to Fitzwilliam on 16 March 1792:

> You seem to dread the prevalence of Paine's opinions (which in most parts I detest as much as you do) while I am much more afraid of the total annihilation of all principles of liberty and resistance, an event which I am sure you would be as sorry to see as I. We both hate the two extremes equally, but we differ in opinions with respect to the quarter from which the danger is most pressing.[46]

Whatever the reason, by May 1793 Malmesbury was forlornly claiming that the party was 'dispersed and broken' – a fact demonstrated by Fox's tiny muster of just fifty votes in the king's speech debate.

Fox was looking an increasingly lonely figure – not that you would know it from the Austrian painter Karl Anton Hickel's massive canvas in the National Portrait Gallery, which shows Pitt in full rhetorical flow in the Commons, with Addington in the Speaker's chair and Fox, Sheridan and the great lawyer Thomas Erskine apparently surrounded by supporters on the opposition benches. The drift continued as Pitt persuaded Lord Loughborough to defect and become Lord Chancellor in January 1793. Then Windham set up his own grouping, the 'third party', together with twenty-six others; and in January 1794 Portland announced that as far as he, the Whig leader in the Lords, was concerned, hostility to the war was over. That summer, four more former opposition members joined the newly enlarged Cabinet, including Portland as Home Secretary and Windham as Secretary at War.

At first Fox's much-diminished band were resilient. They had plenty to rail against. Grey urged parliamentary reform, Sheridan tabled motions condemning the arrest of several supposedly Jacobin members of the Society of the Friends of the People, Fox declaimed against the arrest and deportation of the Scottish radicals Thomas Muir and Thomas Fyshe Palmer, and when a new round of trials of twelve radicals began in 1794, Erskine represented them for no fee and won their acquittal. In the Commons, though, there were no such victories. After the king's coach came under attack on the way to the state opening of parliament in 1795, Pitt had no difficulty driving through yet more repressive legislation in the shape of the Seditious Meetings and Treasonable Practices Acts, which introduced a penalty of seven years' deportation for even campaigning in favour of reform. Grey grew despondent, arguing that the Fox group's constant exertions, which 'only subjected [them] to daily insult', were fruitless, as they did not even bring 'any benefit to the country'. Some politicians delight in being in a minority of one. Indeed, in one episode of solitary opposition to a government measure, Pitt the Elder had said that he appeared in the Commons as Eve did in the garden, single and naked, yet not ashamed. Fox, who was as sceptical about hard work as he was about the value of parliamentary attendance, was not of this stamp, and at a dinner at his nephew's home Holland House in 1797 decided on a determined policy of secession from parliament. What his Westminster constituents made of this withdrawal – he spent the next four years in Surrey – we cannot know, but it meant that the opposition was even more diminished, with Grey, now forty-six, and Sheridan and George Tierney, who were both still in their early thirties, taking the lead.

Fox's original complaint had been that Pitt was just a royal puppet, but in 1801 Hanoverian history repeated itself. For just as George III had undermined his ministers over Fox's India Bill of 1783, so now, having found out from Loughborough that Pitt intended to legislate for Catholic emancipation in Ireland, the king told Windham at his levee on Wednesday, 28 January that 'he should consider any person who voted for it, as personally indisposed towards him',[47] and let another know that he would reckon any such person 'my personal enemy'. Fox was mightily amused to see the poacher poached, but Pitt had more backbone to him in 1801 than Fox had had in 1783 and marched out of the government – along with Grenville, Windham, Spencer, and his closest Commons ally and most regular drinking companion, the Scotsman Henry Dundas (who had been in one form of ministerial office or another ever since 1766).

The government now fell into the lap of Henry 'Doctor' Addington, the former Speaker now turned courtier–premier whose distinguishing virtue, to the king's mind, was his opposition to Catholic emancipation. In reality Addington was no more suitable for the post than Bute had been, but to be fair, Pitt had left him a prickly legacy. The country was financially and physically exhausted by war. There had been two more years of famine, and a very unpalatable peace treaty had to be signed with Napoleon. Yet on 18 May 1803, just a year after the Treaty of Amiens, Britain was back at war.

Pitt had pledged that he would not go into open opposition, but Addington faced twin opponents in the shape of Fox's 'old opposition' and a 'new opposition' led by Pitt's brother-in-law Grenville, who had been a peer since 1790, plus Windham, Spencer, Grenville's brother Thomas, his nephew Lord Temple and their relative Charles Williams Wynn, all of whom sat together in the Commons on a bench below the gangway. Grenville was pulled in alternating directions – towards Pitt in favour of the war against France, towards Fox in favour of Catholic emancipation – but as Addington's problems worsened, Grenville was under pressure to enter into alliance with one or the other in order to remove the vacillating premier. In 1804, frustrated by what Pitt called the 'tardiness, languor, and imbe-cility of ministers in every thing',[48] he, Grenville and Fox found themselves in agreement that successful prosecution of the war demanded a new administration, and forced the issue: but when Addington resigned, personal animosities rapidly got in the way of any further accord. Sheridan refused even to be in the same room as Grenville; Tierney and Erskine, who wanted a whole new approach to the war, thought the mere removal of the premier alone was too paltry an ambition; Grenville refused to join a new ministry *without* Fox; and the king refused to coun-tenance a ministry *with* Fox. George's only option was to re-summon Pitt, who formed a ministry with the dregs of the non-aligned on 10 May 1804.

For Pitt, the next eighteen months were ones of increasing loneliness, ill health and disappointment. He had always preferred a small coterie of friends to a large party, but now his circle was dwindling. His most enduring companion, his brother-in-law Edward Eliot, had died in 1797, and his close friendship with Henry Dundas, now Viscount Melville, had soured. His phenomenal consumption of alcohol and concomi-tant gout, as well as constant headaches and a persistent stomach

complaint, had weakened his tall, bony frame. He was unequivocally married to politics, and it was politics on the grand scale
that delivered a blow from which he was not to recover.
For although his supporters might toast him as the 'pilot who
weathered the storm', when Napoleon routed Britain's allies, the
Austrian and Russian forces, at Austerlitz on 2 December 1805,
even victory at Trafalgar was scant consolation as Pitt saw his
grand European plan fall into pieces. Within seven weeks, on
23 January 1806, the 46-year-old Prime Minister was dead.

Fox, who became Foreign Secretary in the new Government
of All the Talents that was formed under Grenville on Pitt's
death, was not to last much longer. For much of the year he was
ill with dropsy, and on 7 August went through the hideous experience of being tapped. Never a man for religion of any kind, he
allowed occasional readings from the Book of Common Prayer
to please his wife, with whom he had made a pact that whichever
of them was to go first, the other was to 'stay by all the time and
to try and look gay and cheerful'. At 5.45 p.m. on 13 September
he died at the duke of Devonshire's house in Chiswick.

It was said that when the Speaker announced the plan to
raise a memorial to Pitt, 'the silence was deathlike, and several of
the hardiest oppositionists said it was like an electrical shock . . .
and that they could hardly breathe'.[49] A state funeral was
organized and he was soon interred close to his parents in
Westminster Abbey. But Fox, who had scarcely been in office
for eighteen months out of his thirty-eight years in the
Commons, was equally missed. Although his funeral was private,
the Cabinet and more than a hundred MPs attended, and if
anything the mourners outnumbered those who had turned
out for Pitt.

The two men were made in very different moulds. Pitt could
be austere, aloof, business-like. Wilberforce reckoned that he did
not particularly make friends, and members commented that

when he entered the Commons he would barely acknowledge others. It is easy to speculate on his reasons for remaining so private. He certainly preferred the company of men, and while there is no evidence that he was homosexual, he was certainly homosocial. Fox, by contrast, had a magnanimity about him that could thaw even the harshest critic. When a furious shopkeeper thrust a hangman's noose in his hand during one of his Westminster elections, Fox responded not with anger but with wit, refusing to accept the gift, as he was sure it must be a family relic. But there were also similarities. Both men had a well-tuned ear for the Commons mood – although Fox was more prepared to speak against it – and both had that particular parliamentary poise that can render an acerbic insult all the more effective for being elegantly put. Both had their views dramatically altered by events. Pitt started out a convinced Whig, a supporter of liberty for Wilkes and for America, but moved steadily towards a benevolent monarchism and eventually adopted repressive measures to stem republicanism. Fox, originally no great enthusiast for parliamentary reform, Catholic emancipation or the abolition of slavery, was by the end of his life a fierce advocate of all three. Events in America and France had politicized them both, and rescued both Toryism and Whiggery from decline into mere campaigns for personal advancement. And both men's lives ended on a downbeat. To Pitt, desperate to defeat Napoleon, Austerlitz had been a crushing blow; Fox, equally determined to secure a peace, had failed to get Talleyrand to the table.

The irony that the two men should die within months of each other was not lost on anyone, especially when their tombs were placed just inches apart in the Abbey. In the words of Sir Walter Scott, whose lengthy poem *Marmion, a Tale of Flodden Field*, was published in 1808 with addresses to several of his friends interpolated into the epic story of Tudor chivalry:

415

These spells are spent, and, spent with these
The wine of life is on the lees;
Genius, and taste, and talent gone,
For ever tombed beneath the stone,
Where taming thought to human pride
The mighty chiefs sleep side by side.
Drop upon FOX'S grave the tear,
'Twill trickle to his rival's bier;
O'er PITT'S the mournful requiem sound,
And Fox's shall the notes rebound.
The solemn echo seems to cry,—
'Here let their discord with them die.
Speak not for those a separate doom,
Whom Fate made Brothers in the tomb;
But search the land of living men,
Where wilt thou find their like agen?'

Such was the very special sense of personal honour felt by the ruling class that although duelling had long been illegal, MPs and peers were regular combatants. Here the Secretary for War, Viscount Castlereagh, confronts the Foreign Secretary, George Canning, on Putney Heath in September 1809.

13

Honourable Members

A LITTLE AFTER EIGHT on the morning of Saturday, 21 March
1829, Arthur Wellesley, the distinguished and rather proper 61-
year-old duke of Wellington, appeared at Battersea Fields in
south London, primed to fire a pistol at the earl of Winchilsea.
The issue ostensibly involved religion and politics, but was really
about honour and credibility. The arch-Protestant earl had written that 'under the cloak of some coloured show of zeal for the
Protestant religion' Wellington had 'an insidious design for the
infringement of our liberties and the introduction of Popery into
every department of the State'.[1] In other words, the duke was a
liar, a hypocrite and a crypto-Catholic. This was a fiercely
provocative imputation, especially against the background of the
duke's highly controversial and rather recent support for
Catholic emancipation. But most peers would have casually
dismissed these comments as no more than political banter from
a frothy lightweight, certainly not grounds for insisting on a duel.
Winchilsea had a reputation for bombastic ranting in the Lords,
as though he were 'shouting to a mob on a windy day upon
Pennenden Heath'.[2] Wellington's colleagues might also have
pointed out to the duke that despite his successful military career

he was a notoriously bad shot, especially since an artillery explosion in the Royal Ordnance had irremediably damaged his hearing and balance. Furthermore, the duke was a long-time and outspoken opponent of duelling: it had cost him too many able young officers.

Most importantly, though, Wellington was taking an enormous risk, not just with his life, but also with his career. For every aspect of duelling was illegal, including issuing a challenge, attending a duel, assisting the combatants and firing a weapon (whether one hit one's opponent or not). Monarchs had constantly bemoaned the practice. In addition to the common law offences of affray and assault under which a duellist might be arrested, there was a wealth of legislation: the Stabbing Act of 1604; the Coventry Act of 1682 (named after an MP whose nose had been slit open following a dispute in the Commons); the Black Act of 1723; and, most recently, the Malicious Shooting or Stabbing Act of 1803. All pointed, albeit obliquely, to the law's central contention that, in the words of Sir Edward Coke, 'to kill a man in a duel is murder'. And the duke was no mere private individual; he was the Prime Minister. If he were discovered in the act he could face imprisonment, and if he were to slay his opponent that would be a felony, punishable by execution.

On the other hand, to let the insult stand would be tacitly to accept the imputation of dishonesty; and, as suing for defamation was not yet widely thought of as an effective recourse, the duke's only means of proving his sincerity was to throw down the gauntlet.

So Wellington issued the challenge and appointed the Secretary at War, Sir Henry Hardinge MP, as his second. There was an element of farce to the proceedings. Wellington and Hardinge were so nervous of being caught that they leaped into a ditch to hide from some early morning labourers; when Hardinge was marking out the distance at which the two combatants should stand, Wellington insisted that Winchilsea be placed away from another ditch lest he 'tumble in'; and when it came to the moment when the seconds would normally load the pistols, the attending doctor did the honours as Hardinge had lost his left hand at Waterloo and Viscount Falmouth, the earl's second, was shaking uncontrollably. When Hardinge gave the command to shoot, Winchilsea refused to raise his arm to fire, so Wellington deliberately shot wide, catching the earl's coat, whereupon Winchilsea shot in the air. It was all over in a few bathetic moments. The earl tendered an apology, which the duke sniffily accepted. Within less than fifteen minutes of arriving they had both hastened back into town, honour satisfied. By lunchtime, having briefly broken the news to his friend the diarist and Tory hostess Mrs Arbuthnot, Wellington was at his desk considering the merits of setting up a Metropolitan Police Force.

Wellington's risk paid off politically. Although the duel was public knowledge within days and cartoonists and satirists lampooned him with glee, he got his apology, public opinion swung behind him, and on 13 April he got his Catholic Emancipation Bill through Parliament.

Wellington was neither the only nor the first Prime Minister to defend his honour with the duelling pistol. The younger Pitt had accepted a similar challenge on Saturday, 26 May 1798 from the Foxite Irish MP George Tierney, who had vigorously attacked Pitt's plans for the Royal Navy. In the lively Commons debate the day before, Pitt had accused Tierney of opposing his plans 'from a desire to obstruct the defence of the country',[3] which was tantamount to an accusation of treason. When Pitt not only refused to withdraw the comment but reiterated it, and when Pitt's friend the Speaker Henry Addington pointedly failed to pull Pitt up on his un-parliamentary jibe, Tierney felt he had no choice but to issue a challenge. So, gathered on the Sunday afternoon close to a recently used gibbet on Putney Heath with their two seconds and the Speaker, both MPs shot, twice, at twelve paces, and (deliberately) missed. Again, according to the quaint code of duelling, honour was restored.

Pitt had not been as fortunate as Wellington. George III made it clear that he expected that 'what has happened will never be repeated . . . Public characters have no right to weigh alone what is due to their country,'[4] and MPs expressed outrage. William Wilberforce, who was doubly scandalized both that there had been a duel and that it had taken place on a Sunday, threatened to force a Commons debate on the matter. As he wrote in his diary, 'this late incident more illustrates the character and exposes the selfishness of the system of modern honour, than any transaction that ever happened'.[5] Pitt took to his bed for several weeks.

Yet there was a hefty dollop of hypocrisy in the public condemnations. For however much monarchs and society decried the practice, parliamentary attempts to bring in water-tight anti-duelling laws failed for more than two centuries, and well into the nineteenth century juries and judges alike refused to convict duellists brought to court.

Thus, more than a century before Wellington and Winchilsea faced each other at Battersea, in 1712 two members of the House of Lords, Charles, 4th Baron Mohun, and James, 4th duke of Hamilton, were both killed as a result of a duel over Mohun's wife's considerable inheritance. Mohun had a long history of duelling. His father had died in a duel; he himself had fought his first duel in 1692 against the earl of Cassilis; and the following year, despite clear evidence that he had held the army officer Richard Hill under an armlock while his second ran Hill through, he was outrageously acquitted when tried by the Lords. Even more extraordinarily, the Lords again acquitted him in 1697 following another duel in Leicester Square, for which his second, the earl of Warwick, was found guilty of manslaughter. It is scarcely surprising that following the mutual murders of

Mohun and Hamilton, Queen Anne opined that 'the impious Practice of duelling requires some speedy and effectual remedy,'[6] and the whole of polite society nodded its ready assent. But Anne's hope was to remain unfulfilled. There was a well-supported campaign led by two MPs, the cringingly shy dramatist Joseph Addison and his friend and fellow writer Sir Richard Steele, in the *Tatler* and the *Spectator*, and seven years later an anti-duelling Bill was carried through the Commons, but the Lords imperiously and resolutely struck it down.

There were also at the end of the eighteenth century still plenty of people who saw duelling as an essential bulwark of society. The philosopher Jeremy Bentham defended it and Samuel Johnson argued its merits in no uncertain terms, telling Boswell that

> in a state of highly polished society, an affront is held to be a serious injury. A duel must be fought upon it; as men have agreed to banish from their society one who puts up with an affront without fighting a duel . . . He . . . who fights a duel, does not fight from passion against his antagonist, but out of self-defence; to avert the stigma of the world, and to prevent himself from being driven out of society.[7]

In one of his observations at least, Johnson was right: his England in the eighteenth and nineteenth centuries was a highly polished society. It was also perfectly mirrored in parliament. By definition the hereditary peers were the representatives of long-established British and (after 1801) Irish families. But in large measure the Commons came from the same pool. So 883 of the 5,034 MPs elected between 1734 and 1832 were the sons of British peers, 452 were baronets and 64 were Irish peers; and between 1790 and 1820 every House of Commons had roughly 170 scions of the nobility and 94 baronets. Indeed, it was considered a virtue that so many sons of peers should sit in the Commons as a form of training. As Philip Stanhope, Viscount Mahon, who sat as an MP before succeeding to his father's earldom, argued in 1832: 'I do think it of the highest importance, if we are to have a House of Lords at all, that those who are to compose it should be trained in the habits of business.'[8] For him the Commons was the training ground for the senior house.

Besides the sons of peers, more than half of all MPs were following in the footsteps of a close family relative, and some families were parliamentary dynasties. In the 98 years between 1734 and 1832, 21 Mannerses, 17 Townshends, and 15 Bullers, Finches and Fitzroys apiece were elected, and 382 seats were held by members of just 31 families. Many had had the same education, too: of the 2,143 MPs elected between 1790 and 1820, nearly half had attended one of six schools (Eton, Westminster, Harrow, Winchester, Rugby and Charterhouse), with 400 passing through Eton alone, and 950 of them had been to Oxford or Cambridge.

Formed within such a tight circle, and with such a strong sense of parliamentary succession, parliament retained a very traditional concept of honourable behaviour; and, thanks to the presence of so many senior army and navy officers, its unpublished rule-book still reflected the medieval concept of chivalry, with its emphasis on physical courage, military prowess, gallantry and loyalty. It was the gentlemanly code of the Elizabethans, which stressed courtesy towards women and protection for the vulnerable, and abjured cowardice. According to this code, many things could impugn a man's honour and bring about his downfall, so that imputations of treason, sedition, adultery, dishonesty, cowardice, cruelty or sexual deviance could all provoke parliamentary ire. Evidence of infidelity or financial ruin was by definition scandalous, and although many examples of cuckoldry and concupiscence were cheerfully ignored while known only within the narrow circle of supposedly polite society, the moment a story became open knowledge, the shutters of public humiliation and shame descended. Transgressors could be not just ignored or excluded, but actively hounded out of society. Every politician considered himself a gentleman, and every gentleman would have averred with Mowbray in Shakespeare's *Richard II*: 'Mine honour is my life: both grow in one. Take honour from me and my life is done.'

It all seems very high-minded. But several contemporary thinkers were critical of the concept of honour as it worked out in practice, not least because so many members of the ruling élite considered the code of honour to apply only to their social equals. The radical philosopher and archdeacon of Carlisle, William Paley, complained in 1785:

> Profaneness, neglect of public worship or private devotion, cruelty to servants, rigorous treatment of tenants or other dependents, want of charity to the poor, injuries done to tradesmen by insolvency or delay of payment, with numerous examples of the same kind, are accounted no breaches of honour, because a man is not a less agreeable companion for these vices, nor the worse to deal with in those concerns, which are usually transacted between one gentleman and another.[9]

Paley's point is well made by the case of James Brudenell, who was an MP before succeeding to his father's title as 9th earl of Cardigan in 1837. Cardigan was a deeply unpleasant man who had courted controversy by marrying a divorcee, starting an affair with another woman while his first wife was dying, and leaving his second wife to her own devices in the country while he carried on with a string of mistresses in London. By career a military man and by nature a braggart and a bully, he was censured in a court martial for 'reprehensible conduct' and thrown out of the army in 1834, but two years later gained command of the 11th Hussars (and, notoriously, later went on to lead the Charge of the Light Brigade). In 1841 he was tried in the Lords for killing one of his former officers in a duel. There were few doubts about the facts. He himself said 'I have hit my man' when arrested. But 120 of his peers unanimously resolved that since, while the prosecution had referred to 'Captain Harvey Tuckett', the original indictment had named the victim as 'Harvey Garnet Phipps Tuckett' – by implication, no officer, and hence no gentleman – Cardigan must be innocent. It was, as *The Times* pointed out, a flagrant example of the fact that 'in England there is one law for the rich and another for the poor'.[10]

It was also evidence that the concept of honour that dominated public life right through to the 1840s was riddled with hypocrisy. Yet in the context of Johnson's 'highly polished society' it is not surprising that many senior politicians took to the field. As the duke of Buckingham and Chandos stated after his own duel with the duke of Bedford in 1822: 'A public man's life is not worth preserving, unless with honour.'[11] Never was this more clearly true than during the dandified, paranoid, repressive, 'polished' period between the French Revolution in 1789 and the Great Reform Act of 1832. During these years, while vanity, pride and personal ambition all played their parts in the intricate dances of acceptable social behaviour, the fact that there was no effective legal remedy against a calumny until libel law developed more fully later in the nineteenth century meant that any public figure keen to preserve his reputation against a slight could only have recourse to the duel. Roughly fifteen duels were fought every year between 1785 and 1821 and about thirteen per year between 1822 and 1843,[12] and yet over the three decades between 1803 and 1832 only eleven people were convicted under the anti-duelling laws, of whom six were executed.

It is difficult to be precise about the number of peers and MPs involved in these contests as they were of necessity clandestine affairs. But we know for certain that the roll call of eighteenth- and nineteenth-century parliamentary duellists included, along with William Pitt the Younger and George Tierney, John Wilkes, who first took on Earl Talbot and then was shot in the belly in a later duel by the Secretary to the Treasury, Samuel Martin, in 1763; Richard Brinsley Sheridan, later to become an MP, twice in 1772, defending the honour of the woman he then married; the radical James Paull, three times with different opponents; the earl of Shelburne, who was hit in the groin by Colonel Fullarton in 1780; Charles James Fox and the Scot William Adam; the MPs for Ludlow (Richard Herbert) and for Newcastle (John Butler), who both fought Irish parliamentarians; the dukes of Buckingham and of Bedford, who fought each other over the 'corrupt' support Grenvillites like Buckingham had given to Lord Liverpool's ministry; Lord George Beresford, who fought his losing parliamentary opponent in 1830; and Daniel O'Connell, who was so full of remorse for killing his challenger John D'Esterre that he paid D'Esterre's daughter a monthly allowance for more than thirty years.

Things were even more rumbustious in Irish politics. John Slattery was killed by Stephen Moore in 1726 in a duel fought with pistols and swords, and three years later Samuel Boyse was badly wounded in a similar affair. In the space of just three years, 1773–5, John Scott narrowly avoided a duel with Benjamin Chapman, but then fought James Cuffe; George Ogle was nearly killed; the two candidates for mayor of Galway fired at each other at just five yards; Francis Mathew was shot in the leg; and Sir John Colthurst was killed by Dominick Trant. And there were countless parliamentary duelling recidivists. Ogle fought again in 1803, as did John Scott on four further occasions, despite being Chief Justice of the King's Bench; Isaac Corry killed a man in 1784 and in 1800, as Irish Chancellor of the Exchequer, took to the field with Henry Grattan; David Walsh fought once in 1764 and again against the diminutive and witty John Philpott Curran (who in turn notched up duels against Captain St Leger, the Attorney-General John Fitzgibbon and the Chief Secretary Robert Hobart); Marcus Patterson, Chief Justice of the Common Pleas, wounded three men in encounters; Sir Edward Newenham fought three times; and John Egan fought five duels, three of them during the Cork election of 1783.

But the doyen of the Irish parliamentary duellists, racking up twelve encounters, was Beauchamp Bagenal, for fifteen years the irascible MP for Carlow. On one occasion he challenged his relative Beauchamp Harvey Bagenal, after which they sat down to a hearty breakfast together. In 1773 he fought the Chief Secretary Colonel Blacquiere and deprived him of some of his hair and his hat. Nor did he mellow with time. Aged sixty, Bagenal took on a neighbour whose pigs had destroyed his flowerbeds, insisting on this occasion that the challenge be held in the afternoon and that he be allowed to take aim seated, on account of his advancing years. The neighbour was badly wounded and Bagenal's chair was shot to pieces.

Duelling did finally lay down its pistols – or at least pass into desuetude. Henry Rich MP commented in 1842: 'It is to the honour of the younger public men of the day, that none of them of any note, or with very few exceptions, have been engaged in a duel. They have amidst all the heat of the last twelve years' debates, preserved their honour, their courage and their consciences unsullied, without this vulgar appeal.'[13] He wasn't quite right. The aristocratically named Grandey Fitzhugh Berkeley duelled in 1836, Charles Vane, the 3rd marquess of Londonderry defended the Tory party's honour against Henry Grattan (junior) in 1839 and Sir Robert Peel was twice very nearly enticed onto the field of combat in the 1830s. But by the middle of Victoria's reign duelling had ceased as a political means of proving one's honour, and late nineteenth-century playwrights like Dion Boucicault openly laughed at the very notion.

Even at its zenith, though, duelling was not the only recourse for those suffering the slings and arrows of outrageous fortune.

At seven-thirty on the morning of 12 August 1822, a Monday, a tall, handsomely slim, 53-year-old Irish aristocrat dispatched his wife's maid Mrs Robinson from their bedroom in his country seat in North Cray in Kent to summon his physician, Mr Bankhead. He was clearly very distressed and his wife, Emily, thought she had hidden all the pistols, knives and razors in the house, but as she briefly stepped into her dressing room, he scrabbled around for a weapon. He found a small penknife and, just as the doctor appeared, he stabbed himself in the neck, declaring: 'Bankhead, let me fall upon your arm; 'tis all over.' As the blood gushed from his carotid artery, he slipped and died.

Suicide was a major scandal in the early nineteenth century. English common law had treated what it termed *felo de se* as a crime for centuries, and the post-mortem penalty was severe. The right hand was separated from the body, which was buried after dark in unconsecrated ground with a stake through it and without liturgy or obsequy, and the suicide's property was automatically forfeit to the crown, leaving wife and family disgraced, homeless and penniless.

In this case the horror was exacerbated by the identity of the suicide; for the aristocrat in question, the marquess of Londonderry (or, as he was normally known, Lord Castlereagh), was not only a personal friend to Wellington and the new king, George IV, but for a decade had served as Foreign Secretary and Leader of the House of Commons. That he should deliberately, in sound mind, take his own life was for a man at the heart of the establishment to challenge the very foundations of the state and its established church. For it was not just the law but, in Shakespeare's words, the Almighty that 'had fixed his canon against self-slaughter'.

And yet Castlereagh's choice of exit was not unique, nor indeed particularly unusual. Indeed, the roll call of senior late eighteenth- and early nineteenth-century parliamentary suicides is striking. John Pardoe MP in 1796, William Crosbie MP in 1798 and Sir Godfrey Webster MP in 1800 all took their own lives. George Barclay MP attempted to do so in 1806. William Eden MP, the son of Lord Auckland, drowned himself in 1810 and the former MP Sir William Erskine dispatched himself in Lisbon in 1813.

These were not all cases of public figures facing shame and humiliation. Pardoe shot his brains out during his wife's funeral, a victim of grief. The case of Sir Samuel Romilly, one of the best-liked politicians of his day, was similar. Son of a Soho jeweller, Romilly had been a successful barrister before being drafted into the predominantly Whig Government of All the Talents and (since he was not yet an MP) into parliament as Solicitor-General in 1806. His was not a lengthy ministerial career, as the administration swiftly collapsed, but thereafter Romilly applied himself as a backbench member to the reform of the criminal law, especially the death penalty. He had significant success, abolishing it for theft from the person and winning the much-coveted Westminster seat in 1819. Only a few months later his adored wife died. He was so visibly devastated that he was kept under constant supervision, but when briefly left unattended at his Russell Square home on 2 November 1818 he slit his throat.

Others, however, clearly took their lives expressly to avoid obloquy and scandal. A typical instance was that of Richard Trench Chiswell, who had inherited the estate of his unmarried uncle Richard Chiswell in 1772 and his father's in 1790, and had made his own fortune as a merchant banker. In keeping with the Chiswell family tradition of bookselling, he was a renowned antiquary and bequeathed his journals to the Bodleian Library at Oxford. But he also sought political office, first standing for

Haslemere in 1761 but only managing finally to get elected when he purchased the seat of Aldborough in Yorkshire from the duke of Newcastle for £30,000. Soon after the 1796 election he found himself in severe financial difficulties and by the end of the year he had lost much of his fortune speculating in the East Indies. On 3 February 1797, virtually bankrupt, he shot himself.

James Paull similarly succumbed to fear of financial ruin, although – or perhaps because? – he had started life with little. The son of a Scottish tailor, he moved to India, acquiring in Lucknow both a fortune and a passionate hatred of the governor-general, Lord Wellesley (Wellington's brother), before returning to Britain and entering parliament in 1805 as MP for Newtown on the Isle of Wight. The fiery Paull soon became part of the opposition and a friend of Charles James Fox, William Cobbett, Sir Francis Burdett and Sir Samuel Romilly, but when he was abandoned by the Whig aristocracy in the November 1806 and May 1807 elections he stood in the most fiercely contested seat in the country, Westminster. In the first election the two seats were taken by the Whig playwright Richard Brinsley Sheridan and the Tory Sir Samuel Hood, and after losing his vexatious appeal Paull managed to fall out with more of his Whig supporters. At this point he insisted on a duel with the new leading Whig candidate, Burdett, which ended in both of them being badly wounded but nonetheless returning from their assignation in Wimbledon in the same carriage. Burdett came top of the poll with 5,134 votes; Paull, with just 269, came last. Devastated, wounded, politically isolated and facing financial ruin, Paull languished for a year. Then, on 14 April 1808, he went gambling in Pall Mall and blew 1,600 guineas in a single night. The next day, at home in Charles Street in Westminster, he took a knife to his right arm and then to his throat.

Bankruptcy was not the only brand of ruin a public figure might fear enough to take his own life. Lord Graves was the tall, amiable, portly and unaffected MP for, successively, Okehampton, Windsor and Milborne Port, and later served as Commissioner of Excise. So attuned was he to the possibility of dishonour that when in 1830 he learned that his wife, from whom he was separated, intended to divorce him and that people believed his acquiescence in her affair with the king's brother, the duke of Cumberland, had been bought at a hefty price, he dropped a note to Lady Graves and, after failing to turn up to dinner with his brother-in-law the marquess of Anglesey, took his own life. The coroner determined that 'the deceased died by a wound inflicted by himself on his throat, in a sudden fit of delirium'. The *Gentleman's Magazine* put it more adroitly: 'It appears too probable that his Lordship fell a victim to his own nice sense of honour.'[14]

A similarly 'nice sense of honour' bore heavily on John Calcraft the younger, who was an MP for nearly thirty-five years between 1786 and 1831. Having served for thirty-two of those years as a Whig, in 1828 he accepted the job of Paymaster of the Forces in the Tory government – only to fall out with the Tories in 1831 when he voted for the second reading of the Reform Act, a division that was won by a single vote. In the certain belief that everyone on all sides of the House now detested him as a rat who had, in Winston Churchill's later phrase, 're-ratted', Calcraft too took his own life.

Such intense sensitivity to damaged self-esteem is intrinsic to public life. It is not just that others have to believe in you; you have to believe in yourself. To a public figure, shame, dishonour, disgrace and humiliation are matters not just of embarrassment but of personal destruction; indeed, a mere intimation of mediocrity or an acute sense of straightforward political failure can have similarly devastating effect.

In 1815 another leading Whig was found lying in a pool of blood, a razor by his side. Unlike Paull, the second Samuel

Whitbread was no outsider; but, as the son of a brewer and merchant, albeit a very successful one, he never enjoyed so assured a place in society as the landed gentry who formed the backbone of the Whigs. Nevertheless, as MP for Bedford since 1790, Whitbread was a respected campaigner for religious toleration and the abolition of slavery. He advocated parliamentary reform and a national education system, tried to introduce a national minimum wage, and after Fox's death was the Whig leader in the Commons. He was also so passionate a supporter of the theatre that when the Theatre Royal, Drury Lane burned down he put up thousands of pounds for its rebuilding. As his friend Romilly put it, he was 'the promoter of every liberal scheme for improving the condition of mankind, the zealous advocate of the oppressed, and the undaunted opposer of every species of corruption and ill-administration'.[15] Above all, though, he was a dedicated and very public follower of Napoleon. This was not an easy case to argue in bellicose Britain, so it was no surprise that on returning one night from the Commons he complained to his wife: 'They are hissing me. I am become an object of universal abhorrence.'[16] When Bonaparte abdicated in 1814, Whitbread was plunged into such a deep depression that he resigned his seat to his son William. On 6 July the following year, twelve days before the battle of Waterloo, with Napoleon on the run, he came downstairs to his dressing room and drew a razor across his throat. Drury Lane Theatre was dark for the night.

Each of these suicides occurred in very different circumstances, but the coroners returned very similar verdicts. Despite Chiswell's having left a suicide note expressly referring to his financial speculation as the cause of his taking his own life, the coroner's inquest found that he was insane. The fact that Paull was buried at the society church of St James's Piccadilly suggests that he too was not posthumously expunged from society but regarded as having not been in his right mind when he took his life. So too the original reports on Whitbread's death suggested that he had died from a fit of 'apoplexy', but the coroner's court brought in a verdict of 'insanity'. In each case the coroner and jury were doing the MPs and their families a favour, preferring to believe that the victim was a madman rather than a criminal and thereby protecting him from ruin. That the individual should risk eternal wrath was one thing, but to bring certain financial ruin on one's surviving dependants was quite another.*

This may well explain a mystery about the death of Castlereagh. As with Paull, Romilly, Whitbread and Chiswell, the jury of Castlereagh's neighbours who came to inspect the dressing room, the knife and the noble corpse on the day of his demise wrote off his death not as suicide but as an act of insanity. Following suit, all the nineteenth- and twentieth-century biographical accounts of his death place a heavy emphasis on his state of mind. They cite the duke of Wellington, who thought him 'very low, out of spirits and unwell' at the Cabinet on 7 August,[17] and wrote that when he saw him on the tenth he was 'bordering on insanity'. They quote Hamilton Seymour's letter to Castlereagh's half-brother Sir Charles Stewart (written a week *after* Castlereagh's death), saying that the Foreign Secretary wandered his gardens at Cray 'melancholy and dejected in his manner', held his hand on his head and said that he was 'quite worn out here. Quite worn out – and this fresh load of responsibility is more than I can bear.'[18] The conclusion all Castlereagh's biographers draw is that it was mental illness that led to his suicide. Delusional, depressive, insane, he took his own life because (as they cite him saying of himself), 'my mind is, as it

---

* Many Whigs, indeed, did not subscribe to the high church theology on suicide; it may be that for men such as Paull, Calcraft and Whitbread one's honour among the living was far more important than one's standing with the Almighty.

were, gone'.[19] However, these accounts all ignore other possibilities.

What if he was in fact perfectly sane? Two factors suggest that this may indeed have been the case. First, Castlereagh maintained that there were plots against him, possibly including by Wellington himself. Historians have suggested – along with Wellington – that this merely proves he was suffering from paranoia. But we know from Harriet Arbuthnot, who described herself as Castlereagh's 'dearest and best friend', that on 5 August her MP husband Charles talked to Castlereagh about some anonymous letters Stewart had received, which Castlereagh immediately presumed to refer to him. When she met him later that day, 'he took my hand and entreated me in the most earnest manner to tell him if I had ever heard anything against his honour or character'. The next day he went further, confessing that three years earlier he had received an anonymous letter about a visit he had made to a brothel. As she put it, 'he actually fancied the purport of this letter was to accuse him of a crime not to be named, and this notion could not be put out of his head'.[20]

Most importantly, there is the question of what Castlereagh said to his other close friend, the king. For on 9 August Castlereagh confided in George that he thought he was being blackmailed for the same crime as Percy Jocelyn, the aristocratic bishop of Clogher, who had absconded a month earlier, having been caught *in flagrante delicto* with a Grenadier Guardsman called John Moverley in the back room of the White Lion public house off the Haymarket in central London and having attempted to flee down the street, only to be caught by an excitable crowd with his trousers round his ankles. If Castlereagh had done something similar, it was indeed 'a crime not to be named' and Castlereagh would have been right to have horses in readiness. Buggery was a capital offence. Only voluntary exile in France or Italy could protect him.

It was also true that Castlereagh had plenty of enemies. Indeed, he had accumulated them with almost wanton disregard. Originally elected to the Irish parliament as MP for Down in the most expensive Irish election to date as an Independent with Whig sympathies, he had travelled an enormous distance politically, alienating his erstwhile dissenting friends and supporters by hitching his wagon to that of the Tory Prime Minister William Pitt. In Irish eyes he had compounded his sin by forcibly repressing the Irish rebellion of 1798, while serving as Acting Chief Secretary for Ireland, and by being the prime architect of the much-derided 1801 Act of Union. The fact that he and Pitt resigned when the court blocked the promised emancipation of Catholics availed him little. His fellow Irishmen held him responsible for this English treachery.

Castlereagh served as Secretary for War and the Colonies in Pitt's last ministry from 1805 to 1806, and returned to the same post a year later in the duke of Portland's rudderless administration, during which Castlereagh developed an antipathy to his Cabinet colleague and successor as Foreign Secretary, George Canning, so fierce that it led to a duel fought on Putney Heath on 21 September 1809. Canning, who had never shot a pistol in his life, ended up with a bullet in his thigh, but such was the sense of outrage that two members of the Cabinet should resort to such illegal means of resolving their differences that they both resigned.

Castlereagh's re-entry into government for the fourth time as Liverpool's Foreign Secretary re-invigorated his old enemies and brought him new ones. There were many repressive ministers in the early nineteenth century, but few could beat Henry Addington, the former Prime Minister and now a very security-conscious Home Secretary. Castlereagh's problem was that since Addington now sat alongside Portland as Lord Sidmouth in the Lords, he, as both Leader of the House and Foreign Secretary, was the main spokesman for the government in the Commons. His own foreign policy was radical and inspired, but he had to defend the government's extremely controversial domestic policies, all of which flew in the face of the radical views he had once promoted. If anyone needed evidence of the brutalism at the heart of the government, the 'Peterloo Massacre' of 16 August 1819 provided it: hussars were sent in to quell a demonstration in support of parliamentary reform in St Peter's Fields in Manchester, killing eleven people and wounding several hundred more. It was Sidmouth's policy; but it was Castlereagh who had to defend it in the Commons.

Thus the poet Shelley satirized the whole government, but reserved his sharpest vitriol for Castlereagh:

> I met Murder on the way –
> He had a face like Castlereagh –
> Very smooth he looked, yet grim;
> Seven bloodhounds followed him.
> All were fat; and well they might
> Be in admirable plight,
> For one by one, and two by two,
> He tossed them human hearts to chew
> Which from his wide cloak he drew.

Castlereagh felt the opprobrium and the imputation of dishonour acutely. It was the same sensitivity that had driven him to fight Canning. And now, with enemies surrounding him in parliament and rumours stalking the streets, he felt such passionate fear of discovery as a homosexual, or at least as having had one homosexual experience (he told Mrs Arbuthnot a garbled tale of a visit to a brothel when he had dallied with a woman who turned out to be a man), that he decided to preserve his honour and take his life. Unlike today, when suicide is often taken as a confirmation of our worst suspicions, in Castlereagh's time society would stiffen every sinew after a suicide to cover up the truth. It was one thing to be hated. It was quite another to dice with eternity. In today's terms, of course, Castlereagh suffered from mental illness. Mental instability ran in his family; his nephew went mad in 1862 and spent the last ten years of his life under lock and key. But that did not make Castlereagh's own decision to take his own life for fear of exposure illogical.

Few people genuinely like being hated or ostracized, though some public figures make the best of a bad lot and pretend to enjoy the attention. Others take a perverse pleasure in daring society to think the worst of them, and yet others again frame their whole political persona out of a feigned brutalism. In Castlereagh's time, within the narrow confines of such a tiny community of people, such obloquy was virtually unsustainable. There was no place to hide.

There were those who managed to survive general opprobrium, though they often had to take themselves out of public view for a time at least. The truly hideous William Pole Wellesley, nephew of the duke of Wellington and son of the Cabinet minister Lord Maryborough, managed to ride out several bouts of scandal. Through his exorbitant spending and his reckless adultery he dispatched both his wife and her fortune and racked up massive debts; having abducted his own children, he spent some time in exile and was arrested for contempt of court before being narrowly acquitted by the Commons Committee of Privileges. Living at the favour of his cousin the 2nd duke of Wellington, he found his way into the Lords and died an earl in 1857. So too Christopher Atkinson, MP for Hedon, was convicted of perjury in 1783, but contrived to get himself pardoned and, having neatly changed his name to Savile, was re-elected for his old (rotten borough) seat in 1796 and 1802; and John Fenton Cawthorne, expelled from the Commons in 1796 for malversation of military monies, got back in eleven years later. In some cases it was not the initial misdemeanour that led to a man's complete undoing. In 1818 Henry Fitzgerald de Ros, who does not seem to have spoken at all during his two-year term in the Commons, was caught having sex with Harriet Spencer. He disowned the child she bore him and accused her of being 'as common as the street'. While a reputation as a roué was not necessarily a fatal blow to social standing, dishonesty at the gaming tables was not so easily brushed aside. In 1837, having inherited the oldest title in England as 22nd Baron de Ros, he was caught cheating at cards and lost the libel case he then brought. That finally did for him socially. His barbed epitaph was provided by the Tory wit Theodore Hook: 'Here lies the premier baron of England, patiently awaiting the last trump.'[21]

Parliament, the mirror of Johnson's 'highly polished society', retained an image of itself as the embodiment of honourable deportment throughout the late eighteenth and early nineteenth centuries. It sought to abide by a strict set of mostly unwritten rules that harked back to an era of chivalry and martial prowess, even though the religious foundation that had once underpinned parliamentary mores was weakening. The social rule-book might be applied differently to peers and to commoners, but little deviation from the norm was allowed and miscreants were dealt with robustly. With the unstoppable prolif- eration of newspapers and satires, a new era of societal scrutiny was beginning in which MPs had either to prove their honour or accept their disgrace. Politicians now feared less the monarch's wrath or the executioner's blade and more the public's scorn, humiliation and ostracism. Few now begged for their lives, but many lamented, like Cassio in *Othello*: 'O! I have lost my repu- tation. I have lost the immortal part of myself, and what remains is bestial.'

The IRISH PATRIOTS.

Two eighteenth-century supporters of Irish parliamentary autonomy, Henry Grattan and Henry Flood, should have been allies, but in October 1783 they very nearly came to blows in the Irish House of Commons. Flood called Grattan a 'mendicant patriot'; Grattan called Flood an 'insufferable egotist'. The personal abuse is said to have gone on for two hours.

14

Ireland

IF EXCESSIVE PATRIOTISM HAS infected the history of the British parliaments, the same could be said in spades of the body that sat in Ireland. At key instances the historical records are scant and the facts are disputed, and unionist and separatist polemicists have filled in the gaps with so much grouting that it is now difficult to differentiate fact from fiction. Even the arrival of the English in Ireland towards the end of the twelfth century is fraught with controversy. For when the Gael Dermot MacMurrough, king of Leinster, was forced out of Ireland in 1166 by his enemies, he invited the Welsh marcher lord Richard de Clare, earl of Pembroke, known as 'Strongbow', to help him seize back his own lands and also take the rest of Ireland. After four years of war they had taken control of Dublin, Waterford, Wexford and Leinster, and Strongbow had married MacMurrough's daughter Aiofe. When MacMurrough died in May 1171 and Strongbow succeeded to his lands, Henry II, king of England, feared that the Irish–Norman kingdom-in-the-making might move against him and in October set sail with an invasion force. He met little resistance and was soon accepted as overlord by much of Ireland, Strongbow being allowed to remain king of Leinster. But Henry's intervention raised the central question of whether Ireland had been conquered or had voluntarily surrendered its sovereignty and could therefore reclaim its autonomy at will.

Henry Monck Mason, the founder of the nineteenth-century Irish Society, was unambiguous in his belief in Ireland's oppression and ability to manage its own affairs. He declared that 'from the first *invasion of Ireland** by Henry II and ever since there has existed a parliament in that country – a legislative assembly, possessing the usual powers of such a meeting';[1] but this was historical grouting on a grand scale. True, since 1188 the king had met in 'common council' with his Irish barons, much as he did with his English ones. The Great Charter had been extended to Ireland in 1217, and there was a series of meetings throughout the thirteenth century that bore some resemblance to a parliament. In June 1264, for instance, a meeting termed a 'parliament' was held at Castledermot at which twenty-six knights adjudicated on the relative rights of the archbishop of Dublin and the king. But when the supporters of Maurice Fitzgerald (the 'Geraldines') seized the royal justiciar, Richard de la Rochelle, on 6 December 1264, the civil war that broke out was brought to an end not by another parliament but a baronial assembly in April 1265. Although a statute on weights and measures was agreed with the assent of the council, the magnates and 'the whole community of Ireland' in 1269, neither the 1264 nor 1265 assemblies was 'legislative', and it is clear that, far from there being a fixed concept of what counsel the king must take, the king and his appointed deputies in Ireland summoned assemblies regularly but on an ad hoc basis.

By the end of the thirteenth century the experimental nature of these gatherings was manifest. As usual, money was at

* Italics added.

the root of them. For, just as in England the king could only raise monies by consent, so when King John wrote in 1204 to all the clergy and faithful of Ireland for financial aid to defend his realm against the French, it was clear that it was entirely voluntary. Likewise, when Edward I needed money for the war in Gascony in 1254 he sent agents to Dublin to meet with prelates and magnates to agree a subsidy. On this occasion there was some form of representation from Irish cities, but assent was granted by the magnates on behalf of their tenants. The next time the crown sought Irish support, though, the king had a tougher time, for when his Chancellor (and later bishop of Emly) Thomas Cantok met with the 'barons and magnates of Ireland as well as the faithful community of the same' in Dublin on 28 January 1292,[2] the commoners (*de vulgo*) kicked up a fuss and persuaded the others that if a fifteenth were to be forthcoming it would have to be extracted from their debtors first.

Three years later Edward I appointed Sir John Wogan, the Welsh lord of Picton in Pembrokeshire, as his justiciar in Ireland and the experimentation continued. Wogan adjudicated as many Irish cases as possible in a newly created Court of the Justiciar without resorting to English courts, he called parliaments almost annually, and in 1297 he summoned not just the archbishops, bishops, abbots, priors, earls, barons and magnates, but the sheriffs of ten counties and the seneschals of the five liberties,[3] plus two knights from each to be elected 'by the assent of his county or liberty'. Not only were these the first commoners in an Irish parliament, but the summons specified that they were to have 'full power from the whole community of the county and liberty etc. to do and receive etc.',[4] the 'etc.' implying that the concept of *plena potestas* known in England was a well-known formula in Ireland as well.

Some have invested this parliament with the same historical significance as the English 'Model Parliament' of 1295.

History is not so tidy, though; far from establishing a pattern, Wogan was winging it. He was conscious that Ireland was disputatious. Native Gaels and Anglo-Normans were at each other's throats, the Irish church had already split itself off from Canterbury, and the archbishop of Armagh, Nicholas MacMolissa, was so opposed to the appointment of Anglo-Normans that when the diocese of Meath fell vacant in 1287 he excommunicated the choice of the local clergy, Thomas St Leger, and attempted to put Walter de Fulburn in his place. The pope eventually found in favour of St Leger and Fulburn had to make do with the bishopric of Waterford, but the rows continued as Waterford had just been vacated by Fulburn's brother Stephen, who had controversially just been made archbishop of Tuam. These episcopal shenanigans were mirrored in wider Irish society, so Wogan sought to settle the ethnic disputes by gathering together everyone who might matter in a 1297 parliament that was expressly summoned to the Holy Trinity Priory in Dublin to 'establish peace more firmly'.[5] The result was a new prohibition on marauding private armies. Felons escaping with plunder were to be arrested. And Englishmen were banned from 'having the hair of the head half-shaved and preserving and allowing the hair at the back of the head to grow long, which they call the "culan", conforming themselves to the Irish in both habit and face'.[6] Two years later Wogan took another experimental step, including representatives of those cities and boroughs which depended on foreign merchants in the summons to a parliament that would consider new rules on foreign coinage; and in 1300 he extended the summons to all the counties and boroughs.

The composition of parliament did not really settle until the latter part of the fourteenth century, when the attendance of the commons in the shape of two knights each for the counties and boroughs within the royal jurisdiction became permanent from about 1370 and the lower clergy began to attend a year later. The four archbishops were nearly always summoned, but neither they nor their multitudinous bishops (fluctuating in number between twenty and twenty-eight) were regular attendees. Indeed, the archbishop of Tuam ignored summonses as a matter of course, and the archbishop of Armagh was often accompanied by only the bishop of Meath from his own province. As for the heads of the religious houses, the parliament of January 1375 included nine Cistercian abbots, six heads of houses of regular canons and the prior of the knights of St John of Jerusalem at Kilmainham, but by 1449 the regular attendees had dwindled to just six. Even the Irish peerage remained a floating concept for much longer than in England: a list from 1310 includes eighty-seven magnates, yet in 1324 just the three earls of Ulster, Kildare and Louth and fourteen lords in total are mentioned, while in 1375 the number leaped back up to forty-two and three years later was back down to twenty-eight. It seems that it was not until 1460, when Thomas Bathe demanded that Henry VI grant him his rightful seat in parliament as Lord of Louth, that a concept of an exclusive list of Irish peers was accepted.

All of which illustrates a simple fact: although Wogan's improvisations hint at a degree of Irish autonomy, Ireland was no different from subjugated Scotland or Gascony. The king could legislate directly for Ireland, his Irish subjects could petition him directly in London, his Irish ministers could be charged in Westminster, and his lawless subjects could be dragged to England to be arraigned.

Ostensibly, the primary role of the Irish parliament at this point was still the exercise of justice as a high court. Petitions were considered: the earl of Kildare had antagonized the archbishop of Dublin by quartering a hundred kerns (foot-soldiers) on his land; a chaplain called Alan McKinnery sought the king's forgiveness for a string of trespasses; the tenants of

Colmanstown wanted a cut in their rent. But two main issues exercised the parliament and successive justiciars, or lieutenants as they were increasingly termed: the English–Irish apartheid and financial demands from London. For much of Ireland was under the *de facto* if not *de jure* rule of the Irish chieftains, and English writ ran little further than the area around Dublin surrounded by a fortified ditch, known as the Pale. Moreover, all Irishmen other than the occasional Gaelic bishop or abbot were barred from parliament, which consequently reflected almost entirely the interests of the immigrant English, as witnessed most remarkably by the statutes of the Kilkenny parliament summoned by Lionel, duke of Clarence and earl of Ulster, in 1366, which sought to undo the steady intermingling of native Irish and English colonists. Intermarriage was banned by statute, as was interracial adoption; Irish pastimes like 'horling' and 'coiting' were to be suppressed in favour of good old English archery; Irish minstrels were banned from English areas as subversives; the English language was made mandatory for all non-Irish; English common law would supplant Irish march law; and the Irish were banned from English churches and cathedrals. This was an English parliament for the English in Ireland, and although Richard II made a half-hearted attempt to include Gaelic lords in 1395, the plan was soon forgotten.

Financial questions, as ever, loomed large. During Sir William of Windsor's two bouts as Lieutenant in 1369–72 and 1374–6, the Irish complained that he was so eager to secure subsidies from them that he summoned seven parliaments and five great councils, solely to discuss money. Indeed, he was so determined to get his way in parliament that he imprisoned unhelpful representatives and even called parliament to the tiny, isolated village of Ballydoyle near Cashel in 1371 in the hope that discomfort would speed debate. After another unhelpful parliament in January 1375, the aged Edward III sent Sir Nicholas

Dagworth to a parliament in Kilkenny; when he returned empty-handed, Windsor issued writs commanding sixty representatives to appear before the king in England to assent to taxation. Several towns and counties refused to give their representatives any such authority, claiming that it was against 'the liberties, privileges, rights, laws and customs of the land of Ireland',[7] and that it was only out of respect for the king that they would agree to attend. After discussion of this response in the Good Parliament of 1376, Dagworth was again dispatched to Ireland with a commission to arrest the miscreants, only to have his commission revoked by the dying king. Part of the Irish objection to these financial exactions lay in the fact that while the king maintained that he needed Irish cash to pay for the security of the English communities in Ireland, the money disappeared into royal coffers in Westminster; so when the earl of March was appointed Richard II's Lieutenant in 1379 and his contract guaranteed that any income he raised from Ireland would stay with him, the crown finally got an Irish subsidy. It was an innovation reinforced by repetition, the same deal applying on the appointment of Lieutenants Philip Courtenay in 1383 and the duke of Gloucester in 1393.

By the start of the fifteenth century it was rare for a year to pass without a Lieutenant summoning a parliament, which became the arena in which the persistent divisions in Irish society were played out – divisions that went beyond the central rift between English and Irish. When James Butler, who succeeded his father as 4th earl of Ormond at the age of fifteen in 1406, was appointed Lieutenant in his own right in 1420, he was well placed to provide a far more broadly based Irish leadership than his predecessors as he spoke Gaelic and his lineage included many Gaelic families. One family, though, was immune to his charms. For the man he replaced as Lieutenant was the military hero John Talbot (later earl of Shrewsbury), whose younger brother Richard was the archbishop of Dublin. The Talbot–Ormond feud that was to dominate the politics of Ireland for two decades had probably started with Talbot's exaction of an ancient fine from Ormond; in any event, when Ormond became Lieutenant he removed all Talbots from the administration, got parliament to condemn Talbot's lieutenancy and complained to the king that the Talbots had systematically persecuted him. The archbishop retaliated with accusations of treachery and attacks on Ormond's lands. Over the years the pendulum of power swung between the two families, with Archbishop Talbot twice becoming Irish Chancellor (1423–6 and 1426–41) and Ormond assuming the reins of government when Talbot was briefly removed from the chancellorship in 1426. In 1428 parliament got involved in the dispute again, sending a petition supporting Ormond to the king, who at the same time was hearing claims that Ormond had been burning down churches and that the archbishop had illegally imprisoned the earl's son. The feud continued to fester until in 1441 archbishop and earl came to a temporary agreement that saw Ormond back in government. But within a year the archbishop was up in arms again, attacking Ormond in the Westminster parliament of 1442 for packing the Irish parliament with his own household staff, and supporting new charges of treason and necromancy. The English Privy Council responded with a stern rebuke to both men, but it was only later in the decade, with the marriage of Ormond's daughter Elizabeth to Shrewsbury's son John, that the feud was finally drawn to a close.

In Holy Trinity Cathedral, Dublin, on 24 May 1487, a ten-year-old boy who claimed to be Edward IV's lost nephew the earl of Warwick was crowned Edward VI, king of England and Ireland – and promptly held a parliament. The impostor's real name was Lambert Simnel and he was the son of an Oxford organ-builder, but for Irish Yorkists such as Henry VII's

Lieutenant, Gerald Fitzgerald, the 8th earl of Kildare, he was a rallying point for an invasion aimed at ousting the Tudor king. Within weeks two thousand German mercenaries supplemented the Irish force of four thousand led by Kildare's brother Thomas Fitzgerald and John de la Pole, the earl of Lincoln, which landed in England on 5 June, but defeat came swiftly in a single battle at Stoke Field on 16 June, at which both Thomas Fitzgerald and Lincoln were slain.

This left Henry with a problem, for it was bad enough when the Irish were at loggerheads with one another, but if the Irish were going to start meddling in English matters the crown would have to pay far closer attention. At first Henry showed leniency. Simnel was given a job in the royal kitchens. The big issue, though, was what to do about Kildare, the sitting – and Yorkist – Lieutenant. For when Edward IV had attempted to give the governorship of Ireland to Henry, Lord Grey of Ruthin, Kildare had mustered so strong an Irish opposition that he was able to call his own parliament and effectively force Grey to retire to England. Since then the earl had built up a dense family network of support, marrying the daughter of Baron Portlester, marrying his sister to Conn Ó Néill, chief of Tyrone, and securing important Irish peers and chiefs for five of his daughters. Moreover, Kildare had a ferocious temper. To remove him as Lieutenant could cause havoc. In the end Henry opted for discretion. Sir Richard Edgecombe was sent to Dublin in 1488 to secure new oaths of loyalty – and Kildare, reappointed, bowed the knee.

His show of loyalty did not last long. In 1491 he and his cousin the earl of Desmond supported the next Yorkist conspiracy, led by Perkin Warbeck, who claimed to be Edward IV's son Richard, duke of York. This time Henry determined on a policy of complete control of Ireland. In the course of seeing off this, Warbeck's first venture in Ireland, Kildare was sacked and Sir James Ormond, the illegitimate brother of Thomas Butler, the

7th earl, was put in his place, a series of now lost articles were promulgated at an unconventionally summoned parliament at Drogheda in September 1493, and on 12 September 1494 the astute military leader Sir Edward Poynings was appointed deputy Lieutenant to the infant Prince Henry and sent to Ireland with 650 troops. At first a penitent Kildare supported Poynings and helped him cut a deal, but when Poynings suspected him of working with the Gaelic chieftains behind his back he had him arrested, attainted and shipped back to London. This provoked Kildare's brother James to lead another Geraldine rebellion, which Poynings soon suppressed, but it is a measure of Kildare's strength and value to the crown that within two years he was pardoned, allowed to marry the king's cousin (his first wife having died) and reappointed Lieutenant.

By then Henry had a trump card in his hand, which the monarchy would continue to use for the next two centuries. For in the parliament in Drogheda that had agreed Kildare's attainder, Poynings had secured forty-nine statutes, which among other things declared that the statute law of England pertained in Ireland and should therefore 'be accepted, used and executed within this land of Ireland'.[8] This new 'Poynings' Law' further stipulated that no parliament could be held in Ireland without the king's express permission, and that any parliament could only consider such legislation or matters as the king thought meet and proper. 'If', it specified, 'any parliament be holden in that land hereafter contrary to the form and provision aforesaid, it be deemed void and of none effect in law.' By its own hand the Irish parliament became little more than a rubber stamp. For Henry this was a godsend, as henceforth even a mighty Irish peer like Kildare, without whose cooperation as Lieutenant royal authority could not properly be exercised, could be legally restrained by the crown in London. True, there would be times when the monarch would resent the corresponding restriction

Poynings' Law inadvertently imposed on the crown by giving a defined role to the Lieutenant and Irish council in requesting a parliament and suggesting its business. Poynings' Law was suspended, for instance, when Thomas Fitzgerald (known as Silken Thomas because his troops wore silken fringes on their helmets) forswore his allegiance to Henry VIII on 11 June 1534 because he thought his father Gerald, the 9th earl of Kildare, had been executed in London, attacked Dublin Castle and had the archbishop of Dublin, John Allen, murdered. In retribution, Henry's forces seized Fitzgerald's castle at Maynooth in 1535 and put the whole garrison to death in the sarcastically named 'Maynooth pardon'; and although Silken Thomas himself surrendered in July 1535 on the understanding that he would be guaranteed free passage to London where he could plead for mercy, he and five of his uncles were executed at Tyburn.

This suspension of Poynings' Law conveniently enabled the king entirely to circumvent the Irish council, enabling Henry and Thomas Cromwell, backed up by an additional 340 troops based in the Pale, to force the Irish parliament that gathered in May 1536 to enact the king's supremacy over the Irish church, establish the succession on the descendants of Anne Boleyn, declare anyone who called Henry a heretic or schismatic a traitor, and deprive the pope of the first fruits of Irish dioceses. Despite the fact that the spiritual peers had a clear majority, the only murmur of discontent came from the proctors of the clergy, who, according to the Vice-Treasurer, Sir William Brabazon, 'somewhat do stick in divers of these acts'.[9] Thus the main elements of the Irish Reformation were enacted without demur. But when the parliament gathered again in September there were more objections to two Bills introducing a form of income tax and suppressing the monasteries, and in May 1537 the lords spiritual united with the lower clergy in blocking both measures. This time Brabazon reckoned the bishops were the main culprits as the proctors' opposition was 'a crafty cast devised between their masters the bishops and them';[10] so over the coming months Henry set about bullying George Browne, the recently appointed archbishop of Dublin, and Edward Staples, the bishop of Meath, into backing his plans. Finally, in October 1537, Henry got his way. The clerical proctors were dismissed from parliament, thirteen monasteries were abolished and a new anti-Catholic oath of allegiance was required of all Irish office-holders. By the end of 1541 the remaining parliamentary abbots had surrendered their houses. Even Henry's great military ally and occasional Treasurer of Ireland John Rawson was forced to relinquish the Hospitallers' priory at Kilmainham in exchange for a new parliamentary title as Viscount Clontarf. The capstone of the project was then added with the help of the new Lord Deputy, Anthony St Leger, and the Irish Speaker, Sir Thomas Cusack, in the shape of the 1541 Act of Kingly Title, which annexed the Irish crown to that of England and declared the whole of Ireland to be subject, as one nation, to the king. With Poynings' Law suspended, the monarch's power in Ireland was total. Since its imposition and suspension were both willingly agreed by the same parliament, it is clear that body was at best a timid beast.

The Tudor years continued to prove Ireland's parliament timid. In 1557, in due obedience to Queen Mary (and surrounded by a judicious number of English troops under the new Lord Deputy, the earl of Sussex), it joined Hugh Curwin, her new Lord Chancellor and archbishop of Dublin, on its knees in abject contrition for its sinful renunciation of the pope. But three years later, in equally due obedience to Elizabeth, it enacted her reinstatement of the Reformation. Surprisingly, there were few changes in the episcopal ranks. Mary had Archbishop Browne demoted to the office of prebendary, removed the bishops of Kildare and Leighlin, and deprived bishop Staples – who complained to Cecil that he had been 'driven almost to begging, thrust out of my house, cast from estimation and made a jesting stock among monks and friars, nor any cause was laid against me, but for that I did marry a wife'.[11] But Elizabeth removed no Irish bishops prior to the January 1560 parliament, allowing even the new Marian bishops of Meath and Kildare, William Walsh and Thomas Leverous, to remain in place until they refused parliament's new oath of supremacy. True, she created nine additional shire seats in the Commons and seats were found for a few loyal Protestants; but the men who attended parliament in 1560 were probably largely the same who had attended in 1557, and yet they happily stood on their collective head for successive monarchs twice in the twinkling of a coronet.

Ireland's *people*, by contrast, were anything but cowed. Indeed, the reason for parliament's startling flexibility in the matter of religious reform may well lie in the fact that most Irish barely expected to be ruled in the matter by either crown or parliament. The legislation in Ireland allowed for the liturgical use of Latin and in large parts of the country the crown held little sway. In England the apparatus of the state, its magistrates, sheriffs and courts, could enforce the new religion; but in Ireland, beyond the narrow sliver of the Pale, such royal authority was a pipedream. So parliament could aver its 'godly' faith, but the people would maintain their rebellion by quietly saying mass, making pilgrimages and adhering to the pope.

Moreover, parliament itself was more an occasionally useful tool of royal authority than a settled Irish institution. In her long reign Elizabeth summoned only two further parliaments, each of which sat for just a few weeks, in 1569–71 and 1585–6. The first of these was occasioned by another bout of Gaelic infighting, which had seen the rebellious Gaelic chief of Tyrone, Shane O'Neill, overthrown and decapitated. In response to the dangerous collapse of order, the Lord Deputy Sir Henry Sidney had a threefold plan – seize the Tyrone lands in Ulster for the crown by a parliamentary Act of Attainder, deprive the Gaelic chiefs of 'coign and livery', their traditional source of revenue,* and start a new process of colonizing Munster. Such a concatenation of ideas alienated not just Gaels but the occupants of the Pale as well, so Sidney got just part of what he sought from parliament. He left with a stinging rebuke, and called the Irish in general 'a sort of barbarous people, odious to God and man, that lap your [English] blood as greedily as ours'.[12] The next parliament fourteen years later was summoned by a new Lord Deputy, Sir James Perrott, who had made his name in Ireland initially as the vindictive first president of Munster who had sent eight hundred rebels to the gallows. He returned in 1585 a hardened soldier, determined to bring peace, if necessary by force. He had other ideas, too, seeking the imposition of the same anti-Catholic measures that had just been agreed in England, and demanding further reform of revenue gathering. Having alienated both the new English colonialists and the old-established English families alike, he left with little more than another Act of Attainder and a sharp lecture from the Speaker, Nicholas Walsh, on the constitutional liberties of Ireland.

Elizabeth's final years were absorbed in a ferocious bout of Irish blood-letting, unleashed by the formerly loyal Hugh O'Neill, earl of Tyrone, and Hugh O'Donnell, another Gaelic chieftain, who together led a nine-year rebellion that forced a reluctant queen to send eighteen thousand English troops to Ireland under the earl of Essex. Although the chiefs were defeated at Kinsale in 1602, the war left the English parliament so debilitated by its cost that a relatively generous peace was made with the Ulster lords, whom the new King James tolerated, much as he

---

* Coign and livery was the ancestral right of an Irish chief to sequester goods for his household and quarter his troops on his subjects in times of war.

had the Scottish chieftains, while depriving them of their lands. By 1607 the slow war of attrition over land rights with the new Lord Deputy, Sir Arthur Chichester (whose brother's severed head had been kicked around like a football by Tyrone's troops in 1597), led Tyrone, Hugh's brother Rory O'Donnell and about ninety followers to seek support in Spain for a new war, but when the Spanish force was lost in the battle of Gibraltar the earls remained in exile, their abandonment of Ulster leaving room for a new plantation of Protestant English settlers.

James was no keener to call an Irish parliament than Elizabeth. Indeed, the Irish parliament was almost entirely irrelevant throughout the Stuart era, and there were just seven general elections throughout the seventeenth century.[13] The 1613 session was about as addled as that in Westminster the following year. Chichester's strong Protestant convictions had led him to deprive Catholics of office by requiring them to swear the oath of supremacy for the first time, and he had had the elderly Catholic bishop of Down and Connor, a Franciscan called Conor O'Devany, executed for treason in 1612. Believing that bringing Ireland to the Protestant faith was the most sacred and important job of work he could do, he then sought parliamentary approval for further anti-Catholic measures and created a flock of new borough seats so as to guarantee a Protestant majority in the parliament that he summoned for 1613. The Catholic members, led by Sir John Everard, would have none of it. When it came to the election of Speaker in Dublin Castle on 18 May, Everard was nominated and was immediately planted in the Speaker's chair, whereupon the Protestants proceeded to elect Sir John Davies in his stead. When Everard refused to budge, the tellers simply deposited Davies in his lap until they managed to drag him away. The Catholic members attempted to storm out, but when they found the doors were locked, vented their fury in vociferous complaint. When at last they were allowed out, one

Catholic member, John Talbot, declared: 'Those inside the house are no house.'[14] The Catholic boycott was to last a year, until Chichester caved in, relinquishing some of the new seats and withdrawing the anti-Catholic legislation in exchange for a cash subsidy. Perhaps the most important repercussion of the 1613 session was a re-alignment of the old allegiances. Now the 'old English' were ranging themselves with what was left of their co-religionist Gaelic lords against the Protestant bishops and 'new English' colonialists. In Chichester's eyes, this was to choose Barabbas over Jesus.

James's son was no keener on Irish parliaments than his father, preferring to rule Ireland through strong deputies and summoning parliament only twice, in 1634 and 1640, both times in search of cash. The initiative for the first of these parliaments sprang not from Lord Deputy Thomas Wentworth but from a collection of loyal Catholic peers of old English stock such as Richard de Burgh, 4th earl of Clanricarde (and earl of St Albans), who had been brought up in England, married Sir Francis Walsingham's daughter Frances and spent twelve years as president of Connacht, and Richard Nugent, earl of Westmeath, who – being 'turbulent, [and] unmindful of his majesty's great favour to him'[15] – had fought against the creation of Protestant seats in 1613. This group now suggested a deal with the crown: £40,000 a year for three years in exchange for the redress of a series of grievances compiled in two documents akin to the Petition of Right, known as the 'Matters of Grace and Bounty' and the 'Graces'. The petitioners and the crown alike wanted the matter settled in a parliament, which was duly called for 14 July 1634. Wentworth, infused with Laudian theology and aware of Clanricarde's connections at court, was not unhappy with the suggestion of some leniency for the Catholics, so while the new English Protestants gave him a mild headache in this first session (to which he had persuaded the city of Dublin to send him as a burgess), he was still able to get a handsome subsidy through. When it came to a second session later that year, though, he was less forthcoming on the 'Graces' and refused to countenance Clanricarde's key demand – guaranteed protection for the mostly Catholic landowners in Connacht – so the Puritans and the Catholics were soon equally disaffected with the crown. This gave Wentworth a pronounced migraine in the form of a Commons defeat by nine votes, whereupon the remaining Graces were shelved and Wentworth dissolved parliament. He had achieved his aim of raising money, but he had managed to alienate virtually the whole population.

By 1640, though, Charles urgently needed more funds for his war against the Scottish Covenanters; so in March Wentworth, who had been summoned back to London in September 1639 as Charles's closest adviser and promoted to Lord Lieutenant of Ireland and earl of Strafford in January 1640, summoned another parliament. As in 1634, the first session passed off well enough, with four subsidies of £45,000 each agreed. But when Strafford, sick with dysentery and gout, returned to England for the Short Parliament, matters soured. In sessions in June and October Strafford's successor Christopher Wandesforde found it impossible to keep order. First Catholics and Puritans combined to reduce the subsidies to £12,000 each, at which point Wandesforde tore the offending pages out of the *Commons Journal*. Then they determined to impeach Strafford and the bishop of Derry, John Bramhall, leading Wandesforde to prorogue parliament before dying, exhausted, in December.

No parliament was to be convened again in Ireland until the Restoration, but as the armed Irish uprising against the authority of the Long Parliament and the Scottish Covenanters gathered force under Owen Roe O'Neill, the Catholic clergy and nobility created their own parliamentary body, the Kilkenny

Confederation, which first met in the house of a great-grandson of Hugh O'Neill, Robert Shee, on 24 October 1642. Although this body used the same franchise as parliament, the Confederates refused to use the term lest they be thought to usurp the authority of the king (to whom they counted themselves loyal). Accordingly they determined to sit as one house and expressly referred to their presiding officer, the lawyer Sir Nicholas Plunkett, as Chairman rather than Speaker. In November the Confederation elected a supreme council of twenty-four to run Ireland, with the Catholic Richard Butler, Viscount Mountgarrett, as its first president. Soon the war was essentially religious, and the Confederation was divided between the competing demands of the new Florentine papal nuncio, Archbishop Giovanni Rinuccini, who sought a complete purgation of Protestants from Ireland, and Charles I's appointed Deputy, James Butler, the 12th marquess of Ormond, with whom a treaty was eventually signed guaranteeing religious freedom in Ireland in exchange for support for the royalist cause – in January 1649, just before Charles's execution. Demoralized at the rejection of his purist policy, Rinuccini departed just as Prince Rupert's royalist fleet landed at Kinsale in February. The Long Parliament had been scandalized into action in 1642 by tales of hundreds of thousands of Protestant colonialists being murdered in Ulster, but now, threatened with an Irish–royalist invasion, the English parliament girded its Puritan loins with yet greater vigour and within months Oliver Cromwell was brutally en route for Ireland, intent on its complete and ultimate subjugation.

Although no medieval Irish parliament had been involved in deciding the royal succession when the English king was formally entitled 'lord of Ireland', Henry VIII's creation of the kingdom of Ireland intimated a closer parallel with the English bond of monarch and parliament, so it seemed only fair that the

Cromwellian republic should properly be ended by an Irish parliament. So Richard Cromwell's fall initiated a sequence of events that led to the parliament's recall. First his brother Henry resigned as Lord Deputy; then Sir Charles Coote, who had seized Galway from the Confederates in 1652, took Dublin Castle from Sir Hardress Waller; Roger Boyle, Lord Broghill, the president of Munster, rallied to Charles II; and Coote, as president of Connacht, engineered a Convention, which sat briefly in early 1660 and demanded that the king summon a full parliament with legislative authority independent from England, and that he restore the Church of Ireland. On 14 May 1660 Charles II was acclaimed king of Ireland, and the following year a parliament was summoned, which proved generous in granting new customs and excise duties and a perpetual hearth tax.

Charles's new Irish government, led by the reappointed Lord Deputy Ormond (now a duke) and Broghill (now earl of Orrery), faced more difficulty in undoing the work of the Long and Rump Parliaments, which had barred Catholics from voting or sitting in parliament and redistributed large amounts of Irish land. An Act of Uniformity was passed, which bore down heavily on all dissenters and re-established the Church of Ireland, and a new set of bishops was appointed, including the Laudian Bramhall as archbishop of Armagh and Jeremy Taylor as bishop of Down and Connor. As for the property issue, the very fact that the 1662 Act of Settlement had to be supplemented by a further 1665 Act of Explanation was proof that the former's attempt to hand land back to old English and 'innocent Catholics' had satisfied nobody. The issue was to rankle throughout the rest of the century, as Charles II summoned no Irish parliament and James II did not do so until he had already fled London and 'vacated' the throne. The resulting body, nicknamed the 'Patriot Parliament' by Charles Gavan Duffy in the late nineteenth century, consisted almost entirely of Catholics loyal to James and drove through legislation demanding the full restitution of Catholic lands, but it was to prove a nugatory exercise; Westminster demanded that henceforth all Irish MPs take oaths abjuring the pope, and William III's Irish parliament of 1692 (summoned once he had secured victory in yet another bloody Irish war) abolished all the 'Patriot' acts and even destroyed all records of the 1689 meeting.

The views of the misanthropic maverick nineteenth-century historian J. A. Froude might seem to invite dismissal. After all, he himself reckoned that 'we Froudes have a way of our own of laying hold of the stick by the burnt end, and making the worst rather than the best of everything'.[16] But his views on eighteenth-century Ireland still have a resonance. He rightly excoriated the Church of Ireland bishops for their exaggerated and unnecessary attacks on nonconformists and reckoned that they were the cause of more mischief than anyone. For good measure he added that for fifty years there was nobody in the Irish parliament 'deserving to be called eminent' and that its 'periodic agitations were without purpose'.[17] In all honesty he had a point. Yes, there were occasional moments of rhetorical brilliance. William Conolly, the son of an innkeeper, who prospered thanks to the redistribution of the lands of James II's former supporters, was an impressive Speaker from 1715 to 1729. There were even a few who had interesting, largely nationalist, things to say. Building on the work of the Galway lawyer Patrick Darcy, who had played an important role as a Catholic in the 1634 and 1640 parliaments and had stated in his 1641 *Argument* that no parliament but an Irish one could properly legislate for Ireland, the wealthy Dubliner William Molyneux, MP for Dublin University from 1692 until his death in 1698, similarly argued for Irish legislative autonomy in his *Case of Ireland Being Bound by Acts of Parliament in England, Stated*. Molyneux's assertion that 'to tax me without consent is little better, if not at all, than downright robbing me' would soon reverberate in America.[18] But, even allowing for the relative lack of documentary evidence, these admittedly significant contributions were exceptions in a period of stale, compromised and unrepresentative Irish parliamentary politics.

Having said all that, the 1692 parliament was no pushover. By now Poynings' Law had been subverted on several occasions by the procedural innovation of 'Heads of Bills', whereby the Irish Commons would draw up a broad outline of Bills that would be acceptable to them before the Irish and English councils had their say, but King William wanted to return to a crown-driven model for both money Bills and ordinary legislation. The tussle ended with an important compromise. The Commons would automatically grant a token supply Bill in each session of parliament in acknowledgement of the royal prerogative, but, importantly, no grant of supply would last more than two years, so parliament would have to be called at least biennially. For the first time in its modern history the Irish parliament would begin to form a tradition, its membership would remain steady and it would acquire a corporate memory.

What hampered the Dublin body, though, was its uncompromising Anglicanism and its steady stream of anti-Catholic legislation, which saw foreign education banned, Catholics denied arms or horses, Catholic lawyers deprived of a living and, in 1704, a fierce new penal code. There was a sort of method in the madness, as while the revolutionary cause had been defeated it still relied on papal support, so Catholicism could be seen as a real threat. But anti-Catholic measures hardly endeared Catholic subjects to their Protestant king. Anglican adherents of the inadequately led Church of Ireland were in a tiny minority, so the idea that this parliament was in any sense representative was arrant fiction. Yet the pattern of anti-Catholic legislation continued well into the eighteenth century. To make matters worse, in

1728 Catholics were even deprived of the vote. This sense of Protestant, English-facing ascendancy also infected matters not directly related to religion. When the Irish House of Lords claimed in 1713 that it alone had the right of ultimate judgment as highest court of appeal for Irish legal cases, partly basing its argument on the belief that Ireland had not been conquered by Henry II and that the medieval Irish chiefs had merely volunteered their allegiance to him, it tried to commit the barons of the Irish Exchequer to prison for contempt, for having attempted to enforce the judgment of the Westminster House of Lords in a land dispute;* but in response Britain simply passed a Declaratory Act antagonistically entitled the 'Dependency of Ireland on Great Britain Act' denying any autonomy to the Irish legislature, and acknowledging *force majeure* Dublin acquiesced.

The Dublin parliament of the seventeenth and early eighteenth centuries was, then, in large measure, as Jonathan Swift put it, a 'lousy p–t'[19] – or in the words of the twentieth-century Protestant historian Edmund Curtis, 'a shackled and spiritless legislature' supporting an 'irresponsible government ruling in English interests'.[20] Yet even the shackled can occasionally rebel. When Walpole granted a patent for new copper coinage for Ireland without any consultation in Ireland itself, the furious national campaign was led from outside parliament by Swift's scabrous *Drapier's Letters*, and soon even the archbishop of Armagh, Hugh Boulter, was condemning the coinage, despite his fierce adherence to the policy of imposing English bishops like himself on the Irish church – and parliament forced Walpole to cancel the patent.

* The Irish Court of Exchequer heard a case between Maurice Annesley and his cousin Hester Sherlock over some lands in County Kildare in 1709 and found for Annesley. Sherlock then appealed to the Irish House of Lords and Annesley invoked his right of appeal in the Westminster House of Lords.

It was not till the middle of the century, though, that Ireland started to dance to a more assertive democratic tune. The resurgence started with the double-headed Dublin by-election of 1748–9. On 16 August 1748 Alderman Sir James Somerville, one of the city's two MPs, died, followed the next May by his colleague Alderman Nathaniel Pearson. Since the writ could not be moved for the by-election until parliament next sat, which was not until October 1749, the city was subject to a lengthy campaign. The first candidate to enter the fray, while there was still just one vacancy, was James Digges Latouche, a wealthy scion of a Dublin banking family who had campaigned with an aggressively anti-Catholic Dublin apothecary and physician called Charles Lucas against the self-perpetuating corruption of the Dublin city authorities. But within a week Latouche had an establishment opponent in the shape of Alderman Sir Samuel Cooke, and on the same day, much to Latouche's annoyance, Lucas also joined the campaign trail in his own right. All politicians like to think themselves tireless campaigners, but Lucas truly was, touring the city guild meetings, publishing his own weekly newspaper, *The Censor*, and churning out lengthy pamphlets and addresses to the electorate full of constitutional encomiums peppered with tawdry attacks on his opponents. Like Darcy, Molyneux and Swift, he rejected the claim that Ireland was a conquered colony dependent on Great Britain and declared: 'It must now be confessed that there was no general rebellion in Ireland, since the first British invasion, that was not raised or fomented by the oppression, instigation, evil influence or connivance of the English.'[21] His stream of publications continued to flow throughout the winter of 1748–9, and when on Pearson's death he and Latouche rejoined forces in a combined effort to take both seats, there was a distinct chance that they might both win.

The aldermanic party had its answer ready, though. On

Thursday, 12 October, the day after parliament had assembled, Sir Richard Cox MP, who had described Lucas during the campaign as a Jacobin and 'the offspring of an Irish popish priest',[22] charged him with incendiary and potentially treasonable libels, and the Commons decided that Lucas should answer for himself at a special committee. At its first meeting Lucas refused to answer questions lest he incriminate himself, but when he arrived the following Monday at the parliament house, he was accompanied, like an Irish Wilkes, by an adoring crowd. The committee ploughed on regardless, reporting to the Commons that his publications promoted sedition and insurrection. Under threat of arrest and fearful that his supporters would rise in anger, Lucas fled the country, his place taken on the anti-aldermanic ticket by Thomas Read. The nineteen-day ballot ended on Saturday, 11 November with Cooke a mere 44 votes ahead of Latouche, who took the second seat ahead of the other aldermanic candidate, Charles Burton. The establishment had voted in force against Latouche and Read – and they had one more throw of the dice, as Burton challenged the result and the Commons cynically ousted Latouche by 112 votes to 60. Despite being pursued for seditious libel, Lucas returned to Ireland a decade later with a pardon from George III in his pocket and stood again for Dublin in 1761. This time his brand of constitutional nationalism bore fruit and he was elected alongside a new opponent, the merchant James Grattan.

By the time Lucas died in 1771, after a decade as MP, the world of Irish politics was changing. The lopsided balancing act that saw a tiny group of Anglicans, many of them English sojourners or absentee landlords, led by an unpopular Lord Deputy or Lieutenant, dominate the vast mass of Catholic and Presbyterian Irish, was becoming unsustainable, and just as the American colonies looked to the theories of Darcy and

Molyneux, so young Irishmen looked to American and French ideas for inspiration.

The first off the blocks was Henry Flood, the (widely considered illegitimate) son of the Lord Chief Justice of the King's Bench for Ireland. Prone to intermittent bouts of priggish self-righteousness and naked ambition, Flood first entered parliament in a by-election in November 1759, lost his seat two years later and started to make his mark as an oppositionist MP when he managed to get re-elected in another by-election for Callan in 1762. Flood had hoped that Ireland's fortunes would improve under a new administration when Pitt the Elder appointed Viscount Townshend as the new Lord Lieutenant in 1767; but when Townshend introduced new excise duties, expanded the army and prorogued parliament early to avoid censure, Flood became convinced that Ireland's liberties were being undermined and led the opposition with vim. When Townshend was replaced, though, Flood entered into protracted negotiations with the new Lord Lieutenant and landed himself the well-paid position of Vice-Treasurer. This unprincipled volte-face understandably infuriated his erstwhile allies and, notwithstanding his support for a string of oppositionist causes, which in November 1781 finally led the government to dispense with his services, forever tarnished his reputation.

It was a strange moment to step into opposition again. The North government was foundering in Westminster, and in Ireland a strong 'patriot' movement had formed around James Grattan's son Henry, who had so abruptly fallen out with his establishment-minded father by consorting with radicals such as Gervase Parker Bushe and Hercules Langrishe MP that he was disinherited. When Grattan entered parliament in 1775, though, it was not on his own initiative, but by invitation, and rather suddenly: when Francis Caulfeild, MP for Charlemont, died in

November 1775 his brother Lord Charlemont nominated Grattan to take his place. Elected on 11 December, he made his maiden speech four days later. It must have been an odd event, for every account of a Grattan speech reports how strangely he behaved. As one put it, 'he bent his body to the ground; swung his arms over his head, up and down and around him; and added to the grotesqueness of his manner a hesitating tone and drawling emphasis'.[23] Yet oddness was no bar to political success (Grattan himself, indeed, said of Chatham that he was 'very great and very odd'[24]), and with Flood now in government, Grattan became leader of the oppositionists, declaring in January 1780 that his great campaign was to 'strain every nerve to effectuate a modification of the Law of Poynings . . . [and] to secure this country against the illegal claims of the British parliament'.[25] He launched his campaign less than a month after North's government collapsed, striding into parliament on 16 April 1782 to move a motion declaring the Irish parliament's independence, and being cheered all the way.

At great moments politicians often strain language beyond its sticking point, but having trained himself in the rhetoric of the ancients, Grattan liked a neat turn of phrase, and he spoke now with energy and skill. 'I am now to address a free people', he started:

> I found Ireland on her knees, I watched over her with a pater-nal solicitude; I have traced her progress from injuries to arms, and from arms to liberty. Spirit of Swift, spirit of Molyneux, your genius has prevailed! Ireland is now a nation! In that new character I hail her and bowing to her august presence, I say, *Esto perpetua!*[26]

Grattan was fortunate. At Westminster, Rockingham's new government felt cowed by the menacing noises coming from the Irish Volunteer Convention at Dungannon in its pressure for Irish legislative independence, and was anyway more inclined towards reform than North had been. So the time was ripe for Barry Yelverton, the MP for Carrickfergus and newly appointed Attorney-General, to propose 'an act to regulate the manner of passing bills, and to prevent delays in summoning of parliaments', which repealed Poynings' Law and the Declaratory Act and ceded legislative authority to the Irish parliament. In the words of William Lecky, the late nineteenth-century Irish historian turned Unionist MP: 'Without the effusion of one drop of blood, and with singularly little violence or disorder, the whole constitution of Ireland was changed, and a great revolution accomplished, which Burke described without exaggeration as the Irish analogue to the English revolution of 1688.'[27] In fact, Grattan's euphoria and Lecky's assertions were wild exaggerations. This was no democratic nirvana. The vast majority of Irish seats were pocket boroughs, and very few saw open contests. The majority of the population remained unrepresented – and unenfranchised.

It is little wonder that with Grattan enjoying his popularity (the Commons voted him a massive sum of £100,000 in gratitude, of which he accepted £50,000) and making an accommodation with the Fox–North coalition's Irish administration under Robert Henley, 2nd earl of Northington, Flood now came to the fore again, joining the Volunteers in repeatedly calling for urgent parliamentary reform, from which Grattan fought shy. Thus the two men who should have been allies became enemies, competitors for public popularity – and on 28 October 1783 the accumulated bile poured forth on the floor of the Commons. The invective was designed to sting. Flood called Grattan a 'mendicant patriot who was bought by [his] country for a sum of money and then sold [his] country for prompt payment'. In return, Grattan called Flood an 'insufferable egotist' and proceeded:

> We have seen you a violent opposer of Government, and after-
> wards on the most trying questions silent – silent for years, and
> silenced by money; we have seen you haunting this House like
> a guilty spirit, watching the moment when you should vanish
> from the question; or you might be decried hovering about this
> dome like an ill-omened bird of night, with sepulchral note,
> cadaverous aspect and a broken beak, watching to stoop and
> pounce upon your prey; or we have detected you hid behind
> that chair, to avoid a division or feigning infirmities to excuse
> your absence.[28]

He ended that contribution with panache and brutal directness: 'I, therefore, tell you in the face of your country, before all the world, and to your beard, you are not an honest man.'[29] Each man returned to the battle several times, and by the time the exchange finally ended the Commons had witnessed two unmissable hours of tirades. It was all the Speaker could do to have the two men arrested lest they proceed to fight the duel they both demanded.

The permanent fissure in the patriot party that now ensued was not to be healed, even when Grattan moved unambiguously into opposition again in 1785; but by then new voices had joined the call for reform within parliament – Richard Wellesley, the 2nd earl of Mornington, in the Lords and George Ponsonby, MP for Inistioge, in the Commons – and outside it Wolfe Tone and other like-minded young men founded the Society of the United Irishmen, intent on securing complete separation from England. These developments, especially the Society's success in uniting Protestant dissenting and Catholic Irishmen, and the subsequent war with France and consequent threat of a tricoloured Catholic invasion of Ireland, so fretted Pitt's government that successive lords lieutenant used ever more repressive measures. As in England after the French Revolution, habeas corpus was suspended. In 1797 the whole of Ulster was put under martial law. Houses were burned; captured rebels were subjected to torture (including 'pitchcapping', whereby boiling tar was poured on the suspect's head, allowed to cool and then torn off with the accompanying scalp). Grattan, who had been campaigning for the emancipation of Catholics (a measure he lost in parliament in May 1795 by 155 votes to 84 and again in 1796 by 149 to 12) now took his cue from his allies in London. Like Fox in London, he and the patriot Irish withdrew from the Dublin parliament in 1797. Meanwhile the Society, which by this point had some 280,000 sworn members, had been forced underground and Wolfe Tone himself, having been in exile in America since 1795, joined the French army in an attempted landing at Bantry Bay in 1796. The main insurrection, though, came in May 1798, when first the Irish and then another French invasion force, accompanied by Tone, attempted to oust the English. Both sides used exceptional violence, but by October the French were defeated, Tone had been seized and had slit his own throat rather than be executed, and the British had control of Ireland again.

The rebellion of 1798 completely transformed the political landscape. Less than two decades earlier Britain had been prepared to cede limited authority to Dublin. Now, with the rebellion costing far more than the Irish administration could raise, the pressure was to integrate Ireland far more tightly into Britain. The day after he heard of the rebellion, Pitt began pressing for a full union of the two parliaments – an outcome the king too was eager to see. The only concession offered to Irish opponents of the proposal was that such a union could proceed only on the basis of votes in both parliaments, as had occurred with Scotland in 1707.

There was plenty to recommend the plan. Pitt noted that while Rockingham's Irish reforms of 1782 had effectively abolished a constitution, nobody had thought to draft a new one, and others pointed to Britain and Ireland (or at least the Protestant ascendancy in Ireland) sharing the same enemy, the French; so the union project had the backing not only of the newly appointed and very Irish 29-year-old Chief Secretary for Ireland Robert Stewart, Viscount Castlereagh, but of key figures and groups in Ireland. Many Ulster Protestants were indifferent to the fate of the Irish parliament; the corporations of Dundalk and Armagh agreed supportive motions; Edward Cooke, MP for Old Leighlin and under-secretary for the civil department, backed up the new Lord Lieutenant, Charles, Marquess Cornwallis, with a pamphlet explaining the advantages of union; even the Catholic archbishop of Dublin supported it on the presumption that it would entail the emancipation of his co-religionists. This last was a key issue that Cornwallis and Pitt had already spotted, for Cooke could argue that while it would be dangerous to allow Catholics to sit in a Dublin parliament where they might form a majority, it would be safe to allow them to sit in a union parliament because there they would undoubtedly be in a minority. Fatally for Anglo-Irish relations, thanks to George III's intransigent belief that this would be inconsistent with his own coronation oath this was a promise that Pitt was not able to deliver.

But the union had plenty of opponents, too, especially within the Irish parliament. Both the Ponsonby brothers, William and George, argued that it was the incontestable right of the Irish people to have their own legislative assembly, and even the Speaker, John Foster, declared himself vehemently opposed – despite having been Irish Chancellor of the Exchequer, despite having spent more than twenty years as a government loyalist and despite his younger brother William being the royally appointed Anglican bishop of Clogher.

When parliament gathered in Dublin in January 1799 the mood was tense, and on 23 January the Commons voted by 105 to 104 against a proposition that asserted 'the undoubted birthright of the people of Ireland to have a free and independent legislature'. The next day it voted more convincingly against any idea of union, by 111 to 105. Cooke had warned that if an act of union were to be agreed it would have to be 'written-up, spoken-up, intrigued-up, drunk-up, sung-up and bribed-up',[30] and so it was to prove. No more than a score of MPs changed their votes between January 1799 and the following year, but £32,000 was spent out of secret service funds to secure the result. More significantly, though, the government managed to get seventy-five MPs to step down, relinquishing their seats to pro-union members. It is easy to condemn this as corrupt, but Castlereagh undoubtedly thought he was on a campaign against corruption – the corruption endemic in the Irish borough system, which made a parliamentary seat a valuable commodity. So when parliament met on 15 January 1800 it was clear that the crown might get its way. Grattan, who had (ironically enough) bought the parliamentary seat of Wicklow at midnight for £1,200, dramatically turned up in the small hours of the debate, dressed in a Volunteer uniform and so emaciated through illness that he had to totter in on the arms of his friends Arthur Moore and George Ponsonby. Castlereagh nervously watched him take his oath and speak, seated, for two impressive hours on liberty and the evils of the union. He need not have worried: an anti-union amendment fell by 138 votes to 96; a motion to accept a message in favour of a union was carried by 158 to 115; and the two parliaments of Ireland and Britain moved inexorably towards enacting a union based on Ireland contributing to Westminster four bishops, twenty-eight representative peers (each elected for life) and one hundred MPs taking newly created seats. It was a sign of how frayed tempers were becoming that when Isaac Corry, another former Chancellor of the Exchequer, accused Grattan of being a revolutionary, the two men fought a duel.

For many years the Irish parliament had been peripatetic, meeting in a variety of cities and venues. In 1661 it had moved into Chichester House in Dublin, outside the old city borders at College Green, and in 1729, with biennial parliaments now mandatory, the parliament convened in the Bluecoat School in Oxmantown while a new home, the elegant neoclassical Parliament Building, was constructed on College Green, with a magnificent octagonal chamber for the Commons and a grander, rectangular one for the Lords. Less than a century after its opening, on 1 August 1800, the British Bill having already passed its final hurdle in Westminster at the beginning of July, the Irish Bill received royal assent. The next day Speaker Foster closed the session and the parliament and took away both the mace and the Speaker's chair, swearing that whenever the government should come asking for them, he would only restore them to that body to whom they truly belonged, the Commons of Ireland. Grattan struck a melodramatic pose and spoke of Irish independence: 'I sat by her cradle; I followed its hearse.'[31]

We'll join hand in hand all Party shall cease.
And glass after glass shall our Union increase,

In the Cause of Old England we'll drink down the Sun,
Then toast Little Ireland and drink down the Moon!

Satirical prints flourished at the time of the Act of Union with Ireland in 1801. Here George, the prince of Wales, presides at a raucous dinner held on 19 January at Cumberland House, Pall Mall, surrounded by the 'Carlton House set' of his closest allies. All were opponents of the Prime Minister, William Pitt the Younger, and, like him, drank considerably.

Epilogue: The Wisdom of our Ancestors

WHEN THE NEW PARLIAMENT of the United Kingdom of Great Britain and Ireland, or the 'Imperial Parliament' as the press liked to refer to it, gathered on Thursday, 22 January 1801, change was in the air. The House of Lords had sat in the elegant but petite Queen's Chamber ever since the middle ages, remaining there even when Pitt had created an unprecedented eighty-seven new Tory peers and George III complained that the Lords were 'too numerous' at 350. Now they, plus twenty-eight new Irish representative peers and four Irish bishops, were installed in the former Court of Requests or 'Lesser Hall'. Such was the haste with which the new chamber had been prepared that *The Times* noted that although the new building 'has much of grandeur in its appearance' and the vast Armada tapestries had been transferred with the peers, 'there has not been leisure for minute decoration'.[1] For the Commons, St Stephen's Chapel was remodelled (again) to accommodate a hundred Irish MPs; extra seating was installed and the space in the galleries reserved for the public was reduced. With the total number of MPs now standing at 658, it was a cramped affair. The architect of the Union, Viscount Castlereagh, formerly the Westminster MP for Orford but now sitting for his old Irish seat of Down, had to rub shoulders with seventy-five others who swiftly took their seats, including his half-brother Charles Stewart, the radical supporter of emancipation Richard Martin, the Pittite Irish Chancellor of the Exchequer Sir Isaac Corry (who was favourably reported to have 'no brogue' but did have six children, despite never marrying), the leader of the Whig anti-unionists William Ponsonby and, within weeks, Ponsonby's brother George, who was elected in the first United Kingdom by-election and was soon leading the Whig opposition in Westminster.

The government had gone to great pains to make sure that the new intake was onside. Castlereagh's clever successor as Secretary for Ireland, Charles Abbot, kept a detailed list of which Irish MPs and peers turned up, who was for the government and who for the opposition, and what were their 'circumstances'. He reckoned on 55 MPs for, 25 against and 6 'ineffective'.[2] Since 71 Dublin MPs had previously been on the government's books, this was only to be expected. In the Lords the numbers were similar; there was one fly in the ointment, the radical, eccentric and extravagant bishop of Derry, Frederick Hervey – but then, he already had a seat in the Lords as the fourth earl of Bristol. The opening speeches of the new parliament set the tone for future centuries, with ladlesful of self-congratulation. In the Lords, James Graham, the 45-year-old third duke of Montrose, who had been a member of the Commons before he succeeded to his father's dukedom, declared that 'these countries will thus naturally become one; the people, who speak the same language and are governed by the same laws, will thus also become one people'.[3] In the Commons he was outdone by the orotund Sir Watkin Williams-Wynn, who rolled out the rhetoric, pronouncing that

> every fear of the promoters of that grand measure, every menace of its adversaries, has been happily disappointed.

Tumults of the populace, the din of opposition, the mistaken complaints of manufacturers and merchants, old prejudices of the unenlightened, the secret disaffection of those who might incline to listen to the seductions of our perfidious enemies, appear to have been . . . effectually hushed.[4]

Anyone might have been excused for thinking that the constitution was now settled for all eternity, as apart from the composition of parliament not much else had changed since the days of Walpole. Rotten boroughs, electoral bribery and partisan patronage were still the order of the day. Gentlemen's clubs used secret ballots, but not parliament. Some elements of how parliament worked would have been recognizable even to Mauger le Vavasour or Fulk Peyferer. Apart from the Septennial Act's limit on the length of a parliament, the king still decided when parliament sat, adjourned, prorogued or dissolved. Peers still exercised a phenomenal sway over the lower house, directly nominating a hundred or so MPs and influencing the selection of a further 125. What is more, the Prime Minister, the younger Pitt, had been in post since December 1783 thanks to royal favour rather than parliamentary arithmetic, and his Cabinet differed in its composition from that of a Stuart or Tudor Privy Council only by its not including a bishop, consisting as it did of a duke (Portland), a marquess (Cornwallis), five earls (Chatham, Spencer, Westmorland, Camden and Liverpool), three first-time barons (Loughborough, Amherst and Grenville) and just two other MPs (Henry Dundas and William Windham).

Even so, those with a nose for such things might just have detected the faintest sniff of reform in Westminster. The war with revolutionary France was in its eighth debilitatingly costly year. Royal lassitude, Cabinet divisions, and a degree of ministerial incompetence on the part of Pitt's brother-in-law, the Foreign Secretary, and his great mate, the War Secretary, had made it a difficult war to prosecute to victory, so there was an appetite for peace. The debate on the loyal address, which started on 2 February, was remarkably febrile, with those who had opposed the union, such as Charles Grey, now in his fifteenth year as MP for Northumberland, clamouring for Pitt to honour his promise of Catholic emancipation, even as Pitt was secretly battling over the matter with the king. But by the time the two houses voted on Grey's amendment to the loyal address, the only change was that Pitt had resigned, to be replaced (once George had got over another bout of insanity) by the recently re-elected and lugubriously dull Speaker, Henry Addington, of whom the common quip was that as Pitt was to Addington, so London was to Paddington. Whatever its historic pretensions, parliament was clearly still in the monarch's thrall.

What shape was parliament in, 543 years after those fourteen knights had travelled to London in 1258? The House of Lords, still dominated by the great landed families, was supremely self-confident in its pre-eminence. Dukes, marquesses, viscounts, earls and barons knew their place in the established order and expected deference and unquestioning support for the hereditary principle. They presumed to rule. They still thought of themselves alone as the guardians of the common weal, and ceded authority to the Commons on taxation alone. By contrast, the bench of bishops, led by two English archbishops of negligible personal presence, scholarship, administrative ability or moral insight, had reached its spiritual nadir. Only Belby Porteus, the anti-slavery bishop of London from 1787 to 1809, struck much of an ecclesiastical figure in the life of parliament; more typical of the episcopacy as a whole were the profoundly unimpressive Brownlow North, whose forty-nine years as a bishop owed more to his father's earldom and his half-brother's premiership than any spiritual qualifications; the bishop of Durham, Shute Barrington, who happened to be brother to the former Secretary at War; James Yorke at Ely, whose father and brother served as Lord Chancellor; and the archbishop of Armagh, William Stuart, the son of the former premier the earl of Bute. Nepotism, pluralism, absenteeism, a devotion to religious uniformity, ready adherence to the government that had appointed them and complacent disregard for the world around them all made the bishops a tawdry irrelevance.

As for the Commons, although it was now conscious of its own importance and fierce in defence of its own privileges, most of its members never faced a contested election and the House still harboured plenty of scions of the old parliamentary families (including an Egerton, two Thynnes, two Bentincks, three Cokes, a Talbot, a Bathurst, a Pelham, a Walpole, a Petty and a Russell). True, there were also men who had got there by virtue of their convictions rather than their connections; but even they were men of means, as although ministerial office was extremely lucrative and scores had some sort of government pension or emolument, there was at this point no payment for simply being a member of parliament. Even so, some of the most notably effective MPs had come from the growing numbers of the 'middling sort' of families who had never sent a man to parliament before. One ability was valued above all else: the gift of the gab, and many who had it excelled as parliamentary performers, attracting great audiences. Fox was still refusing to attend and was anyway past his best, but Pitt's duelling partner Tierney was as passionate as ever, and Sheridan could deliver a witty speech when he was sober and an even wittier one when drunk. Among the Tories, Pitt could draw blood as few others then or since, George Rose, his patronage secretary, was a thoroughly effective proto-whip, and George Canning, the MP for the rotten borough of Wendover, who described himself as 'an Irishman born in London' and would later be condemned by Grey as the son of an actress and therefore '*ipso facto* disqualified from being Prime

Minister', was already established as a sparkling orator, although still climbing in the foothills of political office.

In large measure, then, this was a parliament that would have been recognizable to a visitor from a century earlier. And yet, far from Westminster there were artisans and working people clamouring for greater rights; and in the coffee-houses and salons of London the concept of MPs as openly elected local representatives was flickering across the mind of the body politic. British aristocrats had been frightened by events across the Channel, though. Witness the mightily wealthy William, Earl Fitzwilliam, nephew and heir to the former Whig Prime Minister the marquess of Rockingham, who vigorously opposed any parliamentary reform, as he thought it would 'frenchify' Britain and he had 'nothing less at heart than to be *frenchified*'.[5] He was not alone. As the concept of democracy took shape in Britain, the Tory lawyer Sir William Grant, MP for Banffshire (described as 'great on the bench, an oracle in Parliament, but like Mrs Siddons a preposterous body in a drawing room'[6]), declared his preference for 'the wisdom of our ancestors', a phrase that soon became a rallying cry for reactionaries who would come to question even the established liberties and constitutional concepts, including habeas corpus, the financial privilege of the Commons, and free speech within and outside parliament.

This battle between ancestral voices and people shouting 'reform, reform, reform' would soon come into sharp focus and would dominate the next two centuries of parliamentary history; but Grant should have known that among the ancestors themselves had been reformers in every generation. And Fitzwilliam might have acknowledged that the ancestral principles of the Imperial Parliament owed much to the man who had first called commoners to parliament in the thirteenth century, Simon de Montfort, a Frenchman.

Notes

Prologue

1 *House of Commons Debates* (*HC*), 15 May 1945, vol. 410, col. 2307.
2 *HC*, 24 Feb. 1920, vol. 125, col. 1624.
3 Bill Cash, *John Bright*, London, Tauris, 2012, pp. 96–7.
4 Henry Hallam, *The Constitutional History of England*, London, John Murray, 1846, vol. 1, pp. 1–2.
5 Thomas Babington Macaulay, *History of England*, London, Longman, 1849, vol. 1, p. 13.
6 *HC*, 22 July 1875, vol. 225, cols 1824–6.
7 E. Hodder, *The Life and Work of the Seventh Earl of Shaftesbury*, London, Cassell, 1886, vol. 3, p. 326.
8 Samuel Pepys, *Diary and Correspondence*, Berkeley, University of California Press, 1981, vol. 7, p. 416, 19 Dec. 1666.
9 *HC*, 4 Apr. 1938, vol. 334, col. 6.
10 *HC*, 27 July 1893, vol. 15, col. 724.
11 Cited in William Kent, *John Burns: Labour's Lost Leader*, London, Williams & Norgate, 1950, p. 367.
12 James Lowther, Viscount Ullswater, *A Speaker's Commentaries*, London, E. Arnold, 1925, vol. 1, p. 235.
13 Cited in David McKie, *Jabez: The Rise and Fall of a Victorian Rogue*, London, Atlantic Books, 2004, p. 85.
14 Edward Maunde-Thomson, ed., *Chronicon Adae de Uske*, Oxford, Oxford University Press, 1904, p. 257.
15 Edmund Burke, *The Works of the Rt Hon. Edmund Burke*, London, Holdsworth & Ball, 1834, vol. 1, p. 180.
16 Christopher Hollis, *Can Parliament Survive?*, London, Hollis & Carter, 1949, p. 36.

17 Nathaniel Wraxall, *Historical Memoirs of My Own Time*, London, Cadell and Davies, 1815, vol. 2, p. 168.

18 Robert Blake, *The Conservative Party from Peel to Churchill*, London, Eyre & Spottiswoode, 1970, p. 277.

Chapter 1: The First Commoners

1 Matthew Paris, *English History from the Year 1235 to 1273, Translated from the Latin by the Rev. J. A. Giles*, London, G. Bohn, 1854, vol. 3, p. 280.

2 H. R. Luard, ed., *Matthaei Parisiensis, Monachi Sancti Albani, Chronica Majora*, vol. 5, p. 621, cited in J. R. Maddicott, *The Origins of the English Parliament 924–1327*, Oxford, Oxford University Press, 2010, p. 223.

3 Paris, *English History from the Year 1235*, vol. 3, p. 279.

4 *Curia Regis Rolls*, XV: 1233–37, no. 2047.

5 Paris, *English History from the Year 1235*, vol. 3, p. 256.

6 See the detailed list of great councils and parliaments in Maddicott, *The Origins of the English Parliament*, pp. 454–72.

7 *Calendar of Patent Rolls*, 1258, p. 645.

8 Lincoln sent Egidius de Gousell, William de Iseny, William de Ingolby and William de Sancto Laudo.

9 *Rotuli Litterarum Clausarum*, vol. 1, p. 132, cited in R. G. Davies and J. H. Denton, *The English Parliament in the Middle Ages*, Manchester, Manchester University Press, 1981, p. 6.

10 William Stubbs, ed., *Select Charters and other Illustrations of English Constitutional History from the Earliest Times to the Reign of Edward I*, Oxford, Clarendon Press, 1913, p. 282.

11 Ibid.

12 The full list of those named in the expenses writ of 1258 is Robert of Cam (or Cambhou), William of Buketon, Simon le Lilling, Mauger le Vavasour, William of Barton, Giles de Gousle, William de Iseny, William de Ingolby, William de Santo Laudo, William le Moyne, Walter de Wassyngley, Simon de Copmanford and Baldwin de Drayton, together with the unnamed knights for Gloucester,

Northampton, Kent, Leicester, Warwickshire, Nottingham, Derby, Buckinghamshire, Devon and Dorset who may or may not have been the same as those on the writ of summons. See Helen M. Cam, 'The parliamentary writs "de expensis" of 1258', *English Historical Review*, vol. 46, no. 184 (Oct. 1931), pp. 630–2.

13 Cited in Andrew H. Hershey, 'The English royal writ and "1258"', *English Historical Review*, vol. 113, no. 453 (1998), p. 841.

14 Paris, *English History from the Year 1235*, vol. 1, p. 335.

15 Henry Hart Milman, ed., *Annals of St Paul's Cathedral*, London, John Murray, 1869, p. 59.

16 H. R. Luard, ed., 'Annales Monasterii de Burton', in *Annales Monastici*, London, Longman, 1864, vol. 1, p. 471.

17 Paris, *English History from the Year 1235*, vol. 3, p. 295.

18 Reginald Francis Traherne, ed., *The Documents of the Baronial Movement of Reform and Rebellion*, Oxford, Clarendon Press, 1973, p. 301.

19 H. R. Luard, ed., 'Annales Theokesberia', in *Annales Monastici*, London, Longman, 1864, vol. 1, p. 102.

20 Ibid., p. 143.

21 In Latin, 'tam ex maioribus quam minoribus': see Stubbs, William, *The Constitutional History of England*, vol. 2, Oxford, Clarendon Press, 1875, p. 101.

22 *Consilium*, with an 's', was regularly used to mean both 'counsel', as in advice, and 'council', the small continuous body of royal advisers which we might better call the king's council. *Concilium*, with a 'c', was generally used to refer to a body specifically summoned on a fixed date and for a limited period. See Albert Beebe White, 'Early instances of concentration of representatives in England', *American Historical Review*, vol. 19, no. 4 (July 1914), pp. 735–50.

Chapter 2: Subjected Thus

1 William Stubbs, *The Constitutional History of England*, Oxford, Clarendon, 1875, vol. 2, p. 102.

2 Henry Hallam, *View of the State of Europe during the Middle Ages*, London, A. C. Armstrong, 1880, vol. 2, p. 31.

3 *The Statutes*, London, Eyre & Spottiswoode, 1870, vol. 1, p. 16.

4 Ibid., p. 71.

5 Sir William Betham, *The Origin and History of the Constitution of England*, Dublin, William Curry, 1834, p. 104.

6 Stubbs, *Constitutional History of England*, vol. 2, pp. 134, 267.

7 Constitutions of Clarendon, cap. 11, cited in R. G. Davies and J. H. Denton, *The English Parliament in the Middle Ages*, Manchester, Manchester University Press, 1981, p. 89.

8 H. G. Richardson and G. O. Sayles, eds, *Rotuli [Parliamentorum Anglie Hactenus] Inediti*, Camden Society, 3rd series, 1935, vol. 51, p. 101, cited in Claire Valente, 'The deposition and abdication of Edward II', *English Historical Review*, vol. 113, no. 453 (1998), pp. 860–1.

9 Cited in Valente, 'The deposition and abdication of Edward II', p. 865.

10 Cited in Ian Mortimer, *The Perfect King*, London, Jonathan Cape, 2006, p. 54.

11 *French Chronicle of London*, London, Camden Society, 1844, p. 86.

12 A. R. Myers, ed., *English Historical Documents, 1327–1485*, vol. 4, London, Eyre & Spottiswoode, 1969, p. 72.

13 Gaillard T. Lapsley, *Crown, Community and Parliament in the Later Middle Ages*, Oxford, Blackwell, 1951, p. 247.

14 *The Anonimalle Chronicle*, cited in Myers, ed., *English Historical Documents 1327–1485*, vol. 4, p. 114.

15 Ibid., p. 118.

16 Ibid., p. 115.

17 Cited in George Holmes, *The Good Parliament*, Oxford, Clarendon Press, 1975, p. 103.

18 John Taylor, Wendy R. Childs and Leslie Watkiss, eds, *The St Albans Chronicle; the Chronica Maiora of Thomas Walsingham, 1376–1394*, Oxford, Oxford University Press, 2003, p. 57.

19 Peter R. Coss, *The Origins of the English Gentry*, Cambridge,

Cambridge University Press, 2003, p. 197.

20 John Stachey, ed., *Rotuli Parliamentorum*, House of Lords (London, 1832), vol. 2, p. 310.

Chapter 3: A House Divided against Itself

1 Jeanne Krochalis and Edward Peters, eds, *The World of Piers Plowman*, Philadelphia, University of Pennsylvania Press, 1982, p. 116.

2 Siegfried Wenzel, trans., *Preaching in the Age of Chaucer*, Washington DC, Catholic University of America Press, 2008, pp. 242–6.

3 Isabella's sigh in *Measure for Measure*, Act II scene 2: '. . . but man, proud man, Drest in a little brief authority, Most ignorant of what he's most assured, His glassy essence, like an angry ape, Plays such fantastic tricks before high heaven As make the angels weep.'

4 Prov. 16: 18, King James Bible.

5 Shakespeare's Bushy in *Richard II*.

6 C. Given-Wilson, ed. and trans., *The Chronicle of Adam of Usk, 1377–1421*, Oxford, Oxford University Press, 1997, p. 29.

7 Cited in Gaillard Lapsley, *Crown, Community and Parliament in the Later Middle Ages*, Oxford, Blackwell, 1951, p. 351.

8 David Preest, trans., and James Clark, ed., *Chronica Maiora of Thomas Walsingham*, Woodbridge, Boydell, 2005, p. 311.

9 Ibid.

10 Lapsley, *Crown, Community and Parliament*, p. 351.

11 Ibid., p. 357.

12 House of Lords, *Report on the Dignity of a Peer*, London, 1820, vol. 1, p. 348.

13 William Stubbs, *The Constitutional History of England*, Oxford, Clarendon Press, 1903 edn, vol. 2, p. 533.

14 In order: Anthony Steel, *Richard II*, Cambridge, Cambridge University Press, 1941, p. 8; Alec R. Meyers, *England in the Late Middle Ages*, Harmondsworth, Penguin, 1952, p. 35; May

McKisack, *The Fourteenth Century, 1307–1399*, Oxford, Clarendon Press, 1959, p. 498.

15 Given-Wilson, *The Chronicle of Adam of Usk*, p. 65.

16 Frank Scott Haydon, ed., *Eulogium Historiarum Sive Temporis*, London, Longman, 1863, vol. 3, p. 409.

17 See A. J. Pollard, 'The Lancastrian constitutional experiment revisited: Henry IV, Sir John Tiptoft and the parliament of 1406', *Parliamentary History*, vol. 14, no. 2 (1995), pp. 103–19.

18 For these details I am grateful to Janet Muir and her treatise *Personnel of Parliament under Henry IV*, which is in the House of Commons library.

19 Cited in Nick Inman, *Politipedia, A Compendium of Useful and Curious Facts about British Politics*, Petersfield, Harriman Press, 2007, p. 246.

20 Whether Clarence was drowned in a butt of malmsey wine, as tradition claims, or his remains were transported to Tewkesbury Abbey in a barrel – as Horatio Nelson's remains were carried in a brandy barrel – remains uncertain.

21 See Alfred John Kempe, *Historical Notices of the Collegiate Church of St Martin-le-Grand*, London, Longman, 1825.

22 Specifically, 34 lords, 84 knights, 170 squires, 65 yeomen, 18 clergy, 17 merchants and 9 others. See J. R. Lander, 'Attainder and forfeiture', in E. B. Fryde and Edward Miller, eds, *Historical Studies of the English Parliament*, vol. 2: *1399 to 1603*, Cambridge, Cambridge University Press, 1970.

23 See S. J. Payling, 'County parliamentary elections in fifteenth century England', *Parliamentary History*, vol. 18, no. 3 (1999), pp. 237–59.

24 John Stachey, ed., *Rotuli Parliamentorum*, House of Lords (London, 1832), vol. 2, p. 355.

25 My translation of 'wyll off craffte sende amonge yow . . . vj or more wyth harneyse fore to sclandre yowre felawschep wyth seying that they be ryotous peple and nott of substance'; see N. Davis, ed., *Paston Letters and Papers of the Fifteenth Century*, Oxford, Clarendon Press, 1971–6, vol. 1, p. 432.

26 See Matthew Davies, 'Lobbying parliament: the London companies in the fifteenth century', *Parliamentary History*, vol. 23, no. 1 (2004), pp. 136–48.

27 See Hannes Kleineke, 'Lobbying and access: the canons of Windsor and the matter of the poor knights in the parliament of 1485', *Parliamentary History*, vol. 25, no. 2 (2006), pp. 145–59.

28 See J. Roskell, *The Commons in the parliament of 1422*, Manchester, Manchester University Press, 1954.

29 See Hannes Kleineke, 'The payment of members of parliament in the fifteenth century', *Parliamentary History*, vol. 26, no. 3 (2007), pp. 281–300.

Chapter 4: The King's Pleasure

1 D. M. Brodie, ed., *The Tree of Commonwealth: A Treatise Written by Edmund Dudley*, Cambridge, Cambridge University Press, 1948, pp. 35, 40, 83.

2 Elizabeth R. Foster, ed., *Proceedings in Parliament: 1610*, New Haven, Yale University Press, 1966, vol. 2, p. 301.

3 John Bale, *Illustrium Maioris Brytanniae Scriptorum*, cited in G. W. Bernard, *The Late Medieval English Church*, New Haven, Yale University Press, 2012, p. 51.

4 Cited in Paul Cavill, *The English Parliaments of Henry VII 1485–1504*, Oxford, Oxford University Press, 2009, p. 30.

5 *Rotuli Parliamentorum* VI, pp. 275–8, cited in Stanley Bertram Chrimes, *Henry VII*, Berkeley, University of California Press, 1972, p. 63.

6 The five peers were John Howard, duke of Norfolk; Thomas Howard, earl of Surrey; Francis, Viscount Lovell (no relation to Sir Thomas Lovell); Walter Devereux, Lord Ferrers; and John, Lord Zouche.

7 Nicholas Pronay and John Cox, eds, *The Crowland Chronicle Continuations, 1459–1486*, London, Yorkist History Trust, 1986, p. 195.

8   Joan Kirby, ed., *The Plumpton Letters and Papers*, Camden
     Society, 5th series, vol. 8, London, Royal Historical Society, 1996,
     p. 63.

9   John Stow and Edmond Howes, *The Annales or General
     Chronicle of England*, London, Thomas Daweson, 1615, p. 479.

10 National Archives, PRO ME, XVI. 332 (*Rotuli Parliamentorum*
     VI.526a).

11 *House of Lords Journal* (*LJ*), vol. 1, 10a, 4 Feb. 1512.

12 *Calendar of State Papers* (*CSP*) *Venice, 1202–1509*, vol. 1, no. 942,
     8 May 1509.

13 *CSP Spain, 1485–1509*, vol. 1, p. 178, 25 July 1498.

14 Kirby, ed., *The Plumpton Letters and Papers*, p. 186.

15 A. H. Thomas and I. E. Thornley, eds, *The Great Chronicle of
     London*, London, Guildhall Library, 1938, p. 348.

16 *CSP Venice, 1520–6*, vol. 3, p. 312, 16 Apr. 1523.

17 William J. Thoms, ed., *John Stow's A Survey of London*, London,
     Whittaker, 1842, p. 127.

18 I am indebted to the work of Alasdair Hawkyard and Maria
     Hayward in 'The dressing and trimming of the parliament
     chamber, 1509–58', *Parliamentary History*, vol. 29, no. 2 (2010),
     pp. 229–37.

19 This was not particularly unusual. Cardinal David Beaton of
     Scotland had eight illegitimate children.

20 Elsie V. Hitchcock, ed., *William Roper's The Lyfe of Sir Thomas
     Moore, Knighte*, Oxford, Early English Text Society, original
     series, vol. 197, 1935, p. 7.

21 Sir Henry Ellis, *Original Letters Illustrative of English History*, 1st
     series, vol. 1, pp. 220–1, cited in Claire Cross, David Loades and
     J. J. Scarisbrick, eds, *Law and Government under the Tudors:
     Essays Presented to Sir Geoffrey Elton*, Cambridge, Cambridge
     University Press, 1988, p. 3.

22 Richard Baker, *A Chronicle of the Kings of England*, London,
     Henry Sawbridge, 1684, p. 270.

23 Edward Hall, *Chronicle; Containing the History of England*,
     London, J. Johnson et al., 1809, p. 656.

24 Richard Sylvester and David Harding, eds, 'William Roper, The Life of Sir Thomas More', in *Two Early Tudor Lives*, New Haven, Yale University Press, 1962, p. 206.

25 Hall, *Chronicle*, p. 657.

26 Cited in Cross et al., eds, *Law and Government under the Tudors*, p. 17.

27 Roger B. Merriman, ed., *Life and Letters of Thomas Cromwell*, Oxford, Clarendon Press, 1902, vol. 1, p. 313.

28 Ibid.

29 In his *New Chronicle of England and France*, cited in S. E. Lehmberg, *The Reformation Parliament, 1529–1536*, Cambridge, Cambridge University Press, 1970, p. 5.

30 Lehmberg, *The Reformation Parliament*, p. 79.

31 PRO SP I/75, fo. 81.

32 Richard Hall, *The Life of Fisher*, Oxford, Oxford University Press, 1921, pp. 69–70.

33 Alan Neame, *The Holy Maid of Kent*, London, Hodder & Stoughton, 1971, p. 137.

34 Hall, *Chronicle*, p. 785.

35 Ibid., p. 788.

36 George Cavendish, *The Life of Cardinal Wolsey*, London, Harding, Triphook & Lepard, 1825, vol. 1, p. 195.

37 J. S. Brewer, ed., *Letters and Papers of Henry VIII*, vol. 4, London, HMSO, 1875, p. 2779.

38 James Gairdner, ed., *Letters and Papers of Henry VIII*, vol. 8, London, HMSO, 1885, p. 326.

39 It was hardly perfect. It guaranteed support for the 'aged, poor and impotent persons . . . of necessity compelled to live by alms', but said that anyone found 'whole and mighty in body and able to labour' should be 'tied to the end of a cart naked and be beaten with whips throughout the . . . town . . . till his body be bloody'.

40 James Gairdner, ed., *Letters and Papers of Henry VIII*, vol. 12, part 1, London, Longman, 1890, no. 976.

41 Hall, *Chronicle*, p. 767.

42 Hall, *Life of Fisher*, p. 68.

43 Lehmberg, *The Reformation Parliament*, p. 13.

44 Gairdner, ed., *Letters and Papers of Henry VIII*, vol. 12, part 1, p. 903.

45 James Gairdner, ed., *Letters and Papers of Henry VIII*, vol. 10, London, Longman, 1887, p. 929.

46 Ibid., p. 816.

47 James Gairdner and R. H. Brodie, eds, *Letters and Papers of Henry VIII*, vol. 20, part 2, London, Longman, 1907, p. 63.

48 S. T. Bindoff, ed., *The House of Commons, 1509–1558*, London, Secker & Warburg, 1982, vol. 1, p. 634.

49 Ibid., p. 635.

50 Hall, *Chronicle*, p. 788.

51 Lehmberg, *The Reformation Parliament*, p. 138.

52 Revd Stephen Reed Cattley, ed., *John Foxe's Acts and Monuments*, London, Seeley & Burnside, 1838, vol. 5, p. 505.

53 Edward Hall, *Union of the Two Noble and Illustre Families*, London, 1550, fos. 231*v*–232*r*.

54 James Gairdner, ed., *Letters and Papers of Henry VIII*, vol. 12, part 2, London, Longman, 1891, p. 952.

55 Member successively for Stamford (1553), Arundel (1559), Boston (1563), Lincolnshire (1563, 1571 and 1572) and Essex (1584, 1586, 1589, and 1593).

56 William Page, ed., 'Houses of Benedictine monks: Abbey of Battle', in *A History of the County of Sussex*, vol. 2, London, Victoria County History, 1973, pp. 52–6.

57 N. Harpsfield, *A Treatise on the Pretended Divorce between Henry VIII and Catharine of Aragon, Westminster*, ed. N. Pocock, London, Camden Society, 1878, pp. 300–1.

58 She also brought back to parliament the prior of the Knights Hospitallers of St John of Jerusalem, Sir Thomas Tresham.

59 Gairdner and Brodie, eds, *Letters and Papers of Henry VIII*, vol. 20, part 2, p. 1030.

60 Sir Henry Ellis, *Hall's Chronicle*, London, J. Johnson, 1809, pp. 864–5.

Chapter 5: An Outward Countenance

1 R. K. Gilkes, *The Tudor Parliament*, London, University of London Press, 1969, pp. 79–80.

2 Gilbert Burnet, *The History of the Reformation of the Church of England*, London, Richard Chiswell, 1680, vol. 2, p. 158.

3 J. G. Nichols, ed., *Literary remains of King Edward VI*, London, J. B. Nichols, 1857, vol. 2, p. 390.

4 John Guy, *Tudor England*, Oxford, Oxford University Press, 1988, p. 210.

5 Cited in Jennifer Loach, *Parliament under the Tudors*, Oxford, Oxford University Press, 1991, p. 94.

6 Sir Thomas Wyatt, the poet and diplomat, also sat as knight of the shire for Kent in 1542.

7 Guy, *Tudor England*, p. 234.

8 In 1552 the diocese was amalgamated with Worcester on Nicholas Heath being deprived.

9 Foxe, John, *Acts and Monuments*, London, n.p., 1583, bk 11, p. 1794.

10 John Strype, *Ecclesiastical Memorials*, Oxford, Oxford University Press, 1822, vol. 3, part 1, p. 245.

11 *CSP Venice, 1555–58*, vol. 6, p. 250, 18 Nov. 1555.

12 Richard Carew, *Survey of Cornwall*, London, T. Bensley, 1811, p. 292.

13 Both cited in Guy, *Tudor England*, p. 319.

14 John Strype, *Annals of the Reformation and Establishment of Religion*, London, John Wyat, 1709, p. 106.

15 Hastings Robinson, ed., *Zurich Letters*, Cambridge, Cambridge University Press, 1842, vol. 1, p. 23.

16 John Strype, *Annals of the Reformation and Establishment of Religion*, Oxford, 1824, vol. 1 part 2, pp. 407, 436.

17 T. E. Hartley, ed., *Proceedings in the Parliaments of Elizabeth I*, Leicester, Leicester University Press, 1981, p. 10.

18 Strype, *Annals of the Reformation*, 1824 edn, vol. 1, part 1, p. 444.

19 *CSP Venice, 1555–8*, vol. 6, p. 111, 15 June 1555.

20 'A Declaration of the Life and Death of John Story', in *Harleian Miscellany*, London, T. Osborne, 1753, vol. 3, p. 100.

21 'Devices', British Library (BL) Add. MS 48023, fo. 45*v*.

22 PRO SP 12/148, fo. 171.

23 Burghley to Francis Walsingham, 8 Sept. 1586, Scottish Collection, vol. 8, p. 701, cited in Sir John Neale, *Elizabeth I and her Parliaments*, vol. 2, London, Jonathan Cape, 1957, p. 104.

24 Cited in Neale, *Elizabeth I and her Parliaments*, vol. 2, p. 110.

25 T. E. Hartley, ed., *Proceedings in the Parliaments of Elizabeth I*, vol. 3, Leicester, Continuum, 1995, pp. 220–1.

26 Heywood Townshend, *Historical Collections*, London, T. Basset and W. Cooke, 1680, p. 230.

27 Ibid., p. 244.

28 Ibid., p. 234.

29 Ibid.

30 John Roche Dasent, ed., *Acts of the Privy Council*, London, Mackie, 1901, vol. 23, pp. 5–6.

31 P. W. Hasler, ed., *The History of Parliament: The House of Commons 1558–1603*, 3 vols, London, HMSO, 1981, vol. 2, p. 396.

32 Townshend, *Historical Collections*, p. 246.

33 Ibid., p. 322.

34 Loach, *Parliament under the Tudors*, p. 39.

Chapter 6: Freeborn Men

1 T. E. Hartley, ed., *Proceedings in the Parliaments of Elizabeth I*, vol. 1, Leicester, Leicester University Press, 1981, pp. 425–34.

2 Ibid., p. 435.

3 *Rotuli Parliamentorum*, 1832, vol. 5, p. 337a.

4 E. V. Hitchcock, ed., *Willam Roper's The Lyfe of Sir Thomas Moore*, Oxford, Oxford University Press, 1935, p. 16.

5 Sir Simonds d'Ewes, *The Journals of all the Parliaments during the Reign of Queen Elizabeth*, London, John Starkey, 1682, p. 66a.

6   Ibid., p. 432.

7   Heywood Townshend, *Historical Collections*, London, T. Basset and W. Cooke, 1680, p. 18.

8   d'Ewes, *The Journals of all the Parliaments*, p. 17a.

9   T. E. Hartley, ed., *Proceedings in the Parliaments of Elizabeth I*, vol. 3, Leicester, Continuum, 1995, p. 22.

10 Sir John Neale, *Elizabeth I and her Parliaments*, vol. 2, London, Jonathan Cape, 1957, p. 246.

11 Ibid., p. 76.

12 Ibid., p. 150.

13 Cited in Jennifer Loach, *Parliament under the Tudors*, Oxford, Oxford University Press, 1991, p. 52.

14 Georgina Galbraith, ed., *Journal of the Rev. William Bagshaw Stevens*, Oxford, Clarendon Press, 1965, p. 276.

15 Louis Jennings, ed., *The Croker Papers*, London, John Murray, 1884, vol. 2, p. 23.

16 A. Aspinall, 'English party organisation in the early nineteenth century', *English Historical Review*, vol. 41, no. 168, p. 404.

17 *The Times*, 26 Dec. 1834.

18 Frank McDonough, *Neville Chamberlain, Appeasement and the British Road to War*, Manchester, Manchester University Press, 1998, p. 126.

19 Edward Arber, *John Milton's Areopagitica*, London, 1869, p. 73.

Chapter 7: The Gathering Storm

1   *Commons Journal (CJ)*, vol. 1, p. 164, 3 Apr. 1604.

2   *CJ*, vol. 1, p. 939a, 30 Mar. 1604.

3   *CJ*, vol. 1, p. 917a, 21 June 1628.

4   King James's letter to the House of Commons, 10 May 1604, in *Memorials of Affairs of State in the Reigns of Queen Elizabeth and King James I*, London, T. Ward, 1725, p. 20.

5   'The Form of Apology and Satisfaction', in J. P. Kenyon, ed., *The Stuart Constitution 1603–1688: Documents and Commentary*, Cambridge, Cambridge University Press, 1986, p. 31.

6 PRO SP 14/8, 93, reprinted in Kenyon, ed., *The Stuart Constitution*, p. 36.

7 G. P. V. Akrigg, ed., *Letters of James VI and I*, Berkeley, University of California Press, 1984, p. 291.

8 P. Croft, ed., *A Collection of Several Speeches and Treatises of the Late Lord Treasurer Cecil*, Camden Miscellany, vol. 29, London, Royal Historical Society, 1987, pp. 255–60.

9 Sir Walter Cope, 'An apology for the late Lord Treasurer', in J. Gutch, *Collectanea Curiosa*, Oxford, Clarendon Press, 1781, p. 122.

10 Joseph Tanner, ed., *Constitutional Documents of the Reign of James I*, Cambridge, Cambridge University Press, 1930, p. 359.

11 Cited in Wallace Notestein, *The House of Commons 1604–1610*, New Haven, Yale University Press, 1971, p. 376.

12 Akrigg, ed., *Letters of James VI and I*, pp. 316–17.

13 James Spedding and Robert Ellis, eds, *The Works of Francis Bacon*, vol. 8, London, Longman, 1858, p. 109.

14 Ibid., p. 362.

15 Thomas Lorkin to Sir Thomas Puckering, 28 May 1614, in *The Court and Times of James I*, London, Henry Colburn, 1848, vol. 1, p. 316.

16 Maija Jansson, ed., *Proceedings in Parliament 1614*, Philadelphia, American Philosophical Society, 1988, p. 31.

17 Wallace Notestein and Frances Helen Relf, eds, *Commons Debates 1621*, vol. 7, New Haven, Yale University Press, 1935, p. 644.

18 Andrew Thrush and John Ferris, eds, *The House of Commons 1604–1629*, Cambridge, Cambridge University Press, 2010, vol. 5, p. 489.

19 *CJ*, vol. 1, p. 497, 25 May 1614.

20 Thrush and Ferris, eds, *The House of Commons 1604–1629*, vol. 3, p. 531.

21 Jansson, ed., *Proceedings in Parliament 1614*, p. 423.

22 Neville sat for Lewes in 1614, Sussex in 1621 and Lewes again in 1624; Wentworth for Yorkshire in 1614, 1621, 1625 and 1628 and Pontefract in 1624; Chute for East Retford in 1614.

23 Samuel Rawson Gardiner, *History of England*, London, Longmans, Green, 1889, vol. 2, p. 251.

24 Godfrey Goodman, *The Court of King James the First*, London, Richard Bentley, 1839, vol. 1, pp. 225–6.

25 Francis Bamford, ed., *A Royalist's Notebook: The Commonplace Book of Sir John Oglander*, London, Constable, 1936, p. 41.

26 Henry Wotton, *Reliquiae Wottonianae*, London, Thomas Roycroft, 1654, p. 77.

27 For a full examination of the personal relationship between Villiers and King James, see David Bergeron, *King James and Letters of Homoerotic Desire*, Iowa City, University of Iowa Press, 1999, which includes the letter from Villiers in which he remembers an occasion at Farnham Castle 'where the bed's head could not be found between the master and his dog'.

28 Roger Lockyer says in his *The Early Stuarts: A Political History of England 1603–1642* (London, Longman, 1999) that Michell was a member of the Commons, but I can find no evidence of this.

29 Notestein and Relf, eds, *Commons Debates 1621*, vol. 2, p. 180.

30 Spedding and Ellis, eds, *The Works of Francis Bacon*, vol. 14, p. 149.

31 Notestein and Relf, eds, *Commons Debates 1621*, vol. 6, p. 372.

32 Even though there was some reconciliation with Lady Coke, it did not prove a happy marriage. John was made Viscount Purbeck, but Frances' first child was almost certainly sired by Sir Robert Howard; she was found guilty of adultery and fled to the Savoy. The saga did not do much for Coke's reputation or his marital affairs, either, as his wife left the marital home with the silver and furniture, never to return.

33 Notestein and Relf, eds, *Commons Debates 1621*, vol. 6, pp. 249–51.

34 Ibid., vol. 2, p. 194.

35 Ibid., vol. 7, appendix, p. 616.

36 Lady Evangeline de Villiers, ed., *The Hastings journal of the parliament of 1621*, Camden Miscellany, vol. 20, London, Royal Historical Society, 1953, pp. 26–7.

37   PRO SP 16/21/105.

38   Notestein and Relf, eds, *Commons Debates 1621*, vol. 1, p. 407.

39   Cited in Lockyer, *The Early Stuarts*, p. 203.

40   Cited in William Cobbett, *The Parliamentary History of England*, vol. 1, London, Curson Hansard, 1806, p. 1327.

41   *CJ*, vol. 1, p. 677, 5 Mar. 1624.

42   *CJ*, vol. 1, p. 82, 11 Mar. 1624.

43   *CJ*, vol. 1, p. 756, 6 Apr. 1624.

44   Menna Prestwich, *Cranfield: Politics and Profits Under the Early Stuarts*, Oxford, Clarendon Press, 1966, p. 448.

45   R. F. Williams, ed., *The Court and Times of Charles I*, London, Henry Colburn, 1849, vol. 1, pp. 103–4.

46   S. R. Gardiner, ed., *Commons Debates 1625*, London, Camden Society, 1873, p. 103.

47   A. B. Grossart, ed., *Sir John Eliot's Negotium Posteriorum*, London, Chiswick Press, 1881, vol. 2, p. 94.

48   Cited in Roger Lockyer, *The Life and Political Career of George Villiers, First Duke of Buckingham*, London, Longman, 1981, p. 304.

49   From the diaries of Sir Thomas Holland, in Bodleian Rawlinson MS D 1100, fo. 3, and John Holles, in BL Harleian MS 6383, fo. 129.

50   Cited in Brian O'Farrell, *Shakespeare's Patron, William Herbert, Third Earl of Pembroke*, London, Continuum, 2011, p. 168.

51   Cited in Lockyer, *The Early Stuarts*, p. 333.

52   Cited ibid., p. 334.

53   William Laud, *The Works of the Most Reverend Father in God, William Laud*, London, William Parker, 1847, vol. 1, p. 101.

54   R. C. Johnson and M. J. Cole, eds, *Commons Debates, 1628*, New Haven, Yale University Press, 1977, vol. 3, p. 405.

55   Ibid., vol. 2, p. 58.

56   Ibid., vol. 3, p. 272.

57   Ibid., p. 406.

58   Cited in Lockyer, *The Early Stuarts*, p. 344.

59   Johnson and Cole, eds, *Commons Debates, 1628*, vol. 4, p. 182.

60 Bodleian Library, Oxford, MS Rawl. B 183, 191.
61 Cited in Harold Hulme, *The Life of Sir John Eliot*, London, George Allen & Unwin, 1957, p. 261.
62 Thomas Carlyle, *Oliver Cromwell's Letters and Speeches*, London, Chapman & Hall, 1845, vol. 2, pp. 74–5.
63 Edward Hyde (earl of Clarendon), *The History of the Rebellion*, vol. 1, Oxford, Oxford University Press, 1843, p. 13.

Chapter 8: The Vertical Turning Point

1 S. R. Gardiner, ed., *Constitutional Documents of the Puritan Revolution*, Oxford, Clarendon Press, 1906, pp. 79, 82.
2 *LJ*, vol. 4, p. 43, 10 Mar. 1629.
3 J. E. Larkin, ed., *Stuart Royal Proclamations*, vol. 2: *Royal Proclamations of King Charles I, 1625–1646*, Oxford, Clarendon Press, 1983, p. 228.
4 D. Macray, ed., *Clarendon's History of the Rebellion*, Oxford, Clarendon Press, 1888, vol. 3, p. 321.
5 *LJ*, vol. 4, p. 81, 5 May 1640.
6 Edward Hyde (earl of Clarendon), *The History of the Rebellion*, vol. 2, Oxford, Oxford University Press, 1888, p. 79.
7 John Rushworth, ed., *Historical Collections of Private Passages of State*, vol. 4, London, 1682, p. 25.
8 J. A. Manning, ed., *Memoirs of Sir Benjamin Rudyerd*, London, T. & W. Boone, 1881, p. 162.
9 H. R. Trevor-Roper, *Archbishop Laud*, London, Macmillan, 1940, p. 401.
10 Ibid., p. 403.
11 William Laud, *The Works of the Most Reverend Father in God, William Laud*, London, William Parker, 1847, vol. 1, p. 94.
12 *CSP Domestic, Charles I, 1628–9*, p. 499, nos. 64–5, cited in Trevor-Roper, *Archbishop Laud*, p. 66.
13 J. P. Kenyon, ed., *The Stuart Constitution 1603–1688: Documents and Commentary*, Cambridge, Cambridge University Press, 1986, p. 192.

14 Ibid., p. 195.

15 Peter Heylyn, *Cyprianus Anglicus*, London, A. Seile, 1668, p. 537.

16 *Edinburgh Review*, 95, Sept. 1828, p. 134.

17 Rushworth, ed., *Historical Collections*, vol. 4, pp. 184, 187.

18 C. Russell, 'The authorship of the bishop's diary of the House of Lords in 1641', *Bulletin of the Institute for Historical Research*, vol. 41, no. 104 (1968), p. 232.

19 Cited in J. R. Tanner, *English Constitutional Conflicts of the Seventeenth Century*, Cambridge, Cambridge University Press, 1961, p. 111.

20 Cited in J. H. Adamson and H. F. Folland, *Sir Harry Vane, his Life and Times 1613–1662*, London, Bodley Head, 1973, p. 165.

21 *Articles of Accusation and Impeachment of the House of Commons, and All the Commons of England against William Pierce*, London, George Tomlinson, 1642, p. 8.

22 Tanner, *English Constitutional Conflicts*, p. 113. The original quotation is from Lord Clarendon's *History of the Grand Rebellion*, Oxford, Oxford University Press, 1705, vol. 1, p. 255.

23 Rushworth, *Historical Collections*, vol. 4, p. 478.

24 Sir Simonds d'Ewes' account, in Willson Coates, ed., *The Private Journals of the Long Parliament 3 January to 5 March 1642*, New Haven, Yale University Press, 1982, p. 10.

25 A. Wood, *Athenae Oxonienses*, 1692, vol. 2, p. 106.

26 Ibid.

27 Hotham later defected to the royalist cause and was deprived of his seat and imprisoned before being executed on 2 Jan. 1645.

28 Cited in Peter Gaunt, *Oliver Cromwell*, Oxford, Blackwell, 1996, p. 49.

29 Sir Samuel Luke, ed., *Letter Books 1644–45*, Bedford, Bedford Historical Society, 1963, vol. 42, p. 324.

30 Worcester College, Oxford, *Putney Debates Record Book*, MS 65.

31 Kenyon, *The Stuart Constitution*, p. 288.

32 *CJ*, vol. 6, p. 111, 4 Jan. 1648 (1649 in modern dating).

33 James I, *Works*, London, James Montagu, 1616, p. 528.

34 Francis Hargrave, *A Complete Collection of State Trials*, London, T. Wright, 1776, cols 1043–4.

35 *CJ*, vol. 6, p. 132, 6 Feb. 1648 (1649 in modern dating).

36 Cited in Blair Worden, *The Rump Parliament 1648–53*, Cambridge, Cambridge University Press, 1977, p. 51.

37 J. T. Rutt, ed., *Diary of Thomas Burton*, London, Henry Colburn, 1828, vol. 3, p. 110.

38 Richard Barber, ed., *Aubrey's Brief Lives*, London, Penguin, 1982, p. 195.

39 Bulstrode Whitelocke, *Memorials of English Affairs*, Oxford, Oxford University Press, 1853, vol. 2, pp. 475, 481.

40 Ibid., p. 470.

41 Thomas Carlyle, *Oliver Cromwell's Letters and Speeches, with elucidations*, New York, Wiley & Putnam, 1845, vol. 2, p. 112.

42 Ibid., pp. 27–8.

43 R. L. Gardiner, *History of the Commonwealth and Protectorate 1649–1660*, London, Longmans, Green, 1901, vol. 2, p. 210.

44 Ibid., p. 212.

45 Ibid., p. 405.

46 Cited in Tanner, *English Constitutional Conflicts*, p. 170.

47 Francis Rous, *The Lawfulnesse of Obeying the Present Government*, London, J. Wright, 1649, pp. 7–8.

48 Carlyle, *Oliver Cromwell's Letters and Speeches*, vol. 3, p. 192.

49 Sir C. H. Firth, ed., *The Memoirs of Edmund Ludlow*, Oxford, Clarendon Press, 1894, vol. 2, p. 55.

50 *Biographica Britannica: Or the Lives of the Most Eminent Persons*, London, 1763, vol. 6, p. 3993. The speech is contested by some.

51 Samuel Rawson Gardiner, *Oliver Cromwell*, London, 1901, pp. 315, 318.

52 Adamson and Folland, *Sir Harry Vane*, p. 469.

Chapter 9: Court and Country

1 Edward Hyde, *The Life of Edward, Earl of Clarendon*, vol. 1, Oxford, Oxford University Press, 1857, p. 225.

2 Arthur Collins, ed., *Letters and Memorials of State . . . Written and Collected by Sir Philip Sydney*, London, T. Osborne, 1746, vol. 2, p. 722.

3 Clarendon to Ormond, 11 Apr. 1663, Bodleian MS Carte 47, fo. 44*v*.

4 Cited in Ruth Paley and Paul Seaward, eds, *Honour, Interest and Power: An Illustrated History of the House of Lords 1660–1715*, Woodbridge, Boydell Press, 2010, p. 143.

5 Henry John Todd, *Memoirs of the Life and Writings of Brian Walton*, London, Rivington, 1821, vol. 2, p. 149.

6 J. P. Kenyon, ed., *The Stuart Constitution 1603–1688: Documents and Commentary*, Cambridge, Cambridge University Press, 1986, pp. 331–2.

7 William Cobbett, *Parliamentary History of England*, vol. 4, London, Bagshaw, 1808, p. 262.

8 C. Robbins, ed., 'Five speeches, 1661–1663, by Sir John Holland MP', *Bulletin of the Institute of Historical Research*, vol. 28, no. 78 (1955), p. 196.

9 Paul Seaward, *The Cavalier Parliament and the Reconstruction of the Old Regime*, Cambridge, Cambridge University Press, 1988, p. 138.

10 T. H. Lister, *The Life and Administration of Edward Earl of Clarendon*, London, Longman, 1838, vol. 3, pp. 302–3.

11 Bodleian MS Carte 45, fos 222, 232.

12 Anchitell Grey, *Debates of the House of Commons 1667–1694*, London, Henry & Cave, 1763, vol. 1, p. 43.

13 Ibid., p. 65.

14 Samuel Pepys, *The Diary*, London, HarperCollins, 1995, vol. 8, p. 93, 3 Mar. 1667.

15 Edward Hyde, *The Life of Edward, Earl of Clarendon*, vol. 2, Oxford, Oxford University Press, 1858, pp. 322–3.

16 William Bray, ed., *Diary and Correspondence of John Evelyn*, London, Henry Colburn, 1850, vol. 2, p. 58.

17 *CSP 1673–75*, p. 168.

18 Cited in Alan Marshall, *The Age of Faction: Court Politics*

1660–1702, Manchester, Manchester University Press, 1999, p. 163.

19 Bodleian MS Carte 221, fo. 52.

20 Anthony Ashley-Cooper, earl of Shaftesbury, *Letter from a Person of Quality*, London, 1675, p. 1.

21 Anthony Ashley-Cooper, earl of Shaftesbury, *Two Speeches*, Amsterdam, 1675, p. 11.

22 Bishop Gilbert Burnet, *History of his own Time*, London, Company of Booksellers, 1725, vol. 2, p. 678.

23 Hartley Coleridge, *The Life of Andrew Marvell*, Hull, A. D. English, 1835, p. 29.

24 Edward Thompson, ed., *The Works of Andrew Marvell, Esq; Poetical, Controversial, and Political*, London, Henry Baldwin, 1776, vol. 1, p. 443.

25 Cited in Paley and Seaward, eds, *Honour, Interest and Power*, p. 27.

26 *CSP Domestic, 1679–1680*, p. 296.

27 Laurence Echard, *The History of England*, London, J. Tonson, 1718, vol. 3, p. 460.

28 Basil Duke Henning, ed., *The House of Commons, 1660–1690*, London, Secker & Warburg, 1983, vol. 1, p. 367.

29 Grey, *Debates of the House of Commons 1667–1694*, vol. 6, p. 347.

30 Wallace Notestein and Frances Helen Relf, eds, *Commons Debates 1621*, New Haven, Yale University Press, 1935, vol. 2, p. 460.

31 Cited in Mark A. Kishlansky, *Parliamentary Selection: Social and Political Choice in Early Modern England*, Cambridge, Cambridge University Press, 1986, p. 34.

32 Ibid., p. 113.

33 Historical Manuscripts Commission (HMC) *15th Report*, 1899, appendix VII, p. 174.

34 Esmond de Beer, ed., *The Diary of John Evelyn*, Oxford, Oxford University Press, 1955, vol. 4, pp. 164–5.

35 HMC *12th Report*, 1890, appendix V, vol. 2, p. 40.

36 Cited in Kishlansky, *Parliamentary Selection*, p. 171.

37 BL Add. MS 11045, fo. 99.
38 T. Birch, ed., *A Collection of the State Papers of John Thurloe*, London, Woodward & Davis, 1742, vol. 5, p. 230.
39 HMC *13th Report*, 1892, vol. 6, p. 13.
40 Cited in K. H. D. Haley, *The First Earl of Shaftesbury*, Oxford, Oxford University Press, 1968, p. 519.
41 Sir Thomas Burnet, ed., *Bishop Burnet's History of his Own Time*, Oxford, Clarendon Press, 1823, vol. 2, p. 250.
42 Cited in E. Lipson, 'The elections to the Exclusion Parliaments', *English Historical Review*, vol. 28, no. 109 (1913), p. 62.
43 *LJ*, vol. 13, p. 745, 21 Mar. 1681.
44 Cited in Haley, *The First Earl of Shaftesbury*, p. 732.
45 Narcissus Luttrell, *A Brief Historical Relation of State Affairs*, Oxford, Oxford University Press, 1857, vol. 1, p. 341.
46 Cited in Tim Harris, *Revolution: The Great Crisis of the British Monarchy, 1685–1720*, London, Allen Lane, 2006, p. 72.
47 Ibid., pp. 98–9.
48 Grey, *Debates of the House of Commons 1667–1694*, vol. 9, p. 30.
49 Ibid., p. 31.
50 Ibid., p. 35.
51 Charles James Fox, *A History of the Early Part of the Reign of James the Second*, London, William Miller, 1808, p. 23.

Chapter 10: Ane Auld Sang

1 Cited in Tim Harris, *Revolution: The Great Crisis of the British Monarchy, 1685–1720*, London, Allen Lane, 2006, p. 388.
2 Cited in Marc Morris, *A Great and Terrible King*, London, Windmill, 2009, p. 252.
3 Ibid., p. 290.
4 The full text is available in Edward J. Cowan, *For Freedom Alone*, East Linton, Tuckwell Press, 2003, pp. 144ff.
5 K. M. Brown et al., *The Records of the Parliaments of Scotland to 1707*, St Andrews, St Andrews University Press, 2007–2012, 1430/12–14.

6   Ibid., 1445/3.

7   Cited in Alan Macdonald, 'Ecclesiastical representation in parliament in post-Reformation Scotland: the two kingdoms theory in practice', *Journal of Ecclesiastical History*, vol. 50, no. 1 (1999), p. 42.

8   Cited in Robert Chambers, *A Biographical Dictionary of Eminent Scotsmen*, Glasgow, Blackie, 1840, vol. 2, p. 66.

9   HMC *Mar and Kellie*, 1930, vol. 1, p. 225.

10 John Rushworth, ed., *Historical Collections of Private Passages of State*, London, 1721, vol. 2, part 1, p. 183.

11 Osmond Airy, ed., *Gilbert Burnet's History of my own Time*, Oxford, Clarendon Press, 1897, vol. 1, pp. 184–5.

12 Cited in Gillian MacIntosh, *The Scottish Parliament under Charles II*, Edinburgh, Edinburgh University Press, 2007, p. 86.

13 George Hill, ed., *The Montgomery Manuscripts (1603–1706)*, Belfast, J. Cleeland and T. Dargan, 1869, p. 432.

14 Ibid.

15 Cited in MacIntosh, *The Scottish Parliament under Charles II*, p. 113.

16 Cited in Christopher Whatley, *Scots and the Union*, Edinburgh, Edinburgh University Press, 2006, p. 232.

17 Ibid., p. 231.

18 George Lockhart of Carnwarth, *Memoirs Concerning the Affairs of Scotland*, London, J. Baker, 1714, p. 172.

19 Sir William Fraser, ed., *The Earls of Cromartie*, Edinburgh, n.p., 1876, vol. 2, p. 21.

20 Cited in Whatley, *Scots and the Union*, p. 274.

21 Ibid., p. 288.

22 HMC *Mar and Kellie*, 1930, p. 254.

23 Cited in P. W. J. Riley, *The Union of England and Scotland*, Manchester, Manchester University Press, 1978, p. 229.

24 Cited in Whatley, *Scots and the Union*, p. 249.

25 Sir John Clerk of Pencuik, *History of My Life*, Edinburgh, Edinburgh University Press, 1892, Scottish Historical Society, series 1, vol. 13, p. 121.

26 The division on the first article of the union on 4 Nov. 1706 saw the following in favour: court 86; *squadrone volante* 24; opposition cross-votes 5; Seafield 1: total 116. Against were 74 country party; 9 court cross-votes: total 83.

27 John Hamilton, Lord Belhaven, *The Lord Belhaven's Speech in Parliament the Second Day of November*, Edinburgh, n.p., 1706, pp. 4–5.

28 Daniel Szechi, ed., *'Scotland's ruine': Lockhart of Carnwath's Memoirs of the Union*, Aberdeen, Association of Scottish Literary Studies, 1995, pp. 177, 144.

29 Ibid., p. 204.

Chapter 11: One Party State

1 Anchitell Grey, *Debates of the House of Commons 1667–1694*, London, Henry & Cave, 1763, vol. 7, p. 286.

2 Cited in Henry Horwitz, *Parliament, Policy and Politics in the Reign of William III*, Manchester, Manchester University Press, 1977, p. 148.

3 Cited ibid., p. 149.

4 Cited in Conte de Maiole, *A Collection of State Tracts, Publish'd on Occasion of the late revolution*, London, 1707, vol. 2, p. 519.

5 *The History and Proceedings of the House of Commons*, London, Richard Chandler, 1742, vol. 6, pp. 230–1.

6 Edward Gibbon, *Memoir of his Life and Writings*, London, Whittaker, 1830, vol. 1, p. 14.

7 John Carswell, *The South Sea Bubble*, Stanford, Stanford University Press, 1960, p. 264.

8 Henry Sacheverell, *The Perils of False Brethren*, London, n.p., 1709, p. 9.

9 I have used relatively conservative figures here for the party allegiances, presuming that some are not properly identifiable.

10 J. H. Plumb, *Sir Robert Walpole*, vol. 1: *The Making of a Statesman*, London, Cresset, 1956, p. 181.

11 Tobias Smollett, *History of England*, London, R. Scholey, 1810, vol. 2, p. 512.

12 Romney Sedgwick, ed., *The House of Commons 1715–1754*, London, HMSO, 1970, p. 28.

13 Cited in Brian Hill, *The Early Parties and Politics in Britain, 1688–1832*, London, Macmillan, 1996, p. 66.

14 HMC *14th Report*, 1896, vol. 9, p. 509.

15 HMC *Egmont Diary*, 1920, vol. 1, p. 86.

16 Edmund Burke, *Works*, London, Rivington, 1815, vol. 2, pp. 300–1.

17 The Revd William Coxe, *Memoirs of the Life and Administration of Sir Robert Walpole, Earl of Orford*, London, Cadell & Davies, 1798, vol. 3, p. 524.

18 Gilbert Burnet, *History of His Own Time*, Oxford, 1833, vol. 5, p. 192.

19 William Pitt, George Lyttelton and Richard Grenville.

20 Cited in Romney Sedgwick, ed., *The House of Commons 1715–1754*, London, HMSO, 1970, pp. 23–4.

21 David Hayton, ed., *The Parliamentary Diary of Sir Richard Cocks, 1698–1702*, Oxford, Clarendon, 1996, p. 51.

22 Philip Dormer Stanhope, earl of Chesterfield, *Characters*, London, Edward and Charles Dilly, 1778, pp. 31–2.

23 BL Add. MS 35407, fo. 280.

24 HMC Egmont Diary, vol. 3, p. 281.

25 The Revd William Coxe, *Memoirs of the Life and Administration of Sir Robert Walpole, Earl of Orford*, London, Cadell and Davies, 1798, vol. 1, p. 40.

26 William Coxe, *Memoirs of the Administration of the Right Honourable Henry Pelham*, London, Longman, Rees, Orme, Brown & Green, 1829, vol. 1, p. 205.

27 Coxe, *Memoirs of the Life and Administration of Sir Robert Walpole*, vol. 1, p. 206.

28 BL Add. MS 35411, fol. 122, Pelham to Newcastle, 7 Sept. 1750.

29 Cited in W. A. Speck, *Stability and Strife: England 1714–1760*, Cambridge, Harvard University Press, 1977, p. 241.

30 Philip Chesney Yorke, *The Life and Correspondence of Philip*

Yorke, Earl of Hardwicke, Cambridge, Cambridge University Press, 1913, vol. 1, p. 383.

31 Sir Nathaniel Wraxall, *Historical Memoirs of My Own Time*, London, Cadell and Davies, 1815, vol. 2, p. 498.

32 Robinson to Pelham, 16 Dec. 1748, Newcastle (Clumber) MSS, University of Nottingham.

33 The Revd Francis Thackeray, *A History of the Right Honourable William Pitt, Earl of Chatham*, London, Rivington, 1828, vol. 1, p. 229.

34 Cited in Bob Harris, *Politics and the Nation: Britain in the Mid-Eighteenth Century*, Oxford, Oxford University Press, 2002, p. 26.

35 John Carswell and Lewis A. Dralle, eds, *The Political Journal of George Bubb Dodington*, Oxford, Oxford University Press, 1965, p. 264.

36 John Tucker to his brother Richard, 16 Dec. 1742, Bodleian MS Don c 105, fo. 200.

37 Cited in Lloyd Charles Sanders, *Patron and Place-hunter: A Study of George Bubb Dodington*, London, Bodley Head, 1919, p. 147.

38 Horace Walpole, *Memoirs of the Reign of King George the Second*, vol. 3, London, Henry Colburn, 1847, p. 84.

39 Horace Walpole, *Memoirs of the Reign of King George the Second*, vol. 1, London, Henry Colburn, 1846, p. 387.

40 HMC *14th Report*, Part IX, 1895, Onslow, p. 516.

41 Cited in Peter Thomas, *The House of Commons in the Eighteenth Century*, Oxford, Oxford University Press, 1971, p. 302.

42 Cited ibid.

43 John Hatsell, ed., *Precedents of Proceedings in the House of Commons*, London, Hansard, 1818, vol. 2, p. 230.

44 HMC *14th Report*, Part IX, 1895, Onslow, p. 503.

Chapter 12: Revolution and Reaction

1 Cited in John Brewer, *Party Ideology and Popular Politics at the Accession of George III*, Cambridge, Cambridge University Press, 1976, p. 47.

2   Peter D. G. Thomas, 'Sir Roger Newdigate's essays on party',
     English Historical Review, vol. 102, no. 403 (1987),
     pp. 394–400.

3   William Butler Yeats, 'The Second Coming' (1919).

4   John Brooke, *King George III*, London, Panther Books, 1974,
     p. 185.

5   John Timbs, *Anecdote Biography*, London, Richard Bentley, 1860,
     p. 58.

6   John Doran, ed., *The Last Journals of Horace Walpole during
     the Reign of George III, from 1771–1783*, London, J. Lane, 1910,
     vol. 1, p. 82.

7   William Winterbotham, *An Historical, Geographical and
     Philosophical View of the American United States*, London, J.
     Ridgway, 1795, vol. 1, p. 429.

8   James Grahame, *The History of the United States of North
     America*, Cambridge, MA, Boston University Press, 1845, vol. 4,
     p. 197.

9   William Stanhope Taylor and John Henry Pringle, eds,
     Correspondence of William Pitt, Earl of Chatham, London, John
     Murray, 1838, vol. 2, p. 269.

10 Edmund Burke, *Speeches*, London, Longman, 1816, vol. 1, p. 2.

11 A. R. Anson, ed., *Autobiography and Political Correspondence of
     Augustus Henry, Third Duke of Grafton*, London, John Murray,
     1898, p. 103.

12 Horace Walpole, *Memoirs of the Reign of King George the Second*,
     vol. 2, London, Henry Colburn, 1847, p. 320.

13 Hagley Hall, West Midlands, Lyttelton papers, vol. 6, p. 260.

14 *London Evening Post*, 25 Feb. 1772.

15 F. L. Bickley, ed., *Diaries of Sylvester Douglas*, London, Constable,
     1928, vol. 1, pp. 237–8.

16 William Cobbett, *The Parliamentary History of England*, vol. 17,
     London, Longman, 1813, pp. 1280–1.

17 *The Parliamentary Register*, London, John Almon, 1776, vol. 3,
     p. 66.

18 Ibid., p. 359.

19 The full text of the letter is included in Peter Whiteley, *Lord North: The Prime Minister who Lost America*, London, Hambledon, 1996, pp. 229–31.

20 Cited ibid, p. 202.

21 William Cobbett, *The Parliamentary History of England*, vol. 22, London, Longman, 1813, p. 1217.

22 George Thomas Keppel, *Memoirs of the Marquis of Rockingham and his Contemporaries*, London, Samuel Bentley, 1852, vol. 2, p. 11.

23 John Milbanke to Rockingham, 28 Dec. 1761, in Keppel, *Memoirs of the Marquis of Rockingham*, vol. 1, pp. 81–2.

24 Philip Henry Stanhope, *History of England*, London, John Murray, 1858, vol. 6, p. 230.

25 Lord Edmund Fitzmaurice, *The Life of William, First Earl of Shelburne*, London, Macmillan, 1912, vol. 1, pp. 140–1.

26 James Prior, *Memoir of the Life and Character of the Rt Hon. Edmund Burke*, London, Baldwin, Cradock & Joy, 1826, vol. 2, p. 232.

27 HMC *Carlisle*, 1897, p. 506.

28 Lewis Namier, ed., *The House of Commons, 1754–1790*, London, Secker & Warburg, 1985, vol. 4, p. 457.

29 Whiteley, *Lord North*, p. 212.

30 Cited in L. G. Mitchell, *Charles James Fox*, Oxford, Oxford University Press, 1992, p. 29.

31 J. Wright, ed., *The Speeches of the Rt Hon. Charles James Fox in the House of Commons*, London, Longman, 1815, vol. 2, p. 130.

32 William Cobbett, *The Parliamentary History of England*, vol. 23, London, Longman, 1814, col. 1209.

33 N. Wraxall, *The Historical and the Posthumous Memoirs of Sir Nathaniel William Wraxall 1772–1784*, London, Bickers, 1884, vol. 3, pp. 195–6.

34 Cited in William Hague, *William Pitt the Younger*, London, HarperCollins, 2004, p. 151.

35 William Cobbett, *The Parliamentary History of England*, London, Longman, 1815, vol. 24, col. 389.

36 George Pretyman Tomline, *Memoirs of the Life of the Right Honourable William Pitt*, London, John Murray, 1821, vol. 1, p. 303.

37 Lord Chatham to Tomline, 4 Feb. 1821, cited in Hague, *William Pitt the Younger*, p. 166.

38 BL Add. MSS 60487B, Aug. 1789, cited in Mitchell, *Charles James Fox*, p. 110.

39 William Cobbett, *The Parliamentary History of England*, vol. 28, London, Longman, 1813, p. 351.

40 William Cobbett, *The Parliamentary History of England*, vol. 29, London, Longman, 1813, p. 826.

41 Wright, ed., *The Speeches of the Rt Hon. Charles James Fox*, vol. 4, p. 199.

42 Edmund Burke, *Reflections on the Revolution in France*, ed. J. C. D. Clark, Stanford, CA, Stanford University Press, 2001, p. 66.

43 Philip Francis to Edmund Burke, 19 Feb. 1790, in Holden Furber, ed., *The Correspondence of Edmund Burke*, Cambridge, Cambridge University Press, 1965, vol. 6, p. 86.

44 Burke, *Reflections on the Revolution in France*, ed. Clark, pp. 250–1.

45 Cited in Hague, *William Pitt the Younger*, p. 289.

46 E. A. Smith, *Whig Principles and Party Politics: Earl Fitzwilliam and the Whig Party, 1748–1833*, Manchester, Manchester University Press, 1975, pp. 134–5.

47 James Howard Harris, third earl of Malmesbury, ed., *Diaries and Correspondence of James Harris, First Earl of Malmesbury*, London, Richard Bentley, 1845, vol. 4, p. 2.

48 John Ehrman, *The Younger Pitt*, vol. 3: *The Consuming Struggle*, London, Constable, 1996, p. 635.

49 Ibid., p. 830.

Chapter 13: Honourable Members

1 Arthur Wellesley, *The Dispatches of Field Marshal the Duke of Wellington*, London, John Murray, 1838, vol. 5, pp. 527, 531, 533–8.

2 Christopher Hibbert, *Wellington: A Personal History*, London, HarperCollins, 1997, p. 274.

3 W. Hathaway, ed., *The Speeches of the Right Honourable William Pitt*, London, Brettell, 1806, vol. 3, p. 300.

4 George III, 30 May 1798, in Philip Henry Stanhope, *The Life of the Right Honourable William Pitt*, London, John Murray, 1867, vol. 3, appendix, p. xiv.

5 Robert Isaac Wilberforce and Samuel Wilberforce, *The Life of William Wilberforce by his Sons*, London, John Murray, 1838, vol. 2, p. 286.

6 William Cobbett, *The Parliamentary History of England*, vol. 6, London, T. C. Hansard, 1810, col. 1173.

7 James Boswell, *The Life of Samuel Johnson*, London, Henry Baldwin, 1791, vol. 1, p. 166.

8 *HC*, 18 Mar. 1832, vol. 11, col. 421.

9 William Paley, *Moral and Political Philosophy*, 1785, quoted in Charles Moore, *A Full Inquiry into the Subject of Suicide, to Which are Added (As Being Closely Connected with the Subject) Two Treatises on Dueling and Gaming*, London, Rivington, 1790, vol. 2, p. 264.

10 *The Times*, 17 and 18 Feb. 1841.

11 *Annual Register*, London, 1822, p. 82.

12 Antony Simpson, 'Dandelions on the Field of Honor', *Criminal Justice History*, 9 (1988), pp. 99–185.

13 *Edinburgh Review*, Apr.–July 1842, vol. 75, pp. 443–4.

14 *Gentleman's Magazine*, Mar. 1830, vol. 147, p. 268.

15 Sir Samuel Romilly, *The Life*, London, John Murray, 1842, vol. 2, p. 378.

16 Roger Fulford, *Samuel Whitbread, 1764–1815: A Study in Opposition*, London, Macmillan, 1967, p. 304.

17 Wellesley, *The Dispatches of Field Marshal the Duke of Wellington*, vol. 1, p. 255.

18 Sir Archibald Alison, *Lives of Lord Castlereagh and Sir Charles Stewart*, Edinburgh, Blackwood, 1861, vol. 3, p. 181.

19 Ibid., p. 180n.

20 Francis Bamford and the duke of Wellington, eds, *The Journal of Mrs Arbuthnot 1820–1832*, London, Macmillan, 1950, vol. 1, p. 178.

21 *Quarterly Review*, vol. 168, 1889, p. 149.

Chapter 14: Ireland

1 Henry Monck Mason, *Essay on the Antiquity and Constitution of Parliaments in Ireland*, Dublin, W. Folds, 1820, p. 5.

2 Cited in James Lydon, ed., *Law and Disorder in Thirteenth Century Ireland*, Dublin, Four Courts Press, 1997, p. 131.

3 The counties were Dublin, Louth, Kildare, Waterford, Tipperary, Cork, Limerick, Kerry, Connacht and Roscommon; the liberties were Meath, Wexford, Carlow, Kilkenny and Ulster.

4 Translation in Lydon, ed., *Law and Disorder in Thirteenth Century Ireland*, p. 149.

5 Cited in Lydon ed., *Law and Disorder in Thirteenth Century Ireland*, p. 125.

6 Sir William Betham, *Dignities, Feudal and Parliamentary*, London, Thomas & William Boone, 1830, vol. 1, pp. 270–1.

7 Cited in Art Cosgrove, ed., *A New History of Ireland*, Oxford, Oxford University Press, 1987, vol. 2, p. 373.

8 Goddard James Butler, ed., *Statutes at Large, Passed in the Parliaments held in Ireland, 1310–1761*, Dublin, George Grierson, 1765, vol. 1, pp. 56–7.

9 *CSP Henry VIII*, vol. 2, p. 316.

10 Ibid., p. 439.

11 Staples to Cecil, 16 Dec. 1558, in Evelyn Philip Shirley, *Original Letters and Papers in Illustration of the History of the Church in Ireland*, London, Rivington, 1851, pp. 87–8.

12 Cited in Brian Farrell, ed., *The Irish Parliamentary Tradition*, Dublin, Gill and Macmillan, 1973, p. 83.

13 In 1613, 1634, 1640, 1661, 1689, 1692 and 1695.

14 Padraig Lenihan, *Consolidating Conquest: Ireland 1603–1607*, Harlow, Pearson Education, 2008, p. 71.

15 S. S. Brewer and William Miller, eds, *Calendar of the Carew Manuscripts, 1603–23*, London, HMSO, 1974, p. 275.

16 W. H. Dunn, *James Anthony Froude: A Biography, 1818–1856*, Oxford, Clarendon Press, 1961, vol. 1, p. 184.

17 J. A. Froude, *The English in Ireland in the Eighteenth Century*, London, Charles Scribner's, 1906, vol. 1, pp. 657–8.

18 William Molyneux, *Case of Ireland Being Bound by Acts of Parliament in England, Stated*, Dublin, Augustus Long, 1749, p. 59.

19 H. Williams, ed., *The Correspondence of Jonathan Swift*, Oxford, Oxford University Press, 1963, vol. 2, p. 463.

20 Edmund Curtis, *A History of Ireland*, London, Methuen, 1950, p. 296.

21 Henry Holmes, ed., *The Political Works of Charles Lucas*, Dublin, Henry Holmes, 1785, vol. 2, p. 123.

22 Richard Cox, *The Cork Surgeon's Antidote against the Dublin Apothecary's Poison*, cited in Sean Murphy, 'Charles Lucas and the Dublin election of 1748–1749', *Parliamentary History*, 1983, vol. 2, no. 1, p. 101.

23 George Henry Jennings, *An Anecdotal History of the British Parliament*, London, Horace Cox, 1899, p. 191.

24 Stephen Lucius Gwynn, *Henry Grattan and his Times*, London, Harrap, 1939, p. 33.

25 Henry Grattan, *Miscellaneous Works*, London, Longman, 1822, p. 143.

26 Daniel Madden, ed., *The Speeches of the Rt Hon. Henry Grattan*, Dublin, James Duffy, 1853, p. 70.

27 William Lecky, *History of Ireland in the Eighteenth Century*, London, Longman,1913, vol. 2, p. 317.

28 Gwynn, *Henry Grattan and his Times*, p. 170.

29 Cited in James Kelly, *That Damn'd Thing Called Honour: Duelling in Ireland, 1570–1860*, Cork, Cork University Press, 1995, p. 135.

30 Cited in John C. Whale, ed., *Edmund Burke's Reflections on the Revolution in France*, Manchester, Manchester University Press, 2000, p. 62.

31   Lord Henry Brougham, *Historical Sketches of Statesmen who Flourished in the Reign of George III*, London, Charles Knight, 1839, vol. 1, p. 265.

Epilogue: The Wisdom of our Ancestors

1   *The Times*, 21 Jan. 1801.
2   Abbot later became Speaker. His lists are in PRO 30/9/134.
3   *Parliamentary Register*, 2 Feb. 1801, vol. XIV, p. 13.
4   Ibid., p. 32.
5   E. A. Smith, *Whig Principles and Party Politics: Earl Fitzwilliam and the Whig Party, 1748–1833*, Manchester, Manchester University Press, 1975, p. 242.
6   *The Diaries of Sylvester Douglas, Lord Glenbervie*, London, Constable, 1928, vol. 2, p. 129.

Bibliography

General

Baker, Richard, *A Chronicle of the Kings of England*, London, Henry Sawbridge, 1684

Betham, Sir William, *Dignities, Feudal and Parliamentary*, vol. 1, London, Thomas & William Boone, 1830

— *The Origin and History of the Constitution of England*, Dublin, William Curry, 1834

Blake, Robert, *The Conservative Party from Peel to Churchill*, London, Eyre & Spottiswoode, 1970

Cash, Bill, *John Bright*, London, Tauris, 2012

Echard, Laurence, *The History of England*, London, J. Tonson, 1718

Froude, James Anthony, *History of England from the Fall of Wolsey to the Death of Elizabeth*, 12 vols, London, n.p., 1856–70

Gardiner, Samuel Rawson, *History of England*, 10 vols, London, Longmans, Green, 1883–9

— *History of the Great Civil War, 1642–1649*, 4 vols, London, Longmans Green, 1886–1901

Hall, Edward, *Chronicle; Containing the History of England*, London, J. Johnson et al., 1809

Hallam, Henry, *The Constitutional History of England*, 3 vols, London, John Murray, 1846

Hargrave, Francis, *A Complete Collection of State Trials*, London, T. Wright, 1776

Hatsell, John, ed., *Precedents of Proceedings in the House of Commons*, 2 vols, London, Hansard, 1818

Hill, Brian, *The Early Parties and Politics in Britain, 1688–1832*, London, Macmillan, 1996

The History and Proceedings of the House of Commons, London,

Richard Chandler,1742

Jennings, George Henry, *An Anecdotal History of the British Parliament*, London, Horace Cox, 1899

Jones, Clyve, ed., *A Short History of Parliament*, Woodbridge, Boydell Press, 2009

Macaulay, Thomas Babington, *History of England*, 5 vols, London, Longman, 1849–56

Moore, Charles, *A Full Inquiry into the Subject of Suicide, to Which are Added (As Being Closely Connected with the Subject) Two Treatises on Dueling and Gaming*, vol. 2, London, Rivington, 1790

Silvester, Christopher, *The Literary Companion to Parliament*, London, Sinclair-Stevenson, 1996

Smith, G. Barnett, *History of the English Parliament*, 2 vols, London, Ward, Lock, Bowden and Co., 1892

Smith, Robert, ed., *The House of Lords*, London, Memorial Society of Great Britain, 1994

Smith, Robert, and Moore, John S., eds, *The House of Commons*, London, Memorial Society of Great Britain, 1996

Stanhope, Philip Henry, *History of England*, 6 vols, London, John Murray, 1858

Stubbs, William, *The Constitutional History of England*, 3 vols, Oxford, Clarendon Press, 1875

The History of Parliament Trust publications

Bindoff, S. T., ed., *The House of Commons, 1509–1558*, London, Secker & Warburg, 1982

Cruickshanks, Eveline; Handley, Stuart; and Hayton, David, eds, *The House of Commons, 1690–1715*, Cambridge, Cambridge University Press, 2002

Hasler, P. W., ed., *The History of Parliament: The House of Commons 1558–1603*, London, HMSO, 1981

Henning, Basil Duke, ed., *The House of Commons, 1660–1690*, London, Secker & Warburg, 1983

Namier, Lewis, ed., *The House of Commons, 1754–1790*, London, Secker & Warburg, 1985

Roskell, J. S.; Clark, Linda; and Rawcliffe, Carole, eds, *The House of Commons, 1386–1421*, Stroud, Alan Sutton, 1992

Sedgwick, Romney, ed., *The House of Commons, 1715–1754*, London, HMSO, 1970

Thrush, Andrew, and Ferris, John, eds, *The House of Commons 1604–1629*, Cambridge, Cambridge University Press, 2010

Medieval

Bernard, G. W., *The Late Medieval English Church*, New Haven, Yale University Press, 2012

Brand, P., 'Petitions and parliament in the reign of Edward I', in I. Clarke, ed., *Parliament and People: Parliament in the Middle Ages*, Edinburgh, Edinburgh University Press, 2004

Butt, R., *A History of Parliament: The Middle Ages*, London, Constable, 1989

Cam, Helen M., 'The parliamentary writs "de expensis" of 1258', *English Historical Review*, vol. 46, no. 184 (Oct. 1931), pp. 630–2

Clark, I., 'Magnates and their affinities in the parliaments of 1386–1421', in R. H. Britnell and A. J. Pollard, eds, *The McFarlane Legacy: Studies in Late Medieval Politics and Society*, Stroud, Alan Sutton, 1995

Coss, Peter R., *The Origins of the English Gentry*, Cambridge, Cambridge University Press, 2003

Davies, Matthew, 'Lobbying parliament: the London companies in the fifteenth century', *Parliamentary History*, vol. 23, no. 1 (2004), pp. 136–48

Davies, R. G., and Denton, J. H., *The English Parliament in the Middle Ages*, Manchester, Manchester University Press, 1981

Davis, N, ed., *Paston Letters and Papers of the Fifteenth Century*, Oxford, Clarendon Press, 1971–6

Denton, J. H., and Dooley, J. P., *Representatives of the Lower Clergy in Parliament 1295–1340*, Woodbridge, Boydell Press, 1987

'The earliest known knights of the shire: new light on the parliament of April 1254', *Parliamentary History*, vol. 18, no. 2 (1999), pp. 109–30

Fryde, E. B., and Miller, Edward, *Historical Studies of the English Parliament*, vol. 1: *Origins to 1399*, Cambridge, Cambridge University Press, 1970

Given-Wilson, C., ed. and trans., *The Chronicle of Adam of Usk, 1377–1421*, Oxford, Oxford University Press, 1997

Holmes, George, *The Good Parliament*, Oxford, Clarendon Press, 1975

Kishlansky, Mark A., *Parliamentary Selection, Social and Political Choice in Early Modern England*, Cambridge, Cambridge University Press, 1986

Kleineke, Hannes, 'Lobbying and access: the canons of Windsor and the matter of the poor knights in the parliament of 1485', *Parliamentary History*, vol. 25, no. 2 (2006), pp. 145–59

— 'The payment of members of parliament in the fifteenth century', *Parliamentary History*, vol. 26, no. 3 (2007), pp. 281–300

Lander, J. R., 'Attainder and forfeiture', in E. B. Fryde and Edward Miller, eds, *Historical Studies of the English Parliament*, vol. 2: *1399 to 1603*, Cambridge, Cambridge University Press, 1970

Lapsley, Gaillard T., *Crown, Community and Parliament in the Later Middle Ages*, Oxford, Blackwell, 1951

McFarlane, K. B., *The Nobility of Later Medieval England*, Oxford, Clarendon Press, 1973

McKisack, May, *The Fourteenth Century, 1307–1399*, Oxford, Clarendon Press, 1959

— *The Parliamentary Representation of the English Boroughs during the Middle Ages*, Oxford, Oxford University Press, 1932

Maddicott, J. R., *The Origins of the English Parliament 924–1327*, Oxford, Oxford University Press, 2010

— *Simon de Montfort*, Cambridge, Cambridge University Press, 1994

Meyers, Alec R., *England in the Late Middle Ages*, Harmondsworth, Penguin, 1952

Milman, Henry Hart, ed., *Annals of St Paul's Cathedral*, London, John Murray, 1869

Morris, Marc, *A Great and Terrible King*, London, Windmill, 2009

Mortimer, Ian, *The Perfect King*, London, Jonathan Cape, 2006

Myers, A. R., ed., *English Historical Documents, 1327–1485*, London, Eyre & Spottiswoode, 1969

Paris, Matthew, *English History from the Year 1235 to 1273, Translated from the Latin by the Rev. J. A. Giles*, 3 vols, London, G. Bohn, 1854

Payling, S. J., 'County parliamentary elections in fifteenth century England', *Parliamentary History*, vol. 18, no. 3 (1999), pp. 237–59

Pollard, A. J., 'The Lancastrian constitutional experiment revisited: Henry IV, Sir John Tiptoft and the parliament of 1406', *Parliamentary History*, vol. 14, no. 2 (1995), pp. 103–19

Powell, J. Enoch, and Wallis, K., *The House of Lords in the Middle Ages*, London, Weidenfeld & Nicolson, 1968

Prestwich, Michael, *The Three Edwards: War and State in England, 1272–1377*, 2nd edn, London, Routledge, 2003

Pronay, Nicholas, and Cox, John, eds, *The Crowland Chronicle Continuations, 1459–1486*, London, Yorkist History Trust, 1986

Richardson, H. G., and Sayles, G. O., *The English Parliament in the Middle Ages*, London, Hambledon, 1981

— *Parliaments and Great Councils of Medieval England*, London, Stevens & Sons, 1961

Riess, Ludwig, *The History of the English Electoral Law in the Middle Ages*, trans. with additional notes by K. L. Wood-Legh, Cambridge, Cambridge University Press, 1940

Roskell, J., *The Commons in the Parliament of 1422*, Manchester, Manchester University Press, 1954

— *Parliament and Politics in Late Medieval England*, 3 vols, London, Hambledon, 1983

Steel, Anthony, *Richard II*, Cambridge, Cambridge University Press, 1941

Strype, John, *Ecclesiastical Memorials*, vol. 3, Oxford, Oxford University Press, 1822

Taylor, John; Childs, Wendy R.; and Watkiss, Leslie, eds, *The St Albans Chronicle; the Chronica Maiora of Thomas Walsingham, 1376–1394*, Oxford, Oxford University Press, 2003

Traherne, Reginald Francis, ed., *The Documents of the Baronial Movement of Reform and Rebellion*, Oxford, Clarendon Press, 1973

Valente, Claire, 'The deposition and abdication of Edward II', *English Historical Review*, vol. 113, no. 453 (1998), pp. 852–81

Wedgwood, Josiah C., 'John of Gaunt and the packing of parliament', *English Historical Review*, vol. 45, no. 158 (1930), pp. 623–5

White, Albert Beebe, 'Early instances of concentration of representatives in England', *American Historical Review*, vol. 19, no. 4 (July 1914), pp. 735–50

Tudor

Alford, Stephen, *Kingship and Politics in the Reign of Edward VI*, Cambridge, Cambridge University Press, 2002

Bossy, J., 'The mass as a social institution, 1200–1700', *Past and Present*, vol. 100, no. 1 (1983), pp. 29–61

Brewer, J. S., ed., *Letters and Papers of Henry VIII*, London, HMSO, vol. 4, 1875

Brigden, Susan, *New Worlds, Lost Worlds*, London, Viking, 2001

Brodie, D. M., ed., *The Tree of Commonwealth: A Treatise Written by Edmund Dudley*, Cambridge, Cambridge University Press, 1948

Cavendish, George, *The Life of Cardinal Wolsey*, 2 vols, London, Harding, Triphook & Lepard, 1825

Cavill, Paul, 'Debate and dissent in Henry VII's parliaments', *Parliamentary History*, vol. 25, no. 2 (2006), pp. 160–75

— *The English Parliaments of Henry VII 1485–1504*, Oxford, Oxford University Press, 2009

Chrimes, Stanley Bertram, *Henry VII*, Berkeley, University of California Press, 1972

Coke, Dorothea, *The Last Elizabethan, Sir John Coke*, London, John Murray, 1957

Condon, Margaret, 'Ruling elites in the reign of Henry VII', in Charles Ross, ed., *Patronage, Pedigree and Power in Later Medieval England*, Gloucester, Alan Sutton, 1979

Croft, P., ed., *A Collection of Several Speeches and Treatises of the Late Lord Treasurer Cecil*, Camden Miscellany, vol. 29, London, Royal Historical Society, 1987

Cross, Claire; Loades, David; and Scarisbrick, J. J., eds, *Law and Government under the Tudors*, Cambridge, Cambridge University Press, 1988

d'Ewes, Sir Simonds, *The Journals of all the Parliaments during the Reign of Queen Elizabeth*, London, John Starkey, 1682

Duffy, E., *The Stripping of the Altars: Traditional Religion in England 1400–1580*, New Haven and London, Yale University Press, 1982

Elton, G. R., *The Parliament of England, 1559–1581*, Cambridge, Cambridge University Press, 1986

— *The Tudor Constitution: Documents and Commentary*, Cambridge, Cambridge University Press, 1960

Foster, E. R., *The House of Lords, 1603–1649: Structure, Proceedings and the Nature of its Business*, Chapel Hill, University of North Carolina Press, 1983

Freeman, T. S., '"The reformation of the church in this parliament": Thomas Norton, John Foxe and the parliament of 1571', *Parliamentary History*, vol. 16 (1997), pp. 131–47

Fryde, E. B., and Miller, E., eds, *Historical Studies of the English Parliament*, 2 vols, Cambridge, Cambridge University Press, 1970

Gilkes, R. K., *The Tudor Parliament*, London, University of London Press, 1969

Graves, M. A. R., *Elizabethan Parliaments, 1559–1601*, London, Longman, 1987

— *The House of Lords in the Parliaments of Edward VI and Mary I: An Institutional Study*, Cambridge, Cambridge University Press, 1981

— *Thomas Norton: The Parliament Man*, Oxford, Blackwell, 1994

Gunn, S. J., *Cardinal Wolsey: Church, State and Art*, Cambridge, Cambridge University Press, 1991

— 'The courtiers of Henry VII', *English Historical Review*, vol. 108, no. 426 (1993), pp. 23–49

— *Early Tudor Government, 1485–1558*, Basingstoke, Macmillan, 1995

— 'Sir Thomas Lovell: a new man in a new monarchy', in John L. Watts, ed., *The End of the Middle Ages*, Stroud, Alan Sutton, 1998

Guy, John, *Tudor England*, Oxford, Oxford University Press, 1988

Haigh, Christopher, ed., *The Reign of Elizabeth I*, London, Macmillan, 1984

Hall, Edward, *Union of the Two Noble and Illustre Families*, London, n.p., 1550

Hall, Richard, *The Life of Fisher*, Oxford, Oxford University Press, 1921

Hartley, T. E., ed., *Proceedings in the Parliaments of Elizabeth I*, 3 vols, London and New York, Leicester University Press, 1981–95

Hawkyard, Alasdair, and Hayward, Maria, 'The dressing and trimming of the parliament chamber, 1509–58', *Parliamentary History*, vol. 29, no. 2 (2010), pp. 229–37

Hirst, D., *The Representative of the People? Voters and Voting in England under the Early Stuarts*, Cambridge, Cambridge University Press, 1975

Hitchcock, Elsie V., ed., *William Roper's The Lyfe of Sir Thomas Moore, Knighte*, Oxford, Early English Text Society, original series, vol. 197, 1935

Hutchinson, Robert, *Thomas Cromwell: The Rise and Fall of Henry VIII's Most Notorious Minister*, London, Weidenfeld & Nicolson, 2007

Hutton, R., *The Rise and Fall of Merry England: The Ritual Year, 1400–1700*, Oxford, Oxford University Press, 1994

James, M. E., 'At a crossroads of the political culture: the Essex Revolt, 1601' in *Society, Politics and Culture: Studies in Early Modern England*, Cambridge, Cambridge University Press, 1986

Jardine, Lisa, and Stewart, Alan, *Hostage to Fortune: The Troubled Life of Francis Bacon*, London, Victor Gollancz, 1998

Jones, N. L., *Faith by Statute of Parliament and the Settlement of Religion, 1559*, London, Royal Historical Society, 1982

Knowles, D., *The Religious Orders in England*, vol. 3: *The Tudor Age*, Cambridge, Cambridge University Press, 1959

Lehmberg, S. E. *The Reformation Parliament, 1529–1536*, Cambridge, Cambridge University Press, 1970

— *Sir Walter Mildmay and Tudor Government*, Austin, Texas University Press, 1964

Leland, John, *The Itinerary of John Leland in or about the Years 1535–1543*, ed. L. Toulmin Smith, London, Centaur, 1964

Loach, Jennifer, *Parliament and the Crown in the Reign of Mary Tudor*, Oxford, Oxford University Press, 1986

— *Parliament under the Tudors*, Oxford, Oxford University Press, 1991

Loades, D. M., *The Reign of Mary Tudor: Politics, Government and Religion in England, 1553–1558*, London, Benn, 1979

Luckett, D. A., 'Crown patronage and political morality in early Tudor England: the case of Giles, Lord Daubeney', *English Historical Review*, vol. 90, no. 437 (1995), pp. 578–95

MacCaffrey, Wallace, *The Shaping of the Elizabethan Regime*, London, Jonathan Cape, 1969

MacCulloch, Diarmaid, *Thomas Cranmer*, New Haven and London, Yale University Press, 1996

Neale, J. E., *Elizabeth I and her Parliaments*, 2 vols, London, Jonathan Cape, 1953–7

Neame, Alan, *The Holy Maid of Kent*, London, Hodder & Stoughton, 1971

Nichols, J. G., ed., *Literary Remains of King Edward VI*, 2 vols, London, Roxburghe Club, 1857

Pollard, A. F., 'The Reformation Parliament as a matrimonial agency and its national effects', *History*, vol. 21, no. 83 (1936), pp. 219–29

Powell, J. Enoch, and Keith Wallis, *The House of Lords in the Middle Ages*, London, Weidenfeld & Nicolson, 1968

Rebholz, R. A., *The Life of Fulke Greville, First Lord Brooke*, Oxford, Oxford University Press, 1971

Roskell, John S., *The Commons and their Speakers in English Parliaments, 1376–1523*, Manchester, Manchester University Press, 1965

Scard, Margaret, *Tudor Survivor, The Life and Times of William Paulet*, Stroud, History Press, 2011

Simmons, T. F., ed., *The Lay Folks Mass Book*, London, Early English Text Society, original series, 71, 1879

Skinner, Q. R. D., *The Foundations of Modern Political Thought*, vol. 2: *The Age of Reformation*, Cambridge, Cambridge University Press, 1978

Snow, Vernon F., 'Proctorial representation and conciliar management during the reign of Henry VIII', *Historical Journal*, vol. 9, no. 1 (1966), pp. 1–26

Starkey, David, 'The age of the household: politics, society and the arts, *c.*1350–*c.*1550', in S. Medcalf, ed., *The Later Middle Ages*, London, Methuen, 1981

— *The Reign of Henry VIII: Personalities and Politics*, London, George Philip, 1985

Thurley, S., *The Royal Palaces of Tudor England: Architecture and Court Life, 1460–1537*, New Haven and London, Yale University Press, 1993

Williams, P., *The Tudor Regime*, Oxford, Oxford University Press, 1979

Wood, A. C., ed., *Memorials of the Holles Family, 1493–1656 by Gervase Holles*, London, Camden Society, 3rd series, 55, 1937

Wood, Robert L., 'Politics and precedent: Wolsey's parliament of 1523', *Huntington Library Quarterly*, vol. 40, no. 4 (1977), pp. 297–312

Wootton, D., 'Francis Bacon: your flexible friend', in J. H. Elliott and L. W. B. Brockliss, eds, *The World of the Favourite*, New Haven and London, Yale University Press, 1999

Stuart

Adamson, J. H., and Folland, H. F., *Sir Harry Vane, His Life and Times 1613–1662*, London, Bodley Head, 1973

Airy, Osmond, ed., *Gilbert Burnet's History of my own Time*, 2 vols,Oxford, Clarendon Press, 1897

Akrigg, G. P. V., *Jacobean Pageant*, London, Hamish Hamilton, 1962

— ed., *Letters of James VI and I*, Berkeley, University of California Press, 1984

Ashley-Cooper, Anthony, earl of Shaftesbury, *Letter from a Person of Quality*, London, n.p., 1675

— *Two Speeches*, Amsterdam, n.p., 1675

Bamford, Francis, ed., *A Royalist's Notebook: The Commonplace Book of Sir John Oglander*, London, Constable, 1936

Bergeron, David, *King James and Letters of Homoerotic Desire*, Iowa City, University of Iowa Press, 1999

Bray, William, ed., *Diary and Correspondence of John Evelyn*, 2 vols, London, Henry Colburn, 1850

Brewer, S. S., and Miller, William, eds, *Calendar of the Carew Manuscripts, 1603–23*, London, HMSO, 1974

Burnet, Gilbert, *The History of the Reformation of the Church of England*, 2 vols, London, Richard Chiswell, 1680

Carlyle, Thomas, *Oliver Cromwell's Letters and Speeches*, 3 vols, London, Chapman & Hall, 1845

Carpenter, Edward, *The Protestant Bishop, Being the Life of Henry Compton*, London, Longman, 1956

Coates, Willson, ed., *The Private Journals of the Long Parliament 3 January to 5 March 1642*, New Haven, Yale University Press, 1982

Coleridge, Hartley, *The Life of Andrew Marvell*, Hull, A. D. English, 1835

Croft, Pauline, *King James*, London, Palgrave, 2003

Cust, Richard, *Charles I, A Political Life*, Harlow, Pearson, 2005

de Beer, Esmond, ed., *The Diary of John Evelyn*, 4 vols, Oxford, Oxford University Press, 1955

de Villiers, Lady Evangeline, ed., *The Hastings journal of the parliament of 1621*, Camden Miscellany, vol. 20, London, Royal Historical Society, 1953

Feiling, K., *A History of the Tory Party, 1640–1714*, Oxford, Oxford University Press, 1924

Firth, Sir C. H., *The House of Lords During the Civil War*, London, Longmans, Green, 1910

— ed., *The Memoirs of Edmund Ludlow*, 2 vols, Oxford, Clarendon Press, 1894

Foster, Elizabeth R., ed., *Proceedings in Parliament: 1610*, 2 vols, New Haven, Yale University Press, 1966

Fox, Charles James, *A History of the Early Part of the Reign of James the Second*, London, William Miller, 1808

Gardiner, R. L., *History of the Commonwealth and Protectorate 1649–1660*, 4 vols, London, Longmans, Green, 1901

Gardiner, S. R., ed., *Commons Debates 1625*, London, Camden Society, 1873

— *Constitutional Documents of the Puritan Revolution*, Oxford, Clarendon Press, 1906

Gaunt, Peter, *Oliver Cromwell*, Oxford, Blackwell, 1996

Goodman, Godfrey, *The Court of King James the First*, 2 vols, London, Richard Bentley, 1839

Grey, Anchitell, *Debates of the House of Commons 1667–1694*, London, Henry & Cave, 1763

Grossart, A. B., ed., *Sir John Eliot's Negotium Posteriorum*, London, Chiswick Press, 1881

Haley, K. H. D., *The First Earl of Shaftesbury*, Oxford, Oxford University Press, 1968

— *Politics in the Reign of Charles II*, Oxford, Oxford University Press, 1985

Harris, Tim, *Restoration: Charles II and his Kingdoms*, London, Allen Lane, 2005

— *Revolution: The Great Crisis of the British Monarchy, 1685–1720*, London, Allen Lane, 2006

Hayton, David, ed., *The Parliamentary Diary of Sir Richard Cocks, 1698–1702*, Oxford, Clarendon Press, 1996

Hill, George, ed., *The Montgomery Manuscripts (1603–1706)*, Belfast, J. Cleeland and T. Dargan, 1869

Holmes, Geoffrey, *Politics in the Age of Anne*, London, Hambledon Press, 1987

Horwitz, Henry, *Parliament, Policy and Politics in the Reign of William III*, Manchester, Manchester University Press, 1977

Hulme, Harold, *The Life of Sir John Eliot*, London, Allen & Unwin, 1957

Hyde, Edward (earl of Clarendon), *The History of the Rebellion*, 3 vols, Oxford, Clarendon Press, 1807

James I, *Works*, London, James Montagu, 1616

Jansson, Maija, ed., *Proceedings in Parliament 1614*, Philadelphia, American Philosophical Society, 1988

Johnson, R. C., and Cole, M. J., eds, *Commons Debates, 1628*, New Haven, Yale University Press, 1977

Jones, David Lewis, *A Parliamentary History of the Glorious Revolution*, London, HMSO, 1988

Jones, J. R., *Country and Court, England 1658–1714*, London, Edward Arnold, 1978

— *The First Whigs*, Oxford, Oxford University Press, 1961

Kenyon, J. P., ed., *The Stuart Constitution 1603–1688: Documents and Commentary*, Cambridge, Cambridge University Press, 1986

Kishlansky, M. A., *Parliamentary Selection: Social and Political Choice in Early Modern England*, Cambridge, Cambridge University Press, 1986

Kyle, K. R., *Parliament, Politics and Elections, 1604–1648*, Cambridge, Camden Society, 2001

Larkin, J. E., ed., *Stuart Royal Proclamations*, vol. 2: *Royal Proclamations of King Charles I, 1625–1646*, Oxford, Clarendon Press, 1983

Laud, William, *The Works of the Most Reverend Father in God, William Laud*, 7 vols, London, William Parker, 1847–60

Lipson, E., 'The elections to the Exclusion Parliaments', *English Historical Review*, vol. 28, no. 109 (1913), pp. 59–85

Lister, T. H., *The Life and Administration of Edward Earl of Clarendon*, 3 vols, London, Longman, 1838

Lockyer, Roger, *The Early Stuarts: A Political History of England 1603–1642*, London, Longman, 1999

— *The Life and Political Career of George Villiers, First Duke of Buckingham*, London, Longman, 1981

Luke, Sir Samuel, ed., *Letter Books 1644–45*, vol. 42, Bedford, Bedford Historical Society, 1963

Manning, J. A., ed., *Memoirs of Sir Benjamin Rudyerd*, London, T. &

W. Boone, 1881

Marshall, Alan, *The Age of Faction: Court Politics 1660–1702*, Manchester, Manchester University Press, 1999

Miller, John, *The Stuarts*, London, Hambledon, 2004

Notestein, Wallace, *The House of Commons 1604–1610*, New Haven, Yale University Press, 1971

Notestein, Wallace, and Relf, Frances Helen, eds, *Commons Debates 1621*, New Haven, Yale University Press, 1935

Paley, Ruth, and Seaward, Paul, eds, *Honour, Interest and Power: An Illustrated History of the House of Lords 1660–1715*, Woodbridge, Boydell Press, 2010

Prestwich, Menna, *Cranfield: Politics and Profits Under the Early Stuarts*, Oxford, Clarendon Press, 1966

Robbins, C., ed., 'Five speeches, 1661–1663, by Sir John Holland MP', *Bulletin of the Institute of Historical Research*, vol. 28, no. 78 (1955), pp. 189–202

Russell, C., 'The authorship of the bishop's diary of the House of Lords in 1641', *Bulletin of the Institute of Historical Research*, vol. 41, no. 104 (1968), pp. 229–36

Sacheverell, Henry, *The Perils of False Brethren*, London, n.p., 1709

Seaward, Paul, *The Cavalier Parliament and the Reconstruction of the Old Regime*, Cambridge, Cambridge University Press, 1988

Sharpe, Kevin, *Faction and Parliament*, London, Methuen, 1978

Smith, D. L., *The Stuart Parliaments, 1603–1689*, London, Hodder Arnold, 1999

Speck, W. A., *Tory and Whig: The Struggle in the Constituencies*, London, Macmillan, 1970

Spedding, James, and Ellis, Robert, eds, *The Works of Francis Bacon*, 8 vols, London, Longman, 1858

Swatland, A., *The House of Lords in the Reign of Charles II*, Cambridge, Cambridge University Press, 1996

Tanner, Joseph, ed., *Constitutional Documents of the Reign of James I*, Cambridge, Cambridge University Press, 1930

— *English Constitutional Conflicts of the Seventeenth Century*, Cambridge, Cambridge University Press, 1961

Trevor-Roper, H. R., *Archbishop Laud*, London, Macmillan, 1940

Vallance, Edward, *The Glorious Revolution*, London, Little Brown, 2006

Whitelocke, Bulstrode, *Memorials of English Affairs*, 2 vols, Oxford, Oxford University Press, 1853

Williams, R. F., ed., *The Court and Times of Charles I*, 2 vols, London, Henry Colburn, 1849

Witcombe, D. T., *Charles II and the Cavalier House of Commons*, Manchester, Manchester University Press, 1966

Worden, Blair, *The Rump Parliament 1648–53*, Cambridge, Cambridge University Press, 1977

Eighteenth century

Alison, Sir Archibald, *Lives of Lord Castlereagh and Sir Charles Stewart*, vol. 3, Edinburgh, Blackwood, 1861

Anson, A. R., ed., *Autobiography and Political Correspondence of Augustus Henry, Third Duke of Grafton*, London, John Murray, 1898

Aspinall, A., 'English party organisation in the early nineteenth century', *English Historical Review*, vol. 41, no. 163 (1926), pp. 389–411

Bamford, Francis, and the duke of Wellington, eds, *The Journal of Mrs Arbuthnot 1820–1832*, 2 vols, London, Macmillan, 1950

Black, J., *Parliament and Foreign Policy in the Eighteenth Century*, Cambridge, Cambridge University Press, 2004

Brewer, John, *Party Ideology and Popular Politics at the Accession of George III*, Cambridge, Cambridge University Press, 1976

Brooke, John, *King George III*, London, Panther, 1974

Brougham, Lord Henry, *Historical Sketches of Statesmen who Flourished in the Reign of George III*, vol. 1, London, Charles Knight, 1839

Burke, Edmund, *Reflections on the Revolution in France*, ed. J. C. D. Clark, vol. 2, Stanford, Stanford University Press, 2001

— *Speeches*, vol. 1, London, Longman, 1816

— *Works*, vol. 2, London, Rivington, 1815

Cannon, J., *Aristocratic Century: The Peerage of Eighteenth Century England*, Cambridge, Cambridge University Press, 1984

Carswell, John, *The South Sea Bubble*, Stanford, Stanford University Press, 1960

Carswell, John, and Dralle, Lewis A., eds, *The Political Journal of George Bubb Dodington*, Oxford, Oxford University Press, 1965

Coxe, Revd William, *Memoirs of the Life and Administration of Sir Robert Walpole, Earl of Orford*, 3 vols, London, Cadell & Davies, 1798

Doran, John, ed., *The Last Journals of Horace Walpole during the Reign of George III, from 1771–1783*, vol. 1, London, J. Lane, 1910

Douglas, Sylvester, *The Diaries of Sylvester Douglas, Lord Glenbervie*, 2 vols, London, Constable, 1928

Ehrman, John, *The Younger Pitt*, 3 vols, London, Constable, 1959–96

Fitzmaurice, Lord Edmund, *The Life of William, First Earl of Shelburne*, 2 vols, London, Macmillan, 1912

Fulford, Roger, *Samuel Whitbread, 1764–1815 : A Study in Opposition*, London, Macmillan, 1967

Furber, Holden, ed., *The Correspondence of Edmund Burke*, vol. 6, Cambridge, Cambridge University Press, 1965

Gibbon, Edward, *Memoir of his Life and Writings*, 3 vols, London, Whittaker, 1830

Gilmour, Ian, *Riots, Risings and Revolution*, London, Pimlico, 1993

Hague, William, *William Pitt the Younger*, London, HarperCollins, 2004

Harris, Bob, *Politics and the Nation: Britain in the Mid-Eighteenth Century*, Oxford, Oxford University Press, 2002

Hathaway, W., ed., *The Speeches of the Right Honourable William Pitt*, vol. 3, London, Brettell, 1806

Jones, Clyve, ed., *A Pillar of the Constitution: the House of Lords in British Politics, 1640–1784*, London, Hambledon Press, 1989

Keppel, George Thomas, *Memoirs of the Marquis of Rockingham and his Contemporaries*, 2 vols, London, Samuel Bentley, 1852

Large, D., 'The decline of "the party of the crown" and the rise of parties in the House of Lords, 1783–1837', *English Historical Review*, vol. 77 (1963), pp. 669–95

Marsh, Charles, *The Clubs of London; with Anecdotes of Their Members, Sketches of Character, and Conversations*, London, Henry Colburn, 1828

Mitchell, L. G., *Charles James Fox*, Oxford, Oxford University Press, 1992

O'Gorman, F., *Voters, Patrons and Parties: The Unreformed Electorate of Hanoverian England*, Oxford, Clarendon Press, 1989

O'Toole, Fintan, *A Traitor's Kiss, The Life of Richard Brinsley Sheridan*, London, Granta, 1997

Pearce, Edward, *The Great Man: Sir Robert Walpole, Scoundrel, Genius and Britain's First Prime Minister*, London, Jonathan Cape, 2007

— *Pitt the Elder: Man of War*, London, Pimlico, 2011

Plumb, J. H., *Sir Robert Walpole, The Making of a Statesman*, 2 vols, London, Cresset, 1956

Romilly, Sir Samuel, *The Life*, 2 vols, London, John Murray, 1842

Sanders, Lloyd Charles, *Patron and Place-hunter: A Study of George Bubb Dodington*, London, Bodley Head, 1919

Sedgwick, Romney, ed., *The House of Commons 1715–1754*, London, HMSO, 1970

Smith, E. A., *Whig Principles and Party Politics: Earl Fitzwilliam and the Whig Party, 1748–1833*, Manchester, Manchester University Press, 1975

Speck, W. A., *Stability and Strife: England 1714–1760*, Cambridge, MA, Harvard University Press, 1977

Stanhope, Philip Dormer, earl of Chesterfield, *Characters*, London, Edward & Charles Dilly, 1778

Stanhope, Philip Henry, *The Life of the Right Honourable William Pitt*, 3 vols, London, John Murray, 1867

Taylor, William Stanhope, and Pringle, John Henry, eds, *Correspondence of William Pitt, Earl of Chatham*, vol. 2, London, John Murray, 1838

Thackeray, Revd Francis, *A History of the Right Honourable William*

Pitt, Earl of Chatham, 2 vols, London, Rivington, 1828

Thomas, Peter, *The House of Commons in the Eighteenth Century*, Oxford, Oxford University Press, 1971

— *John Wilkes: a friend to liberty*, Oxford, Clarendon Press, 1996

— 'Sir Roger Newdigate's Essays on Party', *English Historical Review*, vol. 102, no. 403 (1987), pp. 394–400

Tomline, George Pretyman, *Memoirs of the Life of the Right Honourable William Pitt*, 2 vols, London, John Murray, 1821

Turbeville, A. S., *The House of Lords in the Age of Reform, 1784–1837*, London, Faber, 1958

Walpole, Horace, *Memoirs of the Reign of King George the Second*, 3 vols, London, Henry Colburn, 1846

Whale, John C., ed., *Edmund Burke's Reflections on the Revolution in France*, Manchester, Manchester University Press, 2000

Whiteley, Peter, *Lord North: The Prime Minister who Lost America*, London, Hambledon, 1996

Wilberforce, Robert Isaac, and Wilberforce, Samuel, *The Life of William Wilberforce by his Sons*, vol. 2, London, John Murray, 1838

Wraxall, N., *The Historical and the Posthumous Memoirs of Sir Nathaniel William Wraxall 1772–1784*, 5 vols, London, Bickers, 1884

Wright, J. ed., *The Speeches of the Rt Hon. Charles James Fox in the House of Commons*, vols 2 and 4, London, Longman, 1815

Yorke, Philip Chesney, *The Life and Correspondence of Philip Yorke, Earl of Hardwicke*, vol. 1, Cambridge, Cambridge University Press, 1913

Scotland

Balfour-Melville, E. W. M., 'Burgh representation in Early Scottish parliaments', *English Historical Review*, vol. 59, no. 233 (1944), pp. 79–87

Brown, K. M. et al., eds, *The Records of the Parliaments of Scotland to 1707*, St Andrews, St Andrews University Press, 2007–12

Chambers, Robert, *A Biographical Dictionary of Eminent Scotsmen*, 2 vols, Glasgow, Blackie, 1840

Clerk of Pencuik, Sir John, *History of My Life*, Edinburgh, Edinburgh University Press, 1892, Scottish Historical Society, series 1, vol. 13

— *A Letter to a Friend, Giving an Account how the Treaty of Union Has Been Received Here*, Edinburgh, n.p., 1706

Collins, Arthur, ed., *Letters and Memorials of State . . . Written and Collected by Sir Philip Sydney*, 2 vols, London, T. Osborne, 1746

Cope, Sir Walter, 'An apology for the late Lord Treasurer', in J. Gutch, *Collectanea Curiosa*, Oxford, Clarendon Press, 1781

Duncan, A. A. M., 'The early parliaments of Scotland', *Scottish Historical Review*, vol. 45, no. 139 (1966), pp. 36–58

Fraser, Sir William, ed., *The Earls of Cromartie*, 2 vols, Edinburgh, n.p., 1876

Hamilton, John, Lord Belhaven, *The Lord Belhaven's Speech in Parliament the Second Day of November*, Edinburgh, n.p., 1706

Lockhart of Carnwarth, George, *Memoirs Concerning the Affairs of Scotland*, London, J. Baker, 1714

Macdonald, Alan, *The Burghs and Scotland in Parliament c. 1550–1651*, Aldershot, Ashgate, 2007

— 'Ecclesiastical representation in parliament in post-Reformation Scotland: the two kingdoms theory in practice', *Journal of Ecclesiastical History*, vol. 50, no. 1 (1999), pp. 38–61

MacIntosh, Gillian, *The Scottish Parliament under Charles II*, Edinburgh, Edinburgh University Press, 2007

Rait, Sir Robert S., *The Parliaments of Scotland*, Glasgow, Maclehose, 1924

Riley, P. W. J., *The Union of England and Scotland*, Manchester, Manchester University Press, 1978

Szechi, Daniel, ed., *'Scotland's ruine': Lockhart of Carnwath's Memoirs of the Union*, Aberdeen, Association of Scottish Literary Studies, 1995

Whatley, Christopher, *Scots and the Union*, Edinburgh, Edinburgh University Press, 2006

Ireland

Bradshaw, B., *The Irish Constitutional Revolution of the Sixteenth Century*, Cambridge, Cambridge University Press, 1979

Burns, R. E., *Irish Parliamentary Politics in the Eighteenth Century*, 2 vols, Washington, Catholic University of America Press, 1989–90

Cosgrove, Art, ed., *A New History of Ireland*, 2 vols, Oxford, Oxford University Press, 1987

Curtis, Edmund, *A History of Ireland*, London, Methuen, 1950

Farrell, Brian, ed., *The Irish Parliamentary Tradition*, Dublin, Gill & Macmillan, 1973

Froude, J. A., *The English in Ireland in the Eighteenth Century*, 2 vols, London, Charles Scribner's, 1906

Grattan, Henry, *Miscellaneous Works*, London, Longman, 1822

Gwynn, Stephen Lucius, *Henry Grattan and his Times*, London, Harrap, 1939

Haslam, J. C., *A Miniature History of the Irish Parliament, from the earliest times to the Act of Union in 1800*, London, Cassell, 1888

Holmes, Henry, ed., *The Political Works of Charles Lucas*, vol. 2, Dublin, Henry Holmes, 1785

James, F. G., 'Illustrious or notorious? The historical reputation of Ireland's pre-union parliament', *Parliamentary History*, vol. 6, no. 2 (1987), pp. 312–25

Kelly, James, *That Damn'd Thing Called Honour: Duelling in Ireland, 1570–1860*, Cork, Cork University Press, 1995

Lecky, William, *History of Ireland in the Eighteenth Century*, 2 vols, London, Longmans, 1913

Lenihan, Padraig, *Consolidating Conquest: Ireland 1603–1607*, Harlow, Pearson Education, 2008

Lydon, James, ed., *Law and Disorder in Thirteenth-Century Ireland: The Dublin Parliament of 1297*, Dublin, Four Courts, 1997

MacNeill, J. G. Swift, *The Constitutional and Parliamentary History of Ireland till the Union*, Dublin, Talbot, 1917

Madden, Daniel, ed., *The Speeches of the Rt Hon. Henry Grattan*, Dublin, James Duffy, 1853

Mason, Henry Monck, *Essay on the Antiquity and Constitution of Parliaments in Ireland*, Dublin, W. Folds, 1820

Molyneux, William, *Case of Ireland Being Bound by Acts of Parliament in England, Stated*, Dublin, Augustus Long, 1749

Moody, T. W., 'The Irish parliament under Elizabeth and James I: a general survey', *Proceedings of the Royal Irish Academy*, 45C (1939–40), pp. 41–81

Murphy, Sean, 'Charles Lucas and the Dublin election of 1748–1749', *Parliamentary History*, vol. 2, no. 1 (1983), pp. 93–111

O'Flanagan, James Roderick, *Annals, Anecdotes, Traits, and Traditions of the Irish Parliaments, 1172 to 1800*, Dublin, M. H. Gill, 1893

Richardson, H. G., and Sayles, G. O., *The Irish Parliament in the Middle Ages*, Philadelphia, University of Pennsylvania Press, 1952

—— *The Irish Parliament in the Middle Ages. Etudes présentées à la Commission internationale pour l'histoire des assemblées d'Etats*, new edn, Philadelphia: University of Pennsylvania Press, 1964

—— 'The Irish parliaments of Edward I', *Proceedings of the Royal Irish Academy*, 38C (1928–9), pp. 128–47

Shirley, Evelyn Philip, *Original Letters and Papers in Illustration of the History of the Church in Ireland*, London, Rivington, 1851

Watt, J. A., 'The first recorded use of the word "parliament" in Ireland?', *Irish Jurist*, new series, vol. 4 (1969), pp. 123–6

Picture Acknowledgements

Every effort has been made to trace copyright holders. Any who have been overlooked are invited to get in touch with the publishers.

Images in the text

p. 14: *Civitatis Westmonasteriensis pars*, view of part of the city of Westminster, 1647, engraving by Wenceslaus Hollar: Getty Images.

p. 32: Seal of Simon de Montfort, 1208–65: copy.

p. 54: 'How the knights guarding Jesus in the sepulchre told their masters and the princes of the law that Jesus had risen', detail of a page from the Holkham Bible Picture Book, English illuminated manuscript, *c.*1320–30, British Library, MSS Add. 47682, fo. 35v: © The British Library Board.

p. 82: Thomas Chaucer, 1436, brass rubbing from Ewelme Parish Church, Oxfordshire, from *English Church Monuments AD 1150–1550* by Frederick Herbert Crossley, 1921.

p. 116: Execution of John Fisher, engraving from *Review of Foxe's Book of Martyrs* by William Andrews, 1826: © Interfoto/Alamy.

p. 152: Queen Elizabeth I in parliament, sixteenth-century engraving: private collection/The Bridgeman Art Library.

p. 188: *The Pillory Triumphant*, detail of an engraving after Jefferyes Hamett O'Neale, 1765: © The Trustees of the British Museum.

p. 208: *The description of Giles Mompesson late Knight censured by Parliament the 17th of March, Anno 1620*, 1621, detail of an anonymous engraving: © The Trustees of the British Museum.

p. 242: *The World turn'd upside down . . .* , 1647, anonymous title-page engraving of a verse satire by John Taylor: British Library/The Bridgeman Art Library.

work, 15th century, from *Facsimiles of Irish Manuscripts*, vol. III, plate xxxvii: © The National Archives, Kew; tomb of Sir William Disney, *c*.1350, St Peter's Church, Norton Disney, Lincs.: © Richard Croft.

'The empty throne', parliament recognizes Bolingbroke as the king of England under the name of Henry IV, 1400–5, illumination from *La Prinse et mort du roy Richart* (*Book of the Capture and Death of King Richard II*), British Library: UIG via Getty Images; *Four Gentlemen of High Rank Playing Primero*, 16th-century oil painting by the Master of the Countess of Warwick: © The Right Hon. Earl of Derby/The Bridgeman Art Library; 'An Act for the Attainder of Thomas Earl of Strafford for High Treason', 10 May 1641, Parliamentary Archives, HL/PO/PB/1/1640/16&17C1n23; *George Villiers, 1st Duke of Buckingham*, *c*.1616, oil painting attributed to William Larkin: National Portrait Gallery, London, © Stefano Baldini/The Bridgeman Art Library; execution of Robert Tresilian, illumination from the Froissart Chronicles, 1470–5: Bibliothèque nationale de France, ms fr. 2646.

'Wheel of Fortune', Rochester Cathedral, 13th-century fresco: © Paul Hillman; *Lord Cromwell, Wearing the Order of St George*, school of Hans Holbein, 16th century: ©The Trustees of the Weston Park Foundation Foundation/The Bridgeman Art Library; *Execution of Charles I* (detail), anonymous engraving, *c*.1649: Getty Images; *Oliver Cromwell*, unfinished 17th-century portrait miniature by Samuel Cooper: private collection/The Bridgeman Art Library; *The Seven Bishops committed to the Tower in 1688*, anonymous oil painting of Archbishop William Sancroft and Bishops Thomas Ken, John Lake, William Lloyd, Jonathan Trelawny, Francis Turner and Thomas White, *c*.1688: © National Portrait Gallery, London; 'Lenthall runns away With his mace to the Army', Royalist playing card, 1660–5: © Images Asset Management Ltd/Alamy.

The Crimson Bedchamber by Sir John Baptist de Medina, 17th-century oil painting of a group of gentlemen with musical instruments, traditionally said to depict the Cabal ministry of Charles: left to right, Thomas Clifford, Henry Bennet, George

Villiers, Anthony Ashley-Cooper, John Maitland: Private Collection/ De Agostini Picture Library/The Bridgeman Art Library; *The Solemn Mock Procession of the Pope, Cardinalls, Jesuits and Fryers & co Through the City of London on 'Queen Elizabeth's Day 17th November, 1679'*, broadside after Francis Barlow, 1680: private collection/The Bridgeman Art Library.

Second section

Whipping list, 1703: © Northamptonshire Record Office; *A Whig Toast. A Tory Sentement*, satirical print attributed to Isaac Cruikshank, *c*.1795: ©The Trustees of the British Museum.
'The Downsitting of Parliament', coloured engraving from Henry Abraham Chatelain's *Atlas Historique*, 1720, but engraved earlier and representing the Scottish parliament in session *c*.1680: © National Museums Scotland; *S—th Pilgrims on their Journey to St Stephens Chapel in Obediance to the Order of their High Priest*, anonymous satire, 1784: © The Trustees of the British Museum; *The Irish House of Commons in 1780: Henry Grattan urging the claim of Irish Rights*, detail of an oil painting by Francis Wheatley, 1780: © Leeds Museums and Galleries (Lotherton Hall)/The Bridgeman Art Library; articles of Union between England and Scotland, House of Lords Record Office, 1707: Houses of Parliament/ The Bridgeman Art Library.
Sir Robert Walpole addressing his Cabinet, watercolour by Joseph Goupy, 1723–42; British Museum/The Bridgeman Art Library; *Arthur Onslow*, ink drawing by George Townshend MP, 1751–8: © National Portrait Gallery, London; *Death of the Earl of Chatham*, 18th-century oil painting attributed to John Singleton Copley (in fact Chatham died a month later): Mead Art Museum, Amherst College / Bequest of Herbert L. Pratt (Class of 1895) / The Bridgeman Art Library; *Thomas Pelham-Holles, 1st Duke of Newcastle-under-Lyne and Henry Clinton, 7th Earl of Lincoln*, portrait by Sir Godfrey Kneller, *c*.1721: © National Portrait Gallery, London.

An Election Entertainment, oil painting by William Hogarth, 1755: courtesy of the Trustees of Sir John Soane's Museum, London / The Bridgeman Art Library; *Procession to the Hustings after a Successful Canvass* by James Gillray: © Courtesy of the Warden and Scholars of New College, Oxford / The Bridgeman Art Library; *View of the Hustings*, satirical print by James Gillray, 1806: © Courtesy of the Warden and Scholars of New College, Oxford / The Bridgeman Art Library; 'Bankhead, let me fall upon your arm. 'Tis all over!': Castlereagh commits suicide; *Two Pair of Portraits*, satirical print by James Gillray, 1798: Getty Images.

William Pitt addressing the House of Commons, oil painting by Anton Hickel, 1793: De Agostini/Getty Images.

Index

abbeys and abbots (14th–16th
    centuries), 106–7, 145–9; *see also*
    dissolution of the monasteries
Abbot, Charles, 476
Abbot, George, archbishop of
    Canterbury, 222–3, 235, 236
Abercorn, James Hamilton, 6th earl
    of, 296
Abingdon, 304
Act for the Advancement of True
    Religion (1543), 156
Act for the Assurance of the Queen's
    Power (1563), 176
Act of Security: (1696), 346; (1703),
    347
Act of Settlement (1701), 347
Act of Supremacy: (1534), 138;
    (1559), 173, 174, 177; (1669),
    343, 344
Act of Union: (1707), 18, 334–53;
    (1801), 18, 436, *474*, 475
Acton Burnell, 27, 57, 58–9
Acts of Attainder, 105 *and n*, 108–9,
    118, 120–1
Acts of Pains and Penalties, 368
Acts of Uniformity, 157, 161, 385
Acworth, George, 183–4
Adair, James, 396
Adam, William, 402, 427
Adam of Usk, 27, 91
Adamson, Patrick, archbishop of St
    Andrews, 335
Addington, Henry *see* Sidmouth,
    Lord
Addison, Joseph, 423
'Addled' Parliament (1614), 218–21
Agincourt, battle of (1415), 99, 100,
    103

Aislabie, John, 358–60
Albany, John Stewart, duke of, 330
Albany, Robert Stewart, duke of, 328
Albemarle, George Monck, duke of,
    275, 283, 305, 342
Alcock, John, bishop of Ely, 119, 120,
    124
Alcock, John, mayor of Canterbury,
    140–1
Aldborough, 431
Allen, John, archbishop of Dublin,
    451
Alexander II, of Scotland, 321
Alexander III, of Scotland, 326
Alexander IV, Pope, 47, 48
Alford, Edward, 226
Aliens Acts, Scotland: (1705), 348–9;
    (1793), 409–10
Allestry, Roger, 300
Allington, William, 106
Ambrose, William, 77
America, 380; colonies, 392–3, 395–8,
    400; Stamp Act (1765), *386*,
    390–1, 392–3, 395
American War of Independence
    (1775–82), 397–8
Amersham, 300
Amherst, Jeffery, Baron, 477
Anabaptists, 262
Anglesey, Arthur Annesley, earl of,
    311
Anglesey, Henry Paget, marquess of,
    432
Anglo-Dutch War, Third (1672), 291
Angus, Archibald Douglas, earl of,
    330, 336
Annandale, Robert Bruce, 5th Lord
    of, 322

Anne, Queen, 19, 346, 347–8, 349, 352, 361, 362, 363, 364, 367, 368, 423
Anne of Cleves, 139
Anne of Denmark, 223
Annesley, Maurice, 462*n*
Apology and Satisfaction, 213–14
Apparel Act (1532), 144
Appellate Jurisdiction Act (1876), 80
Appleby, 404
Apsley, Sir Allen, 23
Arbuthnot, Charles, 435
Arbuthnot, Harriet, 421, 435, 437
Arden, Richard, 403
Argyll, Archibald Campbell, 9th earl of, 310
Argyll, Archibald Campbell, 10th earl of, 321
Argyll, Archibald Campbell, marquess of, 8th earl of, 340, 341, 342
Argyll, John Campbell, 2nd duke of, 348
Arlington, Henry Bennet, 1st earl of, 283, 286, 288, 290
Arminianism, 236, 239, 243, 244, 247, 253
Arminius, Jacobus, 235
Armstrong, Sir Thomas, 309
Arran, James Hamilton, duke of Châtelherault, 2nd earl of, 330, 331, 332
Arran, James Hamilton, 3rd earl of, 331
Arthur, Prince of Wales, 123
Articles of Perth (1621), 339
Arundel, 227
Arundel, Henry FitzAlan, 19th earl of, 159
Arundel, Richard FitzAlan, 11th earl of, 85, 87
Arundel, Thomas, archbishop of Canterbury, 86, 87, 89, 94
Arundel, Thomas Howard, 21st earl of, 238
Arundell of Wardour, Henry, 3rd

Baron, 297, 306
Ashe, Edward, 259
Ashe, James, 259
Ashe, John, 259
Ashley, Edith, 163
Ashley Cooper, Anthony *see* Shaftesbury, earl of
Ashmead-Bartlett, Sir Ellis, 24
Aiscough, William, bishop of Salisbury, 104
Aske, Robert, 150
Askew, Anne, 168
Asquith, Herbert Henry, 23
Astor, Nancy, Viscountess, 16
Atholl, John Murray, duke of, 350, 351
Atholl, John Murray, marquess of, 320
Atholl, Walter Stewart, earl of, 328
Atkinson, Christopher, 438
Atterbury, Francis, bishop of Rochester, 367, 375
Attorney-General, 218 *and n*
Aubrey, John, 269
Audley, Sir James, 45
Audley, James Touchet, 7th Baron, 121
Audley, John, 6th Baron, 119
Audley, Thomas, 1st Baron Audley of Walden, 134, 135–6, 137, 140, 170
'Auld Alliance', 323, 327, 329, 330
Aumale (Albemarle), count of, 45
Austerlitz, battle of (1805), 414, 415
Austin, Michael, 24
Ayala, Pedro de, 123
Aylmer, John, bishop of London, 180
Aymer de Valence, bishop of Winchester, 46

Babington plot (1586), 179
Bacon, Anne (née Cooke), 173, 218
Bacon, Sir Francis, 124, 197, 214, 216, 217–18, 224–5, 227–8
Bacon, Sir Nicholas, 173, 195–6, 218
Badlesmere, Bartholomew de, 44
Badlesmere, Giles de, 43, 44

Badlesmere, Gunceline de, 44
Bagenal, Beauchamp, 428
Bagenal, Beauchamp Harvey, 428
Baginton, Warwickshire: Church of
    St John the Baptist, 92
Bagnall, Sir Ralph, 164
Bagot, William, 92
bailiffs, 78
Bainbridge, Robert, 199
Balcarres, Colin Lindsay, earl of, 319
Baldwin, Stanley, 205
Balfour, Jabez Spencer, 25
Ball, Father John, 84
Balliol, Edward, 326
Balliol, John, 351–2
Ballydoyle, 446
Balmerino, John Elphinstone, Lord,
    351
Banbury, 180; battle of (1644), 259
Bank of England, 357, 359
Banks, Sir John, 300–1
Bannockburn, battle of (1314), 64,
    325
Banqueting Hall, Whitehall, 267
Baptists, 262
Barbon, Praisegod, 271
Barclay, George, 430
Barclay, Robert, 341
'Barebone's Parliament' (1653),
    271–2
Barkstead, John, 277
Barlow, William, bishop of Bath and
    Wells, 154
baronetcies/baronets, 26, 217, 423
barons: 13th century, 32, 33, 34–6,
    37–8, 39, 45, 47, 49, 56, 57, 72,
    321; 14th century, 61–2, 63–5, 67,
    68, 71, 75, 77; 15th century, 98,
    107; in Scotland, 321, 322, 323,
    327, 329, 333
Barré, Colonel Isaac, 390–1, 396, 399,
    400
Barrington, John, Viscount, 372
Barrington, Shute, bishop of
    Durham, 478–9
Basset, Fulk, 46–7

Basset, Gilbert, 47
Basset, Sir Philip, 45, 46
Bath, William Pulteney, earl of, 365,
    369, 371, 373, 376
Bathe, Thomas, 445
Batoni, Pompeo: Frederick, Lord
    North, 393
Battle Abbey, 146
Baynard, Robert, 78
Baynards Castle plot (1615), 222, 234
Bayon (or Bayen), Thomas, 113
Beaton, David, cardinal archbishop of
    St Andrews, 330, 331
Beaton, James, archbishop of
    Glasgow, 335
Beauchamp, Edward Seymour,
    Viscount, 210
Beauchamp, Giles de, 71
Beauchamp, Lord John, 86
Beaufort, Henry, bishop of
    Winchester, 92, 93, 101, 102–3,
    106, 107
Beaufort, Joan, 92
Beaufort, John, 92
Beaufort, Margaret, 124
Beaverbrook, Max Aitken, Lord, 205
Beckford, William, 390
Bedford, 142, 433
Bedford, Francis Russell, earl of, 178
Bedford, John, duke of, 101, 102, 103
Bedford, John Russell, 6th duke of,
    426, 427
Bedford, John Russell, earl of, 160,
    163, 167, 173
Beefsteak Club, London, 369
Belasyse, John, Baron, 297–8, 306
Belfast East, 25
Belhaven, John Hamilton, 2nd Lord,
    351–2, 353
Bell, Robert, 174, 181, 185, 197
Bennet, Sir Henry see Arlington, earl
    of
Bennett, Thomas, 298, 299
Benson (or Boston), William, abbot
    of Westminster 147
Bentham, Jeremy, 423

Bentinck family, 479

Bere, Richard, abbot of Glastonbury, 147

Beresford, Lord George, 427

Berkeley, Grandey Fitzhugh, 428

Berkeley Castle, 88

Berwick, Pacification of (1639), 246

Berwick, Treaties of: (1357), 326; (1560), 331, 332

Betanson, Thomas, 120

Betham, Sir William, 59

Beverley, 258

Bigod, Hugh, 38, 48

Bill of Rights (1688), 200, 317

Birch, Colonel John, 286, 288

Birch, John, 372

Bird, John, vicar of Dunmore, 163

Birgham, Treaty of (1289), 322

bishops: 13th century, 37, 39, 45, 46, 47, 48, 60–1; 15th century, 106–8; 16th century, *116*, 126, 127–8, 133*n*, 134–6, 141, 146–7, 153–4, 156–7, 160, 163, 164–6, 175–8; 17th century, *242*, 243, 246, 247, 252–6, 258, *280*, 283–5, 294–5, 298, 310, 311, 312, 314, 316–17; 18th century, 478; in Scotland, 319, 320–6, 327, 332, 333, 335–40, 342, 344

Bisse, James, 183

Black Acts: (1584), 336; (1723), 420

Black Rod, *152*, 256*n*

Blackburn, Peter, bishop of Aberdeen, 337

Blackfriars, London, parliaments: (1523), 126, 127–31; (1529), 132–5

Blacquiere, Colonel, Chief Secretary, 428

Blagge, George, 142

Blagrave, Daniel, 277

Blake, Robert: *The Conservative Party from Peel to Churchill*, 30

Blanche of Castile, Queen, 37

Bletchingley, 160

Blount, Sir George, 177

Blunt, Sir John, 357–8

Boleyn, Anne, 42, 137, 138, 451

Bolingbroke, Henry *see* Henry IV

Bolingbroke, Henry St John, 1st Viscount, 363, 365, 367

Bolingbroke, Oliver St John, 1st earl of, 260

Bond, Dennis, 372

Bonham, Sir Thomas, 170

Boniface of Savoy, archbishop of Canterbury, 46–7, 48, 51

Bonner, Edmund, bishop of London, 149, 157, 160, 163, 164, 176, 177

Book of Common Prayer, 155, 157, 160–1, 174, 196, 198–9, 285–6

books, licensing of, 200–1

Boscawen, Edward, 304

Boscawen, Admiral Edward, 380

Boscawen, Hugh, 315

Bosworth Field, battle of (1485), 102, 105, 118

Bothwell, James Hepburn, 4th earl of, 334

Boucicault, Dion, 428–9

Boughton Malherbe, 43; St Nicholas' Church, 43*n*

Boulter, Hugh, archbishop of Armagh, 462

Bourchier, Sir John, 276

Bower, Robert Tatton, 23

'Boy Patriots', 370, 371

Boyse, Samuel, 427

Brabazon, Roger, 62

Brabazon, Sir William, 451–2

Bradshaw, John, 267, 276

Bramber, 194

Bramhall, John, archbishop of Armagh, 457, 459

Bray, John, Baron, 169

Bray, Sir Reynold, 124

Brembre, Nicholas, 85

Brentford, battle of (1642), 261

Brewer, John, 356

Brewers' Company, 112

Bridges, Giles, 224

Bridges Act (1530), 143

Bridgwater, 378

Bridgwater, John Egerton, 3rd earl of, 310

Bright, John, 16–17

Brinton, Thomas, bishop of Rochester, 74, 83–4

Bristol, 114, 192, 264

Bristol, George Digby, 2nd earl of, 283, 286

Bristol, John Digby, 1st earl of, 231, 238

British Gazette, 205

British Worker, 205

Broderick, Sir Allen, 23

Broghill, Roger Boyle, Lord *see* Orrery, earl of

Broke, Thomas, 142, 194

Bromley, Henry, 200

Brooke, Thomas, 97

Brooks's club, 405

Browne, Sir Anthony *see* Montagu, Viscount

Browne, George, archbishop of Dublin, 452

Browne, Richard, 264

Bruce, Edward, 325

Brydges, John, 140

Buchan, John, 29

Buckingham, 140, 145, 300, 305

Buckingham, George Villiers, 1st duke of, 223–5, 228, 230–1, 232–5, 236–7, 238–9, 240

Buckingham, George Villiers, 2nd duke of, 287, 289–94, 296–7, 298, 305, 307, 314, 317; *The Rehearsal*, 289

Buckingham, Henry Stafford, 2nd duke of, 108

Buckingham and Chandos, Richard Temple-Grenville, 1st duke of, 413, 426, 427

Buckinghamshire, 110, 210, 305

buggery, 435

Buggery Act (1533), 144

Bull, Frederick, 396

Buller family, 424

Burdett, Sir Francis, 203–4, 431

burgesses (borough freemen): 13th–14th century, 49–51, 53, 59, 62–3, 65, 72, 78; 15th century, 98, 100, 113–14; 16th century, 144–5, 167

Burghersh, Henry, bishop of Lincoln, 67

Burghley, Mildred Cecil (née Cooke), Baroness, 173, 184

Burghley, William Cecil, 1st Baron, 160, 167, 173, 174, 179–80, 184–6, 194, 226, 453

Burghley House, 185

Burgoyne, John, 30, 383–4

Burke, Edmund, 7, 20, 27, 393, 399, 401, 402, 407, 408–10; *Reflections on the Revolution in France*, 408

Burley, Simon, 86

Burley, William, 111–12

Burnell, Robert, bishop of Bath and Wells, 57–9

Burnet, Alexander, archbishop of Glasgow, 343

Burnet, Gilbert, bishop of Salisbury, 295, 304, 314, 343, 368

Burnley, 25

Burns, John, 24–5

Burton, Charles, 464

Burton-upon-Trent, abbey of: annals, 47

Bury St Edmunds, 103, 114

Bush, Paul, rector of Winterbourne, 163

Bushe, Gervase Parker, 465

Bussy, Sir John, 86–7, 88

Bute, John Stuart, earl of, *188*, 201, 381, 388, 389, 392, 395, 400, 479

Butler, John, 427

Butler, Richard ('Rab'), 23

Butler, Theobald Walter, Baron, 42

Byford, Lewis, bishop of Bangor, 95

Byng, George, 405

Byng, Admiral John, 378, 379

CABAL ministry, 290–4

Cabinet, 169*n*, 367

Cabot, Sebastian, 196
Cade, Jack: rebellion (1450), 104
Cadogan, William, Baron, 365
Caerlaverock, siege of (1300), 44
Caernarvon Castle, 68
Caesar, Sir Julius, 213, 217, 219
Calais, 142, 145, 194
Calcraft, John, the younger, 432, 434*n*
Calderwood, David, 337
Callaghan, James, 19–20
Callington, 243
Calne, 172, 397
Calvin, John/Calvinism, 235, 246,
    311, 332, 338
Cambridge, 253
Cambridge, John, 78
Cambridgeshire, 110, 111
Camden, John Pratt, earl of, 477
Canning, George, *418*, 436, 479
Canterbury, 140
Cantilupe, Walter de, bishop of
    Worcester, 46, 47, 48, 49
Cantok, Thomas, bishop of Emly, 443
Cardigan, James Brudenell, 9th earl
    of, 425–6
Carew, John, 276
Carew, Sir Peter, 167–8
Carew, Richard, 168
Carleton, Dudley, 214, 216
Carlisle, 97, 399
Carlisle, Charles Howard, earl of, 293
Carlow, 428
Carlton Club, 23
'Carlton House Set', *474*
Carlyle, Thomas, 240, 277
Carmarthen, 165
Carmarthen, Francis Osborne,
    marquess of, 403
Carmarthenshire, 26
Carnarvon, James Brydges, earl of, 364
Caroline, Queen, 370
Carrick, Robert Bruce, earl of, 323
Carson, Sir Edward, 24
Carteret, John, Lord, 373–4, 375, 376
Cassilis, John Kennedy, 7th earl of,
    422

Castledermot, Ireland: 'parliament'
    (1264), 442
Castlemaine, Barbara Villiers,
    countess of, 287
Castlereagh, Robert Stewart,
    Viscount, *418*, 429–30, 434–8,
    470, 471, 475–6
Castle Rising, 300, 355
Caswall, Sir George, 359–60
Catesby, Sir William, 120
Caulfeild, Francis, 465
Cavendish, John, Lord, 372, 401, 405
Cavendish, William *see* Devonshire,
    dukes *and* earls of
Cawdray, Richard, 105
Cawley, Will, 277
Cawthorne, John Fenton, 438–9
Cecil, David, 184
Cecil, Mary (née Cheke), 184
Cecil, Richard, 184
Cecil, Robert *see* Salisbury, earl of
Cecil, William *see* Burghley, 1st Baron
Censor, The, 463
Chalgrove, battle of (1643), 261
Chaloner, Thomas, 270, 277
Chamberlain, Austen, 26
Chamberlain, Joseph, 24
Chamberlain, Neville, 19, 205–7
Chambers, John, abbot of
    Peterborough, 149
Champernon, Sir Arthur, 167, 169
Chancellor of the Exchequer, 361*n*
Chapman, Benjamin, 427
Charlemont, James Caulfeild, 1st earl
    of, 465–6
Charles I, 14, 19, 221, 229–30, 231–3,
    234–8, 240–1, 243, 245–51, 252,
    256–9, 260, 261, 262, 263–7, 276,
    281, 367; and Ireland, 456, 457,
    458; and Scotland, 338–41, 342
Charles II, 269, 270, 276, 277, *280*,
    281–9, 291–308, 309, 310, 317,
    368, 459; and Scotland, 342–4
Charles IV, of France, 65
Charles Louis, Elector Palatine, 256
Châtelherault, duke of *see* Arran,

James Hamilton, 2nd earl of
Chatham, William Pitt (the Elder),
   earl of, 201, 369, 374–81, 388,
   389, 392, 393, 395, 399, 405, 406,
   465, 466
Chaucer, Geoffrey, *82*, 86, 92
Chaucer, Thomas, *82*, 92–3, 96, 97,
   100, 104
Cheke, John, 160, 184
Chester, 145
Chesterfield, Philip Stanhope, 4th
   earl of, 371–2, 382
Cheyne, Sir Thomas, 141
Chichester, Sir Arthur, 455, 456
Chippenham, 371
Chipping Wycombe, 300
Chisholm, William, bishop of
   Dunblane, 335
Chiswell, Richard Tench, 430–1, 433,
   434
Christie, Thomas, 311
Christmas, Thomas, 120
Chudleigh, Thomas, 308
Churchill, John *see* Marlborough,
   duke of
Churchill, Sir Winston, 16, 19, 205,
   278, 432
Chute, Sir Walter, 220–1
Cinque Ports, 50, 141
civil wars (1642–51), 259–66, 268–9
Clanricarde, Richard de Burgh, 4th
   earl of, 456–7
Clare, John Holles, 1st earl of, 250
Clare, John Holles, 2nd earl of, 261
Clare, Richard de, 48
Clarence, George Plantagenet, duke
   of, 102, 106
Clarence, Lionel, duke of, 446
Clarence, Lionel of Antwerp, 1st duke
   of, 100, 102
Clarendon, Edward Hyde, earl of,
   247, 249, 252, 254, 255–6, 277,
   281–3, 286, 287–9, 290, 317
Clarendon, Henry Hyde, 2nd earl of
   (*formerly* Lord Cornbury), 288,
   314

Clarke, Edward, 232–3
Clayton, Sir Robert, 357
Clement V, Pope, 63
Clement VII, Pope, 132
Clement, Gregory, 270, 276
Clere, Sir John, 194
clergy, 183–4; *see also* abbeys and
   abbots; bishops
Clerk of Penicuik, Sir John, 248, 352
Cleveland, 23
Cleveland, Barbara Palmer, duchess
   of, 299
Clifford, Thomas, 1st Baron Clifford
   of Chudleigh, 290, 291–2, 294
Clive, Robert, 380
Clontarf, John Rawson, Viscount, 452
Close Rolls: (1237), 51; (1242), 39;
   (1258), 40
Clotworthy, Sir John, 252, 264
Cobbett, William, 431
Cobham, Eleanor, 103
Cobham, Richard Temple, Viscount,
   369
'Cobham's Cubs', 369, 370, 375, 380,
   389
Cochrane, Admiral Thomas, 204
Cockayne, John, 111
Cockermouth, 97
Coke, Lady Bridget (née Paston), 225
Coke, Sir Edward, 55, 225–6, 227,
   228, 229, 231, 233, 237, 240, 420
Coke, George, bishop of Hereford,
   255
Coke, Sir John, 255
Coke family, 479
Colchester, 77, 120
Colepeper, Sir John, 254, 256
Colthurst, Sir John, 427
Commons, House of: 13th–14th
   centuries, 72–9; 15th century,
   93–5, 98, 99, 109, 110; 16th
   century, 156–9; 18th–19th
   centuries, 423–4; attendance fees,
   parliamentary (15th century),
   113–14; and discipline, 195–6,
   200; divisions, 131 *and n*;

Commons, House of (*cont.*)
elections, 109–12, 114, 212, 371; last member of royal family to enter, 257; *see also* burgesses; freedom of speech; knights; Speakers
Company of Scotland, 346
Compton, Henry, bishop of London, 310, 311, 312, 314, 316
Compton, Sir Thomas, 223
Comyn, John, the younger, 324, 325
Congregationalists, 262
Conolly, William, 460
Conventicle Acts (1648, 1664), 286, 296
'Convention Parliaments': (1660), 275; (1689), 314, 315–16
Convocations of Canterbury, 61, 133 *and n*, 135
Convocations of York, 61, 133
Conway, General Henry, 392
Cook, Hugh, abbot of Reading, 148
Cook Islands, 17
Cooke, Sir Anthony, 160, 171, 173, 174, 218
Cooke, Edward, 470–1
Cooke, Sir Samuel, Alderman, 463, 464
Coote, Sir Charles, 459
Coote, Sir Eyre, 380
Cope, Anthony, 180, 198–9
Copley, Thomas, 178, 195
Corbett, Miles, 277
Corfe Castle, 300
Cornbury, Lord *see* Clarendon, 2nd earl of
Cornwall, 41, 155, 168
Cornwall, Charles Wolfran, 399
Cornwall, duke of *see* Frederick Louis, Prince of Wales
Cornwallis, Charles, Marquess, 398, 470, 477
coroners, 109
Corrupt Practices Acts (1854, 1883, 1885), 26
corruption, 20, 25–6, 355, 356–61, 364, 371–2
Corry, Isaac, 427, 471–2, 476
Coryton, William, 244, 245
Coss, Peter R.: *Origins of the English Gentry*, 78
Costyn, Geoffrey, 78
Cotton, John Hinde, *354*
Court of Chancery, 210, 211
Courtenay, Sir Henry, 108
Courtenay, Humphrey, 108
Courtenay, James, 177
Courtenay, Sir John, 108
Courtenay, Peter, bishop of Exeter, 108
Courtenay, Philip, 108
Courtenay, Lieutenant Philip, 447
Courtenay, Sir Philip, 108
Courtenay, Sir Walter, 108
Courtenay, William, bishop of London/archbishop of Canterbury, 75, 86
Courtenay, William, marquess of Exeter, 139
Courtenay, Sir William, 167, 169, 177
Courtenay family, 107–8
Covenanters, 247, 262, 283, 284, 291, 307, 340, 341, 342, 344
Coventry, *54*, 157
Coventry, Sir William, 288
Coventry Act (1682), 420
Coverdale, Miles: Great Bible, 139
Cox, Richard, bishop of Ely, 149
Cox, Sir Richard, 464
Craggs, James, 358, 359
Craggs, James, the younger, 358, 359
Cranfield, Sir Lionel *see* Middlesex, earl of
Cranmer, Edmund, archdeacon of Canterbury, 153
Cranmer, Thomas, archbishop of Canterbury, 137, 141, 153, 154, 157, 160, 161, 166, 194
Crawthorne, Matthew, 109
Crean, Eugene, 24
'Creeping Parliament' (Scotland, 1571), 335

Crepyn, Ralph, 60
Crewe, Mrs Fanny, 404
Crewe, Sir Randolph, 218, 236
Croker, John, 204
Cromwell, Henry, 459
Cromwell, Oliver, *242*, 253, 254, 262–3, 265, 268–71, 272–3, 274, 277–8, 341, 342
Cromwell, Richard, 273–4, 459
Cromwell, Thomas, 118, 131–2, 133, 136–40, 143, 144, 150, 156, 158, 170, 171, 185, 194, 458
Crosbie, William, 430
Crowe, Sackville, 224
Cuffe, James, 427
Culloden, battle of (1745), 375
Cumberland, 97
Cumberland, Ernest, duke of, 432
Curll, Walter, bishop of Winchester, 258
Curran, John Philpott, 428
Curtis, Edmund: *A History of Ireland*, 462
Curwin, Hugh, archbishop of Dublin, 452
Curzon, Sir John, 300
Cusack, Sir Thomas, 452

Dacre, Francis Lennard, 14th Baron, 260
Dafydd, son of Gruffydd, 56, 58, 59
Dagworth, Sir Nicholas, 446–7
Dalrymple, Sir John, 320
Dalrymple of Stair, Sir James, 345
Dalton, James, 171, 179
Danby, Thomas Osborne, earl of, 288, 294, 295–6, 299, 302–4, 312, 313, 315
Dance, Sir Nathaniel: *Frederick, Lord North*, 394
Dannett, Thomas, 179
Danvers, Sir John, 268
Darcy, John, 69, 70–1
Darcy, Patrick, 460, 463, 464
Darcy, Thomas, 1st Baron, 140
Darien Scheme, 346, 349

Darknall, Robert, 140
Darley, Henry, 259
Darley, Richard, 259
Darnley, Henry Stuart, Lord, 334
Darrell, William, 184
Dashwood, Sir Francis, 202, 388
David I, of Scotland, 326
David II, of Scotland, 327
David II, bishop of St Asaph, 95
Davies, Sir John, 181–2, 183, 455
Day, George, bishop of Chichester, 160, 163
Deasy, John, 25
Declaration of Arbroath (1320), 325–6, 351
Declaration of Breda (1660), 276, 282, 285
Declaration of Indulgence (1662), 286
Defoe, Daniel, 351
de la Mare, Sir John, 75
de la Mare, Sir Peter, 73–6
Deloraine, Henry Scott, earl of, 349
Denbigh, William Feilding, earl of, 260
Denison, Evelyn, 15
Derby, 300
Derbyshire, 172
Dering, Edward, 253
Derwentwater, James Radcliffe, earl of, 372
Desborough, John, 274
Desmond, James FitzGerald, 8th earl of, 449
Despenser, Hugh, 45, 49, 52, 66, 79
Despenser, Hugh, the younger, 64, 66, 79
D'Esterre, John, 427
Devon, 107, 155, 177
Devonshire, Georgiana Cavendish, duchess of, 400, 406
Devonshire, Henry Courtenay, 7th earl of, 126
Devonshire, Hugh Courtenay, 2nd earl of, 107
Devonshire, Thomas Courtenay, 5th earl of, 108

Devonshire, Thomas Courtenay, 6th earl of, 108
Devonshire, William Cavendish, 1st duke of, 299, 312
Devonshire, William Cavendish, 3rd duke of, 376
Devonshire, William Cavendish, 4th duke of, 372, 374, 379
Devonshire, William Cavendish, 6th duke of, 205
Devonshire, William Cavendish, 3rd earl of, 299
Devonshire, William Cavendish, 4th earl of, 311
d'Ewes, Sir Simonds, 257
Digges, Sir Dudley, 224
Digges, Thomas, 179
Disney, Sir William, 43–4n
Disney, Sir William (son), 43–4n
Disraeli, Benjamin, 22, 23
dissolution of the monasteries, 136–7, 145, 168
Dixwell, John, 276–7
Dodington, George Bubb, 379
Dolben, Gilbert, 314
Dolben, John, bishop of Rochester, 303
Dolben, John, MP, 363
Doncaster, 186
Donne, John, 183
Dorchester, Henry Pierrepoint, marquess of, 261, 290
Doreward, Sir John, 99
Dorset, 99
Dorset, Lionel Sackville, 1st duke of, 202
Douglas, Alexander, 341
Dover, 301; Treaty of (1670), 291
Dover, Henry Carey, earl of, 260
Dowdeswell, William, 389
Down, 436
Downing, Sir George, 277
Downton, 137, 140
Drake, Sir Francis, 183
Drake, Sir William, 300
Draper, Cresheld, 300–1

Droitwich, 265
Dublin: Chichester House, 472; Holy Trinity Cathedral, 448; Holy Trinity Priory, 444; Parliament Building, 472
Dudley, Edmund, 117–18, 124–6
Dudley, John, 124
Dudley, William, bishop of Durham, 124
duelling, 418, 419–23, 426–9, 436
Duffy, Charles Gavan, 459
duke (title), 61
Duket, Laurence, 60
Dunbar, battles of: (1296), 323; (1650), 273
Dunblane, Peregrine Osborne, Lord, 300, 302
Duncombe, Edward, 218
Dundas, Henry see Melville, Viscount
Dundee, John Graham, Viscount, 319, 321
Dunfermline, Alexander Seton, 3rd earl of, 345
Dunning, John, 397
Duppa, Brian, bishop of Winchester, 284
Durham, 186
Durham, County, 248

Earle, Giles, 371
East India Bill (1783), 402, 412
East India Company, 357, 395–6
Eden, William, 430
Edgecombe, Sir Richard, 449
Edgehill, battle of (1642), 259, 260
Edinburgh: Parliament Hall, 327; Parliament House, 340; riots (1558), 331
Edmonds, Captain Piers, 226–7
'Edmund Crouchback' see Lancaster, 1st earl of
Edmund of Langley, duke of York, 88
Edward, the Black Prince, 72, 75
Edward I, 32, 48, 49, 50, 51, 53, 55–63, 78, 102, 145, 323–4, 443
Edward II, 61, 62, 63–8, 77, 325

Edward III, 61, 62, 66, 67, 68–75, 78–9, 287, 297, 326, 446
Edward IV, 101–2, 106, 107, 108, 111, 114, 118, 119, 121, 123, 448, 449
Edward V, 102, 106
Edward VI, 20, 146, 153, 155, 156–7, 159, 160, 161, 172, 330
Edward of Caernarvon, 322
Edward the Confessor, St, 65, 69; shrine to 34, 37, 53, 55, 99
Egan, John, 428
Egmont, John Perceval, 2nd earl of, 378
Egyptians Act (1530), 143
Eleanor of Provence, 36, 37, 45
Eliot, Edward, 413
Eliot, Sir John, 233–4, 239–40, 244, 245
Elizabeth I, 19, 20, 42, 150, *152*, 169–87, 190–1, 195, 196–7, 198, 200, 209, 211, 214, 215, 218, 331, 332–3, 452, 453, 454, 455
Elizabeth of Bohemia, 222
Elizabeth of York, 121, 123
Ellesmere, Thomas Egerton, Baron, 211, 212
Ellis, Sir William, 300
Elyot, Sir Thomas, 134
Empson, Sir Richard, 117–18, 124–6
Erasmus, Desiderius, 129
Erle, Sir Walter, 256
Erpingham, Sir Thomas, 88
Errol, Francis Hay, 9th earl of, 336
Erskine, Thomas, 411, 413
Erskine, Sir William, 430
Esher Palace, 133–4, 137
Espléchin, Treaty of (1340), 69
Essex, 99, 305
Essex, Arthur Capell, 1st earl of, 306, 309
Essex, Robert Devereux, 2nd earl of, 209, 226, 454
Essex, Robert Devereux, 3rd earl of, 258–9, 261, 263
Euripides: *The Suppliant Women*, 207
Euston, George Fitzroy, Lord, 405

Evelyn, George, 301
Evelyn, John, 292, 301
Everard, Sir John, 455
Evesham, battle of (1237), 51–2
Exchequer, 70 *and n*
Excise Act (1767), 388–9
Exclusion Bills: (1641), 281; (1679–81), 23, 306, 307
Exeter, 158, 167
Exeter, Henry Courtenay, earl of, 126
Exeter, Thomas Beaufort, duke of, 93
Eyles, Sir John, 372
Eyre, Robert, 300

Fabyan, Robert, 133
Fagg, Sir John, 80, 295
Fairfax, Ferdinando, 2nd Lord, 259, 262, 263
Fairfax, Mary, 289
Fairfax, Sir Thomas, 259, 263, 265, 275, 289
Falkirk, battle of (1298), 324
Falkland, Anthony Cary, Viscount, 314–15
Falkland, Henry Cary, Viscount, 283
Falkland, Lucius Cary, Viscount, 252, 253, 254, 256
Falmouth, Edward Boscawen, 4th Viscount, 421
Farrelly, Paul, 189
Farnham, 141
Fauconberg, Thomas Belasyse, 2nd Viscount, 293, 310
Fauconer, Sir John de, 97
Fauconer, William, 97
Fawkes, Guy, 235
Feckenham, John, abbot of Westminster, 149, 175
Felton, John, 239
Fenner, Edward, 199
Fenwick, Sir John, 367
Ferrar, Robert, bishop of St David's, 165
Ferrers, George, 194–5
feudal aids/dues/revenues, 123 *and n*, 125, 129, 214

Fiennes, Nathaniel, 256, 259
Fife, Robert Stewart, earl of, 328
Finch, John, 244, 247–8, 250, 253, 303
Finch family, 424
Finland: Eduskunta, 17
Fisher, Hayes, 24
Fisher, John, bishop of Rochester, 116, 134–5, 138, 140, 141, 143
Fisher, Robert, 138
Fitz Eustace, Philip, 90
Fitzgerald, Maurice, 442
Fitzgerald, Thomas ('Silken Thomas'), 449, 451
Fitzgibbon, John, 428
Fitz John, Elias, 77
Fitz Peter, Geoffrey, 50
Fitzroy family, 424
Fitzwarin, Fulke, 42–3
Fitzwilliam, William, 4th earl, 410, 480
Five Mile Act (1665), 286
Fleetwood, Charles, 274
Fleetwood, Sir Miles, 231, 244
Fleetwood, William, 179
Fleetwood, Sir William, 210
Flemyng, William, 140
Fletcher, Andrew, of Saltoun, 347, 351
Fleury, Cardinal André-Hercule de, 367
Flodden Field, battle of (1513), 329
Flood, Henry, 440, 465, 466, 467
Foreign Wines Act (1531), 143–4
Forest Charter (1217), 53, 62
Forrester, Sir George, 339
Fortescue, Sir John, 210–12
Foster, John, Speaker, 470, 472
Foster, Reverend John, 183
Foster, William, bishop of Clogher, 470
Fox, Charles, 195
Fox, Charles James, 317, 388, 400–16, 427, 431, 467
Fox, Edmund, 195
Fox, Henry, Lord of the Treasury, 376, 377, 389, 400, 401
Fox, Sir Stephen, 302

Foxe, John 143; Book of Martyrs, 166
Foxe, Richard, bishop of Winchester, 128
Frampton, Robert, bishop of Gloucester, 312
France, 34, 69, 94–5, 99, 100, 129, 378, 380, 381, 412, 413, 414, 415; 'Auld Alliance' with Scotland, 323, 327, 329, 330
Francis, Philip, 409
François II, of France, 331–2, 333
Franklin, Benjamin, 390
Fraser, William, bishop of St Andrews, 322–3
Fraunceys, David, 61
Frederick II, Holy Roman Emperor, 222
Frederick V, Elector Palatine, 222
Frederick Louis, prince of Wales, duke of Cornwall, 370, 378, 379, 387
freedom of speech, 21, 189–94, 195–6, 197, 199–200, 205–7
French Revolution, 204, 407–9, 426
Frescheville, Ranulf de, 61
Freurs, William, 140
Frewen, Accepted, archbishop of York, 284
Frewen, Thankful, 284
Froude, James Anthony, 460
Fulburn, Stephen de, archbishop of Tuam, 444
Fulburn, Walter de, bishop of Waterford, 444
Fullarton, Colonel William, 427
Fuller, Nicholas, 216
Fuller, Robert, abbot of Waltham Holy Cross, 149
Fuller, Rose, 390

'Gagging Acts' (1795, 1817), 21, 204
Gardiner, Samuel Rawson, 277–8
Gardiner, Stephen, bishop of Winchester, 141, 160, 163, 164, 166
Gargrave, Sir Thomas, 193

Garroway, William, 315
Garth, Charles, 390
Gatton, 114, 178, 195
Gaveston, Piers, 63–4, 65
Geddes, Jenny, 246
Geddie, John, 345
Gee, Sir Orlando, 356
Gee, Richard, 356
General Assembly (Scotland), 335–6, 337
Gentleman's Magazine, 384, 432
George I, 359, 364–5, 366, 367
George II, *354*, 370, 373, 375, 376, 379–80
George III, *188*, 201, 380–1, 387–8, 391, 392, 397, 401, 402, 403, 404–5, 407, 411, 412, 422, 464, 469, 470, 475, 478
George IV (and as prince of Wales), 401, 405, 406, 429, 435, *474*
George V, 278
Germain, George Sackville, Lord, 397
Gibbon, Edward, 360
Gibbon, Edward (grandson), 360
Gibbs, Vicary, 24
Giffard, Walter, archbishop of York, 53
Gifford, George, 140
Giggs, Ryan, 189
Gille, Thomas, 114
Gisors, John de, 60
Gladstanes, George, bishop of Caithness, 337
Gladstone, William Ewart, 24
Glanvill, John, 230
Glastonbury Abbey, 145, 146
'Glorious Revolution' (1688), 16, 316–17, 363
Gloucester, 49, 51, 165; Abbey, parliament at (1407), 96; Cathedral, 147
Gloucester, Henry, duke of, *280*
Gloucester, Humphrey, duke of, 101, 102, 103–4, 112
Gloucester, Richard, duke of, 102–3
Gloucester, Thomas of Woodstock, duke of, 85, 86, 447
Gloucester, William, duke of, 346
Gloucestershire, 110
Glyn, John, 264
Glyndwr, Owain, 27, 93, 95
Glynn, John, 259
Godfrey, Sir Edmund, 297, 298
Godolphin, Sidney, Earl, 307, 348, 362
Goffe, William, 276–7
Golden Act (1592), 336
'Good Parliament' (1376), 76, 79, 83, 84, 110, 193, 447
Goodman, Godfrey, bishop of Gloucester, 223, 255
Goodwin, Sir Francis, 210, 211
Goodwin, Sir Fred, 189
Gordon, Alexander, bishop-elect of Galloway, 332
Gordon, George, 1st duke of, 319
Goring, Sir George, 229
Gostwick, John, 194
Gousle, Giles de, 40
Gowrie, William Ruthven, earl of, 335
Grafton, Augustus FitzRoy, 3rd duke of, 384, 393
Graham, Sir Robert, 328
Grant, Sir Archibald, 372
Grant, Sir William, 480
Grantham, 114, 300
Grattan, Henry, 427, *440*, 465–9, 471, 472
Grattan, Henry, the younger, 427
Grattan, James, 465
Graves, Thomas, 2nd Baron, 431–2
Gray, Sir Thomas, 88
Great Bedwyn, 224
Great Boke of Statutes, The, 194
Great Charter (1215), 18, 27, 35, 45, 53, 62, 70, 237, 442
Green Ribbon Club, 298, 302, 304
Gregory IX, Pope, 51
Gregory X, Pope, 57
Gregory, Robert, 184
Gregory, William, 303
Grenville, George, 201, 369, 372, 380, *386*, 388, 389–92, 394, 395, 399, 412, 413, 477

Grenville, John, 97
Grenville, Thomas, 413
Grey, Anchitell, 260, 300
Grey, Charles, 409, 411, 412, 478, 479–80
Grey, Lady Jane, 149, 161
Grey, John, 301
Grey, Richard de, 45
Grey of Codnor, Henry, Lord, 111, 119
Grey of Ruthin, Henry, Lord, 449
Grey of Warke, Baron, 304, 309
Grey of Wilton, Lord, 211
Grimsby, 113
Grimston, Sir Harbottle, 250, 276, 281
Grindal, Edmund, archbishop of Canterbury, 160
Grosseteste, Robert, bishop of Lincoln, 37, 46
Grosvenor, Sir Richard, 228
Grosvenor, Thomas, 404
Guardians (Scotland), 322–3, 324, 327, 328
Guildford, Francis North, earl of, 394
Gunter, Colonel Robert, 24
Gwynn, Nell, 289, 307

habeas corpus, 21, 204, 278, 368, 409
Habeas Corpus Act (1679), 20, 304
Hackett, Sir Andrew, 305
Hackwell, William, 183
Haddington, Thomas Hamilton, 6th earl of, 352
Hales, Robert, Lord Treasurer, 85
Halifax, 272
Halifax, Charles Montagu, Baron, 362
Halifax, Edward Wood, Viscount, 19, 205–6
Halifax, George Savile, 1st marquess of, 293, 306, 310, 315, 316
Hall, Arthur, 197–8, 199
Hall, Edward, 140, 142, 148, 150, 151
Hall, Joseph, bishop of Norwich, 255
Hallam, Henry: *Constitutional History of England*, 18; *View of the*

State of Europe . . ., 58
Halteby, John de, 78
Hamilton, Anne, duchess of, 344
Hamilton, James, bishop of Argyll, 332
Hamilton, James, 1st duke of, 265, 341
Hamilton, James, 4th duke of, 346, 350, 351–2, 353, 422
Hamilton, James, 2nd marquess of, 338
Hamilton, John, archbishop of St Andrews, 332
Hamilton, Patrick, abbot of Fearn Abbey, 331
Hamilton, Sir Patrick, of Little Preston, 339
Hamilton, William, 320
Hamilton, William Douglas, 3rd duke of, 343, 344, 345
Hamond, John, abbot of Battle Abbey, 146
Hampden, John, 247–8, 250, 254, 256, 259, 260, 261, 316
Hampden, John (grandson), 314
Hampshire, 172
Harbord, William, 298, 299
Harclay, Sir Andrew, 65
Hardinge, Sir Henry, 420–1
Hardwicke, Philip Yorke, earl of, 375, 376, 380, 399
Harley, Edward, 264
Harley, Robert, 351, 363
Harpsfield, Nicholas, 148
Harrington, John, 160
Harrington, William Stanhope, Lord, 373
Harrison, Thomas, 270, 276
Haselrig, Sir Arthur, 256, 258, 272–5
Haslemere, 97
Hastings, Sir Edward, 172
Hastings, Sir Francis, 172
Hastings, George, 25
Hastings, Warren, 407
Hatton, Christopher, 180
Hatton, Sir William, 225

Hayman, Mary, 154
Hayman, Sir Peter, 244, 245
Haynes, Hezekiah, 302
Healy, Tim, 24
Heath, Nicholas, archbishop of York, 160, 175, 176
Helyun (*or* Helion), Sir Walter de, 59
Hemming, John, 189
Heneage, Sir Thomas, 146, 199
Henri IV, of France, 220, 231
Henrietta Maria, Queen, 231, 259
Henry II, 39, 42, 441–2
Henry III, *32*, 33, 34–41, 46, 48–9, 51, 52–3, 55, 56, 59, 127
Henry IV (Henry Bolingbroke), 85, 86, 87–9, 90, 91, 92, 93–9, 110, 118, 192
Henry V, 91, 97, 99–100, 101
Henry VI, 100–2, 103–5, 107, 114, 155, 445
Henry VII, 102, 108, 117, 118–26, 129, 144–5, 448–50
Henry VIII, 18, *116*, 118, 125–51, 155–6, 165, 167, 168, 194, 200, 210, 330, 451–2, 458
Herbert, Sir Edward, 243, 256
Herbert, Sir John, 213
Herbert, Richard, 427
Herbert, Sir William, 219
Hereford, Humphrey de Bohun, earl of, 64–5
heresy trials, 139
Hertfordshire, 300
Hervey, Frederick, bishop of Derry, 476
Hesse, Dr Fritz, 206
Hethe, Hamo, bishop of Rochester, 67
Hewson, John, 277
Heytesbury, 114, 172
Hickel, Karl Anton: *The House of Commons, 1793–94*, 410
Hill, Richard, 422
Hindon, 114, 137, 140, 177, 183
Hoare, Samuel, 206
Hobart, Sir James, 125
Hobart, Sir Miles, 244

Hobart, Robert, Chief Secretary, 428
Hoby, Sir Edward, 182, 193–4
Hoghton, Sir Henry, 383
Holgate, Robert, archbishop of York, 153, 163
Holland, Henry Rich, 1st earl of, 259
Holland, Sir John, 286
Holles, Denzil, 244, 250, 256, 259, 261, 263, 264, 265, 276, 299
Hollis, Christopher: *Can Parliament Survive?*, 29
honour, 18th-century concept of, 424–6
Hood, Samuel, 1st Viscount, 406, 431
Hook, Theodore, 439
Hooker, John, 158
Hooper, John, bishop of Gloucester, 165, 168
Hopton, Sir Ralph, 261
Horne, Robert, bishop of Winchester, 160, 172, 184
Hoskins, John, 219, 220–1
Hotham, Sir John, 258
Houblon, Sir James, 357
Howard, Charles, 398–9
Howard, General George, 392
Howard, Lord Henry, 209–10
Howard, Robert, 314
Howard of Escrick, Edward, Lord, 248, 270
Howson, John, bishop of Durham, 238–9
Hughes-Hallett, Colonel F. C., 25
Hull, Kingston upon, 258, 296
Hulme: St Benedict's Abbey, 147
Hume, Sir Patrick, of Polwarth, 345
Hundred Years War, 100
Hungerford, Thomas, Speaker, 84
Hungerford, Sir Thomas, 108
Hungerford, Walter, Speaker, 100
Hungerford, Sir Walter, 184
Huntingdon, 40
Huntingdon, George Hastings, 4th earl of, 172
Huntingdon, Henry Hastings, 3rd earl of, 172

Huntly, George Gordon, 4th earl of, 332, 336
Hurleston, Ralph, 199
Hyde, Anne, 287, 292n
Hyde, Edward see Clarendon, earl of
Hyde Abbey, 147
Hywel ap Gruffydd ap Iorwerth, 68

Iceland: the Althingi, 17
Île de Ré expedition (1628), 236–7, 239
'Illiterate Parliament' (1404), 54
Ingersoll, Jared, 390
Innocent IV, Pope, 35
Innocent VIII, Pope, 124
Iorwerth, 68
Ipswich, 78
Ireland, 441–72; Act of Kingly Title (1541), 452; Act of Union (1801), 18, 436, 474, 475; anti-Catholic legislation, 461–2; assemblies (13th century), 442; Catholic emancipation, 412, 421; Catholic rebellion (1641), 254–5; and Charles I, 456–8; and Charles II, 459–60; conspiracies and impostors (15th century), 448–50; Court of the Justiciar, 443; and the Cromwells, 458–9; and Elizabeth I, 452–5; first Act of Parliament (1216), 17; and James I, 455–6; and James II, 459–60; the Pale, 446, 451; parliaments, 443–8, 471–2; peerage, 445; 'Poynings' Law', 450–1, 452; see also Dublin; Grattan, Henry
Ireton, Henry, 263, 265, 276
Irish Home Rule Bill, 24
Irish Rebellion (1798), 436
Irish Society, 442
Isabella, Queen, 65–6, 67, 69
Islip, John, abbot of Westminster, 147

Jackson, Richard, 390
Jacob, Captain Richard, 301

James I (VI of Scotland), 26, 209, 210, 211, 212–17, 220, 221–3, 226, 227, 228, 229, 230, 231, 234, 235, 246, 334–5, 336, 337–8, 454–5; Bible 235
James I, of Scotland, 328
James II (and as duke of York), 280, 287, 291, 292, 295, 299, 305, 306, 308, 312–16, 317, 319–20, 345, 346, 355, 361, 368, 459, 460
James II, of Scotland, 328, 329
James III, of Scotland, 329
James IV, of Scotland, 123, 329
James V, of Scotland, 329–30
James VI, of Scotland see James I (VI of Scotland)
James the Steward, 324
Janssen, Sir Theodore, 359
Jeffreys, Sir George, 355
Jewel, John, bishop of Salisbury, 175; Apology of the Church of England, 175
Jewish Naturalisation Act (1753), 376–7
Jews, 51, 53, 56, 59
Jocelyn, Percy, bishop of Clogher, 435
John, King, 35, 40–1, 42–3, 46, 50–1, 442
John de Eselington, 41–2
John de Letewell, 41–2
John de Twynne, 41–2
John of Balliol, 323, 324
John of Gaunt, 73, 74–6, 84, 87, 92, 100, 110
John of Wigton, 61–2
Johnson, Dr Samuel, 423, 439
Johnson of Sciennes, William, 352–3
Johnston, Sir Patrick, Lord Provost, 351
Jones, John Gale, 203
Juxon, William, archbishop of Canterbury, 267, 284

Katherine of Aragon, 127, 132, 141, 162
Keighley, Henry of, 62–3

Keilway, Francis, 184

Keith, George, 4th Earl Marischal, 338

Kemp, Cardinal John, archbishop of Canterbury, 103, 107

Ken, Thomas, bishop of Bath and Wells, 316–17

Kenilworth Castle, 37, 66

Kent, 43, 141, 181

Kentwode, Sir John, 75

Keppel, Frederick, bishop of Exeter, 389

Kett, Robert: rebellion, 159

Kidderminster, Richard, abbot of Winchcombe, 146

Kildare, Gerald Fitzgerald, 8th earl of, 449

Kildare, Gerald Fitzgerald, 9th earl of, 451

Kildare, Thomas FitzJohn Fitzgerald, 2nd earl of, 445

Kilkenny, Ireland, 446, 447

Kilkenny Confederation/ Confederates, 457–8, 459

Killiecrankie, battle of (1689), 321

Killigrew, Henry, 184

Killigrew, John, 184

Killigrew, John (son), 184

Killigrew, Sir Robert, 219

Killsby, William, 69, 71

Kilmainham, Ireland: Hospitallers' priory, 452

Kilsyth, James Livingstone, Viscount, 351

Kincardine, Alexander Bruce, 4th earl of, 351

King, Henry, bishop of Chichester, 284

King's Lynn, 122, 157, 361, 364

Kingsmill, George, 172

Kingsmill, Henry, 172

Kingsmill, John, 172

Kingsmill, Sir Richard, 172

Kingston, Sir Anthony, 167, 168

Kingston, Sir William, 142

Kipling, Rudyard, 205

Kiston, Abbot, of Peterborough, 146–7

Kitchin, Anthony, bishop of Llandaff, 176

knights: 13th century, 38, 39–44, 45, 47–8, 49, 52, 53, 58, 59; 14th century, 62, 63, 65, 72, 76–8; 15th century, 96, 97, 99, 100, 110, 111, 113; 16th century, 144–5

Knole, Palace of, Kent, 128–9

Knollys, Sir Francis, 160, 171

Knollys, Sir William, 173, 174, 212

Knox, John, 332, 334, 336, 340

Knyvet, John, 73

Lagos, battle of (1759), 380

Lambe, John, 238

Lambert, General John, 269, 275

Lamberton, William, bishop of St Andrews, 324

Lambeth Palace, London, 15, 46

Lancashire, 141

Lancaster, 95, 96, 145

Lancaster, Edmund Plantagenet, 1st earl of ('Edmund Crouchback'), 35

Lancaster, Henry Plantagenet, 3rd earl of, 66

Lancaster, Thomas Plantagenet, 2nd earl of, 63, 64–5

Land Qualification Act (1711), 368

Langley, Thomas, 94, 99

Langport, battle of (1645), 263

Langrishe, Hercules, 465

Larke, Joan, 129

la Rochelle, Richard de, 442

Lashbrook, Lewis, 184

Latimer, Edward Osborne, Viscount, 302

Latimer, Hugh, bishop of Worcester, 165–6

Latimer, William, Lord Chamberlain, 74, 75

Latouche, James Digges, 463, 464

Latton, John, 140

Laud, William, archbishop of
Canterbury, 235–6, 238–9, 246,
250–1, 252, 253, 255, 271, 284,
339
Lauderdale, John Maitland, 1st duke
and 2nd earl of, 283, 290, 291,
320, 342–3, 344–5
Launceston, 231
lay subsidies, 62*n*
Layton, Sir William, 206
Lecky, William, 467
Lee, Edward, archbishop of York, 147
Lee, Dr George, 371
Lee, Rowland, bishop of Coventry
and Lichfield, 195
Lee, Thomas, 140
Lee, Walter, 184
Leeds, 272
Legett, Richard, 111
Leicester, Sir Peter, 383
Leicester, Robert Dudley, earl of, 182,
185–6
Leicester House set, 379, 381
Leicestershire, 97, 172
le Lilling, Simon, 40
Lemons, Sir James, 111
Lennox, Esmé Stewart, duke of, 222
Lennox, Matthew Stewart, 4th earl of,
334, 335, 336
Lent parliament (1300), 62
Lenthall, William, 256–7, 271
Lepton, John, 226
le Rous, Roger, 59
le Scrope, Richard, archbishop of
York, 89, 93
Lesley, John, bishop of Ross, 335
Leslie, David (later Lord Newark), 262
le Vavasour, Maud, 42, 43
le Vavasour, Mauger, 33, 40, 42, 43,
44, 48, 477
le Vavasour, Sir Robert, 42
Levellers, 270
Leven, Alexander Leslie, earl of, 262
Leverous, Thomas, bishop of Kildare,
453
le Waleys, Henry, 59–60

Lewes, 125; battle of (1264), *32*, 49
Lewis, Sir William, 264
Lewknor, Edward, 199
Leybourne, Roger, bishop of Carlisle,
125
libel law, 426
Licensing Act (1737), 207
Lilburne, John, 270
Lilburne, Robert, 270
Lincoln, 40, 302; parliament (1301),
62
Lincoln, John de la Pole, earl of, 121,
449
Lincolnshire, 110, 111
Lindsay, David, bishop of Edinburgh,
246
Lindsay, David, bishop of Ross, 336,
337
Lindsay, Patrick Lindsay, 6th Lord,
333
Linlithgow, 333
Liskeard, 114, 225
Littleton, Sir Edward, 243, 288, 304
Liverpool, Robert Jenkinson, 2nd earl
of, 204, 436, 477
Livesey, Sir Michael, 277
Llewelyn ap Gruffydd, 49, 51, 56
Lloyd, Sir Robert, 224
Lloyd George, David, 26
lobbying, 109, 112–14
Lockhart, George, of Carnwarth, 349,
350, 351
Logan, Sir John, 24
Lollards, 100, 329
Londonderry, Charles Vane, 3rd
marquess of (*formerly* Charles
Stewart), 428, 434, 476
Long, Walter, 244, 264
'Long Parliament' (1640–60), 21, 248,
254–5, 270–1, 275, 282, 314–15,
341, 457, 458
Longland, John, bishop of Lincoln,
127
Lord Chamberlain, 207
Lord Chancellor of England, 15, 57*n*,
152

Lords, House of: 14th–15th centuries, 72, 73, 77, 95; 17th century, 219, 226, 227, 228–9, 230, 231, 237, *242*, 252 *and n*, 256, 266, 268; 18th century, 26, 363; as court of appeal, 79–80
Lords of the Congregation (Scotland), 332
Loudon, John Campbell, 1st earl of, 340
Loughborough, Lord *see* Rosslyn, 1st earl of
Lougher, Robert, 183
Louis XVI, of France, 409
Louth, John de Bermingham, 1st earl of, 445
Love, Sir William, 286
Lovell, Francis, 1st Viscount, 120–1
Lovell, Sir Thomas, 113, 119–20, 121
Lowther, James, 25
Lowther, Sir James, 404
Lowther 'dynasty', 97–8
Lucas, Charles, 463, 464
Ludlow, 114, 195, 427
Ludlow, Edmund, 274, 277
Lumley, Richard, Baron, 312
Lusignans from Poitou, 34, 37
Luttrell, Narcissus, 309
Lymryk, Thomas, 113
Lynn, East Anglia, 77
Lyons, Richard, 74, 75
Lyttelton, George, 369, 370, 380

Maastricht Treaty, vote on (1993), 20
Macaulay, Thomas Babington, 18–19, 252, 317; *History of England*, 18
Macclesfield, Charles Gerard, 2nd earl of, 309
Macclesfield, Thomas Parker, earl of, 372
McKinnery, Alan, 445
MacMolissa, Nicholas, archbishop of Armagh, 444, 445
MacMurrough, Aiofe, 441
MacMurrough, Dermot, king of Leinster, 441

Maddicott, J. R.: *The Origins of the English Parliament*, 39
Maesygarnedd, John Jones, 276
Magna Carta *see* Great Charter
Mahon, Viscount *see* Stanhope, 5th earl
Maldon, 77
Malicious Shooting Act (1803), 420
Mallory, Melchisedech, 198
Mallory, William, 229
Malmesbury, James Harris, earl of, 410
Man, Isle of: the Tynwald, 17
Manchester, 272
Manchester, Edward Montagu (Viscount Mandeville), 2nd earl of, 248, 256, 262, 263, 276, 283
Manners, Frances, marchioness of Buckingham, 223
Manners, Oliver, 177
Manners family, 424
Mansell, Sir Robert, 224, 233
Mansfield, James, 405
Mar, John Erskine, earl of, 334, 350
March, Edmund Mortimer, 3rd earl of, 74, 76, 89, 93, 447
Marchmont, Patrick Hume, earl of, 352
Margaret de Leveland, 43
Margaret of Anjou, 101, 105–6, 107, 109, 123
Margaret of Scotland, 322
Margaret Tudor, 123, 329
Marie Antoinette, Queen, 408
Marlborough: parliament (1267), 52, 53
Marlborough, John Churchill, duke of, 313, 362
Marshall (*or* Beche), Thomas, abbot of Colchester, 148
Marsham, Charles, 404
Marston Moor, battle of (1644), 262
Marten, Henry, 259, 269, 270
Martin, Richard, 476
Martin, Richard (lawyer), 182, 216
Martin, Samuel, 202, 427

Martin, Thomas, 183
'Martin Marprelate', 200–1
Marvell, Andrew, 21, 296; *An Account of the Growth of Popery and Arbitrary Government*, 296
Mary, Queen of Scots, 179–80, 185, 197, 209, 330, 331, 334, 336
Mary I, 19, 20, 142, 146, 149, 155, 161–9, 171, 175, 195, 200, 452
Mary II, 19, 312, 315–16, 321, 361
Mary of Guise, 330, 331
Mary of Modena, 292, 308, 313, 347, 367
Maryborough, Lord, 438
Mason, Henry Monck, 442
Massie, Edward, 264, 266
Massingham, Thomas de, 77
Master of the Rolls, 218*n*
Mathew, Charles, 183
Mathew, Francis, 427
Matthew, Tobias, 177
Maurice, Prince, 259
Mautravers, William, 52
Maynard, Sir John, 264
Mayne, Simon, 276
'Maynooth pardon' (1535), 451
Maynwaring, Roger, bishop of St David's, 237, 253
Mayo, County, 25
Meal Tub plot (1679–80), 305
Melbourne, William Lamb, 2nd Viscount, 205
Melton, William, archbishop of York, 67
Melville, Andrew, 335, 344
Melville, Henry Dundas, Viscount, 412, 413, 477
Mercers' Company, 113
Merchant Shipping Bill (1876), 22
Merchant Shipping Survey Bill (1871), 22
'Merciless Parliament' (1387), 86, 87, 92
Meres, Sir Thomas, 287, 303
Merke, Thomas, bishop of Carlisle, 89, 90

Merrick, Sir John, 259
Michaelmas parliament (1259), 47
Michell, Francis, 224, 225, 227, 228
Michiel, Giovanni, 167
Middlesex, 41, 203
Middlesex, Lionel Cranfield, earl of, 227, 230, 231, 233
Middleton, Charles Middleton, 2nd earl of, 307
Milborne Port, 359
Mildmay, Sir Walter, 180
Militia Bill (1642), 258
Milne, Alex, 319
Milton, John, 201, 297; *Areopagitica*, 201, 207
Minorca, 378
'Model Parliament' (1295), 18, 27, 55, 60–2
Mohun, Charles, 3rd Baron, 295
Mohun, Charles, 4th Baron, 422–3
Moleyns, Adam, bishop of Chichester, 103, 112–13
Molyneux, William, 460–1, 463, 465; *Case of Ireland Being Bound by Acts of Parliament in England, Stated*, 460–1
Mompesson, Sir Giles, 26, *208*, 224, 226, 227
Monarch, HMS, 378
Monck, General George *see* Albemarle, duke of
Monks of Medmenham (club), 202
Monmouth, 145
Monmouth, James Scott, 1st duke of, 291, 305, 307, 310
monopolies, 181–2, *208*, 224–5, 226, 228
Montagu, Anthony Browne, 1st Viscount, 141, 175, 176
Montagu, Henry Pole, 1st Baron, 139
Montagu, Ralph, 299
Montagu, Richard, bishop of Chichester, 235, 236, 238, 253; *A New Gag for an Old Goose*, 235
Montfort, Henry de, 49, 52
Montfort, Peter de, 40, 45, 49, 52

Montfort, Simon de, earl of Leicester, 21, *32*, 36–8, 47–53, 56, 480; seal of, *32*

Montgomery, Sir James, 319, 321

Montgomery, Philip Herbert, earl of, 222

Montgomery, Robert, archbishop of Glasgow, 336

Montrose, James Graham, 3rd duke of, 476

Montrose, John Graham, 3rd earl of, 338

Montrose, James Graham, 1st marquess of, 341, 342

Moore, Arthur, 471

Moore, John, archbishop of Canterbury, 402

Moore, Stephen, 427

Moray, James Stewart, earl of, 334

Moray, John Randolph, earl of, 326

Martin, Richard, 476

Mordaunt, Baron *see* Peterborough, Henry Mordaunt, 2nd earl of

Mordaunt, John, 113

More, Sir George, 183

More, Sir Thomas, 118, 129–30, 132, 134, 136, 138, 144, 147, 148, 192–3

Morning Advertiser, 25

Mornington, Richard Wellesley, 2nd earl of, 468

Morrice, Sir William, 287

Morrison, Sir Richard, 160

Mortimer, Edmund *see* March, earl of

Mortimer, Roger, 49, 51, 52, 66, 67, 68, 69

Morton, James Douglas, 4th earl of, 334, 335

Morton, Cardinal John, 123

Morton, Thomas, 113

Morton, Thomas, bishop of Durham, 255

Morton, Thomas de, 77

'Morton's fork', 124

Mountgarrett, Richard Butler, Viscount, 458

Moverley, John, 435

Mowbray, Thomas *see* Norfolk, 1st duke of

Much Wenlock, 114, 177

Muir, Thomas, 411

Mytton, John, 26

Napoleon Bonaparte, 204, 412, 414, 433

Naseby, battle of (1645), 263

Neale, Sir John, 174

Neile, Richard, bishop of Lincoln, then Winchester, 219–20, 238–9

Neville, Alexander, archbishop of York, 86

Neville, Christopher, 220–1

Neville, Edward, 139

Neville, George, archbishop of York, 102, 106, 107

Neville, Sir Henry, 182, 219

Neville, John, 74, 75

'New Model Army', 263, 265

Newbury, battle of (1643), 261, 263

Newcastle, Thomas Pelham Holles, duke of, *354*, 372–5, 376–7, 378–81, 382, 383, 388, 395, 399, 431

Newcastle, William Cavendish, marquess of, 262

Newcastle under Lyme, 164

Newcastle upon Tyne, John Holles, duke of, 373

Newdigate, Sir Roger, 387–8

Newenham, Sir Edward, 428

Newport, Isle of Wight, 252

newspapers, 439; and free speech, 204–6

New Zealand, 17

Nichol, Anthony, 264

Nicholas IV, Pope, 444

Nicoll, Anthony, 247

Nicolson, Harold, 206

Nine Years War (1688–97), 356

Norfolk, Roger Bigod, 5th earl of, 62

Norfolk, Thomas Howard, 3rd duke of, 138, 139, 140–1, 142

Norfolk, Thomas Howard, 4th duke of, 179, 199, 209
Norfolk, Thomas Mowbray, 1st duke of, 85, 87, 93, 104
Norris, John, 112
Norris, Lord, 304
North, Brownlow, bishop of Winchester, 478
North, Frederick, Lord, 30, 203, 393–6, 397–9, 400, 401–2, 403, 404, 466, 467
North Briton, 188, 201, 202
Northampton, 49
Northampton, Henry Howard, 1st earl of, 213, 217, 218, 221
Northampton, James Compton, 3rd earl of, 259–60
Northampton, Spencer Compton, 2nd earl of, 259
Northampton, William de Bohun, 1st earl of, 71
Northampton, William Parr, marquess of, 159
Northamptonshire, 124
Northington, Robert Henley, 2nd earl of, 467
Northleigh, Henry, 300
Northumberland, 41, 88, 248, 368
Northumberland, Algernon Percy, 10th earl of, 282
Northumberland, John Dudley, duke of, 159, 160, 161
Norton, Margaret (née Cranmer), 178
Norton, Thomas, 174, 178–9, 198
Norwich, 410
Nottingham, 259
Nottingham, Charles Howard, 1st earl of, 213
Nottingham, Daniel Finch, 2nd earl of, 314
Nottinghamshire, 110
Noy, William, 224, 240

Oates, Titus, 297
O'Connell, Daniel, 427
O'Connor, T. P., 24, 29
Octavians, 336
O'Devany, Conor, bishop of Down and Connor, 455
O'Donnell, Hugh, 454
O'Donnell, Rory, 455
Ogilvie of Inchmartin, Sir Patrick, 339
Oglander, Sir John, 223
Ogle, George, 427
Oglethorpe, Owen, bishop of Carlisle, 175–6
Okehampton, 300
Okey, John, 277
Oldhall, Sir William, 104
Olliphant, Patrick, Lord, 350
Ó Néill, Conn, chief of Tyrone, 449
O'Neill, Owen Roe, 457
O'Neill, Shane, chief of Tyrone, 453
Onslow, Sir Arthur, *82*, 100, 366, 381–2, 383
'Ordinances' (1311), 64, 65, 66
ordinaries, 136*n*
Orford, Admiral Edward Russell, earl of, 362
Orleton, Adam, bishop of Hereford, 66, 67, 79
Ormesby, William, 78
Ormond, James Butler, 1st duke of, 288, 290, 310, 458, 459
Ormond, James Butler, 4th earl of, 447
Ormond, Sir James, 449–50
Ormond, Thomas Butler, 7th earl of, 449
Orphans Bill (1695), 356
Orrery, Roger Boyle, earl of, 459
Osborne, Sir Thomas *see* Danby, earl of
Ossory, Thomas Butler, 6th earl of, 290
Our Seamen: an Appeal (1873), 22
Overbury, Sir William, 223–4
Owen, John, bishop of St Asaph, 255
Owen, Morgan, bishop of Llandaff, 253, 255

Owen, Sir Roger, 218, 219
Oxford, 140, 232, 306; assembly (1258), 38, 39, 40, 44–5, 46
Oxford, Henry de Vere, earl of, 228
Oxfordshire, 93, 110

Paget, Sir William, 155, 161
Paine, Thomas: *Rights of Man*, 408, 410
Pakelesham, William de, 77
Pakington, Robert, 142–3
Paley, William, archdeacon of Carlisle, 425
Palmer, Thomas Fyshe, 411
Papillon, Thomas, 301
Pardoe, John, 430
Paris, Matthew: *English History from the Year 1235 . . .*, 33, 36, 39, 42, 46
parliament: first use of word, 39
'Parliament of Bats' (1426), 103
'Parliament of Dunces' (1404), *54*
Parry, Sir Thomas, 213, 219
Paston, John, 225
Paston, Sir John, 111
'Patriot Parliament' (1689), 459
Patterson, Marcus, 428
Paulet, Thomas, 140
Paulet, Sir William, 137, 159
Paull, James, 427, 431, 433–4
Paxton, Sir William, 26
Pearson, Nathaniel, Alderman, 463
'Peasants' Revolt' (1381), 84–5
Pease, J. A., 24
Peckham, Edmund, 169
Peckham, Henry, 167, 169
Peckham, Robert, 169
Peel, Sir Robert, 205, 428
Pelham, Henry, *354*, 372, 373–4, 375, 376, 377, 378, 383
Pelham, Peregrine, 258
Pelham of Laughton, Thomas, Lord, 373
Pembroke, 183
Pembroke, Aymer de Valence, 2nd earl of, 64

Pembroke, Henry Herbert, 2nd earl of, 159
Pembroke, Richard de Clare, earl of ('Strongbow'), 441
Pembroke, William Herbert, 3rd earl of, 222–3, 234
Penrith, 97
Penryn, 184
Pepys, Samuel, 23, 300
Perceval, John, Viscount, 366
Percy, Harry, 88, 90
Percy, Thomas, 86
Percy family, 88
periodicals, licensing of, 201
Perne, Christopher, 184
Perrers, Alice, 72, 74, 75, 76
Perrot, Sir John, 167, 169
Perrott, Sir James, Lord Deputy of Ireland, 454
Perth: Blackfriars Church, 328; parliament (1606), 337
Peterborough, Henry Mordaunt, 2nd earl of (Baron Mordaunt), 311
Peterborough Abbey/Cathedral, 147, 149
'Peterloo massacre' (1819), 204, 437
Petition of Right (1628), 237–8, 240, 261
Petre, Sir William, 140, 150
Petre, William, 4th Baron, 297, 306
Pewterers' Company, 113
Peyferer (or Payforer), Fulk, 43–4, 48, 477
Phelips, Sir Edward, 210, 220
Phelips, Sir Robert, 229, 233
Philip I, of Spain, 162, 163, 164, 167, 168
Philip II, of Spain, 177–8
Philippa of Lancaster, 95
Philips, Sir John, 389
Pickering, Colonel John, 263
Pierrepoint, William, 295, 260, 261, 276
Piers, William, bishop of Bath and Wells, 255, 284
Piggott, Sir Christopher, 212

Pilgrimage of Grace (1536), 143, 150, 155

Pilkington, Alice (née Kingsmill), 172

Pilkington, James, bishop of Durham, 172

Pilye, Robert, 122

Pitt, Thomas, Lord, 404

Pitt, Thomas, of Boconnoc, 369

Pitt, William, the Elder *see* Chatham, earl of

Pitt, William, the Younger, 19, 399, 402–8, 409–16, 421–2, 427, 436, *474*, 475, 477–8, 479; and Ireland, 468, 469–70

Place Bill (1713), 19

Player, Sir Thomas, 302, 303

playing card monopoly, 182

Plimsoll, Samuel, 21–2

Plumpton, Sir Robert, 120

Plunkett, Sir Nicholas, 458

pocket boroughs, 26

Pole, Sir Geoffrey, 139

Pole, Cardinal Reginald, 20, 143, 164, 175, 211

Pollard, Sir John, Speaker (1553), 162

Pollard, Sir John, Speaker (1555), 167, 168, 169

Pollard, Richard, 140

Pollexfen, Henry, 314

Ponet, John, bishop of Winchester, 153–4, 163

Ponsonby, George, 468, 470, 471, 476

Ponsonby, William, 470, 476

Pontefract, 97

Poole, Sir Henry, 300

Pope, Thomas, 140

Popham, Henry, 97

Popham, Sir John, 97, 103

Popham, Sir John de, 97

Popish Plot (1678), 297, 298

Porteus, Belby, bishop of London, 478

Portland, William Cavendish-Bentinck, duke of, 402, 403, 404, 410, 411, 436, 477

Portman, William, 140

Portsmouth, 275

Portsmouth, Louise de Kérouaille, duchess of, 307

Potter, Thomas: *Essay on Woman* (with Wilkes), 202

poundage duty, 100 *and n*, 121, 232, 243

Powis, William Herbert, earl of, 297, 306

Powle, Henry, 304, 314

Powys, Thomas, 404

Poynings, Sir Edward, 450

'Poynings' Law', 450, 451, 452, 461, 466, 467

praemunire, 133, 141

Presbyterianism/Presbyterians, 245, 246, 261, 262, 263, 264, 265, 266, 269, 270, 272, 275, 276, 282, 284, 286, 299, 302, 311, 319

Preston, 145; battle of (1648), 265; election of 1768, 383–4

Preston, John de, 78

Prices of Foreign Hats Act (1529), 143

Pride, Colonel Thomas, 266, 268, 276

Prideaux, John, bishop of Worcester, 258

'Pride's Purge', 260, 266

Privy Council, 169 *and n*, 173, 184, 200, 215, 367

'Provisions of Oxford' (1258), 38, 39, 44, 46, 52–3

'Provisions of Westminster' (1259), 48, 51, 52

Prynne, William, 266, 288

publishing: and freedom of speech, 200–7

Puckering, Sir John, 170, 185, 199

Pulteney, William *see* Bath, earl of

Purcell, Henry, 308

Puritans, 174, 178, 196, 200, 212, 218, 235

purveyance, 216

Pym, John, 229, 235, 247, 248, 249, 250, 251, 252, 254, 256, 257, 259, 261–2

Quaker Act (1662), 286
Quakers, 304
Quebec, 380, 390
Queensberry, James Douglas, duke of, 347, 348, 349, 350, 351, 352, 353
Quiberon Bay, battle of (1759), 380

Raby Castle, 250
Radcot bridge, battle of (1387), 85
Rainsborough, Colonel Thomas, 265
Ralegh, Sir Walter, 182
Ramsay of Balmain, Sir David, 352–3
Rastell, John, 138
Read, Thomas, 464
Redman, Richard, bishop of St Asaph, 119
Reform Act (1832), 17, 18, 19, 426, 432
Reform Club, London, 23
Reformation, 160, 175
Reformation Acts (1560), 334
'Reformation' Parliament (1529–36), 133–44, 147, 170
Rente, Thomas de, 78
Report on the Dignity of a Peer, 90
Restoration (1660), 201, 260, 277, 280, 282, 289, 296
Reynolds, Edward, bishop of Norwich, 284
Reynolds, Thomas, bishop of Hereford, 176
Reynolds, Walter, archbishop of Canterbury, 67, 89
Rich, Henry, 428
Rich, Richard, 1st Baron, 172
Richard, 3rd duke of York, 100–1, 104, 105, 107, 192
Richard II, 14, 84–91, 92, 99, 110, 315, 446
Richard III, 102, 108, 118, 119, 120, 123–4
Richmond, Charles Lennox, 3rd duke of, 399
Ridgway, Sir Thomas, 213–14
Ridley, Nicholas, bishop of London, 165–6
Rinuccini, Archbishop Giovanni, 458

Riot Act (1714), 360, 368
Rizzio, David, 334
Robert I (Robert the Bruce), 322, 324–6, 327, 351
Robert II, of Scotland, 324n, 327
Robert III (John Stewart, earl of Carrick), 327–8
Robert de Cam (or Cambhou), 40
Robert the Bruce see Robert I
Robert the Steward, 324n, 326
Roberts, William, bishop of Bangor, 284
Robinson, George, 372
Robinson, Thomas, 377
Rochester, 25
Rochester, Laurence Hyde, earl of, 307, 313
Rochester Cathedral, 83–4
Rockingham, Charles Watson-Wentworth, 2nd marquess of, 381, 386, 388, 389, 391, 392, 393, 395, 397, 400, 401, 410, 466, 469, 480
Roger de Bachewurth, 41
Roger de la Dune, 41
Rogers, Sir Edward, 167–8
Rogers, Sir Richard, 184
Rokesley, Gregory de, 59
Rolle, Henry, 243
Rolle, John, 243
Rolt, Edward, 371
Romilly, Sir Samuel, 430, 431, 433, 434
Roos, Lady, 301
Roper, William, 129
Ros, Henry Fitzgerald, 22nd Baron de, 439
Rose, George, 479
Rosebery, Archibald Primrose, 1st earl of, 351
Rosebery, Archibald Primrose, 5th earl of, 278
Rosse, General Charles, 359
Rosse, John de, bishop of Carlisle, 67
Rosslyn, Alexander Wedderburn, 1st earl of (formerly Lord Loughborough), 411, 412, 477

Rotherham, Thomas, archbishop of
York, 119
Rothermere, Harold Harmsworth, 1st
Viscount, 205
Rothes, John Leslie, 6th earl of, 339,
340, 352
Rothesay, David, duke of, 328
rotten boroughs, 26, 265, 438–9, 477,
479
Rous, Francis, 247, 271–2
Rudyerd, Benjamin, 233, 237, 249
Rugge, William, bishop of Norwich,
147, 160
'Rump Parliament' (1648), 268, 269,
270, 275, 282
Rupert of the Rhine, Prince, 259, 262,
458
Rushock, Thomas, bishop of
Chichester, 86
Russell, Elizabeth (née Cooke), 173
Russell, Edward, 312
Russell, John, Lord, 173
Russell, William, Lord, 298, 309
Ruthven raiders, 335
Rye House Plot (1683), 309, 316

Sacheverell, Reverend Henry, 363, 364
Sacheverell, William, 298
Sackville, Sir Edward, 229
Sackville, George, 202
Sadleir, James, 26
Sadleir, John, 26
Sadler, Ralph, 140, 180
St Albans, 309; Abbey, 146; battle of
(1455), 100
St Germans, 233
St John, Sir Alexander, 260
St John, Sir Anthony, 260
St John, Sir Beauchamp, 260
St John, Elizabeth, 277
St John, Henry see Bolingbroke, 1st
Viscount
St John, Oliver, Baron St John of
Bletsoe, 260
St John, Oliver, 249, 253, 260, 261,
277

St John, Oliver (son), 260
St John, Oliver (lawyer), 260
St Leger, Anthony, 452
St Leger, Captain, 428
St Leger, Nicholas, 199
St Leger, Thomas, 444
St Martin's le Grand church, London,
105, 107
St Paul's Cathedral, 15, 47, 172
St Stephen's Chapel, Westminster, 14,
34, 157
Salcot, John, abbot of Hyde, 149
Salisbury: parliament (1297), 62;
Treaty of (1289), 322
Salisbury, James Cecil, 3rd earl of,
293, 297, 306
Salisbury, Margaret Pole, 8th countess
of, 139
Salisbury, Robert Cecil, earl of, 118,
182, 184, 186–7, 194, 209–10, 212,
215–17
Salisbury, William Montagu, 1st earl
of, 71
salt monopoly, 181
Saltash, 249
Sancroft, William, archbishop of
Canterbury, 308, 312, 316
Sandford, Francis, 308–9
Sandwich, Edward Montagu, 1st earl
of, 263, 283
Sandwich, John Montagu, 4th earl of,
202
Sandys, Sir Edwin, 172, 213–14, 220,
227, 228, 231, 240
Sandys, Miles, 172
Sandys, Samuel, 373
Sauchieburn, battle of (1448), 329
Saunderson, Colonel Edward, 24
Savoy, Peter de, 45
Savoy Palace, London, 215
Sawyer, Sir Edmund, 212
Say, Will, 277
Saye, William Fiennes, Viscount, 259
Scarborough, 178, 196
Scilly Isles, 278
Scory, John, bishop of Hereford, 163

Scotch Militia Bill (1708), 368
Scotland, 58, 69, 261–2, 319–53; 'Auld Alliance' with France, 323, 327, 329, 330; and Charles I, 338–42; and Charles II, 341–4; Covenanters, 283, 291, 307, 340–1, 342, 344; parliament, 326–7, 328–30, 333–4, 340–3, 348; Reformation (1560), 245–6, 333; Union with England, 27, 213–14, 227, *318*, 338, 345–53; *see also* Calvin/Calvinism; Mary, Queen of Scots; Presbyterianism
Scott, John, 427
Scott, Thomas, 268, 273, 276
Scott, Sir Walter, 415–16
Scottish Convention of Estates (1689), 319–21, 341
Scottish National Covenant (1638), 246
Scougal, Patrick, bishop of Aberdeen, 344
Scrope, Henry, 3rd Baron Scrope of Masham, 91
Scrope, Richard, Baron Scrope of Bolton, 91, 119
Scrope, William, earl of Wiltshire, 91
Seafield, James Ogilvy, earl of, 353
secretaries of state, 358*n*
Seditious Meetings and Treasonable Practices Acts (1795), 411
Selden, John, 243, 244, 245
Semple, John, 341
Septennial Act (1715), 365, 368, 477
Seton, Alexander, Lord, 337
Seven Years War (1756–63), 379, 393, 399
Seymour, Canon, 113
Seymour, Sir Edward, 288, 303, 310, 314, 315
Seymour, Sir Francis, 233, 247–8, 249
Seymour, Hamilton, 434
Seymour, Thomas, Lord High Admiral, 156, 158
Shaftesbury, Anthony Ashley Cooper, 1st earl of, 283, 290, 291, 292, 293, 294–5, 297, 298, 299, 302, 303, 305–8, 317; *Letter from a Person of Quality*, 294
Shaftesbury, Anthony Ashley Cooper, 7th earl of: on Plimsoll, 22
Shakespeare, William: *Cymbeline*, 127*n*; *Hamlet*, 429; *A Midsummer Night's Dream*, 146; *Othello*, 439; *Richard II*, 99, 425; *The Tempest*, 127*n*; *The Winter's Tale*, 127*n*
Sharp, James, archbishop of St Andrews, 343–4
Shee, Robert, 458
Shelburne, William Petty, 2nd earl of, 400, 401, 402, 427
Sheldon, Gilbert, bishop of London, 284, 286, 288
Sheldon, Sir Joseph, 302
Shelley, Percy Bysshe: 'The Mask of Anarchy', 437
Sheppard, Thomas, 212
Sherborne, Robert, bishop of Chichester, 125
Sherborne Castle, siege of (1642), 261
Sheridan, Richard Brinsley, 407, 409, 410, 411, 412, 427, 431
sheriffs: 13th century, 38, 40, 41, 47–8, 50, 443; 14th century, 63, 79, 109–10; 16th–17th centuries, 195, 211, 233, 305, 307; 18th century, 371
Sherlock, Hester, 462*n*
Shinwell, Emanuel ('Manny'), 23
Shippen, William, 359
Shirley, Dr Thomas, 80, 295
'Short Parliament' (1640), 248, 249, 281, 457
Shrewsbury: parliaments, 56, 57, 58–60 (1283), 87 (1398)
Shrewsbury, Anna Talbot (née Brudenell), countess of, 289, 293
Shrewsbury, Charles Talbot, 12th earl of, 293, 312
Shrewsbury, Elizabeth Talbot (née Butler), countess of, 448

Shrewsbury, Francis Talbot, 11th earl of, 293
Shrewsbury, John Talbot, 1st earl of, 447
Shrewsbury, John Talbot, 2nd earl of, 448
Shropshire, 177, 218
Sibthorpe, Robert, 236
Sicilian Vespers (1282), 220
Sicily, 35–6, 37
Sidmouth, Lord (Henry 'Doctor' Addington), 204, 410, 412, 413, 421–2, 436, 437, 478
Sidney, Algernon, 271, 309
Sidney, Henry, 312
Sidney, Sir Henry, Lord Deputy of Ireland, 453–4
Silverman, Sydney, 21
Simnel, Lambert, 121, 448, 449
Skinner, Robert, bishop of Oxford, 255, 284
Skipworth, Patrick, 111
Slattery, John, 427
Smalley, Edward, 198
Smith, Sir Thomas, 170
Smollett, Tobias, 364
Society of the United Irishmen, 468, 469
Solicitor-General, 218*n*
Somers, John, Lord, 362
Somerset, Edmund Beaufort, 4th duke of, 101, 104–5, 109
Somerset, Edward Seymour, duke of, Lord Protector, 155–7, 158–60, 178, 184
Somerset, Robert Carr, earl of, 222, 223–4, 227
Somerset, William Seymour, 2nd duke of, 261
Somerville, Sir James, Alderman, 463
Somery, Roger de, 45
'Sons of Liberty', 396
Sophia, Electress of Hanover, 347
Southampton, Henry Wriothesley, 2nd earl of, 226–7, 228
Southampton, Thomas Wriothesley, 1st earl of, 137, 159
Southampton, Sir William Fitzwilliam, 1st earl of, 141
Southamptonshire, 97
South Sea Company, 357–9, 369
Southwood, Julius Elias, Baron, 205–6
Spain, 221–2, 229–31, 233, 234, 272, 371; War of the Spanish Succession (1701–14), 348, 357, 362
Speakers, 15, 20, 74, 76 *and n*, 77, *82*, 84, 86, 93, 97–8, 99–100, 103, 104, 106, 109, 112, 113, 117–18, 119–20, 125, 129, 130, 131, 162, 170, 185, 187 *and n*, 191–2, 193, 198*n*, 210, 218, 244, 256–7, 276, *280*, 303, 355–7, 381–2, 399, 411, 454; first, 73–4, 77
Speaker's House, 15
Spectator, 201, 423
Spencer, George, 2nd Earl, 412, 413, 477
Spencer, Harriet, 439
Spicer, William, 181
Spragge, Admiral Sir Edward, 301
Stabbing Acts (1604, 1803), 420
Stace, Thomas, 78
Stafford, 194
Stafford, Sir Humphrey, 120–1
Stafford, Ralph de, 1st earl of, 70
Stafford, Thomas, 120–1
Stafford, William Howard, Viscount, 297, 306
Stamford, 160, 184
Stamford, Henry Grey, earl of, 260
Stamp Act (1765), *386*, 391–2, 395
Standish, Sir Frank, 383
Standish, Henry, bishop of St Asaph, 141
Stanford, William, 194
Stanhope, Charles, 359, 360
Stanhope, Sir Edward, 182
Stanhope, James, 1st Earl, 361, 365–6
Stanhope, Sir John, 213
Stanhope, Michael, 182

Stanhope, Philip *see* Chesterfield, 4th earl of

Stanhope, Philip, 5th Earl (Viscount Mahon), 424

Stanley, James, bishop of Ely, 134

Stanley, James Smith (Lord Strange), 383

Stapledon, Walter, bishop of Exeter, 67

Staples, Edward, bishop of Meath, 452

Stapleton, Sir Philip, 259, 260, 261, 264

Star Chamber, 21, 191 *and n*, 200

State Bed, 15

Stationers' Company, 21, 200

Statute in Restraint of Appeals (1533), 137

Statute of Gloucester (1278), 59

Statute of Jewry (1275), 59

Statute of Merchants (1283), 58

Statute of Mortmain (1279), 59

Statute of Religious Men (1279), 59

Statute of the Exchequer (1275), 59

Statutes of Westminster (1275, 1285, 1290), 56, 58, 59

Steele, Sir Richard, 423

Stephens, Richard, 200

Steward, George, 206

Stewart, Alasdair, 328

Stewart, Charles *see* Londonderry, 3rd marquess of

Stewart, Esmé, 334

Stewart, Murdoch, 328

Stewart, Walter, 328

Stewart or Stuart family, 324*n*

Stillington, Robert, bishop of Bath and Wells, 119

Stirling Bridge, battle of (1297), 324

Stoke Field, battle of (1487), 121, 449

Stokesley, John, bishop of London, 143

Stone, George, archbishop of Armagh, 202

Stonehouse, Sir George, 269

Stonor, Francis, 177

Story, John, 177–8, 195

Stourton, William, 99

Strafford, Thomas Wentworth, earl of, 233, 237, 238, 249–50, 281, 456, 457

Strangways, Giles, 260

Strangways, John, 260

Strangways, Sir John, 255, 260

Strangways, Thomas, 260

Strangways, Wadham, 260

Stratford, John, archbishop of Canterbury, 67, 69–72, 79

Stratford, Robert, bishop of Chichester, 69, 70–1

Strickland, Walter, 259

Strickland, Sir William, 259

Strickland, William, 178, 196–7

Strode, William, 244, 256

Stuart, James Francis Edward, 347, 367

Stuart, William, archbishop of Armagh, 479

Stubbs, Bishop William, 55, 60, 90–1

Sudbury, Simon, archbishop of Canterbury, 85

Suffolk, Alice Chaucer, duchess of, 104

Suffolk, Edmund de la Pole, 3rd duke of, 121

Suffolk, Mary Tudor, duchess of, 210

Suffolk, Michael de la Pole, earl of, 85

Suffolk, Thomas Howard, 1st earl of, 213

Suffolk, William de la Pole, 1st duke of, 101, 103

suicides, 429–35, 437–8

Sunderland, Charles Spencer, 3rd earl of, 358, 359, 360, 362, 365–6, 373

Sunderland, Robert Spencer, 1st earl of, 306

Sunderland, Robert Spencer, 2nd earl of, 307, 310, 312

Surrey, 305

Surrey, Henry Howard, earl of, 209

Surrey, John de Warenne, 6th earl of, 323

Surrey, John de Warenne, 7th earl of, 64
Sussex, 125
Sussex, Thomas Radclyffe, 3rd earl of, 452
Sutton, Sir Robert, 372
Swift, Jonathan, 462, 463; *Drapier's Letters*, 462
Swinfen, John, 288
Sword Blade Company, 360
Swynford, Katherine, 92
Sydney, Thomas Townshend, Lord, 403

Tailboys, Walter, 111
Tailors' Company, 112–13
Talbot, John, 177
Talbot, John (Irish MP), 456
Talbot, Richard, archbishop of Dublin, 448
Talbot, William, 1st Earl, 427
Talleyrand, Charles-Maurice de, 415
Tanner, Dr Charles, 24
Tatler, 201, 423
Taunton, 137, 140
Tavistock, 218, 247
taxation: 14th century, 72, 73, 75, 76–7, 84; 15th century, 93, 95, 96–7, 98, 100, 123; 16th century, 123, 126, 129–31; 17th century, 215–17, 228, 247–8; 18th century, 368; *see also* feudal aids; tonnage
Taylor, Jeremy, bishop of Down and Connor, 459
Taylor, John, bishop of Lincoln, 163
Tea Act (1773), 396
tea trade, 395–6
Temple, Lord Richard *see* Buckingham and Chandos, 1st duke of
Temple, Sir Richard, 3rd baronet, 286
Temple, Richard Grenville-, 2nd Earl, 201, 369, 380, 389
Temple, Thomas, 172
Temys, Thomas, 142

Test Act (1673), 291–2, 293, 298, 310, 311
Test Bill (1675), 294–5, 299
Teviot, Thomas Livingston, 1st Viscount, 350
Tewkesbury, battle of (1471), 102, 108, 109
Tewkesbury Annals, 41, 51
Thatcher, Margaret, 19–20
theatre: censorship, 207
Theatres Act (1843), 207
Theobalds, Hertfordshire, 185, 215, 232
Thetford, 145
Thirlby, Thomas, bishop of Ely, 176
Thirty-Nine Articles (1563), 178
Thirty Years War (1618–48), 232
Thomas, Sir Edmund, 371
Thorisby, Thomas, 122
Thornborough, John, bishop of Bristol, 213
Thornton, William, abbot of St Mary's, York, 147
Thorpe, Thomas, 109
Thorpe Hall, Peterborough, 277
Throckmorton, Anthony, 173
Throckmorton, Clement, 173
Throckmorton, George, 173
Throckmorton, Sir George, 143, 160, 172
Throckmorton, Job, 180, 199, 201
Throckmorton, John, 169, 173
Throckmorton, Sir John, 173
Throckmorton, Kenelm, 173
Throckmorton, Sir Nicholas, 167–8, 173
Throckmorton, Sir Robert, 173, 177
Throckmorton, Sir Thomas, 173
Thynne family, 479
Tierney, George, 412, 413, 421–2, 427, 479
Times, The, 205, 426, 475
Tiptoft, Sir John, 93, 94, 95, 111, 192
Titulus Regius statute, 118, 120, 121
Tone, Wolfe, 468, 469
Tonge, Israel, 297

tonnage duty, 100 *and n*, 121, 232, 243
Topcliffe, Richard, 184
Tories, 314, 315, 356, 357, 361, 362, 363–4, 365, 366–7, 370–1, 377, 380, 387
Totnes, 114
Tournai, siege of (1340), 69
Tower of London, 15, 48
Towers, John, bishop of Peterborough, 255
Townshend, Charles, 390, 395
Townshend, Charles, 2nd Viscount, 361, 365, 373
Townshend, Lord Charles, 26
Townshend, George, 3rd Viscount, 365
Townshend, Reverend Lord Frederick, 26
Townshend, John, 405
Townshend family, 424
Towton, battle of (1461), 101, 105, 108, 123
trade laws, 143–4; *see also* monopolies
Trades Union Congress, 205
Trafigura (company), 189
Trant, Dominick, 427
Treasons Bill (1534), 143
Treby, Sir George, 315
Tregony, 189
Tresham, Thomas, 109
Tresham, William, 103, 104
Tresilian, Robert, 85–6
Trevor, Edward, 355
Trevor, Sir John, 355–7
Triennial Acts, 249, 278, 287 (1641), 365, 368 (1694)
Trussell, William, 67
Tucker, John, 379
Tuckett, Harvey Garnet Phipps, 426
Tuddenham, Sir Thomas, 104
Tunstall, Cuthbert, prince-bishop of Durham, 150, 161, 176
Turner, Francis, bishop of Ely, 314
Turnham Green, battle of (1642), 261

Turnor, Edward, 357
Tweeddale, James Hay, 2nd marquess of, 347, 350, 352
Tweeddale, John Hay, marquess of, 345
Tyler, Wat, 84–5
Tyrone, Hugh O'Neill, earl of, 454, 455, 458
Tyrrell, Sir James, 121

Ullswater, James William Lowther, Viscount, 97–8
Ulster, Richard Óg de Burgh, 2nd earl of, 445
Upton, John, 247
Utrecht, Treaty of (1713), 26, 363

Valentine, Benjamin, 244
Vane, Sir Henry, 250, 251, 259, 270–1
Vane, Sir Henry (younger), 251, 253, 254, 259, 273–5, 278–9
Vaughan, John, 287, 288
Vaughan, Stephen, 137
Vavasour, John, 113
Vavasour family, 42; *see also* le Vavasour
Verney, Edmund, 169
Verney, Captain Edmund, 25
Verney, Sir Edmund (d. 1642), 260
Verney, Sir Edmund (d. 1649), 260
Verney, Francis, 169
Verney, Ralph, 260
Vernon, Richard, 111
Vernon, Thomas, 360
Vertue, John, 120
Vesey, John, bishop of Exeter, 160, 163
Victoria, Queen, 19
Villiers, Christopher, 224
Villiers, Sir Edward, 224
Villiers, Lady Frances (née Coke), 225
Villiers, Francis, 296
Villiers, George *see* Buckingham, duke of
Villiers, Sir John, 225
Voltaire, 378

Wake, Thomas, 67
Wakefield, battle of (1460), 101
Wales/the Welsh, 26, 27, 34, 35, 36, 38, 68, 93, 94–5, 96, 145, 441
Wallace, Sir William, *14*, 324
Waller, Edmund, 260, 288
Waller, Sir Hardress, 260, 266, 459
Waller, Thomas, 260
Waller, Sir William, 259, 260, 261, 264, 266, 302
Wallingford Castle, 93
Walpole, Galfridus, 372
Walpole, Horace, 378, 379, 382
Walpole, Horatio, 372
Walpole, Sir Robert, 207, 361, 363, 364, 365–7, 368–9, 370–2, 373, 374, 378, 462
Walsh, David, 427–8
Walsh, Nicholas, 454
Walsh, William, 200
Walsh, William, bishop of Meath, 453
Walsingham, Sir Francis, 171, 179, 456
Walsingham, Thomas, 76, 90
Walter de Bibbeworthe, 41
Waltham Abbey, 145
Walton, Brian, bishop of Chester, 284
Walton, Valentine, 277
Wandesforde, Christopher, 457
War of Jenkins' Ear (1739), 370
War of the Spanish Succession (1701–14), 348, 357, 362
Warbeck, Perkin, 125, 449
Warburton, William, bishop of Gloucester, 202
Ward, Mary, 269
wardship, 216
Wareham, 160
Warenne, John de *see* Surrey, earls of
Warham, William, archbishop of Canterbury, 122, 128, 135, 136
Warner, Sir Edward, 167–8
Warner, John, bishop of Rochester, 258, 284
Wars of the Roses (1455–87), 100, 101–9, 118–22, 192
Warwick, 180, 181

Warwick, Edward Plantagenet, 17th earl of, 121
Warwick, Edward Rich, 6th earl of, 422
Warwick, Guy de Beauchamp, 10th earl of, 64
Warwick, Richard Neville, 16th earl of, 101, 106
Warwick, Admiral Robert Rich, 2nd earl of, 258–9
Warwick, Thomas de Beauchamp, 12th earl of, 85
Washington, George, 398
Watson, Thomas, bishop of Lincoln, 176
Webster, Sir Godfrey, 430
Wellesbourne, Agatha, 154
Wellesley, Richard Wellesley, 1st Marquess, 431
Wellesley, William Pole, 438
Wellington, Arthur Wellesley, 1st duke of, 205, 419–21, 422, 429, 435, 438
Wellington, Arthur Wellesley, 2nd duke of, 438
Wells, 183; Cathedral, 147
Welsh *see* Wales
Wenlock, 140
Wenlock, John, 109
Wentworth, Barbara, 153
Wentworth, Paul, 190, 197, 199
Wentworth, Peter, 189–91, 198–200, 216
Wentworth, Sir Peter, 270
Wentworth, Thomas (Recorder of Oxford), 216, 220, 221
Wentworth, Thomas *see* Strafford, earl of
Wesley de Cobain, Samuel, 25
West, Nicholas, bishop of Ely, 141
Westbury, 114, 142
Westmeath, Richard Nugent, earl of, 456
Westminster, Palace of, 15, 33–4; St Stephen's Chapel, Westminster, *14*, 34, 157

Westminster Abbey, 15, 34, 37, 53, 55, 69, 73, 89, 149, 284, 308; Henry VII Chapel, 147; shrine to Edward the Confessor, 34, 37, 53, 55, 99

Westminster Hall, *14*, 34, 48, 88, 308, 312

Westmorland, 41, 97

Westmorland, John Fane, 10th earl of, 477

Westmorland, Ralph Neville, 2nd earl of, 113

Westmorland, Ralph Neville, 3rd earl of, 119

Weston, Sir Richard, 141

Weymouth and Melcombe Regis, 378

Whalley, Edward, 276–7

Wharton, Philip, 4th Baron, 297

Wharton, Thomas, earl of, 362

Whigs, 16, 205, 307, 309, 311, 314, 315, 316, 357, 358, 361–71, 377, 379, 387–8, 379, 405, 407

Whitbread, Samuel, the younger, 432–4

Whitbread, William, 433

White, John, bishop of Winchester, 171

White, Thomas, bishop of Peterborough, 312

Whitelocke, Bulstrode, 268, 269–70, 281

White's club, 405

Whitgift, John, archbishop of Canterbury, 180

Whiting, Richard, abbot of Glastonbury, 148

Whittocksmead, John, 113

Widdrington, Sir Thomas, 268

Wilberforce, William, 21, 400, 414, 422

Wildman, John, 314

Wilkes, John, *188*, 201–3, 395, 405, 415, 427; *Essay on Woman*, 202

Wilkes, Sir Thomas, 181

William, son of Reyner, 41

William III, 19, 312–14, 315–17, 319, 320, 345, 346, 355–6, 361, 362, 367, 368, 460, 461

William de Valence, 37, 44, 46

William of Barton, 40

William of Buketown (*or* Boketown), 40

Williams, John, bishop of Lincoln/archbishop of York, 232, 233, 235, 253, 255

Williams, John, bookseller, *188*

Williams, Thomas, 193

Williams-Wynn, Sir Watkin, 476–7

Willoughby, Lord, 303

Wilmington, Spencer Compton, earl of, 372–3, 374, 378

Wilson, Thomas, 171, 173–4

Winchelsea, 300

Winchelsey, Robert, archbishop of Canterbury, 62, 63

Winchester, 46

Winchilsea, George Finch-Hatton, 10th earl of, 419, 421

Windebank, Sir Francis, 250

Windham, William, 410, 411, 412, 413, 477

Windsor, Sir William of, 446

Wingfield, Sir Robert, 182, 211

Winnington, Sir Francis, 303

Winwood, Sir Ralph, 219

Wishart, George, 331

Wishart, Robert, bishop of Glasgow, 323–4

Wogan, Sir John, 443, 444

Wogan, Thomas, 277

Wollstonecraft, Mary: *A Vindication of the Rights of Woman*, 408

Wolsey, Cardinal Thomas, 128–38, 143, 144, 146

women, votes for, 17, 20

Woodstock, 177

wool industry, 98, 143, 182

Wootton Bassett, 114, 281

Worcester, 49; battle of (1651), 269, 273

Worcestershire East, 25

Wotton, Sir Edward, 212

Wotton, Sir Henry, 223

Wraxall, Sir Nathaniel, 30
Wray, Sir Cecil, 406
Wren, Sir Christopher, 369
Wren, Matthew, bishop of Ely, 253, 255, 284
Wright, Robert, bishop of Coventry and Lichfield, 255
Wriothesley, Sir Thomas see Southampton, earl of
Wroth, Sir Robert, 172, 183
Wroth, Sir Thomas, 160, 172
Wyatt rebellion (1554), 163, 168
Wyatt, Sir Thomas, 163
Wykeham, William, bishop of Winchester, 75
Wykes, Thomas, 52
Wyndham, Sir John, 121
Wyndham, Sir William, 367
Wynn, Charles William, 413
Wynter, Thomas, 129

Yarmouth, 77
Yeats, W. B.: 'The Second Coming', 388
Yelverton, Barry, 467
Yelverton, Sir Christopher, 131, 216
Yelverton, Henry, 216
Yonge, Thomas, 192
York, 40, 114, 248, 294; parliaments: (1268), 53; (1298), 53; (1314), 64
York, duke of see Edmund of Langley; James II; Richard of York
Yorke, James, bishop of Ely, 479
Yorkshire, 40, 88
Yorktown, battle of (1781), 398
Young, Thomas, MP for Bristol, 104–5
Young, Thomas (secretary), 205

Zouche, William de, 70

Parliament: The Biography
Volume 2: Reform

Chris Bryant

OVER THE LAST two hundred years parliament has witnessed and effected dramatic and often turbulent change. Political parties rose – and fell. The old aristocratic order passed away. The vote was won for the working classes and, eventually, for women. The world was torn apart by two extraordinarily bloody global wars. And individual politicians were cheered for their altruism or bravery and jeered for their sexual or financial misdemeanours.

This second volume of Chris Bryant's majestic *Parliament: The Biography* has a cast of characters that includes some of British history's most famous names: the Duke of Wellington, Sir Robert Peel, Gladstone, Disraeli, Lloyd George, Churchill and Thatcher. Its recurring theme is reform and innovation, but it also lays bare an obsessive respect for the past and a dedication to evolution rather than revolution that have left us with a fudged constitution still perilously dependent on custom, convention and gentlemen's agreements.

This is riveting, flawlessly researched and accessible popular history for anyone with an interest in why modern Britain is the nation it is today.